HOOSIERS IN HOLLYWOOD

David L. Smith

Indiana Historical Society Press
Indianapolis 2006

©2006 Indiana Historical Society Press. All rights reserved.

Printed in Canada

This book is a publication of the
Indiana Historical Society Press
450 West Ohio Street
Indianapolis, Indiana 46202-3269 USA
www.indianahistory.org

Telephone orders 800-447-1830
Fax orders 317-234-0562
Online orders @ shop.indianahistory.org

The paper in this publication meets the minimum requirements of
American National Standard for Information Sciences—Permanence of Paper for Printed Library Materials,
ANSI Z39.48-1984. ∞

Library of Congress Cataloging-in-Publication Data

Smith, David L. (David Lee), 1929–
    Hoosiers in Hollywood / David L. Smith.
        p. cm.
    Includes bibliographical references and index.
    ISBN 0-87195-194-0 (alk. paper)
        1. Motion picture actors and actresses—Indiana—Biography. 2. Motion picture producers
and directors—Indiana—Biography. 3. Television actors and actresses—Indiana—Biography.
4. Television producers and directors—Indiana—Biography. I. Title.

PN1993.5.U7415S65 2006
791.4302'80922772—dc22

                                                                        2005057952

Most photos are in the author's collection.

Parts of the section discussing Ken Maynard in David L. Smith's book, *Hoosiers in Hollywood*, pages 354-60, were previously published in Raymond E. White's chapter, "Ken Maynard: Daredevil on Horseback" in the book *Shooting Stars: Heroes and Heroines of Western Film*, edited by Archie P. McDonald (Bloomington: Indiana University Press, 1987), pages 20–41, and used without attribution. The Indiana Historical Society Press apologizes for this oversight.

For Lucy Ann
The brightest star in my heaven

CONTENTS

FOREWORD ix
INTRODUCTION xi
ACKNOWLEDGMENTS xv
BEGINNINGS xvii
    C. Francis Jenkins of Richmond and the invention of
    the motion picture projector

THE SILENT ERA

CHAPTER 1   Leading Men 1
    J. Warren Kerrigan, Monte Blue, John Bowers,
    Charlie Murray, Victor Potel, Tom Santschi

CHAPTER 2   Leading Ladies 38
    Edna Goodrich, Valeska Suratt, Rose Melville,
    Alice Terry, Louise Fazenda, Ann Christy,
    Julanne Johnston

THE SOUND ERA

CHAPTER 3   LEADING MEN 71
    Clifton Webb, Ole Olsen, Norman Foster,
    James Dean, Steve McQueen, Red Skelton,
    Brendan Fraser, Greg Kinnear

CHAPTER 4   LEADING LADIES 127
    Marilyn Miller, Louise Dresser, Carole Lombard,
    Marjorie Main, Betsy Palmer, Anne Baxter,
    Florence Henderson, Shelley Long, Vivica Fox

CHAPTER 5   FAMILIES 202
    The Benhams, The Geraghtys, The Seegar Sisters,
    The Bennetts, The Lane Sisters, The Jacksons

CHAPTER 6   SUPPORTING PLAYERS 231

CHAPTER 7   TARZANS 315
    Elmo Lincoln, James Pierce, Denny Miller

CHAPTER 8   DISNEY HOOSIERS 331

CHAPTER 9   COWBOYS 343
    Buck Jones, Ken Maynard, Allan "Rocky" Lane,
    Max Terhune, Chubby Johnson, Steve Clark,
    Kenneth MacDonald, Tex Terry, Fred Gamble,
    Major Gordon W. "Pawnee Bill" Lillie

CHAPTER 10   DIRECTORS 381
            Al and Ray Rockett, Lambert Hillyer,
            Tim Whelan, Clifford Smith, Mack V. Wright,
            Ray Enright, Howard and Kenneth Hawks,
            George Seaton, Robert Wise, Sydney Pollack

CHAPTER 11   SCREENWRITERS AND NOVELISTS 411

CHAPTER 12   MUSICIANS AND COMPOSERS 433

CHAPTER 13   BEHIND THE SCENES 475

CHAPTER 14   NONNATIVES 489

APPENDIXES   OSCAR WINNERS AND NOMINEES 515
            SOAP HOOSIERS 518
            MOVIES SHOT IN OR ABOUT INDIANA . . 522
            HOOSIERS ON THE
                HOLLYWOOD WALK OF FAME 525
            OTHER PLAYERS 526
            COUNTY BY COUNTY LIST 532

INDEX 540

When you meet Professor David Smith for the first time, you immediately learn two things. First, he's clearly a scholar, but one whose knowledge is derived not only from books but also from people and personal experiences over a lifetime. Second, he's passionate about his home state of Indiana and the people whose lives it spawned or touched.

When David told me of his opus, *Hoosiers in Hollywood*, I jumped at the opportunity to write the Foreword. Why me? It was always my dream to make movies. The seven plus years that I lived in Indiana gave me an understanding of the heartland of America necessary, in my humble opinion, to make films for the widest possible audience. As they say in Hollywood, "It's the stuff dreams are made of." My Hoosier experience has enabled me to make my own dream come true.

During the years I lived in Bloomington, I was inspired by others who were there on the Indiana University campus at the very same time and before each made his or her respective trek to "La-La Land": actor Kevin Kline; television broadcaster Jane Pauley; Oscar-winning composer Howard Ashman; Oscar-winning screenwriters Steve Tesich and Bruce Joel Rubin; writing/directing team Angelo Pizzo and David Anspaugh; noted Jazz critic and king-pin jazz disc jockey Michael Bourne; all followed by "The Flash" aka actor John Wesley Shipp. In the pages that lie ahead, Dave has amassed an incredible number of facts as well as a wealth of anecdotes and quotations. For the first time, Indiana's contributions to the arts and to the entertainment industry are documented and preserved for generations of proud Hoosiers to come.

Who knew that at the time of the invention of motion pictures, before there was Thomas Edison, there was C. Francis Jenkins of Richmond, Indiana?

Who knew that Ma Kettle hailed from Acton, Indiana?

Who knew that Hollywood's coolest man alive in the 1950s, James Dean, first learned how to be cool in Indiana? A once-in-a-lifetime fluke, you say? Then how do you explain that Hollywood's coolest man alive during the 1960s–1970s, Steve McQueen, also came from Indiana? This tome proves it—Indiana is cool.

Living in Bloomington, I did know all about the music and legend of Hoagy Carmichael and the fact that the piano he used to compose "Stardust" at The Book Nook (later, The Gables) was still there when my friends and I dropped in for stroms and chocolate malts in the early 70s. It was only later that I learned that Indiana's having spawned one of the top music talents in history was no aberration. Indiana has also given the world Cole Porter (yes, and Michael Jackson, too!).

Hoosier influence in Hollywood spans the generations, affecting every aspect of entertainment. From vaudeville and the silent movies to rock n' roll and soap operas, Indiana's talented men and women were some of the most respected in front of and behind the camera and the microphone. Academy Award-winning Anne Baxter (who played the villainous Zelda the Great on the *Batman* television series, Academy Award-nominated Clifton ("Stars & Stripes Forever") Webb, and the immortal comedian Red Skelton were a few of the Hoosiers who conquered Hollywood in decades past, while

Brendan Fraser and Greg Kinnear are making their creative marks today. Three silver screen Tarzans (including the very first) and three of the most famous movie cowboys of all time hailed from Indiana. And some of the most important directors in film history can claim the same. It doesn't matter what part of the arts and entertainment world is your personal favorite, within these pages you'll discover how many artists and stars call our Hoosier land home. A fan of 1970s old television series will learn that Joyce DeWitt of *Three's Company* spent a significant part of her life in this state. Karl Malden may be known for *The Streets of San Francisco*, but he spent far more of his life on the streets of Indiana.

So the next time you're thinking of visiting Hollywood to search for stars, don't bother. Stay in Indiana and don't go looking any farther than your own backyard. From Richmond to Rushville, Gary to Goshen, Bloomington to Beech Grove, Muncie to Michigan City, Kokomo to Peru, Winchester to Vincennes, or Indianapolis to Evansville, for over a century it's been Hoosiers who have paved the way for Hollywood's Walk of Fame.

Michael Uslan
President, Branded Entertainment
Executive Producer of *Batman* for motion pictures and television
2005

"When I was in London, an interviewer asked me where I came from: I simply replied, 'Indiana,' and he at once said, 'Oh of course, that accounts for it.' I take delight in the fact that I was born in Indiana. So many wonderful people come from there."
—Marilyn Miller (Marilynn Reynolds of Evansville), Ziegfeld and film musical star

"You know, the funniest thing . . . I knew Cole Porter in Peru . . . he was a Peru boy too . . . but I'd been working in 'Fifty Million Frenchmen' quite a while before I realized he was the composer of the thing. Indiana's a swell place and I'm coming back some day."
—John "Ole" Olsen (Peru), vaudeville and film comedy star

"I think probably the first picture that I made where I did something that was fun for me was 'The Crowd Roars.' I'd been driving for a little while. I knew all the great drivers. We had about eight Indianapolis drivers working in the picture and we had fun all the way through it."
—Howard Hawks (Goshen), director

Grand Theater.
INDIANA HISTORICAL SOCIETY, BASS PHOTO CO.
COLLECTION, A-135

"Of course I loved Ma Kettle . . . and I always thought of Ma as a real person—that I could get in my car and go out in the country and visit. I don't think I could have ever played that part if I hadn't lived on a farm in Indiana."
—Marjorie Main (Marybelle Tomlinson of Acton), vaudeville, Broadway, and film actress

"I feel I was in a neighborhood in Indianapolis where one inevitably grew up with gangs. We would break into lock-up shops . . . that kind of thing. I mastered two skills in Indianapolis, how to steal hubcaps and shoot pool."
—Steve McQueen (Beech Grove), highest paid actor of the 1960s and 1970s

"Crosby asked me what my name was . . . I told him, and his wife Hazel recognized my name as an Indiana name. She was from Indiana too. 'My God,' she said, 'are you a Hoosier?' I admitted I was. 'I'm a Hoosier too,' she crowed. 'Nobody has to be ashamed of being a Hoosier.' 'I'm not.' I said, 'I never knew anybody who was.'"
—Kurt Vonnegut Jr. (Indianapolis), from his book Cat's Cradle.

English Hotel and Opera House.
INDIANA HISTORICAL SOCIETY, BASS PHOTO CO.
COLLECTION, A-136

A surprising number of people from the Hoosier State were important figures in the development and maturation of the motion picture industry. Their contributions began with the invention of the first motion picture projector, continued through the silent era and the advent of sound, and are an important presence in the industry today. Hoosiers have reflected a people's character, ideals, and traditions in a medium whose tremendous power has shaped American society.

Indiana, with the National Road running through its heartland, excellent rail service, and central location, became an early transportation hub. Medicine shows and circuses crisscrossed the state. By the 1800s the state was hosting numerous theatrical touring companies. The Grand Theater opened in 1875. It was built by three brothers, James, George, and John Dickson. In 1910 it was remodeled and opened as B. F. Keith's. Indianapolis businessman and politician William H. English built the English Opera House in 1880. The

Park Theater.
INDIANA HISTORICAL SOCIETY, BASS PHOTO CO.
COLLECTION, 6451

Bijou Theater.
INDIANA HISTORICAL SOCIETY, BASS PHOTO CO.
COLLECTION, 217080-F

Alhambra Theater.
INDIANA HISTORICAL SOCIETY, BASS PHOTO CO.
COLLECTION, 6079

larger was the English Opera House with a seating for two thousand and an elaborate Egyptian-style setting. The English featured such talent as Sarah Bernhardt, Oscar Wilde, Ethel Barrymore, and Otis Skinner. Theater headliner Lily Langtry appeared at the Park Theater in Indianapolis in 1883.

Hoosiers from South Bend to Evansville were exposed to the best that vaudeville and the legitimate stage had to offer. Vaudeville theaters and opera houses opened in almost every city in the state. When motion pictures arrived, Indiana embraced the new medium enthusiastically. The state's first movie theater, the Bijou, opened in Indianapolis in 1906. The Alhambra, the first theater dedicated solely to films (and the first with a balcony) opened in the capital city in 1913. In 1916 Robert and Herman Lieber, with A. L. Block, organized a group that built the Circle Theater on Monument Circle in downtown Indianapolis. It was followed by a building boom of movie theaters throughout the state.

Author Dan Wakefield noted that "Creativity sparks others' creativity and tradition begets inspiration." Indiana has produced a remarkable variety of theatrical artists, perhaps because of the diversity of its landscapes, from the hills of Brown County in the south, to the dunes on the shores of Lake Michigan in the north. From the steel factories of Gary to the remarkable "Athens of the Prairie" in Columbus, this diversity has produced artists with diverse talents. There are composers, from the sophisticated melodies and lyrics of Peru's Cole Porter to the homespun, jazzy tunes of Bloomington's Hoagy Carmichael. There are actors, from the cosmopolitan Clifton Webb of Indianapolis to Acton's raucous Marjorie Main. There are writers, from literary giants Booth Tarkington and Theodore Dreiser to the "Hoosier Poets" James Whitcomb Riley and Kin Hubbard.

In the beginning, only a comparatively few people put films together. Today, after more than a century of creative development, a wide range of creative personnel contribute to the shape of a film, and Hoosiers have made major contributions in all areas of filmmaking. Many times Hoosiers have worked together to change the face of the entertainment industry.

In 1921 the two top moneymakers on Broadway had talented Hoosiers to thank for their success. Marilyn Miller of Evansville appeared in one of her biggest hits, *Sally*. At the same time, Noble Sissle of Indianapolis cowrote and starred in *Shuffle Along*, a political satire about behind-the-scenes shenanigans in colored "Jimtown." These vastly disparate productions each featured a show-stopping song. Miller sang Jerome Kern's "Look for the Silver Lining," and Sissle wrote the lyrics for Eubie Blake's tune, "I'm Just Wild about Harry." These shows created an impact that shaped American musical comedy, especially in the movies, for decades to come. Miller starred in three early musical films, and Sissle made film history by appearing in a sound film with his partner, Blake, in 1923, four years before Al Jolson made *The Jazz Singer*.

In 1934 Howard Hawks of Goshen, Indiana, cast his second cousin, Carole Lombard of Fort Wayne, in an unusual breakthrough film, *Twentieth Century*. The film spawned "The Screwball Comedy" genre, and Hawks's mentoring of Lombard's comedy talents launched her screwball comedy career. The film, costarring John Barrymore, was based on a play by Charles Bruce Millholland of Economy, Indiana.

Robert Wise of Winchester, Indiana, was the editor of two screen masterpieces: *Citizen Kane* and Hoosier Booth Tarkington's *The Magnificent Ambersons*. Among the actors in *The Magnificent Ambersons* were Anne Baxter from Michigan City and Richard Bennett from Deacon's Mills. Wise went on to become one of the industry's greatest directors. He gave Muncie's James Edwards and Beech Grove's Steve McQueen their first roles. In 1966 he directed McQueen in *The Sand Pebbles*, which was McQueen's only Oscar-nominated role.

In this book, the reader will find these and many other stories about Hoosiers working together to advance the art of theater and motion pictures. Why did so many Hoosiers have such a great impact on the world of theater and film? Kentland's George Ade gave this clue:

Circle Theater.

> Because Indiana is not overbalanced by city population and is not cowed by arrogant wealth and has a lingering regard for the cadences of the spellbinder, an old-fashioned admiration for the dignified profession, and local pride in all styles of literary output, the Hoosier has achieved his peculiar distinction as a mixed type . . . a puzzling combination of shy provincial, unfettered democrat and Fourth of July orator. He is a student by choice, a poet by sneaking inclination and a story-teller by reason of his nativity.

And so over the years, Hoosier students, poets, and storytellers have made their way to Hollywood—the Mecca for those with stories to tell and talents to be showcased. There are so many Hoosiers who found fame in the motion picture industry, that some inevitably will be absent from this compilation. The author has done his best to uncover native Hoosiers who have contributed in some fashion to the motion picture industry, as well as those who spent much of their formative years in the state.

Due to space limitations, it was impossible to list filmographies for all of the people covered in this book. Filmographies can be found at The Internet Movie Database—www.imdb.com.

ACKNOWLEDGMENTS

This book is dedicated to several people. First, my mother who named me after a child movie star (Davey Lee) and who told me about a silent film star named Monte Blue who was raised in the Knightstown Soldiers and Sailors Home just as she was. Second, to my father whose diverse taste in movies can be discerned by his favorite actors, Charles Laughton, W. C. Fields, and Jaques Tati.

To my wife, Lucy Ann, who made it possible for me to pass English Grammar at Indiana University and a little later made it possible for me to finish this book with a modicum of grammatical errors.

To our three children—all of whom, along with my wife, share my affinity for motion pictures. Steve, who actually reads the book before he sees the movie; Dan, whose knowledge of motion picture history never ceases to amaze me. "Florence Vidor? Oh, she was King Vidor's wife, right?" And to Chris, who was a big help in my research in Los Angeles and whose favorite stars are Fred Astaire, Irene Dunne, and Lucille Ball.

And to our seven grandchildren—Amanda, Emily, Jordan, Jacob, Zachary, Justin, and Sean, who try valiantly to comprehend my fascination with yesterday's movies, while I, in turn, try to appreciate their fondness for today's movies.

Others who contributed to the making of this book include Chuck Anderson, Jim Ashton, Ross Barbour, Kelly Bergman, Tove and Richard Blue, Bonnie Britton, John and Mary Bromfield, Howard Caldwell, David Chierichetti, Minard Coons, Annie Corley, Donald Davidson, Bill and Adrienne Flower, Beth Fowler, Melissa Galt, Wes Gehring, Gloria Gresham, Dorothy West Hagemeier, Terry Harbin, James Harlan, Jackie Holl, Maria Williams Hawkins, Michael Dann Hayes, Katrina Baxter Hodiak, Barbara Blue Hoelter, Dell Jones, Bob King, Regina Kramer, Nancy Kriplen, Conrad Lane, Al Lazure, Edward A. Leary, Shelley Long, Carter Manny, Daniel Mast, R. Maturi, Elizabeth McCloud, Mike McCormick, John McElwee, George McWhorter, Kim Milanowski, Denny Miller, Betsy Neylon, Betsy Palmer, Mike Pitts, Buck Rainey, Duncan Schiedt, Robert Schreiber, Miriam Seegar, Doug Shortridge, Barbara Stodola, Larry Stout, Charles Stumpf, Jeri Taylor, Michael E. Uslan, Joseph Vance, Fred Vollrath, Robert Williams, Jo Ann Worley, Robert Young.

Organizations to which I am grateful include Academy of Motion Picture Arts and Sciences (The Margaret Herrick Library); Allen County Historical Society (Randy Elliot); Ball State University Library; Daviess County Historical Society; Garrett Historical Society; Greentown Historical Society; Indiana Historical Society (Ray Boomhower, Kathy Breen, Paula Corpuz, Rachel Popma, Susan Sutton, and David Turk); Indiana State Library; Indiana University Alumni Association (Max Skirvin); Indianapolis Star/News; Jay County Historical Society; Library of American Broadcasting (Suzanne Adamko); La Porte County Historical Society; Madison Jefferson County Library; Michigan City Historical Society; Michigan City Public Library; New Albany Floyd County Public Library (Betty C. Menges); Northern Indiana Center for History; Rushville Public Library; Simpson College and the Simpson Magazine; University of Wyoming American

Heritage Center, the Anne Baxter Collection (Leslie C. Shores and Ann M. Guzzo); Valparaiso University (Mel Doering); and Wayne County Historical Museum (Jim Harlan).

C. Francis Jenkins.

C. FRANCIS JENKINS, *RADIOMOVIES, RADIOVISION, TELEVISION* (WASHINGTON, D.C.: JENKINS LABORATORIES, 1929)

C. Francis Jenkins and his Lens—disk Radiomovies Transmitter.

C. FRANCIS JENKINS, *RADIOMOVIES, RADIOVISION, TELEVISION* (WASHINGTON, D.C.: JENKINS LABORATORIES, 1929)

C. Francis Jenkins, born just north of Dayton, Ohio, in 1868, moved to Fountain City, Indiana, when he was two years old. His father, Amasa Jenkins, opened a jewelry store in Richmond. He had one brother, Atwood. Jenkins spent his childhood days in the Wayne County area and attended Earlham College in Richmond. He left Richmond, accepting a position as a stenographer with the Treasury Department in Washington, D.C., and eventually enrolled at the Bliss School of Electricity there. While a student there in 1894, he met Thomas Armat, who was trying to perfect a device for showing motion pictures on a screen. Jenkins had been working on the same idea. His first efforts began in 1890 when he said, "I began work on mechanisms for recording and reproducing motion."

Jenkins had already obtained a patent on a camera he called "The Phantascope." He and Armat formed a partnership and began experimenting to improve the Phantascope projector, using the "beater" intermittent movement, invented by the Frenchman Georges Demeny in 1893. This movement, in which an eccentrically mounted roller pulled on the film once per turn, proved to be a quantum leap in projector design. Their first major public showing of the machine was at the Cotton States Exposition in Atlanta, Georgia, in September 1895.

The showing was not as successful as Jenkins and Armat hoped. They were trying to sell something no one knew anything about. Discouraged, Jenkins returned to Richmond to attend his brother's wedding, taking one of the three projectors they had built and some film. He made arrangements to have an exhibition in his brother's jewelry store. Unfortunately, there was no electricity in the store. The only current in reach was the trolley wire that passed by the door. He attached a wire to the trolley wire and brought it into the store. He placed his machine on the counter of the store and hung a bed sheet on the opposite wall. On Tuesday evening, October 29, 1895, the arc began to sputter and out from the wall stepped a girl who began to do the "Butterfly Dance." The dancer was Annabelle, a vaudeville favorite whom Jenkins had filmed in the backyard of his Washington boardinghouse. He paid her five dollars for the performance. Those present were witnessing one of the first moving-picture exhibitions in the world.

After the film stopped, the small group of people began to ask one another what they had seen. The original Annabelle was seen but she was certainly not present. Some went to look behind the screen to see what kind of trickery this was. However, the wall was solid. The machine was examined, but they could not understand what they had just experienced. The next day the *Richmond Telegraph* published a story with headlines, "Phantascope: A Wonderful Invention . . . Jenkins Jewelry Store the Scene of a Splendid Exhibition Last Night."

The newspaper article tried to describe how the device worked. "The strip passes before the lens at the rate of almost twenty miles an hour, giving a complete picture, with the changing expression of countenance and every movement of the figure as in life. The pictures presented upon the canvass last night at Jenkins' jewelry store were all life size, and those fortunate enough to see them were enraptured at the wonderful and beautiful effects seen. This is the invention of Mr. Jenkins, and he has a fortune in it." And so it was that Hoosiers were among the first in the nation to see moving pictures. A total of twenty or more guests witnessed the demonstration in the Jenkins and Company Jewelers storeroom. According to the *Richmond Palladium*, among those present were Demas Coe of the *Palladium*, Strick Gillilan, George Eggemeyer, Doctor J. H. Kinsey, Amasa Jenkins, and Atwood Jenkins. The reception of the invention in Richmond was much more appreciated than the demonstration in Atlanta.

This showing, however, marked the parting of the ways for Jenkins and Armat. The two fell into a dispute about each other's contributions and dissolved the partnership. Armat bought out Jenkins's interest in the invention and then sold it to Thomas Edison. Edison at this point had never projected moving pictures. His pictures could only be seen through "peep-hole machines." Edison and his people had been working on a projector but had never been able to perfect one. Edison's people urged Armat to allow Edison to take credit for the machine. "In order to secure the largest profit in the shortest time, it is necessary to attach Mr. Edison's name in some prominent capacity to this new machine." Thus Edison sold the invention as his own.

Under this arrangement, Jenkins was never fully credited with his part in the development of motion pictures, and to this day his contributions to the industry are little known. Edison changed the name of the projector to "The Vitascope" and first used it for a paying audience on April 20, 1896, at Koster and Bial's Music Hall in New York City. Jenkins had given public demonstrations of his projection machine as early as 1891. The Vitascope proved to be essentially the prototype of the modern projector. Jenkins was also instrumental in the development of television. He was able to send a crude forty-eight-line image on a six-inch square mirror from Anacosta, Virginia, to Washington, D.C., in 1925. It was a blurry picture and was a mechanical device rather than an electronic one. Nevertheless, it was a picture; no small achievement for this lone inventor from Indiana.

Jenkins began to sell television receivers in 1928. Several thousand people paid $85 to $135 for one of his sets. There was not much to see. There were no stations other than Jenkins's own experimental station W3XK in Wheaton, Maryland. Jenkins helped organize and was the first president of the Society of Motion Picture Engineers (SMPE). In 1931 it was reported he was seriously ill. His illness lingered, and he died on June 6, 1934, at the age of sixty-six. At his death he held more than four hundred patents, some seventy-two directly related to radiovision, radiomovies, and television.

Today Richmond, Indiana, boasts the best archives in the nation for this largely forgotten inventor.

BIBLIOGRAPHY

Croy, Homer. *How Motion Pictures Are Made*. New York: Harper and Brothers, 1918.

Everson, George. *The Story of Television: The Life of Philo T. Farnsworth*. New York: Arno Press, 1974.

Fielding, Raymond. *A Technological History of Motion Pictures and Television: An Anthology from the Pages of the* Journal of the Society of Motion Picture and Television Engineers. Berkeley: University of California Press, 1967.

Lewis, Tom. *Empire of the Air: The Men Who Made Radio*. New York: Burlingame Books, 1991.

Lloyd, Ann, and David Robinson, eds. *The Illustrated History of Cinema*. New York: Macmillan, 1986.

Ramsaye, Terry. *A Million and One Nights: A History of the Motion Picture*. 1926. Reprint, New York: Simon and Schuster, 1964.

Rawlence, Christopher. *The Missing Reel: The Untold Story of the Lost Inventor of Moving Pictures*. New York: Atheneum, 1990.

Richmond Item, June 7, 1934.

Richmond Palladium, June 6, 1934.

Spehr, Paul C. *The Movies Begin: Making Movies in New Jersey*. Newark, N.J.: Newark Museum, 1977.

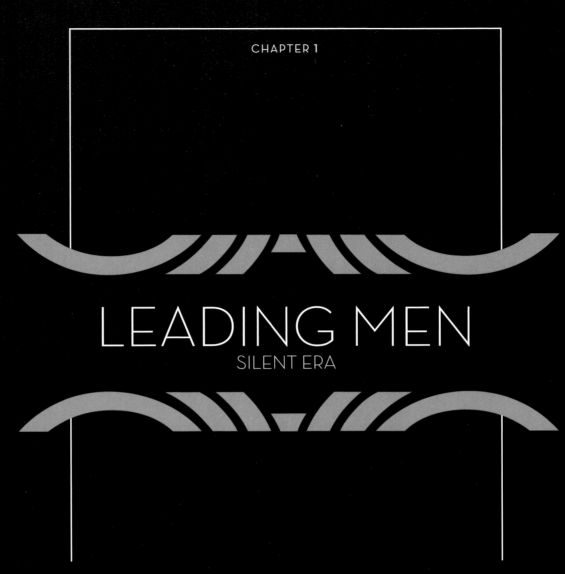

CHAPTER 1

LEADING MEN
SILENT ERA

For a number of years after that day in 1896 when Thomas Edison began showing moving pictures for profit, the industry was unorganized and the films were uninspiring. This did not stop the public from enjoying them. Just the novelty of seeing pictures move attracted huge audiences. The first films were produced in New Jersey and Chicago. It was in Chicago that J. Warren Kerrigan of New Albany, Indiana, started a film career that made him the movies' first matinee idol.

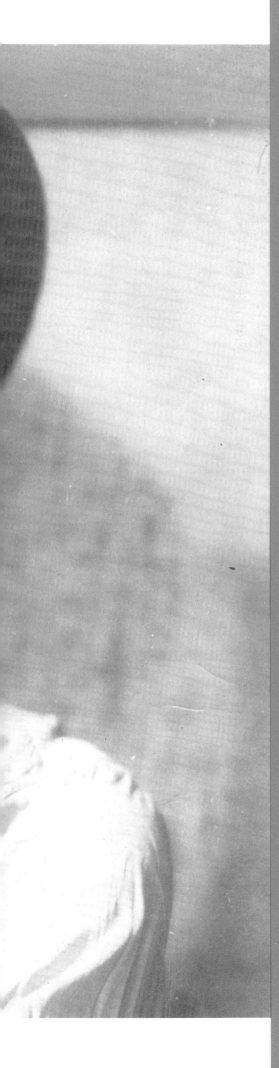

J. WARREN KERRIGAN

"The Great God Kerrigan": The First Matinee Idol

When Harold Lloyd was an extra at Universal, J. Warren Kerrigan was a star. Lloyd remembered him well. "Kerrigan was a tremendous figure in those days. He was a wonderful individual, big, handsome, had a Roman-type nose," said Lloyd. "I think he would be good today with the appearance he had. He was certainly the star of that lot." Kerrigan had many "firsts" to his credit. He could legitimately lay claim to the fact he was the movies' first matinee idol, the first Western star, and the first leading man in motion pictures who was known to be gay.

Shortly after the Civil War, John Kerrigan from Ireland married Sarah McLean from Canada and settled in Louisville, Kentucky, where six of their children were born. In 1880 the Kerrigans moved across the Ohio River to New Albany, where John had obtained a job as a clerk in a warehouse. Two years later on July 25, 1882, Sarah bore twin sons, Wallace and George Warren. George soon became known as "Jack." The twins were not identical. Wallace had red hair and Jack's hair was brown.

Jack was a fragile child. Sarah said, "For a year I carried this boy around on a pillow. He was delicate and I never knew when I might lose him." Little did she know that Jack would grow into a handsome, barrel-chested man standing more than six feet tall and weighing more than two hundred pounds. Jack became his mother's favorite, and an impenetrable bond developed between them. Death was the only thing that would separate them.

As a boy on the streets of New Albany, Jack harbored a secret ambition to become a great actor. His mother wanted him to be a minister; his father wanted him to be an accountant. An older brother thought he might make a great prize-fighter because of his physique. But Jack was delicate and imaginative and was often called a dreamer. He recalled that as a child in New Albany, "I often went into the woods and acted and declaimed to my heart's content, thinking all along what a shame it was there was no one around to appreciate my talent."

He managed to attend the University of Illinois briefly and then went back to New Albany, where he began to work as a clerk in his father's company. He said he survived the tedium by building "tunnels among the empty dry-goods boxes, where no one could find me, and there spent most of my time reading." He was determined that this foray into the business world would not deter him from achieving his goal.

Perhaps Jack's dream was fueled by the fact that his only sister had become an actress. Kathleen (her birth name was Catherine) first appeared on stage at age seventeen. She was a big hit as "Truth" in the play *Everywoman*, which was a popular stage play of that era. In 1894 she married Morton John Stevenson. In 1900 at age eighteen, Jack made his stage debut with Kathleen in *Sam Houston*, directed by actor, director, writer, and producer Clay Clement.

Clement had little faith in Jack's acting ability but gave him the part of Houston's son as a favor to Kathleen. In a week's time, J. Warren (as he was now known) was playing not only the Houston son but also doubling as an Indian chief. The play, and especially J. Warren, was a hit. By 1906 Kathleen had divorced Stevenson and married her leading man, Clay Clement. In 1906 Clement took *Sam Houston* to Broadway. It was one of three plays on Broadway in which Kathleen appeared. Her biggest Broadway success was in *Laugh, Clown Laugh*, which was a David Belasco production and opened at the Belasco Theater on November 28, 1923. Her costars were Lionel Barrymore and Vaughn De Leath. J. Warren never made it to Broadway.

Kerrigan struck out on his own before *Sam Houston* made it to Broadway. He joined the Spooner Stock Company in New York and appeared in a juvenile role in *Brown of Harvard*, which played in Louisville in 1908. The *Louisville Post* said, "Warren Kerrigan was the recipient of considerable applause from his numerous friends in the audience, and although not an experienced actor, at times forcing an effect, has an excellent stage presence and will in time develop his natural talent." He followed this play with appearances in *The Master Key* and *The Road to Yesterday*, touring with these plays in all the major cities.

While the latter play was on stage in Chicago, a representative of the Essanay Company offered him a chance to appear in motion pictures. Most respectable actors of that day did not want to associate with this new upstart medium, and Kerrigan at first scoffed at the idea, saying, "I thought it cheapened a man to be seen entering a five-cent house." However, Kerrigan's mother was frail and sick and he noted, "The principal inducement which moved me to make this decisive step was the fact that my mother was at that time in ill health, and by leaving the road for a permanent engagement in Chicago, I might be near her and personally care for her until her complete recovery."

In 1910 he joined the Essanay Company in Chicago and threw himself into the new flickers, determined to get to the top. Kerrigan, who had posed for several New York illustrators, was already known as "The Gibson Man," presumably because he was at least as handsome as Charles Dana Gibson's "Gibson Girl." He was with Essanay for one year, making several one-reelers. Two of those released in 1910 were *The Hand of Uncle Sam* and *A Voice from the Fireplace*. He turned down an offer from Selig, preferring to stay with Essanay. However, when the American Film Company (known by its nickname Flying A) made him an offer to go to California, he accepted, realizing that the weather would benefit his mother's health. For three years he played the lead in every picture released by American, at the rate of two a week.

Shortly after the move to California, Kerrigan was making enough money to bring his mother, sister, and twin brother out West to join him. Kathleen's husband, Clay Clement, died in 1910 of uremic poisoning. His brief obituary in the *New Albany Daily Ledger* stated that "Mr. Clement has often spent his summer vacation in this city where he is widely known and extremely popular." Clay Clement Jr., Kathleen's

J. Warren Kerrigan as a young man.

(Opposite page) J. Warren Kerrigan and Lois Wilson in *The Covered Wagon* (1923).

(Previous page) J. Warren Kerrigan in *Thundering Dawn* (1923).

stepson, became a well-known Broadway and motion picture actor and was a founding member of the Screen Actors Guild.

John Kerrigan, the patriarch of the family, died in New Albany in 1914. Kerrigan moved his family into what was dubbed "The Kumfy Kerrigan Cottage." The house was built by Kerrigan in the Cahuenga Pass between Hollywood and the San Fernando Valley. This situation was considered a valuable asset at the time. The Flying A executives hailed the arrangement as a symbol of homespun values.

Thanks to Kerrigan's connections, Wallace secured a job as Mary Pickford's production manager. He later worked for Universal and then became an executive with the United States Costume Company. Kathleen acted in at least seven films between 1914 and 1931 and wrote two screenplays that were made into films in 1916 and 1923.

In Santa Barbara, Flying A built screenland's first real movie studio with stages, cutting rooms, and back lots. The company also built a granite-and-glass palace largely funded by profits from Kerrigan's films. Word soon spread through the trades that Kerrigan had become so popular that he soon would appear in something other than "wild and woolley West plays."

J. Warren Kerrigan (left) and Ernest Torrance in *The Covered Wagon* (1923).

In spite of his prolific screen appearances, Kerrigan was not widely known until after a national publicity campaign. The star system was just coming into being when *Photoplay* magazine conducted a contest to see who the most popular actors were. Kerrigan won a silver cup in that 1913 contest. Since most of his one-reelers were Westerns, he could legitimately lay claim to the fact he was the movies' first cowboy matinee idol. By 1914 he was listed as one of the ten major leading men in the business. *Photoplay* dubbed him "The Great God" Kerrigan, and the name stuck. He began to distance himself from Westerns and starred in light comedies, historical parts, and drawing-room melodramas with equal success.

In June 1914 *Photoplay*'s prestigious popularity contest named him the most popular star, outdistancing his nearest rival by almost one hundred thousand votes. At the peak of his popularity Carl Laemmle enticed Kerrigan to Universal Pictures. Kerrigan said he made the move because "Universal presented possibilities in the art of production unequalled by any other company. They furnish better stories, encourage better acting and produce on a much larger scale than any other company engaged in making moving picture drama." In 1914, when he appeared in *Samson*, he was the highest-paid actor in the world and had enough clout to get his sister a part in the film and also was able to improve his brother's position in the industry. Wallace was appointed manager of the Universal Ranch. Mack V. Wright, who became a Western actor/director, was born in Princeton but grew up in New Albany. Wright looked up the Kerrigans when he went to California. He said, "Wally was in charge of the Universal ranch. [He] offered me a job on the ranch and I accepted."

Kerrigan had an almost fatal accident while filming *Samson*, during a scene in which he was supposed to slay a lion with his bare hands. He had rehearsed the scene with a big African lion a number of times and was confident that he could manage the animal. The director arranged that at the moment Kerrigan opened the lion's jaws with his hands, the camera would stop a few moments while the lion was drugged for the struggle. The animal came out snarling, and as rehearsed Kerrigan took its jaws in his hands. When the physician pricked the lion with a hypodermic needle, it quivered, roared, and sprang on Kerrigan, pinning him to the ground. As the lion raised its paw to deliver a deathblow, Kerrigan closed his eyes, but the director shot the beast through the heart while two cowboys riddled him with bullets to the head. Kerrigan was dragged from beneath the dead animal soaked with the lion's blood and his own. The incident is reminiscent of fellow Hoosier Elmo Lincoln's tussle with a lion while shooting the first *Tarzan* film. Lincoln was more fortunate as he was carrying a huge knife and managed to kill the lion himself.

With stardom, Kerrigan was inevitably put in the spotlight. In May 1914 the Motion Picture Blue Book reported, "In spite of his good looks, Warren Kerrigan does not care for girls. He is seldom seen with women. He says he loves the ladies devotedly . . . and then adds, 'when they leave me alone.'" Also in 1914 Kerrigan became the first film star to author an autobiography, dedicating the thousand copies of the book to "My Mother." Sarah was an industry fixture, the first in a long line of film-star mothers to become characters almost as well known as their children. In another era, fellow Hoosier Clifton Webb's mother became a celebrity in her own right, appearing everywhere with her son.

Sarah was the head of the house, reading her son's scripts and discussing his interpretations, his makeup, and the details of his action. Kerrigan once stated that at the end of each working day he looked forward to heading home and working in his flower garden, "where my best friend in the world . . . my dear mother . . . is waiting for me." Kerrigan's bachelorhood worked to his advantage. *Moving Picture Weekly* named him tops in its 1916 popularity poll.

In 1916 he starred in *Langdon's Legacy*, and it was the first of several films in which his costar was Lois Wilson. It also happened to be a film based on fellow Hoosier Meredith M. Nicholson's novel. Wilson had no theater experience. She found herself in the movies after winning a Universal Pictures beauty contest in her home state of Alabama. She was named "Miss Universal" and, along with Kerrigan, helped Laemmle open Universal City on March 15, 1915. Wilson thought highly of Kerrigan, saying, "At times, when I was uncertain about small bits of business, Mr. Kerrigan came to my rescue and assisted me in every possible way."

Kerrigan was now getting 100 to 150 letters a day from all over the world, and he tried to answer every one. He said, "If my friends from the screen think enough of me and my work to take the trouble to write me commending it, the very least I can do is to acknowledge their kind letter in as friendly a spirit as they showed in the first place."

Although Kerrigan was described as effeminate offscreen, he was an avid outdoorsman. He had an assortment of guns, fishing rods, and tackle. He liked nothing better than cooking his own breakfast and sleeping out under the stars. He had no qualms about shooting game with his trusty Remington and once trailed a deer for four days.

Two events virtually shattered his career. One was the fact (although not well known at that time) that his secretary, a young actor named James Vincent, was actually his lover. Vincent lived in the same house with Kerrigan, his mother, sister, and brother. Kerrigan's homosexuality was a known fact to those in the industry. Director Allen Dwan told Peter Bogdanovich of an incident while he was directing Kerrigan in an early one-reel Western, *The Poisoned Flume*. Dwan said that he and the rest

J. Warren Kerrigan in *Captain Blood* (1924).

of the crew knew Kerrigan was gay. One scene called for the villain to hold Kerrigan's head underwater, facedown in a flume. Dwan admitted to prolonging the scene to make Kerrigan stay underwater as long as possible. When he came up, spitting and coughing, the whole crew had a good laugh at the expense of the effete leading man. Later when Kerrigan became a powerful figure in the industry, he saw to it that Dwan was out of work for a considerable period of time.

The other event that led to Kerrigan's demise was World War I. When other stars were enlisting, he publicly refused, saying, "I am not going to war. I will go, of course, if my country needs me, but I think that first they should take the great mass of men who aren't good for anything else, or are only good for the lower grades of work. Actors, musicians, great writers, artists of every kind . . . isn't it a pity when people are sacrificed who are capable of such things . . . of adding to the beauty of the world?" His words were printed and circulated nationwide. *Photoplay* ran an editorial that dubbed him one of the beautiful slackers. His fans were stunned. J. Warren Kerrigan had self-destructed.

In 1917 Kerrigan formed his own company and made ten features from 1917 to 1920. They were not good films, and he was almost forgotten from 1920 to 1923. His career was revitalized in 1923 when director James Cruze was searching for a leading man for the epic six-reel western, *The Covered Wagon.* Cruze tried to get John Barrymore, but he was not available. He settled for Kerrigan, casting him opposite former leading lady and old friend Wilson. Wilson adored Kerrigan and was very close to his family. While Kerrigan was on location for *The Covered Wagon* in the Snake River valley on the borders of Utah and Nevada, Sarah died. It was a tremendous blow.

When the film was released, Kerrigan was criticized for his makeup, which made him stand out against the rough, tanned faces of the cowboys, and his tight-fitting costume that was completely wrong for his figure. Wilson was criticized for always looking so immaculate. In spite of this, *The Covered Wagon* was an unparalleled success and was considered to be almost a documentary. The sweeping scenes of the cattle drive, the endless line of covered wagons, the prairie fires, fights with Indians, and a buffalo hunt brought greatness to the film. The *New York Times* said, "And the best part about the photoplay is that it is a motion picture. Its scenes speak to you."

The Covered Wagon is a film of major importance. As the first epic Western, it acted as a powerful stimulant to the faltering Western genre and was one of the most financially successful films ever made. Later, it was mercilessly copied. The picture was a triumph for Cruze and for Western pictures, and the actors were overwhelmed by the magnitude of the film itself. However, Kerrigan's career was not restored as a result of this film.

Kerrigan had one more chance as the lead in *Captain Blood.* The year was 1924, and it was the last film for which he received credit. It was a big picture, and Kerrigan was resplendent in the swashbuckling costumes of that era, complete with long curls, moustache, and goatee. Unfortunately, Kerrigan's image on the screen was much too effete. The costumes with the lace-trimmed sleeves and the long-haired wigs did not help. Again the picture was a success, but it did not serve to rejuvenate his career. Some reports indicate he was so despondent after the loss of his mother that he no longer had the desire to be a movie star. The *Indianapolis News* in 1932 stated, "Two years ago Kerrigan returned to New Albany for a short visit. He said he was out of the movies 'because there is no demand for me.'"

However, he never lost his love for the industry entirely. Although he was financially secure, from time to time he took bit parts or even served as an extra in a movie. The last few years of his life he was in ill health. He contracted pneumonia and died at his home in Balboa Beach, California, on June 9, 1947, at the age of sixty-seven. He was survived by his twin Wallace, two other brothers, Robert and Edward, and sister Kathleen.

BIBLIOGRAPHY

Brownlow, Kevin. *The War, the West, and the Wilderness.* New York: Alfred A. Knopf, 1979.

Fenin, George N., and William K. Everson. *The Western: From Silents to Cinerama.* New York: Bonanza Books, 1962.

Garbicz, Adam, and Jacek Klinowski. *Cinema, the Magic Vehicle: A Guide to Its Achievement,* vol. 1. New York: Schocken Books, 1975.

Indianapolis News, March 1, 1932.

The Internet Broadway Database. http://www.ibdb.com/.

The Internet Movie Database. http://www.imdb.com/.

"J. Warren Kerrigan in 'Landon's Legacy.'" *Moving Picture Weekly* (January 1916).

Katchmer, George A. *Eighty Silent Screen Stars: Biographies and Filmographies of the Obscure to the Well-known.* Jefferson, N.C.: McFarland and Company, 1991.

Katz, Ephraim. *The Film Encyclopedia.* New York: Perigee Books, 1979.

Kerrigan family. 1880 U.S. Census. Floyd County, Indiana.

Louisville Post, December 19, 29, 1908.

Mann, William J. *Behind the Screen: How Gays and Lesbians Shaped Hollywood, 1910–1969.* New York: Penguin, 2001.

Menges, Betty C. Letter to the author. August 30, 2000.

New Albany Ledger, February 21, 1910, December 28, 1918, January 1, 1919.

New Albany Tribune, June 10, 1947.

1910 Index to Floyd County, Indiana Census.

Pratt, George C. *Spellbound in Darkness: A History of the Silent Film.* Greenwich, Conn.: New York Graphic Society, 1966.

Ramsaye, Terry. *A Million and One Nights.* 1926. Reprint, New York: Simon and Schuster, 1964.

"Serials, Stunts, and Six-Guns!" *Screen Thrills Illustrated* (February 1963).

The Silents Majority. http://www.silentsmajority.com/.

Slide, Anthony. *Silent Players: A Biographical and Autobiographical Study of One Hundred Silent Film Actors and Actresses.* Lexington: University Press of Kentucky, 2002.

MONTE BLUE

From Orphans' Home to International Stardom

n 1915 director D. W. Griffith finished a film that would change motion pictures forever. *The Birth of a Nation* was a turning point in motion picture history and more than one Hoosier was there, working behind the scenes as well as in front of the camera. Despite the fact the story the film was based on was nothing more than racist propaganda, it became a launching pad for bigger and better things for the industry as well as a launching pad for the film career of Hoosier Monte Blue.

In the fall of 1895 a young mother, facing financial disaster after the death of her husband, a Civil War veteran, traveled from Indianapolis to an orphans' institution in Henry County to admit the two youngest of her four sons. One of the boys, eight-year-old Gerard Montgomery Blue, spent seven years at the home and there received his first taste of what became his chosen profession: acting. During his long career as an actor, Blue appeared in approximately 250 films. From his beginnings in 1915, Blue became an internationally known silent-film star, appearing as a leading man with such notable actresses as Clara Bow and Gloria Swanson. When his stardom dimmed with the advent of talking pictures, he turned his career around and worked steadily as a character actor in both films and television. "I've lived enough lives for seven men," Blue later reflected. "I have no regrets."

Born in Indianapolis on January 11, 1887, Blue loved to sit and listen to his father, William Jackson Blue, tell stories about his experiences as a Union soldier during the Civil War, where he served four years with the Twenty-seventh, Seventieth, and Thirty-third Indiana volunteer infantries. After the war, the senior Blue worked as a scout for William F. (Buffalo Bill) Cody. Rupert Blue, former Surgeon General of the Army, and Rear Admiral Victor Blue were kinsmen. William Blue's death on January 9, 1895, from injuries he suffered during a railroad accident in Illinois left his family nearly penniless. Unable to care for her four children, Lousetta Springer Blue decided to place her two youngest boys—Monte and Morris—in the care of the Indiana Soldiers' and Sailors' Orphans Home in Knightstown.

Founded in 1865, the state-run home provided care and education to both orphaned and destitute children of Civil War Union army veterans. In the application for admission she filled out for her children, Lousetta Blue wrote, "I have no home nor income and am unable to make a living in my poor health." Morris Blue stayed at the

Monte Blue.
MGM

(Previous page) Monte Blue and Raquel
Torres and her sister in White Shadows in
the South Seas (1928).
COURTESY OF THE ACADEMY OF MOTION PICTURE ARTS
AND SCIENCES

home for seven years, leaving at the age of seventeen to find work to help support his mother. Monte remained at the Knightstown facility for a total of seven years and three months, leaving in January 1903.

Blue enjoyed life at "The Home." He and his brother played in the school band, and Monte, who eventually would reach six feet, three inches and weigh 185 pounds, played on the football team. J. B. Vandaworker, the director of the school band, took them on tours. Blue enjoyed touring with the band and the football team. Particularly memorable was a trip to a Grand Army of the Republic (GAR) national encampment in Philadelphia. Blue recalled: "We paraded down Broad Street. Our band came to a halt right in front of the stand. President William McKinley and Vice President Theodore Roosevelt were reviewing the parade. 'Teddy' came down to our Soldiers' and Sailors' Orphans Home Band and shook hands with us. I can remember him saying to us, 'Bully Boys!'"

It was at the Knightstown institution that Blue made his stage debut in a playlet, Goldilocks and the Three Bears. "I played the Mama Bear. I guess I got the part because I was so big," he said. While at the home he also "took his degree" in practical printing. When he left the home just nine days short of his sixteenth birthday, Blue found a job at the Indianapolis News, where his old mentor, J. B. Vandaworker, was director of the Newsboys' Band. Blue delivered papers, worked as a printer's devil, and played drums in the band. To further his education, he enrolled in high school night classes at Manual Training School.

Then he followed in his father's profession and worked on the railroad. Years later, when a reporter suggested that the life of an actor was a strenuous one, Blue laughed and said: "Do you know what I call hard work? Shoveling coal on a locomotive all through a winter night when it's so cold you don't dare leave the door open or the cold air would kill your fire. Open the door, throw in a shovel of coal, shut the door . . . repeat that over and over again." Blue worked for what was known as the Big Four Railroad until he was in a wreck near Ludlow Falls, Ohio, where he broke both legs, both arms, and several ribs. He spent the next eighteen months in St. Vincent Hospital in Indianapolis. He was a little more than eighteen years old when he was discharged from the hospital. "My mother, who had been opposed to the job all along, begged me to quit and I did," said Blue.

Blue then moved to Benton Harbor, Michigan, where he worked for the Baker-Vawter Steel Company for several months. He heard there were jobs in coal mining in Wilkes-Barre, Pennsylvania, and started working in a mine there. One day while working the mine, Blue and six others were caught in a cave-in and trapped for thirty-six hours in total darkness. He decided to quit coal mining and move west.

Blue's way west was filled with boxcar rides, handouts, and fights with bums. He lived in "tramp jungles" until he got to Wyoming, where he found a ranch job in Big Piney country on the Bar S Ranch. He learned to ride, but after a year he became restless and headed for Flat Head Indian country in Montana. There he punched cattle for the Flying V Ranch for one season. With two of the cowhands, he joined the Ringling Brothers Circus and got a job as a horseman with Zeller's Zouaves. In the spring of 1910 he became a clown for the circus. He eventually took off for the state of Washington, where he got work in a lumber camp north of Index, Washington. He became proficient with an ax, but working conditions were ter-

Monte Blue, Mae Murray, and an
unidentified man in a scene from
Peacock Alley (1922).

rible and he began campaigning for better conditions for lumber-
jacks. Finally, because of this activity, he was escorted out of town by
the city police.

Blue got a job on the *Henry Lindstrom*, a lumber ship sailing the
Pacific coast. Sailing was not to his liking, so he deserted in San Francisco with $18 in his pocket. He managed to hop a Southern Pacific
train and rode on top of the diner. He said he "inhaled his food
through the ventilator." In Los Angeles he got a job as a roust-a-bout
at the Whiting Mead-Wrecking Company in May 1912. A few months
later he was laid off. He walked the streets, mooching dimes and eating free lunches in cheap saloons. He slept anywhere he could. Then
one of his "bum" friends suggested he try to get a job at the motion
picture studios. They needed laborers. Blue walked the long, weary
miles from the hobo district to Hollywood. In front of the D. W.
Griffith studio he found a lot of would-be actors carrying cigar boxes
with their makeup in them, waiting for a call. Blue waited five days,
sleeping nights in a nearby eucalyptus grove and begging food from
local people. When it was announced that the studio wanted a day
laborer, the "actors" faded away. Blue walked up in his dirty clothes
and was hired. He was assigned to dig trenches and later to clear away a
grove of fig trees. Being a former axman, he had no problem clearing
the trees. He was making $1.50 a day.

Blue became involved in a "labor dispute" while working and successfully fought off three men. According to an *Indianapolis Times* article, he used a handy two-by-four. "When I finished," he said, "there was considerable wreckage strewn around, but I was intact." Director Griffith witnessed the fight and asked Blue to work on his new film, *The Absentee.* "My role was to quell a mob," Blue recalled. After that film he worked as an extra and a stuntman on Griffith's *The Birth of a Nation.* "I'd put on a blue uniform and fight with the Union army," Blue said of his experience on the film. "Then I'd change into gray and a slouch hat and move over to the Confederate trenches. They'd give me boots and a saber and I would be in the Rebel cavalry. Then another change of costume, and I'd be leading the Northern artillery to a change of position."

When Griffith finished *The Birth of a Nation* in 1915 and started on his epic *Intolerance,* Blue again became a stuntman but also was an assistant to Griffith. In his book, *Adventures with D. W. Griffith,* Karl Brown, an assistant cameraman on many Griffith films, said:

> Griffith used dozens of assistants, each in charge of a unit of this or that. Then there was Monte Blue, who stuck so close to Griffith all through the battle, because Monte gave the signals to the various unit directors scattered through the crowds. Crowds, plural, because we had one attacking crowd on the ground to storm the walls and another on the walls to defend them. Monte presented a

Monte Blue and Florence Vidor in
Main Street (1923).

very war-like appearance because he wore two heavy .45 revolvers, one on each hip, with a number of different-colored flags under one arm. The revolvers were loaded with blanks, and they were for signaling purposes only. A yellow flag meant one thing, a red one another, a green something else. Monte was a very busy man.

Intolerance marked Blue's second film and first screen credit. He was a strike leader. He also fought a hand-to-hand duel with an enemy warrior atop an eighty-five-foot wall and had to fall off the wall into a safety net. He was paid an additional $3.50 for the stunt. After *Intolerance*, Blue continued to work for Griffith in the same capacities—stuntman, errand boy, and extra. Griffith put him on a two-day guarantee, which assured him of $10 per week and then fretted because his discovery was "so damn tall." Standing 6 feet, 3 inches in the days of stationary cameras and diminutive feminine stars, Blue was somewhat of a misfit.

Due to the box office failure of *Intolerance*, there was no more work for Blue with Griffith. The experience with Griffith helped him find work as a stuntman, riding horses over cliffs, stalling cars on railroad tracks, and escaping from burning buildings. One stunt job called for Blue to do stunts for the famous magician Harry Houdini. Houdini was making a film called *The Grim Game* (1919), and Blue was to do a stunt in an airplane for him. Houdini had an aversion to planes and did not even come to the airfield when the sequence was shot. Blue said:

Monte Blue and Lillian Gish in *Orphans of the Storm* (1921).
COURTESY OF THE ACADEMY OF MOTION PICTURE ARTS AND SCIENCES

I had dressed to match his costume perfectly. The man who was to fly the plane had it rolled out in front of the corrugated hangar and was waiting. As I stepped out of the studio car the pilot yelled to me: "Come on Monte, let's go up and warm 'er up!" I ran over to the plane. But just as I was stepping into the cockpit the telephone alarm bell rang. The pilot had the engines running and was about to taxi around for the start when the man on the telephone waved to me and said: "The studio is calling you." I unbuckled my belt.

As I climbed out of the plane the pilot said, "OK I'll take her up and get her ready." I went to the telephone. Over the telephone the wardrobe man said: "I just want to check your costume again to be sure." That was done. I then went outside to find that everyone was looking up to the sky. I looked too. The pilot of that plane seemed in trouble. The plane was acting like a roller coaster . . . up, then down, getting lower all the time. Finally it skimmed over the hangar and crashed into a ditch. It burst into flames. That was the end for the plane and the pilot. I talked with Houdini afterward and he said to me: "Something told me not to get in that plane."

Three years after *The Birth of a Nation*, Blue was getting occasional supporting roles. In 1918 he appeared in ten films, including a serial, two Mary Pickford features, and two films for Cecil B. DeMille, including the famous *The Squaw Man*, first filmed by DeMille in 1914. Blue made an impression on DeMille just as he had on Griffith. DeMille used him in *Something to Think About* in 1920 and *The Affairs of Anatol* with Gloria Swanson in 1921. Finally, Griffith called Blue back to work for him in *Orphans of the Storm*, also in 1921. This film starred the famous Gish sisters—Lillian and Dorothy. Blue had worked with Lillian in *The Birth of a Nation* and *Intolerance*. He was cast as Danton, a hero in the

French Revolution, who attempts to save Lillian's character from the guillotine. Before filming began, Blue searched libraries for stories about his character's life in France. "I read every line I could find," he recalled. "I read the 'French Revolution' over and over again."

Blue's expertise with horses served him and others well during filming. In one scene an extra ran the wrong way and found herself in the wrong place as a hundred galloping horses bore down upon her. Seeing the woman collapse on the fake cobblestone street, Blue leaned out of his saddle at full gallop and plucked the woman off the ground to safety. "It was the greatest feat of horsemanship I ever expect to see," said Harry Carr, a worker on a number of silent films, who wrote about the incident in the magazine *Smart Set.*

Blue received good reviews for his work in *Orphans of the Storm* and as a result was chosen to be Mae Murray's leading man in *Peacock Alley* (1922). This film was made in New York, where Blue renewed an acquaintance with a Follies girl named Tove Danor. Danor was the daughter of a well-known Norwegian actress, and her real name was Tove Rosing Janson. Danor was also a model for Harrison Fisher's famous magazine cover drawings that appeared on the covers of *Cosmopolitan* magazine. Blue divorced his first wife, Gladys Erma Blue, in 1923. Shortly after the divorce, he married Danor. Their union produced two children, Barbara Ann, who became a nurse and did her graduate work at Methodist Hospital in Indianapolis, and Richard Monte, who became an electrical engineer. Famed cowboy Tom Mix, who had become good friends with Blue, was godfather to both children. When Mix died in 1940, Blue delivered the formal Masonic service and also served as a pallbearer along with director John Ford.

In 1923 Blue signed a contract with Warner Brothers, where he eventually became one of that company's, and one of the film industry's, most valuable stars. In the eight years he was under contract to the studio, Blue had thirty-five starring roles. He became world famous with wide-ranging roles from light comedy to a race driver to a boxer. One of his favorite roles was that of Dr. Will Kennicott in the 1923 version of Sinclair Lewis's *Main Street.* With his success, Blue tried to erase his mother's early hard life by buying her a home in Indianapolis and surrounding her with luxuries until her death in 1926.

In 1928 Blue was loaned out to MGM to do a film called *White Shadows in the South Seas.* It was to be directed by famed documentary director Robert Flaherty, but Flaherty became disenchanted with the film and W. S. Van Dyke stepped in and finished the film. Blue said of the film: "That was a black shadow certainly for me. We were on location in the South Seas when sound came in. We returned with an outdated silent film." Blue's home studio, Warner Brothers, was the developer of sound film. MGM, not to be outdone, tacked on a musical background and dubbed in one word of dialogue for Blue's character. Unfortunately, MGM hired a high-voiced actor in New Jersey to record the word. It disillusioned the public about Blue's speaking voice, and producers were leery for years about casting him in sound film.

Blue took a course in "voice culture" to prepare himself for the talkies. He then made a reel for a news service, and the technician who recorded it exclaimed, "What a voice! It's the best I've recorded in a year." Word spread, and studios were soon dickering for Blue's services. In 1929 he starred in five films for Warner Brothers and appeared in the studio's all-star variety film, *Show of Shows.* After his

Monte Blue.

(Opposite page) Monte and Tove Blue with autograph that reads: "To Jean and Dod . . . Your friendship has meant a great deal . . . Monte and Tove."

contract with Warner Brothers ran out, he took a world cruise. When he returned he found the stock market crash had taken its toll. His investments had failed, and he was broke.

Hollywood in 1932 no longer looked upon him as a star. He was forty-two years old and said, "I looked in the mirror and saw I was no Little Lord Fauntleroy. I decided to build my new career on a rock instead of sand. So I started out at the bottom as an extra. I was in the awkward stage between stardom and character parts." After a time he managed to get regular work in Westerns and serials, usually playing the villain. He worked with such Western stars as Randolph Scott, Buster Crabbe, Gene Autry, Roy Rogers, fellow Hoosier Ken Maynard, and others. His old friend Cecil B. DeMille cast him in *The Plainsman*, *Union Pacific*, and *Northwest Mounted Police*.

In 1942 Blue returned to his old studio, Warner Brothers, as a contract player. The roles were not that big, but every so often he managed to land a good one like that of the sheriff in the Bogart classic, *Key Largo* (1948). His last role of any significance was that of Geronimo in *Apache* (1954). He was happy to play an Indian, as he did many times, since he was one sixteenth Cherokee on his father's side.

Blue's wife, Tove, whom he called "Jimmy," died on March 23, 1956, in Santa Monica. She was fifty-five. He married Indiana artist Betty Jean Munson Mess in 1959. Blue was always very active in the Masons, and he, Harold Lloyd, and six other Shriners met on Lloyd's yacht and came up with the idea of a "Crippled Children's Hospital" supported by the Shriners. Blue was also active in the Elks and the Optimist International, and during his last years he did advance work for the Shrine Circus. While he was working as an advance man for the Hamid-Morton Circus in Milwaukee, he collapsed in his hotel room and died of a coronary attack complicated by influenza on February 18, 1963.

Monte and Tove's son Richard had two children, Richard and Tove Diane. Richard is a law enforcement officer with the Los Angeles Police Department, and Tove Diane has followed in the footsteps of her famous grandfather by working in the motion picture industry as a sound specialist.

Scene from *Key Largo* (1948) with (left to right) Claire Trevor, Monte Blue, Lauren Bacall, and Lionel Barrymore.

After Blue's death, his wife, Betty, moved to Seminole, Florida, where she established "The Monte Blue Memorial Foundation of Arts for the Handicapped." In 1984 she said, "People bring scrapbooks to me all the time to show me their collections on Monte. I am sorry I don't know their names, there are too many of them."

Despite some monumental setbacks, remorse was never in Blue's heart. He always considered Indianapolis his home, and his first stop when he came back to visit was the Knightstown Home. He loved to visit there and give inspirational talks to his fellow "orphans." "Of course I have memories. Wonderful memories," said Blue. "I keep them here in my heart, to feed on when the spirit begins to flag. I never discuss them with others, because they would be bored, and because it's the present that's important anyway."

Blue remained a "dyed-in-the-wool" Hoosier to the end. He said, "Oh I can stand up and sing 'California Here I Come' with a lot of gusto, but when the band plays 'Back Home Again in Indiana,' something as big as a potato gets in my throat and I can't do a thing but fight back the nostalgia that seems to take me in hand every time I hear it."

BIBLIOGRAPHY

Admittance Records. Knightstown Soldiers' and Sailors' Children's Home, 1895. Knightstown, Indiana.

Behlmer, Rudy. *W. S. Van Dyke's Journal: White Shadows in the South Seas, 1927–1928.* Lanham, Md.: Scarecrow Press, 1996.

Blue, Betty. Letter to the author. July 10, 1984. Seminole, Florida.

Blue, Tove, and Richard. Interview with the author. April 2001. Los Angeles, California.

Brown, Karl. *Adventures with D. W. Griffith.* New York: DeCapo Press, 1976.

Carr, Harry. "Untold Tales of Hollywood." *Smart Set* (March/May 1930).

Eames, John Douglas. *The MGM Story: The Complete History of Fifty Roaring Years.* New York: Crown Publishers, 1976.

Gish, Lillian. *The Movies, Mr. Griffith, and Me.* Englewood Cliffs, N.J.: Prentice-Hall, 1969.

Hoelter, Barbara. Interview with the author. March 2000. Independence, California.

The Home Journal (monthly publication of the Indiana Soldiers' and Sailors' Children's Home). (November 1941).

Indianapolis News, November 14, 1929, February 20, 1932, August 10, 1948, December 17, 1949, January 21, 1953, July 22, 1955, May 4, 1959.

Indianapolis Star, July 29, 1923, February 20, 1927, February 19, 1943.

The Internet Movie Database. http://www.imdb.com/.

Katchmer, George A. *Eighty Silent Film Stars: Biographies and Filmographies of the Obscure and the Well-Known.* Jefferson, N.C.: McFarland and Company, 1991.

"Knightstown Home Greets Monte Blue." *Public Welfare News* (March 1938).

Leibman, Roy. *From Silents to Sound: A Biographical Encyclopedia of Performers Who Made the Transition to Talking Pictures.* Jefferson, N.C.: McFarland and Company, 1998.

Pitts, Michael R. "The Career of Monte Blue." *Classic Film Collector* (1973).

Ragan, David. "The Ups and Downs of Monte Blue." *Indianapolis Star Magazine,* January 2, 1949.

Truitt, Evelyn Mack. *Who Was Who on Screen.* New York: R. R. Bowker Company, 1984.

Monte Blue near Monument Circle in Indianapolis (1950s).

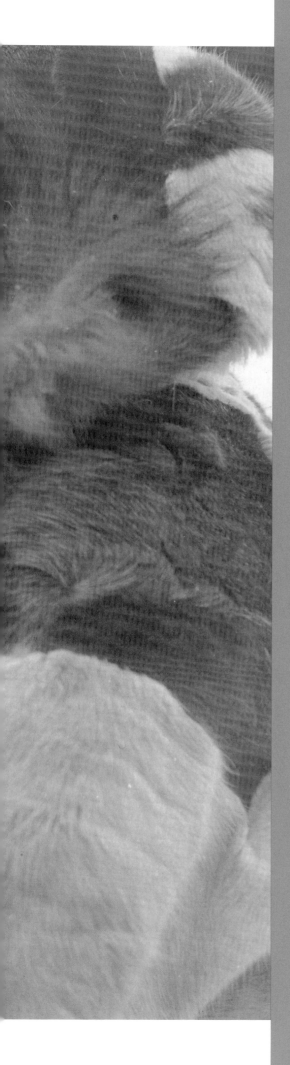

JOHN BOWERS
Stardom to Tragedy

Although it has never been officially recognized, it has long been accepted that the Norman Maine character in the 1937 film *A Star Is Born* was based on the life of John Bowers. Certainly the plot of *A Star Is Born* is filled with incidents that parallel the life and death of Bowers.

John Elehue Bowersox was born in Garrett, Indiana, on December 25, 1885. Most reports list him as being born in 1899, but the birth records in De Kalb County, Indiana, show John E. Bowersox being born fourteen years earlier than most published accounts indicate. His father, George A. Bowersox, was a railroad engineer who moved to Indiana from Ohio. His mother, Ida Bowersox, was born in Maryland. Thais Heinzerling of Garrett, who is ninety-one-years-old, was not around when Bowers was growing up in Garrett, but she remembers many things about him and his family. She thought Bowers was a very attractive man. "He looked like one of those men in an Arrow Collar ad."

After spending his boyhood in Garrett, Bowers went to Huntington, Indiana, to attend Huntington Business College. While in Huntington, he became interested in the theater and began to participate in amateur theatricals in the town. He decided to forego a business career for a life on the stage and left Huntington to join a stock company, in which he slowly gained experience and finally advanced to the lead in *The Student Prince*. Bowers appeared on the New York stage under the direction of William A. Brady, a Broadway theatrical producer who later became involved in the motion picture industry.

Under Brady's guidance, Bowers made his Broadway debut in *Little Miss Brown* at the Forty-eighth Street Theater on August 29, 1912. In 1914 he was the leading man in *Life*, which ran for 161 performances at the Manhattan Opera House. In 1916 he appeared in *Rich Man, Poor Man* again at the Forty-eighth Street Theater. It ran for forty-four performances and was his last appearance on Broadway. This same year his father, George A. Bowersox, died, and John returned to Garrett for his father's funeral.

Bowers began his career in films in an uncredited role in the 1914 Tom Mix film, *In the Days of the Thundering Herd*. (This date lends credence to the fact he was born in 1885. If he had been born in 1899, he would have been only fifteen years old at this time.) Within two years he had dropped the "ox" from his name and was the love interest opposite Mary Pickford as Allan Walton, "the handsome boarder," in the 1916 film *Hulda from Holland*.

His good looks and easy manner made him an established leading man by the early 1920s. Bowers married actress/writer Beulah Poynter during his early film career. He regularly played opposite some of Hollywood's major female stars. His most frequent costars were Pauline Frederick, Mary Miles Minter, and his second wife, Marguerite de la Motte.

Bowers was extremely busy in the late teens and early twenties, making eleven feature films in 1918 and a total of thirty-four films from 1919 to 1923. In 1919 Samuel Goldwyn announced a formation within Goldwyn Pictures of a separate unit, Eminent Authors Inc. Goldwyn hired a stable of prominent writers including Rex Beach, Mary Roberts Rinehart, and Gertrude Atherton. One of the first pictures for this new unit was *Out of the Storm*, based on Atherton's novel, *The Tower of Ivory*. Bowers played the leading man, John Ordham.

Bowers's film success enabled him to buy a yacht. His love of the sea was such that whenever he was not working, he was aboard the *Uncas*. The yacht was moored at Balboa, and Bowers loved to paint and do the necessary repairs himself. The *Uncas* was described as a "palatial yacht" with all kinds of expensive accouterments. He loved to race, and in 1919 he took the yacht to Honolulu for a race. No record can be found when he and his first wife divorced, but Rita, as he called her, was with him on the yacht in 1919.

About 1920 Bowers was driving in Hollywood and came upon a bad automobile accident. He stopped and helped get a family—mother, father, and daughter—out of the car. As they were being put into an ambulance, he asked the girl's name. "Marguerite de la Motte," someone said. "Probably a movie actress." De la Motte was just starting her film career, having made her first film two years earlier in 1918, and Bowers had never heard of her. Three days after the accident, her mother died. A few months later her father died from injuries received in the same crash. De la Motte was only eighteen at this time, and she and her brother were put under the guardianship of a manager who promptly mismanaged their money.

In 1922 Bowers was the title character in *Quincy Adams Sawyer*, which featured an all-star cast including Lon Chaney, Blanche Sweet, Louise Fazenda, and Elmo Lincoln. That same year Goldwyn began testing actors for the lead role in Hoosier Lew Wallace's *Ben-Hur*. Although Bowers and fellow Hoosier Buck Jones were tested, the part went to Ramón Novarro.

In 1923 Bowers was cast opposite de la Motte in *What a Wife Learned*. Much to his surprise, he discovered she was the one he helped rescue in the automobile accident. He also discovered that her credit was exhausted due to huge bills run up by her financial manager. Bowers took charge. He had the guardianship papers annulled, rearranged her expenditure allowance, began managing her earnings, and advised her on her motion picture contracts. Most likely he saw to it that she was in as many movies with him as possible, because they eventually made twelve films together.

In 1923 Bowers was thirty-eight and de la Motte was twenty-one. In spite of their age difference, Bowers was smitten with Midge, as he called her. Although de la Motte was not anxious to marry, Bowers pursued her relentlessly and built a three hundred-thousand-dollar home in the San Fernando valley, hoping this would convince her to

John Bowers.

(Previous page) John Bowers and Anne Cornwall in *The Heart of the Yukon* (1927).

be his wife. A movie magazine of that day headlined a story on the couple—"A Three-Hundred-Thousand-Dollar Gamble." A photo with the story shows the couple in front of a castle-like structure "looking over the plans of the new home." Finally on December 12, 1924, they were married in San Bernardino. A few years after their marriage, the couple returned to Indiana, where they were given a "great reception" at the Royal Theater in Garrett.

In 1925 Bowers was cast opposite Vincennes, Indiana, native Alice Terry in *Confessions of a Queen*. Terry had jump-started her career in 1921 opposite Rudolph Valentino in *The Four Horsemen of the Apocalypse*. *Confessions of a Queen* was directed by the greatly respected Swedish director, Victor Sjostrom. Although Bowers made seven features in 1927, the year sound was introduced, Hollywood's transition to the talkies nearly ended his career. A movie magazine article of that day stated, "Yet another old star of the silent screen is coming back in talkies, Marguerite de la Motte is the heroine of a Western called 'Shadow Ranch.' I have had no news of her husband, John Bowers, making a talkie comeback, but hear that Warner's made a test of him recently and upon that will depend his immediate future."

His future in sound films proved to be bleak. While his wife made films through 1934, Bowers appeared in just three sound films. In the 1929 film, *Say It with Songs*, he played a handsome surgeon who saves

John Bowers rescues Blanche Sweet in
Quincy Adams Sawyer (1922).
PHOTOPLAY MAGAZINE

(Top) John Bowers on his yacht *Uncas*.

(Bottom) Sheet music for a song from *The Way Out* (1918).

the life of child star Davey Lee, thereby enabling Al Jolson to get back together with his wife. In 1929 he had a minor role in *Skin Deep*. His last sound film was *Mounted Fury* (1931), a Western in which he played an alcoholic. Bowers by this time was well on his way toward becoming an alcoholic in real life. By 1932 he was forty-seven years old, there were no acting jobs for him, his beloved Midge divorced him, and he was a has-been.

Bowers had always been interested in aviation and was a good friend of Charles A. Lindbergh. Bowers and Douglas Fairbanks were both aviation enthusiasts, and Bowers's scrapbook shows several photos of Charles and Anne Morrow Lindbergh with the two actors. During his unemployment, he began to devote more time to aviation and yachting, spending an increasing amount of time on his yacht *Uncas*. Bowers invested heavily in aviation companies and suffered large financial reverses in the stock market crash. In 1934 he returned to Indiana to take care of his ailing mother. Ida was living in Syracuse, where his father had died in 1916. While living with his mother, he offered his help and knowledge to the Wawasee Yacht Club. He sailed in several races on Lake Wawasee and taught locals and visiting vacationers the art of sailboating.

He began writing short stories and several were published. In addition, Bowers wrote a highly praised serial for the *Garrett Clipper*, the newspaper of his birthplace. The first episode of this serial, entitled "Middle West," was published in the *Clipper* on March 9, 1936. The introduction read:

> Mr. Bowers was born in Garrett and lived here until he was a young man, when he joined a troupe of actors and began an acting career. He later entered moving pictures and rose rapidly in the profession. He is a member of the Bowersox family, well-known in Garrett for many years. This product of John Bowers' pen will be of particular interest to Garrett, inasmuch as many Garrett residents are mentioned in the story, and the scene is laid in this locality.

The story ran every weekday in the *Clipper* through August 17, 1936. While writing this serialized novel, he began work on a book, "The Lore of Lake Wawasee," but it was never finished.

His fellow Hoosiers were deeply impressed with Bowers. He could talk for hours about American or English literature, could speak French fluently, had a great deal of knowledge about aircraft, and liked to take apart and reinstall motors in boats, autos, and airplanes. He liked to take long walks through the Indiana countryside and continued his daily regimen of exercises every morning and afternoon, keeping his six-foot frame strong and muscular.

In 1936 Ida died, and Bowers returned to Hollywood to live with his sister, Mrs. R. W. Bonyea. He told his friends in Syracuse that he was going to attempt a screen comeback and if he was unsuccessful, he would go into aviation or sailing. He left Indiana feeling confident that he would find something to do in California, where he had once made and spent a fortune. His old friend Henry Hathaway was directing a picture on Catalina Island, and according to Hathaway, Bowers came to him and said, "I've got to have a job." Hathaway explained the company was shooting only exteriors on the island and using few actors. Then Bowers asked for a major role. "I know I could handle it," he pleaded. Hathaway told him to telephone the studio after he

John Bowers and Priscilla Dean in
The Danger Girl (1926).

returned to the mainland. Bowers told him, "This is the last time I'll ask for a job."

Hathaway invited him to have dinner with members of the company and then paid Bowers's steamer fare and gave him money for a taxi back to Hollywood. When he left the company, Bowers said, "Well, this is the last time you'll ever see me. You'll have a real life picture. I'm going to jump overboard." The next morning Bowers rented a small sailboat at Santa Monica and went out into the ocean alone. On November 17, 1936, Bowers's body was washed ashore at Malibu Beach. On November 18, 1936, *Variety*'s obituary stated, "The body of John Bowers, star of silent pictures, was washed ashore today at Malibu Beach. A deputy sheriff friend identified the body and disclosed that the actor had declared his intention to commit suicide by getting into a boat and 'sailing away into the sunset.' A man resembling Bowers rented a boat Sunday (15). It was found later empty and adrift."

The most widespread report was that Bowers ended his life by walking into the Pacific Ocean at Malibu. His suicide was reportedly witnessed by writer Adela Rogers St. Johns, who was an uncredited writer for *A Star Is Born* in 1937. Obviously no one could have witnessed Bowers's suicide since he went out alone in a boat. St. Johns mentions nothing about the incident in her autobiography. She was one of the principal writers of the screenplay for *What Price Hollywood?* in 1932, before Bowers's death. It had a similar story line but did not end with the hero drowning.

In her autobiography, Colleen Moore tells a story about her first husband, John McCormick, the movie producer. After divorcing Moore in 1930, he lived in a house next to St. Johns at Malibu Beach. One day, drunk and despondent, McCormick began swimming out to nowhere. Moore said, "Adela was in her study on the second floor and just happened to look out. She saw John and ran down to the beach calling for help. Jack [John] Gilbert, who had a house on the other side of St. Johns, ran to her, and they rowed out and pulled John in just as he was going down." Moore claimed St. Johns used this for the 1937 version of *A Star Is Born*. Moore also claimed a statement she made about McCormick inspired the line, "This is Mrs. Norman Main" at the end of *A Star Is Born*.

It is likely that the plotline of *A Star Is Born* was a composite of the lives of McCormick, John Barrymore, John Gilbert, and Bowers. All were alcoholics, but Bowers was the only one who actually committed suicide. The circumstances were changed because apparently a suicide by walking into the ocean was considered to be more dramatic than renting a boat and jumping overboard. Remakes of *A Star Is Born* in 1965 and 1976 used essentially the same plot.

Bowers was survived by his sister, Mrs. R. W. Bonyea, his brother Charles, and an aunt and cousins who lived in Syracuse and Garrett. It is sad to think that today Bowers is remembered primarily as the inspiration for a plotline that was so fascinating that it was used in three films. He is so thoroughly forgotten that most film reference books do not even list his name. Yet he was one of the most popular silent leading men of his day. He became an overnight star and then almost as quickly faded into obscurity, leading to a tragic and premature death.

John Bowers and Marguerite De La Motte.

BIBLIOGRAPHY

All Movie Guide. http://www.allmovie.com/.
Anderson Daily Bulletin, November 18, 1936.
Auburn Evening Star, November 18, 1936.
Bell, Caroline. "A Three-Hundred-Thousand-Dollar Gamble." Unidentified movie magazine in author's collection.
Brownlow, Kevin. *The Parade's Gone By.* Berkeley: University of California Press, 1968.
Garrett Clipper, March 9–August 17, 1936, November 18, 1936.
Garrett Clipper and Evening Star, October 1, 2002.
The Internet Broadway Database. http://www.ibdb.com/.
The Internet Movie Database. http://www.imdb.com/.
Katz, Ephraim. *The Film Encyclopedia.* New York: Perigee Books, 1979.
Marill, Alvin H. *Samuel Goldwyn Presents.* South Brunswick, [N.J.]: A. S. Barnes and Company, 1976.
Moore, Colleen. *Silent Star.* Garden City, N.Y.: Doubleday and Company, 1968.
1900 Census. De Kalb County, Indiana. Town of Garrett.
Parish, James Robert. *The Hollywood Death Book.* Las Vegas, Nev.: Pioneer Books, 1992.
Syracuse (Ind.) Journal, November 19, 1936.
Variety, November 18, 1936.

CHARLIE MURRAY

Slapstick with Mack Sennett

Charlie Murray.

n an interview in 1915 for a magazine titled *The Lens Squirrel*, Charlie Murray told of his beginnings.

I was born at an early age from poor but honest folks, just as the sun was casting its gleaming rays over the Whitewater Valley at Laurel, Indiana. I was pronounced a healthy, robust child, and I have proven this statement as I have been with the Keystone Company seven months and am still able to navigate. Being a good policeman [referring to his being a Keystone Cop], I have to fall for everything.

Actually, Murray was born on June 22, 1872, on a farm in the Whitewater valley between the towns of Laurel and Metamora. As a youngster, Murray had quite a reputation in Franklin County, where he was labeled as being the most mischievous youth the town of Laurel ever produced.

The Murray family lived in an old brick farmhouse "halfway up the hill on the street that leads to the Connersville Road," and Charlie fell under the spell of the footlights when he staged shows in an old barn on the farm. Charlie went to school in Laurel intermittently until he was about thirteen years old. Charlie did not like school, but he did like life on the farm in Indiana. It is said that of his four brothers and two sisters, Charlie wailed the loudest when his father, Isaac Murray, announced that he was closing the Murray store in Laurel and moving to Cincinnati.

Moving to Cincinnati did not improve Murray's school attendance, and he constantly thought up ways to skip school in order to be near the theaters. He sold newspapers, making it a point to be around the stage doors when the actors entered and left. Finally, after making himself obnoxious with his constant hanging around, he landed a job as an extra in a play at the old Haviland Theater on Central Avenue. The next thing the family knew, Murray had left town with the John Robinson circus. In the circus he was a clown, a Roman charioteer, and a trick rider. While Murray was traveling with the circus, his parents left Cincinnati and moved to Muncie, Indiana. Murray recuperated in Muncie after being injured while performing with a skating Shetland pony. The pony stepped on his chest with his skates.

After recovering from his injury, he was doing a show in Centerville, Indiana, when he met a young man named Ollie Mack (his real name was Oliver Trumball). The two formed a stage partnership, caricaturing Irishmen, calling themselves Murray and Mack. They played successfully together in a number of musical-comedy productions for more than twenty-one years. Although they met with great success as a team, they occasionally split up to take individual roles. Murray married Boa Hamilton in 1906, and they were in several dramas together. They were booked in Los Angeles in 1909 at the Belasco Theater in a production of *The College Widow* and again in Toledo, Ohio, in 1910 in a production at the Arcade Theater.

The team of Murray and Mack broke up when Murray decided to try for a film career. In 1912 a friend told Murray that he could be perfect for the movies. However, movies were looked upon as a step down from vaudeville. In an interview with the *Columbus Dispatch* in 1915, Murray said, "We were afraid acting in five-cent movies would jeopardize our engagements next season. No company would engage a man or woman who had appeared in a plebeian movie." But Murray had nothing better to do at the time, so he went down to the Biograph Studio. There were long lines of people trying to get a job, and Murray was about to leave when director Dell Henderson, an old friend, spotted him. "Hello Murray, what are you doing here?" Murray told him, and Henderson said, "You are just the man I want; make up for a jealous husband." Murray said, "Well, having played that part in real life for five years, I was exactly suited for the part." Murray received twenty-five dollars for the part.

Of film acting Murray said, "My first impression of the picture game was a picnic . . . nobody worked hard . . . we just loafed through the pictures until the director called for action and then I was on my toes with the necessary pep to enliven the scenes." Murray made five

Louise Fazenda, Harry Booker, and Charlie Murray in a Keystone Comedy in 1917.

hundred comedies known as "split reelers." It was during this time that he had a chance to work with legendary director D. W. Griffith. Unlike most directors, Griffith rehearsed everything before the cameras rolled. Even with this handicap, the split reelers were completed at the rate of several each week.

When Mack Sennett began producing his famous Keystone Cop comedies, Murray was one of the first actors whose services he obtained, becoming part of the famous chase scenes, careening around Hollywood streets in a specially built patrol car. "Fatty" Arbuckle, Chester Conklin, and Hank Mann joined Murray and other early comedians in this eight-foot-high automobile monstrosity. In short order a progression of stars—Charlie Chaplin, Marie Dressler, Gloria Swanson, and Will Rogers, to name a few—were working for Sennett. Murray costarred with Chaplin in a number of one-reel shorts. In 1914 he played a Keystone Cop in *Tillie's Punctured Romance*, the first successful feature comedy and the film that made Chaplin a star. Later Murray would say, "I never lived until I broke into the movies. For twenty years I lived out of a trunk. Now the trunk is pensioned . . . it's a great old friend and I still have it."

In his early cinema days Murray was famous for his chin whiskers and patented grimace. His most famous characterization was that of an Irishman named Kelly. But since his face was like a "map of Ireland," even when not playing that role he was invariably cast as someone named Hogan, Clancy, Riley, or McFadden. Sometimes the likable Irishman from Indiana was the star of the film; other times he was just a member of the supporting cast. Wherever he was cast, he was satisfied. The inborn desire to be an actor made Murray happy in any role he was given, and his attitude attributed to his success in the film business.

Working on the same lot with Murray was Louise Fazenda from Lafayette, Indiana. Murray and Fazenda were teamed in several of Keystone's Triangle comedies. Two of the best were *The Great Vacuum Robbery* (1915) and *Bucking Society* (1916). In the former, Edgar Kennedy and Fazenda decide to rob a bank by crawling down the hot-air channel and sucking the bank notes from the vault with a vacuum cleaner. Murray, as a detective in a female disguise, and his assistant played by Slim Summerville, chased Fazenda and Kennedy in and out of rooms, through skylights, and over rooftops until they were caught.

Everybody liked Murray. Arbuckle was especially fond of him, and somehow Murray got away with calling him, "My child, the fat." Murray was known as the "court jester" of the Keystone lot. In the slapstick days at Keystone, Murray and the other players were expected to perform any stunt that was "reasonable." Seldom were stuntmen used. Murray almost lost his hearing in a stunt that had a bomb being thrown at him. It exploded too close to him and he was rendered deaf; fortunately, his hearing gradually returned.

Murray reached his peak of popularity in the 1920s and early 1930s in a series of films about two feuding friends, "The Cohens and Kellys." Murray played Kelly, and comedian George Sidney played Cohen. These were all short films, and the characters were roughly based on the characters in the hit Broadway play, *Abie's Irish Rose.* His talking-picture debut came in 1930 with two films released just days apart: *Clancy in Wall Street* and *The Cohens and Kellys in Scotland.* In 1932 Murray and Sidney opened as the stars of *Abie's Irish Rose* at the

Charlie Murray in *Her Second Chance* (1926).

Alcazar Theater in San Francisco. Murray played Patrick Murray, and Sidney played Solomon Levy.

Their last film together was *The Cohens and Kellys in Trouble* in 1933. By that time new comedians such as the Marx Brothers, Wheeler and Woolsey, and Laurel and Hardy were coming of age and doing well in films. Murray was sixty-one years old, and he decided it was about time to retire. He had earned hundreds of thousands of dollars during his film career and, unlike some new stars, invested it wisely. He was extremely generous and contributed regularly to many down-and-out fellow troupers.

Murray visited his family and relatives in Muncie on a regular basis. His brothers, Asher and Carver, were usually in charge of the old-fashioned Murray reunion. They liked to call it "The Murrays of Muncie." Usually present were Charlie's other brothers, Bob and Ed, and a sister, Hattie Krise, who lived in Fort Thomas, Kentucky. Murray's daughter, Henrietta McQuade, who lived in Jacksonville, Florida, was frequently present with her two children.

In 1941 Murray came down with a severe cold, which developed into pneumonia. He died July 29, 1941, in Hollywood. He was sixty-nine. At his bedside was his wife, Boa, with whom he had celebrated their thirtieth wedding anniversary in May of that year. Henrietta was their only child.

BIBLIOGRAPHY

All Movie Guide. http://www.allmovie.com/.

Edmonds, Andy. *Frame-Up! The Untold Story of Roscoe "Fatty" Arbuckle.* New York: William Morrow and Company, 1991.

Indiana Biographical Dictionary: People of All Times and All Places Who Have Been Important to the History of the State. 2nd ed. 2 vols. St. Clair Shores, Mich.: Somerset Publishers, 1999.

Indianapolis News, July 30, 1941.

The Internet Movie Database. http://www.imdb.com/.

Katchmer, George A. "Everyone's Favorite Comedian." *Classic Images* 170 (August 1989).

Lahue, Kalton C. *World of Laughter: The Motion Picture Comedy Short, 1910–1930.* Norman: University of Oklahoma Press, 1966.

Liebman, Roy. *From Silents to Sound: A Biographical Encyclopedia of Performers Who Made the Transition to Talking Pictures.* Jefferson, N.C.: McFarland and Company, 1998.

New York Times, July 30, 1941.

Sennett, Mack. *King of Comedy.* Garden City, N.Y.: Mercury House, 1954.

Yallop, David A. *The Day the Laughter Stopped: The True Story of Fatty Arbuckle.* New York: St. Martin's Press, 1976.

Charlie Murray in *Down Memory Lane* (1949).

VICTOR POTEL
Slapstick and More

Victor Potel (1922).

Victor Potel along with fellow Hoosiers Louise Fazenda and Charlie Murray achieved fame in the slapstick comedies of Mack Sennett. While Murray and Fazenda are better known, Potel's career lasted more than thirty-seven years, during which he displayed an amazing versatility as a busy character actor.

Potel was born in Lafayette, Indiana, on October 12, 1889, in a little house on Ferry Street between Eighth and Ninth streets. His parents, Dr. and Mrs. Christian Potel, became alarmed at the rate of his growth as a young man. They were fearful of his health and kept him indoors most of his youth. He grew into a tall, lanky man, reaching the height of six feet and one inch. In those days this was unusually tall.

His primary education was in a Lutheran school in Lafayette, followed by enrollment at Lafayette High School. Although in high school he was remembered for his artistic talent, there was nothing to suggest at that time that he would become a rough-and-tumble slapstick comedian. His father died when he was a young man, and Potel turned to painting for a livelihood.

After two years as a painter, Potel moved to Chicago, where he was employed as an interior decorator. A little later he was offered a position at Marshall Field and Company. It was while he was working at Marshall Field that he attracted the attention of G. M. "Bronco Billy" Anderson. Anderson was about to produce a series of films for Essanay in Chicago about Hank and Lank, characters patterned after the cartoon strip, *Mutt and Jeff.* Anderson had already found his "Jeff" in the person of Augustus Carney. He was trying to find a tall, lanky actor to play Lank when he discovered Potel walking down the street. Anderson knew immediately that this was his "Mutt" character. The first film in this series was a comedy titled *A Dog on Business*, released by Essanay on September 7, 1910. The second Hank and Lank film was *Joy Riding* and was released on September 17, 1910. Nine Hank and Lank films were made (all of them split-reel films), with most of them shot in Chicago. Others were shot on the road at various locations. The films were all short and filled with good clean fun. Potel quit his job at Marshall Field and went West with Anderson and his Essanay troupe in 1910. Once Potel and Carney's box-office appeal was established, they created new characters to fit into the Snakeville comedy series that began in 1911. This series was largely based on rural humor. Snakeville was a mythical village that provided the setting for many of

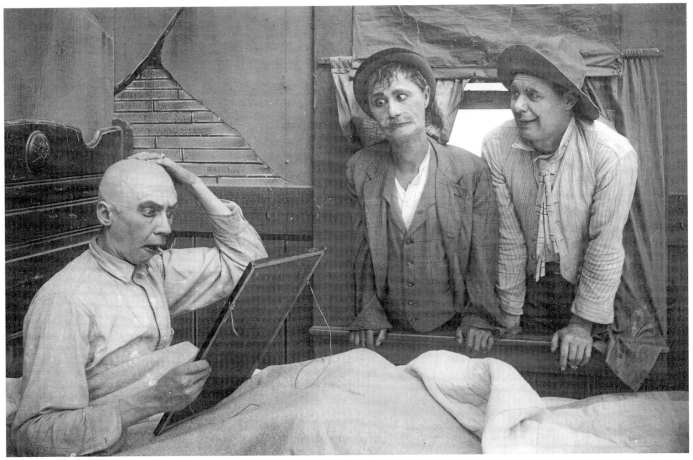

Victor Potel (left) in the "Snakeville" comedy series, circa 1914–15.

the Essanay comedies. Potel also appeared in some of Bronco Billy's Westerns while he was working on the Snakeville series.

One of the characters created in the new Snakeville series was Carney's Alkali Ike. This characterization became so popular that it led to a series of Alkali Ike films. When Carney left the Snakeville series in November 1913, Snakeville really came into its own. Potel appeared in at least ninety-three Snakeville comedies.

In 1915 the director of the Snakeville series, Roy Clements, moved to Universal. Potel left, too, joining Clements in a series at Universal that was a takeoff on the Snakeville comedies, becoming a part of what was described as "The Joyous Trio," which included Margaret Joslin as Sophie Cutts, Harry Todd as Mustang Pete, and Potel as Slippery Slim. Potel moved to Keystone in August 1916 but stayed only a short time. His *Variety* obituary claims he was a Keystone Cop, but that is not true. He worked in Sunshine Comedies for about six months, then set up his own shop, the Victor Potel Homespun Comedy Company, but found more work in features working for all the big studios—Metro, Paramount, Ince, Goldwyn, First National, and United Artists. The advent of sound did not deter Potel. He continued on the screen without a break.

His comic talents were in demand, and he found steady work, eventually appearing in more than two hundred films. He became a member of Preston Sturges's official stock company, appearing in *The Great McGinty* (1940), *Christmas in July* (1940), *The Lady Eve* (1941), *Sullivan's Travels* (1941), *The Palm Beach Story* (1942), *The Miracle of Morgan's Creek* (1944), *Hail the Conquering Hero* (1944), and *The Great Moment* (1944). He was uncredited in some of these films, while in others he had a nice supporting role. When Sturges directed his last film in 1947, Potel was in the cast. In *The Sin of Harold Diddlebock*, he was Professor Potelle, a seal trainer. Using a variation of his real name for a character he was playing was something he did on a regular basis.

He was a particular favorite with Western directors, appearing in at least thirty-six Western films over the course of his career. He played opposite such Western stars as Bronco Billy, Tom Mix, Gary Cooper, Buster Crabbe, and Ken Maynard.

One of his more memorable comic portrayals was that of Crowbar, the Indian in *The Egg and I* (1947). In it he worked with a fellow Hoosier, Marjorie Main (Acton, Indiana). After Potel's death, the Crowbar character proved to be so popular that it was continued in the *Ma and Pa Kettle* series with a variety of other actors portraying the role.

Potel returned to Lafayette in the late 1920s as a guest of his uncle, Chris Stocker, who was a retired hotel manager. While there he visited many spots where he played as a boy and renewed a number of boyhood acquaintances. Lafayette friends remembered Potel as a big, good-natured youth, always full of fun and perpetually congenial.

He died in Hollywood on March 8, 1947, at age fifty-seven, after a brief illness. He was survived by his wife, Mildred. He was busy to the end, completing five feature films in 1947.

BIBLIOGRAPHY

Banta, Ray. *Indiana's Laughmakers: The Story of Over Four Hundred Hoosiers; Actors, Cartoonists, Writers, and Others.* Indianapolis: PennUltimate Press, 1990.

Brown, Barry. "Ben Turpin." *Films in Review* (October 1977).

Indianapolis News, March 11, 1932.

Kiehn, David. *Slapstick* (June 2002).

Lahue, Kalton C. *World of Laughter: The Motion Picture Comedy Short, 1910–1930.* Norman: University of Oklahoma Press, 1966.

New York Times, March 10, 1947.

Truitt, Evelyn Mack. *Who Was Who on Screen.* New York: R. R. Bowker Company, 1984.

Twomey, Alfred E., and Arthur McClure. *The Versatiles: A Study of Supporting Character Actors and Actresses in the American Motion Picture, 1930–1955.* New York: Castle Books, 1969.

Variety, March 12, 1947.

Victor Potel (right) as Lem the stagecoach driver with Jeanette MacDonald in *The Girl of the Golden West* (1938).

TOM SANTSCHI
The Kokomo Cowboy

A young Tom Santschi.

I ndiana has provided more than its share of Western supporting players. Many of the early Western films featured Hoosier actors, and one of the earliest was Tom Santschi. Film historian William K. Everson calls Santschi "the first recognizable villain type" for his role in the 1914 version of *The Spoilers.*

Santschi was born Paul William Santschi in Kokomo, Indiana, on October 14, 1878. Many sources state that he was born in Lucerne, Switzerland, a myth promoted by Santschi himself. An article in a 1915 *Motion Picture* magazine has the heading "Paul W. Santschi." It quotes him as saying, "I was born at Lucerne, the city beautiful of the first republic of Europe."

However, the 1880 census for Elkhart County shows John and Anna Santschi living there with their three children, Augusta, William, and Bertha. John's occupation is recorded as barber. The records show William (with no mention of Paul being his first name) listed as being two years old at that time. Santschi's father is listed as being born in Switzerland and his mother in New York. All three children were born in Indiana. Exactly how the family arrived in Indiana is unknown.

Throughout his career Santschi was a very private person who did not give interviews or did not answer fan mail. He once stated that he would answer the last one if it was better than all the others. Because Santschi would not talk about himself unless it was about his role in a film, biographers and researchers have had a difficult time finding out much about his background.

Some sources state that he was taught the watchmaking trade by his father, which contradicts census records that state his father was a barber. Possibly the studio publicity department assumed that if the father came from Switzerland, he most likely would be a watchmaker. We do know that Santschi became an accomplished piano player, but he did not read music and apparently was self-taught. He had a passion for automobiles and loved to take his friends for high-speed rides, frequently reaching speeds of eighty miles per hour, which was very fast in those days. He loved to hunt. Later in life, when he could afford it, he became a big-game hunter. He was a good horseman, and this helped him land his Western movie roles.

At some point the family moved to Saint Louis. Santschi is quoted as saying that he considered Saint Louis his home. He launched his career from there, barnstorming around the country with a variety

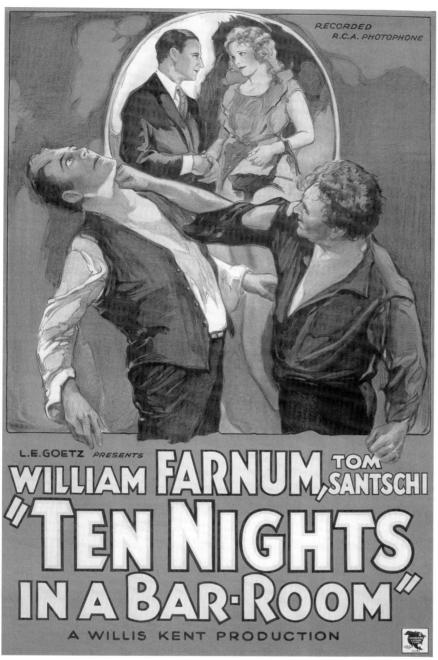

of theater companies for nearly twenty years. When times got rough, he doubled as a piano player. Although his first film appearance is a source of controversy, he was among the earliest actors on the screen. Some sources list his first film in either 1906 or 1907, when the center of the movie industry was on the East Coast. Santschi joined the Selig Polyscope Company and was one of the original group that moved to California in 1908 when Selig became the first motion picture company in that state. This was the beginning of motion pictures when pictures were measured by feet instead of time. A film one thousand feet long was considered a "special."

Probably because of his size and looks, Santschi evolved into playing mostly villains. He was more than six feet tall and weighed more than two hundred pounds. He had light-brown hair and blue eyes and developed a cold, hard stare that was extremely menacing. He became a convincing villain and is generally regarded as the first film actor to achieve notoriety as such.

Santschi's offscreen personality, however, was calm and pleasing. He was always cordial and modest but was not a "mixer." He had a few close friends and was very loyal to those he trusted. He was an intelligent actor who studied his parts intensively, practiced his athletic stunts, and always worked to stay in shape.

Santschi started in films before the star system began. In the beginning, actors' names were not listed. However, it was not long before the public demanded to know the names of their favorite performers. One of these was Kathlyn Williams. Santschi was cast opposite her in 1913 in one of the earliest film serials ever made, *The Adventures of Kathlyn*. Years later, Hoosier Carole Lombard said that her favorite actresses as a youth were serial queens Kathlyn Williams and Pearl White.

In the Selig pictures Santschi was as much an animal tamer as an actor. He and Williams had several narrow escapes while shooting scenes with wild animals. In an interview, he stated it was impossible to govern an animal entirely by kindness.

> You may have a beast ten years and be ever so kind to it. But you cannot allow it to escape punishment always. Wild animals take advantage of an easy trainer. They are like spoiled children. No man's life would be safe with them if he attempted to govern by kindness only. I am strongly against cruelty to wild animals by travelling them in boxes and keeping them cooped up in small cages, but truth compels me to say that in training animals it is impossible to be as kind as one might wish.

The film that brought Santschi the most notoriety and made him a featured player was released in 1914. It was the film version of Rex Beach's *The Spoilers*. This story became so popular that there were three remakes of it after Santschi's original version. The highlight of this film, as it was in all the remakes, was a fierce brawl between the villain (Santschi) and the hero (William Farnum). In the 1942 remake John Wayne and Randolph Scott staged the knock-down, drag-out fight. The big difference in these two films was that the Wayne-Scott fight was slickly staged, benefited from sharp editing, used breakaway furniture and innumerable doubles, and was physically an impossible battle. The Santschi-Farnum fight may have looked clumsy, but it was real.

Santschi recalled that prior to the fight scene, Farnum suggested that they make it real and not an obviously staged fight, which was common in those days. Both men were about the same size, with Santschi being a bit taller, and the fight was a classic. Costar Williams could not watch the fight because it was so brutal, and some scenes were so vicious they were edited out. Santschi reported that he took a blow to the mouth, which loosened several teeth. He fell over a typewriter, wrenched his back, and suffered several bruised ribs. One source reported that both men had to stay in a hospital several days to recuperate.

The Spoilers was a remarkable film in many ways. It ran close to ninety minutes, managed to avoid confusion despite a multiplicity of characters, created a realistic picture of a muddy, brawling, gold-mining town, and was the first Western to build deliberately to a grand-scale, hand-to-hand fight as its climax. It set a precedent for screen fights and scenario construction and today is considered one of the landmarks of screen history. It was the best film the Selig company ever produced.

Tom Santschi.

After seeing Santschi perform, it is obvious he was a natural actor. He had none of the overacting stage gestures that many of that day, including Farnum, possessed. This made him all the more real to movie audiences and all the more convincing as a cold, calculating, conniving, cigar-smoking (one of his trademarks) villain.

Santschi was multitalented. In addition to being an accomplished musician and big-game hunter, he was also a director and writer. He directed and starred in several of his own vehicles and wrote a series of two-reel Westerns for Pathe. Even though he was identified mostly as a movie bad man, he also starred in a number of films as a hero. His rugged physique was ideally suited for outdoor roles, and due to his popularity and dependability, he worked for many studios, appearing in features for Selig, Pathe, Goldwyn, First National, Universal, and Fox. In 1918 he was the leading man opposite Colleen Moore in the film version of James Whitcomb Riley's poem, "Little Orphant Annie."

Shortly before his death, he engaged in another movie brawl with Farnum in an early talkie, *Ten Nights in a Bar-Room* (1931). He died in Hollywood on April 9, 1931, at age fifty-three from high blood pressure. He was truly one of the industry's early pioneers, appearing in more than 275 silent films, many of which were one- and two-reelers.

BIBLIOGRAPHY

All Movie Guide. http://www.allmovie.com/.

1880 Census. Elkhart County, Indiana.

Everson, William K. *The Bad Guys: A Pictorial History of the Movie Villain.* New York: Citadel Press, 1964.

———. *A Pictorial History of the Western.* Secaucus, N.J.: Citadel Press, 1969.

"The Expressions of Tom Santschi: Hero of Wild Animal and Western Films." *Picture Show Magazine* (August 13, 1921).

Franklin, Joe. *Classics of the Silent Screen: A Pictorial Treasury.* New York: Citadel Press, 1972.

Indiana Biographical Dictionary: People of All Times and All Places Who Have Been Important to the History of the State. 2nd ed. 2 vols. St. Clair Shores, Mich.: Somerset Publishers, 1999.

The Internet Movie Database. http://www.imdb.com/.

Katchmer, George A. "One of the Best: Tom Santschi." *Classic Images* 70 (July 1980).

Liebman, Roy. *From Silents to Sound: A Biographical Encyclopedia of Performers Who Made the Transition to Talking Pictures.* Jefferson, N.C.: McFarland and Company, 1998.

McClure, Arthur F., and Ken D. Jones. *Western Films: Heroes, Heavies, and Sagebrush of the "B" Genre.* New York: A. S. Barnes, 1972.

Ramsaye, Terry. *A Million and One Nights.* 1926. Reprint, New York: Simon and Schuster, 1964.

Roat, Albert L. "Paul W. Santschi." *Motion Picture* (November 1915).

Spears, Jack. *Hollywood: The Golden Era.* South Brunswick, N.J.: A. S. Barnes and Company, 1971.

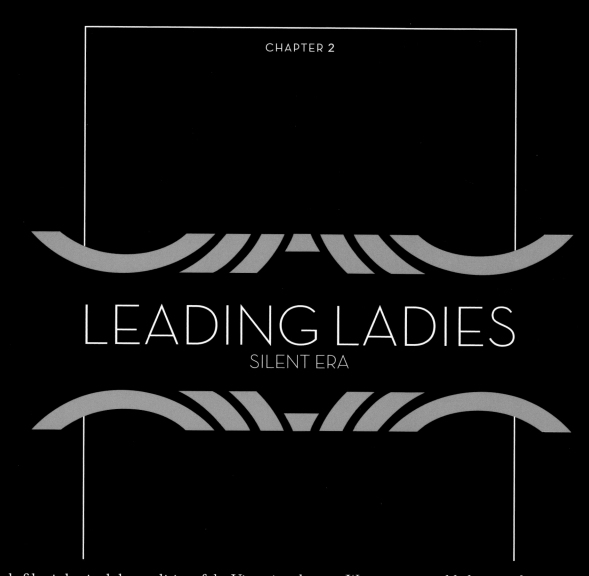

CHAPTER 2

LEADING LADIES
SILENT ERA

Early film inherited the qualities of the Victorian theater. Women were noble beings whom men were expected to place on pedestals. It was the function of the hero to save the heroine from a fate worse than death. Most of the early silent stars from Indiana fell into that category. Alice Terry, Julanne Johnston, and Ann Christy were all as pure as the driven snow.

However, when a little known actress named Theodosia Goodman became Theda Bara, the era of the erotically destructive woman began. They were called Vamps after the famous Sir Philip Burne-Jones's painting, *The Vampire*. Rudyard Kipling's poem, published the same year the painting went on view, was entitled *The Vampire*. Bara's first film in 1914 was *A Fool There Was*, and it was a smash hit. Terre Haute's Valeska Suratt, already a stage star, was called to Hollywood to become the second best-known movie Vamp.

When Hollywood found that women could be funny as well as pristine and erotic, Louise Fazenda of Lafayette and Fort Wayne's Carole Lombard became an integral part of the rough and tumble slapstick shorts churned out by Mack Sennett.

Shortly after the turn of the century, Indiana's earliest female star emerged. Edna Goodrich started her theatrical career long before motion pictures as a popular medium were introduced.

EDNA GOODRICH

Floradora Girl to Goldwyn Girl

Edna Goodrich in *American Maid* (1917).
CULVER SERVICE

I n 1900 the first theatrical sensation of the new century was the British musical comedy *Floradora.* It was the story of a young woman seeking romance and restoration of a stolen inheritance. Its sextet of chorines became the rage of London and New York. Edna Goodrich was one of the ladies of this chorus. When they sang "Tell Me Pretty Maiden" ("Are there any more at home like you?"), audiences were entranced.

Goodrich was born in Logansport, Indiana, on December 22, 1883. Her father, A. S. Stephens, was a coffee merchant in Logansport. Goodrich decided she wanted to be an actress and went on stage while still in her teens. In 1901 she was performing in New York in the chorus of *Floradora* when America's leading architect and the designer of Madison Square Garden, Stanford White, caught the show. White built a magnificent rooftop apartment with spectacular gardens, which his wife never visited, and threw many parties and entertained many chorus girls there.

With Goodrich in the Floradora girl lineup was sixteen-year-old Evelyn Nesbit. White immediately took notice of Nesbit and asked Goodrich, who was already acquainted with White, to bring Nesbit and meet him in his tower apartment for lunch. Nesbit's mother balked, but Goodrich convinced her that White was a gentleman and that he could be very good for her daughter's career. Nesbit and Goodrich dined with White and another man in the tower. After the meal, White gave the girls a tour of the studio, which contained multiple rooms and floors and displayed valuable paintings and gorgeous lighting. On the second floor there was a huge room filled with White's sketches, drawings, and paintings, and hanging in the center of the room was a plush red-velvet swing.

White invited Nesbit to swing. She hopped on the seat and swung as high as she could, laughing brightly. White persistently pursued Nesbit, and when he offered to pay for her dental work, her mother once again was reluctant to accept. However, after meeting him, she finally agreed. Eventually, Nesbit became White's mistress, staying with him until Harry K. Thaw came into her life. Against everyone's advice, she married Thaw, and the final result was murder. Thaw killed White on June 25, 1906, ending a series of events set in motion by Goodrich convincing Nesbit to lunch with White.

In 1908 Goodrich married fellow actor Nat C. Goodwin but divorced him two years later. In 1913 she came to Indianapolis as the star of *Evangeline*, a play based on the Henry Wadsworth Longfellow poem. The general manager of the production was Tarkington Baker, formerly the dramatic editor of the *Indianapolis News*, and his assistant Theodore Vonnegut, both Indianapolis natives.

While performing in London in 1914, Goodrich was spotted by Samuel Goldwyn, who at that time was working for Jesse Lasky and was constantly on the lookout for talent. Goldwyn described Goodrich as follows: "Miss Goodrich had three assets at this time. She was beautiful; she had created a sensation on the London stage, and she had recently joined the recession of wives of the late Nat Goodwin." Goldwyn signed Goodrich to a contract, and she made her first picture in 1915, *Armstrong's Wife*. Her costar was Thomas Meighan. She was paid five thousand dollars with the understanding that if the film was successful, the Lasky Company would have the first option on her second film.

Cecil B. DeMille was assigned to work with Goodrich in another 1915 film called *The Golden Chance*, which was to star Wallace Reid. However, after working with her briefly, he wired Goldwyn, "Goodrich too cold." Goldwyn said that time "refused to thaw her," and he came to the conclusion that some actresses who are magnificent on stage simply do not come across on camera. As a result, Goodrich's movie career was brief. She made a total of eleven films from 1915 to 1918. One of her last films was *Her Husband's Honor* in 1918, which was based on a story by Maibelle Heikes Justice, who must have known Goodrich because she was also from Logansport.

In 1916 Goodrich made *The House of Lies*, directed by William Desmond Taylor. Six years later Taylor was murdered, a crime that remains unsolved to this day. Thus, Goodrich had connections to two of the most notorious crimes of the century. She died on May 26, 1971, in New York City at the age of eighty-eight.

BIBLIOGRAPHY

Goldwyn, Samuel. *Behind the Screen.* New York: George H. Doran Company, 1923.

Higham, Charles. *Cecil B. DeMille.* New York: Charles Scribner's Sons, 1973.

Indianapolis News, September 27, 1913.

Indianapolis Star, September 7, 1913.

The Internet Movie Database. http://www.imdb.com/.

Vazzana, Eugene Michael. *Silent Film Necrology: Births and Deaths of Over Nine Thousand Performers, Directors, Producers, and Other Filmmakers of the Silent Era.* Jefferson, N.C.: McFarland and Company.

Edna Goodrich.
THE OLIVER MOROSCO PHOTOPLAY

VALESKA SURATT

A Vamp to Rival Theda Bara

In the early 1900s, Valeska Suratt's frequent visits to her parents' home at 1634 N. Ninth Street in Terre Haute, Indiana, brought hordes of curiosity seekers hoping to catch a glimpse of the famous New York stage and vaudeville star. Suratt had purchased the home for her parents from the wealth she had earned in the entertainment world. She had a vibrant singing voice to complement her skills as an actress and was a headliner for American vaudeville founder Benjamin F. Keith. She was known as the "Original Gibson Girl," "The Belle of Broadway," and "Vaudeville's Dynamic Force." With this kind of fame and talent, her entry into motion pictures was only a matter of time.

Suratt was born on June 28, 1882, in Owensville, Indiana, one of five children born to Ralph, a blacksmith, and Anna Suratt. At age four, she moved with her parents to Terre Haute. She sang in the choir at the Central Presbyterian Church and as a teenager worked for the Albert LeClear Photography Studio. Later, she and her sister, Leah, opened a hat shop in the Hotel Deming in Terre Haute. At age eighteen she got a job in the millinery department at the William H. Block department store in Indianapolis, earning five dollars a week. She was always interested in theater, and one of the first items she bought with her own money was a ninety-eight-cent poster of Ziegfield star Anna Held.

Wanting a career on stage, she left Indianapolis for Chicago and moved in with a girlfriend. One evening they attended a party at the Wellington Hotel, where she met Grand Duke Boris of Russia, who invited her to lunch the next day. During the luncheon he asked, "What is it that you would rather do than anything else in the world? Is there anything you want very much?" She did not hesitate, "Yes, I want to go on the stage." The grand duke immediately wrote her a check for ten thousand dollars and handed it to her. He saw her home and then disappeared from her life forever.

This unlikely story was published in *Photoplay* magazine. Another version of Suratt's sudden wealth involved a lottery ticket. Supposedly Leah bought a twenty-five-cent ticket in a Honduras lottery and won one thousand dollars. Valeska borrowed from her sister's winnings and took off for New York City. Neither story may be true, but the fact is she left Terre Haute in early 1904 to go to Chicago to study music and voice culture. While there she met comic Billy Gould, who had just lost his partner and was looking for a new one. Suratt had no experience, but Gould saw potential in the handsome, lithe brunette who could wear clothes as though they were part of her. Gould began coaching her and developed a wisecracking act with the two of them in evening dress. The act, which included exotic dancing by Suratt and an apache dance by the couple, was a hit, and Suratt and Gould were soon married. In 1905 the *Terre Haute Star* reported that Suratt and Gould went to South Africa, where they were a hit on stage. After their South African tour, they went to London.

Eventually they made their way back to the United States and wound up in New York City. On December 3, 1906, Suratt appeared on Broadway in *The Belle of Mayfair* opposite Jack Gardner. Suratt no longer needed Gould, and they split in 1908. Suratt formed her own company and embarked on a solo vaudeville career in an act called "The Belle of the Boulevards," in which she sang, danced, and displayed her figure in a variety of stunning costumes. By 1909 she was advertising herself as "Vaudeville's Greatest Star" and "The Biggest Drawing Card in New York."

Sime Silverman wrote in *Variety* (November 20, 1909), "In the show world Valeska Suratt occupies a little niche all to herself. There is no one who can look as Miss Suratt does when costumed as only she can dress." In 1910 she starred in her own thirty-three-minute minirevue at Hammerstein's Victoria Theater entitled *Bouffe Variety*. Her leading man was Fletcher Norton, who later became her husband. They did a comedy routine, "When Broadway Was a Pasture." The show closed with her as a bride. The success of her revue convinced Suratt that she could leave vaudeville, and from that time on, her chief claim to fame was as a sultry and exotic leading lady in a series of melodramas. On April 25, 1910, she opened on Broadway in an original play entitled *The Girl with the Whooping Cough*. She returned to musicals in *The Red Rose*, which opened on Broadway on June 22, 1911.

In 1913 she starred in *Black Crepe and Diamonds*. *Picture World* magazine stated that forty thousand dollars were in hanging pieces and costumes alone for this vehicle. During the production she became friends with two performers who were a brother-sister act, Jesse and Blanche Lasky. In 1910 Blanche married Samuel Goldfish (later changed to Goldwyn), who was entering the motion picture business. He asked Jesse to join him. The Jesse L. Lasky Feature Play Company made its first movie, *The Squaw Man*, in California with Cecil B. DeMille directing. Shortly after the film premiered, Lasky asked Suratt to join him in the film business. However, she did not want to give up vaudeville and turned him down.

Lasky continued to pursue her. Finally she relented and signed a contract with Lasky giving him exclusive rights to her acting services from November 1, 1914, through November 30, 1916. She insisted that the contract allow her to select all her own costumes, as well as those of her supporting players. She went to Los Angeles to make her first film for Lasky and Goldfish. In *The Immigrant*, released in 1915, Suratt played a comely Russian girl defiled by a depraved contractor. It received rave reviews.

Fort Lee, New Jersey, was the movie capital of the country at this time and was the site for the 1915 Fox film, *A Fool There Was*, starring Theda Bara as a conscienceless hussy. Bara at the time was an obscure extra; however, with the release of the film, she became an overnight celebrity. The term "vamp" originated from a painting entitled *The Vampire*, which inspired Rudyard Kipling to write a poem with the same

Valeska Suratt.

(*Previous page*) Valeska Suratt.

title. Hollywood borrowed the opening line of the poem "A Fool There Was" and created the term vamp to apply to a woman who uses her charm to seduce and exploit men. Fox thought Suratt would make a perfect vamp and lured her away from Lasky's Paramount studios with a big contract.

Suratt's debut film for Fox was *The Soul of Broadway*, which even integrated part of her vaudeville act. The film was a triumph and added to the national "vamp craze." From 1915 to 1917 Suratt had top billing in a series of similar films, usually wearing outlandish costumes and pictured in elaborately designed futuristic sets. The titles of her films clearly indicated their appeal: *Jealousy*, *The Victim*, *A Rich Man's Plaything*, *She*, *The Siren*, *The Slave*, *The Straight Way*, *Wife Number Two*, and *The New York Peacock*. At the time, she was known as "the only great vaudevillian who has gone into the movies." *New York Peacock*, released in 1917, was her last film. The vamp craze was ending and by 1919 even Bara's career faded. Suratt's film career had ended as suddenly as it had begun, and she decided to return to her first love, the stage. She married Norton, and they put together several minirevues for Hammerstein's. Their production of *The Purple Lady* was the first full-length play ever to appear in a New York vaudeville house.

Valeska Suratt.

After the play folded, she approached showman Eddie Darling with an idea for a dramatic sketch. "I'm calling it 'The Purple Poppy,'" she said. "You see, I'm identified with the color purple." Much against Darling's objections, she opened her tour in the Middle West. Suratt was right, and the play was successful. Although the color purple became permanently identified with her, she did not relegate herself to just one color. One of her most successful stage appearances was in the title role of *Scarlett*, which had an extended engagement at the Palace Theater in New York, playing a cabaret singer loved by a Society type. She also appeared in a sketch called *Jade*. It was a story about a girl who, finding a piece of jade, must give herself to its masculine owner.

Suratt reached the peak of her career in 1920 when, as "The Dynamic Force of Vaudeville," she headlined at the Palace. *Variety* said, "There are two wonders in vaudeville. They are Eva Tanguay and Valeska Suratt." *Variety* went on to say that Suratt "wore her clothes as a flower its petals." Her costumes and hats were regularly shipped to Terre Haute by the trunkload. The four upstairs bedrooms of her parents' house and a big attic were used for Suratt's "storage." She continued to headline in vaudeville through most of the 1920s. She appeared in an original musical revue, *Spice of 1922*, on Broadway and shattered Al Jolson's crowd record at the Winter Garden in New York in *Spice* in 1924. She again triumphed at the Winter Garden in 1929 in *The Frolics of 1929*.

She donated liberally to charities. Her favorite was the Red Cross, and she sent at least five hundred dollars weekly to the organization throughout World War I. She lived in an apartment in New York that was described by an interviewer in 1916 as follows: "We sat in her gorgeous sitting room flanked by Egyptian Placques of white and gold and crimson, sphinxes of marble, and a great bronze Bubastic sitting on her haunches, between royal figures in basalt of Ises and Osiris that were dim and impending against the dark lavender hangings which warm and soften her walls in the winter time." She loved to entertain and "likes to have everyone she can think of to dinner every night." She also financially supported some of her sisters' children.

Suratt became a student of the Bible and in 1927 collaborated with Mirza Ahmad Schrab, an Arabic scholar, to write a screenplay that she called *Mary Magdalene*. She gave it to fellow Hoosier Will Hays, who gave it to DeMille for evaluation. When DeMille's *The King of Kings* was released, she recognized some of the scenes as being from her script, and she sued DeMille for one million dollars. When the plagiarism case came to court, Hays and Suratt were witnesses. Hays stated that it was piracy and that "this is the greatest outrage ever done to a woman." A professor of literature from Columbia University confirmed the fact that original material from Suratt's script appeared in the film.

The judge examined the script written by DeMille's scenarist, Jeannie MacPherson, and stated that "only 11 incidents of similar scenarios" were in the movie. DeMille issued a statement to the press that read, "I have always been under the impression that Matthew, Mark, Luke and John were the first to write the story of Jesus Christ. If Mirza Ahmad Schrab was its author, and pre-dates them, the record will have to be changed." The case was thrown out of court. Suratt was emotionally drained by the litigation, and some said that show business forces blacklisted her after this case. At any rate, vaudeville was fading fast, and Suratt's career had come to an end.

Suratt disappeared from public view for years. When she resurfaced, her fortune was gone, and she was living as a recluse and religious zealot in a small New York hotel. Author Fannie Hurst sponsored a benefit for her, but Suratt soon frittered away the proceeds. The Hearst Publishing Syndicate asked for her biography, but when it was submitted, the publisher dismissed it saying, "Valeska thought she was the mother of God." In early 1961 she was discovered living in a Washington, D.C., nursing home, where she died on July 2, 1962. She is buried next to her mother and sister in Terre Haute's Highland Lawn Cemetery.

BIBLIOGRAPHY

Bacon, George Vaux. "Valeska Suratt of Terre Haute." *Photoplay* (March 1916).

Blum, Daniel C. *A Pictorial History of the American Theater, 1960–1985.* New York: Crown Publishers, 1986.

Card, James. *The Seductive Cinema: The Art of Silent Film.* New York: Alfred A. Knopf, 1994.

Gilbert, Douglas. *American Vaudeville: Its Life and Times.* 1940. Reprint, New York: Dover Publications, 1968.

Higham, Charles. *Cecil B. DeMille.* New York: Charles Scribner's Sons, 1973.

The Internet Broadway Database. http://www.ibdb.com/.

The Internet Movie Database. http://www.imdb.com/.

"Lasky Secures Valeska Suratt." *Picture World* (November 21, 1914).

Slide, Anthony. *The Vaudevillians: A Dictionary of Vaudeville Performers.* Westport, Conn.: Arlington House, 1981.

Terre Haute Star, February 12, 1905.

Terre Haute Tribune-Star, November 5, 12, 19, 1995.

Vazzana, Michael Eugene. *Silent Film Necrology: Births and Deaths of Over Nine Thousand Performers, Directors, Producers, and Other Filmmakers of the Silent Era.* Jefferson, N.C.: McFarland and Company, 1995.

ROSE MELVILLE
"Sis Hopkins"

From 1891 to 1918 a minister's daughter from Terre Haute, Indiana, was responsible for creating and perpetuating a stage character that became a national sensation. Rose Melville was the daughter of Jacob and Carolyn Smock. After Jacob and Carolyn married in 1841, they went to work helping Jacob's father, William, on his farm in Raccoon Township in Parke County. By 1857 they had accumulated substantial real estate holdings and decided to go into Baptist missionary work.

The Smocks moved to Terre Haute, where Jacob became the pastor of the Missionary Baptist Church. Eventually the couple had six children, the last of which was Rosa, born January 30, 1873, when Jacob was forty-nine years old. Six years after Rosa's birth, Carolyn died. Since his two sons had already left home, Jacob and his four daughters moved into the St. Clair House, a hotel at 202 Wabash Avenue.

In 1881 Jacob married Dinah Wilson and moved the family to 403 Willow Street. The girls all were infatuated with the theater, and Josephine (who began using Pearl Melville as her stage name) was the first to join a touring theater group. Maud and Ida soon followed. By 1886 the three sisters had formed the Melville Sisters Stock Company. When Josephine married actor Walter Baldwin, the company became the Walter Baldwin Stock Company.

While her sisters were on the road, Rosa attended school at St. Mary-of-the-Woods and later, Franklin College. In the summer of 1889 she visited her sisters on tour in Zanesville, Ohio, and replaced an ill male actor. She immediately became "stage-struck" and decided to pursue a career in the theater. She did not reenroll at Franklin and went on the road, playing sixteen different characters over the next two years.

In 1891 Rosa (who now began calling herself "Rose") and Ida left the stock company to strike out on their own. Ida married Samuel Y. Young, an aspiring playwright. Young wrote a play, *Zeb*, for his new wife and her sister. It was about an unpolished Appalachian hillbilly girl named "Sis Hopkins." The play became very popular and led to an appearance at New York's Garden Theater for $150 a week. The sisters were billed as "The Two Jays from Indiana" and were now Broadway stars. "Siseretta Hopkins" became larger than the play that created her. The character established a new theater genre associated with rural Appalachian comedy as much as the Hatfields, McCoys, and Li'l Abner.

THE
FOOLISH BOOK
A MAGAZINE OF WIT AND HUMOR
EDITED BY
"SIS HOPKINS"

Vol. III, No. 18.   Nov., 1904

PUBLISHED MONTHLY
At 35 West 21st Street, New York

Grant E. Hamilton ⎰ Publishers for
W. J. Merrill   ⎱ Arkell Co.

(MISS ROSE MELVILLE)

TITLE REGISTERED AS A TRADE-MARK

Price 10 cents
Subscription, $1.00 per year

Entered as second-class matter, May 1, 1903, at the
Post-office at New York (N. Y.), under the
Act of Congress of March 3, 1879.

Copyright, 1904, by Arkell Co.

ROSE MELVILLE IN HER CHARACTER "SIS HOPKINS"

After Jacob died in 1895, Ida quit the play and sold all rights to the characters to Rose, who had already taken on the major role. Sis Hopkins was becoming an institution and was featured in several other plays with Rose always appearing as Sis, a naïve young girl who was the subject of romantic pursuits and youthful fantasies. Sis's lament, "There ain't no sense in doin' nuthin' for nobody that won't do nuthin' for you!" became a national mania. Rose became so associated with the role that audiences refused to accept others in the lead role. Rose returned to Terre Haute in 1900 and again in 1905, portraying Sis Hopkins. On her last visit, she complained the role was "getting stale," but audiences were still enchanted by the character.

On June 12, 1910, Rose married Frank Minzey. Minzey wrote a song, "Siseretta," which made the best-seller lists. A *Sis Hopkins* magazine was published regularly, encompassing more than eighty issues. The Minzeys moved to Lake George, New York, but Rose could not escape Sis Hopkins. Rose made at least nineteen films, portraying Sis Hopkins in all of them. These were shorts turned out by Biograph, Keystone, Fox, and Goldwyn studios. In 1916 she made a feature-length silent film as Sis in *She Came, She Saw, She Conquered.*

After at least five thousand performances in which she appeared before five million spectators, Rose retired in 1918, having sustained her popularity past her forty-third birthday. The next year Hollywood made a Sis Hopkins movie with Mabel Normand in the title role. Another screenplay was produced in 1941 starring Judy Canova as Sis. Costarring with Canova was Indiana native Charles Butterworth.

Rose died on October 8, 1946, at the Minzey estate named Highwood, overlooking Lake George. Rose's nephew, Walter Baldwin Jr., became a noted character actor, appearing on Broadway and in more than forty motion pictures.

BIBLIOGRAPHY

Terre Haute Tribune-Star, March 9, 1997, March 12, 1999.

Truitt, Evelyn Mack. *Who Was Who on Screen.* New York: R. R. Bowker Company, 1984.

Vazzana, Eugene Michael. *Silent Film Necrology: Births and Deaths of Over Nine Thousand Performers, Directors, Producers, and Other Filmmakers of the Silent Era.* Jefferson, N.C.: McFarland and Company, 1995.

(Opposite page) Rose Melville as her character "Sis Hopkins."
COURTESY OF MIKE MCCORMICK

ALICE TERRY

From Vincennes to Valentino

Alice Terry never liked making movies; it was a chore to be completed as quickly as possible in order to enjoy the excitement of living. At the height of her fame, a year or two after her marriage to director Rex Ingram, she said she was always anxious to find an excuse to take a break from filming. She told *Photoplay* in September 1923, "I am content when leaving the studios to lock Alice Terry in the dressing room and become Mrs. Rex Ingram."

She was born Alice Frances Taaffe on July 24, 1899, on a farm on the outskirts of Vincennes, Indiana. Her father, Martin Taaffe, was a farmer from County Kildare, Ireland. Her mother, Ella Thorn, had French blood. Alice was the youngest of three children. The others were Edna, who was to be a close companion to her in later years, and a brother. Shortly after her birth, the family moved into Vincennes, residing in a cottage that formerly stood at the corner of Seventh and Perry streets south of the Hall Brothers Grocery store.

The family moved to Los Angeles in 1905, when Alice was five years old. Her father was killed in an accident, and her mother, left with three children and a small income, returned to Vincennes. When Alice was about fifteen, the family went back to California, settling in Venice. While she was in high school, the family moved to Santa Monica, where she completed high school. Enid Markey, who was the first Jane to Hoosier Elmo Lincoln's Tarzan, lived in the same building as the Taaffe family and convinced Alice to try for a job at Thomas Ince's studio, Inceville.

She was successful in obtaining bit parts but said, "I felt so small and miserable, always looking over stars' shoulders so that the camera would pick me up and the company would get its seven-dollars-and-fifty-cents worth of me every day, that I gave it up and went into the cutting-room at Lasky's." She stayed in film editing for two years, but the work began to get on her nerves and she decided to be an extra again. Although she got small parts, she had no confidence at all in her acting ability. Charlotte Arthur, a fellow extra, recalled some years later, "Alice Terry, with whom we at once made friends, whose name was Taaffe in those days and whom everyone called Taffy. She was very poor and very Irish and very simple and nice . . . and very plump . . . and nobody thought she had a chance. She couldn't act. Well . . . Rex Ingram taught her how to do that."

In 1916 she was in *Not My Sister*, and *Photoplay* (September 1916) wrote, "She is an added starter and looks very promising." However, film work was never anything very important in her life. Her friend Claire Du Brey got both of them positions in the Universal stock company starting at twenty-five dollars a week, but Alice stayed at Ince because she liked a boy there.

In 1917 Reginald Ingram Montgomery Hitchcock, a budding director who changed his name to Rex Ingram, selected Alice for a bit part. Alice recalled how it all began. "One day when I was feeling completely cowed and unusually wretched, Mr. Ingram walked across the lot, turned his head, straightened out his eyebrows, and looked right through me. I thought he was going to have me arrested for trespassing. But he didn't. He gave me a part!"

Shortly thereafter, Ingram left to join the Royal Flying Corps in Canada. When he returned in 1918, he called Alice one day to pose for a sculpture. Ingram had attended art school in Ireland, where he was born, and was an accomplished sculptor. Later when Ingram was hired by Metro, he helped Alice get a bit part in the film he was directing. Unfortunately, Ingram was rather harsh with Alice, and she walked off the set crying. The next morning he called and apologized, telling her he had another part for her.

He began to realize she had talent, and she knew he was an exceptional director. He offered her the lead in his film *Hearts Are Trumps*. She turned it down saying, "I can't. I haven't had enough experience in the playing of important roles like that." Ingram replied, "You're the right type, and you can leave the acting instructions to me." Finally she consented. It was at this point he suggested her name be changed to Alice Terry.

Terry recalled another important change for her at about this same time.

Alice Terry.

(Previous page) Alice Terry and Rudolph Valentino in *The Four Horsemen of the Apocalypse* (1921).

COURTESY OF THE ACADEMY OF MOTION PICTURE ARTS AND SCIENCES

> I was putting make-up on one day and there was a blonde wig and I put it on and it looked so silly. Just then Rex came in and said, "Leave that on," and I thought, "Oh no, I can't do that part," but I kept it on. And it felt so silly. We didn't see the rushes for about three days as we were on location. We went into the projection room and I had a terrible headache and I had been taken out of pictures before so I wasn't too confident about myself. When I appeared on the screen I looked so different and from that time on I never got rid of the wig. I was stuck with it. I didn't feel like myself and my freckles didn't seem to show. My skin looked whiter and there was a different person there. If I ever had to rehearse I always put the wig on or I couldn't do it.

Thus began a lifelong relationship of trust and respect. Ingram respected not only Terry's acting, but he was also very open to her suggestions regarding both direction and business. He said, "If Alice had been married to someone else when I met her, I think I would promptly have engaged her as my business manager."

The year 1921 was a fortuitous one because Ingram cast Terry with a little-known leading man named Rudolph Valentino in *The Four Horsemen of the Apocalypse.* Of her coupling with Valentino, Terry said, "Valentino and I had worked together on many a set for $7.50 a day, and Valentino was playing small parts. I couldn't imagine why Rex should wish to gamble so recklessly with two unknown extra people, although none of us knew at that time that 'The Four Horsemen,' far from the story angle alone, was to prove so popular with the public." Ingram again made her a blonde stating, "This time she had to wear the blonde wig for contrast. She played opposite Rudolph Valentino, and as a balance for his Latin swarthiness, she had to be blonde." The film solidified Ingram as a major director and rocketed both Terry and Valentino to stardom. The film was released in December 1919. The *Los Angeles Times* said, "Alice Terry is emotionally triumphant in her role." The film got rave reviews.

While attending the New York release of *The Four Horsemen of the Apocalypse*, it suddenly dawned on Ingram just how miserable he was without Terry by his side. He said, "I called her up on the telephone right away. And from 3,000 miles away I asked her to marry me!" They were married in an adobe mission in Pasadena on Saturday, November 5, 1921. On Monday morning they went right back to work on *The Prisoner of Zenda.* By this time Terry was known as a golden-haired beauty, and she appeared in a blonde wig for most of her movie career. An article in *Photoplay* magazine in 1926 provides an insight into Terry's image and personality. The interviewer states:

> Her coloring was exquisite, and of the Dresden-doll, pink-and-white tonality. Her dancing blue eyes and the mobile corners of her small, sensitive mouth indicated the presence of a bubbling sense of humor. Her voice, almost contralto, made her pronounced Middle-Western accent seem smooth and melodious.

Some of Terry's friends speculated that she may not have pursued her career had it not been for Ingram. She was described as "a most capable housewife who did not allow her career to interfere with her domestic chores." She was certainly not consumed with a burning ambition to get to the top and stay there at all costs. She and Ingram were best friends. She was his favorite actress, and he was her favorite director. She seemed to be at her best under his guidance. The two worked side by side, with Terry offering advice and assistance on his movies. It was apparent she was more than an actress to him. Ingram said of her, "I know that if I ask her advice on matters artistic or pertaining to business, I will get counsel as mature and as valuable as an expert could give. Alice has keen eyes and a keen mind. She observes things closely and stores them away in her head."

In 1921 *The Conquering Power* was released with Terry in the title role and Valentino as her cousin, Charles. She received the only star billing above the title. This was the last film in which Valentino and Terry were to star together. Ingram became disenchanted with Valentino and decided to promote another actor's career. Ingram directed two features with Ramón Novarro as Terry's leading man. Both were released in 1923. *Where the Pavement Ends* and *Scaramouche* were popular hits, and Novarro became a star.

In 1924 Terry and Ingram settled on the French Riviera. Ingram was tired of the Hollywood studio system and longed for a studio of his own. He acquired the Victorine Studios in Nice and went to work on his first film with his own company. Being from Ireland, Ingram was more comfortable living in Europe. Terry, the shy little girl from Indiana, stayed at her husband's side far away from the land she had known as home. The first Ingram film shot in Europe was *The Arab,* starring Terry and Novarro. It was the first time she did not wear a blonde wig. To many fans she looked like a blonde Alice masquerad-

Alice Terry and Rex Ingram.

ing as someone else. *The Arab* was not a huge success.

In 1925 Terry returned to the states to make four pictures, working for the first time in four years with a director other than her husband. She made two films at Paramount with director Henry King, *Any Woman* and *Sackcloth and Scarlet.* She then made two at MGM. Reginald Barker directed *The Great Divide*, and Victor Sjostrom directed *Confessions of a Queen.* In the latter film, fellow Hoosier John Bowers was Prince Alexei to her Queen Frederika. Terry was back in Europe under Ingram's direction for two 1926 features—*Mare Nostrum* and *The Magician. Motion Picture World* (February 27, 1926) reviewed *Mare Nostrum* and said, "Alice Terry, always beautiful, never looked more stunning than as Freya, and superbly handles this role." Later Terry would say, "I feel that 'Mare Nostrum' was the only film I ever did really. I will never get another part like that, I will never like a part better and I will never have the luck I had on that."

In 1927 Terry again returned to the states to make *Lovers?*, which reunited her with Novarro. It was directed by John M. Stahl. Then she returned to Europe to make her last screen appearance in *The Garden of Allah*, playing Domini to Ivan Petrovich's Boris. Sadly, her final screen appearance was not well received. She seemed content to retire from screen acting without a murmur of protest or regret. The Ingrams continued to live in Europe, with Rex concentrating on painting and sculpture. In 1931 he directed *Baroud*, a tale of Arab life and love, for which he had a particular fascination. Several years earlier he and Terry had adopted an Arab boy, Kada-Abd-el-Kader.

Ingram not only directed *Baroud* but also starred in it. Terry worked as his codirector on the production. This was not the first time she served in this capacity. Many times in the past she had taken over the

Alice Terry and Henry Kolker in *Any Woman* (1925).

direction of a film when Ingram became upset or discouraged. *Baroud* was released in the United States in 1933 as *Love in Morocco.* It did not receive good reviews. It was evident the coming of sound did not suit either of them.

The years spent in Nice were "heady" days for Ingram, but by 1934 the couple was living in Cairo. However, Terry soon moved to California, while Ingram wandered around in North Africa for two years, writing his first novel. He returned to the states before the outbreak of World War II, but his precious collection of art was left in Cairo and could not be retrieved until after the war. He took an extended trip to Cairo in 1947 and regained his treasures but returned to California in ill health.

The Ingrams lived in North Hollywood with Terry's sister, Edna, and her husband. In 1950 Ingram entered a hospital to have some tests and X-rays. He asked her to pick him up the next day and told her to pick out something for her birthday. However, by the time she arrived home, the hospital called to say he was unconscious. Terry was at Ingram's bedside when he died on July 22, 1950. Terry never made another film, and she lived in seclusion with her sister in the house that she and Ingram bought in the 1930s. She entered the spotlight briefly in 1951 when she instigated a lawsuit over the film *Valentino.* She sued for $270,000 in damages from Edward Small of Small Productions and Columbia Studios for portraying her as having had a clandestine relationship with Valentino both before and after her marriage. The case was settled in her favor, and she accepted a substantial out-of-court settlement. She died on December 22, 1987, thirty-seven years after she lost her beloved husband.

Alice Terry.

BIBLIOGRAPHY

"Alice Terry No Longer a Blonde." *Movie Weekly* (May 3, 1924).

Bodeen, DeWitt. "Rex Ingram and Alice Terry, Part 2." *Films in Review* (March 1975).

"The Life Story of Alice Terry." *Movie Weekly* (June 6, 1925).

Lussier, Tim. "The Lifelong Love Affair of Reginald Hitchcock and Alice Taaffe." 1999. Silents Are Golden. http://www.silentsaregolden.com/articlesessays.html.

O'Leary, Liam. *Rex Ingram, Master of the Silent Cinema.* [London?]: British Film Institute, 1993.

Robinson, Selma. "Alice Terry as Seen through the Eyes of Her Director/Husband." *Picturegoer Magazine* (1924).

Slide, Anthony. *The Idols of Silence.* South Brunswick, N.J.: A. S. Barnes and Company, 1976.

———. *Silent Players: A Biographical and Autobiographical Study of One Hundred Silent Film Actors and Actresses.* Lexington: University Press of Kentucky, 2002.

"You Never Know Your Luck." *Photoplay* (January 1926).

"What Do They Earn Today?" *Photoplay* (September 1923).

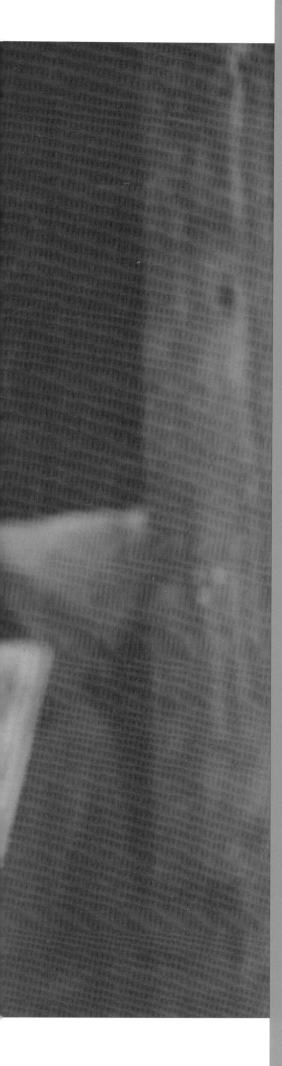

LOUISE FAZENDA

Mack Sennett Clown to Character Actress

Louise Marie Fazenda traveled a long way from Indiana to glamorous Tinseltown, yet she never tried to completely brush all the hay out of her hair. In an interview for the *Indianapolis Star Magazine* in 1939 she said, "I'm a Tippecanoe County farm girl, and proud of it. My parents took me off to California when I was a mighty small fry, but I'm still a Hoosier. I still have relatives living in Lafayette. Wish I had time to visit them." During her film career, Fazenda did visit her Schilling relatives in West Lafayette and made a personal appearance at the old Family Theater, which later became the Mars Theater.

Fazenda was born on the old Schilling farm near Lafayette on June 17, 1896, the daughter of Jose Altamar and F. Nelda Schilling Fazenda. Nelda, whose family was of Dutch ancestry, was a native of Chicago who moved to California as a young girl. Jose was born in Mexico and was of mixed Italian, French, and Portuguese heritage. Nelda was thirty-nine years old when she became pregnant, and Louise was to be an only child. During her pregnancy Nelda and her new husband decided to visit her brother at the Schilling homestead, and Louise was born there. The Fazendas stayed in Lafayette for three years, until Jose heard about oil being discovered in Los Angeles. He thought he might find work as a cooper building oil tankers.

The Fazendas moved to the Mexican section of Los Angeles when Louise was three years old. Her father did not find work as a cooper and decided to follow the family tradition by opening a grocery store. Louise worked in the store after school and during vacations. The family attended all denominations of churches when Louise was young, and as a result Louise had a lifelong interest in religion. Her family attended Baptist, Presbyterian, Catholic, Episcopalian, and occasionally Buddhist places of worship. Jose had been a Buddhist. Later he became very involved in the Unity faith and was very active in the Unity Church in the San Fernando Valley.

Louise graduated from Los Angeles High School in 1913. She then briefly attended St. Mary's Convent in Los Angeles. Louise said, "We were a typical Edna Ferber family. I was with older people all of the time. After school I hitched up an old horse and delivered the groceries. In films I later portrayed many of the types who came into Dad's store." Louise was always a strong girl. Her father reared her as he would rear a boy. She learned to ride a horse expertly, had no fear of the wilderness, and slept in the mountains wrapped in a blanket.

Louise Fazenda and Victor Potel (Lafayette) in *Quincy Adams Sawyer* (1922).

(Previous page) Louise Fazenda looking at a World War I German hand grenade.

Louise Fazenda and the Louise Fazenda doll.

She could broil trout over a campfire and could throw a diamond hitch over a packsaddle.

When she was about fourteen a friend, Pearl Elmore, a character actress, urged her to try her luck in the movies and offered to introduce her to Charles Farney at Universal. Fazenda thought she would like to earn some Christmas money, so she went to Farney. He hired her to play an Indian squaw in *A Romance of the Utah Pioneers.*

Although she never got before the camera all day, she was paid two dollars at the end of the day and decided then that movies would be her career. In 1914 and 1915 she was trained in the art of comedy by Max Asher, producer of Universal's Joker Comedies. When nothing else was available, she did stunt work, mastering a three-story leap without nets. Recalling her stunt work she said, "My first close call was a fire scene. I was doubling for the star and appeared at the 2nd story window of a burning hotel screaming and jumping up and down. I did it so well the flames burned the hair on one side of my head and part of my dress. As I leapt from the window, the straw they had used to start the fire caught on my foot and I became a fiery broomstick as I sailed down into the dirt."

Comic great Ford Sterling saw her stunt work and arranged an interview with Mack Sennett. She became affiliated with Sennett's Keystone Studio beginning in 1915. Her first assignment was frolicking on the beach as a Sennett "Bathing Beauty." She made remarkable progress at Sennett. In 1917 *Motion Picture* magazine called her the "star comedienne of Mack Sennett's aggregation, and perhaps the most popular 'slap-stick' actress in Hollywood." Years later Fazenda would recall, "In those days, a picture was not written . . . it started with some girls gathered around a policeman then someone socked him, then everyone ran, and, from there on, nature and the camera took their course."

Fazenda had the gift of grimace and a good sense of pantomime. She was also able to withstand the rough-and-tumble of slapstick comedy. The studio people soon realized that Fazenda could ride, swim, and shoot, and, in addition, she was fearless. In 1915 when Mabel Normand, the reigning comedy queen at Keystone, started fussing with Sennett about making classier films he replied, "I'll send for Fazenda." Like Normand, Fazenda was able to develop a depth of character in her portrayals that brought them warmth—a quality that usually was not present in cold-water seltzer slapstick.

Her appearance on-screen belied her good looks. She wore ridiculous costumes, covered her face with pancake makeup, and pulled her hair back tight with pigtails sticking out in several places. Sennett maintained that Fazenda could get a laugh just by making an appearance. Sometimes known as "The Judy Canova of her day," Fazenda's early image was that of a rowdy country bumpkin. Film critic James Agee said of her, "the perennial farmer's daughter and the perfect low-comedy housemaid, primping her spit-curl; and how her hair tightened a good-looking face into the incarnation of rampant gullibility." As the years progressed, her range broadened, and she appeared in leading as well as character roles. In private life, however, she was a cultured and beautiful woman.

In 1915 Sennett was shooting *A Game Old Knight* with Charlie Murray from Laurel, Indiana, and Polly Moran. Moran became ill, and the desperate studio asked Fazenda to step into the part. The two Hoosiers

Louise Fazenda as the spinster in *A Sailor's Sweetheart* (1927).

hit it off so well that the studio decided to use them again. Fazenda and Murray became a team and appeared together in several two-reel comedies, such as *Bombs!*, *The Judge*, *His Precious Life*, and *Maggie's First False Step*. Fazenda gave memorable portrayals in these shorts as the quintessential country bumpkin, wearing a calico dress, with a lone spit curl bouncing in the middle of her forehead and four tight pigtails flapping in the breeze. Sennett later had her trademark pigtails insured for ten thousand dollars.

In addition to Murray, Fazenda appeared with several other leading Keystone comics, including Mack Swain, Chester Conklin, Ford Sterling, and Roscoe "Fatty" Arbuckle. In 1917 she married film director Noel Mason Smith. They were separated six years later, and in 1926 she obtained a divorce on grounds of desertion. In 1920 she left Keystone Comedies to start her own production company. When she could not obtain financial backing, she went into vaudeville, touring in 1921 and 1922.

When she returned to Hollywood, she generally played comedy caricatures such as gawky girls, country spinsters, and once, a lady blacksmith, giving each of these portrayals her own comic twist. No one could do it better. Fazenda regularly received letters from women who felt a kinship to her. She said, "There are girls who can't imagine themselves in Norma Talmadge's place, she is so beautiful, but when they see things turning out well for me on the screen, it cheers them up, for they can visualize themselves in my place."

One of Fazenda's funniest films was *A Pest in the Storm Country*. It was showing in the Tower Theater in Los Angeles, where Hal B. Wallis was the manager. He ran the film five straight weeks, not so much because the public wanted it, but because the girl fascinated him. Two years later he met her and a romance blossomed.

In 1927 she was making a speech before the National Press Club in Washington, D.C., and closed her talk with this statement: "In fact, I have such a big appreciation of newspapermen that I think I'll marry one when I get back to California." The six thousand people in the Press Club audience as well as those in the radio audience did not realize she was saying "yes" to a proposal of marriage by Wallis, who had been a California newspaperman and was then a studio publicity agent. Louis Ludlow, former representative from Indiana, was president of the Press Club at that time and said later, "Miss Fazenda put over a scoop right under our eyes and ears."

Fazenda first met Wallis when she was making *The Lighthouse by the Sea*, which starred Rin Tin Tin. Wallis was a publicist for the studio. In the early 1920s Fazenda's parents moved to Hollywood. Her father had already retired when she and Wallis became a twosome. Wallis stated that they did not like the idea of Fazenda, an established star, going with a struggling young publicist. Fortunately Fazenda did not see it that way, and she and Wallis were married in 1925 in Fazenda's home, where they took up residence. At that time Wallis could not afford to buy a house. Fazenda's father passed away before the wedding took place.

As Wallis became more and more successful as a producer, he and Fazenda bought some land in the San Fernando Valley so they could be closer to the studio. They built an English-style down-home American farm and built a small cottage for Fazenda's mother on the property. They planted orchards of walnut and apricot trees and bought more and more land. Wallis stated that they built their fortune together, developing and increasing their incomes by putting the land to use, growing quality produce.

Fazenda and Wallis longed for a child, but it seemed not to be. Several years before her marriage to Wallis, Fazenda was playing an especially rough scene in a slapstick comedy when another actor pulled a chair from beneath her just as she was about to sit down. She went down hard and was carried from the studio in pain. A doctor examined her and told her she would recover but it was doubtful she could ever become a mother. After a recuperation period, she went back to work a much sadder clown than before.

Fazenda said, "I prayed for a baby. It was the one request I wanted to have granted more than anything else in the world. After I married Hal, I hoped more than ever; but time went on and I thought of it only occasionally. Then came my trip to Quebec, and my visit to this marvelous old church." She was speaking of the shrine of St. Anne de Beaupre in Quebec. "It was just about twilight, and a dead hush spread over everything. I felt that I was alone with God; alone to pour out the hunger of my starved soul, in the quiet beauty of that little old chapel," Fazenda recalled. A short time later she became pregnant with her son, Brent. He was the couple's only child.

Marriage did not derail Fazenda's career. She continued making films to the end of the silent era, including a reunion with her old Hoosier screen beau, Murray, with whom she made two features, *Vamping Venus* (1928) and *Noah's Ark* (1929). The latter was an epic directed by the great Michael Curtiz. In 1928 she costarred with W. C. Fields in a remake of *Tillie's Punctured Romance*, playing Tillie.

Louise Fazenda.

She became so concerned about the appearance required for her comedy roles that when she came home from the studio wearing her costume and makeup, she would sneak in a side door and change before Wallis could see her. She said, "I'm just an old fashioned wife with modern ideas, like an old fashioned house with modern plumbing . . . comfortable but convenient." She was an excellent cook and often prepared dishes for her friends and neighbors. Besides cooking, she enjoyed writing poetry and collecting antiques. She was also quite a businesswoman and loved to build and sell houses, and she hired and supervised the workmen. She also designed houses, including a duplex that she and Wallis lived in for several years.

Although Fazenda had no trouble making the transition to sound, she was making fewer pictures by its advent. She had a well-modulated voice and delighted her faithful audiences with sound films such as *The Show of Shows* (1929), *The Cuban Love Song* (1931), *Alice in Wonderland* (1933), and *Wonder Bar* (1934). She appeared in several musicals, including *No, No, Nanette*, *Viennese Nights*, and *Rain or Shine* with another fellow Hoosier, Joe Cook. Her husband was with Warner Brothers, which also happened to be Fazenda's home studio. Wallis produced many classic films such as *Dark Victory, The Adventures of Robin Hood, Yankee Doodle Dandy*, and *Casablanca*. He was nominated eleven times for an Academy Award, winning for *Casablanca*. He also produced six films in which his wife appeared.

Fazenda's last film was *The Old Maid*, released in 1939 and starring Bette Davis and Miriam Hopkins. She left the screen with no regrets,

Louise Fazenda and Nat Pendleton in *Swing Your Lady* (1938).

remarking that she preferred the spontaneity and camaraderie of the early Hollywood years. In a letter in 1979, her son Brent said, "The film colony made her nervous in later years. She spoke frequently about how much fun the early days of the film industry were. It became less personal." After her retirement she was always reluctant to talk about her screen career. When the *Indianapolis Star* interviewed her in 1949 she said she was willing to talk about anything but that.

Fazenda apparently was not entirely happy being a comic. In a *Photoplay* magazine article in 1931 she said she wanted to play a serious role, which she did in a film entitled *The Mad Parade.* Her fear in taking on dramatic roles was that people would laugh when they saw her come on the screen. Those fears, however, were unfounded, and she demonstrated her versatility in both comedies and dramas in the later years of her career.

In the mid-1950s the Hollywood Chamber of Commerce installed a "Walk of Fame," honoring those artists who helped create the aura that made the city world famous. The first eight stars were dedicated in September 1958 and placed in the sidewalk on the northwest corner of Hollywood Boulevard and Highland Avenue. Fazenda was included in that first series of eight stars. Just four years after she witnessed her star being put in the "Walk of Fame," she died in Beverly Hills on April 17, 1962, of a cerebral hemorrhage. She and Wallis had been married thirty-four years. In 1966 Wallis married actress Martha Hyer. He died on October 5, 1986, at age ninety-seven.

Fazenda never forgot her roots as witnessed by the fact that she and Wallis managed an active farm for a number of years on their San Fernando Valley property. Living on the farm, she frequently said that it "was the life she was meant for." She was living proof of the old adage, "You can take the girl out of the country, but you can't take the country out of the girl." This self-described "Tippecanoe County farm girl" brought delight to the world with her warm and humorous portrayals on the silver screen.

In retirement Fazenda was an astute businesswoman who managed her large properties and amassed a collection of paintings and sculptures that would have made a museum envious. She also gave to many charities and became somewhat of a social activist. During World War II she helped bring Jewish refugees to a safe haven in Baja, California. At her funeral, Rabbi Morton Bauman said of her, "She was not one who knew only the flippancies of life but one who knew life in all dimensions." She also helped more than a half dozen families financially, most of whom were her relatives. "They're Fazendas," she explained.

Wallis said this of her in his autobiography: "Louise Fazenda is not forgotten. Her gift of laughter endeared her to a generation of filmgoers. Her caring ways left a legacy of devoted friends. This warmhearted, generous woman gave so much of herself to the crippled children at UCLA hospital that a memorial fund has been set up in her name. I cherish her memory."

BIBLIOGRAPHY

Agee, James. *Agee on Film.* 2 vols. New York: McDowell, Obolensky, 1958.

Carlisle, Helen. "Duckling or Swan? What Has the Change Meant to Louise Fazenda?" *Movie Weekly* (September 27, 1924).

Indiana Biographical Dictionary: People of All Times and All Places Who Have Been Important to the History of the State. 2nd ed. 2 vols. St. Clair Shores, Mich.: Somerset Publishers, 1999.

Indianapolis News, April 12, 1932.

The Internet Movie Database. http://www.imdb.com/.

Lang, Harry, and Jeanne North. "She Wants to Thrill Us to Laughter! Tears!" *Photoplay* (1931).

Liebman, Roy. *From Silents to Sound: A Biographical Encyclopedia of Performers Who Made the Transition to Talking Pictures.* Jefferson, N.C.: McFarland and Company, 1998.

Louise Fazenda, birth certificate, Tippecanoe County, Indiana.

"Louise Fazenda's Life Story." MGM Publicity Department, 1935.

MacCann, Richard Dyer, comp. *The Silent Comedians.* Metuchen, N.J.: Scarecrow Press, 1993.

Meredith, Edith. "The Miracle of Louise Fazenda's Baby." *Photoplay* (August 1933).

New York Times, April 18, 1962.

Ragan, David. "At Home with Fazenda." *Indianapolis Star Magazine*, April 24, 1949.

Roberts, Katherine. "The Lady Can Take It." *Collier's Magazine* (June 11, 1938).

The Silents Majority. http://www.silentsmajority.com/.

Silverman, Stephen M. *Funny Ladies: The Women Who Make Us Laugh.* New York: Harry N. Abrams, 1999.

Torrence, Bruce T. *Hollywood: The First Hundred Years.* New York: Zoetrope, 1982.

Wallis, Brent. Letter. November 2, 1979. San Francisco, California.

Wallis, Hal, and Charles Higham. *Starmaker: The Autobiography of Hal Wallis.* New York: Macmillan and Company, 1980.

West Lafayette Journal and Courier, April 18, 1962.

ANN CHRISTY
Harold Lloyd's Choice

Ann Christy.

Hoosiers Ann Christy and Julanne Johnston both proudly achieved the coveted distinction of being named a Wampas Baby Star. The Baby Star promotion was the result of an idea by the Western Associated Motion Picture Advertisers, founded in 1920, to recognize future stars. Unfortunately, neither Johnston nor Christy fulfilled the Wampas prophecy. Each starred in a classic film opposite one of the major stars of the day, after which their film careers went nowhere.

Christy was born Gladys Cronin on May 31, 1905, in Logansport, Indiana, to David and Laura Cronin. Her father was a steamfitter in the Pennsylvania Railroad shops. She and her sister, Leonora, were raised on a farm. Gladys fed the chickens, milked the cows, and did all the other chores associated with farming. She began her stage career by putting on shows in her own backyard in Logansport. Her admission fee was a collection of pins, pencils, and broken dishes.

When she entered Logansport High School, she majored in art. She was a member of the art staff for her school yearbook and won many prizes for her pencil and charcoal sketches. Shortly after graduating from high school in 1922, she married Ed Harvey, the son of a Logansport attorney. The couple moved to South Bend briefly and then moved to California. The Harveys were renting an apartment from an employee of the Christie Film Company and upon his recommendation, Gladys was hired, becoming a regular in "Christie comedies."

It was at this point she changed her name. Since she was working for Al Christie, she changed the spelling and took that as her last name. Her first feature film was in the title role of *The Kid Sister*, released in 1927 and in which she played the sister of Marguerite de la Motte, who was Hoosier John Bowers's wife. About this time Harold Lloyd began looking for a "typical New York girl" for the leading lady in his next film, *Speedy*, which was being shot in New York. For some reason, he thought that Christy, a farm girl from Logansport, was perfect for that image.

In 1928, the same year *Speedy* was released, Christy was chosen to be one of thirteen "baby stars" by Wampas. *Speedy* received very good reviews. The *New York Times* described the final chase scene in the film as "the best thing of its kind that has been put on the screen" and stated that Christy was "an attractive partner in the picture." Christy played the love interest of Harold "Speedy" Swift (Lloyd), a good-natured,

baseball-crazy guy who sets out to save his girl's grandfather from the designs of big-business gangsters. Babe Ruth had a featured role in the film. The director, Ted Wilde, received an Academy Award nomination for his work on the film. It was Lloyd's last silent film.

This was the biggest role Christy would ever have. She was supposed to costar again with Lloyd in his first two sound films, but she was replaced by another Wampas Baby, Barbara Kent. Her next appearance was with Jack Holt and Nancy Carroll in a supporting role in *The Water Hole.* It was the last film she made at Paramount, but she went on to work with several other companies. In 1929 she was Hoot Gibson's leading lady in *The Lariat Kid* for Universal. She also starred in *Just Off Broadway* opposite Donald Keith.

Christy appeared in several feature talkies in the early thirties, as well as a number of shorts such as *Big Ears,* which was an "Our Gang" comedy. She was also in a number of Mack Sennett shorts, including the first Bing Crosby short film. She was in four films in 1930, including the lead in *The Fourth Alarm.* She suffered a delay in her film career when she was involved in a serious automobile accident in 1930. She recovered but made only a few shorts and two more features. Her final film was *Behind Stone Walls* in 1932.

It is not known when she was divorced from Harvey, but she retired from the screen in 1932 after marrying wealthy Texas rancher Robert Moore Jr. They lived on his 500,000-acre ranch, which was featured in an *Architectural Digest* article. Christy became interested in historical

Ann Christy, studio publicity shot, circa 1926–27.

Ann Christy and Harold Lloyd in *Speedy* (1928).

buildings and bought and restored the Tombstone, Arizona, home of Virgil Earp, brother of the famous Wyatt. The Moores had two sons. She died of a heart attack in Vernon, Texas, on November 14, 1987.

BIBLIOGRAPHY

Banta, Ray. *Indiana's Laughmakers: The Story of Over Four Hundred Hoosiers; Actors, Cartoonists, Writers, and Others.* Indianapolis: PennUltimate Press, 1990.

Indianapolis News, March 10, 1932, April 28, 1959.

Indianapolis Star, July 13, 1927.

Liebman, Roy. *The Wampas Baby Stars: A Biographical Dictionary, 1922–1934.* Jefferson, N.C.: McFarland and Company, 1995.

"Obituaries." *Classic Images* (January 1988).

Schickel, Richard. *Harold Lloyd: The Shape of Laughter.* Boston: New York Graphic Society, 1974.

Uselton, Roi A. "The Wampas Baby Stars." *Films in Review* (February 1970).

JULANNE JOHNSTON

Sharing a Flying Carpet with Douglas Fairbanks

Julanne Johnston.
LYMAN POLLARD, HOLLYWOOD

Julanne Johnston appeared to be on her way toward joining the ranks of the top Hollywood stars when she was chosen by Douglas Fairbanks to be his princess in *The Thief of Bagdad.* Unfortunately, it was not to be. Although she received good notices for her performance, she never appeared in any other films of the caliber of that spectacular 1924 classic.

Julanne (sometimes listed as Julianne) Johnston was born in Indianapolis, Indiana, on May 1, 1900. She took early training to become a dancer and began appearing with the famous Ruth St. Denis dancers. Later she entered vaudeville and did some local theater work. Her first appearance in a film was as an extra in Cecil B. DeMille's *Joan the Woman* in 1917. She eventually graduated to Fox comedies but was still primarily being cast as a dancer in movies until the early 1920s.

Johnston began to receive billing in pictures such as *Seeing It Through* (1920), *The Madness of Youth* (1923), and *Tea: With a Kick!* (1923). The latter film also featured Hoosiers Louise Fazenda and Victor Potel. During the filming of *Seeing It Through* and *Tea: With a Kick!*, she became friends with Zazu Pitts. This friendship led to the formation of a ladies club called "Our Club." The honorary president of the club was Mary Pickford.

After the release of *Robin Hood* in 1922, Fairbanks was looking for something to equal or top this tremendously successful film. He found it in *Thief of Bagdad* and began looking for a leading lady. Fairbanks had signed a striking brunette, Evelyn Brent, to a contract, and although no announcement had been made about her first film, publicity shots were made with her in oriental costumes, suggesting the setting for *Thief of Bagdad.* Rumors began to fly that Fairbanks was romantically involved with Brent. Pickford, Fairbanks's wife, got wind of the rumor and ordered Brent off the Pickfair lot.

Fairbanks then chose Johnston to portray the ravishingly beautiful princess. Critics agreed she was a good choice. The *New York Times* said, "Julanne Johnston makes a stunning Princess." *Motion Picture* magazine stated, "Douglas Fairbanks might have searched every kingdom and he would never have found a lovelier princess for his magical 'Thief of Bagdad' than the fair Julanne Johnston. She is the image of every fairy princess in every fairytale come true."

Thief of Bagdad opened at the Liberty Theater in New York City, which was transformed into an Arabian Nights Miracle for the opening. The walls of the theater were hung with paintings by Pagany—

PICTURE·PLAY
OCT. 1924   MAGAZINE   25 Cents

JULANNE JOHNSTON

THEY WANT TO BE BAD TO BE GOOD   AND   HOW THE STARS BRING UP THEIR CHILDREN

Julanne Johnston sleeping on bed with Douglas Fairbanks and Anna May Wong in a scene from *The Thief of Bagdad* (1924).

enlargements of his exquisite illustrations for *Arabian Nights*. In the lobby there were tapestries, incense, rugs and silks, Turkish coffee, and a caravan of oriental singers chanting songs of welcome. Outside a crowd of five thousand gathered, and when Fairbanks, Johnston, and Pickford arrived, they were nearly crushed. The first reviews vindicated Fairbanks's proclamation that this was his greatest achievement. The special effects stunned the audiences. Johnston was part of the magical illusions conceived by Fairbanks and his production staff for the film. The *New York Times* said, "There are some wonderfully well-worked out effects, and even to an experienced eye the illusion is in nearly every instance kept up to a state of perfection."

One of the best illusions was that of the "flying carpet." The *Times* reviewer told how it was done. "The carpet had a steel frame and steel cross-strapping underneath. When the drum winch began to turn, the whole thing, with Fairbanks and Miss Johnston sitting cross-legged on it, rose before the eyes of the suitably astonished spectators and thin wires pulled it toward the window." On the next shot, which was outside the window, an eighty-foot boom was used. Johnston did not participate in this shot. A double was used.

In recognition of her success in *Thief of Bagdad*, Johnston was selected as a Wampas Baby Star in 1924. Some of the other "Babies" chosen with Johnston that year were fellow Hoosier Carmelita Geraghty, Clara Bow, and Dorothy Mackaill. The Wampas Baby Stars was a promotion sponsored by the Western Associated Motion Picture Advertisers. Founded in 1920, the organization selected a group of promising stars annually. It was a much sought-after honor to be a Baby Star.

After *Thief of Bagdad*, Johnston was featured in beautiful color on the cover of the October 1924 issue of *Picture-Play* magazine. The magazine mentions the fact that she had gone to Europe and "was having a beautiful time sightseeing and studying dancing in Berlin and Paris in addition to working on 'Garragan.'" *Garragan* was a German film released in 1924. She appeared in two more European films, *The Prude's Fall* (1924), shot in England, and then another German film, *Stadt der Versuchung Die* (1925). She then returned to America, where she was cast as the leading lady in *Dame Chance* in 1926. She was scheduled to play the lead opposite Reginald Denny in *The Missourian*, but the film was never made. After this her leading roles virtually disappeared.

As her roles diminished in size and frequency, her good friend Colleen Moore stepped in and helped her get work. Johnston appeared with Moore in *Twinkletoes* (1926), *Her Wild Oat* (1927), *Oh Kay!* (1928), and *Synthetic Sin* and *Smiling Irish Eyes* (both in 1929), both written by Rushville, Indiana, native Tom Geraghty.

Julanne Johnston.

In 1926 Johnston was invited to San Simeon for one of William Randolph Hearst's famous weekend parties. Moore, who accompanied her, described the event. "Mr. Hearst's secretary phoned to say the private train . . . not a private car, mind you, but a private train . . . would be leaving at seven o'clock Friday night and for us to be at the Southern Pacific Railway station at six-thirty." On board the train were Hedda Hopper, Constance Talmadge, King Vidor, Adolphe Menjou, Bebe Daniels, Jack Pickford, Jack Gilbert, Irving Thalberg, Norma Shearer, and MGM director Carey Wilson with his wife (from Rushville, Indiana) Carmelita Geraghty Wilson. A little after midnight the train was put on a siding at San Luis Obispo. The next morning after breakfast aboard the train, the group climbed into a fleet of limousines to drive along the Pacific Ocean to the great castle on the hill. Moore recalled that going up the hill she saw "a large herd of buffalo racing up the mountain, followed by zebras and deer. Ibex and gnu roved around. We even passed two large giraffes." There were about fifty people in all, and Johnston and Moore were assigned to a guesthouse that held twelve people. This was the first of Moore's many visits to San Simeon. There is no word as to whether or not Johnston was ever invited back.

In Johnston's last few films she was little more than an extra and was sometimes uncredited. Although she had made the transition into talkies, her roles were essentially bit parts. One of her last screen appearances was a bit part in *Bolero* (1934), which featured a rising actress by the name of Carole Lombard. Johnston married David Rust, an executive in an automobile accessory company, and retired to the life of a socialite in posh Grosse Pointe, Michigan. She had two daughters and a son (the latter preceded her in death). Johnston died on December 26, 1988, in Grosse Pointe.

BIBLIOGRAPHY

All Movie Guide. http://www.allmovie.com/.

Carey, Gary. *Doug and Mary: A Biography of Douglas Fairbanks and Mary Pickford.* New York: E. P. Dutton, 1977.

The Internet Movie Database. http://www.imdb.com/.

"Julanne Johnston Plays Another Leading Role." *Movie Weekly* (May 3, 1924).

Liebman, Roy. *From Silents to Sound: A Biographical Encyclopedia of Performers Who Made the Transition to Talking Pictures.* Jefferson, N.C.: McFarland and Company, 1998.

———. *The Wampas Baby Stars: A Biographical Dictionary, 1922–1934.* Jefferson, N.C.: McFarland and Company, 1995.

Moore, Colleen. *Silent Star.* Garden City, N.Y.: Doubleday and Company, 1968.

New York Times, March 19, 1924.

"Our Portrait Gallery." *Motion Picture* (August 1924).

"Over the Teacups." *Picture-Play* (October 1924).

Tibbetts, John C., and James M. Welsh. *His Majesty the American: The Cinema of Douglas Fairbanks.* South Brunswick, N.J.: A. S. Barnes and Company.

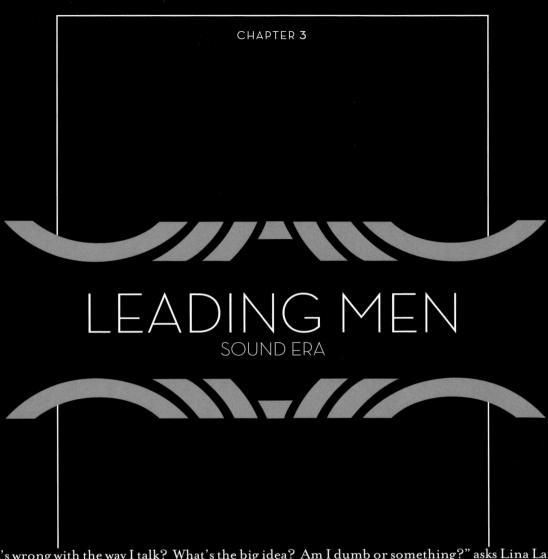

CHAPTER 3

LEADING MEN
SOUND ERA

"What's wrong with the way I talk? What's the big idea? Am I dumb or something?" asks Lina Lamont, the speech-challenged silent star of *Singin' in the Rain*, played by Jean Hagen (Elkhart, Indiana).

Many who enjoyed silent films through the 1920s were apprehensive about the approach of sound. It wasn't just the studio moguls who were worried about the revolution of the industry. Many movie-goers had become so accustomed to silent film, they didn't want it changed in any way.

Today it is difficult for many to understand how the audiences of the presound era had come to love its silence. Moviegoers were used to sitting in beautiful movie palaces or cozy neighborhood houses watching the silent film masterpieces. Their favorite stars did not speak. The audience could only imagine the sound of their real voices.

When audiences did hear a star's voice for the first time, many were inevitably disappointed. Some stars were unable to weather the transition. Hoosiers J. Warren Kerrigan and Charlie Murray did not become stars of the sound era. John Bowers made only three sound films before his career faded. Others saw their careers advance with sound. Buck Jones and Ken Maynard became even bigger stars in sound films. Monte Blue's leading man status had just about peaked when sound was introduced. However, his perseverance and versatility produced a longevity that carried him all the way into television.

Some Hoosiers used sound to great advantage. Clifton Webb's voice ideally matched his suave, sardonic wit. Red Skelton easily transferred his unique personality from radio to the movies.

CLIFTON WEBB

Mabelle and Me

"He was at this time in his late fifties, a tall elegant man with good features and thick waving dark hair only sufficiently greying to add to the distinction of his appearance . . . he had taken great pains to adopt the manner of speech as spoken in England and you had to have a very sensitive ear to catch now and then an American intonation. . . . He was well-favored, bright, a good dancer, and an asset at any party. He took an immense amount of trouble to make himself agreeable to aging women . . . using everyone as stepping stones to his social advancement. He was a snob without shame." W. Somerset Maugham's description of Elliott Templeton in his novel *The Razor's Edge* was also a perfect description of Clifton Webb. Webb's offscreen persona was much the same as his on-screen performances. He played Clifton Webb exceptionally well. This lack of range usually hurt actors, but audiences were enchanted with Webb's urbane, caustic, and arrogant personality.

From the mid-forties to the early sixties, moviegoers vicariously enjoyed Webb's superiority. There is no trace of his Hoosier roots in the sardonic, suave, witty, and dandyish character he played and lived. Webb may have acquired much of his theatrical air and talent from the time he was in his mother's womb. Mabel A. Parmelee was a stagestruck young woman who attended the performances of every stock company that ever played in Indianapolis. She was a feisty, headstrong woman who dreamed of "lace tablecloths and fine dresses" and whose fondest wish was to become an actress. She even changed the spelling of her name from Mabel to the more dramatic "Mabelle." Webb said, "In Indianapolis, where she was queen of a front-porch court, Mabelle exercised the lisp and flutter with devastating effect." When a tall, dark, and handsome stranger hit town, Mabelle was intrigued. It was whispered that "he had something to do with railroads." As Webb described it: "A little later, against the background of an eminently fashionable dance, one Mr. Jake Grant Hollenbeck was presented to Miss Mabelle Parmelee. He looked at her dance card, saw it was full, and frowned with disappointment. She tossed the card elegantly over her left shoulder and made a silent wish. Then Mr. Hollenbeck smiled and then Miss Parmelee smiled." She informed her parents: "I'll marry Jake Hollenbeck or die!" On January 18, 1888, she married Hollenbeck, and her dreams of being an actress ended. On November 19, 1889, she gave birth to a son at their home at 305 N. Mississippi Street in Indianapolis. She named

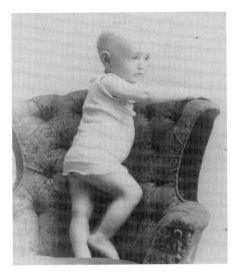

Clifton Webb as a baby.
ELITE STUDIO, INDIANAPOLIS

(Previous page) Clifton Webb in *Sitting Pretty* (1948).

Clifton Webb in Tom Sawyer costume.

Clifton Webb.

him Webb Parmelee Hollenbeck. She would call her son by his first name all her life.

The Hollenbecks later moved to a house on Pennsylvania Street, near North Street, in Indianapolis. Although Webb Parmalee Hollenbeck was not to remain in Indiana for long, his family had deep roots in the state. The Hollenbecks were from Dutch stock, who originally settled in New York State. Jacob's father, Jacob Wesley Hollenbeck, was a well-known superintendent of the city yards on East Market Street in Indianapolis and represented one of the old pioneer families of Indiana. Jacob W.'s grandfather settled with his family in Scott County, Indiana, as early as 1817. Jacob W. and two of his brothers were in the Union army during the Civil War. James P., the oldest son, served in the Eighty-second Indiana Infantry and was killed at the Battle of Chickamauga. In 1854 Jacob W. married Eliza A. Nichols, a granddaughter of William Nichols, who was one of the oldest pioneers of Scott County. From this union, Jacob G. was born.

Although Mabelle liked to boast that both sides of Webb's family included clergymen, lawyers, doctors, and college presidents, the truth was that both sides of the family were in the railroad profession. Jacob G. began working at age nineteen in the Indianapolis office of the Big Four Railroad. When he retired in Missouri, he was assistant traffic manager for the Missouri Pacific Railroad Company. Mabelle's father, Dave Parmelee, was a railroad conductor. It is possible this similarity in professions in both families led to the meeting of Jacob and Mabelle.

After Webb's birth, Mabelle continued to see as many plays as possible in Indianapolis. Jacob never accompanied her. He cared nothing for the theater and was concerned that Mabelle's love of the theater might be transferred to their son.

He had cause to worry. When Webb was three years old and Jacob was away at work, Mabelle impetuously boarded a train bound for New York City with the child in tow. Upon their arrival, she immediately enrolled him in dancing, acting, and music lessons. She apparently knew that her husband would never agree to such training. Her solution was to leave her husband and raise her child as she wished.

Eventually, Jacob located his wife and son in New York. An arrangement was made where Mabelle and her child were allowed to stay in New York. Jacob was a well-paid railroader and was able to support Mabelle and Webb in what he thought would be a brief New York adventure. However, Mabelle had other ideas and wanted to stay in New York, where she could vicariously participate in the theater through her son.

When Webb was seven, an agent saw him performing in an acting class and recommended that Webb audition at the Children's Theater, housed in the Carnegie Lyceum. Mabelle was delighted when Webb won the role of Cholly Boutonniere in an old play called *Brownies*. Webb flitted about the stage in this role until the theater changed productions after four seasons.

In 1898, when Webb was nine years old, his parents divorced. That same year Jacob, who by this time had been transferred to Saint Louis, married Ethel Brown of that city. A short time later Mabelle remarried as well. Webb's stepfather, Green Raum Jr., worked in a copper factory. The family took up residence at 101 West Seventy-seventh Street in New York City. From the onset Webb disliked his stepfather, and their relationship became increasingly strained.

By age ten, in spite of the fact that he was becoming tall and angu-
lar, Webb won the role of Oliver in the Children's Theater version
of *Oliver Twist.* After one season as Oliver, he played Arthur, a young
nephew of Richard the Lionhearted, imprisoned in the Tower of
London. He was now a mainstay of the Children's Theater, and he was
next cast as a southern boy whose father was fighting in the Civil War,
followed by a role in *Rags to Royalty*, which was the Children's Theater
version of *The Prince and the Pauper.*

Webb was now a teenager, and Mabelle wanted Webb to stretch his
talents as far as possible. Although he had attended a public school
(No. 87 in New York), most of his schooling was from private tutors.
He studied portrait painting with Robert Henri and became a talented
painter. His acting career was also progressing nicely. At age fourteen
he had his own one-man show. He continued to take dancing lessons,
and Mabelle saw that he was tutored in French, German, and Italian.
He took piano lessons and was composing concertos at age sixteen.

As Mabelle's divorce proceedings got under way, Webb and
Mabelle decided that it was time to change his name. Some reports
state that he took the name Clifton after appearing in Clifton, New
Jersey. However, as Webb described it:

> The name Webb I liked. The sensible thing seemed to be to keep
> it as a surname and find another that went well with it. I found a
> pencil and paper and started to write down every name I could think
> of, from Abraham to Zachariah. We arrived in due course at the
> C's . . . Charles, Charlemagne, Clayton, Clinton . . . none of them

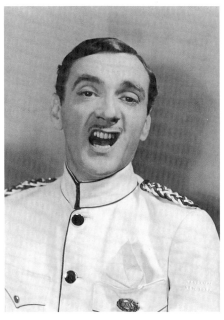

Clifton Webb.

Clifton Webb and Anne Baxter (Michigan
City) in *The Razor's Edge* (1946). Both were
nominated for Best Supporting Oscars for
this movie. However, only Baxter won.

appealed to me. I wanted something with rhythm. For no particular reason I wrote down Clifton Webb. Clifton Webb . . . pum-tee-pum . . . Clifton Webb . . . "I think that does it," I said. "How right you are, dear," Mabelle said. "It will look nice in lights."

Webb studied opera with Victor Maurel, and the seventeen-year-old made his grand opera debut in *Tosca* at the Boston Opera House. He eventually mastered twenty-eight operatic roles in French, Italian, and German and became a member of the Aborn Opera Company. Mabelle was now the mainspring of his life.

At age eighteen, also in Boston, Webb was a baritone and played in the French opera *Mignon*, playing the rather important role of Laerte, the actor. With his mother at his side, Webb went up and down the eastern seaboard for the next two years, singing in *Tales of Hoffman*, *La Boheme*, and *Madame Butterfly*. His last opera appearance was as the witch in *Hansel and Gretel*.

In 1913 he made his debut as a professional dancer on Broadway. *The Purple Road* was an operetta set in Napoléon's court. Webb played Destris, the dancing master to Josephine. His limp-wristed minuets were met with gales of laughter. But Webb was not a buffoon; his dancing was amazing, and he created unique and humorous dances. As Webb began to concentrate on dancing and move away from opera, Mabelle opened a theater called Follies Mariguy. She apparently was not very successful, because in 1914 when Webb was sued for nonpayment of singing lessons by Maurel, he complained that Mabelle "took all he earned."

About this time, Vernon and Irene Castle were doing tangos and cakewalks in restaurants, tearooms, and supper clubs in New York. The public loved this departure from the long-reigning popularity of the waltz. Bonnie Glass already was a noted dancer when she saw Webb in *The Purple Road*. She asked him to go to a nightclub with her to see if they danced well together. After they finished their trial dance, the manager of the club came to their table and asked if he could hire them. This was all the encouragement they needed, and they immediately formed a partnership.

Glass and Webb became immensely popular, and Webb quickly became known as one of the best dancers in America. Mabelle was always looking to make more money and, at her suggestion, she and Webb opened a dance school, which brought them into contact with the cream of New York society. Webb gave lessons, and Mabelle served as secretary and manager of the Webb Dance Studio. Eventually, Glass was partnered with Rudolph Valentino, and Webb found a new partner in Mae Murray. However, they did not get along well, and their partnership was short-lived.

When Mabelle accepted an invitation from decorator Elsie de Wolfe to stay at her home, the Villa Trianon in Versailles, she and Webb embarked on what would be the first of at least forty trans-Atlantic crossings. They came back to New York, where Webb appeared as a dancing comedian in a 1914 Al Jolson show, *Dancing Around*. Webb's roles at this time of his career could best be described as eccentric and effeminate.

In 1916 he was introduced to fellow Hoosier Cole Porter when he was cast in Porter's Broadway vehicle, *See America First*. Unfortunately, it was not a hit. "I played a cowboy and an autumn flower. Others had

Clifton Webb.

roles not so believable," Webb remembered. This was the beginning of a long and close friendship between Webb and Porter. In 1928 Webb appeared in a Porter revue, *The Ambassadeurs*, for which Porter wrote a song especially for Webb—"Looking at You." The revue was a hit. In 1937 Porter sustained compound fractures to both legs in a fall from a horse, which required a lengthy recuperation. Webb urged him to return to work. Porter promised Webb he would and finished the score for *You Never Know*, which opened with Webb as the star in February 1938.

In his early stage roles, Webb frequently portrayed a plaything of society. He had become concerned about the effect of his portrayals on the public, once asking a reporter, "Do you find me offensive? You know it is a risky part. Men especially hate that sort of person." His last role of this type was in 1924 in *Parasites*. Webb resumed his dancing career with Mary Hay, the wife of Richard Barthelmess, a well-known movie star. When Webb and Hay opened a new nightclub, Ciro's, with their act, they were a big hit. They soon rivaled Fred and Adele Astaire in popularity and in the eyes of the critics. Their dancing, without departing from rhythmic perfection, had odd quirks that made them a highly amusing pair.

Clifton Webb's mother Mabelle.

Barthelmess did not want his wife to restart her career and was unhappy and a little jealous about her teaming with Webb. However, when she provided "proof" that Webb was not interested in women, he calmed down. Hay and Webb, with the ever-present Mabelle, sailed for Europe with Mary Pickford's brother Jack and his wife. Webb danced briefly with the Dolly Sisters in Paris, where they had opened a new nightclub, "Les Acasias." Webb and Hay were a hit in Europe and had a wild time with the Pickfords.

On their return, Mabelle told the press, "My son and Mary Hay! It is perfectly ridiculous! Why, he is in Great Neck week-ending with Dick Barthelmess, now. So you see, he hasn't broken up any home." "Yes," she continued, "Clifton and Mary danced together for two months abroad, and they were a great hit. But as for romance, that is absurd. My son will never marry. I am his best pal. Certainly I was with them all the time, not that they needed a chaperone, but I am never parted from my son." Hay and Barthelmess separated and eventually divorced.

Clifton Webb and his mother Mabelle.

Webb was now one of Broadway's highest paid stars. In 1930 he performed a crowd-pleasing snake-hips dance with Libby Holman in *Three's a Crowd*. In 1933 he was with fellow Hoosier Marilyn Miller in *As Thousands Cheer*. His impersonations of Mahatma Gandhi, Douglas Fairbanks Jr., and Noël Coward were the hit of the show. This brought him to the attention of Hollywood. Although he had made several nondescript silent films in the 1920s, it was not until 1935 that Hollywood finally offered him star billing in a film.

Webb was to be groomed by MGM to be a dancing star in the same vein as Fred Astaire. Unfortunately, his arrival in Hollywood gave the moguls at MGM second thoughts. Webb arrived wearing a top hat and white gloves with Mabelle on his arm and trailing his fancy-cut French poodle on a leash. He also brought along his parrot Goo-Goo. The picture, *Elegance* (in which he was to play opposite Joan Crawford), was put on hold. Hollywood in 1935 was not ready to make an obvious homosexual a star. Tired of waiting, and seeing the handwriting on the wall, Webb tore up his contract and left Hollywood. The film was never made.

He returned to New York, where he accepted a role in *And Stars Remain*, which opened on Broadway in 1936, playing opposite fellow Hoosier Richard Barbee (Lafayette) and Helen Gahagan Douglas. Webb remained active on Broadway, appearing in Cole Porter's *You Never Know* with old friend Libby Holman in 1938. This was followed in 1939 with *The Importance of Being Earnest* and finally Coward's *Blithe Spirit*, which ran from 1941 to 1943. Webb was now more of an actor than a musical-comedy star.

In 1943 Otto Preminger came to Los Angeles with a group of friends to see *Blithe Spirit*. Preminger was about to produce a film called *Laura*. He had never seen Webb before, and he was struck by his performance. "That's the man to play Waldo Lydecker," he said. When Preminger informed Darryl Zanuck of his intention to cast Webb, Zanuck said he would have to see a screen test. Webb, still sour over his past experiences with Hollywood, refused and suggested they film him on stage doing his bit in *Blithe Spirit*. Zanuck said, "I'm not filming some damned play." However, Preminger was so sure Webb was the right choice for the part that he arranged a filming of Webb's big monologue. Zanuck and others were still not sure if Webb was the right choice, but Preminger was determined. He signed Webb and took over the direction of the film after Rouben Mamoulian was dismissed.

Apparently Hollywood in 1944 was ready to take on an effeminate and unlikely leading man. Webb was fifty-five years old in 1944, but he was still handsome (though undeniably gray), thin, and just under six feet tall. Webb's "debut" in *Laura* was a hit, as was the film itself. He was nominated for a best supporting actor Oscar, his career path took a new turn, and he was on his way toward becoming a major film star.

Clifton Webb and Ginger Rogers in *Dreamboat* (1952).

Two years later, in 1946, he was cast as Elliott Templeton in *The Razor's Edge* and received his second Oscar nomination for best supporting actor. In 1948 he was offered a change of pace as the urbane, acerbic babysitter Mr. Belvedere in *Sitting Pretty*. He was nominated for a best actor Oscar for this film, and it launched him into a series of roles showcasing his arrogant personality. He played Mr. Belvedere in two sequels, as well as an ironic angel in *For Heaven's Sake* and an eccentric professor in *Dreamboat*. Webb even became a father figure in *Cheaper by the Dozen*, *Elopement*, and *The Remarkable Mr. Pennypacker*. "I've destroyed the formula completely," he said. "I'm not young, I don't get the girl in the end and I don't swallow her tonsils, but I have become a national figure."

In 1950, when Webb starred in the real-life story of the Gilbreth family in *Cheaper by the Dozen*, his costar was Myrna Loy. She was not the first one who had problems with Webb's scene-stealing antics, but in spite of this, they became good friends, and Loy was frequently invited to Webb's house for parties. Loy said, "Mabelle, who looked like Clifton in drag, held court. Mabelle was the quintessential stage mother, her son's promoter, adviser, and inseparable companion since his youthful Broadway years. They used to say Clifton and Mabelle were Hollywood's happiest couple. Everybody went to their house. He was very social and very dear in his way . . . it just had to be his way." When in America, Coward also frequently stayed at Webb and Mabelle's house on North Rexford Drive in Hollywood. Coward was amused with Webb's jolly but formidable mother, who "would willingly dance the can-can for you . . . her version . . . at the age of nearly ninety."

When Mabelle died of heart disease on October 18, 1960, Webb was devastated. He had thought her to be indestructible. For the first time in his seventy-one years, he had to face the future without Mabelle. Coward said, "Poor Clifton is still, after two months, wailing and sobbing over Mabelle's death. As she was well over ninety, gaga, and had driven him mad for years, this seems excessive and over-indulgent. I feel sorry for him but he must snap out of it." When Webb continued to lament the passing of his mother, Coward said sharply, "It must be tough to be orphaned at seventy-one."

Webb made only one movie after the death of his mother. In 1962 he was cast as a priest in Leo McCarey's last film, *Satan Never Sleeps.* For the first time Webb did not use much makeup, had a simple hairstyle in keeping with his character, and wore an oversized costume to appear thinner than the nineteen pounds he lost for the role. The film was not a success, but Webb's performance was moving and effective, suggesting that his acting range had never been fully exploited.

After this film Webb retired, leaving the studio where he was recognized as "one of the most consistent money-makers in Fox history." He began having health problems and was treated by famed surgeon Michael DeBakey in 1963 for an abdominal aneurysm. In 1965 he suffered an intestinal block. He began work on an autobiography, *Mabelle and Me,* but it was never finished. On October 13, 1966, Webb died from a heart attack at his Rexford Drive home. His secretary, Helen Matthews, said, "I don't think Clifton could face the thought of another anniversary of his mother's death." He was interred next to his mother in the Sanctuary of Peace in the Abbey of Psalms Mausoleum at Hollywood Forever Memorial Park.

BIBLIOGRAPHY

Eells, George. *The Life That Late He Led: A Biography of Cole Porter.* New York: G. P. Putnam's Sons, 1967.

Frischauer, Willi. *Behind the Scenes of Otto Preminger: An Unauthorized Biography.* New York: William Morrow and Company, 1974.

Holland, Larry Lee. "Clifton Webb." *Films in Review* (April 1981).

Indianapolis News, December 28, 1936, October 14, 1966.

Indianapolis Star, April 19, 1931, October 27, 1940.

Kotsilibas-Davis, James, and Myrna Loy. *Myrna Loy: Being and Becoming.* New York: Alfred A. Knopf, 1987.

Lesley, Cole. *Remembered Laughter: The Life of Noël Coward.* New York: Alfred A. Knopf, 1976.

Mann, William J. *Behind the Screen: How Gays and Lesbians Shaped Hollywood, 1910–1969.* New York: Viking, 2001.

Marchant, William. *The Privilege of His Company: Noël Coward Remembered.* Indianapolis: Bobbs-Merrill, 1975.

Pierce, Max. "Sitting Pretty . . . The Talented Mr. Webb." *Films of the Golden Age* (Summer 2000).

Shipman, David. *The Great Movie Stars: The International Years.* New York: St. Martin's Press, 1972.

Thomson, David. *A Biographical Dictionary of Film.* 3rd ed. New York: Alfred A. Knopf, 1994.

Tierney, Gene, and Mickey Herskowitz. *Self-Portrait.* New York: Wyden Books, 1978.

Webb, Clifton. Interview. 1949. Biography Resource Center. Academy of Motion Picture Arts and Sciences, Beverly Hills, California.

————. "Mabelle and Me." Unpublished autobiography, circa 1962–63. Author's collection.

OLE OLSEN

"May You Laugh as Long as You Live"

Ole Olsen and Chic Johnson.
© 1941, UNIVERSAL PICTURES

Schoolmates who knew him described Ole Olsen's early life as "one round of hilarity after another." During his days at Peru and Wabash high schools, he gained a reputation as a "genius for sheer nonsense that was unmatchable." Folks in Wabash were so impressed with his wit as a youth that in 1909 they made him the right honorable "jokist" of the *Sycamore*, which was the high school annual. He was president of his junior class and a member of the orchestra and the football team.

Wabash High School's class poet wrote of Olsen,

Ole's Ha! Ha's! are noted.
And should always be quoted
To make your hearts joyous and light.

John Sigvaard Olsen was born on March 15, 1891, in Peru, Indiana. Three months after his birth, Cole Porter was born there. When Olsen was playing in *Fifty Million Frenchmen*, he said, "You know, the funniest thing . . . I knew Cole Porter in Peru. He was a Peru boy too, but I'd been working in 'Fifty Million Frenchmen' quite a while before I realized he was the composer of the thing."

Olsen, like Porter, wanted to excel musically in his youthful days after high school. In 1910 he went to Indianapolis and attended the Metropolitan School of Music, which later became Arthur Jordan Conservatory, where he studied the violin. Money was scarce, and he helped pay his way by pumping organs in a church and by working in the conservatory lunchroom. He earned his first money from music by singing in a nickelodeon located near the Hotel Washington. He said he was "a tenor, just short of being a soprano." After trying to master the violin, he decided his gifts might be elsewhere. He enrolled at Northwestern University but did not stay much more than a year.

While at Northwestern he met three other young men who had tastes for music and comedy similar to his own. They started a vaudeville quartet and began playing in cafes and hotels in Chicago, calling themselves "The College Four." In 1914 he met Chic Johnson, a member of a band Olsen was playing with. When the band broke up, Olsen and Johnson formed a vaudeville act. Although they really did not have a set act, the duo found themselves booked into a small Chicago nightclub as part of *Mike Fritzol's Frolics*. When it came time for them

to go on, they pushed a piano onstage. Johnson seated himself at the keyboard and began to plunk out a ragtime tune. The pair began to exchange "patter"—mostly insults—and the famous "Olsen and Johnson" team began to emerge.

They appeared on the Pantages vaudeville circuit, and as their popularity increased their salaries rose to $250 a week between them. Encouraged by their success, Olsen and Johnson worked continually to make their act zanier than ever. Their efforts paid off, and they reached the apex of vaudeville when they signed with the Keith-Orpheum circuit. They were billed as "Two Likable Lads . . . Loaded with Laughs," and their salary reached new heights. They were in vaudeville for twenty-five years and made appearances in nearly every town on the circuit, including Indianapolis. Whenever Olsen was in town, he would visit the Busy Bee dairy lunch and give passes to all the employees. The reason for this generosity, according to Olsen, was "that lunchroom was the site of the flicker palace where I made my first dollar singing."

In 1930 Warner Brothers signed Olsen and Johnson for their film debut in *Oh Sailor, Behave*. They played two sailors on the lookout for a crook with a wooden leg who had robbed a navy storehouse. Their zany method of detecting the crook was to aim peashooters at the legs of anyone they suspected. This film featured the pair's famous "Laughing Song."

While making films, they appeared in another wacky revue, *Monkey Business*. They relied greatly on sight gags, many borrowed from the Keystone Cops, Laurel and Hardy, the Three Stooges, and the Ritz and Marx brothers. They even tried their hand at radio, appearing on

Ole Olsen in *Ghost Catchers* (1944).

Rudy Vallee's program. The sight gags got plenty of laughs from the studio audience.

In 1933 Olsen and Johnson went back to Chicago and starred in *Take a Chance.* When this revue closed, they took off for England and Australia, touring in the revues *Tip Toes* and *Tell Me More.* Then once again they were called to make films. Republic signed them to a two-picture deal for *Country Gentlemen* (1936) and *All Over Town* (1937).

However, the best was yet to come. In 1938 their most chaotic conglomeration of lunatic routines came together for the smash stage hit *Hellzapoppin.* From the moment of their entrance in a clownish automobile, there is no relief. The show was a helter-skelter assembly of all their low comedy gags accompanied by ear-splitting sound. It consisted of two acts with twenty-five scenes, during which the audience was bombarded with bananas and eggs. When the lights went out, the audience was immersed in rubber snakes and spiders. The show ran on Broadway for a record-breaking 1,404 performances.

In 1941 Universal attempted to translate *Hellzapoppin* to film, and it generally succeeded in transferring most of the Broadway show's original gags. Due to the success of *Hellzapoppin*, Universal produced *Crazy House* (1943) and *Ghost Catchers* (1944). These films were not nearly as successful, but the team's last film, *See My Lawyer* (1945), was their worst. The film industry was incapable of sustaining the cyclonic pace of these two madcap comedians.

This was not the end of Olsen and Johnson. They returned to

Broadway in 1944 in *Laffing Room Only*. Olsen's son, J. C. Olsen, had just been discharged from the service and joined his father as a gag writer, photographer, and appointment keeper.

In 1949 Olsen and Johnson appeared as a summer replacement for Milton Berle. The show was called *Fireball Fun for All*. Regulars included singer Bill Hayes and comedian Marty May, as well as two newcomers: June Johnson, daughter of Chic, and J. C. Olsen, son of Ole.

Olsen and Johnson played in the gambling casinos of Las Vegas for a while, but both men were elderly and suffering serious health problems. Johnson died on February 28, 1962, and Olsen died on January 26, 1963. They both were born less than a year apart, were of Swedish ancestry, attended Northwestern University, entered show business as musicians, suffered from kidney problems, and died at the age of seventy-one, less than a year apart. Both are buried in Palm Memorial Gardens in Las Vegas.

At the time of his death, Olsen had two sisters living in Indiana, Olga Young of Peru and Mrs. John Barnard of Bloomington. In 1963, the year of his death, the Ole Olsen Memorial Theater was established in Peru. One of Olsen's daughters, Moya Lear, keeps in touch with the theatrical group and is invited to performances. She lives in Nevada and often sends good-luck telegrams to the theater.

Olsen's niece, Gwen Werner, still lives in Peru and is an enthusiastic supporter and contributor to the theater. Werner says she remembers happy times with her uncle Ole at family gatherings, where he was as much a prankster in real life as he was before his audiences. He lived his life in keeping with a line always used at the end of his vaudeville shows. Olsen would turn to Johnson and say, "May you live as long as you want," to which Johnson would reply, "And may you laugh as long as you live."

BIBLIOGRAPHY

Indiana Biographical Dictionary: People of All Times and All Places Who Have Been Important to the History of the State. 2nd ed. 2 vols. St. Clair Shores, Mich.: Somerset Publishers, 1999.

Indianapolis News, March 7, 1932, January 26, 1963.

Indianapolis Star, March 16, 1937, December 30, 1952, October 30, 1987.

Indianapolis Times, January 27, 1963.

The Internet Broadway Database. http://www.ibdb.com/.

The Internet Movie Database. http://www.imdb.com/.

Maltin, Leonard, ed. *Leonard Maltin's Movie Encyclopedia.* New York: Penguin Putnam, 1994.

Slide, Anthony. *The Vaudevillians: A Dictionary of Vaudeville Performers.* Westport, Conn.: Arlington House, 1981.

Stumpf, Charles. "Olsen and Johnson, the Zaniest of Zanies." *Classic Images* 294 (December 1999).

NORMAN FOSTER
Actor, Director, Producer

Norman Foster.

Before starting a stage career in 1925, Norman Foster was known as just plain "Nick" to his schoolmates in Richmond, Indiana. Garland "Nick" Hoeffer was born in Richmond on December 13, 1900, to C. Foster and Blanche Cummins Hoeffer. Blanche was born and raised in Middletown, Indiana, wrote poetry, and published a book of poems titled *Blue Water*. Nick's grandfather, Reverend Charles W. Hoeffer, was a former cowboy and pastor of the Seventh Street Christian Church in Richmond. Nick went through grade school in Richmond and attended Morton High School. While in high school he became active in dramatics and secured a leading role in the school production of *H.M.S. Pinafore*. After graduation from high school, he enrolled at the Carnegie Institute of Technology in Pittsburgh.

Leaving college, he went to New York City to try his luck on the stage. He took the stage name of Norman Foster for his first professional work in *The Goose Hangs High*. Later, he appeared in *The Poor Nut*, *Just Life*, and *Sure Fire*. His first hit was as the barker's boy in *The Barker*, by Crawfordsville native Kenyon Nicholson. *The Barker* ran for more than six months at the Biltmore Theater in New York and then played London. During rehearsal for *The Barker*, Foster met a young French actress named Claudette Colbert. Colbert was twenty-five at the time and had never spoken a word of English until she was fourteen. A romance blossomed, and they were secretly married in London in March 1928. The couple kept the marriage a secret because Colbert's mother once asked Foster the meaning of the word "threshold" and then told him never to cross hers. More than a year passed before anyone knew of the marriage, including Colbert's mother. The marriage might have been hidden indefinitely if Walter Winchell had not mentioned it in his column. Even after the announcement, Colbert continued to live in her mother's apartment.

After *The Barker* came *The Racket* at the Ambassador Theater in New York, in which Foster played a reporter, a profession he was well acquainted with from his one-year stint at the *Richmond Palladium*. He never lost his love of reporting, and after going on stage, his hobby was going with reporters to cover "big news." He also began to dabble in writing plays.

Foster's next stage success was *June Moon*, and it was his performance in this production that led Paramount to sign him to a contract as one of its featured players. His first two films, *Gentlemen of the Press* (1929)

Norman Foster and Claudette Colbert
in *Young Man of Manhattan* (1930).
PARAMOUNT PICTURES

and *Young Man of Manhattan* (1930), also starred his wife. In 1931 he made two pictures with fellow Hoosier Carole Lombard, *Up Pops the Devil* and *It Pays to Advertise.* (The primary supporting actor in these two films was Richard "Skeets" Gallagher of Terre Haute.) As a result, both Foster and Colbert became close friends of Lombard. Foster and Colbert were divorced in 1935.

In the early thirties Foster was listed as one of the ten most promising actors in the cinema. He made at least forty-six films before he turned his talents to directing and producing. In 1935 he was cast as the lead in the first sound version of Edward Eggleston's (Vevay, Indiana) *The Hoosier Schoolmaster.* In 1936 he made his directorial debut with *I Cover Chinatown.* He joined Twentieth Century Fox that same year as a director and spent several years turning out B mysteries and melodramas, many of which he wrote or cowrote, including many of the best Charlie Chan and Mr. Moto pictures.

Foster had written radio scripts for Orson Welles, and the two men had a strong professional relationship. In the early 1940s Welles asked Foster to direct a Mercury production called "My Friend Benito" in Mexico, but the production was shut down, and he was assigned to

Welles's *Journey into Fear* in 1942. There was some controversy over who really directed that film, Welles or Foster. Welles later said, "I was on the set and decided the angles; from then on, I often said where to put the camera, described the framings, made light tests. I designed the film but can't be called the director. It's Norman Foster's film." Foster continued his association with Welles by appearing on screen in Welles's never-completed *The Other Side of the Wind* in the 1970s.

Foster's other directorial efforts include *Rachel and the Stranger*, *Kiss the Blood Off My Hands* (both 1948), *Father Is a Bachelor* (1950), and *Navajo* (1952). He worked for Walt Disney putting together such television shows as *Davy Crockett, King of the Wild Frontier* (1954), *The Nine Lives of Elfego Baca* (1959), and *The Sign of Zorro* (1960). His last film was *Brighty of the Grand Canyon* in 1967. In the 1970s he attempted to resume his acting career with a role in the television series *Cannon*.

He was married to actress Sally Blane, sister of Loretta and Polly Ann Young, from 1939 until his death from cancer in Santa Monica on July 7, 1976. He and Blane had two children.

BIBLIOGRAPHY

Anderson Daily Bulletin, July 4, 1932, August 7, 1939.

Bogdanovich, Peter. *This Is Orson Welles.* New York: HarperCollins, 1992.

Brady, Frank. *Citizen Welles: A Biography.* New York: Charles Scribner's Sons, 1989.

Indiana Biographical Dictionary: People of All Times and All Places Who Have Been Important to the History of the State. 2nd ed. 2 vols. St Clair Shores, Mich.: Somerset Publishers, 1999.

Indianapolis News, March 3, 1932.

The Internet Movie Database. http://www.imdb.com/.

Maltin, Leonard, ed. *Leonard Maltin's Movie Encyclopedia.* New York: Penguin Putnam, 1994.

Tapert, Annette. *The Power of Glamour: The Women Who Defined the Magic of Stardom.* New York: Crown Publishers, 1998.

Norman Foster and Charlotte Henry in *The Hoosier Schoolmaster* (1935), written by Hoosier Edward Eggleston.

RED SKELTON

The Clown Prince

In June 2001 eighty-nine-year-old Dorothy West Hagemeier vividly recalled her schoolgirl relationship with a schoolmate who would later be described as "one of the greatest clowns of the twentieth century." Hagemeier went to Tecumseh School in Vincennes, Indiana, with Red Skelton and two of his brothers. Tecumseh was on Second Street across from the Catholic school. There were five Dorothys at the school, so Dorothy was forced to use her middle name, Irene. She did not care for the name, and Skelton knew it. She remembered particularly that in the second and third grades, Skelton would follow her out after school and yell "Irene!" at the top of his lungs. She said she would turn around, and he would "turn his whole face wrong side out." He knew it made her mad, but she said, "He was only there to make you laugh."

She said everyone knew Skelton. "He didn't tease maliciously, and he had the reddest hair I've ever seen in my life." Hagemeier said there was a house across from the school that they called "The Dummy House." This is where they sent people who got in trouble or fell behind in their studies. She said, "He spent a lot of time there, but he was anything but dumb." She remembered Skelton standing on his head on the railroad tracks and spinning around.

Hagemeier said the Skeltons lived in a poor section of Vincennes called "Oklahoma" in the north part of town. Hagemeier recalled Vincennes in those days was a "class" town. The north side was tough, the south was French, the southeast was German, and the east was just being developed. Hagemeier remembered that two of the Skeltons, Chris and Paul, were both very tough boys. She did not like them. One of the last times she saw Skelton as a youngster was when she spotted him and his two brothers as she was walking home. She crossed the street to keep from speaking to them. Later when Skelton became famous, she remembered he set up Chris in a cleaning business in Lawrenceville, about nine miles from Vincennes.

She remembered Skelton as a teenage usher at the Moon Theater in Vincennes. She also remembered him being in a medicine show in Vincennes. It was set up on Main Street by the lumber company. Hagemeier's girlfriend, Mary Jane Hess, dated Skelton for a while.

After Skelton left Vincennes and became famous, Hagemeier met him again unexpectedly, while serving as a volunteer guide for the historic Old Cathedral in Vincennes. She was inside one day when she noticed a solitary figure at the door. Realizing it was Skelton, she walked up to him and introduced herself. He remembered her, and they spent at least an hour talking about the old days in Vincennes. Hagemeier said he was alone except for a driver who was sitting in a car outside.

Skelton had been appearing at the Indiana State Fair and decided impulsively to drive to Vincennes and try to talk to the priest, Father Doll, who had been a friend to him as a youngster. This was shortly after Skelton's son, Richard, had died. Unfortunately, Father Doll was out of town that day. Hagemeier asked if he wanted to see the monsignor, and Skelton replied, "No I just came to see Father Doll." He made it clear he just wanted to get in and out of town without a big fuss.

Hagemeier asked Skelton how his wife, Georgia, was, and he said, "Not feeling very good right now." Skelton commented that the church seemed much smaller than he remembered. Hagemeier said, "Well after all Red, you've been to the Vatican." She recalled that Skelton took a picture of the three statues in front of the church, and they spent a nice quiet time reminiscing. After bidding farewell and watching him drive away, Hagemeier thought, "This is the same Red that used to torment the life out of me and now I watch him in my living room."

Richard Bernard (Red) Skelton was born on July 18, 1913, in Vincennes, Indiana. His father, Joseph Elmer Skelton, was born in Princeton, Indiana, and his mother, Ida M. Fields, was born in Harvard, Nebraska. They were married on April 13, 1905, in Knox County. Their first child was Joseph Ishmal, followed by Chris and Paul. Red's father was reputed to have been a circus clown at one time, though evidence of this is slim. It may have been that he met his Nebraska-born wife while touring as a clown.

Joseph was a lineman for the phone company and a grocer. When he died at age thirty-five, the 1913 obituary was headlined, "North End Grocer Dies Suddenly." In order to keep her family together, Ida became a cleaning woman for several Vincennes establishments. This meant Red was frequently left in the care of his brothers. As is the case with older brothers, Skelton endured the taunts, teasing, and bullying that helped toughen him and thus prepare him for the rough road ahead. When Skelton began to entertain ideas about entering show business, he tried to get his brother Paul to go along with him. A few years after Paul's death, Skelton recalled, "I wanted Paul to go into show business with me because he played the piano. My mother played the piano. But he didn't want to go into show business, so I went in alone. I wish he had gone with me."

Some accounts state that Skelton left Vincennes to join a medicine show in 1923. However, there is documentation that he was performing in Vincennes in 1929. If he left Vincennes at an early age, he must have returned rather frequently. Skelton has always credited Clarence Stout as his hometown mentor. Stout, a songwriter and producer, put Skelton in his minstrel shows as early as 1929. He gave the young Skelton tips on timing, stage presence, and how to effectively deliver a joke. Skelton also learned his first dancing steps from Stout's daughter, who was a dancing teacher.

By 1930, when he was not quite seventeen, Skelton was playing in burlesque. He began hanging out at the Pantages Vaudeville Theater in Kansas City, hoping to substitute for an act that failed to show. When he did manage to get on stage, he was not a big hit. In fact, the head

Red Skelton.

(Previous page) Red Skelton as Clem Kaddidlehopper.

S.C. JOHNSON AND SON INC.

"I'm not used to this courage business, but I'll catch on!" Ben (Red Skelton) tells wife Martha (Jean Hagen) doubtfully.

M-G-M's "HALF A HERO"

Copyright 1953 Loew's Incorporated   Country of Origin U.S.A.   7   Property of National Screen Service Corp. Licensed for display only in connection with the exhibition of this picture at your theatre. Must be returned immediately thereafter.   53/499

Scene from *Half a Hero* (1953) with Red Skelton and Jean Hagen (Elkhart).
© 1953, LOEW'S INC.

usherette, fifteen-year-old Edna Stillwell, complained to her manager that Skelton should not be allowed on stage. Skelton became enamored of Stillwell and tried to date her. She initially brushed him off, but Skelton persevered, and they finally began to date. According to Stillwell, "We went together about six weeks before we were married."

On June 1, 1931, the eighteen-year-old Skelton and the sixteen-year-old Stillwell became man and wife. Stillwell paid the two dollars for the marriage license since Skelton was broke, and they headed to Saint Louis, where he was to be the emcee of a Walkathon. Skelton later said, "We raised each other. We didn't have anybody else to turn to."

More than any other person in his life, Stillwell would be the guiding force that made Skelton a star. She wrote material for him, managed his career, taught him how to dress, and encouraged him to qualify for his high school diploma. When they were divorced in 1943, he retained her as his manager and head writer.

By 1934 they were tired of doing Walkathons and gave vaudeville a try. They were a comedy team on the vaudeville circuit with Stillwell both appearing in and writing the act. She said, "I was the no-talent part of Red's act. But we couldn't afford to hire another girl. And Red had to have someone to bounce his routines off. So I stooged for him."

Skelton began to serve as an emcee for vaudeville shows as well as do his comic bits in them, eventually earning two thousand dollars per week. One of his funniest routines was his doughnut-dunking bit. Stillwell got the idea when she saw a man dunking a doughnut in a diner. When Skelton made his first film in 1938, *Having Wonderful Time*, the doughnut-dunking sketch was featured.

On August 17, 1937, Skelton made his national radio debut on Rudy Vallee's popular *Fleischman's Hour.* Vallee was known to spot talent and give them their big break on his show. The folks back home in Vincennes were especially proud because many of Skelton's jokes were written around his hometown. A deluge of fan mail brought him back to Vallee's show again. A local newspaper reported, "Red Skelton gave his hometown the sort of publicity that money couldn't buy." During his first appearance, Skelton had jokingly referred to Evansville as a "suburb of Vincennes." The primary reason for this joke was the fact that Evansville's Joe Cook was a guest on this same radio program. The second Vallee program again had Skelton and Cook as guests, and Cook used the opportunity to get back at Skelton. The *Vincennes Sun-Commercial* ran a front-page article headlined "Red Skelton to Pursue Feud with Joe Cook on Air Tonight."

In 1938 Skelton returned to Indiana, where he played at the Lyric Theater in Indianapolis and was honored at the Indianapolis Press Club. On January 7, 1939, he made his first appearance on *Avalon Time*, a radio show sponsored by Avalon cigarettes. Stillwell followed, making her first appearance on February 18, 1939. *Avalon Time* was a musical comedy/variety show, featuring country stars such as Red Foley and Curt Massey. Other comics were guests on the show, such as Terre Haute's Bill Thompson, who became the mainstay on the *Fibber McGee and Molly* show, originating such characters as "The Old Timer," "Wallace Wimple," and "Horatio K. Boomer." Skelton, however, quickly became the top comic on the show.

Red Skelton with Leon Ames (Portland) (left) and Marilyn Maxwell (Fort Wayne) in *The Show-Off* (1946).

Later in 1939, when he returned to Vincennes for a visit and trib-ute, Skelton not only was a top radio comic and a movie star, but he also had just entertained President Franklin D. Roosevelt at one of his birthday theater parties in Washington, D.C. Stillwell was a big hit with the locals in Vincennes. The paper said, "Mrs. Skelton was practically a 'native daughter' by the time she said her 'good-byes.' Vincennes warmed immediately to her gracious and cultured charms. All agreed she was the girl for 'our boy.'"

Raleigh cigarettes offered Skelton his own show on NBC in 1941. This was his chance to develop a full line of comedic characters. "Clem Kadiddlehopper," "Willy Lump-Lump," "Junior," "the Mean Wid-dle Kid," and others made their debut for the national radio audi-ence. At the same time, Skelton was under contract to MGM studios and appeared in his first starring role in *Whistling in the Dark* (1941). The movie was so successful it spawned two sequels, *Whistling in Dixie* (1942) and *Whistling in Brooklyn* (1943).

Their marriage unraveled as Skelton's star climbed. Perhaps the fatherless, impoverished child who was now a movie and radio star allowed his fame to go to his head. He bought expensive clothes in bulk, and the ranch he and Stillwell built had a large swimming pool, though neither of them could swim. There was talk of infidelity as well. On December 28, 1942, Stillwell filed for divorce. Skelton knew, however, he could not function without Stillwell. She agreed to stay as his manager/writer. When Skelton was about to remarry in April 1944, his fiancée, showgirl Muriel Morris, suddenly backed out, stat-ing, "Choose between your ex-wife and me!" Skelton could not sever his ties with Stillwell, and the marriage was called off.

In June 1944 Skelton reported for induction into the army. He went through basic training at Fort MacArthur and then Camp Rob-erts in California. His younger inductees referred to the thirty-one-year-old Skelton as "Pops." Later, he would joke about being the only name performer to both enter and exit the service as a private. He did not attempt to pull any strings to get an officer's commission, and he did not attempt to go into special services as a military entertainer. He wanted to be a regular GI.

However, even without asking, Skelton was transferred to the army's Special Service School at Washington and Lee University in Virginia. He became an entertainment specialist and was expected to perform regularly for late-night officers' club meetings. During a two-week furlough in 1945, he returned to the West Coast and married MGM starlet Georgia Davis, whom he nicknamed "Little Red." Davis also was bothered by Skelton's close ties with Stillwell. When Skelton returned to California to marry Davis, Stillwell had even accompanied him on the cross-country trip.

Shortly after the marriage, Skelton's troop ship left for Italy. He was under great stress on ship as well as on shore. He commented, "I have done 41 shows in 6 days, about 8 a day." He had no privacy on the ship and was constantly bombarded with requests for performances and auto-graphs. He finally found a small pantry where he could bunk by himself. He said, "This little closet I sleep in is sure nice; they can't find me for autographs. . . . I'd go on deck for some air but some bastard would rank me into a show." Finally, in April 1945 he suffered a "breakdown." He was sent home on a hospital ship and spent the rest of his military career recuperating at the army hospital at Camp Pickett in Virginia.

Red Skelton in *Merton of the Movies* (1947).
© 1947, LOEW'S INC.

When Skelton returned to Hollywood in early 1946, a film he made just before he entered the service, *Ziegfeld Follies*, was released. The timing was excellent. He received very good reviews for the film that featured his "Guzzler's Gin" routine. He quickly resumed his weekly radio show and was again busy at MGM making movies. Yet problems began to surface in his marriage to Davis, possibly because of Stillwell's constant proximity. Stillwell had arranged for the couple to live in the Wilshire Palms, a luxury residential project that was co-owned by Skelton and Stillwell. Stillwell and her new husband, Frank Borzage, lived there as well. Stillwell, however, continued to control her ex-husband's purse strings and most of his schedule. Davis lived on an allowance dictated by Stillwell, and Skelton would not even cash a check without Stillwell cosigning. Skelton did not trust himself with money, having given away too much and frittered much away in bad investments. Stillwell had invested his income in oil wells and real estate, making them both rich.

Davis persistently tried to get Stillwell removed from the picture. This led to some bitter arguments and brief separations, after which they would always reconcile. On May 5, 1947, Davis gave birth to a daughter, Valentina Marie. On June 14, 1948, she gave birth to Richard Freeman, thus satisfying Skelton's wish for a son. In 1949 Stillwell divorced Borzage, blaming it on her all-consuming focus on Skelton's career.

Red Skelton and Nobu McCarthy on *The Red Skelton Show* (1959).
CBS TELEVISION NETWORK

While Skelton's first love was his radio series, he turned out some very popular movies. Two of his best were released in 1948, *The Fuller Brush Man* and *A Southern Yankee*. Buster Keaton, who was a behind-the-scenes adviser to Skelton on the movie set, was frustrated that Skelton did not put more effort into his films. Keaton felt Skelton had great potential for the movies, but he gave more of his attention to his radio series. That attention paid off, as Skelton was always near the top of the Hooper ratings. The only show to top his regularly was that of Bob Hope.

In 1951 television was just beginning, and Skelton decided to jump into the new medium. This devotion and attention to television led to the winding down of his movie career. Television was very demanding in the early days, with thirty-nine weeks of new programs instead of the twenty-five or twenty-six of today. Thus, there was little time for making movies. He signed a contract for seven years with NBC for more than five million dollars. The amount was staggering at that time. His program won several Emmys and was ranked high in the ratings for nineteen seasons.

Skelton's marriage to Davis continued to be filled with stress, partly because of Skelton's workaholic nature. He had a nonstop need to be creative in whatever free time he had. He painted, composed music, wrote, and even became fascinated with the art of bonsai, the shaping of dwarfed trees and shrubs. He had little time for the children. There were separations, and Skelton would move out and stay at a hotel for a while. Davis, a strong Catholic, would not even think about divorce.

Perhaps helping the marriage but hurting his career, Stillwell was beset with health problems and could not continue to devote as much time to the comedian. Skelton started periodic binge drinking, and Davis was diagnosed as an alcoholic. Things got so bad that MGM dropped him. It was clear Skelton preferred television now to the movies. NBC dropped his show, but CBS picked it up.

Red Skelton with his wife Georgia and their children Valentina and Richard.
NBC PHOTO

In January 1957 Skelton's nine-year-old son Richard was diagnosed with leukemia. Doctors told them the boy's life expectancy was only five months to a year. Skelton was unable to do his next television show, but returned the next week bolstered by twenty thousand letters and telegrams from fans. After suffering through daily blood transfusions, Richard died on May 10, 1957, less than two weeks before his tenth birthday.

In 1962 Skelton made one of five appearances at the Indiana State Fair. Since CBS was airing his show, he visited the CBS affiliate, WISH-TV, for an interview. While there, he posed for photos, looking in the viewfinder of a television camera. As he was leaving, he walked by a small room at the back of the studio where several engineers were eating lunches they had brought from home. He went into the room, sat down on the couch, and stayed for some time conversing with the stunned and delighted engineers.

In 1963 he returned to Vincennes, where he helped dedicate a new bridge over the Wabash River named in his honor. The city fathers declared it to be Red Skelton Day, and there was a big parade and a charity concert appearance by the comedian. At the show he pledged $10,000 to the orphans and needy of Knox County. He quipped, "With the toll from the bridge, I should make it back in no time."

In 1969 daughter Valentina presented the Skeltons with their first grandchild, Sabrina. The following year Skelton wrote a children's book, *Gertrude and Heathcliffe*, which included the dedication, "To my daughter, Valentina, who laid a golden egg named Sabrina."

Davis became more involved in Skelton's management. She took over many of the duties held by Stillwell and was always present in the wings when he was performing. She was the one who broke the news to him when CBS canceled his television series in 1970, despite the fact it was very highly rated. His shows were skewing old, and CBS wanted a younger audience to enhance advertiser appeal. NBC took him back, but the series was not successful.

The family moved to Palm Springs, and Skelton began spending more time painting his beloved clown pictures. Years later, a single clown canvas could sell for $80,000. His lithographs earned more than $2.5 million per year. He kept busy appearing in Las Vegas, at state fairs and colleges, and in cameo appearances in movies such as *Those Magnificent Men in Their Flying Machines.*

He began writing daily love letters to Davis. He wrote a letter the first thing every morning so that she would have it waiting for her when she awakened. Each year he had them leather-bound into a book that he gave to her. Despite this seeming devotion, Skelton became romantically involved with a woman twenty-five years younger, and in 1971 he filed for a divorce.

The other woman was Lothian Toland, daughter of the great cinematographer Greg Toland. He married Lothian in 1973. In 1976, afflicted with ill health, having suffered a heart attack and a mysterious blood disease, Davis took her own life. Exactly eighteen years to the day that Richard had died of leukemia, she picked up a .38-caliber revolver, walked into the garden, and shot herself in the head.

For the rest of his life, Skelton continued to perform while receiving many honors. He was given an honorary doctorate by Ball State University in 1986 and was inducted into the National Academy of Television Arts and Sciences' Hall of Fame in 1989 and the National Comedy Hall of Fame in 1993. He performed as often as he was able. He contracted pneumonia and died on September 18, 1997. He never forgot the words of his mother, Ida M. Skelton, who admonished him as a young boy in Vincennes, "Son, don't take life too seriously. You'll never get out of it alive."

BIBLIOGRAPHY

Buxton, Frank, and Bill Owen. *The Big Broadcast, 1920–1950.* Rev. ed. New York: Viking Press, 1972.

Gehring, Wes D. *Seeing Red: The Skelton in Hollywood's Closet.* Davenport, Iowa: Robin Vincent Publishing, 2001.

Hagemeier, Dorothy West. Telephone interview with the author. June 25, 2001. Vincennes, Indiana.

Hay, Peter. *MGM: When the Lion Roars.* Atlanta, Ga.: Turner Publishing, 1991.

Higham, Charles. *Merchant of Dreams: Louis B. Mayer, MGM, and the Secret Hollywood.* New York: D. I. Fine, 1993.

Indianapolis Star, March 20, 1999.

Lackmann, Ron. *The Encyclopedia of American Radio.* New York: Checkmark Books, 2000.

Marx, Arthur. *Red Skelton.* New York: E. P. Dutton, 1979.

JAMES EDWARDS
Leading Man and Social Crusader

James Edwards in *A Member of the Wedding* (1952).

© 1952, COLUMBIA PICTURES CORP.

James Edwards was born in Muncie, Indiana, on March 6, 1918 (another source says 1916). He was the eldest of the eight children of Valley and Annie Edwards. Valley was an outstanding entertainer who toured the country as a member of several quartets. The other Edwards children included a doctor, four athletes, a nurse, a soprano soloist, and a daughter with a business degree. Annie worked as a domestic eight hours a day, raised her children, and completed a four-year degree in missionary leadership at the Chicago Baptist Institute. She was vice president of the Indiana State Baptist Convention Auxiliary and president of the Northern Indiana District Baptist Association Auxiliary.

Edwards was just six years old when he went on tour with his father. He thought he might someday become a poet, a singer, or a writer. When he was nine years old, his family moved from Muncie to Hammond, where he graduated from high school. He briefly enrolled at Indiana University, then transferred to Knoxville College in Tennessee. He majored in psychology and received his degree in 1938. He returned to Hammond and worked for the Pullman Standard Car Company. He joined the Congress of Industrial Organizations and for several years was group grievance chairman.

Edwards moved to Chicago and went to night school at Northwestern University. He studied voice and piano and was cast in the leading role in a campus production of *Death Takes a Holiday*. This made him decide on a stage career. However, World War II interfered. He attended Officers' Candidate School and was commissioned a second lieutenant. He was discharged as a first lieutenant in 1946.

A wartime automobile accident disfigured Edwards's face, and he had to undergo plastic surgery. During his long rehabilitation, he decided to take courses in public speaking to boost his confidence and resocialize himself. He went back to Northwestern University, where he studied drama and began to participate in student productions. Later he appeared with the Skyloft Players in Chicago, performing in such plays as *The Little Foxes*, *Skin of Our Teeth*, and *The Petrified Forest*.

Edwards believed he could make it on the New York stage. He was given the opportunity to audition to understudy the role of Charles Brett in the Broadway-bound play *Deep Are the Roots*. Deciding to look his best, he came to the audition wearing a purple zoot suit, a yellow coat, a yellow feather in his hat, a long watch chain dangling from his pants pocket, and a flashy necktie. Director Elia Kazan looked him over and

James Edwards in *The Steel Helmet* (1951).

asked him to remove the yellow coat. Edwards did not get the part. Sometime later he auditioned again with Kazan, and this time Kazan gave him the role of the understudy in *Deep Are the Roots.* Edwards later assumed the role of the war hero and toured in the play, winding up on the West Coast. While in California he decided to pursue film work. In 1949 he was cast by fellow Hoosier Robert Wise as the young prize-fighter in *The Set-Up,* giving a striking, memorable performance.

After working in another play on the West Coast, Edwards was visited by fledgling producer Stanley Kramer, who was looking for an actor to play the lead in *Home of the Brave* (1949). This was the first post-war film to focus on American racism. Edwards shone in the role. He was the precursor for the kind of hero Sidney Poitier would become in the 1950s. Many thought this success would lead to full integration in Hollywood. However, it did not happen.

Edwards's talents were not utilized. In spite of his critically acclaimed performances in *The Set-Up* and *Home of the Brave,* he did not make another film until 1951, when he appeared in *The Steel Helmet.* He seemed to fall into a category where producers would cast him primarily as a military man. As a result, he was in uniform in such films as *Bright Victory* (1951), *Battle Hymn* (1957), *Men in War* (1957), *Pork Chop Hill* (1959), and *The Manchurian Candidate* (1962).

Edwards never hesitated to speak out on causes he believed were right. In 1951 he refused to testify before the House Un-American Activities Committee against actor Paul Robeson. Edwards's refusal no doubt influenced the way some movie executives thought about him. That same year he also spoke out against the television series *The Amos 'n Andy Show*, stating that "for the sake of 142 jobs which Negroes hold down with the 'Amos 'n' Andy Show,' 15 million more Negroes are being pushed back 25 years by perpetuating this stereotype on television." In 1953 he spoke out against rumors that had labeled him as a heavy drinker, a womanizer, and an arrogant and difficult person to work with.

In 1955 Edwards appeared in two dramas on television. In "D. P.," on *The General Electric Theater*, he portrayed an American soldier stationed in Germany, whose bitterness was mellowed when he became the surrogate father of an orphaned black boy. In "Toward Tomorrow," on the *Du Pont Cavalcade Theater*, he played the young Ralph Bunch, struggling with the idea of whether or not to attend college. Edwards's career began to decline, and in 1958 he was a supporting player in *Anna Lucasta.* He was in a low-budget film, *Night of the Quarter Moon*, in 1959 and was one of Elizabeth Taylor's bohemian friends in *The Sandpiper* (1965). His next-to-last appearance was as the general's valet in *Patton* (1970).

Edwards died on January 4, 1970, in San Diego, California, of a heart attack.

James Edwards and George C. Scott in *Patton* (1970).

© 1970, 20TH CENTURY-FOX FILM CORP., LTD.

BIBLIOGRAPHY

Bogle, Donald. *Blacks in American Films and Television: An Encyclopedia.* New York: Simon and Schuster, 1989.

Hicks, Luther. *Great Black Hoosier Americans.* N. p.: Luther C. Hicks, 1977.

Indianapolis Star, November 13, 1949.

The Internet Movie Database. http://www.imdb.com/.

Jones, Ken D., Arthur F. McClure, and Alfred E. Twomey. *Character People.* South Brunswick, N.J.: A. S. Barnes, 1976.

MacDonald, J. Fred. *Blacks and White TV: African Americans in Television since 1948.* 2nd ed. Chicago: Nelson-Hall Publishers, 1992.

WILLIAM MARSHALL

"Blacula"

Born in Gary, Indiana, on August 19, 1924, William Marshall became a leading actor on stage and screen. Despite the fact he appeared in many major Broadway productions and feature films, he is best known for his 1972 portrayal of African Prince Mumuwalde, who, after being bitten by Count Dracula, became the blaxploitation hero Blacula. He reprised the role in 1973 in *Scream Blacula Scream!* These two films made him a cult figure but did not prevent him from appearing in a diverse selection of roles the rest of his career.

After graduation from Gary Roosevelt High School, Marshall moved to New York City, where he studied acting. He made his Broadway debut during World War II when, as a private, he appeared in the U.S. Army Air Forces production of *Winged Victory*. The writer and director was Moss Hart, and the music was by Private David Rose. Other privates in the cast were Red Buttons, Lee J. Cobb, John Forsythe, and Kevin McCarthy. Marshall went on to appear in four more Broadway productions. Along with James Earl Jones, Canada Lee, and William Warfield, he was in *Set My People Free* in 1948. In 1949 Marshall appeared in Maxwell Anderson's *Lost in the Stars*. He was Cookson in the 1950 production of *Peter Pan*, which starred Jean Arthur and Boris Karloff. In 1951, largely thanks to his booming voice, he was cast as God in the revival of *The Green Pastures*.

Marshall made an auspicious film debut in 1952 in *Lydia Bailey*, playing the towering deep-voiced leader of the Negro Republicans, a Haitian called King Dick. Although the film focused on a white hero and heroine, Marshall completely stole the picture. He remained busy in the 1950s in such films as *Demetrius and the Gladiators* (1954), *Something of Value* (1957) (with Sidney Poitier), and *Sabu and the Magic Ring* (1957), in which he played a genie.

Although Marshall was a confident, polished, and sophisticated actor with an unusual mixture of physical strength and sharp intelligence, important film roles seldom came his way.

Marshall was very busy as a television actor, appearing in many shows between 1959 and 1979. He also made several notable stage appearances, portraying such outstanding African Americans as Paul Robeson and Frederick Douglass. He taught acting workshops on several college campuses and was the director of the Mufandi Institute in Watts in the 1960s. Marshall was featured as Judge Marcus Black in the 1977 television series *Rosetti and Ryan*, and in 1981 he starred in a television production of Shakespeare's *Othello*.

On behalf of his grandchildren, Marshall ventured into children's television as King of Cartoons in the children's series *Pee-Wee's Playhouse* from 1987 to 1991. He had a cameo role as a riverboat gambler in the 1994 Mel Gibson film *Maverick.* He continued to make feature films through 1996. He retired from films and entered a nursing home in Los Angeles, a victim of Alzheimer's disease. He died of complications from the disease on June 11, 2003.

William Marshall and Vonetta McGee in *Blacula* (1972).
© 1972, AMERICAN INTERNATIONAL PICTURES

BIBLIOGRAPHY

The African American Registry. http://www.aaregistry.com/.
Bogle, Donald. *Blacks in American Films and Television: An Encyclopedia.* New York: Simon and Schuster, 1989.
The Internet Broadway Database. http://www.ibdb.com/.
The Internet Movie Database. http://www.imdb.com.
"William Marshall." *Classic Images* (August 2003).

STEVE MCQUEEN
The King of Cool

He became an international superstar and was the most celebrated and highest-paid film actor of the 1960s and 1970s. He was king of the box office, headed his own production company, and was ranked thirtieth in a list of the top one hundred movie stars of all time (*Empire Magazine*). All this belies his background.

Terrence Steve McQueen was an unwanted child and virtually abandoned by his mother. He was almost deaf in one ear, was dyslexic, ran with gangs, stole for the fun of it, hated school, and ran away from home to join a circus at age fourteen. In spite of all this, McQueen said, "I'm out of the Midwest. It was a good place to come from. It gives you a sense of right or wrong and fairness, which I think is lacking in our society."

McQueen was born in Beech Grove, Indiana, on March 24, 1930. His mother, Julian Crawford, was a rebellious, pleasure-loving teenager. It was the Roaring Twenties, and Julian was the embodiment of the flapper. At the age of sixteen she left her little suburb of Beech Grove and went to Indianapolis. There she met Bill McQueen, who she later described as "dashing and romantic." Bill was a daredevil stunt flier and impressed the teenager with tales of his adventurous life. When it was discovered Julian was pregnant, Bill married her, but left her after six months.

Steve McQueen would later say, "My father named me after a one-armed bookie pal of his, Steve Hall. He must have had a weird sense of humor." As it turned out, the name was the only thing Bill left young Steve. Steve searched for his father for years, and although he came close to finding him, they never got a chance to meet face to face.

In an interview in London in 1969, McQueen was asked what he would do if he could meet his father right then. His first reply was, "I'd probably kill him." Then after a pause for reflection he said, "No, that's the wrong thing to say. I wouldn't kill him . . . I'd feel sorry for him because he missed out on me, on me growing up, as much as I missed out on him. He was foolish in what he did."

The young and beautiful Julian found it difficult to deal with life after becoming a mother and being abandoned by her husband. She decided to take her son from their Beech Grove home to live with his great-uncle, Claude Thompson. Thompson had a working hog farm in Slater, Missouri, and had not been affected by the depression. Julian dropped her three-year-old son at the farm and left. He had now been abandoned by both his parents.

Although Thompson ruled with an iron fist, he was the closest thing to a father that McQueen would ever know, and he developed an emotional bond with the boy. They would ride into town together, and McQueen was enlisted to help with the chores around the farm, getting up in the dark, and as he later recounted, "milked cows, worked the cornfield, cut wood for the winter . . . there was always plenty to do. I came to love and understand animals and to feel that in a few ways they are superior to human beings. When I'd get lazy and duck my chores, Claude would warm my backside with a hickory switch. I learned a simple fact: you work for what you get."

McQueen learned that his uncle was a stern but generous man whose word was as good as gold. McQueen said, "He was a very good man. Very strong. Very fair. I learned a lot from him." McQueen was rewarded for his diligence on the farm. He had his own room and went to Saturday matinees in downtown Slater. He said, "Westerns were my favorite. I used to bring my cap pistol and fire at the villains."

On McQueen's fourth birthday, Thompson gave him a red tricycle. "That started my racing fever," he recalled. "There was a dirt bluff behind the farm and I'd challenge the other kids in the area. We'd race for gumdrops. I usually reached the top first. Got some skinned knees, but I sure won a lot of gumdrops."

McQueen started school in Slater at age six but did not like it. Learning was difficult. It was not until years later he found he suffered from dyslexia and from a hearing loss brought on by a mastoid infection before the days of antibiotics. He learned to fish and hunt from Thompson and loved both. He was living a rather idyllic life on the farm when suddenly Julian came back to Slater. She had remarried and decided it was time for her son to join her in Indianapolis.

Although Thompson hated to see the boy go, he did not fight it. As they were leaving for Indianapolis, Thompson called McQueen aside and said, "Here, I want you to have this to remember me by." He gave McQueen a gold pocket watch. Inside was the inscription, "To Steve . . . who has been like a son to me." The eight-year-old wiped the tears from his eyes and left with his mother.

McQueen never liked to talk about his early life: "My early life I try not to think about too much." In Indianapolis he escaped his callous and domineering stepfather by running wild on the streets. He described it as "doin' a little stealin'." He added, "It was a bad scene, man." Then as if to offer an excuse, "I feel I was in a neighborhood in Indianapolis where one inevitably grew up with gangs." Describing his activity he said, "We would break into lock-up shops . . . that kind of thing. It wasn't that we did this in terms of money . . . because we were never short of money . . . but as a relief from boredom." He later recalled mastering two skills in Indianapolis: "how to steal hubcaps and shoot pool." He would be an avid and skilled pool player the rest of his life.

On McQueen's twelfth birthday, his mother and her new husband decided to move to Los Angeles. (McQueen's new stepfather was a man named Berri. McQueen never did know his stepfather's first name.) After the family's arrival in Los Angeles, Julian, becoming disillusioned with her volatile husband, began to drink as an escape from her unhappy life.

By this time McQueen was well on his way to becoming a delinquent, spending even more time on the streets with various gangs. When McQueen was caught for the second time stealing hubcaps off

Steve McQueen.

(Previous page) Steve McQueen in The Hunter (1980).

a Cadillac, Julian decided to send him to the California Junior Boys' Republic in Chino.

Before she committed McQueen to the school, however, Julian decided to swallow her pride and call Thompson, who agreed to take the boy back. When McQueen returned to Slater, he found Thompson had remarried. His new wife was named Eva, and when McQueen arrived dirty and starving, Eva immediately fed him and then made him take a bath. Thompson was happy to have his "son" back, but warned McQueen that the first time he got in trouble he would be sent back to his mother. McQueen knew that meant reform school.

In 1944 a traveling circus came to Slater. McQueen was always fascinated with circuses. A man selling pencils at the circus told the fourteen-year-old he could make big money selling pencils. McQueen left Slater without saying good-bye to anyone, including Thompson, who was heartbroken and searched for days before giving up.

McQueen's stay with the circus was short lived, and he returned to California to his mother and his hated stepfather. However, his relationship with his stepfather had not improved, and McQueen again found himself involved in the gang scene. After each problem with the law, his stepfather would beat him. Finally, after a severe beating McQueen told him, "You lay your stinkin' hands on me again and I swear I'll kill ya."

That was the end of McQueen's stay with Julian and Berri. He was sent to the Boys' Republic in Chino. McQueen arrived at Chino on February 6, 1945. He was not popular with the other boys at the facility, got into a number of fights, and tried to run away more than once. Finally, he met a man who would change his life. One of the counselors, a Mr. Panter, started to get through to McQueen. McQueen soon realized what Panter said made sense. "He was sayin' some straight things . . . and I began to listen," said McQueen. Panter reminded McQueen of his uncle Claude. Panter told him he had a chance to be somebody special someday. Eventually, through Panter's efforts, McQueen became a role model at the school.

Steve McQueen with his first wife, Neile Adams. They were married from 1956 to 1972.

In 1946 Berri died, and McQueen's mother moved to New York, where she met a cinematographer named Victor Lukens. She moved in with him and sent for McQueen. Although he was doing well at Chino, the thought of going to live in New York excited him. When he arrived in New York and gave his mother an awkward kiss, he realized she was drunk. After they arrived at her apartment, he was assigned to share a room with another man downstairs. It was at this point that he totally wrote off his mother, decided to forgo his high school education, and hit the streets of New York on his own at age sixteen.

McQueen joined the merchant marines, deserted in the Dominican Republic, went to Cuba, worked as a towel boy in a brothel, and finally joined the U.S. Marines in 1947. He was honorably discharged in 1950 and decided to go back to New York. He was about to go to a tile-setting school on the GI Bill when the girl he was dating at the time asked him to go with her to the Neighborhood Playhouse, where she was taking acting lessons. He was introduced to Sanford Meisner, a highly respected drama teacher and director. Meisner was impressed with McQueen, and in no time McQueen was in drama school.

Two years later he won a scholarship to the Uta Hagen-Herbert Berghof School and got his first paid acting job. He got other jobs and went on tour with several shows. After finding himself back in New York without a job, he decided to audition for the prestigious Actors Studio.

He auditioned for Lee Strasberg with a scene from *Golden Boy*. Hundreds auditioned, but only five were accepted. McQueen was one of the five.

McQueen's first part in a major film came about because of a confluence of incidences that all seemed to have a Hoosier flavor. In 1956 fellow Hoosier Robert Wise gave McQueen a bit part in *Somebody Up There Likes Me*. The lead actor was Paul Newman in a role that was meant for James Dean, who had just died. Somehow McQueen felt the part in that movie belonged to him. But it was not McQueen that originally impressed Wise—it was McQueen's future wife, dancer/actress Neile Adams. Wise saw her performance in *Pajama Game* and asked her to come to Hollywood for a screen test. She did, and Wise cast her in his film *This Could Be the Night*. Adams managed to get McQueen introduced to Wise.

Wise remembers his first meeting with McQueen: "He came in, in a sport jacket, kind of gangly and loose and he had a little cap. A little bill around the top of his head. I guess it was his cocky manner somehow, not fresh, but just nice and cocky and a bit full of himself that just caught my eye and I cast him in this small part. It was the part of some kid on a rooftop fighting back in New York."

Steve McQueen in the television series *Wanted: Dead or Alive* (1958–61).

After this brief fling at the movies, McQueen went back to New York, but he was miserable all by himself and called Adams and told her he was coming to Hollywood to marry her. McQueen said, "I didn't have the price of a flight to California, so I had to pawn my gold pocket watch . . . the one my Uncle Claude had given me. I loved that ol' watch. But I loved Neile more." When he arrived in California, he told Adams he wanted to be married at Capistrano, "where the swallows are." When they arrived at the mission a nun informed them that there was no way they could be married that night. The banns had to be published, and that would mean a three-day delay. McQueen told the nun, "All right then, we'll live in sin." They got in the car, and McQueen drove furiously toward San Clemente. Two highway patrolmen stopped them for speeding. McQueen told them, "Really, all we want to do is get married." The patrolmen took them to a Lutheran minister they knew. The minister opened up his church, and they were married with the two patrolmen as their witnesses.

Eventually the couple returned to New York, where he managed to get roles in television shows such as *Studio One*. McQueen did some summer stock and managed to get in the national tour of *Time Out for Ginger*, which starred Melvyn Douglas. He got a chance to read for the part of John Drew Barrymore's boyhood chum in a movie called *Never Love a Stranger*. He got the part, but it was a low-budget B movie and not much came of it. However, a television series called *Trackdown* was about to spawn a spin-off about a bounty hunter. McQueen had appeared in one episode in which he played Josh Randall, the bounty hunter. McQueen's agent asked that he be considered for the lead in the new series, but the casting department turned him down. McQueen's agent then went directly to Dick Powell, whose company (Four Star Productions) produced *Trackdown*, and begged Powell to audition McQueen.

Powell, who spent a number of years in Indianapolis singing for Charlie Davis and his band, decided to take a look at McQueen. The new series was to be the first to feature a "heavy" as a lead. A bounty hunter is a loner and is disliked by the bad guys and the good guys. Powell knew he had to find someone who had appeal even though his character might be unsympathetic. Powell said, "If he's some big, aggressive football type, your audience will turn against him. I need a guy who looks tough but with a boyish appeal behind the toughness and a hint of menace underneath." Powell decided McQueen had those qualities. In Josh Randall, McQueen found a character in which he could play himself. He was a loner. He was an adult who had never quite grown up. He was tough, stubborn, and yet vulnerable. McQueen decided to fight for whatever he thought was right for this character. He fought for script changes, costumes, and cast members. He was not well liked by his coworkers, but he molded the character in his own image. *Wanted: Dead or Alive* became his ticket to success.

William F. Nolan, a writer for *Wanted: Dead or Alive*, tells of an incident when McQueen refused to say a line because he thought it was not right. After Nolan rewrote it, McQueen said somewhat apologetically, "Sometimes I get spiky. They say I'm nuts to worry about every line of a show like this. Just a cheap western series. Grind 'em out. Assembly line stuff, right? Wrong, I tell 'em. You do a thing, you go all the way. Which means I give every scene my best shot. Every line counts. If it doesn't, then how come I'm out here in my funny hat making a damn fool of myself?" In spite of his seeming dedication to his art, McQueen was never comfortable being an actor. Much later in his career, he would say, "I'll tell ya, in my own mind, I'm not sure acting is a thing for a grown man to be doing."

After Hoosier rebel James Dean was killed in a car crash in 1955, he received two posthumous nominations for Oscars for *East of Eden* and *Giant*. His fan following grew larger, and Hollywood was looking for his successor. McQueen bore a resemblance to Dean, both physically and in the rebel image he exuded. This similarity surely helped launch his screen career. McQueen even borrowed some of Dean's mannerisms at the start of his acting career.

Since he had a steady income now, McQueen decided to renew his search for his father. He and Adams traced his father to the Silverlake area in California and left messages at every bar and pool hall imploring anybody who knew of Bill McQueen's whereabouts to call. Finally, a woman called who identified herself as Bill McQueen's lady friend—only she called him Terry McQueen. This was the first time McQueen knew his father's name was also Terrence. The McQueens drove to the woman's apartment, where she told them Terry had died three months earlier. McQueen said, "You know, although I never met him, I felt a real sense of loss. I talked to some of the people who lived with him. They say he saw me on TV and said I might have been his boy, that I had the McQueen look." Before they left, the woman gave McQueen a photograph of a man who was his mirror image. She also gave him a silver lighter with the initials TMcQ.

McQueen's career began to take off. He had made one feature just before he started on *Wanted: Dead or Alive*. It was a low-budget horror film called *The Blob*. After that, McQueen vowed never to do another low-budget film. Fortunately, director John Sturges saw McQueen and recommended him to Frank Sinatra. Sinatra took a look at McQueen on *Wanted: Dead or Alive* and put him in his next film, *Never So Few*. McQueen made such an impression that Sturges cast him in *The Magnificent Seven*. It took a lot of doing to get out of his contract with *Wanted: Dead or Alive*, but he finally managed to leave after three years of trying to sustain both a television and a film career.

In 1963 McQueen made *The Great Escape*, and his performance made it clear he was a major star. *Life* magazine described him as "an oddball

Steve McQueen in *The Great Escape* (1963).

Steve McQueen in *The Sand Pebbles* (1966).

who combines the cockiness of Cagney, the glower of Bogart and the rough-diamond of Garfield." He became a star primarily because of his presence on the screen. The camera loved McQueen—the body language, the face, the raised eyebrow, the look across the camera. Here was someone with no literary or artistic background who stood out because of something that might be termed pure animal instinct.

In 1966 McQueen reached the apex of his career when Wise asked him to star in *The Sand Pebbles.* McQueen was perfect for the part of Jake Holman and received his first and only nomination for a best actor Oscar. Concerning his work with McQueen, Wise said, "Of all the stars whom I worked with, I think Steve knew better what worked for him on the screen than any other. He had such a sense of what he could register, and that helped a lot in terms of shaping the character and the script."

During the filming of *The Getaway* in 1972, McQueen became involved with his costar, Ali McGraw. This ended his marriage with Adams. He married McGraw in 1973, and the marriage lasted four years. Shortly after the divorce, McQueen saw a pretty young girl's picture in a fashion magazine. He tracked Barbara Minty down, and, although they became a couple, they were not married until January 19, 1980, after McQueen had been diagnosed with cancer.

After finishing what would be his last picture, *The Hunter*, he became short of breath and was coughing consistently. He attributed his condition to "a cold I caught in Chicago. I just haven't been able to get

"The Reivers," William Faulkner's Pulitzer Prize-Winning Novel, is now a film!

Steve McQueen **plays** Boon in "The Reivers"

co-starring
Sharon Farrell, Will Geer, Michael Constantine, Rupert Crosse, Mitch Vogel

An Irving Ravetch-Arthur Kramer Production·In Association with Solar Productions
Executive Producer-Robert E. Relyea · Music by John Williams · Screenplay by Irving Ravetch and Harriet Frank, Jr.
Based on the Novel "The Reivers" by William Faulkner · Produced by Irving Ravetch · Directed by Mark Rydell
Panavision®& Technicolor.®A Cinema Center Films Presentation. A National General Pictures Release.

rid of it." A short time later, McQueen collapsed while at his ranch. Doctors at Cedars-Sinai Medical Center in Los Angeles ran a full battery of tests and discovered a malignant tumor in his right lung. It was inoperable, and it was usually caused by exposure to asbestos, a material used in his racing clothes and even on a mask he wrapped around his mouth underneath his helmet. McQueen died on November 7, 1980, clutching a Bible Billy Graham had given him. He was in Juarez, Mexico, where he had gone to seek alternative treatments for his cancer.

Three years later Steve's son, Chad McQueen, who had become an actor, helped dedicate the Steve McQueen Recreation Center at the Boys' Republic in Chino. Because he had requested that he be cremated, Steve McQueen never had a grave site, but the inscription on the bronze plaque at Chino would have suited him just fine:

> Steve McQueen came here as a troubled boy but left here as a man. He went on to achieve stardom in motion pictures but returned to this campus often to share of himself and his fortune. His legacy is hope and inspiration to those students here now, and those yet to come.

A memorial service was held at McQueen's ranch in Santa Paula, California, on November 9, 1983. In attendance were his three wives, Adams, McGraw, and Minty, his two children, Terry and Chad, and six close friends. At the end of the service a group of planes piloted by some of McQueen's aviator friends flew over in a missing-man formation. The vacant spot was for the boy from Beech Grove, Indiana. They dipped their wings once, then headed out over the Pacific, where McQueen's ashes were scattered.

Perhaps McQueen summed up his own life best in 1963, when he said, "When I did 'The Great Escape,' I kept thinking, if they were making a movie of my life, that's what they'd call it: 'The Great Escape.'"

BIBLIOGRAPHY

"The Bad Boys Break Out." *Life*, July 12, 1963.

Indianapolis News, April 23, 1979, October 10, November 8, 1980.

The Internet Movie Database. http://www.imdb.com/.

Keyser, Michael, with Jonathan Williams. *A French Kiss with Death: Steve McQueen and the Making of* Le Mans. Cambridge, Mass.: Robert Bentley Publishers, 1999.

Leeman, Sergio. *Robert Wise on His Films.* Los Angeles: Silman-James Press, 1995.

New York Times, November 8, 1980.

Nolan, William F. *McQueen.* New York: Berkley Books, 1984.

Spiegel, Penina. *McQueen: The Untold Story of a Bad Boy in Hollywood.* Garden City, N.Y.: Doubleday and Company, 1986.

"Steve McQueen Plays the Tough-Guy, Good-Guy Game." *Look*, January 27, 1970.

Terrill, Marshall. *Steve McQueen: Portrait of an American Rebel.* New York: Donald I. Fine, 1993.

Toffel, Neile McQueen. *My Husband, My Friend.* New York: Atheneum, 1986.

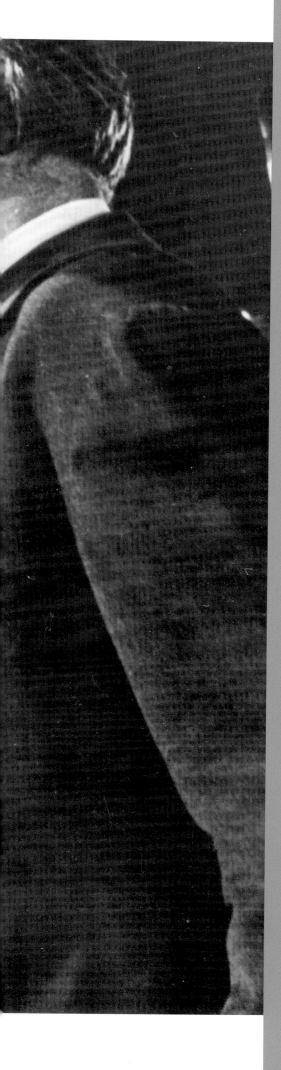

JAMES DEAN
Hoosier Rebel

Several Indiana stars have met untimely deaths. John Bowers of Garrett, a silent-screen star who could not make the transition to sound, committed suicide by renting a boat and jumping into the Pacific Ocean. His life and death served as the basis for the film *A Star Is Born.* Cowboy star Buck Jones of Vincennes successfully bridged the gap between silent and sound films and was moving from leading man to more mature roles when his career ended with the horrific fire at the Cocoanut Grove Night Club in Boston. Carole Lombard of Fort Wayne was perhaps at the peak of her career at age thirty-three when her plane crashed into a Nevada mountain. She was on her way back to Hollywood after completing a hugely successful war-bond drive in Indianapolis.

However, the most famous death of all was that of James Dean, whose promising career had barely begun when he was killed in an automobile accident. Today, Dean has been immortalized as an eternal symbol of youthful rebellion and is an icon for young people, as well as those who yearn to recapture their youth. Gwyn Steinbeck, former wife of the author of *East of Eden*, Dean's first major film, said, "For many of these youngsters without emotional roots, without a basic faith, Dean has become a substitute Christ. As such, they are even trying to resurrect him."

Visits to Dean's grave in Fairmount, Indiana, have become as much a part of celebrity mythology as trips to Graceland. His life and death have inspired films and plays (*September 30, 1955* and *Come Back to the Five and Dime, Jimmy Dean, Jimmy Dean*). The aunt who raised him, Ortense Winslow, said, "There wasn't anything very different about him . . . except his ability to take you along with his feelings." Dean made just three major films, and he took the whole world along with him. One critic described him as an "American farm boy with the eyes of an injured animal and the innocent grace of a captive panther."

James Byron Dean was born on February 8, 1931, in Marion, Indiana, in a house at Fourth and McClure streets. He was given the first name of the attending physician, James Emmick. His middle name, some sources say, came from the poet Lord Byron, and Dean always believed his mother named him after the poet. However, it is not likely that either his mother or father had ever heard of Byron. Dean's father had a friend named George Byron Fiest, and the name probably came from him.

Dean's father and mother, Winton and Mildred Dean, were both native Hoosiers. When Jimmy was almost three, his father quit his

James Dean.

James Dean.

(*Previous page*) James Dean and Raymond Massey in *East of Eden* (1955).

job as a dental technician at Marion's Veterans Hospital and moved the family to Fairmount. They moved to the farm of Winton's sister Ortense and her husband, Marcus Winslow. The Deans lived in a small cottage along Back Creek, a small stream that ran through the Winslow farm. Winton tried his hand at raising bullfrogs, but there was not much of a market for frogs' legs during the Depression years, so the Deans returned to Marion. Winton returned to work at the hospital. A year later, in 1935, Winton was transferred to the Sawtelle Veterans Hospital near Santa Monica, California.

Mildred was interested in the theater, and she made a little cardboard theater for Jimmy and herself. Together they would engage in a fantasy world of their own devising. A favorite game was the "Wishing Game." Jimmy would go to bed and place a slip of paper under his pillow. When he was asleep, his mother would remove the paper and read his wish. If it was at all possible, she tried to make it come true the following day. She arranged for Jimmy to have dancing and music lessons. He adored his mother.

Mildred kept in touch with the folks back home in Indiana, sending frequent photos of young Jimmy to Winton's parents in Fairmount. A friend from Fairmount, who visited the Deans in 1938, reported that Mildred said, "I don't want Jimmy to grow up out here. I've even been thinking about going back home to Indiana. Everything's so artificial here. I want my Jimmy to grow up where things are real and simple." Tragically, her wish would come true in another year.

Jimmy was almost nine years old when his mother began to complain about severe abdominal pain. An operation revealed she had uterine cancer. In May 1940 Winton wrote to his mother in Fairmount to tell her that Mildred was dying and she should come immediately. Emma Dean went to California, and seven weeks later, on July 14, 1940, Mildred died at age twenty-nine. Emma told Winton, "Now, I want you to think this thing over carefully. If you see fit to let Jimmy come back to Fairmount, Ortense and Marcus would like to take him in. They'll raise him for you if you want."

Later Winton said, "I was deep in debt with doctor's bills, X-rays, radium treatments and everything else. I was alone without anyone to look after the boy when I was at work. I had to get my feet under me again." Winton sold his car to pay for his wife's last operation and could not even afford to go to the funeral in Fairmount.

Jimmy rode the train back to Fairmount with his grandmother and his mother's body. Practically speaking, he was an orphan because he would see his father only occasionally the rest of his life. The Winslows put Jimmy to work on their large farm in Fairmount. They provided a stable upbringing for their young charge.

Dean's education in Fairmount was unspectacular, though he liked the change in schools from Brentwood Public School in California to Fairmount. His grades improved, and he had help from his older "sister," Joan, the Winslows' daughter.

Adeline Brookshire (later Nall) came to Fairmount High School in 1940, the same year Dean came back from California. She said the grade school students would come over and see dress rehearsals of the plays the high school students were doing. In this way Dean got to see two plays a year. In junior high school he went to Brookshire and asked her to coach him in his WCTU (Woman's Christian Temperance Union) reading, "Bars." He used a chair as a prop for the reading, but when it was time to perform, the chair was not allowed. He refused to compete.

In spite of his aunt's insistence that there was not anything different about him, Dean was not the average Hoosier schoolboy in the eyes of his peers. Sue Hill, a high school classmate, recalled, "We watched Jimmy with a little awe, but felt he was explosive and not part of the community." Hill's twin sister, Shirley, added, "His dramatic ability awed us, but his artistic capability in oils and his basketball and baseball talents gave him peer acceptance and popularity in spite of his individuality."

Another classmate and debating partner, Barbara Leach, said that "audacious" would be the best way to describe Dean. "He was a little more daring," said Leach. As a senior, she remembered a Halloween party in a barn at which Dean tried to pour cider from the loft into the open mouths of the kids below. Leach recalled that during their debates, if Dean could not find documentation to back up a particular point, he faked it. "I lived in dread that he would be found out and the good name of Fairmount High ruined," she said.

Like most Hoosier schoolboys, Dean learned to play basketball at an early age. Rex Couch, a friend from Dean's youth, said that the Winslow barn was known as the county's basketball center. "Every Sunday, there were anywhere from ten to thirty-five guys playing there. At an early age, Jimmy was playing with guys much older than he was," Couch said. The barn also served as a place to perform trapeze stunts. Dean lost his two front teeth while trying a stunt his uncle had shown him and wore false teeth the rest of his life.

At the beginning of Dean's senior year at Fairmount High, he was the basketball team's top scorer, although he was only five feet, seven-and-a-half inches tall and weighed just one hundred forty-six pounds. Fairmount went into the sectional tournament as an underdog but managed to beat Van Buren High and Mississinewa, two teams that had defeated them during the regular season. In the final they faced Marion, a much larger school. Although they lost, Dean was the game's star with fifteen points, a high for both teams. He also was on the baseball team and participated in track and field, where he was a hurdler and pole-vaulter.

James Dean.

Although he was known for his athletic prowess in high school, Dean's real love was dramatics. Brookshire chose *You Can't Take It with You* as the senior play. Dean was not cast in a leading role because Brookshire knew that no one besides Dean could play the eccentric Russian ballet instructor. Classmate Joyce John said, "Quite often he was late for practice and sometimes didn't show up at all. He had quite a temper and would walk out of practice if things didn't suit him. He was disruptive . . . but he was good!"

The highlight of Dean's senior year at Fairmount was when he won the Indiana state championship in the Indiana Dramatic Speaking Contest for his reading of Dickens's "A Madman's Manuscript" from *Pickwick Papers*. Dean and Brookshire went to Longmont, Colorado, representing Indiana in the national meet. At the Marion depot where they left by train, the band played, the cheerleaders yelled, and Dean began to bawl. In Longmont, Dean placed sixth out of twenty-two contestants. Brookshire said, "I can still remember seeing him huddled in his seat during the finals, heartsick that he was out of the running."

When he finished high school, Dean decided to go to Santa Monica to live with his father and stepmother, intending to study drama at UCLA. Unfortunately, he discovered that living with his father was not all that pleasant. Winton Dean thought that being an actor was not a "manly profession" and "the movies were full of pantywaists." Dean also found that UCLA was too expensive for an out-of-state student. He decided to enroll in Santa Monica Junior College, obtain his residency, and then apply to UCLA. He got into the Santa Monica Theater Guild, becoming a stage manager and sometimes actor.

In 1950 Dean made a three-week trip back to Indiana with his father and stepmother. While there, he visited the campus of Indiana University, where Brookshire was working on her master's degree in speech and theater. Dean told Brookshire he did not feel his year at Santa Monica Junior College had been very useful to him. She took him to see Dr. Lee Norvelle, chairman of the theater department. Norvelle told Dean he would be delighted to have him at Indiana University, but he also told Dean that he believed all theater majors should get a teaching certificate as a hedge against not succeeding as an actor. Dean did not want to hear this and decided against attending the university. He went back to California and transferred from Santa Monica to UCLA.

Dean did not make much progress at UCLA, although he did manage to appear in several plays. He made frequent trips into Hollywood, hoping to get some kind of a part. He discovered that actor James Whitmore was conducting an off-campus workshop, and he dropped out of UCLA and enrolled in Whitmore's class.

In 1951 Dean was cast in a radio series called *Alias Jane Doe.* The star of the series was Pleasant Lake, Indiana, native Lurene Tuttle. Later, when Tuttle was named to the board of advisers of the James Dean Foundation, she met Brookshire in New York in 1956. Tuttle told Brookshire she remembered when Dean first worked in *Alias,* he would let each sheet of the script flutter to the ground after it was read. The rest of the cast laughed at him for it, but Brookshire said that was exactly what she taught Dean to do.

After getting a few bit parts in several movies, Dean made a surprise visit to his old hometown. He looked up Brookshire and asked if she could arrange for him to speak at a convocation of the student body. He talked for ninety minutes, telling about his experiences in commercials, his first movie role in *Fixed Bayonets,* and his visits to bullfights in Mexico. He even gave a bullfighting demonstration, using a student as the charging bull. He directed a rehearsal of the junior play at Brookshire's request and used it to demonstrate some of the acting techniques he learned from Whitmore.

It was at Whitmore's suggestion that Dean moved to New York City. This atmosphere gave him more freedom to express his individuality. The *Marion Leader-Tribune* of January 19, 1952, said, "Friends of Jim Dean, Fairmount High School graduate in 1949, will have a chance to see him on TV today in a play scheduled to begin at three P.M." The play was *I Remember Mama,* and Dean's part was so small he was not identified. Although he began to get other television parts, he was barely surviving when he got a job as a stunt tester on the television show *Beat the Clock.* The producers were amazed at how he was able to control his body. His athleticism allowed him to perform all the stunts with ease.

In July 1952 Dean received notice that he had been accepted into the Actors Studio. He had auditioned with fellow actress Christine

James Dean with Winslow farm in background (1955).
DENNIS STOCK/MAGNUM PHOTOS INC.

White, and they were both accepted. This was unusual because most aspiring actors have to audition several times before they are accepted. Unfortunately, Dean and Lee Strasberg, the resident guru of the Actors Studio, did not get along. Strasberg was devastating in his critiques of actors, and Dean refused to bow to this type of instruction. He left the studio after a short time and never felt he learned much of value from "the Method."

Dean made his Broadway debut on December 3, 1952, in *See the Jaguar*, playing a young man whose mother kept him in a cage and who was more animal than boy. It closed after five performances, and Dean went back to doing television programs and was cast in a *Studio One* play, *Sentence of Death.* In it he worked with East Chicago native Betsy Palmer. During rehearsals for this play, they discovered they were both from Indiana. They were teamed again a week later in "Death Is My Neighbor," a *Danger* episode. Dean was getting enough work now to afford his own apartment. Palmer said, "All he had was a mattress. I gave Jimmy blankets, pillows, and sheets for his first apartment on Sixtysixth street." She went on to say, "Both being from Indiana drew us together. We were good friends, and actually . . . briefly . . . lovers. Friendship was more important than the sexual part. Nurturing was really the thing about our relationship. He was a lost lamb. I never felt he would live to be old. Something hovered around him, an air of 'I've got to get this done quick.' He was a skyrocket, a comet." Dean and Palmer dated steadily for nine months. "He would come to my place and I would cook for him. He had no money. His agent would take Jimmy's money." Of their breakup she said, "We had a stupid falling out. You know we both were so young. I always felt he had an inclination for being quite reckless."

Dean got his first big break in 1953 when he was cast as Bachir, an Arab boy, in the play *The Immoralist*. Costarring were Geraldine Page and Louis Jourdan. Once Dean got the part, he set out on his Royal Enfield motorcycle for Indiana. This was in November, and he had to travel through snow, ice, and freezing temperatures, but he arrived in time for Thanksgiving. He worked on his part while on the farm. He also drove to Marion to see WBAT radio announcer and sportscaster Bill Fowler, whom he had known from his days on the high school basketball team. He told Fowler of his part in *The Immoralist* and asked, "Do you want to interview me?" Fowler said he made several ten-minute tapes of their conversations. "I sure wish I knew what happened to those tapes," he lamented. Fowler's wife said the tapes had been erased. No one thought they were worth saving.

Dean made his way back to New York, and shortly after *The Immoralist* opened, screenwriter Paul Osborn (Evansville) recommended Dean for the part of Cal Trask in *East of Eden*. Osborn was a well-known scenarist and author. He had written the popular play, *On Borrowed Time*, which eventually was transferred to the screen, and wrote screenplays for such major films as *The World of Suzie Wong* and *Sayonara*. He was hired to write the screenplay for *East of Eden* from John Steinbeck's novel. According to Elia Kazan, Osborn brought Dean to his attention:

> Paul Osborn, who was writing the screenplay, said I should have a look at the young man playing the bit part of an Arab in a play at the John Golden Theater. I wasn't impressed with James Dean. . . . I'd begun to think about Brando again . . . but to please Osborn, I called Jimmy into Warners' New York offices for a closer look. When I walked in, he was slouched at the end of a leather sofa in the waiting room, a heap of twisted legs and denim rags, looking resentful for no particular reason. I didn't like the expression on his face, so I kept him waiting. I also wanted to see how he'd react to that. It seemed that I'd out-toughed him, because when I called him into my office, he'd dropped the belligerent pose. We tried to talk, but conversation was not his gift, so we sat looking at each other. He asked me if I wanted to ride on the back of his motorbike. I didn't enjoy the ride. He was showing off . . . a country boy not impressed with big-city traffic. When I got back to the office, I called Paul and told him this kid actually was Cal in "East of Eden"; no sense looking further or "reading" him. I sent Dean to see Steinbeck. . . . John thought Dean a snotty kid. I said that was irrelevant; wasn't he Cal? John said he sure as hell was, and that was it.

After Dean arrived in Hollywood, he and Kazan were heading toward the studio when Dean said, "Can we stop here a minute? My father lives in there." Kazan stopped, and Dean went in and got his father. Kazan said, "Out came a man as tense as Jimmy was, and they hardly could look at each other. They could hardly talk; they

James Dean and actress Pier Angeli at a Hollywood party (1954).

(Opposite page) James Dean in *Giant* (1956).

mumbled at each other, I don't know what the hell Jimmy stopped to see him for, because in a few minutes he said, 'Let's go.'"

Dorothy Kilgallen mentioned in her column that Dean was Indianapolis native Clifton Webb's protégé. There was no basis for this rumor. However, after *East of Eden* premiered and Hedda Hopper had refused to attend because of a disastrous early encounter with Dean, Webb told Hopper he had just seen an extraordinary performance and that regardless of her justifiable distaste for Dean, she should arrange a private screening. After she saw the film at a Warner Brothers private screening, Hopper exclaimed, "such power, so many facets of expression, and so much sheer invention." She now called Dean "the brightest new star in town."

Shortly before the premier of *East of Eden*, Dean and Dennis Stock, a photographer, went to Fairmount to explore Dean's roots. They stayed five days while Dean posed in several locations around town, including the high school. But this time he made no effort to contact Brookshire. When Brookshire tracked him down, he launched into a tirade of complaints about the "bunch of leeches" who followed him around. Brookshire was hurt by this experience.

After *East of Eden* was released, Dean went home to Fairmount again. However, when the *Marion Leader-Tribune* wanted to interview him, he refused. He felt that the local paper had given him insufficient coverage while he was on his way up. Instead of talking to the paper, he invited Fowler to dinner at the Winslow home.

Dean's next film paired him with a director who was a lot like him. Nicholas Ray threw himself into his work much in the same way Dean did. Ray had so much confidence in Dean that he encouraged him to improvise and asked him to collaborate. The result was *Rebel without a Cause*, a film that was shaped by and built around Dean. Costar Natalie Wood said, "He used to come on the set and watch the scenes, even when he wasn't in them. He was that interested in the whole picture and not just his part."

Rebel without a Cause had a theme that was popular during the fifties—lack of communication as it applied to misunderstandings between parents and children. The film hit a nerve, not just because of the subject matter, but due to Dean's intensity, charm, and hypnotic appeal.

When Dean accepted the part of Jett Rink in Edna Ferber's *Giant*, he encountered a director who was very different from Ray. George Stevens did not allow actors to follow their instincts, and throughout the making of *Giant*, Dean complained endlessly about Stevens's abuse of his talents. Dean felt the picture was going too big in an artificial way. In particular, he wanted the portrayal of Rink as an old man to be quite different from what it was turning out to be. He also felt that he was being sacrificed for Elizabeth Taylor and Rock Hudson. In spite of this, Dean overshadowed everything in the film. His performance earned him his second Oscar nomination (posthumously). His first nomination was for *East of Eden*.

Actress Carroll Baker gave this account of how she received the news of Dean's death as she and the cast of *Giant* were looking at the almost finished film:

On Friday, September 30, around six o'clock, Elizabeth, Rock and
I and a small group were watching the rushes. George Stevens was

behind us at this desk by the controls. The projection room was dark. The phone rang. The soundtrack screamed to a halt. The picture froze. The lights shot up. We turned and looked at George. The phone dangled in his hand. He was white and motionless. Death was present in that room. Slowly and with great effort, his voice coming from a long and distant tunnel, George said, "There's been a car crash. Jimmy Dean has been killed." I went numb.

A number of years after his death, Dean's family in Fairmount signed a contract with CMG Worldwide, an Indianapolis marketing and licensing firm. Dean's image is now reproduced on coffee mugs, commemorative plates, official calendars, greeting cards, a line of hats, leather jackets, red windbreakers, boots, and western wear. Mourners still come to Fairmount for the annual James Dean Festival to celebrate his life and visit his grave site. At Cholame, California, at the intersection of Highways 41 and 46, cars with license plates from all over the country stop to look and to stand on the spot where Dean died and was swept into legend.

BIBLIOGRAPHY

Adams, Leith, and Keith Burns, eds. *James Dean: Behind the Scenes.* New York: Citadel Press, 2001.

Beath, Warren Newton. *The Death of James Dean.* New York: Grove Press, 1986.

Corliss, Richard. "Byron Meets Billy Bud." *Time*, August 22, 1994.

Dalton, David. *James Dean: American Icon.* New York: St. Martin's Press, 1984.

———. *James Dean: The Mutant King.* New York: Dell Publishing Company, 1974.

Fowler, Beth. Interview with the author. December 3, 2001. Marion, Indiana.

Frome, Shelly. *The Actors Studio: A History.* Jefferson, N.C.: McFarland and Company, 2001.

Gehring, Wes. *James Dean: Rebel with a Cause.* Indianapolis: Indiana Historical Society Press, 2005.

Giant: The Making of an Epic Motion Picture. VHS. Special Collector's Edition. Warner Brothers, 1996.

Hamblett, Charles. "James Dean Dead: Idol of Youth." *Picture Post* (October 1, 1956).

———. "James Dean: The Name Goes Marching On." *Picture Post* (October 8, 1956).

Hedda Hopper Collection. Margaret Herrick Library. Academy of Motion Picture Arts and Sciences, Beverly Hills, California.

Holley, Val. *James Dean: The Biography.* New York: St. Martin's Press, 1995.

Movie Life (October 1956).

Palmer, Betsy. Interview with the author. May 3, 2003. New York.

Stott, William, with Jane Stott. *On Broadway: Performance Photos.* Austin: University of Texas Press, 1978.

FRED WILLIAMSON

It's "Hammer" Time

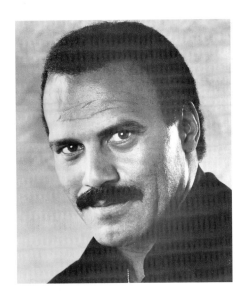

Fred Williamson.

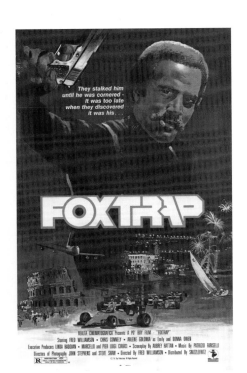

Fred Williamson was born in Gary, Indiana, on March 5, 1938, and graduated from Froebel High School. He decided he wanted to be an architect and enrolled at Northwestern University. However, when he went out for the football team, he met coach Ara Parseghian, became a star on the team, and became an All-Pro defensive cornerback, earning the nickname "The Hammer" because of his hard hitting. He graduated from Northwestern in 1959 with a degree in architecture. He was drafted by the NFL, played for the Oakland Raiders and the Kansas City Chiefs, and had the distinction of playing in Super Bowl I.

After his pro career, Williamson headed for Hollywood. Almost immediately after his arrival in 1972, he was cast as the lead opposite Diahann Carroll in *Julia*. He was in *M*A*S*H* (1970) as Captain Oliver Harmon "Spearchucker" Jones and worked with Liza Minnelli in *Tell Me That You Love Me, Junie Moon* (1970). He became interested in producing and directing and started his own company, Po'Boy Productions, in 1974. He has directed or starred in at least forty films. He also did television and was nominated for an Emmy for a role in *Police Story*.

Williamson's quick wit has made him a favorite on shows such as *Politically Incorrect*. When Quentin Tarantino came to him to ask him to be in his movie *From Dusk till Dawn* (1996), he could not believe Tarantino was a fan: "When he first told me, I didn't believe him . . . until he started quoting lines from all the movies. It was a fantastic compliment."

In 1996 Williamson returned to his hometown, along with costars Pam Grier, Jim Brown, and Richard Roundtree, to shoot a new film. It was called *Original Gangstas*. He was the producer of the film and saw it as an opportunity to bring the generations together. He said, "The bad guys in the film are Rap artists . . . and on the other side there's the music of The Dells and The Temptations."

In 2004 Williamson was featured in *Starsky & Hutch* with Ben Stiller and Owen Wilson. He played their boss, Detective Doby. He hopes this movie will open the doors for larger Hollywood roles.

BIBLIOGRAPHY

Hurkos, Stephany. "Biography—Fred Williamson." http://www.stephanyhurkos.com/fred_biography.htm.

The Internet Movie Database. http://www.imdb.com/.

Ramos, Steve. "It's Hammer Time Again." http://www.citybeat.com/archives/1996/issue223/film1.html.

BRENDAN FRASER

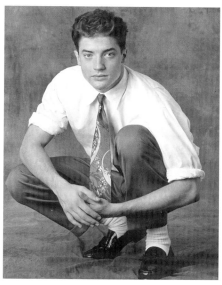

Brendan Fraser in *School Ties* (1992).
© 1992, PARAMOUNT PICTURES. PHOTO BY KARIN EPSTEIN

Brendan Fraser is the last of four sons born to Canadians Peter and Carol Fraser. Since his birth in Indianapolis on December 3, 1968, he has not stopped moving. His father, who worked with the Canadian Foreign Service, just happened to be stationed in Indianapolis when Brendan was born. Brendan and his three older brothers spent most of their youth living in Canada and Europe. The family moved shortly after Fraser's birth, and he found himself continually having to start all over again. "My family moved every two or three years, and I was always the new kid. I had no real consistency in my life. In my deepest soul, I longed to be a part of a community, to have a place to go. It was much like an actor's life, having to constantly redefine myself." Perhaps due to this longing, he once came back to Indianapolis just to see the city of his birth. When he arrived, he said, "Everyone was playing basketball all over the town." He had come to Indianapolis when the Gus Macker charity basketball tournament was in full swing.

Fraser attended schools in Holland, London, Seattle, Ottawa, and Toronto. He learned French in Ottawa and Dutch in the Hague and developed a love of art through visits to museums in the countries where he lived. "Growing up, there wasn't much television to watch, and when there was, it was often old black and white silent movies, like Buster Keaton," he recalled. From an early age, Fraser grew to appreciate these silent comedians as well as the circus clowns whom he was frequently taken to see on school outings. "I saw a lot of physical comedy, which is probably how I learned to appreciate it. It didn't have to be in English for me to get the joke."

It was in England at age twelve, where he was first exposed to the vibrant London theater scene, when the acting bug really bit. "I was struck by make-believe, everyone participating in a story, really believing in it. I wanted to be up there." As an eighth grader in Seattle he made his first stage appearance in a production of *The Pirates of Penzance.* "On opening night, I charged down the staircase onstage, shouted, 'Unhand my daughter!' and tripped, and my cape landed over my head. I could hear the laughter from the audience. I became very angry with myself. I asked, 'What am I doing here?' And then I realized I was enjoying myself more than anything I'd ever done in my life. I was ready for anything."

At thirteen his parents sent him to Upper Canada College, an exclusive boarding school in Toronto. It was at boarding school that he decided to become an actor. "I felt I knew what was really important to me, and it wasn't what people expected to be important. Acting was considered a frivolity. Their attitude was like, 'Get a real job, son.' I was expected to make high marks in subjects that would make money."

At Upper Canada College Fraser had his first working connection to the theater as a stage manager and ticket seller. At age eighteen he enrolled at the Actors' Conservatory at Seattle's Cornish College of the Arts. There he performed Shakespeare and other classical productions in local theaters and received a bachelor of fine arts in 1990. "After I graduated, my father thought that I might get a job as a weathercaster at the local TV stations, because that's about how good he thought I was. I just happened to have higher standards. My mother supported me and adored what I did."

Among the early influences in his career at the time was the actor, pantomimist, and clown, Bill Irwin. "I used to see him perform in Seattle. To my mind, he embodied everything that was talent and creativity. You couldn't categorize what he did or who he was," said Fraser.

Although Fraser was awarded a scholarship to attend graduate school at Southern Methodist University, he never made it there. Instead, he used his mother's car to drive down the coast and seek his fortune in Hollywood. He did not have long to wait. He was given a small role in *Dogfight*, a film starring River Phoenix. He said Phoenix was so gracious, and he "was able to see an infinite possibility in that man's gaze. I admired his work."

Brendan Fraser in *Airheads* (1994).
© 1994, 20TH CENTURY FOX.
PHOTO BY MERIE W. WALLACE

Fraser's agent managed to get him small roles in two made-for-television movies and a couple of television pilots. Fraser's career quickly took off. Within a year he was starring in two feature films of vastly different styles. In the first of these movies, *School Ties*, a critically praised drama about anti-Semitism at a private prep school, he was part of an ensemble cast that included up-and-comers Matt Damon, Ben Affleck, and Chris O'Donnell. Fraser was overwhelmed by the others in the cast. He said, "It was movie acting, and I came from the theater. All I knew came from a book by Michael Caine about toning it down for the movies." But Fraser more than held his own. Not long after *School Ties*, he made *Encino Man*, a mindless but enjoyable film in which Fraser played a frozen caveman who is unearthed by two teenagers, one of whom is the goofy Pauly Shore.

"I was twenty-three and had just finished shooting 'School Ties,'" Fraser recalled, "and I was fighting against doing 'Encino Man.' But I was happy to be working at that time and to be honest, I was thinking more about paying the rent. I also realized that the careers I admired were built on diversity. Starting off you need to have a calling card that will say 'I can do this and I can do that—extremes from the sublime to the ridiculous.'" This attitude led to other roles in films such as *With Honors* (1994), *The Scout* (1994), and *The Passion of Darkly Noon* (1995). He had only been in the business six years, and he was making $10.5 million per film.

In 1997 Fraser was cast to play *George of the Jungle*. Although intended primarily for younger viewers, the writing, as well as Fraser's portrayal, was done so adults also found the movie entertaining. The success of *George of the Jungle* helped spur the development of a number of live-action adaptations of cartoons.

Fraser followed *George of the Jungle* with another adaptation of a Jay Ward cartoon about the Canadian Mountie Dudley Do-Right. This time his choice was largely personal; his great-grandfather had been a member of the Royal Canadian Mounted Police. "As an old man I would have regretted not making a Mountie movie if I had the chance," said Fraser.

In 1993 he met Afton Smith at a July Fourth barbecue at Winona Ryder's house. Five years later, they were married. He said, "I feel safe with her because of the strength that our relationship gives us in completing aspects of our souls. She has hands that are unafraid." Afton is named after the Robert Burns poem *Afton Water.* He smiled when asked about her description in the media as a former actress. "The press refuses to let that go, but that's not a world she is in now. She has immense knowledge of the craft and she's so incredibly well read. Maybe in the future she'll go into producing. We don't have to meddle in one another's intrinsic endeavors, but we are supportive of one another. We're a very young couple and we're trying to have a life, to settle into who we are towards one another. I think that she will definitely surprise me delightfully in the years to come with the professional choices that she chooses to make." They are the parents of two sons: Griffin Arthur Fraser, born in September 2002, and Holden Fletcher Fraser, born in August 2004.

Fraser seems to have no doubt he has made the right choices, even if they seem strange to some. His work in the remake of the Dudley Moore movie, *Bedazzled*, had him playing seven different roles. Harold Ramis, who directed the film, said, "I knew from his previous work that Fraser could go very broad and also be subtle and serious, as well as dashing and heroic. He manages to combine his vulnerability with his hunkiness. He can be completely goofy without compromising his dreamboat quality or his dignity."

Fraser's paycheck for the sequel to the hit *The Mummy* was reportedly $12.5 million. In just nine years in Hollywood, he has made nearly thirty movies, encompassing everything from comedy to drama. He received critical praise for his dramatic role opposite Ian McKellan in *Gods and Monsters.* In 2001 he appeared on the London stage in *Cat on a Hot Tin Roof.* Fraser has had an eclectic and diverse career that has brought him to the brink of superstardom. "I know how lucky I am," Fraser has said. "I'm living the dream that I imagined. I believe you have a responsibility to comport yourself in a manner that gives an example to others. As a young man, I prayed for success. Now I pray just to be worthy of it."

Brendan Fraser and Sarah Jessica Parker in *Dudley Do-Right* (1999).

BIBLIOGRAPHY

Indianapolis Star, September 27, 2002.

Lynch, Lorrie. "In Tune with Himself." *USA Weekend* (October 24–26, 2003).

Rader, Dotson. "I Was Ready for Anything." *Parade Magazine* (July 30, 2000).

Wohl, Alexander. "The Devil and Brendan Fraser." *Biography* (August 2000).

GREG KINNEAR

Greg Kinnear on the set of his talk show
Later with Greg Kinnear (1994).
©NBC PHOTO BY ALICE S. HALL

Greg Kinnear was born in Logansport, Indiana, on June 17, 1963, the youngest of three sons of Edward and Suzanne Kinnear. Like fellow Hoosier Brendan Fraser, Kinnear's father was in the foreign service. Unlike Fraser, who left Indiana as an infant, Kinnear did not leave Logansport until he was nine years old. It was then that Edward accepted a position with the United States State Department and became a career diplomat. Like Fraser, young Kinnear moved frequently because of his father's career. He lived in such places as Washington, D.C., Beirut, and Greece.

While living in Beirut, Kinnear used to hear gunfire regularly. "It escalated every night and, along with the machine-gun fire, we started hearing explosions. Then we had a couple of hits very close to where we lived. The last few weeks we stayed inside our house sitting on the floor listening to the BBC by candlelight. That's how we got the signal that we were being evacuated." He made his first appearance on camera when news reports covered the evacuation of Beirut's St. George Hotel.

For the next six years the Kinnear family lived in Greece where, at an American school in Athens, he met a teacher who changed his life. Her name was Mrs. Pinopoulos. He said, "She was the first one to get me interested in performance. She went out of her way to be encouraging. Because of her, I quickly got involved in anything that was performance oriented." It was in Athens where he first ventured into the role of talk show host with a radio show, *School Daze with Greg Kinnear.* He said:

> I was a sophomore in Athens and the throne had been handed to me from another gentleman who had graduated. And I remember coming to school on Monday and people saying, "Wow, wow, that was really cool, you on the radio and all." I remember thinking, Wow, that's nice. Somebody was acknowledging me, and they certainly weren't going to acknowledge me in sports because I was okay in a lot of things but not great. I was average across the board. To be above average and stand out because of that little radio show was certainly an indication that maybe there was a future somewhere in entertainment.

In 1981 Kinnear returned to the United States and entered the University of Arizona at Tucson. "All I could see myself doing was

Greg Kinnear and Harrison Ford in *Sabrina* (1995).
© 1995 BY PARAMOUNT PICTURES CORP.

either acting, or television and radio journalism." He started as a drama major but said, "One day a professor came out and informed the class, in a very sobering way, that less than 1 percent of us would ever be able to make a living as an actor." It was then that he switched to broadcast journalism.

He admitted he was not a good student. "I was always explaining why my term papers were never on time. I think that's where I got my acting training. If I'd put as much effort into writing papers as I did into justifying my failures, I'd probably be running a Hollywood studio today instead of working for one." In 1985 he graduated with a degree in broadcast journalism and headed for Los Angeles. He had no luck getting a job in show business, so he took a job as a purchasing agent in a Fremont, California, electrical supply house. "I sat in a windowless shack, ordering copper wire no. 2. But after six months, I felt that wasn't to be my destiny." He managed to land a job as a marketing assistant with Empire Entertainment, promoting cheap exploitable movies such as *Space Sluts in the Slammer* and *Assault of the Killer Bimbos.*

He auditioned to be an MTV VJ but was not chosen. He was creator and coexecutive producer for the Fox television series *Best of the Worst,* which aired from 1990 to 1991. He moved from there to a television job for the cable network Movietime, interviewing celebrities. He said, "I was bad, but I had the sense that maybe I'd arrived where I was meant to be." Eventually Movietime became E! The Entertainment Network, and in 1991, when the network started looking for a host for a new talk show, he was chosen.

The new show was *Talk Soup,* and Kinnear endeared himself to his fans by screening highlights of various trash talk shows. His success

Scene from *As Good As It Gets* (1997) with
Cuba Gooding Jr.

with *Talk Soup* attracted the attention of a lot of people. He received
calls from Fox (when Chevy Chase bombed), Disney (exploring sitcoms and talk shows), Rob Reiner (for a syndicated interview show),
and CBS (which wanted him for the post–David Letterman slot). "My
life became like 'Let's Make a Deal,'" said Kinnear. "You just don't
want the booby prize." He finally took the door marked NBC, where
Bob Costas had given up his late night show in 1994. Kinnear was
given his own late night show, *Later with Greg Kinnear*. Again his brand of
glib humor and his boyish good looks made the show a hit.

In 1995 Lafayette, Indiana, native Sydney Pollack decided to
remake Billy Wilder's 1954 movie *Sabrina*. Pollack cast Harrison Ford
in Humphrey Bogart's role as the older and more sensible brother.
He cast Kinnear in William Holden's role as the carefree, playboy
brother. Both brothers romanced the chauffeur's daughter, played
by Julia Ormond. Although Kinnear did not win the girl and the
film got mild reviews, he did win the hearts of critics and moviegoers.
Critic Gene Siskel said, "Greg Kinnear is the surprise of this version,
quite convincing as the playboy object of Sabrina's affection before
she falls for his workaholic brother."

Kinnear said he will always be "eternally grateful" to Pollack for
casting him in *Sabrina*. Thanks to that movie, he had now crossed the
line between broadcast journalism and acting. He said, "I didn't feel
like the line between the two was that wide. And I found out with time
that it wasn't." He began to get other movie offers and starred in *Dear
God* (1996) and *A Smile Like Yours* (1997). These were not well received
and did not bring him major stardom. However, because of the good
comments surrounding his movie work, he left his NBC show in 1996
to concentrate on movies.

Kinnear's big break came when he was cast as Jack Nicholson's gay neighbor in *As Good as It Gets.* He said that when he first received the script from director James L. Brooks, he recognized it as "something truly extraordinary." He had no trepidations about playing a gay artist. "The character was everything I could hope for: a man with integrity who's pitted against a horror of a human being, Nicholson." Even before its Christmas 1997 release, the film was generating Oscar buzz. Kinnear was nominated for a best supporting actor Oscar, a Golden Globe, a National Board of Review Award (which he won), and others. Nicholson and Helen Hunt won best actor Oscars and Golden Globes.

Kinnear began getting roles, appearing in such hits as *You've Got Mail* (1998), *Nurse Betty* (2000), and *We Were Soldiers* (2002). He took on the challenging role of television star Bob Crane in *Auto Focus* (2002) and then switched back to comedy in the Farrelly brothers production of *Stuck on You* (2003), in which he played the conjoined twin of Matt Damon.

On May 1, 1999, in Sussex, England, he married his longtime companion, British model-turned-writer Helen Labdon. A daughter, Lily, was born in 2003. In September 1999 Kinnear and his wife visited Logansport and found that his boyhood home at 3001 S. Pennsylvania Avenue was for sale. Real estate agent Judy McNarny showed Kinnear through his old house and reported he was unaffected by his fame. "He was fun and charming," she said. After visiting his home, the couple went to Lake Wawasee, where Kinnear's family owned a cottage, and the Sycamore Drive-In, which he patronized as a boy. They went in and ordered dessert. Sixteen-year-old waitress Alyssa Rosomme asked him, "Has anybody ever told you that you look like Greg Kinnear?" He gave her an autograph.

A complimentary description of Kinnear and his home state appears in the movie *Dear God*, when a character utters this line referring to him: "Oh he's a nice guy, he's from Indiana."

BIBLIOGRAPHY

Indianapolis Star, September 21, 1999.

Los Angeles View, December 22–28, 1995.

New York Post, December 1997.

Siskel, Gene. "Splendid Holiday Fare and a Fair Remake." *TV Guide*, December 21, 1996.

Tatum, Charles. "C'Mere Kinnear." *Tribute Magazine* (December 1997).

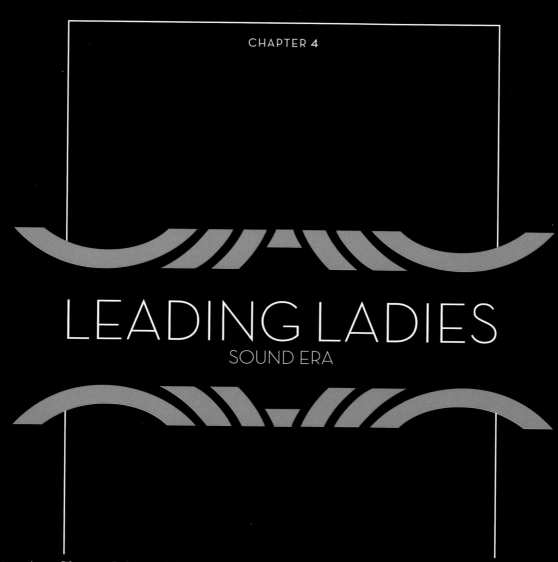

CHAPTER 4

LEADING LADIES
SOUND ERA

Hoosiers Ann Christy, Julanne Johnston, Valeska Suratt, and Alice Terry did not make the transition into sound pictures. Others who started in silent films had their careers enhanced by sound. Carole Lombard, Louise Dresser, and Louise Fazenda easily moved into "the talkies."

In the beginning, female sound stars were groomed to fit into several categories. Some, like Evansville's Louise Dresser, were bred to portray self-sufficient women in tales of emancipation and social rights. Others, such as Fort Wayne's Carole Lombard, were preened to flit about in sophisticated love stories and carry off risqué innuendoes without offending the audience.

Those with musical talent, such as Evansville's Marilyn Miller, appeared in musicals usually based on their stage successes. The coming of sound was potentially a boon to many who were stars of the musical theater. Miller was a huge star for Ziegfeld and was the toast of Broadway for years before sound pictures. Now sound made it possible to hear this astounding talent. Unfortunately, it was discovered that many talented stage performers simply did not come across well in an intimate medium like film.

Great musical stars such as Miller, Gertrude Lawrence, and Mary Martin were unable to deliver the goods on the big screen.

MARILYN MILLER

Ziegfeld's Most Dazzling Star

In March 1936 Marilyn Miller stopped at a little shop on Fifth Avenue in New York City and said to her companion, "I must have that frock." The friend asked, "For a special occasion?" "Very special. I'm going into the hospital tomorrow." "And you want to wear the frock when you leave?" "Yes, when I leave. I want to be buried in it. I am certain I won't leave the hospital alive." Three weeks later on April 7, 1936, the thirty-seven-year-old Miller died at Doctor's Hospital in New York from complications from a sinus infection that caused her temperature to rise as high as 108.

In her day she was the acknowledged "Queen of Musical Comedy." Florenz Ziegfeld said she was "the greatest box office attraction in the country." Critic John Mason Brown called her "a Degas figure turned American . . . a Titania of the jazz age." She was born Marilynn Reynolds (her first name was a tribute to her maternal grandparents, Mary and Lynn Thompson) on September 1, 1898, in Evansville, Indiana, at 622 Southeast Second Street. She was the fourth and last child of Edwin D. Reynolds and the former Ada Thompson. She had two sisters, Ruth, the eldest, then nine years old, and Claire, who was seven. Her only brother, Edwin Jr., was three years old when she was born. She was the first member of her family to be born outside of the state of Tennessee. Both her mother and father were descended from Irish and Scottish immigrants who had settled in Tennessee at the end of the eighteenth century.

Edwin was a lineman for the Cumberland Telephone Company and installed some of the first phone systems in the rural South and the Midwest. He traveled a lot, and while he was on the road his family lived with Ada's mother in Memphis. Yellow fever broke out in Memphis, and a pregnant Ada fled in panic with her three children three hundred miles north to Evansville, where her husband was working. The family arrived at Edwin's temporary lodging above a corner grocery store, in time to hastily summon a doctor for Marilyn's birth.

Ada was the singing and dancing darling of the Thompson family and apparently passed on her talent to her children. Claire was an accomplished pianist who played by ear, and Ruth and Edwin were versatile singers and dancers. Since her own ambitions for a career in show business had not been realized, Ada, a prime example of a stage mother, decided to prepare her children for entertainment careers. Edwin did not share his wife's dreams. In fact, he threatened to leave her if she ever dared let them perform. Edwin's threat fueled Ada's determination to succeed, and she put together an act for Ruth and Claire, becoming their manager, choreographer, costume designer, and makeup artist. She was able to secure a few bookings from ads in *Billboard* magazine, playing mostly beer gardens and amusement parks. About this time Edwin was promoted and was reassigned to Nashville, Tennessee, but Ada did not want to move. Edwin left and Ada and the children never saw him again. She later filed for divorce on grounds of desertion.

Now the family's welfare depended entirely on the success of its theatrical endeavors. Ada added Edwin Jr. to the act. He worked up a routine performing black dialect songs that were in vogue then. The act was never a headline attraction, but it was generally well received. Although Marilyn was too young to be a part of all this, she literally grew up in a trunk. Her crib was the top drawer of the family's wardrobe trunk. Once she began to walk, she was in everyone's way. She was the only one in the troupe who was not paying her own way. Something had to be done and the only solution was to send Marilyn to Memphis to stay with her grandmother, Mary Thompson. Ada's twin brother, Leon, who was a printer, and his wife Louise lived with Mary. They had no children so they offered to share the responsibility of bringing up Marilyn.

Marilyn lived in Memphis about four years, developing a distinct southern drawl to her speech. On the Memphis streets, her only playmates were the children of black servants. The difference in color was meaningless to Marilyn, and this attitude never changed when she became an adult. In fact, if it had not been for her black friends, she might never have become famous. She always credited a young black boy, who brought coal to her house and built the fire on chilly mornings, as her first rhythmic inspiration. While waiting for the fire to start burning, he danced—shuffling, tapping, and buck-and-winging. This was magical to Marilyn, and before long she was matching him step for step.

Marilyn Miller.

(Previous page) Marilyn Miller.

Meanwhile, Ada married Oscar "Caro" Miller, a former letter carrier who was three years her junior. After abandoning his postal career for the theater, Miller acted, danced, sang, and performed acrobatics in everything from vaudeville and circuses to minstrel shows and Gilbert and Sullivan operettas.

Caro took over the act and created something he called The Four Columbians. Although he had the children all use the name Miller so as to create the impression they were a family, he never took steps to become their legal guardian. He was a strict disciplinarian, and Ruth and Claire were terrified of him. Edwin, however, was rebellious and was eventually sent to Memphis to live with his grandmother and Marilyn. The new act, the Columbian Trio, dressed in red, white, and blue satin costumes.

When Ada returned, the adorable four-year-old Marilyn demonstrated some of the dance steps she had learned from her black friends. It did not take long for Ada to decide to take Marilyn with her.

The years from 1905 to 1913 were the golden years of vaudeville, and Marilyn's career began during a frenzied bidding war for talent. There were two thousand vaudeville theaters in the United States, and the nickelodeon, a new entertainment wonder, was just being introduced. Marilyn's first nickelodeon experience was of a ballerina pirouetting across a stage. Afterward, she exclaimed to her mother, "If

I had a costume that would bounce up and down, I could be just like that pretty lady." Ada promptly made a tutu for her daughter. She was such a picture of sweetness that her sister Ruth compared her to a lump of sugar. This evolved into her lifelong nickname, "Lumpy."

Caro was against putting Marilyn in the act, thinking she was much too young. However, he allowed her to dress in costume and watch from the wings. During one show, on August 20, 1903, when the Columbians were taking their bows, Marilyn rushed to the center of the stage. The audience started to laugh, and Marilyn curtsied and launched into her ballerina imitation. The crowd applauded, and Marilyn's career was launched.

Marilyn became known as "Mademoiselle Sugarlump" and eventually became one of "The Five Columbians." She insisted that she and her sisters were "as happy as the day is long. More pains were taken over our education than is devoted to most children. We were treated as very important young ladies!" There is no question, however, that they were subjected to a lot of hardships, catching trains at unearthly hours of the night, dressing or undressing in the cellars of old, dusty theaters, and practicing and practicing until, according to Marilyn, "I was too tired to know what I was doing, or why."

Marilyn was proud to be born a Hoosier, saying, "When I was in London, an interviewer asked where I came from. I simply replied, 'Indiana,' and he at once said, 'Oh, of course. That accounts for it.' I take delight in the fact I was born in Indiana. So many wonderful people come from there." In an interview with the *Indianapolis News* she recalled the time she returned to her native state. "One of my most amusing experiences on the stage occurred about five years ago when the Columbians joined a summer 'Uncle Tom's Cabin' company, playing under a tent in Indiana. Father played Uncle Tom, and I insisted on playing Little Eva, although I was engaged to play one of the angels. It didn't last long but it was exciting." Marilyn reported that the *Uncle Tom* troupe finally broke up. "While we were playing Rushville, the treasurer absconded with the funds. They found him in Crawfordsville. He had started a new 'Uncle Tom's Cabin' troupe. So the Columbians went back into vaudeville!" Marilyn's last visit to Evansville was at the Grand Theater in 1910, when she came with her family on a vaudeville tour.

Marilyn's journey to Broadway began in 1911. Once Marilyn was in her teens and had grown to what was to be her full height, slightly more than five feet, Caro thought she could pass for sixteen, the minimum working age in the big cities. When they played Chicago, however, he was served with a subpoena and fined $250. The penalty convinced him to take the act abroad, where the child labor laws were not so strict. Between 1911 and 1914 the act traveled extensively throughout Europe. During the tour Ruth and Claire fell in love with two American tourists, and the two couples were married in London.

Marilyn had also fallen in love. The object of her affection was a twenty-one-year-old dancer named Frank Carter. However, it was a one-sided romance because she had never met Carter, she had only watched him perform at the London Hippodrome. "I was too young for him to pay any attention to me, but I thought him wonderful." She and Carter would meet again when she was older.

When Caro booked the family in The Lotus Club in London, they were noticed by Lee Shubert. Shubert was an American producer who

Marilyn Miller in *Sally* (1929).
FIRST NATIONAL PICTURES

was on one of his frequent talent hunts overseas. Shubert caught the act in the midst of Marilyn's Bert Williams routine, in which she was dressed in a white satin suit with her long curls topped by a silk hat. Although Shubert thought she was not the most beautiful girl he had ever seen, he realized she had great audience rapport and seemed to be enjoying herself immensely. Shubert offered Caro a guaranteed salary of $75.00 a week for Marilyn to appear in his Winter Garden in New York, and he immediately accepted. Marilyn was not quite sixteen, but Caro did not inform Shubert of her age. The production in which Marilyn appeared at the Winter Garden was *The Passing Show of 1914*. Marilyn's main job was to offer impressions of some of the stars and personalities of the day. In addition, Lee and J. J. Shubert asked twenty-seven-year-old Sigmund Romberg to write a song for Marilyn. He wrote "Omar Khayam" for her, and when he heard her sing it for the first time, he knew she would be a star. After *The Passing Show* opened, *Cosmopolitan* magazine said, "[Marilyn's] voice is phenomenal, in high soprano notes as well as in the almost baritone range brought into play by her uncanny bits of masculine impersonation. Here is an original sort of ingenue who lives still in the blissful age of innocence."

In February 1915 *The Passing Show of 1914* came to the Murat Theater in Indianapolis. In an interview in the *Indianapolis News* titled "One More Hoosier Star," Marilyn said, "I was destined to be born in Memphis, Tennessee, but destiny and yellow fever drove my mother northward, a fugitive, to Evansville, Indiana. So it is that Evansville has the honor of being my birthplace."

As a result of her hit in *The Passing Show of 1914*, she was elevated to star billing before it was over. When *The Passing Show of 1915* was produced, Marilyn was the headliner, and her reviews were even more enthusiastic. In the summer of 1916 the Shuberts produced *The Show of Wonders* with Marilyn as the star. She received a standing ovation on opening night, led by Lillian Russell and Diamond Jim Brady. One day during rehearsals, the ballet master slipped and accidentally struck Marilyn in the nose. Although the blow was severe enough to splinter a tiny bone, the eighteen-year-old Marilyn laughed it off.

Billie Burke, the wife of Flo Ziegfeld, happened to catch Marilyn in *The Show of Wonders* and encouraged her husband to sign Marilyn for his next edition of the *Follies*. It so happened that Ziegfeld had lost Olive Thomas, who had married Jack Pickford, Mary's brother, and who had a much publicized romance with Ziegfeld, leaving an opening in the *Follies* of 1918. He discovered that Marilyn's contract with the Shuberts did not expire until 1919. Ziegfeld's lawyers discovered that the contract had been signed by Caro because Marilyn was a minor. He had assumed since he was married to Ada he was Marilyn's legal guardian. However, this was not the case. As a result the contract was void, and Marilyn signed with Ziegfeld.

The Ziegfeld Follies of 1918 opened at the New Amsterdam Theater on June 18. In addition to Marilyn, the cast included Will Rogers, Eddie Cantor, W. C. Fields, and that darkly handsome man she had secretly admired in London, Frank Carter. She was teamed with him in a number called "A Dream Dance," and their romance began. On opening night, eight taxicabs were needed to carry all her flowers home. The *New York Globe* said, "Marilyn Miller, radiant with smiles and grace of exuberant adolescence, seems to dance for the sheer joy of dancing. What makes her still more delightful is the fact that she is the only dancer who has a voice of any real quality."

During the First World War, Marilyn did quite a lot of volunteer work and was a terrific seller of Liberty Bonds. After the war President Woodrow Wilson met with Marilyn and complimented her on her war work. A few weeks later she received a bronze medal with the president's signature and "Well Done!" on the other side. Years later in the Second World War, another Hoosier would receive praise from the president for her war effort. Carole Lombard followed in the tradition of Miller in serving her country.

Before the 1919 *Follies* opened, Miller and Carter were married. Ziegfeld was livid with Carter, firing him from the *Follies* and swearing that he would never work in any Ziegfeld production again. Carter was quickly signed by the Shuberts. He was a hit, and both of their careers were now booming.

In the spring of 1920 Miller fell in love with a customized Packard touring car. She wanted to buy it, but Carter said it was too expensive. The price was $10,000. However, their first wedding anniversary was coming up so Carter bought the car, ordering the monogram, "MM & FC," on all the doors. He gave his last performance in Wheeling, West Virginia, and telephoned Miller who was in Philadelphia. He did not mention the new car but said he was leaving immediately for Philadelphia. Miller tried to persuade him to wait till daylight. He told her not to worry, he would be careful. While traveling at sixty-five miles an hour, he misjudged a sharp curve and slammed on the brakes. The Packard spun, hit an embankment, and flipped over. He was killed instantly. Eddie Cantor, a longtime friend of both, was asked to break the news to her. Catching Miller before she left the theater, he said, "Marilyn, you're a terrific performer. You sing, you dance, you have youth. No matter what ever happens, you'd be the kind of trouper who'd go on." He said Miller whirled around from her dressing table and said, "Eddie! Frank is dead!" Somehow she managed to get through every performance until the season closed.

Miller's next big hit was the musical comedy *Sally*, which opened in New York on December 21, 1920. The hit song from this show, which became forever identified with Miller, was not written for *Sally*. Jerome Kern wrote it for a proposed musical based on Lafayette, Indiana, native George Barr McCutcheon's book *Brewster's Millions*. Although *Brewster's Millions* was made into a film three times, it never made it as a musical. The song was "Look for the Silver Lining," and it next appeared in a small musical, *Good Morning Dearie*, in 1919. But it was Miller who made the song a sensational hit. Dressed in the drab costume of an orphan, she sang the haunting melody in a plaintive, hushed delivery. There was always an awed silence after she finished, and she would have to repeat the chorus after a storm of applause. *Sally* became the biggest Broadway musical hit of its time and turned Miller into the undisputed queen of American musical comedy.

In 1921 *Sally* and *Shuffle Along* were the two top moneymakers on Broadway. The star and cocomposer (with Eubie Blake) of *Shuffle Along* was Indianapolis native Noble Sissle. These two Hoosiers forever changed the face of musical comedy with their disparate, yet groundbreaking productions. *Sally* epitomized the backstage musical plot, with poor Sally eventually becoming a Ziegfeld star and marrying a Long Island millionaire. *Shuffle Along* was a political satire of behind-

Marilyn Miller (second from right) in a
scene from *Sunny* (1930).

the-scenes election shenanigans in Jimtown. The reform candidate
named in the song, "I'm Just Wild about Harry," wins the mayor's
office and the girl. While *Shuffle Along* was a crude production compared to the sophisticated and grand production numbers of *Sally*, the
difference was more than made up with the exuberance of the dancing
and the comedy. These two shows were great influences in shaping
the American musical comedy for decades to come, especially in the
movies.

During the run of *Sally*, Miller met Jack Pickford. Pickford had
been married to Olive Thomas, whose departure from Ziegfeld paved
the way for Miller's big break. Thomas had taken what she thought
were sleeping pills but instead had swallowed poison. Pickford and
Miller were drawn together by the common bond of grief. They were
married in 1922 at Pickfair, the home of Mary Pickford and Douglas Fairbanks. It was a wedding fit for royalty. Newspaper columnists
called it "the social event of the year." Thousands of fans gathered
around the estate, but detectives and professional wrestlers kept them
at bay. Three airplanes flew over the ceremony and dropped fifty bou-
quets of roses. Unfortunately, both Pickford and Miller were volatile
personalities, and the five-year marriage was a series of quarrels and
reconciliations. They were divorced in 1927.

Miller finally severed her ties with Ziegfeld and signed with impresario Charles Dillingham to appear as Peter Pan. She opened in *Peter
Pan* on November 6, 1924. It was her first appearance in a truly dramatic role. Although the audience liked it, the critics were not too
enthusiastic, and it ran only 125 performances. Dillingham assured
Miller that their next venture would be more successful. Their next

production was a new musical, *Sunny*, with music by Jerome Kern and lyrics by Otto Harbach and Oscar Hammerstein II. *Sunny* featured another Hoosier, Indianapolis native Clifton Webb. Webb was featured with Mary Hay as part of an "eccentric" dance team.

Kern's "Who?" and "Sunny" became enormous hits, and Miller was forever associated with both of them. "Who?" was an unusual song since it began with a single note held for two-and-a-quarter measures. It was impossible to use a phrase, so it had to be a single word. Hammerstein came up with the word, "Who?" Kern claimed that the selection of that word was responsible for the song's success. But he also added that Miller was the song's "editor, critic, handicapper, clocker, tout and winner." Miller was asked to make recordings of these and other songs but declined, feeling that her singing was not good enough to stand on its own. In order for people to appreciate her talent, they needed to see and hear all her talents being applied together.

Miller and Webb became good friends, which also meant that she became friends with Mabelle, Clifton's mother. Mabelle and Webb were constant companions, and she accompanied him everywhere. He was an excellent ballroom dancer, and many compared him to Vernon Castle. Miller loved to go out partying with him after the show, even though it meant that Mabelle was always there too.

Things with Dillingham deteriorated, and Miller reluctantly approached Ziegfeld about coming back to him to do a show. Ziegfeld had just the ticket, a new musical called *Rosalie.* They came to an agreement, and *Rosalie* was a hit primarily due to Miller's appeal.

Miller was always a dedicated performer and worked hard at perfecting her routines. Although she suffered blinding sinus headaches, on stage she did not show the slightest sign of discomfort. She possessed an iron will that kept her delicate body floating through the air. *Rosalie* ran forty-two weeks and was very profitable for both Ziegfeld and Miller. However, it did not have the stuff of *Sally* or *Sunny*.

After the show's run had finished in New York, it went on tour. One night when it was playing in Chicago, Miller received a note, saying, "I am in the city on business and would like to see you. Please leave one ticket for tomorrow night at the box office." It was signed "Edwin J. Reynolds." Miller was thirty years old and had never heard from her father. When he came back stage after the performance, he kissed her lightly on the cheek and said, "Hello, daughter." Reynolds told Miller that he had followed her career with pride, but that he could never work up enough courage to see her until now. She had dinner with him several times before he left town. On his last night, he sat in the front row. Miller waved at him during the curtain calls. He waved back and blew her a kiss. She saw that he was crying. She never saw her father again.

By 1929 sound motion pictures were no longer considered a passing fad, and it was time for Miller to make a move into the film industry. First National offered her $100,000 for her first movie and $150,000 for her second. She accepted on the condition that her first film would be her stage hit *Sally* and that she would have approval of the director. When filming began, Miller found she was working harder than on stage. During a stage run, she could sleep until noon if she wished. In films, she had to be at the studio at the break of dawn. She rectified the situation by having an affair with the head of the studio, Jack Warner. Warner Brothers had taken over First National, running it as a separate company. Warner was easy pickings. He had numerous affairs with many stars and starlets. After her affair with Warner had given her new freedom, she discovered that an old flame, Jack Buchanan, was nearby making a movie at the same studio. Warner was married, and she had to sneak around with him, but Buchanan was single and she could go out in public with him.

Meanwhile, it was discovered that Miller's voice was not coming across well on film. Hal Wallis, then studio manager for First National, said, "On stage, her personal magnetism blinded audiences to her lack of vocal talent. She actually had a very thin voice, and we immediately understood why she never made a recording." The highlights of *Sally* (which was photographed primarily in black and white) were the lavish color sequences and Miller's plaintive rendering of "Look for the Silver Lining." *Sally* got good reviews. Although critics who had seen her perform on stage were disappointed, critics who were seeing her for the first time thought she was wonderful.

Miller knew her future at that time was in the movies. She decided she wanted to do another proven vehicle, *Sunny*. She rented a Beverly Hills mansion and started daily training to get in shape for the film. Warner was still a frequent visitor. *Sunny* started production in June 1930. Unfortunately, the moviegoing public had become tired of the plethora of movie musicals, and Warner tried to assuage the public taste by cutting most of the long production numbers in *Sunny*. This meant that the movie was even less like the stage production than *Sally*. The other problem was that the film was totally black and white, and Miller looked much better in color.

After *Sunny*, Miller wanted to get back on the stage. Ziegfeld, who lost everything in the 1929 stock market crash, had come up with the idea of pairing her with Fred and Adele Astaire. The vehicle was to be called *Smiles*. Miller would play a teenage orphan named Smiles. Vincent Youmans was the composer. Miller knew she would have some stiff competition going up against the Astaires, and she hired a dance coach and worked hard to sharpen up her dancing.

Smiles got mixed reviews. Fred Astaire termed it "a shambles" and "a disaster." Miller missed a number of performances due to illness. The official explanation was she had a bad cold, but the truth was that her migraine headaches were worse. She went to an ear, nose, and throat specialist, who performed a minor but delicate operation on her sinuses. This was supposed to make her less susceptible to such suffering.

Smiles cost Ziegfeld more than $300,000 in losses and he was close to bankruptcy again. On the heels of *Smiles* failure was the fact that Miller's film of *Sunny* was playing to half-empty theaters. The public still perceived it as a musical and would have none of it.

Although she had tons of money in savings and investments, Miller was devastated that she now had two flops in a row. She felt her only salvation was in motion pictures. She went to California and took up with Warner once more. Warner signed her to a contract that placed her among Hollywood's highest-paid stars. However, he had an out in that if he became dissatisfied with her personally or professionally, he could terminate the contract.

Miller had hoped to star in *Grand Hotel* after Greta Garbo walked off the set. However, Garbo came back and Miller had to look for

something else. Darryl Zanuck came up with something called *Her Majesty, Love*. It had been a stage hit in Germany. It would give her a musical context without being an actual musical. Miller had a voice in the casting of the film, and she chose her old vaudeville friend, W. C. Fields. Fields was having difficulty finding work, and Miller thought he would be even funnier in sound films than in silents. Warner objected, but Miller insisted. It was the beginning of Fields's successful movie career.

Her Majesty, Love was released in December 1931. It was a box-office disaster, and her contract was abruptly terminated. Warner suddenly became unavailable and would not even return her phone calls. Although it did not do well at the box office, some critics liked it and even said it was her best work yet. Wallis thought her failure was due to the fact that, "The magic she had onstage, that indefinable charm that made up for her tiny voice and moderate acting talent, utterly vanished on camera."

Miller went back to New York. Ziegfeld died of pleurisy in July 1932. Many Broadway performers, including Miller, did not attend the funeral because Billie Burke decided to have him buried at Forest Lawn in California. Miller was still considered a big star, but she could not find what she considered an appropriate vehicle. Old friend Webb wanted her to join him in *Flying Colors*, but she was not interested. Fellow Hoosier Cole Porter tried to get her for *The Gay Divorcee*, which was to be Fred Astaire's first show without his sister, and Earl Carroll wanted her for the next edition of his *Vanities*.

She was very active socially, appearing at Broadway openings and making the rounds of the popular night spots, escorted by a number of different men. She would sleep till noon, since her sinus headaches were most severe during the morning hours. She realized she would soon turn thirty-five and could no longer play an ingenue. Compounding the matter was that the economy was still sluggish, and business on Broadway was so bad almost every theater offered tickets at cut-rate prices.

Finally, she got the break for which she was hoping. A twenty-eight-year-old playwright named Moss Hart had just written a revue called *As Thousands Cheer*. Irving Berlin was writing the music. A longtime fan of Miller's, Hart had dinner with her, offering her the part. She was reluctant, but Webb, who had already signed to be in the show, talked her into it. She got top billing but only a flat $2,500 per week salary.

She needed to get back in shape fast and began rehearsing and dieting, eventually spending several days in the hospital for "overwork." All the work was worth it. When *As Thousands Cheer* opened September 30, 1933, at the Music Box Theater, the audience gave her a standing ovation. Miller and Webb stopped the show nightly with their rendition of an exquisitely staged "Easter Parade." Ethel Waters, fresh from Harlem's all-black shows, startled the audience singing "Supper Time," with the headline "Unknown Negro Lynched by Frenzied Mob" projected on the curtain. Berlin's songs and the three stars made the show an unqualified hit.

After *As Thousands Cheer* had been running several months, Miller's sinusitis and migraine headaches caused her to miss several performances. Each time she returned to the show she would suffer a relapse, and by spring she was wondering how long she could continue in the

(Opposite page) Marilyn Miller in *Her Majesty, Love* (1931).

show. She managed to keep performing until the following July when her contract expired. She decided not to renew it.

On October 4, 1934, she entered into a third marriage. Her new husband was Chet O'Brien, a twenty-five-year-old chorus boy from the cast of *As Thousands Cheer*. Miller was thirty-six. The headlines read, "Marilyn Miller Marries Chorus Boy." In order to counter the bad publicity and to prove that O'Brien was talented, she invested in a new revue called *Fools Rush In*, in which her husband was the choreographer. The revue lasted only fourteen performances, and Miller lost $33,000. Following this fiasco the couple went to California, where MGM was making a film based on the life of Ziegfeld. She was offered a chance to play herself, but when she demanded equal billing with the stars, the deal fell through. She told MGM she would sue them if her name was even mentioned in the film. *The Great Ziegfeld* was a successful film, but Miller was noticeably absent from it.

While in Hollywood, Marion Davies told Miller about a wonderful Beverly Hills doctor who might be able to help her sinus problem. The doctor examined her and told her there was no permanent cure for what she had. Because of inadequate treatment in the past, she had irreversible damage to the tissues lining the sinus and in the underlying bone. Surgery might be performed, however, to relieve her discomfort.

Without asking for a second opinion, Miller checked into a hospital in Los Angeles. Upon her release, she and O'Brien went to Lake Arrowhead to recuperate. At first the operation appeared to be a success. She accepted an invitation from an Indiana friend, Carole Lombard, to attend an informal gathering at her house on Hollywood Boulevard. Also on the guest list was another Hoosier, Alice Terry. Miller was the life of the party. The rugs were pushed back, and Miller danced and sang, doing numbers from many of her shows. After awhile, she became tired and sat chatting with the other guests for hours. No one present had any idea they were seeing Miller's last performance.

She was offered a role costarring with Ray Bolger in *On Your Toes*, but she did not think she was up to the rigid dancing requirements and reluctantly turned it down. This disappointment probably contributed to her failing health. She was again having headaches, nausea, and a lack of energy. She decided to consult one of the currently fashionable "miracle" doctors. Dr. W. Lawrence Whittemore prescribed a series of insulin treatments. Every evening a nurse would come and inject her with insulin and stay at her bedside until morning. But the nurse said, "When I was first called in, she seemed like a very sick, weak, discouraged person. She did not improve. She appeared to be getting weaker."

On March 12, 1936, Miller was taken to Doctor's Hospital in New York. Her sisters, Ruth and Claire, came to visit her. At first Miller was alert and able to receive visitors. However, on March 20 she lapsed into an eleven-day coma. On April 7 she opened her eyes and smiled and then closed her eyes and passed away.

Miller's sister Claire said she died as the result of incompetent medical treatment. The doctor who performed the sinus operation on Miller a year earlier had cut too closely to the membranes surrounding the brain, leaving it very vulnerable to infection. When infection did develop, Whittemore's insulin injections only made her condition worse. Doctor's Hospital stated she died of hyperpyrexia brought on by an acute toxic condition that had developed from a sinus infection and osteomyelitis of the jaw.

In 1949 Twentieth Century Fox released *Look for the Silver Lining* with June Haver as Miller. It was a highly inaccurate but entertaining biographical film. At the end, Bolger is shown watching Miller (Haver) perform from the wings. He says, "Marilyn Miller will go on forever."

Unfortunately, most of those who saw her on stage at the height of her fame are gone now. Only her three motion pictures survive, giving the viewer just a glimpse of her immense talent. These are inadequate, however, because as Miller knew herself, to fully appreciate the depth of her abilities, she had to be seen live, in person, on her beloved stage.

BIBLIOGRAPHY

Astaire, Fred. *Steps in Time.* New York: Harper and Row, 1959.

Aylesworth, Thomas G. *Broadway to Hollywood: Musicals from Stage to Screen.* New York: Gallery Books, 1985.

Bach, Steven. *Dazzler: The Life and Times of Moss Hart.* New York: Alfred A. Knopf, 2001.

Cantor, Eddie, with Jane Kesner Ardmore. *Take My Life.* Garden City, N.Y.: Doubleday and Company, 1957.

Evansville Courier, April 8, 1936.

Fordin, Hugh. *Jerome Kern Collection.* Santa Monica, Calif.: T. B. Harms, 1988.

Foster, Charles. *Stardust and Shadows: Canadians in Early Hollywood.* Toronto: Dundurn Press, 2000.

Gilbert, Douglas. *American Vaudeville: Its Life and Times.* 1940. Reprint, New York: Dover Publications, 1968.

Hall, Gladys. "The Real 'It' Girl." Unidentified clipping, June 7, 1934. Margaret Herrick Library. Academy of Motion Picture Arts and Sciences, Beverly Hills, California.

Harris, Warren G. *The Other Marilyn: A Biography of Marilyn Miller.* New York: Arbor House, 1985.

Indianapolis News, February 27, 1915, March 22, 1932, April 8, 1936, May 20, 1978.

James, Edward T., ed. *Notable American Women, 1607–1950: A Biographical Dictionary.* 3 vols. Cambridge, Mass.: Belknap Press of Harvard University Press, 1971.

Los Angeles Examiner, April 8, 1936, April 24, 1949.

Mizejewski, Linda. *Ziegfeld Girl: Image and Icon in Culture and Cinema.* Durham, N.C.: Duke University Press, 1999.

New York Times, March 25, 1930, April 8, 1936.

Robinson, Alice M., Vera Mowry Roberts, and Milly S. Barranger. *Notable Women in the American Theatre.* New York: Greenwood Press, 1989.

Sennett, Ted. *Warner Brothers Presents: The Most Exciting Years—From the Jazz Singer to White Heat.* Secaucus, N.J.: Castle Books, 1971.

LOUISE DRESSER

Vaudeville Vocalist to Top Character Actress

Louise Dresser.

ouise Dresser achieved her greatest fame as a dependable supporting actress for such stars as Will Rogers (five films), Rudolph Valentino, and Al Jolson. However, before her movie career began, she was a celebrated beauty, a singing star of vaudeville, and a stage actress.

Louise Josephine Kerlin was born in Evansville, Indiana, on October 5, 1878. Her parents, William S. and Ida Shaffer Kerlin, were both born in Terre Haute. The couple moved to Evansville into a house on Locust Street shortly before Louise was born. Her father was an engineer on the old Evansville and Terre Haute Railroad. It so happened that a "train butcher" (someone who sold candies and refreshments) on Kerlin's train was a young man named Paul Dreiser. Dreiser was a very large young man and had to take a lot of taunts because of his weight. Kerlin, however, was always kind to young Dreiser and tried to shield him from his harassers. Little did Kerlin know that years later this act of kindness would greatly benefit his daughter's career.

Louise was interested in the theater at an early age, and the corner of the Kerlin front porch was a favorite stage for Louise and the neighborhood children. One of her favorite childhood memories was the time she produced a play at the neighborhood firehouse. Louise was always director, star, and treasurer of the productions and collected many pins as the price of admission. She also sang in choirs and appeared in any little show that was available in Evansville. Before finishing high school, she moved with her family to Columbus, Ohio. Shortly after the move, her father was killed in a train wreck.

By the time she was fifteen, Louise was a beautiful blonde with a very good voice, longing for a stage career. In order to attain her goal she cut her education short and, equipped with a railroad pass, set out for Boston, where she thought she had a singing engagement. The job turned out to be in a burlesque theater. Reluctantly she donned tights and performed. She supplemented her meager income by singing at a local wax museum.

While on tour in vaudeville, Louise found herself in Chicago, where she was asked by a song-plugging firm to sing two new Paul Dresser songs. Her performance was so impressive that she was asked to talk with Dresser, who happened to be in Chicago that day. She remembered "thinking at the time that I had never seen such a fat man."

Serie d'oro

505

Lon Chaney e Louise Dresser in "Mister Wu"

METRO-GOLDWYN ROMA

Dresser had met a lot of singers who had performed his music. Nevertheless, he began to talk with Louise and found that she was from Evansville. He asked, "Any relation to 'Billy' Kerlin, who ran an engine on the [Evansville and Terre Haute] railroad?" When Louise informed him that she was his daughter, Dresser was astounded. He told her how her father had befriended him. Dresser decided to repay Kerlin for his kindness through his daughter.

"Are you any good as a singer?" "I don't know," she replied. He had her sing two songs and then said, "Your father was my friend and I am going to repay that friendship. From now on you are Louise Dresser, my little sister." He called the drama editor of the *Chicago Tribune* and told him that his little sister was in town and "she wants a page story about herself." He then booked her into the Masonic Temple Roof Garden in Chicago for her professional debut.

Louise was flabbergasted because "[Dresser] hadn't asked my consent, or how I felt about it. It was his idea, his way of thanking my father." She later had the privilege of introducing Dresser's biggest hit, "My Gal Sal." Unfortunately, he did not live to see the success of his last big hit. Dresser remained in touch with her "brother" Paul through the years and was with him when he died in New York in 1906.

Critics described her as "the girl with the pleasing contralto voice." In 1898, at age twenty, she joined the vaudeville company of Ward and Vokes. She played a bit part in *The Governors* and also appeared in the chorus. She received a salary of twenty-five dollars a week. In 1899 she met and later married Jack Norworth. Norworth, a vaudeville monologist who later became a lyricist, is probably best known for writing the lyrics to "Take Me Out to the Ballgame" to Hoosier Albert Von Tilzer's melody. Norworth penned his famous lyrics in 1908, one year after he and Dresser were divorced.

Dresser was in vaudeville until 1906 when she joined Lew Fields in his play *About Town*. The play had an impressive cast that included

Louise Dresser and Helen Cohan in *Lightnin* (1930).

(Top photo) Louise Dresser and Lon Chaney in *Mr. Wu (1927)*.

Norworth, Vernon Castle, and Mae Murray. The next year she was with Fields in *The Girl Behind the Counter*. In 1909 she was given her greatest stage opportunity when she appeared in *The Girls of Gottenberg*, placing her in the ranks of one of the musical comedy favorites of the day. However, she was not happy. She said, "The strangest part of it all to me is that I should have strayed into musical comedy when I always longed to become a real, legitimate actress."

Dresser began to appear regularly on the New York stage in musical comedy and light opera and met Jack Gardner, who played in many musical comedies. They were married in 1908 when he was appearing in *Yankee Prince* with George M. Cohan at the Knickerbocker Theater. After ten years of marriage, they finally managed to appear on stage together, making two tours of vaudeville as headliners, doing musical sketches.

In 1911 Dresser received her first starring role. Her debut was at the English Theater in Indianapolis. This was a tryout for the Chicago premiere of the play *Lovely Liar*. After it opened successfully in Indianapolis, it played at the Olympia Theater in Chicago. Later that same year Dresser appeared in *A Matinee Idol* with DeWolf Hopper. Her understudy was Hopper's wife, Hedda, who later became a well-known columnist. She kept busy in New York, mostly in musical comedies, creating the leading feminine role on Broadway for Montague Glass's *Potash and Perimutter* (1914, 1915). She was in Cohan's *Hello Broadway* (1914) and the Jerome Kern musicals *Have a Heart* (1917) and *Rock-a-bye, Baby* (1918).

Her last trip to Evansville was in 1919 when she came with Gardner and writer Jack Lait to try out a new act at the Grand Theater. She spent much time calling on old acquaintances and seeking out landmarks she had known as a child.

Upon hearing about the burgeoning motion picture industry in California, she and her husband decided to move there in 1920. By 1922 she had moved into silent films, and Gardner had become an executive with the Fox organization. Dresser worked with many of the giants of the silent screen, including Douglas Fairbanks, Rudolph Valentino, Mary Pickford, and John Drew, and gained a reputation as an excellent character actress. In 1925 she received very favorable notices as the Czarina, Catherine II, opposite Valentino in *The Eagle* and as a drunken ex-star in *The Goose Woman*.

In 1927 Indianapolis native Sid Grauman opened the Chinese Theater in Hollywood. Grauman was part of a group that established the Academy of Motion Picture Arts and Sciences, which was formed to benefit the film industry in a variety of ways. The Academy decided to honor those who were considered to be outstanding contributors to the art of motion pictures. The first nominations for best actress were Janet Gaynor, Gloria Swanson, and Dresser, who was nominated for her role in *A Ship Comes In*. She lost to Gaynor for her performance in multiple films—*Seventh Heaven*, *Street Angel*, and *Sunrise*. Dresser was awarded a Citation of Merit for being a runner-up.

Dresser was quite a versatile actress, playing Calamity Jane in *Caught* (1931) and Empress Elizabeth in *The Scarlet Empress* (1934). She had the opportunity to play in at least two Hoosier authors' stories on film, Gene Stratton-Porter's *Girl of the Limberlost* in 1934 and George Ade's *County Chairman* in 1935. The latter film starred Will Rogers. She had previously worked with Rogers in *Lightnin'* (1930), *State Fair* and *Doctor Bull* (1933), and *David Harum* (1934).

Louise Dresser in the stage play *A Plain Man and His Wife* (1933).
WALTER FREDERICK SEELY

Dresser retired from films in 1940, and she and Gardner moved into a modest bungalow in Glendale, California. She divided her time between gardening and promoting charities for the West Coast's professional colony. Gardner died in 1950, and Dresser remained in Glendale. In 1962, when she was eighty-three years old, she was interviewed by the *Indianapolis Star*. She said she was still a Hoosier at heart and was planning to come back for a visit to Terre Haute, where her parents were born. Several years prior to the interview, Dresser gave her collection of scrapbooks, letters, and photos to the Culver Military Academy in Culver, Indiana. There they were put in the Green Room in the Eugene Eppley Memorial Auditorium on the Culver campus. Dresser died following surgery for an intestinal ailment on April 24, 1965, in Woodland Hills, California.

BIBLIOGRAPHY

Blum, Daniel C. *A Pictorial History of the American Theater, 1860–1985.* New York: Crown Publishers, 1986.

Garraty, John A., ed. *Dictionary of American Biography. Supplement 7: 1961–1965.* New York: Scribner, 1981.

Gunn, Elizabeth E. *Music in Indiana.* Self-published, 1928.

Henderson, Clayton W. *On the Banks of the Wabash: The Life and Music of Paul Dresser.* Indianapolis: Indiana Historical Society Press, 2003.

Indianapolis Star, February 21, 1909, February 25, 1932, January 7, 1940, April 1, 1962.

Jones, Ken D., Arthur F. McClure, and Alfred E. Twomey. *Character People.* South Brunswick, N.J.: A. S. Barnes, 1976.

Osborne, Robert. *Sixty Years of the Oscar: The Official History of the Academy Awards.* New York: Abbeville Press, 1989.

Truitt, Evelyn Mack. *Who Was Who on Screen.* New York: R. R. Bowker Company, 1984.

Variety, April 28, 1965.

Louise Dresser.

(Above, left) Louise Dresser and Basil Rathbone in *This Mad World* (1930).

CAROLE LOMBARD

"The Profane Angel"

There was once a little girl from Fort Wayne, Indiana, named Jane Alice Peters. She went to Los Angeles, where she grew up to be very beautiful and very famous. Millions adored her, including "The King of Hollywood," who married her. Her fairy-tale story was the dream of legions of young women during the golden age of movies. For Jane Alice Peters, it was a dream come true. However, it ended in tragedy.

Jane changed her name for the movies to Carole Lombard, taking Carole from a dear friend and Lombard from Harry and Etta Lombard, an Indiana family who had also migrated to California and who were distant relatives. Lombard was born in Fort Wayne, Indiana, on October 6, 1908, the third child and only girl of the former Elizabeth Knight and Frederic Peters. Her parents were from two of Fort Wayne's well established and well-to-do families. The Knights had banking connections in the East. Jim Cheney, Elizabeth's maternal grandfather, was a friend and confidential adviser to Jay Gould and had amassed a large fortune. He was on the directorate of the syndicate that financed the laying of the first transatlantic cable and was an important figure in financing many of the country's first electric light plants.

Cheney's favorite daughter, Alice, married Charlie Knight, and it was certainly common knowledge that Knight had married into money. An interviewer once asked Lombard if it was a fact that her grandfather laid the first transatlantic cable and thus had acquired several lucrative patents. Lombard replied in what became her trademark way of speaking, "No, that was the older guy. The only thing my grandad laid was Grandmother Knight, but he acquired three luscious daughters."

Frederic Peters's father was the founder of the J. C. Peters Hardware Company in Fort Wayne. J. C. also built the Wayne Hotel on Columbia Street in Fort Wayne in 1887. It was the first one hundred-room hotel in the city. Benjamin Harrison and Rutherford B. Hayes stayed there, and William Jennings Bryan spoke from its balcony on October 21, 1896. Frederic apprenticed in the hardware business with his three brothers. The two families knew each other, and Fred started pursuing Elizabeth, or "Bess," the name she preferred. It was a long courtship. Bess teased him with the notion of leaving Fort Wayne, perhaps to pursue a career on stage. She had appeared in a number of Fort Wayne stage productions, displaying her effusive personality.

The courtship was also elongated because Knight wanted Fred to prove himself in business before marriage.

The opportunity came when Fred was groomed for a managerial position with the Horton Manufacturing Company, which made washing machines. Although Fred sustained a devastating injury in an elevator accident at the factory, the permanent impairment of his leg did not alter his marriage plans. The Knight–Peters wedding was a big event in Fort Wayne at the turn of the century.

Frederic Peters Jr. (known as Fritz) was born in 1902, and Stuart Peters was born in 1906. Jane Alice Peters (Carole) came along two years later. She was born in a large house that J. C. had built at the foot of Rockhill Street. Carole's grandfather had actually built two houses side by side in a fashionable section of Fort Wayne. The property was supposed to be an investment, and the houses were to be leased. However, Fred decided to move into the one nearest the St. Marys River. The land sloped gently down to the banks of the river where the Peters children spent hours playing after school and during summer vacation. The house was big enough for each child to have his or her own room. Carole's room was at the top of the stairs.

As the years went by, Fred's gimpy leg began to give him more trouble, and he started to have severe headaches, which doctors said was attributable to the accident. He not only became more introverted but also adopted an air of aristocracy. When he went fishing and hunting, he always wore a Tyrolean hat, and the family gave him the nickname of "Lord Algie."

Carole Lombard.

(Previous page) Carole Lombard and Clark Gable in *No Man of Her Own* (1932), the only movie the two made together.

As in many other American cities, Fort Wayne had an established class system with economic status as the primary measurement. Indianapolis author Booth Tarkington wrote about it in *The Magnificent Ambersons* and *Alice Adams*. If he had written a similar novel about life in Fort Wayne, he would have found the ideal subjects to be the Knights and the Peterses. They were certainly two of the "best" families in that city.

Lombard made her acting debut in Fort Wayne in *Ivanhoe*. The production took place behind the Thieme house on Berry Street. She was a handmaiden to Rebecca. The boys used garbage can lids as shields, court scenes were held in the Thieme barn, and tourneys were performed in the dirt alley. Robert Pollock, who was a boyhood friend of Fritz and Stuart, stated that Carole wanted to play football with the boys at the foot of Union Street in Fort Wayne. Because there were few girls for her to play with on Rockhill Street, she demanded to play with the boys. Pollock said, "Every other afternoon this six-year old blonde would come screeching across the street, demanding a chance to play one of the ends. She was always sent home again."

Her brothers allowed her to play with them and the other boys in other sports and games of "cops and robbers." She developed exceptional rapport with her brothers. They were "pests" and she was "pet." It may have been that this association with boys in her childhood and in her adolescence in Los Angeles made her capable of a better understanding of the male mentality. Years later she would say, "If I have a masculine manner of thinking, I am not sorry for it. It has brought me fine friendships and has made them last."

Although she was an admitted tomboy, she nevertheless went to Trier's Dancing Academy every Saturday for lessons. Twice a month, on Friday night, she went to the Colonial or the Gaiety movie houses

Carole Lombard and Buck Jones (Vincennes) in *Hearts and Spurs* (1925).

in downtown Fort Wayne. Her favorite actresses were Kathlyn Williams, a serial star, and Pearl White, who was famous for her last-minute escapes in serials. She decided then that she wanted to be a movie star. Fortunately, she had a mother who understood. Bess had always enjoyed being on the stage. She longed to move to Indianapolis and made frequent trips there, cultivating a circle of friends. However, Fred would not budge from Fort Wayne.

As Fred's headaches grew worse, even the new "miracle drug" aspirin did not seem to help. His so-called spells terrified Bess, and she became a bundle of nerves. Finally, unable to cope with her husband's illness any longer, Bess took the children on an extended vacation to California and the San Francisco World's Fair. Fred thought it was a good idea for all concerned. It was thought the children would miss one semester of school at the most. Carole's Grandmother Knight agreed to underwrite the trip, and they left Fort Wayne for San Francisco in October 1914. Carole was six years old.

San Francisco proved to be "too damp," and Bess moved the family to Southern California, where they had several "transplanted" Fort Wayne friends. Bess enrolled Carole in a dramatic school for girls.

Shortly after their arrival, Bess was introduced to the Baha'i faith, which taught of the spiritual unity of mankind and the immortality of the soul. One of the tenets was the belief in the total equality of men and women. Bess raised her daughter to believe this.

Bess and the children loved California, and any thought of returning to Indiana completely disappeared. Fred wrote often, sent money regularly, and made several visits. However, he always returned to Fort Wayne on schedule. Grandmother Knight continued to send money for support. Bess thought of finding a job, but with the support she was receiving, it was not necessary. Bess and Fred remained separated the rest of their lives. Neither married again.

While attending grammar and intermediate school, Carole developed an interest in athletics, playing volleyball and tennis, swimming, and winning trophies for broad jumping and running. Her appearances in school plays encouraged Al and Rita Kaufman, neighbors of the Peters, to persuade Allan Dwan, a pioneer motion picture director, to take a look at her.

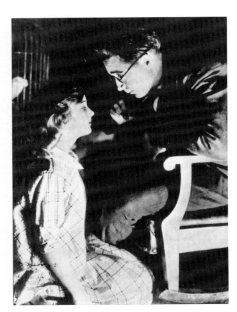

Carole Lombard and Monte Blue in *A Perfect Crime* (1921).

The Kaufmans also were friends with boxer Benny Leonard, who gave the Peters boys boxing lessons. Carole prevailed on her brothers to pass the lessons along to her. One day in 1921 Carole was boxing with the boys in her backyard when Dwan arrived. He was looking for a tomboy to be the kid sister to the leading man in his film *A Perfect Crime*. Coincidentally the leading man was Monte Blue, who was from Indianapolis. Bess knew Blue when he was a teenager in Indianapolis shortly after he left the Indiana Soldiers' and Sailors' Children's Home in Knightstown.

Carole made her motion picture debut with Blue in 1921 when she was twelve years old. However, nothing came of it, and she went back to school where she completed her education at Virgil Junior High School. She left high school to pursue her film career. In 1924 she was asked to audition for Charlie Chaplin for his film, *The Gold Rush*. She was not hired.

She started participating in exhibition ballroom dancing at the Cocoanut Grove in the Los Angeles Ambassador Hotel on Friday nights. One evening in 1925 an executive from Fox Pictures saw the attractive blonde dancing at the hotel and invited her to do a screen test. When the test proved successful, she was offered a contract to appear opposite Edmund Lowe in *Marriage in Transit*, a spy story. Carole received favorable reviews, and before the release of the film Jane Peters adopted the name of Carol Lombard. She would add the *e* later.

Lombard soon discovered that there was an "Indiana Colony" in Hollywood. People from Indiana in the profession helped their fellow Hoosiers get a foothold. Some of the people in the Colony were Richard "Skeets" Gallagher of Terre Haute, Norman Foster of Richmond, Buck Jones of Vincennes, Ken and Kermit Maynard of Vevay, Alice Terry of Evansville, Monte Blue of Indianapolis, John Bowers of Garrett, Raymond Walburn of Plymouth, Charles Butterworth of South Bend, and the Geraghty family of Rushville (Carmelita, screenwriters Maurice and Gerard, and their father Tom, who was a prolific screenwriter in the silent days, penning several movies for Douglas Fairbanks). In addition to the Geraghty brothers, there were a number of people behind the scenes who were Indiana natives. Don McElwaine was an Indiana native and served as a publicist with the

Buck Jones entourage. McElwaine later became a publicist at Pathe, where Lombard worked in the late twenties, and wrote many of her publicity releases. Howard and Kenneth Hawks from Goshen were both directors and Lombard's second cousins.

Jones gave Lombard roles in three of his pictures in 1925. She had bit parts in *Gold and the Girl* and *Durand of the Badlands*. Then Jones gave Lombard her first leading lady role and her first screen kiss in *Hearts and Spurs*. Jones was very fond of Lombard, admiring her ability to hold her own and speak her opinions. W. S. Van Dyke was frequently Jones's director. One day on location for *Hearts and Spurs*, the two men played a practical joke on Lombard. Van Dyke was wearing a gun as a protection against snakes. He loaded it with blanks. When Lombard came out of the makeup truck, Van Dyke and Jones began quarreling as to how the scene was to be shot. In a rage, Van Dyke pulled out his gun and plugged Jones in the chest. Jones, palming catsup, slapped his chest and red oozed out all over his shirt front. He collapsed as Lombard came running to him. She held him, weeping, and shouted for someone to get an ambulance. Then Jones opened his eyes, smiled at her, and began laughing. Realizing what had happened, Lombard dropped his head smartly on the ground and indignantly told both men what they could do with themselves. Her ability to speak her mind directly and bluntly was an unusual and admirable thing in a woman in those days.

Her last film at Fox was *The Road to Glory* (1926), directed by her cousin, Howard Hawks. Her contract was not renewed, and she admitted that "I did feel that I was sadly in need of experience." She remained off the screen until 1927. Part of the reason for this was her involvement in an automobile accident.

Lombard was riding with a friend, Harry Cooper, who was the son of a Los Angeles banker. Another vehicle collided with Cooper's Bugatti roadster, and a splinter of broken glass cut a two-inch wound on her left cheek. There are conflicting reports as to how she overcame this. Some say she had cosmetic surgery. Others say the wound was not that bad and healed without leaving much of a scar. At any rate, it was not difficult to disguise with makeup and proper lighting. Lombard had a photographer snap her from all angles so she could determine how best to be lit. She became an expert on how to light herself to hide the scar.

On the advice of Lonnie Dorsey, a family friend who was employed at the Mack Sennett studios, Lombard did a screen test for the company. She passed the test and started to work for Sennett, "The King of Comedy," in 1927, earning fifty dollars a week. In his autobiography Sennett says, "It was Sally Eilers who brought a young girl named Jane Peters to Keystone. She was a scamp and madcap, much like Mabel (Normand), and we were so struck by her personality that we put her under contract."

Lombard became one of the "Sennett Bathing Beauties," a job which she thoroughly enjoyed. She said, "The theory was if you could 'take' it there, you could do anything." She told an interviewer in 1929, "There won't ever be another Sennett's for laughs. Daphne Pollard and I were in hysterics the whole time. You should have seen that lot when the boys ran riot with water hoses . . . the mess we made off the set was often much worse than the one we did for the benefit of the cameras." It was at Sennett that Lombard met Madelyn

Carole Lombard and her mother Elizabeth Peters, circa 1920.
COURTESY OF ADRIENNE FLOWER

Fields, who became her personal secretary-manager and girl Friday. "Fieldsie" was one of her closest friends.

Lombard did not stay at Sennett very long, but it was long enough to make a good impression. Ruth Taylor, an assistant to Sennett, said in her diary for March 9, 1927, "On the last Sennett set I say there were ten new bathing girls. They looked eager and happy and beautiful. Mr. Sennett says Carole Lombard and Sally Eilers are the pick and they will be great stars some day."

Over the next few years she made films for Pathe, Fox, and Paramount. By 1936 she was making $3,500 a week at Paramount. It was in 1930, when she started her contract with Paramount, that the *e* was officially added to her first name. When large display posters for *Fast and Loose* were printed, Carol had become "Carole." The mistake was not discovered until it was too late to do anything about it. Upon seeing it she said, "What the hell, let's keep it with the 'e.' I don't think I've ever seen it spelled that way and I sort of like it."

Lombard was symbolic of an American type—unspoiled and sporty. She was witty, self-reliant, and managed to achieve independence without toughness. She had a magnetic personality both off screen and on. From her tomboyish Midwest beginnings, she emerged as a beautiful, sophisticated comedienne, managing to develop a character that was a mixture of earthly mannishness and eager surprise. Critic Charles Champlin summarized her in this way, "Well ahead of her time, she was all Woman and all liberated."

Part of her "liberation" was her language. She had no hesitation to use coarse language laced with profanity, a form of expression acquired from her brothers Fritz and Stuart. Fritz had become a buyer for a Los Angeles department store, and Stuart was a trader at a Los Angeles stock brokerage firm. Her acquisition of her vile vocabulary started as a form of defense. She believed she could turn off a lot of would-be romeos with her language. Fritz told how it all began.

> We were at home, both Stuart and I, and Carole came in all upset . . . from the studio where she was working, I suppose. Without beating around the bush, she said she wanted us to teach her all the dirty words we knew . . . when to say them, and what they meant. Now that certainly wasn't anything either Stuart or I wanted to do. We knew all the vile words and I'm sure we used them ourselves often enough, maybe too often . . . but in our own way, and I hope discreetly. We didn't use dirty talk around Carole. For one thing, Mother wouldn't tolerate it. But Sis wouldn't let us off the hook. She'd hit on the idea of discouraging her would-be seducers by swearing at them, and the amazing thing was that she really didn't know very many dirty words . . . anyway, she didn't know what they meant. So we more or less said all right, you asked for it, and started at the beginning. Just getting started was the only embarrassing part. Soon it became a little game and we all relaxed and enjoyed it. I remember that Stuart especially couldn't stop laughing.

Fritz continued, "She memorized all the terms and our definitions like she was studying for a test. And from then on, if some guy made a pass at her or tried to, he'd hear such talk as he just wouldn't

Carole Lombard rehearsing for *Swing High,
Swing Low* (1937) with (left to right)
Charles Butterworth (South Bend), Fred
MacMurray, and director Mitchell Leisen.
©1936, PARAMOUNT PICTURES INC.

expect to come from such a beautiful girl, who was also a nice girl in every way."

The way she talked actually enhanced Lombard's personality. She used her newfound language freely and stopped would-be attackers cold. Word of her brazen language got around the Pathe studio and then began to spread around the town. She realized she had hit upon something and in time refined her technique to use to her advantage in other areas. She soon discovered that after the first shock of hearing a woman swear, men were more likely to relax. She found that she enjoyed talking to men at their own level, and on that level. Her language eventually earned her the nickname, "The Profane Angel."

In 1930 Lombard's Grandmother Knight died, leaving a will that bequeathed ten thousand dollars to Carole and an undisclosed amount to Bess. Carole and her mother returned to the city of her birth in June 1930 for the first time since leaving it. Bess went to Fort Wayne two weeks before Carole, who stopped in the city on her way to Paramount's Long Island studios, where she was to begin production of *The Best People*. Lombard stayed in Fort Wayne four days. She

(*Left to right*) Frederic "Fritz" Peters and his wife, Stuart Peters, Carole Lombard, and her husband, William Powell, on their wedding day, June 26, 1931.

was reunited with her father and a multitude of relatives she barely remembered. A tea party was given in her honor. It became the social event of the season and was talked about for years. She toured the countryside and with her cousins retraced the familiar steps of her childhood. Bess and Fred Peters got together to work out a divorce agreement. Fred wanted Bess to have the freedom to remarry if she should ever consider it. Although Bess made several other trips to Fort Wayne through the years, Carole never returned.

Lombard was now a very busy actress. In 1930 she started shooting *Man of the World* with William Powell at the same time she was shooting *Up Pops the Devil.* Before the latter was finished, she started another picture with Powell, *Ladies' Man.* It was on this film that a romance began to flame in earnest between the two stars.

Powell was married but had been long estranged from his wife. He had never known a girl like Lombard and doubted if another existed. She was fascinated by Powell, who was moody, intellectual, and very proper. Lombard was informal, spontaneous, and loved to dress casually. Powell was an accomplished ballroom dancer; she danced the latest jazz steps. During their courtship Lombard was quoted as saying, "I think marriage is dangerous. It spoils beautiful friendships that might have lasted for years. The idea of two people trying to possess each other is wrong. It must be a friendship . . . a calm companionship which can last through the years."

In spite of Lombard's apparent misgivings, they were married on June 26, 1931, by a Congregationalist minister at her mother's home. Other than Bess, Fritz, and Stuart, only Powell's elderly parents attended. The marriage ended in divorce twenty-eight months later. Lombard said, "Career had little to do with the divorce. We were just two completely incompatible people." They remained on friendly terms the rest of her life.

In 1931 two films were released in which Lombard costarred with Hoosier actors. *It Pays to Advertise* was unique in this respect since the three stars were all from Indiana. Lombard played opposite Norman Foster (real name: Nick Hoeffer) from Richmond, Indiana, and in a major supporting role was Richard "Skeets" Gallagher from Terre Haute. Foster was married to Claudette Colbert, and Lombard and Colbert became good friends. She was reunited with Foster and Gallagher the same year in *Up Pops the Devil.* Both Lombard and Foster received good reviews for these witty comedies.

Carole Lombard and Bing Crosby in *We're Not Dressing* (1934).
©1934, PARAMOUNT PRODUCTIONS INC.

Lombard was always known as a champion of the little guy. She knew every stagehand, propman, wardrobe mistress, and script girl by name, and they loved to work with her. In an interview with Hollywood writer Gladys Hall in 1930 she was asked, "Are you temperamental? You know, walk off sets and things?" She replied, "I do walk off sets but not for the reasons you might suppose. I'm not temperamental about myself. I can take care of myself, all right. But I do get temperamental when I hear some little would-be Napoleon of a director, some little killer-diller of a petty Czar cursing out extras, grips, electricians. I've walked off sets when things like that happen."

In 1934 Lombard appeared opposite Bing Crosby in *We're Not Dressing.* During the shooting, she and Crosby developed a lasting friendship. Crosby enjoyed her "colorful epithets" and described her language as "good, clean and lusty. Her swearing words weren't obscene. They were gusty and eloquent. They resounded, they bounced. They had honest zing!" He was impressed with her forthrightness. "She was the least prudish person I've ever known."

Lombard's career progressed steadily but unspectacularly. A major turning point in her career was a result of contributions by two of her fellow Hoosiers. Director Howard Hawks selected Lombard for the lead opposite John Barrymore for the film *Twentieth Century* (1934). The film was based on a play by Hoosier Charles Bruce Millholland from Economy, Indiana. Millholland wrote a play based on his experiences on the Twentieth Century Limited. He called it *Napoleon of Broadway.* It appeared on Broadway at least three times. Charles MacArthur and Ben Hecht reworked it and titled it *Twentieth Century.*

Working with Hawks and Barrymore turned Lombard into a legitimate actress. Although Hawks had worked with her before, this film would really test her ability as a comedienne. Hawks and Barrymore were both disappointed in Lombard's performance the first few days. Finally Hawks took her aside and told her to quit acting. He said, "He is insulting you, provoking you. What would you do if he tried it off the set?" She replied, "I'd kick him right in the groin." Hawks told her, "We're going back in and make this scene and you kick him, and you do any damn thing that comes into your mind that's natural, and quit acting. If you don't quit, I'm going to fire you this afternoon." She later said that working with Hawks and Barrymore taught her to let go—"to abandon myself to the part." She said, "I hardly recognized myself. I certainly am not the Carole Lombard of the past four years."

The film had become a superior example of sophisticated comedy. It not only showcased the comic acting skills of Barrymore but it also proved that Lombard was a formidable comedienne. After the picture was finished, Barrymore sent Lombard an autographed picture inscribed, "to the finest actress I have worked with bar none." He also surprised the film colony by proclaiming her as "probably the greatest actress I have ever worked with." Barrymore restated his opinion years later, dropping the "probably."

Twentieth Century was the first of Lombard's "screwball comedies," a genre that enjoyed great popularity in the thirties and forties. In 1936 she joined her ex-husband Powell for the classic *My Man Godfrey*, and the next year she did *Nothing Sacred* with Fredric March. These three films are classics of the genre, and as a result, she was forever categorized as the definitive screwball comedienne. Myrna Loy, Katharine Hepburn, Rosalind Russell, Jean Arthur, and Irene Dunne enjoyed success in screwball comedies, but Lombard added a uniqueness and energy to her characterizations that no one would ever match.

According to Richard Schickel, she epitomized a new type of heroine, women who were realists in the company of naïve, fumbling men: "They had a sharper sense of right and wrong, were better students of tactics, and were masters of the mannish wisecrack. In a movie world where women had, prior to the depression, been either innocents or exotics, they were refreshingly down to earth." One wonders what Lombard would have done with the Russell role in *His Girl Friday.* Harry Cohn wanted her for the part, but by this time she was simply too expensive for Columbia Studios.

Lombard had several romances over the next few years. Robert Riskin, who wrote most of Frank Capra's screenplays, was a steady companion. Riskin even tried to convince Capra to cast Lombard opposite Clark Gable in *It Happened One Night.* One evening Lombard and Riskin attended a performance by up-and coming-vocalist Russ Columbo at the Cocoanut Grove. Columbo was immediately smitten with Lombard, sending her flowers and composing a song for her—"Save the Last Dance for Me." Lombard and Columbo became a hot twosome, and their names were linked in most gossip columns. Shortly after they attended a screening of his first starring vehicle, *Wake Up and Dream*, Columbo was killed when an antique pistol he was holding fired. Lombard attended the funeral and broke down sobbing uncontrollably. She was comforted by her brother Stuart and Bing Crosby, both of whom were pallbearers at the funeral.

In 1935, at the age of fifty-nine, Fred Peters died following brain surgery in Fort Wayne. It was a final attempt to alleviate the agony he had suffered since that elevator accident many years ago. Lombard was just recovering from the death of Columbo, and that experience probably led her to a decision not to attend the funeral. There was disappointment in her hometown that its most famous celebrity would not come home for the event. However, Lombard said, "My father is entitled to some dignity and respect in death, and if I were there it would turn into the worst kind of theatrical event."

In 1936 when Universal offered Powell the lead in *My Man Godfrey*, he said he would do it only if Lombard were cast as the female lead. Powell was romantically involved with Jean Harlow at this time. In spite of the gossips hoping for a second Powell-Lombard romance, Powell's insistence on Lombard was strictly based on the fact he knew she would be perfect for the part of the wealthy, spoiled eccentric. He was right. Lombard was a smash in this delightful screwball comedy.

That same year Lombard was one of the people who was in charge of the Mayfair Ball, a big social event in Hollywood. Gable came without his estranged wife, Rhea Langham. Although Lombard was there with Cesar Romero, she and Gable began to talk and then both disappeared. Some time later they came back but not together. This was the beginning of their historic affair.

Lombard had heard all the stories about Gable's philandering. She did love him but was not sure he was husband material. Up to that point Gable had been married to older women. He had been abandoned by his mother when he was ten months old, and he may have

Carole Lombard and (left to right) Groucho Marx, Cary Grant, Lawrence Tibbett, Chico Marx, and Ronald Coleman.

been looking for a mother in his choice of wives. Although Lombard was much younger than Gable, age has little to do with mothering and she felt she could provide the love he was deprived of at such an early age. It was also clear he had never had a wife who was also a pal. She knew she could be that. Lombard learned to tie and cast a fly, to grease the pan for the newly caught fish, and to fire different rifles. She enjoyed shooting skeet and easily became Gable's superior, enjoying getting the better of him. She said, "I'm nuts about skeet shooting. It gets you so that you keep saying 'one more round' and keep on saying it until old sol has run round the clock, likely as not."

When it became increasingly obvious that Gable would play Rhett Butler in spite of his objections, Lombard began to scheme to get the role of Scarlett. It was not to be. After her plans for Scarlett were thwarted, she began concentrating on Gable. Her party girl reputation was dropped almost overnight. She decided that being with Gable was more fun.

When she finished *Nothing Sacred* in 1937, it was decided that when it premiered in Fort Wayne, the city fathers would declare "Carole Lombard Day." Lombard agreed to return to her birthplace, and a triumphant homecoming was planned. The people of Fort Wayne were bitterly disappointed when Lombard changed her mind and went fishing with Gable instead. The ceremony, however, went on without her. The mayor made a proclamation, and Lombard's birthplace and early home at 704 Rockhill Street was dedicated as an historic landmark, complete with an engraved tablet that remains affixed to the house to this day. Over the years the house was converted to apartments and slowly deteriorated. In 1993 Bev and David Fiandt bought the house and restored it. It is now known as the Carole Lombard House and is a bed-and-breakfast. The view from the enclosed porch, where breakfast is served, includes the Carole Lombard Bridge, spanning the St. Marys River, upon whose banks Lombard played as a little girl.

Gable had hoped to end his marriage to Langham quickly. The sticking point was money, and when he thought her demands were exorbitant he decided to bide his time. Instead of the price going down, it went up. Gable might have kept the affair with Lombard going indefinitely had she not reminded him that he had no real power over her, no legal rights. She kept him off balance by indicating she might break it off at any time. Finally, Gable agreed to pay Langham approximately $500,000. The divorce cost him. When a *Photoplay* article in 1939 entitled "Hollywood's Unmarried Husbands and Wives" appeared, it revealed that Lombard and Gable were openly having an affair. It did not affect her career or her popularity. This was a choice coupling similar to that of Douglas Fairbanks and Mary Pickford two decades earlier.

Gable had been living in a house in North Hollywood that he rented from Evansville native Alice Terry and her husband, director Rex Ingram. Lombard had a bachelor apartment she shared with her secretary and adviser Madalynne "Fieldsie" Fields. *Gone with the Wind* was about to start shooting when Gable and Lombard found a forty-three-acre ranch in Encino owned by director Raoul Walsh. The divorce cost Gable some cars and real estate holdings, but he was far from broke. Nevertheless, he did not have the money for the down payment, so Lombard wrote a check to Walsh for $50,000 and began to supervise the construction of their new home.

Carole Lombard.

Carole Lombard.

(Opposite page) Carole Lombard and Clark Gable sitting on the back of a car at their ranch in Encino.

In early March 1939 Gable received his divorce and was free to marry Lombard. The simple rites took place at the First Methodist Church in Kingman, Arizona, on March 29, 1939. It was a town Gable had picked out months before when he was on a hunting and fishing trip. The minister's wife was the bridesmaid, and Gable's friend, neighbor, and studio publicist, Otto Winkler, was best man. Gable was working on *Gone with the Wind* at the time, and the newlyweds returned to Los Angeles immediately after the ceremony.

That summer the couple moved into their new Encino home. It was a white brick, two-story colonial residence with nine rooms and just one bedroom suite. Lombard planned it that way because she did not like to have overnight company. The house was her notion of what a king should have. She supervised every detail with Gable's own taste, comfort, and convenience. It was Early American with quilted wingback chairs, an enormous soft couch, and a huge fireplace. The centerpiece was the gun room with its glass-enclosed display cases.

The couple rarely entertained and was seldom seen at nightclubs. Lombard, however, enjoyed professional tennis and often appeared with Gable at the Los Angeles Tennis Club. Tennis pro Alice Marble was one of her close friends. Lombard shared her husband's enjoyment of the outdoors and was his constant companion on hunting trips. She would pile out of bed at five in the morning, drink some scalding coffee, and go to a duck blind in some God-forsaken wilderness where she would kneel in mud and water, waiting motionless, until a wedge-shaped flight of birds passed overhead. Gable regarded her as a good shot but when she missed, everyone in the party could hear her disappointed "Damn!" About her love of shooting she said, "It's the same with everything I do, I love everything I do. I'm intensely interested in and enthusiastic about everything I do, everything! No matter what I'm doing, no matter how trivial, it isn't trivial to me. I give it all I've got and love it. I love living. I get a kick out of everything I do while I'm doing it."

When *Life* magazine featured Lombard on the cover of the October 17, 1938, issue, she gave world-renowned photographer Alfred Eisenstaedt an exhausting example of her enthusiastic lifestyle. *Life* reported that, "In his travels all over the world, Mr. Eisenstaedt never met a more strenuous, though willing, subject than Miss Lombard, who led him on a merry chase for three days, from home to studio to tennis court, to skeet shoot, to night club, traveling sometimes by automobile, sometimes by motorized scooter."

After *Gone with the Wind* was finished, Lombard attended a private screening with Gable. She immediately knew the picture would be a big hit and was pleased that Gable had done so well. She knew he did not like costume dramas and was reluctant to play Rhett Butler. After she saw the film, she told Gable, "After all your pissing and moaning, this is the part they'll always remember you for."

When elaborate celebrations began shaping up for *Gone with the Wind*, Gable said he would not be a part of them. The organizers desperately wanted him to attend the Atlanta premiere, but he refused to ride on the same plane with David O. Selznick. Lombard knew the appearance was important to his career, and she contacted Paul Mantz, the famous stunt pilot. Mantz knew the president of American Airlines, and a free flight was arranged for Lombard, Gable, Otto Winkler, and a few others.

The first thing Lombard noticed was the premiere was all white. She asked Selznick where was the glorious Hattie McDaniel and Butterfly McQueen? They were not invited. All other major cast members attended with the exception of Leslie Howard, who had flown to England to take part in the war.

Gable was nominated for an Oscar for *Gone with the Wind* but did not win. He already had one for *It Happened One Night*. Lombard desperately wanted to win an Oscar and thought she would get it when she was nominated for *My Man Godfrey*. Louise Ranier won. She was thought to be a sure nominee the next year for *Nothing Sacred*, but Ranier won again. Lombard said, "They don't give awards to comedy performances." It was ironic that her husband had won for what most people would describe as a comedy.

Motherhood was another unfulfilled goal. This meant more to her than winning an Oscar. "If I can have a baby, I'll give up acting. At least for several years." When her longtime secretary, Fieldsie, had a difficult delivery, Lombard kept a bedside vigil and afterward said, "I'd go through it. I'd endure all the pain and all the embarrassment of looking like Oliver Hardy. It would be worth it."

There has been a great deal of speculation as to whether or not the Gable-Lombard marriage would have lasted. It was common knowledge that Lombard had to "watch him like a hawk" because of his predilection for extramarital affairs. Many felt that Lombard was tired of giving and not receiving. Rumors circulated of a split when they put their Encino ranch up for sale in 1941. They later withdrew it from the market, sparking rumors of a reconciliation. Lombard came to believe that a baby would help salvage their marriage. In early 1941 she and Gable went to Baltimore's Johns Hopkins Medical Center where both were examined. It was established there was no reason for the couple's inability to conceive.

Lombard was always looking for new challenges. She had worked for many top directors, including George Stevens, Henry Hathaway, William Wellman, Mervyn LeRoy, and Howard Hawks. However, she greatly admired Alfred Hitchcock and approached him about doing a picture. Hitchcock recalled, "She asked whether I'd do a picture with her. In a weak moment I accepted, and I more or less followed Norman Krasna's screenplay." The film was *Mr. and Mrs. Smith*, released in 1941. It was anything but a typical Hitchcock film.

Later in his famous interview with François Truffaut, Hitchcock said, "I had been quoted as saying that all actors are cattle. When I arrived on the set the first day of shooting, Carole Lombard had had a corral built, with three sections, and in each one there was a live young cow. Round the neck of each of them there was a white disk tied with ribbon, with three names: Carole Lombard, Robert Montgomery, and the name of a third member of the cast, Gene Raymond. I should add that my comment was a generalization, and Carole Lombard's spectacular repartee was her way of kidding me. She probably agreed with me."

In late 1941 Lombard discovered that the Ernst Lubitsch production of *To Be or Not to Be* was having problems. The two stars, Jack Benny and Miriam Hopkins, had an uneasy relationship and Hopkins thought her part was too small. Lombard had always wanted to work with Lubitsch and made it known she was available for the role. Lubitsch told her the part was really not much more than a supporting role. Lombard, however, who read all her own scripts and felt she was a good judge of what would work, believed this could be a great comedy. She also thought Benny was hilarious in *Charley's Aunt*, and working with both Benny and Lubitsch would be delightful. When Lombard was cast, she suggested Lubitsch hire Robert Stack. She had seen Stack give Deanna Durbin her first screen kiss and thought that his good looks might be suppressing a talent for comedy. Gable did not share Lombard's enthusiasm for the film. He did not care for Benny or Lubitsch. Lombard, however, was not to be dissuaded.

After the Japanese bombed Pearl Harbor, MGM volunteered its resources to President Franklin D. Roosevelt. The president's counselors thought a movie star would be the logical spearhead for launching the first national war-bond drive. Louis B. Mayer proposed that the campaign be initiated by either Mickey Rooney or Clark Gable. It was decided that the drive should begin in America's heartland. Since Gable was from Ohio, he was named to lead the bond drive.

There was only one problem—Gable did not want to sell bonds. He said, "I'll help you in any way I can, other than personal appearances. But I hate crowds and don't know how to act when I'm in one. Besides, I'm no salesman." Lombard tried to talk him into it and said she would go with him and help out. When she said she would consider it an honor just to be asked, Gable said, "All right, Maw, consider yourself asked!" Roosevelt was delighted. He remembered how effective Mary Pickford was selling bonds in World War I.

The bond drive was to start at the center of gravity for the U.S. population in 1942—Indianapolis, Indiana. Besides, Indiana was Lombard's home state, and movie czar Will Hays was also from Indiana. When Lombard's efforts to get Gable to go with her proved unsuccessful, she asked her mother to accompany her, promising her she could make a side trip to Fort Wayne. Otto Winkler, MGM's publicist and friend of Gable's, was assigned to accompany mother and daughter.

Lombard, Peters, and Winkler left Los Angeles by train on January 12, heading for Chicago, stopping at Salt Lake City, where Lombard practiced her salesmanship by making an impromptu speech at the train station for defense bonds and stamps. When they arrived in Chicago, Peters took another train for a ride to Fort Wayne for a brief visit. On Wednesday, January 14, Lombard and Winkler took a plane to Indianapolis and were joined there by her mother. On Thursday, Lombard arrived at the statehouse and immediately began selling bonds in the corridor. She later moved into the rotunda and climbed on a table. When she announced she decided she would not give autographs unless a bond purchase was made, the orders started pouring in, and she signed the large red, white, and blue receipts, "Carole Lombard Gable." After her appearance at the statehouse, she was the guest of honor at a reception in the governor's mansion, and that night she went to the rally at the Cadle Tabernacle.

She wore a strapless black velvet gown to make her final sales pitch to twelve thousand people at the Cadle Tabernacle. A number of Lombard's relatives had come down from Fort Wayne for the event. At the time she had three aunts on her mother's side and three aunts and two uncles on her father's side living in Indiana, Illinois, and Michigan. Perhaps the last letter she ever wrote was to Mrs. W. Wright Rockhill, a close friend who lived at 712 Rockhill Street, just

One of the last photos taken of Carole Lombard at the bond rally in Indianapolis in 1942. (Starting from third from the left) Governor Henry Schricker, Lombard, Will Hays, and Eugene Pulliam.

a few doors from the Lombard house. Lombard told Rockhill of her plans to come to Indianapolis, hoping they would meet. At the bond rally she was thrilled to see a large delegation from Fort Wayne in the audience.

Governor Henry Schricker presided over the event, and Elwood's Wendell Willkie was there and made a bond pledge. Sullivan's Hays was with Lombard all day working in defense meetings. Lombard said she was proud to be an American and more grateful than ever to have been born and bred a Hoosier. A black gospel chorus sang the Lord's Prayer. Three military bands and a color guard were in attendance. Although the national anthem had been sung to start the program, Lombard insisted on singing it again at the end of the program, leading the crowd in an a cappella version. After the anthem was finished she said, "This has been a wonderful-memorable day. Nothing could have made me happier than your kind invitation to share it with you and to be in Indianapolis tonight."

Although her bond sale quota was just $500,000, Lombard found she had sold more than two million dollars in bonds—a single day record. She was asked to stay over on Friday to make an appearance at H. P. Wasson Company in downtown Indianapolis to help with additional bond sales but rejected the idea, saying she had to get home to California. Eugene C. Pulliam, publisher of the *Indianapolis Star* and *News*, invited Lombard to his downtown hotel suite to celebrate the success of the rally. At this point she asked Winkler to find what planes were leaving for California on Friday. Peters was startled. She had never flown before and had an aversion to air travel. They already had Saturday reservations on the train. Winkler also preferred the train but Lombard was insistent. She had never been away from Gable more than three days since they were married and besides, she had another picture to start.

Over her mother's protests, Lombard began phoning the airlines pleading for accommodations. Finally she found the Transcontinental & Western Airlines (TWA) had just received cancellations from three passengers on Flight Number 3 to Los Angeles. Peters did not like it. Her numerology beliefs told her it was all wrong. There were three in her party. The flight was number three. Lombard was thirty-three years old, and besides Peters said that flying on January 16 was just "bad luck."

Finally, Winkler suggested they flip a coin. Peters reluctantly agreed. Lombard called tails while Winkler's quarter was in the air. It was tails. The James Todds of Indianapolis, who were friends of Peters, reported that even at the last minute Peters was trying to talk her daughter out of flying. The plane made a stop at Albuquerque, New Mexico, to discharge two passengers and receive others. Nine pilots with military orders boarded, and airport authorities said that all seven nonmilitary passengers would have to be bumped. Lombard would not have it. She had just sold two million dollars worth of defense bonds. Didn't she have the right to stay on the plane? It was finally decided that three extra passengers could be accommodated but all other nonmilitary passengers were bumped. A total of twenty-one people were on board.

The plane made a brief, unscheduled stop at 6:50 p.m. in Las Vegas. At 7:07 p.m. the pilot sent his last radio report, and there was no anxiety in his voice. At approximately 7:20 p.m. the plane

Carole Lombard.

impacted at full cruising speed into the side of Olcott mountain (also known as Table Rock mountain) in Nevada. Flights were directed to fly at ten thousand feet in this area, but Lombard's plane was flying at eight thousand feet at the time of the crash. A series of inquiries followed that showed the plane had been flying off course through restricted air territory. It was a foolish shortcut in an attempt to regain lost time. The hearings also revealed the pilot, Captain Wayne Williams, was fired from TWA in 1933 for alleged carelessness and disregard for regulations. He appealed the dismissal and was rein-stated. The House committee, while attributing the crash directly to Williams's flying course, stated that the accident would never have occurred if TWA had adopted procedures requiring all of its pilots to fly the Spring Mountain Range at ten thousand feet.

Gable had been at home in Encino, planning a surprise home-coming party. The Peters brothers were at the ranch. Having received a telegram from Lombard to the effect she would be late, he had not left home for the air terminal when he received a call from Eddie Mannix, an MGM executive and friend of Gable's. Mannix told him that Lombard's plane went down in Nevada. Gable chartered a plane and flew to Nevada, hoping to find his wife still alive. When he reached Nevada, he learned there were no survivors. He tried to climb to the site of the crash, but the going was too rough. His old friend, Spencer Tracy, chartered a plane and accompanied Gable on his trek, trying to provide some consolation.

A few years before she died, Lombard had provided in her will that she be buried in a white outfit and in a "modestly-priced crypt."

The famed Hollywood couturiere Irene designed a special white gown for her even though the casket was sealed. A private funeral service was conducted at Forest Lawn Memorial Park in Glendale on January 21, 1942. She was buried in a white marble wall crypt. In a nearby alcove lay Russ Columbo, whom Lombard once said was the great love of her life.

It was clear that Gable held himself responsible for Lombard's death. He was in shock for a long time. Writer Adela Rogers St. Johns said, "For months after her death, Clark was almost out of his mind with grief. I'd go to his house and he'd be having dinner alone in the dining room with Carole's dog and Siamese cats at the table. He refused to touch her room and left it just the way it was when she left. I asked, 'Why don't you go out? Why don't you call your old friends like Vic Fleming?' And he'd say, 'Carole used to make the calls when we wanted to go out.'" Rogers St. Johns reminded him how Lombard used to make him laugh. He grinned and said, "One day we were looking at our ranch here in San Fernando Valley and it was beautiful . . . one of those California days. We were just . . . lazy . . . strolling around . . . gabbing and I said, 'Mother, we're awfully lucky, you and I . . . all this and each other . . . anything you want we haven't got?' You know what she said, standing there looking lovely as a dream? She said, 'Well, I could do with another load of manure for the south forty.'"

President Roosevelt sent Gable a telegram. "Mrs. Roosevelt and I are deeply distressed. Carole was our friend, our guest in happier days. She brought great joy to all who knew her and to the millions who knew her only as a great artist. She gave unselfishly of time and talent to serve her Government in peace and in war. She loved her country."

In June 1942 Irene Dunne, a friend of Lombard's who grew up in Madison, Indiana, christened the Liberty ship *Carole Lombard*. Gable, who was a captain in the air force by then, was asked to speak at the launching. He spoke with fists clenched at his sides and openly wept when the champagne bottle was broken across the hull of the ship sliding into the sea. Also present at the christening was Fieldsie, her longtime secretary, and Louis B. Mayer. The *Carole Lombard* served in the Pacific theater throughout the war. The distinguished service certificate was placed in the wheelhouse of the ship. Also in June of that year Governor Schricker named the state's naval air squadron, "The Lombardians." He described Lombard as "a martyr of the war."

Buck Jones, who helped Lombard get started and gave her her first screen kiss, was interviewed shortly after her death. Asked about that first screen kiss, he said, yes, she was the prettiest girl he had kissed or even seen, ever. Ten months later Jones perished in the infamous Cocoanut Grove fire in Boston.

Jack Benny was so shaken by Lombard's death, he canceled his radio program. Years later he would say he only liked three of his movies—*Charley's Aunt*, *George Washington Slept Here*, and *The Meanest Man in the World*. And, he would say, he only loved one—*To Be or Not to Be*.

Lombard's two brothers became estranged from Gable and never spoke to him again. Lombard left her entire estate to Gable with the exception of two annuities for her brothers (each a little more than $8,000) and an $11,000 annuity to Fieldsie. This was no surprise, since Stuart was one of the witnesses who signed Lombard's will in

Carole Lombard in *To Be or Not to Be* (1942), her last film.

1939. Beyond that it was clear the brothers held Gable responsible for both their sister and their mother's death. They were also unhappy with him after hearing rumors that Gable and Lombard had the "fight of their lives" before she left over Gable's lingering affair with an MGM starlet.

Two years before she died, Lombard gave a lengthy interview to Hollywood writer Gladys Hall. She was asked if she feared old age. "There is nothing I am afraid of . . . least of all old age. With age there comes a richness that's divine. Age takes on a beauty everyone can't see, perhaps . . . but I can see it. I don't know of anything in the world more beautiful, more fascinating than a woman ripe with years, rich and lush as velvet with experience, her humor as tangy and flavorous as sun-ripened fruit. If women wouldn't get so self conscious about getting old, they wouldn't get old mentally and then they wouldn't be old at all, only wise and simply divine. I LOVE the idea of getting old."

Gable was too old for the draft, so he joined the Army Air Corps, went through Officers Candidate School, flew several combat missions, and served with distinction being discharged as a major. His friends said they saw a gentleness in him that had not existed before. He became a kinder and more considerate man. He entered into a happy final marriage to his longtime friend Kay Williams. Gable died at age fifty-nine, and four months later his son, John Clark Gable, was born. Kay Gable generously carried out her husband's long-expressed wish to be buried beside his third wife, Jane Alice Peters, of Fort Wayne, Indiana.

Film critic Charles Champlin said of her, "She was breathtakingly beautiful in a day which began by demanding plastic beauty of its heroes and heroines, but what would, I think, have led her on to still greater stardom were the interior qualities, of wit and unaffected worldly wisdom, untrammelled spirits, honesty, directness."

Leonard Maltin summed up her impact as follows, "She swore like a sailor, looked like a million bucks, and when given the chance, outclassed and outacted all the glamour-girls and trained actresses in Hollywood. There was only one Carole Lombard."

BIBLIOGRAPHY

Ankenbruck, John. *Twentieth-Century of Fort Wayne.* Fort Wayne, Ind.: Twentieth Century History of Fort Wayne, 1975.

Biery, Ruth. "Hollywood's Newest Romance." *Photoplay* (June 1931).

Busch, Noel F. "A Loud Cheer for the Screwball Girl." *Life* (October 17, 1938).

Eyman, Scott. *Ernst Lubitsch: Laughter in Paradise.* New York: Simon and Schuster, 1993.

Fort Wayne Journal-Gazette, June 12, 1930, January 22, 1942.

Fort Wayne News-Sentinel, January 17, 1942, July 4, 1942, June 25, 1962, February 23, 1984, June 19, 1993.

Gehring, Wes D. *Carole Lombard: The Hoosier Tornado.* Indianapolis: Indiana Historical Society Press, 2003.

Giddins, Gary. *Bing Crosby: A Pocketful of Dreams.* Vol. 1, *The Early Years, 1903–1940.* Boston: Little, Brown and Company, 2001.

Hall, Gladys. Interviews with Carole Lombard. 1930, 1940. Margaret Herrick Library. Academy of Motion Picture Arts and Sciences, Beverly Hills, California.

Howard, Kathleen. "Gable's Girl." *Photoplay* (February 1937).

Indiana Biographical Dictionary: People of All Times and All Places Who Have Been Important to the History of the State. 2nd ed. 2 vols. St. Clair Shores, Mich.: Somerset Publishers, 1999.

Indianapolis News, February 23, 1932.

Indianapolis Star, December 28, 1943, January 14, 1944.

James, Edward, ed. *Notable American Women, 1607–1950: A Biographical Dictionary.* 3 vols. Cambridge, Mass.: Belknap Press of Harvard University Press, 1971.

Last Will and Testament of Carole Lombard. Book 324, page 314, #211018. Filed August 8, 1939. County of Los Angeles, California.

Maltin, Leonard. *Carole Lombard.* New York: Pyramid Publications, 1976.

McCaffrey, Donald W. *The Golden Age of Sound Comedy: Comic Films and Comedies of the Thirties.* South Brunswick, N.J.: A. S. Barnes and Company, 1973.

Mordden, Ethan. *Movie Star: A Look at the Women Who Made Hollywood.* New York: St. Martin's Press, 1983.

New York Times, January 16, 1942.

Ott, Frederick, W. *The Films of Carole Lombard.* Secaucus, N.J.: Citadel Press, 1972.

Parish, Robert James. *The Hollywood Death Book: From Theda Bara to Rudolph Valentino.* Las Vegas, Nev.: Pioneer Books, 1992.

———. *The Paramount Pretties.* Secaucus, N.J.: Castle Books, 1972.

Rotha, Paul, and Richard Griffith. *The Film till Now: A Survey of World Cinema.* Middlesex, England: Spring Books/Hamlyn Publishing Group, 1967.

Sennett, Mack. *King of Comedy.* Garden City, N.Y.: Mercury House, 1954.

Silverman, Stephen M. *Funny Ladies: The Women Who Make Us Laugh.* New York: Harry N. Abrams, 1999.

St. Johns, Adela Rogers. *The Honeycomb.* Garden City, N.Y.: Doubleday and Company, 1969.

Swindell, Larry. *Screwball: The Life of Carole Lombard.* New York: William Morrow and Company, 1975.

Tapert, Annette. *The Power of Glamour: The Women Who Defined the Magic of Stardom.* New York: Crown Publishers, 1998.

Tornabene, Lyn. *Long Live the King: A Biography of Clark Gable.* New York: G. P. Putnam's Sons, 1976.

Truffaut, François. *Hitchcock.* New York: Simon and Schuster, 1967.

Weis, Elisabeth, ed. *National Society of Film Critics on the Movie Star.* New

MARJORIE MAIN

How Ma Kettle Saved Universal

arjorie Main was the refined, teetotalling daughter of a conservative Church of Christ minister from Indiana, who incongruously carved a niche in motion picture history, playing a series of raucous, rough, and cantankerous women in a career that began in chautauqua, went on to Broadway, and finally, went to motion pictures. Damon Runyan said, "She has a dead pan, square shoulders, a stocky build, a voice like a file, and an uncurried aspect. She has a stride like a section boss. She has bright, squinty eyes and generally starts off looking as if she never smiled in her life, then suddenly she smiles . . . from her eyes out." Her voice was described as "full-throttled and gravel pit," her hair "a bird's nest," with a sack-of-potatoes figure. Off-camera, however, she was more like her real-life role as a minister's daughter. She was soft-spoken, shy, and always very dignified and ladylike.

Mary Tomlinson was born February 24, 1890, "about a mile and a half out of Acton," as she described it. She was the second daughter of native Hoosiers, Reverend Samuel Joseph and Jennie McGaughey Tomlinson. She was delivered by her maternal grandfather, Acton physician Samuel McGaughey. She attended school at Fairland and Shelbyville and made her first stage appearance in a program for her commencement from grammar school. She recited a blood-and-thunder cowboy piece called "Pard and Ruff," in which she played both parts. The recitation ended by having Pard shoot Ruff and then whispering a prayer over his dead body. She liked the sound of the applause she received and decided to pursue more stage work.

She entered an oratory contest and won a fifteen-dollar gold watch and made the decision to take up an acting career. Her puritanical father vehemently opposed her choice and urged her to enroll in a college preparatory class at Franklin College. She spent the 1905–6 school term on campus, stating later that, "I was only there for a year, but I'll never forget those days." While on campus, she became a charter member of what is now the Delta Delta Delta sorority.

She became more determined to go into the theater. Finally, in spite of continuing objections by her parents, she enrolled in the Hamilton School of Dramatic Expression at Lexington, Kentucky. She completed a three-year course there and began teaching drama. She acquired a teaching position at Bourbon College in Paris, Kentucky. About her teaching career she said, "Students liked me too. I got fired. Asked for a raise. They didn't have women's lib then." After a year of teaching, she decided she would move to Chicago and see if she could practice what she was teaching. Not having much luck in Chicago, she went to New York City.

She landed her first professional job on the chautauqua circuit reading scenes from Shakespeare. Her first role was that of Katherine in *The Taming of the Shrew*. She appeared with the company in 1913 at Riverside Park in Indianapolis. Next she joined a stock company in Fargo, North Dakota, and then moved into vaudeville.

She changed her name to Marjorie Main, stating, "I didn't want to use my family's name on the stage because I knew they disapproved. The name I chose was my idea of a name easy to remember." In 1916 she toured in *Cheating Cheaters* with John Barrymore. Two years later she made her Broadway debut in *Yes or No*. Following that, she returned to vaudeville, teaming with W. C. Fields in a skit called *The Family Ford*.

She met a prominent lecturer and psychologist, Dr. Stanley LeFevre Krebs, who was a former minister and was twenty-six years her senior. On November 2, 1921, she married Krebs, gaining a step-daughter (Annabelle), almost her same age. She gave up acting and toured several years with her husband, serving as his secretary. "I like lecturing. My father was a minister and all . . . and I thought it was a nice way to spend your time and see new places." The yearning to perform did not go away, and she drifted back into acting. In 1923 she returned to the New York stage in *A House Divided*. Unfortunately, it lasted only one performance.

In 1927 she was cast as Mae West's aging mother (although she was just one year older than West) in the stage production *The Wicked Age*. In 1928 she appeared opposite Barbara Stanwyck in the long-running stage hit, *Burlesque*. This role required Main to wear tights and pick up her heels, and she played the part with her usual gusto. Also in 1928 she made her Broadway debut in *Salvation*. Two years later she was in another Broadway production, *Scarlet Sister Mary*. In 1931 she appeared on the Broadway stage in *Ebb Tide*.

Her entry into films came in 1931 when she was seen briefly as a town gossip in *A House Divided*. In November 1932 she was back on Broadway playing the role of a servant in the musical, *Music in the Air*. The show was a hit and ran more than a year. During its run she made two more films, *Take a Chance* and *Crime without Passion*. Both of these were filmed at Astoria, Long Island.

When Fox decided to film *Music in the Air*, Main was asked to come to Hollywood to re-create her stage role. She finished the film, made a few other short films, and then the Krebses decided to return to New York. There Main was cast in a drama entitled *Jackson White*. A short time later, it was discovered Krebs had cancer. She took care of him until his death on September 27, 1935. Main admitted that her marriage was not ideal. Toward the end of her life she said, "We pretty much went our own ways, but we was still, in the eyes of the law, man and wife." Main apparently never thought of her marriage in traditional terms. When Krebs died she said, "It was like losing a good friend. Like part of the family."

In his 1994 book, *Hollywood Lesbians*, author Boze Hadleigh features a rather lengthy interview with Main a year before her death that sheds further light on her sexuality. He asked Main, "If you had parents or siblings, would you tell them today?" Main then is quoted as saying, "I wouldn't have to tell 'em. I'd show them. . . . I'd just show up with

Marjorie Main as she appeared when she was on the chautauqua circuit, circa 1912–13.

(Previous page) Marjorie Main and Percy Kilbride in *Ma and Pa Kettle* (1949).
©1949, UNIVERSAL PICTURES INC.

Marjorie Main and Humphrey Bogart in *Dead End* (1937).

my lady friend, and if I'd had it to do all over, I might live with her. I've gotten so used to living on my own, but when I was younger, I'd like to have lived with her." When Hadleigh asked, "Who was she?" Main replied, "someone special." It is known that Main did live for a while with actress Spring Byington, who was a known homosexual. However, Main and Byington did not mix openly with any of the gay crowd in Hollywood.

After Krebs's death, Main felt that returning to the stage would be therapeutic. She said, "Then the dear Lord came to my rescue. I was offered a role in the stage play, 'Dead End.' I played the part of the mother of a young gangster. Night after night, when I wept for his death on the stage, I was crying real tears for my husband. I was able to take out my own personal grief in my work."

Main received rave reviews for her role in *Dead End.* One reviewer referred to her as having a "smoldering intensity." In 1936, after 460 performances in *Dead End*, she left the stage hit to accept a comedy role as Lucy, the cynical Reno hotel keeper in *The Women.* Once again she received glowing notices. When Samuel Goldwyn decided to film *Dead End*, he asked Main to come to Hollywood to re-create her stage role on the screen. The reviews again were highly complimentary. The *Hollywood Spectator* said, "Miss Main is an artist and her contribution to the picture is out of all proportion to the length of her part." *Variety* said, "She is a new and striking type with an interesting screen voice." Many felt she should have been nominated for an Oscar for best supporting actress, but Claire Trevor got the nomination in that category for the same picture.

Her stage work got her another excellent part when *The Women* was filmed in 1939. In 1934 MGM's leading character actress, Marie Dressler, passed away. The studio thought Main might fill the void and signed her to a seven-year contract. In 1940 she appeared opposite Wallace Beery in *Wyoming.* She was cast in a number of roles with Beery that would have gone to Dressler. Unfortunately, Beery and Main never got along. Main said, "Working with Wally Beery wasn't always easy. He never rehearsed his lines, and his odd behavior often un-nerved me." Also in 1940 she played a sacrificing backwoods mother of outlaw Walter Pidgeon in *Dark Command.* In it she made the most of a memorable deathbed scene. She was very effective as a blind prophetess in *The Shepherd of the Hills* in 1941.

In December 1942 Main returned to Indiana to sell bonds for the War Department. When she arrived in Indianapolis on a Wednesday night, about two hundred people were at Union Station to meet her. Olive Tinder of radio station WIRE said, "When Marjorie stepped off the train, she had the most bewildered look on her face for she didn't expect anyone but her family and the committee. They just swarmed over her like bees."

The next morning she sold bonds in the Claypool Hotel lobby. This was an unplanned event, but she sold $1,600 worth of bonds anyway. She went to Shelbyville, Indiana, on Friday of that same week and sold more than $500,000 in bonds. The next night she was at Lowe's Theater in downtown Indianapolis, where she sat in the ticket booth and sold bonds as the admission price. Many people bought a $1,000 bond. Saturday morning she was part of a broadcast from the studios of WIRE. There was a big studio audience present as Main sang at the top of her lungs and joked with the audience. "I'm proud of that Hoosier twang. I've always stuck with it," she said. Main was under contract to MGM studios, but in 1947 Universal asked MGM to loan her to them for the role of Ma Kettle in *The Egg and I.* Claudette Colbert and Fred MacMurray were the stars, but Main and Percy Kilbride stole the movie as the eccentric Ma and Pa Kettle. Main was nominated for an Oscar for best supporting actress. The movie was so successful that Universal decided to make a series of Ma and Pa Kettle movies and asked MGM to borrow her again. Main was not eager to do the series, but she agreed upon MGM's insistence. Since she was on straight salary for the films, she never shared in the wealth they generated (nor in the money MGM charged Universal for her services).

The Kettle films were all shot in black and white at a cost of between $200,000 and $400,000 each. They grossed about $3 million each, saving the day for financially troubled Universal. She made nine Kettle films, including two after Kilbride dropped out of the series. Main wrote much of her own dialogue and created her own costumes and makeup. She was not much for socializing and lived in her dressing room bungalow during the making of the Kettle films, cooking her own meals and never leaving the lot until the picture was finished.

Off the lot she lived alone in a ten-room house in West Los Angeles, doing her own cooking, housework, and laundry. "I don't do it because I'm cheap either, but only because I don't think I could stand to have someone 'do' for me. I've taken care of myself so long, I've got my own ways set. I think it's best to live alone and I like it," she said. "Whenever I want to go, I just pick up and take a trip if I've a mind to,

Marjorie Main, circa 1940.

(Opposite page) Marjorie Main in *Friendly Persuasion* (1956).

5512-520 PUB

Marjorie Main and Walter Pidgeon in
Dark Command (1940).
©1940, REPUBLIC PICTURES CORP.

and live as full a life as I can."

But for a chance meeting the Kettle movies might not have materialized. Main was stricken with a critical illness before she started making them. "It meant a serious operation or probably death in a short time," she recalled. "I thought, 'No, I won't have it, I'm too old for surgery.'" "I was miserable and after leaving the doctor's office I was sitting dejectedly in a cafeteria having coffee. Suddenly a mother and her little daughter came up and asked me for my autograph. The woman thanked me for making her laugh when she saw my pictures. Well she didn't know it, but those simple words bolstered my courage to the point where I was able to go through with the operation."

Main came home to Indiana several times, including an appearance at Keith's Theater in downtown Indianapolis to publicize the opening of *The Egg and I.* Twice Franklin College invited her to homecoming celebrations, but she declined. "I just didn't think my health was up to it, but I'd love to come back some day." In 1965 Robert Reed of the *Franklin Daily Journal* interviewed Main by telephone. "I've got supper on the stove. Just a minute," she told him. "Give my love to everyone. My heart is truly in Indiana."

On April 10, 1975, Main died of lung cancer. She was eighty-five, and few distant relatives remained in Indiana. She had specified that she be buried in Forest Lawn Cemetery in Hollywood Hills next to her husband. "I've been lonely so much of my life and I'd like to be with him in death," she said.

Her last film was *The Kettles on Old MacDonald's Farm* in 1957. "I always thought of Ma Kettle as a real person," she once remarked, "someone I could drive out into the country and see. Ma Kettle was a grand person." Main created one of the most enduring and beloved characters in the history of motion pictures, but she always felt her characterization was a result of her Indiana roots. She said, "I don't think I could have ever played that part if I hadn't lived on a farm in Indiana."

BIBLIOGRAPHY

Ellrod, J. G. *The Stars of Hollywood Remembered: Career Biographies of Eighty-two Actors and Actresses of the Golden Era, 1920s–1950s.* Jefferson, N.C.: McFarland and Company, 1997.

Enslen, Olive. Letter to Hedda Hopper. December 13, 1942. Margaret Herrick Library. Academy of Motion Picture Arts and Sciences, Beverly Hills, California.

Hadleigh, Boze. *Hollywood Lesbians.* New York: Barricade Books, 1994.

Henricks, Sylvia C. "Marjorie Main: 'Good for a Lot of Laughs.'" *Traces of Indiana and Midwestern History* 12, no.1 (Winter 2000).

Hicks, Jim. "Marjorie Main." *Hollywood Studio Magazine* (date unknown).

The Internet Broadway Database. http://www.ibdb.com/.

The Internet Movie Database. http://www.imdb.com/.

Mann, William J. *Behind the Screen: How Gays and Lesbians Shaped Hollywood, 1910–1999.* New York: Viking, 2001.

Parish, James Robert. *The Slapstick Queens.* New York: Castle Books, 1973.

Smith, David. "The Marj That Was Ma." *Indianapolis Star Magazine*, March 12, 1978.

Stumpf, Charles K. "Marjorie Main." Unpublished biography. Author's collection.

Marjorie Main (1953).
©1953, UNIVERSAL PICTURES CO., INC.

ANNE BAXTER

All about Anne

When she was just three years old, a young girl from Michigan City, Indiana, received an extraordinary gift when one of the world's greatest architects built a small theater for her to use. The girl was Anne Baxter, and the architect was her grandfather, Frank Lloyd Wright. Baxter always thought of the gift as "sowing a potent weed," and she went on to become a leading actress of the mid-twentieth century. Wright, once described as "the only architect who achieved the popular status and recognition of a movie star," was pleased, expressing pride at having a granddaughter who achieved the celebrity status he had always enjoyed.

As had fellow Hoosier Carole Lombard, Baxter came from a wealthy family. Her mother was Catherine Wright Baxter, the daughter of the famed architect. Wright spent significant time in Indiana, primarily because two of his children settled in the dunes country on Lake Michigan and the fact that commissions came his way from several sources in the state. Wright designed eight houses built in Indiana. He also designed at least five unbuilt projects for the state, including a fraternity house for Hanover College and an offer that was never accepted to design a campus for the University of Notre Dame.

The Wright children were born in Oak Park, Illinois, where Wright maintained his home-studio for many years. Wright's second son, John Lloyd Wright, became an architect, but his chief claim to fame was his invention of the famous Lincoln Logs for children in 1916. In the early twenties, John was living in Chicago working with his father, when their relationship broke up because his father refused to pay him a salary. His sister, Catherine Wright Baxter, had moved to Michigan City, Indiana, with her husband. She suggested John join them, and he settled in Long Beach, Indiana, in 1923. Long Beach is a lakeside resort community near Michigan City. In 1927 John opened an office in the Warren Building in Michigan City and developed a successful practice there. John designed the City Hall building, several school buildings, and numerous residences and vacation homes for several prominent people who lived at Long Beach. He stayed for twenty-three years, leaving to move to Del Mar, California, where he was an active architect until his death from lung cancer in 1972.

Catherine Wright married Kenneth Stuart Baxter on March 11, 1919. Shortly after their marriage the couple moved to Michigan City, where Baxter became manager of the Sheet Steel Products Company in Michigan City and later worked as a salesman and in public relations for Frankfort Distillers Corporation. Frankfort Distillers manufactured the famous Four Roses brand of bourbon. On January 24, 1920, Catherine gave birth to James Stewart Baxter, who died in his crib when he was five months old. The Baxters' first residence in Michigan City was at 916 Pine Street where, on May 7, 1923, their second child, Anne, was born. Shortly after her birth, the family moved to the Sherman Apartments in Michigan City. In 1926 they moved into a house built by Baxter on the east side of Franklin Street south of Coolspring Avenue.

Anne Baxter and her brother Toby.

Catherine and a friend, Belle Culbert Miller, opened a gift shop in Michigan City. It was located on Eighth Street just off Franklin. In 1929 Kenneth was offered a job with the Seagram and Sons Company. The family moved to White Plains and Chappaqua, New York, before settling in Bronxville. Baxter soon rose to become a top executive in the Seagram Company. In the 1940s Frankfort Distillers sold their Four Roses brand to Seagrams.

Anne was six years old when she left Indiana, but she would later credit the place of her birth and her Midwest upbringing as the primary reason she was chosen for her Oscar-winning role of Sophie in *The Razor's Edge*. "I was brought up right," she said. Her parents were strict Presbyterians who instilled in her a desire to work to the best of her abilities and not accept "the cushion of my birth."

She started appearing in school plays in Michigan City when she was five years old. While in elementary school in New York, the third, fourth, and fifth grade classes produced an operetta, *In Quest of Santa Claus*. The program listed a huge cast of participants, but at the top of the cast list is "Jane . . . In Search of Santa Claus . . . Ann Baxter." In the sixth grade she appeared in *Master Skylark*. The program explained that this play was long and so the most important characters had to be played by two people. Anne was listed as one of two students portraying the lead character.

Anne Baxter in *Swamp Water* (1941).

(Previous page) Anne Baxter and William Eythe in *The Eve of St. Mark* (1944).

In April 1933 Catherine gave birth to a son, Richard Tobin ("Toby") Baxter. Anne was delighted to have a baby brother, but her joy was not to last. Toby died from pneumonia shortly after his third birthday. Anne never had another sibling.

At the age of ten, Anne saw Helen Hayes on stage and decided she wanted to be an actress. She later stated, "I wanted to be an actress because that was the thing I was best at. I knew I could do it. There are a very few things in life that we know we can do." Her mother provided encouragement. She described her mother as a "jack of all trades . . . a human dynamo." Her mother lectured her, "If you want to be an actor, you must stick to it; you must be good at it; and you must make your living at it." She described her father as a man with great enthusiasm for life, possessing supreme ethical sense, unshakable integrity, and lack of guile.

Baxter was "pushed out of the nest" as she described it and told to "fly." At the age of eleven, she commuted from her home on Long Island to New York City on the train alone. She attended a variety of schools whose curriculums were based on the dramatic arts, including Theodora Irvine's School of Theater. She also took private lessons from a teacher named Mary Fisher, whom she greatly respected. She took piano lessons. A recital which featured "the pupils of Cecile Bellaire Van De Carr" took place in June 1936, and Baxter played four pieces.

Baxter made her Broadway debut at age thirteen on September 17, 1936, at the Henry Miller Theater as Elizabeth Winthrop in *Seen but Not Heard*. Shortly after her debut, she was invited to study with the prestigious, strong-willed teacher and actress, Maria Ouspenskaya. Baxter did not always agree with the imperious Russian who followed the Stanislavsky method, and they frequently clashed. Despite this, she continued her training with Ouspenskaya for three years.

Her next acting job was on stage in *There's Always a Breeze*, which opened in Boston in February 1938 and debuted in New York in March 1938 at the Windsor Theater. In October 1938 she was cast with the great Eva Le Gallienne in *Madame Capet*. The summers of 1938 and 1939 were spent at Dennis, Massachusetts, at the Cape Playhouse Stock Company, where she appeared in *Susan and God* and *Spring Meeting*. A little later she auditioned for a role in the Broadway production of *The Philadelphia Story*. She was to play the younger sister of Katharine Hepburn. However, Hepburn accused her of overacting, using too many grand gestures, and missing her comedy cues. Baxter was crushed. However, Shirley Booth stepped in, became a mentor for Baxter, and advised her not to give up.

Anne Baxter, circa mid to late 1940s.

Baxter did not intend to abandon her chosen profession. Instead she decided she was ready for Hollywood. At age fourteen, she managed to get a test with David O. Selznick for *The Adventures of Tom Sawyer* opposite Montgomery Clift. The test was never made because Selznick thought Clift's acne would not look good on the screen. He turned them both down. However, Kay Brown, an agent of Selznick, thought Baxter had possibilities as an actress and arranged another test. As a result of the test and the recommendation by Brown, Baxter was again summoned by Selznick. She recalled her first meeting with Selznick, "I still smart from the first words David O. Selznick ever spoke to me. I had come out to Hollywood at fifteen to make exhaustive tests for his and Mr. Hitchcock's 'Rebecca.' Rooted in panic to Mr. Selznick's plush carpet, I watched him descend on me, bend at the knees, peer glassily at my lips, which promptly froze shut, and say, 'Lemme see your teeth!'" She made a test with Laurence Olivier that she described as "incestuous." The sixteen-year-old Baxter believed that there was no way they could make her up to look twenty years old.

Darryl Zanuck saw her test and signed her to a standard seven-year contract at Twentieth Century Fox starting at $350 per week. After discovering that she was underage, he tried to get out of the contract. But Baxter was determined to stay in Hollywood. Zanuck loaned her out to MGM where she made her film debut in *Twenty Mule Team*, released in 1940. The star, Wallace Beery, complained that she was overacting. She managed to tone down her histrionics to Beery's satisfaction. The result was she did so well in this film that her home studio cast her opposite John Payne in the John Barrymore film, *The Great*

Anne Baxter and George Sanders in *All About Eve* (1950).

Profile, the same year. After she did her first bit in this film with her arms "wildly flailing," Barrymore asked, "Does she have to swim?"

Since she was still of high school age, the studio enrolled her in the Twentieth Century Fox Studio School. After a short stay in the studio school, she enrolled at Los Angeles High School. When she graduated from Los Angeles High School in 1941, she had already appeared in four films. The same year she graduated, she was Amy Spettigue in *Charley's Aunt* opposite Jack Benny and worked with the great French director Jean Renoir in *Swamp Water*. This film did not sit well with the critics, but Baxter received good notices.

In 1942 Baxter was cast in one of her best roles to date, Lucy Morgan in Orson Welles's adaptation of Booth Tarkington's Pulitzer Prize–winning novel, *The Magnificent Ambersons*. Tarkington was from Indianapolis, and the setting for the story was supposed to be his hometown. Baxter and Richard Bennett as Major Amberson were both Indiana natives, as was the film's editor, Robert Wise. Some critics place this film in the same category of greatness as Welles's *Citizen Kane*. Baxter later said, "It was a masterpiece" in the rough cut, but the released version was cut drastically by RKO and did not do well at the box office. Unfortunately, much of what was cut were scenes that featured Baxter. During the shooting of *Ambersons*, Frank Lloyd Wright visited the set. Welles recalled Wright's visits, "The old man used to visit us all the time we were shooting and made withering remarks about the sets. I kept saying, 'But Mr. Wright, we agree with you. That's the whole point.' But he couldn't get over how awful it was that people ever lived in those kind of houses. Oh my God, what a marvelous old man. What an artist, and what an actor!"

In 1944 Baxter gave an outstanding performance as a girl with a false smile and a sick mind in *Guest in the House*. Also in 1944 she made *Sunday Dinner for a Soldier*. Her costar was John Hodiak. A romance blossomed, and they were married in her parents' home on July 7, 1946. A daughter, Katrina, was born July 6, 1951. Shortly after the birth Baxter said, "I'm going to bring up a strong character, let her make her own decisions in life. We hope we can provide the background for a happy, healthy, well-adjusted little girl." Unfortunately, the marriage was a short one. Baxter divorced Hodiak on January 27, 1953. Baxter said, "Marriage between two actors is hell. He never knew just how good he was." Hodiak died of a heart attack two years later, and Katrina was his only child. Katrina followed her parents into theater, appearing in at least one film, *Jane Austen in Manhattan* (1980). She is now involved in directing and acting with local theater groups in the state of Washington.

In 1945 Baxter costarred with Tallulah Bankhead in *A Royal Scandal*. During the shooting Baxter recalled that her grandfather visited her again on the set and, after watching Bankhead at work, remarked, "Not bad for an old dame." Bankhead overheard the remarks and bristled. The next scene called for Bankhead to lightly tap Baxter on the shoulder. Baxter recalled, "But she responded with an uppercut that sent me reeling. Then she smiled sweetly and retired to her dressing room." Baxter recalled 1946 as being "quite a year." She said, "I had married John Hodiak and, through a ridiculous Hollywood series of flukes, got the coveted part of Sophie in 'The Razor's Edge.' I knew about the film . . . they'd tested thirteen girls on and off the Twentieth Century-Fox lot. It never occurred to me they'd even consider me

Anne Baxter.

Anne Baxter and Strother Martin (Kokomo) in *Fools' Parade* (1971).
©1970 COLUMBIA PICTURES INDUSTRIES, INC.

for the part. I'd been sidetracked into sweet-ingenue roles, and from what I'd heard about Sophie, I didn't have a prayer."

When Zanuck began searching for the right Sophie, he found it to be a frustrating experience. No one seemed to fit the part. One Sunday at Zanuck's pool, a friend suggested that Baxter could play the part. Zanuck at first dismissed the idea but then decided to let director Edmund Goulding meet with Baxter to see what he thought. Goulding was impressed enough to give her a test, and she got the part. She always said that she got it because she understood Sophie's background. It was similar to her own—a nice Chicago girl—country-club dances. "I was born fifty miles from Chicago [referring to Michigan City] and went to the same kind of dances. Who could forget a country club named 'The Pottawattomi [*sic*]?'"

Baxter's portrayal of Sophie MacDonald gave the screen one of its most memorable characters of the 1940s. Sophie was a gentle young mother who loses her husband and child in an automobile accident, then becomes a tragic and alcoholic wanton in Paris who an old friend (played by Tyrone Power) unsuccessfully attempts to rehabilitate. The cast was full of highly respected actors—Gene Tierney, Herbert Marshall, and Baxter's fellow Hoosier, Clifton Webb. This film marks the only time two Indiana natives were both nominated for best supporting Oscars for the same film. While Baxter won her first and only Oscar, Webb did not win, losing to Harold Russell for *The Best Years of Our Lives*. However, both Webb and Baxter won Golden Globes for best supporting roles. Webb never won an Oscar.

While *The Razor's Edge* gave Baxter a supporting Oscar, her role opposite Bette Davis in *All about Eve* in 1950 gave her a chance to win a best actress Oscar. It was an unexpected break because actress Jeanne Crain, who was originally cast as Eve Harrington, had to relinquish the part because of a pregnancy. Baxter was very pleased with her performance and with the picture. She said, "I was good, I was respected, I had a great part, the script was superb; the actors were perfect and perfectly cast. Even me, and I wasn't always." As the scheming understudy, Baxter more than held her own against the venerable Davis. On-screen as Eve, Baxter was full of treachery, but offscreen she and Davis became good friends. It was a lasting friendship. Commenting on Baxter's performance, Davis said, "Anne was really playing a double role: one thing on the surface, another underneath. I called it the 'sweet bitch.' Her part was more difficult than mine."

Both Davis and Baxter were nominated for the best actress. Baxter was urged to accept a nomination for best supporting actress but refused, thinking it might be her only chance to win a best actress Oscar. It was believed this split the academy vote, and Judy Holliday won for *Born Yesterday*. Unfortunately, Baxter's career was disappointing after *Eve*.

With rare exceptions, she had little luck in getting roles that utilized her skills as an actress. She did get an important part as Queen Nefretiri in Cecil B. DeMille's *The Ten Commandments* (1956). However, she was widely criticized for her portrayal of the queen as a "sex kitten," even though she acted the role as DeMille had directed.

In 1959 Baxter was in Australia on location for *Summer of the Seventeenth Doll* (later retitled *Season of Passion*), when friends wanted to introduce her to a local rancher. Unfortunately, Randolph Galt was in the Philippines at the time, and Baxter forgot about Galt. On April 9, 1959, Baxter awoke to a phone ringing at 3:00 a.m. It was her mother. "Anne . . . Papa died an hour ago." When asked to speak informally about her grandfather's more private self and his early family days, Baxter later recalled, "Grandfather's roots were so vibrantly American that just speaking about him made you believe all over again in native American space and beauty and tenacity and daring."

At the time of his death, Baxter had developed a relationship with her grandfather that was closer than her mother had ever experienced. Catherine Wright Baxter never forgave her father for leaving her mother. Thus her relationship with her father was always cool. But Baxter was a different story. Having worked hard to gain a celebrity image, Wright was happy to meet and mingle with other celebrities. Nothing pleased him more than to see one of his granddaughters become famous.

As she walked away from the memorial ceremony, still shaking with emotion, she was told she had a phone call. When she answered, a voice said, "This is Ranny Galt." She later reflected, "My grandfather's death had brought a stranger from another world into mine." She agreed to meet Galt for dinner. On February 18, 1960, they were married in Honolulu, the place of Galt's birth. Galt was a Yale graduate and a former air force jet pilot. The Galts had their first daughter, Melissa, on October 5, 1961. Shortly after Melissa's birth, the Galts and Baxter's daughter, Katrina, moved to Australia.

The first years of this marriage were spent on a 36,000-acre ranch 150 miles north of Sydney. They were ten miles from their nearest neighbor, and Baxter found life lonely and hard. In spite of this, she tried to make the best of it by running the household and doing many of the ranch chores. She said, "We make our own electricity. There are no pushbutton kitchens, no frozen foods. Our groceries come by delivery truck twice a week . . . along with the mail. I do all the cooking. Help is hard to get in Australia." Later Baxter wrote a best-selling book, *Intermission*, based on her Australian experience.

When Baxter became pregnant again, it was decided she should have the baby in the United States. The family moved back to California, where Maginel was born on March 11, 1963. Maginel was named after Baxter's favorite aunt, Maginel Wright, a well-known children's book illustrator. Shortly after the birth of Maginel, "Ran," as Baxter called her husband, decided they would not return to Australia. He surprised her by buying an eleven thousand-acre ranch near Grant, New Mexico. Baxter recruited her cousin, Eric Lloyd Wright, to design a three thousand-square-foot adobe home on the ranch land near the Zuni Mountains. Baxter and her three girls moved to New Mexico, but it was apparent the marriage was not working. The couple separated in 1967, and Baxter returned to Hollywood with her three girls to resume her career. Of the split, Baxter said there was "a complete divergence of the way of looking at life." Galt temporarily sidetracked his business interests to come to Hollywood to be with his family, leasing a house near Baxter's two story in Westwood.

Baxter finally divorced Galt on January 29, 1970. Melissa Galt later recalled, "My father was an 'Indiana Jones' type. He tried his hand at cattle ranching in Australia, he did something in Japan, he would boat to Tahiti, work for Signal Oil for a bit. He did pretty much what he felt like." Katrina said, "Ran Galt never did anything small." In later life Galt became a born-again Christian and a missionary. He eventually went back to Australia.

On March 30, 1970, Baxter returned to Broadway as a replacement for Lauren Bacall in *Applause*, the musical version of *All about Eve*. This time she played Margo Channing, the role Davis played in the movie. Despite the fact this was her first Broadway musical, Baxter was a hit in the role, remaining in the musical until July 27, 1972. Penny Fuller, who played Eve Harrington in the musical, compared Bacall's performance with Baxter's. She considered Bacall "a movie star/actress" and Baxter "an actress/movie star." She said, "It was Bacall's charisma and her persona that carried the show when she was in it. And that's not to belittle her acting. It was Anne Baxter's acting, on the other hand, and not charisma, that defined her performance."

On February 28, 1974, Baxter returned to Broadway in two of Noel Coward's one-act plays, *Come into the Garden* and *Song at Twilight*. Her old friend, Hume Cronin, who played opposite Baxter in her second Broadway appearance, *There's Always a Breeze*, in 1938, was her costar along with his wife, Jessica Tandy. The plays ran 140 performances.

Instead of raising her children in glitzy Hollywood, Baxter chose suburban Brentwood, where her three daughters walked to public school and did the usual household chores. Melissa said, "Growing up was boringly normal." She said her mother exposed her daughters to galleries, theaters, and museums. She loved her mother's zest for life, her passion for her work, her ability to speak in front of an audience without butterflies, her love of writing, and her creative energy.

On January 30, 1977, Baxter married Wall Street banker David "Duke" Klee. He died ten months later at age seventy. Baxter kept the Connecticut dream home they had started to renovate and commuted to California for her stage and television work. In 1983 Davis was cast as the lead in a television series, *Hotel*, but was forced to drop out due to illness. Baxter was called and asked if she could report for work immediately as a replacement for Davis. In seventy-two hours she was in Hollywood in another ironic reenactment of the replacement scene in *All about Eve*.

On December 4, 1985, she was walking down Madison Avenue in New York on her way to her hairdresser when she collapsed, suffering from a cerebral hemorrhage. Eight days later, on December 12, she died at age sixty-two in Lenox Hill Hospital without regaining consciousness. She had just signed a contract with the William Morrow publishing house to write a book about her family, tracing her talents from her grandfather. According to her wishes, her ashes are interred under an apple tree in Spring Green, Wisconsin, near the site of her grandfather's famous Taliesin estate.

Anne Baxter and Alfred Hitchcock (1953).

There was no funeral. Her daughters asked that donations be made to the Frank Lloyd Wright Home and Studio Foundation in lieu of flowers. She had recently completed her contract for the *Hotel* television series. *Hotel* costar Connie Selecca said, "I adored her and I loved working with her. Her death is a great loss to me personally and a tremendous loss for the show." Charlton Heston said, "We have lost a remarkable actress and a significant star. Anne was a stimulating actress to work with and a fine woman as well. I will miss her." James Stewart said, "She was purely and delightfully a professional."

She returned to Indiana at least twice, according to childhood friend, Carter Manny. Manny's parents were close friends to the Baxters and stayed in touch with them. In addition, Manny was an apprentice at Taliesin before he became a partner in a large Chicago architectural firm. While a freshman at Harvard in 1938, Manny went to see Baxter open in Boston in *There's Always a Breeze*. In 1946 Baxter's parents returned to Michigan City to visit Frank and Grace Garrettson, who had been their neighbors. A cocktail party was given for the Baxter family, and Anne was in attendance.

In 1982 Baxter attended a fund-raiser for the Frank Lloyd Wright Home Studio in Chicago. She then went to Michigan City where Manny took her to see her place of birth on Pine Street and to the house her father built on Franklin Street. Manny's mother gave a picnic lunch for Baxter and was joined by some of her mother's old bridge club associates. After seeing many of her childhood haunts, Manny remembers Baxter saying, "Oh Carter, you can't go home again." Manny says he believed it was a rather sad experience for her.

Baxter's daughters have pursued different paths. Melissa is an interior designer in Atlanta, Georgia; Maginel is a Catholic nun in a convent in Rome, Italy; and Katrina Baxter Hodiak is involved in community theater as a stage director and actor in Port Orchard, Washington. According to Katrina, her son Tobin (named after Baxter's brother), "can sing, dance and act." After appearing in one movie, Katrina said, "I missed my mother badly. I never saw her enough. I didn't want to do that to my son, so I never pursued a career in the theater."

Today, the daughters rarely communicate. Melissa said, "We have no contact. Mother was the glue that held us together. We have nothing in common. We are three different people." Melissa's greatest regret is that her mother did not live to see her become a successful decorator with her own business. "It would have been neat to have her along."

BIBLIOGRAPHY

The Anne Baxter Collection. University of Wyoming American Heritage Center, Laramie, Wyoming.

Atlanta Business Chronicle, August 31, 2001.

Bawden, J. E. A. "Anne Baxter." *Films in Review* (October 1977).

Baxter, Anne. *Intermission: A True Story.* New York: G. P. Putnam's Sons, 1976.

Bogdanovich, Peter. *This Is Orson Welles.* New York: HarperCollins, 1992.

Chicago Tribune, January 14, 1977.

Donnelly, Paul. *Fade to Black: A Book of Movie Obituaries.* London: Omnibus Press, 2000.

Ellrod, J. G. *The Stars of Hollywood Remembered: Career Biographies of Eighty-two Actors and Actresses of the Golden Era, 1920s–1950s.* Jefferson, N.C.: McFarland and Company, 1997.

Fowler, Karin J. *Anne Baxter: A Bio-Bibliography.* New York: Greenwood Press, 1992.

Galt, Melissa. Interview with the author. December 15, 2002. Atlanta, Georgia.

Gill, Brendan. *Many Masks: A Life of Frank Lloyd Wright.* New York: G. P. Putnam's Sons, 1987.

Goodman, Mickey. "Focus on Design: Melissa Galt." *Points North* (September 2001).

Hall, Gladys. Interview with Anne Baxter. 1953. Margaret Herrick Library. Academy of Motion Picture Arts and Sciences, Beverly Hills, California.

Hodiak, Katrina Baxter. Interview with the author. February 24, 2003. Port Orchard, Washington.

"How Are Hollywood's Children Raised?" *Quick News Weekly*, August 27, 1951.

Indiana Biographical Dictionary: People of All Times and All Places Who Have Been Important to the History of the State. 2nd ed. 2 vols. St. Clair Shores, Mich.: Somerset Publishers, 1999.

Indianapolis News, May 13, 1975.

Indianapolis Star, December 5, 1985, December 13, 1985.

Indianapolis Times, April 24, 1961.

Ingraham, Elizabeth Wright. Interview with the author. December 4, 2002. Colorado Springs, Colorado.

The Internet Movie Database. http://www.imdb.com/.

Jackson, Kenneth T., Karen Markoe, and Arnold Markoe, eds. *The Scribner Encyclopedia of American Lives.* 6 vols. New York: Charles Scribner's Sons, 1998.

Los Angeles Evening Herald Express, February 18, 1960.

Anne Baxter with her grandfather Frank Lloyd Wright and her husband John Hodiak.

Los Angeles Herald-Examiner, February 11, 1960, February 8, 9, 1967.

Manny, Carter. Interview with the author. August 6, 2002. Michigan City, Indiana.

Michigan City, Indiana City Directories. 1921–23, 1925–32.

Michigan City News-Dispatch, December 12, 1985.

Parish, James Robert. *The Fox Girls*. New Rochelle, N.Y.: Arlington House, 1971.

Staggs, Sam. *All about* All about Eve*: The Behind-the-Scenes Story of the Bitchiest Film Ever Made*. New York: St. Martin's Press, 2000.

Stodola, Barbara. *Frank Lloyd Wright and Colleagues: Indiana Works*. Michigan City, Ind.: John G. Blank Center for the Arts, 1999.

———. Interview with the author. August 1, 2002. Michigan City, Indiana.

Tafel, Edgar. *About Wright: An Album of Recollections by Those Who Knew Frank Lloyd Wright*. New York: Wiley, 1993.

Variety, December 18, 1985.

BETSY PALMER

*With James Dean in the Golden Age
of Television*

Betsy Palmer in her debut movie
The Long Gray Line (1955).
©1954, COLUMBIA PICTURES CORP.

When young Rudolph Vincent Hrunek was growing up in his native Prague, Czechoslovakia, shortly after the turn of the twentieth century, he had no idea he would be coming to America, let alone father a child who would become part of a new and magical industry that made pictures move. By the time Hrunek arrived in the United States at age eighteen, motion pictures were catching the public's fancy with increasing rapidity.

One of Hrunek's first jobs in America was with a music store. He did so well that the company sent him to East Chicago, Indiana, to open another store. He set his store up on the first floor of a building that had the East Chicago Business College (ECBC) on the second floor. Marie Love, who grew up in Michigan City, was running the college, which supplied secretaries for the steel mills and oil refineries of that area. Predictably, the man on the first floor and the woman on the second floor noticed each other, were married, and started a family in East Chicago.

Patricia Betsy Hrunek was born November 1, 1926. When she was one year old, the family moved to Hessville, which is a suburb of Hammond. She attended public school there through the fourth grade. The family then returned to East Chicago, where Betsy and her brother Jack completed their elementary education. In 1944 she graduated from East Chicago Roosevelt High School. According to Betsy, "Teachers were always shoving me on stage." She remembers her first stage role in elementary school was that of a blackbird in a huge pie. In high school, she continued to appear on stage in such productions as *Best Foot Forward*. Although she enjoyed her work on stage, she had no plans to become part of the theatrical profession. When she graduated from East Chicago, she enrolled in her mother's secretarial school, but she only lasted six months. "That was a joke. I could write shorthand very well, but I couldn't read it." She decided to enroll in Indiana University extension and take most of the required subjects prior to declaring a major. She worked for the B & O Railroad during the day and attended IU in the evening.

At a loss as to what vocation to pursue, her mother suggested she go to Chicago and take an aptitude test at the YWCA. The test showed that she would be good in personnel work and that she had a "flair for the arts." It was at this point she decided to become a theater major. She enrolled at DePaul University in Chicago. Again, she worked dur-

Betsy Palmer, Walter Hampden (left), and James Dean in "Death Is My Neighbor," an episode on the television series *Danger* (1953).

ing the day, typing scripts at WGN and selling shoes at Marshall Field, and went to school at night. In summer 1949 she went into summer stock, playing in Woodstock, Illinois, with a young Paul Newman.

At this time, Chicago was a reasonably active source for network television programs, and Betsy began getting work doing commercials. One notable job was with the soap opera *Hawkins Falls*, which originated in Chicago. *Hawkins Falls* ran from 1950 to 1955 on NBC. Betsy did commercials for Surf detergent with the primary announcer for the show, Hugh Downs. She decided she could not be Patricia Hrunek anymore because "Nobody could pronounce Hrunek." Her mother got a telephone book and came upon the name Palmer. Her mother thought "Patricia Palmer" had great alliteration. However, when Betsy joined actors' equity, she discovered there was already a Patricia Palmer listed. She decided to use her middle name and thus became Betsy Palmer.

She moved to New York City and, after only five weeks in the city, she was invited to attend a party. Someone at the party asked if she could do a southern accent. She replied that she could. In 1951 she became a cast member for the *Miss Susan* show, which was the first NBC series to originate from Philadelphia. The star was Susan Peters, who had been a paraplegic since 1945. Peters played a paralyzed attorney who returns to her hometown in Ohio. The soap opera aired from 3:00 to 3:15 p.m. every day. It lasted less than a year.

One of Palmer's biggest breaks was her appearance on an ABC television show entitled *Hollywood Screen Test*. The show began in 1948 and was originally hosted by Bert Lytell, then Neil Hamilton. Young talent appearing on the show all were looking for their "big break." In addition to Palmer, some of the program's alumni were Jack Klugman, Martin Balsam, Gene Barry, and Pernell Roberts. In 1952 Palmer joined emcee Todd Russell on a new CBS show, *Wheel of Fortune*. This series was a totally different show than the one hosted by Pat Sajak. The contestants were people who had distinguished themselves as good Samaritans or heroes. It was a summer replacement show in 1952 and 1953.

Betsy Palmer in *The True Story of Lynn Stuart* (1958).

©1958, COLUMBIA PICTURES CORP.

By this time Palmer was living in New York City, and the golden age of television was in full swing. There were many live dramatic shows being produced every week. Palmer began appearing in such shows as *Appointment with Adventure*, *Campbell Soundstage*, *The U.S. Steel Hour*, *Danger*, and *Studio One*. She worked with such up-and-coming directors as Franklin Schaffer, George Roy Hill, Sidney Lumet, John Frankeheimer, Franklin Heller, and producers Worthington Minor and William Dozier. In April 1953 Palmer was cast in a *Studio One* play entitled *Sentence of Death*. Also cast was a young actor named James Dean. They discovered quickly they were both from Indiana. This helped them form a bond, and they became good friends and, for a time, lovers. Dean would come to Palmer's place, and she would cook for him. Jimmy (as she called him) said his agent was very careful with his money and doled it out to him sparingly. When Palmer discovered that all Dean had in his apartment was a mattress, she gave him pillows and blankets.

On September 2, 1953, Palmer and Dean again appeared together in a television drama. This time it was a *Danger* episode entitled *Death Is My Neighbor*. Veteran actor Walter Hampden, with whom Palmer had worked in a previous drama, *The Killer's Club*, was the star of the show. Franklin Heller, who later was the director for *I've Got a Secret*, was the director of the drama.

Dean and Palmer dated for about nine months and then broke up after what she called "a stupid falling out." She said, "It was nothing. We were both so young." Some time after her break with Dean, Palmer met an obstetrician, Dr. Vincent J. Merendino. They were married, and a daughter, Melissa, was born in March 1962. Palmer was married to Merendino for twenty years, divorcing him after playing Nora in Ibsen's *A Doll's House*. She said, "I realized I was very much like Nora." She never married again. In 1953 writer Paddy Chayefsky wrote a play for Philco TV Playhouse. He called it *Marty*. Rod Steiger was Marty, and Nancy Marchand was Clara. Palmer played Virginia. The television production was such a success that it became a highly acclaimed motion picture. Unfortunately, Palmer was under contract to Columbia, and Columbia boss Harry Cohn was contemptuous of a television play being made into a movie and refused to loan her out. The movie featured Ernest Borgnine as Marty, Betsy Blair as Clara, and Karen Steele as Virginia. *Marty* won an Oscar for best picture, and Borgnine won for best actor.

Palmer was now a very busy actress, making appearances on almost all the live dramatic shows on television in the fifties—*Studio One*, *Good-year Playhouse*, *Philco TV Playhouse*, *U.S. Steel Hour*, *Lux Video Theater*, *Kraft Television Theater*, *The Alcoa Hour*, *Armstrong Circle Theater*, and others. She played opposite such actors as Walter Matthau, Ralph Bellamy, Gig Young, Richard Kiley, Richard Basehart, Skip Homeier, and Ed Wynn.

In 1955 Palmer was cast in her first Broadway production, *The Grand Prize.* The leading actors were June Lockhart, Tom Poston, and William Windom. Unfortunately, it had a very brief run. However, that same year she caught the attention of movie director John Ford. Ford met with Palmer in New York and told her he wanted her for the role of Kitty in his next film, *The Long Gray Line.* The production company, Columbia, wanted her to do a screen test. Max Arnow, who was head of casting at Columbia, supervised the test. When he saw her age listed, he decided to "knock off three years." Thus her birth date was changed from 1926 to 1929, and it appears as 1929 in most movie references.

Palmer was signed by Columbia, and later Ford said, "You didn't have to sign with Columbia." Ford had a stock company of players he used frequently. He liked the idea of casting his own people at will. Ford liked Palmer's work and immediately cast her in his next film, *Mr. Roberts.* Her sequences were shot in Hawaii in two weeks. She said she never saw James Cagney, William Powell, or Henry Fonda. She did become friends with Jack Lemmon, and a number of years later she was asked to play Lemmon's wife in *Tribute* on Broadway. Unfortunately, she was already on Broadway at that time appearing in *Same Time Next Year.* She said she would "have loved to play opposite Jack," but it was not to be.

During the shooting of *Mister Roberts*, Ford became ill and had to have gall bladder surgery. Palmer said she visited him while he was recuperating in Hawaii. He showed her his incision and told her, "That's why I'm off the picture." There were reports that Ford wanted to make some changes in *Mister Roberts* that were not in the stage play. Fonda and Leland Hayward were very much against this. Conveniently Ford had his surgery, and Mervyn LeRoy was called in to finish the film.

Palmer's next film was *Queen Bee*, starring Joan Crawford. Palmer had now appeared in three major films, all released in 1955. In 1957 she starred with Fonda in *The Tin Star.* This time she did get to meet and know Fonda. Her next film was *The True Story of Lynn Stuart*, released in 1958. In 1959 she made *The Last Angry Man*, which starred Paul Muni.

In 1956 Palmer accepted two television offers that would change her career dramatically. A game show called *Masquerade Party* had been running since 1952. It was now on ABC with Peter Donald as the host. Palmer was asked to be a panelist, and she accepted. It was easy work and provided a steady income. Another game show, *I've Got a Secret*, had been running since 1952 on CBS and was on its way toward becoming the most successful quiz show in the history of television. It would run fifteen years. The show was hosted by Garry Moore, and the panelists were Bill Cullen, Henry Morgan, Faye Emerson, and Jayne Meadows. Palmer joined the show in 1957, replacing Emerson, and Bess Myerson came aboard in 1958 as a replacement for Meadows. The panel then remained the same until the show's demise in 1967. Palmer left *Masquerade Party* in 1957.

The game show appearances thrust Palmer into the national spot-light. However, she discovered that she was now thought of as a "game show girl" instead of an actress. A little more than a year after her debut on *I've Got a Secret*, she was offered the job of "The Today Show Girl" on NBC. She accepted and appeared on *Today* five days a week while appearing on *Secret* once a week.

In 1958 Palmer was honored by the Sons of Indiana at the Pin-nacle Club in New York as an outstanding Hoosier daughter. For the first time in twenty-eight years, the Sons of Indiana not only allowed a woman to attend the ceremony, but also gave her their supreme honor. Palmer received a gold charm bracelet and a place on the plaque in the Indiana State Capitol, already distinguished by such names as Joe Cook, Ernie Pyle, Gil Hodges, Wendell Willkie, and Herb Shriner. Palmer gave President William Louth a kiss and said, "This is for each and every one of you. This has never happened before and never will again." "Yes it will," said Louth, "You'll win an Oscar." "This is my Oscar," smiled Palmer, "because it's from my family, the sons, daugh-ters, mothers, fathers of Indiana. I hope I will never let you down."

Palmer was now a household name. "All this is great, and I love it. But I just don't feel complete because I don't have enough chances to act." She actually found that her wholesome appearance and spar-kling personality on *Secret* and *The Today Show* worked against her. When she played a lady of easy virtue in the television debut of *Playhouse 90* opposite Jackie Gleason in William Saroyan's *The Time of Your Life*, mail poured in saying, "Betsy! We always thought you were a nice girl. Now we'll never watch you again!"

She decided to leave *The Today Show* in 1959, and NBC promptly signed another Hoosier. Dale, Indiana, native Florence Henderson took over "The Today Show Girl" job after Palmer's departure. Of her resignation from *The Today Show*, Palmer said, "I left to be an actress." She always welcomed the fact she was so accepted by the public, stating that "it gives you a warm feeling to have people you've never seen before come up and call you Betsy and talk to you as if you were a member of their families. I wonder: Do people run up to Julie Harris and call her Julie? I don't think so. If they call her anything, it is Miss Harris. And that's because they have only seen her when she was acting. That's the difference between being a personality and being an actress."

Because of her game show image, her dramatic appearances on television and in feature films had tapered off considerably. She began doing summer stock and made frequent appearances in such venues as The Papermill Playhouse in New Jersey. She appeared in such stan-dards as *The Prime of Miss Jean Brodie*, *The King and I*, *South Pacific*, and *Once More with Feeling*. She returned to Broadway in 1964 in *Roar Like a Dove*. It had a short run, which fortunately made her available to replace Lau-ren Bacall in *Cactus Flower*. Her costar was Lloyd Bridges, who, she said, "Didn't like the stage." After *Cactus Flower*, Bridges never returned to the Broadway stage. Palmer stayed with the play for one year.

In 1976 Palmer was playing in summer stock in Cape Cod. Ten-nessee Williams had just done a rewrite of his play *Summer and Smoke*. He called it *The Eccentricities of a Nightingale*. He was interested in Palmer for the lead. The day before the play opened in Cape Cod, Williams sent Palmer two dozen salmon pink roses. Williams came to see her perform on opening night and visited her in her dressing room after-wards. She said he was very excited and told her, "Baby, you busted

Betsy Palmer and Jim Gerard (WFBM-TV) at the opening of Lafayette Square Shop-ping Center in Indianapolis in 1968.

my balls!" He told her as soon as she finished her summer commitment, they would mount the play. *The Eccentricities of a Nightingale* opened on Broadway on November 23, 1976, and closed on December 12. The critics did not like it. They wanted something new from Williams, not a rewrite of one of his plays. Palmer's last Broadway appearance was in *Same Time Next Year* in 1977. She replaced Ellen Burstyn. Her costars during the run of the play were Don Murray, Monte Markham, and Charles Kimbrough. Interestingly, Kimbrough's aunt was Muncie, Indiana, native, Emily Kimbrough, who wrote *Our Hearts Were Young and Gay.*

Palmer kept busy appearing on stage and keeping up her volunteer work for the Salvation Army. She has worked with the Army for twenty-five years. In 1980 her agent called and asked if she would be interested in a movie to be shot near Crystal Lake in a boy scout camp in New Jersey. Then her agent told her it was a horror film. She thought, "Oh, no, a horror film!" But in spite of her misapprehension, she asked to see the script. It was entitled *Friday the 13th.* After she read it, she thought, "What a piece of junk. No one will ever see this thing." She was told she had to work only ten days and she would be paid $1,000 a day. She decided to go for it, having no idea the film would become a horror classic.

She was asked to do a sequel, *Friday the 13th, Part 2*, in 1981. It was also a big hit. When she was approached to do a third film in the series, she said, "No thanks." The producers decided to use some of Palmer's footage from the first two without her knowledge or permission. Thus, *Friday the 13th, Part 3* and *Friday the 13th, The Final Chapter* use archival footage of Palmer. Thanks to her memorable portrayal of Jason's mother, Pamela Voorhies, in this cult horror series, she now gets fan mail regularly from Japan, South America, Italy, and many other countries. The *Friday the 13th* films brought Palmer to the attention of a whole new generation of fans. She has been invited to attend horror conventions and did accept on two or three occasions.

Betsy Palmer (2003).

In 1988 she joined the cast of *Knots Landing* as Virginia "Aunt Ginny" Bullock. She was on the series until 1990. Today, she keeps busy appearing in television specials and stage appearances. She opened opposite Van Johnson in *Love Letters* in October 2003 in a little theater just outside of New York. She rarely returns to Indiana, but she used to get back to the Midwest, occasionally visiting her brother Jack who lived on their parents' farm in Gobles, Michigan. Jack passed away in spring 2003. Despite her long absence from her home state she maintains, "I'm always happy to say I am a Hoosier!"

BIBLIOGRAPHY

Brooks, Tim, and Earle Marsh. 2nd rev. ed. *The Complete Directory to Prime Time Network TV Shows, 1948–Present.* New York: Ballantine Books, 1981.

Indianapolis Star, October 24, 1958, May 18, 1960.

The Internet Broadway Database. http://www.ibdb.com/.

The Internet Movie Database. http://www.imdb.com/.

Palmer, Betsy. Interviews with the author. May 3, June 11, July 23, 2003. New York.

FLORENCE HENDERSON

Florence Henderson.

(Opposite page) Florence Henderson in *Song of Norway* (1970).

Florence Henderson was the youngest of ten children in a poor Irish Catholic family. At the time of her birth, February 14, 1934, in Dale, Indiana, the country was still in the midst of the Great Depression. Her parents were poor farmers who were barely able to keep their children fed and clothed. Henderson learned at an early age how to survive in adverse conditions. Her mother was musically inclined and began to teach baby Florence how to sing. By the time she was two, she had learned fifty songs. She said, "I spent half my life in church when I was a kid, sight-reading Gregorian chants, singing four-part Masses every Sunday. That's how I learned to sing, that and listening to my mother sing folk songs and country-western music."

Her talent helped the family in its struggle to make ends meet. Henderson was asked to sing in front of wealthy friends and then passed the hat for money. She was uncomfortable with all the attention she received as a youngster and would sometimes close her eyes while singing in order not to have to look at all the people watching her.

Henderson's intellectual ability matched her advanced singing ability, and she entered school early. She remembers attending school with her siblings when she was three or four years old. The Henderson family moved from Dale to Rockport, Indiana, while Florence was still in elementary school. She graduated from St. Bernard's Catholic School in Rockport. When she was not singing for money, she was out in the fields working on the farm. From the age of eight, she was expected to work several hours each day. She also worked as a child cleaning house and babysitting. As a teenager, she worked as a soda clerk at the town's bus station.

Recalling her youth in Indiana, she said, "The highlight of my life was winning a prize for my devil's-food cake at the 4-H fair and getting a trip to the state fair in Indianapolis. I went on one of those crazy rides, and the little money I had slipped down between the floor slats and I saw the 8-foot-4 man who was married to the 2-foot-tall woman. Oh, you can't imagine how exciting it was."

In 1951, just a few months short of her seventeenth birthday, she graduated from St. Francis Academy in Owensboro, Kentucky. She was very involved in music and theater in high school and, thanks to the generosity of a wealthy friend, she was able to study for two years at the American Academy of Dramatic Arts in New York City. When she first arrived in New York, she was in awe of how different the big city

was from her hometown. Dale, Indiana, at that time had a population of about seven hundred.

While studying at the academy in 1952, she auditioned for a Broadway show. *Wish You Were Here* was cowritten by Josh Logan. Henderson was considered for the lead but lost to another girl who had the strong New York accent required for the role. Henderson was cast in the small part of "the new girl" in the show, not a bad showing for an eighteen-year-old attending her first big audition. Richard Rodgers saw Henderson perform in *Wish You Were Here* and was so impressed that he cast her in the leading role of Laurie in the touring company of *Oklahoma.*

A year later when Logan was casting *Fanny,* he remembered Henderson and auditioned her along with people like Maureen O'Hara and Julie Harris. At this time Henderson was twenty years old. She beat out the veterans and was chosen by Logan to play Fanny. *Fanny* opened on Broadway on November 4, 1954. It ran for two years, playing more than eight hundred performances. She credited her good luck in show business to her hometown priest in Indiana. "Father Gerard had kidded me back home in Indiana and said if I would give my first check to their Benedictine order for their new recreation center, they'd pray for me. I said, 'It's a deal.'"

Henderson was now well known and began making guest appearances on such shows as *Coke Time with Eddie Fisher* and *The Ed Sullivan Show.* She also became a regular on a show called *Sing Along.* Her cohost was Bill Hayes, who had a Hoosier connection, graduating from DePauw University in 1947.

In January 1956 she married theatrical manager Ira Bernstein and later that year gave birth to a daughter, Barbara. In 1959 Henderson became a "Today Girl" for NBC's *The Today Show.* She read the news, gave weather forecasts, and occasionally sang. In 1969 her second child, Joseph, was born. She continued on *The Today Show* and began touring in *The Sound of Music* as Maria von Trapp. She continued to make television appearances, becoming a favorite of host Jack Paar, and briefly hosted *The Tonight Show.* In 1963 she gave birth to a son, Robert, and in 1966 she had a daughter, Elizabeth.

In 1968 producer Sherwood Schwartz was about to shoot a pilot for a series about a woman with three daughters who marries a man with three sons. Schwartz's first choice was actress Joyce Bulifant. However, when Henderson came for a screen test, he changed his mind and cast her as the mother of *The Brady Bunch.* After the series ended in 1974, Henderson again went on tour in such shows as *Annie Get Your Gun.* She was also very busy in television. *The Brady Bunch* refused to die, and numerous television specials kept popping up. Three *Brady Bunch* feature films were made in 1995, 1996, and 2002. Fellow Hoosier Shelley Long played Carol Brady in all three films.

In the early 1980s Henderson's marriage to Bernstein began to fall apart. They were divorced, and Henderson went to the Hypnosis Motivation Institute in California for treatment to lift her spirits. It was there she met Dr. John Kappas, whom she married in 1987. In the mid-1980s she had her own cooking/singing/interview show on the Nashville Network called *Country Kitchen.* It ran until 1993. She also made a beauty video entitled *Looking Great, Feeling Great.*

In 1999 she returned to NBC as cohost of *Later Today.* This show followed *The Today Show* and featured news, entertainment, cooking, and fitness regimens. Henderson was featured on the show for two years.

She is still very busy and says she "wants to work as long as possible and bring happiness, laughter, and joy to audiences for years and years to come."

BIBLIOGRAPHY

Indianapolis News, November 30, 1953, July 31, 1975.
Indianapolis Star, May 15, 1958, February 19, 1961.
Indianapolis Times, January 19, 1964.
Johanson, Kristin. "Mini Biography of Florence Henderson."
Lowry, Cynthia. "Hoosier Florence Henderson Wants to Break into Filmdom." *Indianapolis Star Magazine*, January 8, 1967.

SHELLEY LONG

Shelley Long (1987).

"She was a star-struck, fiercely energetic and ambitious kid from Fort Wayne, Indiana, who, behind her glamour queen looks, emerged as someone rather different and quite unexpected . . . the sophisticated comedienne, witty and self-reliant." This might have been a description of Shelley Long, but it was about another star who died seven years before Long was born. Her name was Carole Lombard. Indiana has produced many talented actresses, and Fort Wayne produced two who were remarkably similar in many ways. Lombard as a movie star is not widely remembered today. But for those who do remember her, and see her in the few Lombard films that find their way to television, one can see a kinship between these actresses.

Leonard Maltin calls Long "a savvy comic actress," a description that certainly would have fit Lombard. The first indication that Long might have some acting talent was a school report that stated, "good grades and a lot of enthusiasm for make believe." At an early age she became determined to follow a career in the theater. It was to be a career that garnered many awards, including an Emmy and two Golden Globes.

Shelley Lee Long was the only child of Leland and Ivadine Long. According to a college friend, she was named for actress Shelley Winters. She was born in Fort Wayne's Indian Village neighborhood on August 23, 1949. Her mother and father were both schoolteachers. She attended Kekionga Junior High and South Side High School in Fort Wayne. Her parents were conservative people and that, plus being an only child, put a lot of pressure on her as a youngster. In 1985 Long recalled, "I never had to compete with anyone for my parents' attention, but it also meant that no one was ever there to take that attention away from me when I didn't want it. Being your parents' sole emotional focus is a tremendous responsibility. So I was indulged, and I had more than my share of pressures, both at the same time."

Her first exposure to any kind of a performer was when she saw her first clown at age four. She remembered immediately wanting to be a clown. Her first stage experience was at Indian Village Elementary School where she played Johnny Appleseed's godfather in a fifth-grade play. She took a public speaking class at South Side High School, and her teacher, Robert Storey, quickly became her mentor. He was so impressed with Long that he called her his most talented student. In 1984 he said Long's greatest assets were her "maturity, her willingness to listen to suggestions and her exceptional dramatic instinct."

Shelley Long and Tom Hanks in *The Money Pit* (1986).
©1986, UNIVERSAL CITY STUDIOS INC.

Storey coached Long, molding her into a fine extemporaneous speaker who, in June 1967, won the top award in the original oratory division of the National Forensic League. It was the first time anyone from Indiana had won a major NFL event and the first time in twenty years a female had won the top spot in the division. She gave a speech on sex education in high school. Long has always given Storey credit for inspiring her career. "Mr. Storey saw that I wanted to act, something that wasn't allowed in our speech meets. He knew I felt strongly in pursuing performing, in communicating, in being the channel through which things can flow," Long recalled. In high school she was cast as Mama in the senior class production of *I Remember Mama*. She wanted to major in theater in college, but her parents were against it.

Sally Maier was Long's best friend in high school, and she describes Long as "extremely outgoing. We went through the same fears, traumas and insecurities that other teen-agers go through. We all had our dates and had our hearts broken by people whose names we've forgotten now." Long and Maier remain friends and still call and visit each other periodically. When Maier was married in 1982, Long and her husband flew in for the wedding.

Long was very active in high school. She was a senior class social council member, a member of the National Honor Society, and a member of the Concert Choir. She won a number of honors in speech competitions. Among them were winner of the Outstanding Meterite Trophy and winner of the Drama Humor Trophy.

Since both parents were teachers, they wanted Long to be a teacher. She said this led to "the most serious disagreement I'd ever had with my parents. I had to tell them that I could not accept their advice, that I had to go my own way. And if that meant forgoing their financial support and getting an on-campus job, well, I would do it." She enrolled at Northwestern University in 1967 as a theater major and worked as a cashier in a campus cafeteria at Northwestern.

Her roommate, Ann Ryerson, became her lifelong friend and even appeared in some of Long's movies. Ryerson introduced her to modeling and later to the Second City Improvisational Company in Chicago. Long appeared in several college stage productions, but at the end of her sophomore year she left school and moved a few miles south of Chicago, where she modeled, appeared in commercials, did summer stock, and eventually wrote, directed, and produced educational films. Chicago also was where she married for the first time. She acquired a stepson from that marriage. Today she rarely mentions her first marriage and never mentions her ex-husband's name. "I was 21 years old, when I got married, and my husband was nine years older. He was starting a business at the time and working very hard. I didn't know exactly what I wanted to do, so I thought I'd help him. That's how I got involved writing children's films for *Encyclopedia Britanica*. I did nine of them, and it was a wonderful experience, but in the process my marriage got lost."

After three years of marriage Long received a divorce and returned to show business. She became a cohost and associate producer of *Sorting It Out*, a magazine-format television show in Chicago, and studied improvisational humor for a year and a half with Second City. In 1977 she appeared in *That Thing on ABC*, a pilot for a variety show that never was. She decided to move to Los Angeles in 1977.

She got a small part in *The Love Boat* and made an appearance in *A Small Circle of Friends*. This led to a costar slot in *Caveman* and another in *Losin' It* with a young Tom Cruise. She was cast as Diane Chambers in *Cheers* in 1982. In 1983 she won an Emmy for outstanding lead actress in a comedy series and received nominations in 1984, 1985, and 1986. In 1983 she won a Golden Globe for best performance by an actress in a supporting role in a series. In 1985 she won a Golden Globe for best performance by an actress in a television series.

She did several movies while still a regular on *Cheers*. *Night Shift* (1982), *Irreconcilable Differences* (1984), and *The Money Pit* (1986) were among those squeezed in while doing the series. Her role in *Irreconcilable Differences* brought her another Golden Globe nomination, this time for best performance by an actress in a musical or comedy. Near the end of her tenure on *Cheers*, she made her most successful movie, *Outrageous Fortune*.

The success of her movies encouraged her to leave the television series and concentrate on films. Unfortunately, the films she made after leaving *Cheers* were not as successful as she had hoped. She returned to television in 1993 as the star of *Good Advice*, which ran for nineteen episodes. Another try at a series occurred in 1998 with *Kelly*

Shelley Long in *Troop Beverly Hills* (1989).
©1988, COLUMBIA PICTURES

Kelly, in which she served as coexecutive producer. When she was about to produce *Kelly Kelly*, she asked fellow Fort Wayne native Drake Hogestyn to play her husband. She met Hogestyn when they cohosted the Fort Wayne bicentennial show in 1994. Hogestyn had been a regular on *Days of Our Lives* since 1978. He tried to arrange his schedule to enable him to continue on *Days* and be in *Kelly Kelly* as well. Unfortunately, his schedule made it impossible to accept, and Robert Hays was cast as the husband.

Long continues to be in demand and has made many television appearances in shows such as *Frasier*, *Diagnosis Murder*, *Sabrina, the Teenage Witch*, *Murphy Brown*, and *8 Simple Rules for Dating My Teenage Daughter*. She has made three *Brady Bunch* features in which she plays Carol Brady, the role originated by Dale, Indiana, native Florence Henderson.

She met her second husband, Bruce Tyson, a securities broker, on a blind date in 1979. They were married in October 1981. On March 27, 1985, she gave birth to a daughter, Juliana.

BIBLIOGRAPHY

Fort Wayne News-Sentinel, July 10, 11, 1987.

The Internet Movie Database. http://www.imdb.com/.

Long, Shelley. Internet interview with the author. September 12, 2003.

Monaco, James. *The Encyclopedia of Film*. New York: Perigee Books, 1991.

Ott, Frederick W. *The Films of Carole Lombard*. Secaucus, N.J.: Citadel Press, 1972.

The Shelley Long Asylum. http://www.the-shelley-long-asylum. co.uk/biography_a.html.

VIVICA FOX

Vivica Fox receiving the 2003 Lena Horne "Lady of Soul" award for outstanding career achievement in the field of entertainment.

S hortly after his breakout role as Officer Bobby Hill in *Hill Street Blues*, South Bend native Michael Warren visited Indianapolis. He was at a track meet and recalled, "I remember this wide-eyed little kid coming up. She was very excited to meet me and said she always wanted to be an actress; that was her goal. Her mom wanted her to go to college first, and she was going to do that but she wanted to be an actress." The teenager was Vivica Fox. Warren said he remembered watching her father play basketball in South Bend. In 2000 television producer Steven Bochco cast Warren as a man who runs an inner-city hospital in Los Angeles. The series was entitled *City of Angels.* Bochco informed Warren he had cast a young and upcoming actress as his costar. Her name was Vivica Fox. Warren mused, "Life takes strange twists and turns."

Vivica Anjanetta Fox was born in Indianapolis on July 30, 1964. She is the youngest of four children, growing up with her sister and two brothers. She said, "I lived in a middle-class neighborhood. We lived up the street from the projects . . . across the street from the Methodist Church and I was raised very religious." After graduating from Arlington High School, she enrolled in Golden West College in Huntington Beach, California, graduating with an Associate of Arts degree in social sciences.

She moved to New York and began her slow, steady climb to success, modeling and performing in television shows. She managed to get a recurring role on the soap opera *Generations* from 1989 to 1991 and appeared in other soaps such as *Days of Our Lives* and *The Young and the Restless.* She had small roles in such programs as *Matlock*, *Beverly Hills 90210*, and *The Fresh Prince of Bel-Air.* She was in several failed television shows—*Living Dolls*, *In the House*, and *Out All Night.*

Her first feature film role was as a hooker in *Born on the Fourth of July* (1989). She was still struggling to make ends meet when Wil Smith (the two had remained friends since *Fresh Prince*) recommended her for his next film, *Independence Day* (1996). She said, "I was unemployed, broke. But my parents were extremely supportive; my family lent me money. And I had an acting coach who said your life can change in a day, you've gotta stay focused."

The producers of *Independence Day* had no idea who she was and wanted a bigger name. Smith, however, fought for her to get the part and, as a result, she made her first major film appearance. Good notices led to a quick succession of other films—*Booty Call*, *Batman & Robin*, *Soul Food*, and *Why Do Fools Fall in Love?*

Soul Food was produced by Grammy-winning producer and fellow Indianapolis native, Babyface Edmonds, and his wife, Tracey. Her performance in *Why Do Fools Fall in Love?* as a streetwise hustler garnered some of the best notices of her career. She said, "It's a wonderful time to be an African-American actress. Ten years ago we were all fighting for that one small, token role. Now, we have African-American ensembles, and some of the leads are even female."

In 1997 she was chosen by *People* magazine as one of the fifty Most Beautiful People in the World. Also in 1997 she was Arsenio Hall's wife in the short-lived sitcom, *Arsenio*, on ABC. In 1998 she was the star of a sitcom on the Fox network, *Getting Personal*, for which she was nominated by the NAACP for best actress in a comedy series. Unfortunately, the show ended after one season. Her series with fellow Hoosier Michael Warren also was short-lived.

In July 1999 Fox returned to Indianapolis to accept the Black Expo 1999 Screen Image Award. The crowd gave her a standing ovation. She asked a woman sitting in front if she would stand up. It was her mother. Fox said, "Mama, would you please stand up for me? You have instilled a lot of morals and discipline in me to make me the woman I am. Thank you Mama." Then Fox began to cry in front of the 3,200 people assembled for the award presentation.

Fox continues to be in demand, appearing in such major features as *Boat Trip*, *Kill Bill* (volume 1 and 2), and *Ella Enchanted*. The latter film was directed by Carmel High School and Indiana University grad, Tommy O'Haver. She married singer Christopher Harvest on December 19, 1998. He is better known as rapper Sixx-Nine (his height). After their first meeting at Bar One in Los Angeles, he quickly bought twenty roses from a bar employee and slowly handed them to Fox, one at a time. Two years later Harvest proposed to Fox, and 260 wedding guests gathered for the ceremony at Park Plaza in downtown Los Angeles. Unfortunately, the marriage lasted only a little more than five years.

After her break with Sixx-Nine, she and another rapper, 50 Cent, were a twosome. They eventually went in different directions and Fox, now in her forties, began dating mostly younger men. She said, "If you ask me, Demi Moore is a woman's inspiration. She turned 40 and instead of hiding in a cave, she came back and looks better than ever."

Fox is keeping busy and is enjoying her career. She said, "I've loved to dress up since I was a kid, now I get paid for it."

BIBLIOGRAPHY

Calgary Sun, November 8, 1996, September 21, 1997.
Dunn, Samantha. "Oh Happy Day!" Unidentified magazine article. Author's collection.
Indianapolis Star, July 17, 1999, February 1, 2000.
Star Bios. http://www.tribute.ca/.
Toronto Sun, September 3, 1998.

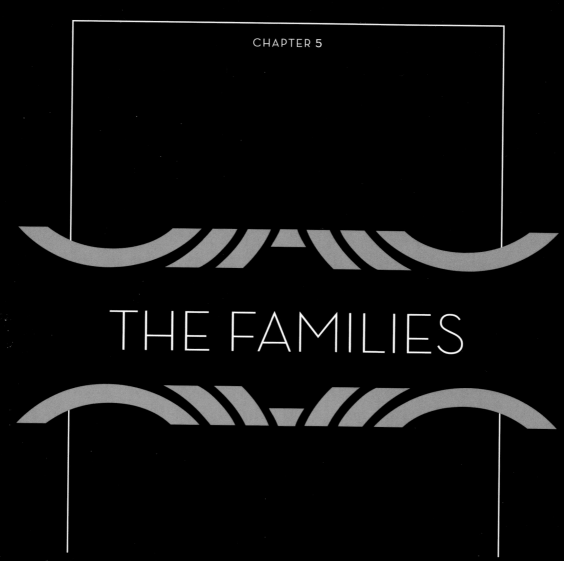

CHAPTER 5

THE FAMILIES

In Japan today there are families of kabuki actors that go back as far as seventeen generations. While the tradition of theater families is not as great as that in Japan, American theater has always had its share of families. There were several Hoosier vaudeville families, including Joe Keaton, his wife Myra, and young Buster. Marilyn Miller's family toured as "The Three Columbians" before she became a star in her own right.

In the early days of motion pictures there were the Barrymores, the Gish sisters, the Talmadge sisters, and Mary, Jack, and Lottie Pickford. More recently, there are the Fondas, the Redgraves, the Carradines, and the Estevez/Sheen family. This chapter will deal with Hoosiers who seem to have had talent "run in their family" and who surely benefited from the fruit of accumulated efforts by their theatrical families.

HARRY BENHAM
and the Benham Family of Actors

At one time the Benham family was among the Thanhouser Film Corporation's most prominent players. The family appeared together and separately in many of that company's leading productions. However, they lacked the sustaining quality that makes so many stars endure. They seemed content to dismiss their film careers as their starring days began to wane.

Harry Benham was born in Valparaiso, Indiana, on February 26, 1884, and was educated in Chicago and Goshen, Indiana. He began his career in light opera and musical comedy and was a matinee idol on the stage early in the century, appearing in fellow Hoosier George Ade's *Sultan of Sulu* and other productions such as *Pinafore*, *Peggy from Paris*, *Woodland*, and *The Gay Musician*.

While appearing on stage, he met and married actress Ethyle Cooke. The couple had two children, Leland and Dorothy. In August 1911 Harry and his family joined the Thanhouser Film Corporation. Harry quickly became one of the leading actors for the company, appearing in light comedy, farce, drama, and society roles. He was very busy from 1911 to 1916 for Thanhouser, appearing in more than sixty films. In 1916 he moved to Universal Studios and was as busy as ever. *The Motion Picture Weekly* of January 1916 has him on the cover. Inside is an ad for *The Man Inside*, starring Edwin Stevens, supported by "that ever popular Universal leading man, Harry Benham."

Ethyle and the two children also were working regularly for Thanhouser and other companies. Ethyle played opposite her husband in a number of films. Leland became a leading player in a series of films for children, appearing in more than twenty films between 1911 and 1915. He also moved to Universal and played opposite his father and sister in a 1916 film, *The Path of Happiness*.

Dorothy also made her film debut for Thanhouser and later appeared in a series of children's films for Universal, produced by the Atlas Film Corporation. Between 1912 and 1915 she appeared in no less than seven films.

Moving on to other studios, Harry appeared for Edward Warren Productions, American Studios, Appolo, Metro, Selznick, Vitagraph, and others. During this period he played opposite such stars as Alice Brady, Marion Davies, and Ina Claire.

By the mid-1920s Harry had faded from the film scene, and the family spent many years in retirement in Wisconsin and Florida. Ethyle died in Waukesha, Wisconsin, on April 20, 1949. In 1953 Harry

The Benham family: Harry, Leland, Dorothy, and Ethyle.
CLASSIC IMAGES, NO. 149 (NOVEMBER 1987)

married Doris Townsend Deppe and died in Sarasota, Florida, on July 17, 1969. He was survived by his second wife and his son. Leland joined the army and served in the Hawaiian Islands. He died in Boynton Beach, Florida, on September 26, 1976. Dorothy married Jack Tutton and remained his wife until her death from Hodgkin's disease in Watertown, Wisconsin, on September 19, 1956.

The family was well known to the moviegoing public during their years of filmmaking, but after they left the screen little was heard of them until the obituaries of Ethyle and Dorothy appeared in the trade papers. By the time Harry and Leland died, they were not given an obituary in any of the trade papers. Once prominent names in the film industry, they passed from the film scene with little notice from the industry they helped pioneer.

BIBLIOGRAPHY

Blum, Daniel. *A Pictorial History of the Silent Screen.* New York: Grosset and Dunlap, 1972.

Doyle, Billy H. "Lost Players." *Classic Images* 149 (November 1987).

"Harry Benham." *Moving Picture Weekly* (January 1916).

Slide, Anthony. *Silent Portraits: Stars of the Silent Screen in Historic Photographs.* Vestal, N.Y.: Vestal Press, 1989.

THOMAS J. GERAGHTY
and the Geraghtys of Rushville

Thomas Jefferson Geraghty started a family film dynasty that became a major influence in several creative aspects of the motion picture industry, beginning with the early silent films and stretching well into the talkies. Geraghty was born in Rushville, Indiana, on April 10, 1881, the son of James and Mary Lynch Geraghty. The Geraghtys were a prolific bunch in Rushville. The 1900 census shows several Geraghty families living there, with a combined number of at least fifteen or twenty. The patriarchs of the families were all born in Ireland.

Geraghty grew up in Rushville. He ran a cigar store and was a sign painter before he went into the newspaper business. He became a reporter and then the editor of the *Rushville Daily Republican.* He married Ethel Carmen De Casseres of Rushville, and they had four children—all born in Rushville—Carmelita, Sheila, Gerald, and Maurice. Geraghty first gained public prominence when he was named best newspaper editor in the state of Indiana. He subscribed to most of the New York papers and modeled his paper after them. The makeup of his paper and the style of his material stood out and caused journalists in much larger markets to take notice.

He gained the acquaintance of most of the famous authors from the golden age of literature in Indiana. Booth Tarkington and George Ade became close friends, and George Barr McCutcheon and Kin Hubbard were also part of Geraghty's circle. Geraghty also interviewed James Whitcomb Riley on more than one occasion. One day in 1910, while in his office at the *Republican,* Geraghty received a letter from Marian G. Scheitlen, the editor of the *New York Herald*, who wanted him to be a staff reporter for his newspaper. He took the position at the *Herald,* and within months he was considered one of the best reporters in New York City. For seven years Geraghty occupied the position of special writer for the *Herald.* His work drew the attention of the *New York Tribune*, and it hired him away from the *Herald.* While in New York he began writing one-reel comedies for Mr. and Mrs. Sidney Drew. Sidney was the uncle of Lionel, Ethel, and John D. Barrymore.

Jesse L. Lasky heard about Geraghty and approached him with an offer to write feature stories for his films. Geraghty's knowledge of small-town life, combined with a thorough newspaper training, helped him considerably in this new field. While at Famous Players-Lasky, Geraghty became a scenario editor and writer for Douglas Fairbanks. This led to a close friendship and an association in which he served as screenwriter and producer of many of Fairbanks's most famous films.

When Famous Players opened its new four-million-dollar studio in Long Island City, Geraghty was put in charge of production and guided the activity of nine production units. After three years in the New York studio, he was sent to London to take a similar position in the Famous Players studio there. After a year in London he returned to New York, supervising and writing for several of the important stars and feature companies. He returned to Hollywood when production was discontinued in the East.

Geraghty became a member of Fairbanks's "court," which met at Pickfair for occasional dinners. Included in the court were several leading directors of that day—Howard Hawks (Goshen, Indiana), Allan Dwan, Raoul Walsh, Victor Fleming, and William Wellman. Geraghty found several Hoosiers in Hollywood who were fellow writers. He and Monte Katterjohn of Boonville, Indiana, were hired at the same time as writers when Geraghty left Lasky to go to the Paralta Studios. Another Hoosier screenwriter, Grover Jones of Terre Haute, became a very close friend.

In 1922 Fairbanks released his version of *Robin Hood.* It was the biggest film Hollywood had ever produced. Credit for the screenplay was given to Elton Thomas, Fairbanks's pseudonym. Although Fairbanks took all the credit for the writing, he had several collaborators, including Geraghty, who participated in many of the script conferences and certainly had a hand in shaping the film.

The association with Fairbanks enabled Geraghty to work for other film stars of the era, such as Gloria Swanson, Mary Pickford, and W. C. Fields. Other Fairbanks films Geraghty wrote were *When the Clouds Roll By* (1919), *The Mollycoddle* (1920), and a sound film, *Mr. Robinson Crusoe* (1932). He cowrote and edited the W. C. Fields film, *It's the Old Army Game* (1926). With Ring Lardner and George M. Cohan, Geraghty wrote the screenplay for *Elmer, the Great* (1933), a very successful Joe E. Brown baseball comedy. Geraghty worked with many Indiana natives throughout his career. In 1920 he wrote the scenario for *Too Much Johnson,* which starred Monte Blue (Indianapolis). In 1923 he adapted George Ade's play *Woman-Proof* for the screen, starring Louise Dresser (Terre Haute). He adapted another Ade story, *Old Home Week,* for the screen in 1925 and also wrote the screenplay for *Sackcloth and Scarlet* in 1925, which starred Alice Terry (Vincennes). Geraghty had the opportunity to write several screenplays for one of the first well-known leading men of the movies, J. Warren Kerrigan of New Albany. He wrote *The Turn of a Card* and *Toby* (adapted from the novel *One Dollar Bid*) in 1918 and *A Man's Man* in 1923. The latter was one of the last films Kerrigan made.

Geraghty also never forgot his hometown. In 1918 the *Rushville Republican* reported, "Tom Geraghty never forgets his home town. A flattering report concerning him which appeared in the Los Angeles Times termed him as 'The Sage of Rushville.' His recent film, 'The American Consul' was based on characters he had known in Rushville. All names were used from Rushville." The article also mentions that "Tom Geraghty and Charlie Fuhr (who wrote for the New Yorker Magazine) are giving a party for all the Rushville folks this week."

In 1918 Fairbanks was quoted in an interview with the *Louisville Herald* as saying, "We have two Indiana boys out here, Ralph Jones of Gas

(Previous page) Carmelita Geraghty and Buck Jones (Vincennes) pose for a publicity shot for *Men without Law* (1930).

Carmelita Geraghty and Tom Mix in
The Last Trail (1927).

City and Tom Geraghty of Rushville. The latter recently remarked that a lot of clever people come from Indiana. The cleverer they are, the quicker they come."

Geraghty and Fairbanks became such good buddies that Fairbanks traveled with Geraghty when his marital troubles with Mary Pickford began. Geraghty and Fairbanks went to Scotland for the Walker Cup golf competition, then took an extended vacation to faraway places with Victor Fleming and Fairbanks's personal trainer, leaving Mary at home. When Fairbanks came up with the idea of doing a modern version of Robinson Crusoe, some felt it was just an excuse to take a South Seas cruise. At any rate, *Mr. Robinson Crusoe* was shot in Tahiti. Fairbanks wrote the story line, and Geraghty helped supervise the production and provided additional dialogue. More than five hundred natives were engaged in supporting roles. The major actors, in addition to Fairbanks, were William Farnum, Earle Brown, and Maria Alba, who played Saturday. (There was no Friday in this version.) The film was made near the end of Fairbanks's career and was not very successful.

In the late 1930s Geraghty went to England to produce British films. He wrote the story for the first British Technicolor film, *Wings of the Morning* (1937), which starred Annabella and Henry Fonda. While in Europe, he was also employed by Mussolini and an Italian company to produce a film based on the history of La Scala opera in Milan. The outbreak of war in Europe caused this project to be abandoned, and Geraghty returned to the United States.

In 1939 Fairbanks died from a massive coronary attack. Pallbearers included Geraghty, Charlie Chaplin, Joe Schenck, and Indianapolis-born Sid Grauman, whose father had dubbed Mary Pickford "America's Sweetheart." Shortly after the Fairbanks funeral, Geraghty visited his hometown of Rushville, renewing old acquaintances and visiting relatives. He then returned to his home in Hollywood, where he was appointed head of the Hollywood Bureau of Censorship of the Office of War Information. It was during his tenure in this position that he became ill and was placed in a private sanatorium in Hollywood, where he died on June 5, 1945. He is buried in Forest Lawn Memorial Park in Glendale, California.

CARMELITA GERAGHTY

Carmelita Geraghty was born in Rushville, Indiana, on March 21, 1901. When her father moved the family to New York, Carmelita was nine years old, and her three siblings were just toddlers. She attended Waddleigh High School in New York and graduated from Hollywood High School after her father moved to the film capital. She got a job as a continuity clerk for Mack Sennett and for a while was one of Sennett's "Bathing Beauties," appearing in a number of Sennett shorts. A publicity release from Sennett during that era states, "Carmelita Geraghty will present one of her flaming Spanish dances and exotic characterizations in the newest picture in the series of All-Star Sennett Comedies upon which production has just begun and in which Alma Bennett, Billy Bevan and Vernon Dent are featured."

When director George Fitzmaurice urged Carmelita to take a part in a feature film, *To Have and to Hold* (1922), she decided to give it a try. Since her father did not want her to become an actress, she at first used a fictitious name. She appeared in a variety of roles throughout the twenties, including the film that was Alfred Hitchcock's debut as a director. *The Pleasure Garden* was filmed mostly in Germany in 1925. Carmelita was cast as a chorus girl who becomes the mistress of a dashing continental playboy. She was the second female lead in this film. In 1927 she had one of her best roles in Mary Pickford's last silent film, *My Best Girl*, playing Pickford's sister, and fellow Hoosier Sunshine Hart (Indianapolis) played Pickford's mother.

Carmelita had her mother's Latin look and was often cast as a Latin type, often adopting a Spanish accent for many of her roles. She later regretted doing the accent so well because that and her appearance caused her some problems getting other roles.

In 1922 the Western Association of Motion Picture Advertisers created a promotion called Wampas Baby Stars, which predicted stars of the future. In 1924 Carmelita was selected as one of the winners. She began her Western career when she costarred with Tom Mix in two

Carmelita Geraghty.
MACK SENNETT COMEDIES. PHOTOGRAPH BY EDWIN BOWER HESSER

films in 1926 and 1927. The next year she was cast with fellow Hoosier Carole Lombard in a short, *The Campus Carmen.*

In an interview in 1930 Carmelita said, "I have been in pictures for quite a few years and I don't think I have any kick coming on my progress. But as yet I haven't done anything that makes me want to stand up and shout to the world." She expressed a desire to become more versatile. "I want to work a little light comedy into my characterizations. I don't mean I want comedy roles as I did enough of those when I was at Mack Sennett's. But I do think it is a good idea to bring some comedy into serious parts." In order to further her versatility, Carmelita believed she should gain some experience on stage. In 1930 she appeared in two stage productions in Los Angeles.

As he was with Lombard, Buck Jones was partial to people who were part of the "Indiana Colony" in Hollywood. In Jones's *Men without Law* (1930), he gave Carmelita the part of a Spanish don's imperiled and imperious daughter. In another Jones film, *The Texas Ranger* (1931), she turns outlaw to avenge the death of her father. She played a dance-hall queen in Ken Maynard's *Fighting Thru* (1930) and was featured in Myrna Loy's first talking picture, *Rogue of the Rio Grande* (1930). She played opposite Ben Lyon in *What Men Want* (1930), and in 1931 she appeared in *Fifty Million Frenchmen*, which featured Cole Porter's music and starred Ole Olsen (with partner Chic Johnson). Porter and Olsen were both from Peru, Indiana. In 1932 Carmelita did a serial, *Jungle Mystery*, with Tom Tyler, in which she played Belle Waldren, a treacherous adventuress. She ended her film career in 1936 with another Latin portrayal in the role of Lolita in another serial, *The Phantom of Santa Fe.*

Carmelita Geraghty.
MACK SENNETT COMEDIES. PHOTO BY GEO. F. CANNONS

After a five-year romance, Carmelita married Carey Wilson, a film writer and producer for MGM, on May 6, 1934. Their closest friends were Norma Shearer, Jean Harlow, and Colleen Moore. The Wilsons were two of a small group who were invited to the wedding and reception of Jean Harlow and Paul Bern in 1932. Wilson was one of the thirty-six founders of the Academy of Motion Picture Arts and Sciences. In 1925 he took over the writing of the screenplay for Hoosier Lew Wallace's *Ben-Hur* from June Mathis and also produced the *Andy Hardy* and *Dr. Kildare* series for MGM.

After her retirement from films in 1937, Carmelita turned to her hobby of painting and worked successfully as a painter for many years. Her style was reminiscent of French impressionism. After her husband's death in 1962, she moved to Paris, where her paintings were featured in several galleries there, including the Weil galleries. She returned to the United States from Paris and was en route to her Los Angeles home when she suffered a heart attack and died in New York City on July 7, 1966. She was survived by her brother, Maurice; sister, Sheila; and a stepson, Anthony. She is buried in the Hollywood Forever Cemetery in Hollywood.

MAURICE AND GERALD GERAGHTY

The brothers Geraghty, like their sister and father, were born in Rushville, Indiana. Gerald was born on August 10, 1906, and Maurice was born on September 8, 1908. The brothers followed in their father's footsteps and became screenwriters and were big contribu-

Gerald Geraghty (left), Anita Stewart, and
Maurice Geraghty.

tors to the Western film, and Gerald received screen credits for many
Gene Autry and Roy Rogers films. The brothers also worked together
on several films, including Gene Autry's first starring film, *The Phantom Empire* (1935), which was an unusual Western because it was really
science fiction. Gerald worked on the screenplay with Wallace Mac-
Donald and Hy Freedman. Maurice, who began his career as a writer
and later became a successful producer and director, commented:

> The first Mascot picture I worked on was the feature version
> of "The Phantom Empire." My brother Gerald had worked on
> the serial version, and together we figured out what transitional
> scenes were necessary to tie it all together as a feature. This was
> Gene Autry's first picture and we worked under the supervision of
> Armand Schaefer, who worked for many years with Autry on and
> off. . . . Gene was chosen because his records were selling sensa-
> tionally and Nat Levine was canny enough to capitalize on that.
> Nobody, not even Levine, expected Gene to make another pic-
> ture, although he had a hold on Gene, just in case. As you know,
> the picture hit big and opened up a whole new era in Westerns, the
> singing, musical Western.

Recalling his days at Mascot, Maurice said, "I was paid $25 a week
and we worked six days a week, from 8:30 to 6:00, and I mean worked.
It was a real sweatshop operation, but jobs were hard to come by at the
time . . . the drag end of the Depression. I was appointed serial story

supervisor . . . we worked in conference, five or six writers. When an episode was blocked out satisfactorily, it was divided up among the writers to be put on paper in synopsis form. Synopses were sent into the executive offices for okay, also screenplays, when written."

Gerald and Maurice both worked on the Hopalong Cassidy films. Maurice was a writer on two Cassidy films, and Gerald was a writer on four of the Cassidy films. Maurice wrote the screenplay for *The Mysterious Rider* (1938), a Zane Grey Western that had Monte Blue in the cast. Gerald and Maurice also worked on the screenplay for the Tom Mix film, *The Miracle Rider* (1935), and Gerald did the screenplay for *King of Dodge City* (1941), starring Tex Ritter.

Gerald wrote not only the first film that starred Gene Autry (*The Phantom Empire*) but also wrote at least twenty other Autry films. He wrote his first Roy Rogers film in 1938 (*Come on Rangers*) and continued to write for Rogers films through 1950. He was given screen credit on at least nineteen Rogers films.

The Falcon was a popular mystery series that starred George Sanders's brother, Tom Conway. Maurice served as producer on eight of these films, while Gerald worked as a writer on at least four. Gerald wrote screenplays for two of Hoosier Allan "Rocky" Lane's Western films and worked with Hoosier directors Ray Enright, Lambert Hillyer, and Mack Wright. Hoosier actors who appeared in Gerald's scripted films included Monte Blue, Robert Paige, Kermit Maynard, Billy Lee, and Elmo Lincoln. He even wrote the screenplay for *Badlands of Dakota*, one of the films in which Frances Farmer starred during her brief Hollywood career.

Both of the Geraghty brothers worked well into the 1950s writing screenplays. In 1956 Maurice wrote the story for Elvis Presley's first film, *Love Me Tender*. He also began to work in television, but his output slowed. He died in Palm Springs, California, on June 30, 1987. Gerald wrote the screenplay for a delightful reunion of all the old-time cowboys in 1950. The film was *Trail of Robin Hood* and starred Roy Rogers and Rex Allen. Allan "Rocky" Lane, Kermit Maynard, Monte Hale, Ray Corrigan, William Farnum, Jack Holt, Tom Keene, and Tom Tyler made cameo appearances in the film. Gerald's last film script was in 1954 for a Rex Allen Western. He had written at least five films for Allen. Gerald died on July 8, 1954, in North Hollywood, California.

BIBLIOGRAPHY

All Movie Guide. http://www.allmovie.com/.

Anderson Daily Bulletin, July 31, 1930.

Bedker, Theodore. "Local Boys Make Good Away from Home." *The Leader*. Undated newspaper clipping. Academy of Motion Picture Arts and Sciences, Beverly Hills, California.

Carey, Gary. *Doug and Mary: A Biography of Douglas Fairbanks and Mary Pickford.* New York: E. P. Dutton, 1977.

"Carmelita Geraghty." *Classic Images* (May 1991).

Chuck Anderson's "Old Corral." http://www.surfnetinc.com/chuck/trio.htm/.

Find a Grave. http://www.findagrave.com/.

Indianapolis Star, June 6, 1945, July 8, 1966.

The Internet Movie Database. http://www.imdb.com/.

Liebman, Roy. *The Wampas Baby Stars: A Biographical Directory, 1922–1934.* Jefferson, N.C.: McFarland and Company, 1995.

Louisville Herald, March 3, 1918.

Mack Sennett Comedies Publicity Release. Academy of Motion Picture Arts and Sciences, Beverly Hills, California.

Moore, Colleen. *Silent Star.* Garden City, N.Y.: Doubleday and Company, 1968.

New York Times, June 6, 1945, July 8, 1966.

Rainey, Buck. *Sweethearts of the Sage: Biographies and Filmographies of 258 Actresses Appearing in Western Movies.* Jefferson, N.C.: McFarland and Company, 1992.

Rushville Republican, February 20, 1918, June 6, 1945, July 8, 1966.

Spoto, Donald. *The Art of Alfred Hitchcock: Fifty Years of His Motion Pictures.* Garden City, N.Y.: Doubleday, 1979.

Tibbetts, John C., and James M. Welsh. *His Majesty the American: The Cinema of Douglas Fairbanks.* South Brunswick, N.J.: A. S. Barnes and Company, 1977.

Tom J. Geraghty biography. Academy of Motion Picture Arts and Sciences, Beverly Hills, California.

Truffaut, François. *Hitchcock.* New York: Simon and Schuster, 1967.

Tuska, Jon. *The Filming of the West.* New York: Doubleday, 1976.

———. *The Vanishing Legion: A History of Mascot Pictures, 1927–1935.* Jefferson, N.C.: McFarland and Company, 1982.

THE SEEGAR SISTERS OF GREENTOWN

Miriam Seegar.

(Above) Dorothy Seegar.

A few years before the start of World War I, four talented sisters were preparing to make their mark in light opera, drama, theater, movies, and television. Helen, Dorothy, Miriam, and Sarah Seegar were the daughters of Frank F. and Carrie Seegar of Greentown, Indiana. A fifth daughter, Mildred, died when she was eight years old. Frank had a thriving hardware business in Greentown. In 1912 a newspaper ad for the hardware store advertised a coal-burning stove and a washing machine and mentioned that Frank also sold ranges, base burners, hardware, pumps, gasoline engines, plumbing, tinning, etc.

Dorothy was the first daughter to enter show business. She had an excellent voice and sang at churches and events in Greentown, frequently accompanied by her sister, Helen, who was an accomplished pianist. Dorothy's solo debut was in 1918 at the dedication service of the newly remodeled Methodist Episcopal Church in Greentown. Her father happened to be on the board of trustees and served on the building committee.

Helen secured a job as secretary to Mr. Peffer, who owned the Redpath Chautauqua Company. She introduced him to Dorothy, and by 1920 Dorothy was singing light opera in *The Gondolier* with the Redpath company. A review stated that she had "a bright future before her in the light opera realm . . . she sings easily and has a flexible voice of pleasing quality."

In March 1921 Dorothy came to Greentown for a performance of *The Climax*, with a road company that staged the play in the new high school auditorium. On January 22, 1925, she gave a recital at the Congregational church in Kokomo. She was on tour at the time and had just completed a two-week engagement in Detroit.

Miriam began appearing in plays at the Greentown schools and was cast as the leading lady in the Greentown High School play of 1922. In 1924 Frank died, and Carrie sold the hardware store and moved her family to Marion, Indiana, where her parents lived. The summer after her father died, Miriam appeared with Dorothy in a production of *The Mikado*. Since there was no part in *The Mikado* for her, Dorothy rewrote it and added the role of Umbrella Boy for fourteen-year-old Miriam. The next summer Miriam appeared in *Sweet Sixteen* with Dorothy and a large chautauqua company. That winter she had a leading role in *Marcheta*, a local production presented in Kokomo.

Miriam finished high school in Marion in 1925, took voice training in New York City, and attended the Petersburg School for Girls in Virginia, where she studied drama. She then spent another season in chautauqua. In summer 1926 she returned to New York. Her first break was in the Broadway production of *The Squall*, starring Blanche Yurka. Miriam stayed with the play for three months. As a result of her performance, she was cast as Annabelle in *Crime*, a show that was to open at the Queen's Theater in London. Since she was underage, she had to be accompanied by her mother.

Miriam was sufficiently impressive in the London show that she was offered a movie contract. She was on the stage at the same time she was shooting movies. Her third film in England was *When Knights Were Bold* (1929) and was directed by fellow Hoosier, Tim Whelan. She said she did not know Whelan was from Indiana until they were talking between scenes. She discovered he was from Cannelton, Indiana, and a romance blossomed between the two Hoosiers. After making three pictures in England, Miriam was cast in the London stage production of *Out Goes She* opposite Ernest Truex. Her stage credits began to mount, and Hollywood took notice. She was signed by Paramount and in 1929 made her first film in Hollywood. *Fashions in Love* costarred Adolphe Menjou but also featured two other Hoosiers, Russ Powell from Indianapolis and Billie Bennett from Evansville. That same year she played opposite Richard Dix in *The Love Doctor*. When Dix left Paramount to star in *Seven Keys to Baldpate*, he requested Miriam as his leading lady. In 1930 she played Hoosier Charlie Murray's (Laurel, Indiana) daughter in *Clancy in Wall Street*.

Helen Seegar.

Miriam was also Vincennes native Buck Jones's leading lady in *The Dawn Trail* (1930). She said that before she was cast in this film, she made it clear that she could not ride a horse and that she was "frightened to death" of them. After shooting began, four men were assigned to lie on their stomachs, each one holding a leg of the horse whenever she was in the saddle. A double did all the riding for her. Despite being uncomfortable around horses, she enjoyed making the film and characterized Jones as "a charming, dear sweet man."

She made another film in 1930 with an actor from Indiana. Leon Waycoff, who later changed his name to Leon Ames, played the role of Judd Brooks in *The Famous Ferguson Case*. Miriam was cast as his wife. During production of the film Miriam discovered that Waycoff had dated Dorothy in high school.

Miriam Seegar and her husband Tim Whelan (Cannelton) shortly after their marriage in 1931.

Miriam made at least sixteen films from 1928 to 1932. Her career was cut short when she married Whelan on May 24, 1931, in Tijuana, Mexico, and in 1933 moved with him to England. The couple lived in England for seven years. During this time Whelan was working with the Kordas (Alexander, Zolton, and Vincent) and had directed several films for them. One of these was the classic, *The Thief of Bagdad* (1940). The credits for this film list Ludwig Berger and Michael Powell as codirectors along with Whelan, who directed most of the action scenes in the film. Shooting began at the Denham Studios in London and in Morocco, but when the war made it impossible to finish the film in Europe, shooting was moved to the United States, where the film was finished on soundstages in Hollywood and on location in the Mojave Desert and the Grand Canyon.

While in England, Whelan directed such films as *The Mill on the Floss*, *Sidewalks of London*, *Q Planes*, and *The Divorce of Lady X*. He is credited

with bringing English stars Vivien Leigh, Laurence Olivier, Charles
Laughton, Geraldine Fitzgerald, and others to the United States.

The couple had two sons, Michael (who was called Johnny) and
Tim Jr. Miriam became an interior designer and worked at this pro-
fession for forty years. Frequently she would run into her old costar,
Adolphe Menjou, who would always urge her to return to acting, stat-
ing that she was "wasting her time." Whelan died from lung cancer on
August 11, 1957.

The oldest Seegar sister, Helen, graduated magna cum laude from
Northwestern University, married Doctor J. C. Stone, and made her
home in Kokomo. Dorothy married Doctor Paul Hatch and continued a successful stage career for some time after her marriage.

Sarah became a Broadway and movie actress and later gained fame
in radio and television. Sara (she dropped the *h* in her first name
when she became an actress) attended elementary schools in London
and Paris. While in England, Miriam was asked to appear in *Three Men
on a Horse*. Miriam said she was not right for the part, but told the producers her sister, Sara, would be perfect. Sara was cast in the production and made her Broadway debut in 1940 in *Horse Fever*, a farce that
starred Ezra Stone. The show folded after three weeks, but Sara and
Stone fell in love and were married two years later. Stone became the
voice of Henry Aldrich on radio, and Sara played several roles over
the next six years in her husband's radio series, *The Aldrich Family*.

The Stones had a son, Josef, and a daughter, Francine Lida. In
1962 Sara appeared as Maude Dunlap in the film version of *The Music
Man*. That same year she was cast as Eloise Wilson, the next-door neigh-

bor in *Dennis the Menace*, opposite Gale Gordon. She was the mother-in-law on *The Red Buttons Show* and on *Occasional Bride*. She appeared on the Sid Caesar, Danny Thomas, and Fred Allen shows and many others.

Under the sponsorship of the American College Theater Festival, Kennedy Center for the Performing Arts, and the Music and Theater Department of the United States Army, Sara served for twenty-three years as adjudicator, lecturer, workshop leader, and guest artist in the theater departments of hundreds of universities and colleges in the United States, South America, Japan, Korea, Greece, and West Germany.

In 1983 Sara came to Indianapolis with her husband at the invitation of Professor Edgar Webb, head of the theater department at Indiana University–Purdue University, Indianapolis. They offered a series of dramatic lessons for the students. Kristina Wagner, who became a regular on *General Hospital* and has appeared in several movies, was one of the students who benefited from their instruction. Their visit was so successful that Webb invited them back in 1986. In their later years the couple lived in Newton, Pennsylvania, where they raised prizewinning purebred Ayrshire dairy cattle. They also were very active in the Bucks County Playhouse in Pennsylvania. Sara died on August 12, 1990, from a brain hemorrhage, and Stone died four years later on March 3, 1994, in an automobile accident.

In 1996 Miriam and Dorothy returned to Greentown and visited their mother's grave and their grandparents' house. They were surprised to see the name "Frank F. Seegar" still on the side of the building where the hardware store was once located. Miriam is the last surviving Seegar sister and lives in Pasadena, California, where she says her grandchildren are just discovering she used to be in the movies.

BIBLIOGRAPHY

Bergan, Ronald. *The United Artists Story*. New York: Crown Publishers, 1986.

Indianapolis News, February 29, 1932.

Indianapolis Times, June 6, 1929.

Katz, Ephraim. *The Film Encyclopedia*. New York: Perigee Books, 1979.

Whelan, Miriam Seegar. Interviews with the author, December 12, 16, 2001. Pasadena, California.

Sara Seegar.

Sara Seegar (upper right) as Mrs. Wilson in the *Dennis the Menace* television series (1962–63).

THE BENNETTS
Richard, Barbara, Constance, and Joan

Richard Bennett in the stage play
Beyond the Horizon (1920).

Despite the lack of theatrical tradition, except for an uncle in his family, Richard Bennett became one of the most celebrated actors in the American theater for more than a half century. In theatrical history, his name ranks alongside John Barrymore, William Gillette, and Francis Wilson as one of the great actors of his age. As well, his wife and three daughters were actresses, with two of the daughters becoming major Hollywood stars.

Charles Clarence William Henry Richard Bennett was born on May 21, 1872, at what was then known as Bennett's Switch, Indiana (later known as Deacon's Mills). He would later brag that his name took up a line and a half in the family Bible. For the sake of brevity, he chose the one name he liked most out of the five that he was christened with. According to Richard's recollection, "Bennett's Switch was between Bunker Hill and Elk River Junction," near Kokomo and Logansport on the banks of the Wabash River, and was named for the whistle-stop junction of a short railroad spur that ran to the Bennett sawmill and homestead.

For generations the Bennetts had been lumber mill operators, first pioneering the frontiers in New Jersey and then migrating to Indiana. It was Richard's grandfather who founded the home and sawmill at Bennett's Switch. He fathered seventeen children and sent nine of them to the Civil War. Only three came back. Richard's father, George Washington Bennett, was one of those. George was a self-ordained preacher, sawmill operator, and three-term sheriff of Howard County.

Although most of the Bennett men were on occasion "hell-fire and brimstone" preachers, it did not prevent them from participating in civic and church theatricals. Richard's uncle Henry was known as a very good amateur actor. Nearby Kokomo had an opera house that brought a variety of attractions to the area, and Richard passed out handbills for the theater in exchange for tickets.

Richard's first experience on stage was at age eight. After watching his uncle Henry playing in a romantic drama at the city hall, Richard and some of his friends decided to do their own production in an empty hayloft. Richard described the scene: "Mother's sheets were utilized for a drop curtain and a couple of pieces of carpet from the waste heap during spring cleaning, made the side drops. An old four-legged table turned upside down with its legs in the air was a ship.

Price of admission was two marbles. I can assure you that I have never played since, before such an enthusiastic and appreciative audience, as at those performances."

Richard had plenty of opportunity to witness real-life melodrama as the son of the sheriff of Howard County. One of his most vivid recollections was about the Monahan gang, a group of hoodlums who robbed freight trains and had murdered four or five travelers. George rounded up and jailed most of the gang, but the ringleader, Doc Kole, was still at large. George lured Kole into a shed and, in true theatrical style, the villain was blasted from several directions and fell dying. George walked over to the mortally wounded Kole and said, "I guess we've got you, Doc." "Yes, you bible-thumping Hoosier bastard!" he said, and then died. Richard always thought that was one of the best exit lines he had ever heard—real or imagined.

Richard's first taste of legitimate drama was in his early teens, when he appeared in a production of *Oliver Twist* as part of a Sunday School entertainment. His first real introduction to the stage came when he played the role of Little Boy Blue in an amateur production of *Little Bo Peep*. At age seventeen, Richard's father apprenticed him to a tailor in Logansport. However, Richard stayed with tailoring only a few months. He began to hang around stage doors, and when an English performer named Joe Coyne came to town in a melodrama, Richard begged him for an audition. Coyne said he had no room in his company and told him to go to New York.

Not quite ready for New York, Richard got together with three other Logansport men and formed a quartet, giving nightly concerts on the street corners of Logansport. Years later, Richard recalled how he finally broke into show business: "'Muldoon's Picnic' was playing in our town. They needed a boy and my friend who gave me the information told me it was a splendid chance for me to go on the stage. I was engaged and did so well I went on the road with the company." He was hired as a musician and sometimes actor.

He eventually met Coyne again, and this time Coyne hired him as a property man and let him double in small roles. Richard had a grueling first year in the theater, but stuck with it. By the age of twenty-four he had established an acceptable reputation as an actor and was regularly employed.

In September 1900 Richard was playing in *The Royal Family*, and in the cast was seventeen-year-old Mabel Adrienne Morrison. From the beginning Richard called her "Mab," and they started dating. By this time Richard was a brilliant, flamboyant, and temperamental matinee idol. He insisted that when they married, she should leave the theater. However, Morrison had her heart set on a career in the theater and refused to give it up. A rejected Richard soon met another seventeen-year-old, and within a week and a half of their meeting, he married Grena Heller. However, Heller and Richard divorced in 1903, and Richard lost no time in returning to Morrison. A compromise was reached, and they were married on November 8, 1903, in Jersey City, New Jersey. When Morrison became pregnant with their first daughter, Constance Campbell Bennett, she reluctantly gave up her acting career and soon gave birth to two more daughters, Barbara Jane and Joan Geraldine. Morrison was determined that her daughters would not follow the acting profession, and Richard agreed that a woman's place was in the home—unless, of course, she wanted to pursue a theat-

Richard Bennett, circa 1930s.

Richard Bennett and his wife Adrienne about to board the *Aquitania* on March 19, 1925.

FOTOGRAMS, NEW YORK CITY

Richard Bennett and Marion Davies in
Five and Ten (1931).

rical career. Naturally, all three daughters became actresses. Barbara,
the middle child, had the briefest career, and Joan, the youngest, had
the longest career. All three girls were given occasional exposure to
the stage, appearing with their father.

In 1913 Richard acquired the rights to a play, *Damaged Goods*, and
adapted, directed, and produced it. It was a daring venture because
it was a controversial study of the devastating social effects of hered-
itary syphilis. After many difficulties, he managed to obtain the
endorsement of several civic and health groups. He addressed clubs,
church groups, and theater audiences, advocating compulsory use
of the Wassermann test in the issuance of marriage licenses. When
Richard brought the play to Indianapolis in October 1913, Hector
Fuller, dramatic editor of the *Indianapolis Star*, attacked the play, saying, "Remembering Mr. Bennett's work as John Sand to 'What Every
Woman Knows,' with Maud Adams . . . or going farther back to his
splendid achievements in 'The Other Girl,' 'The Royal Family,' and
many others which we hold in loving memory . . . we must regret his

present propaganda." Richard replied, "The trouble lies in the fact that people have been so busy with the tango and similar amusements that they have not looked upon such problems as this play presents with enough consideration." He went on to compliment the city, "Indianapolis has unconsciously been a dramatic center, for in my opinion, there is no city where there are more substantial, thinking playgoers than here."

In spring 1914 he received an offer from American-Mutual Film Company to make *Damaged Goods* into a movie with the original Broadway cast. Richard was not impressed with the movies. However, since it was no longer possible to ignore them, he decided to accept the offer. In 1915 Richard appeared in a play by the same author of *Damaged Goods*, Eugene Brieux, entitled *Maternity*. The play was a plea for legalized abortion. It was not successful, but it underscored his dedication to unpopular social causes. In 1916 he starred in another film, *The Valley of Decision*, also for American-Mutual. The cast contained the entire Bennett family, including Richard's sister, Blanche Bennett Hanson.

Despite his early success and lengthy career in films, Richard developed a lifelong disaffection with the industry and the films he made. In a letter to his daughter, Joan, he said, "I have tried to rise to the top in all I've undertaken except in pictures, but after all, that is much like being the champion privy cleaner of Crown Point, Indiana."

In 1919 Richard read a manuscript of a three-act play by Eugene O'Neill, entitled *Beyond the Horizon*. Richard thought it had possibilities, but it was over an hour too long. He made a number of judicious cuts and presented them to O'Neill, but O'Neill refused to cut a word. Richard took him home, they drank all night, and by morning O'Neill had approved all of Richard's cuts. Although irritated with Richard's cutting and rewriting of his lines, O'Neill soon admitted that "Bennett is really a liberal education" and that the experience had made him a better playwright. The play opened on Broadway on February 2, 1920, with Richard playing the principal role of Robert Mayo. He said, "I had to do it all, cast it, cut it, and produce it." O'Neill won the first of his four Pulitzer Prizes for the work.

In her autobiography, *Lulu in Hollywood*, actress Louise Brooks gives a first-person view of the Bennett family. Brooks was a friend and classmate of Barbara Bennett. One morning in 1923 Brooks visited the Bennett apartment on Park Avenue in New York. She said:

> Barbara's beautiful younger sister, Joan, came in with her schoolbooks to study at the secretary by the window. Barbara's beautiful older sister, Constance, had just started her career, but her reputation as the best-dressed, haughtiest actress in movies was already established. All the girls had Richard Bennett's wide cheekbones and finely set eyes, but in character the three daughters did not resemble one another in any way. Constance loved money. During a career that continued to the year of her death, in 1965, she demanded and received a salary equal to that of the top stars. Yet beauty, great acting ability, and a lovely voice could not compensate for the lack of the one attribute without which the rest did not matter: she did not have that generosity, that love for her audience, which makes a true star. What Joan loved was secu-

rity. Her marriages to men powerful in films guaranteed a successful career. Barbara made a career of her emotions. Periods of
work or marriage were terminated by her frightening, abandoned
laughter of despair and failure. Only her death, in 1958, achieved
in her fifth suicide attempt, could be termed a success.

Brooks described that morning as being filled with the usual sibling bickering among sisters and hearing Richard singing "I love life
and I want to live," followed by his entrance in a brocade dressing
gown. He went straight for the liquor cabinet, tossed down a glass of
whiskey, turned to Brooks, and said, "My God, Joan, where did you
get that damned black dress?" Between liquor and poor eyesight, he
often confused Brooks with his daughter Joan. The Bennetts were a
raucous but loving family. However, all was not well with the clan. As
a result of Richard's drinking problems and his many romantic liai-
sons, Morrison instituted divorce proceedings, and she and Richard
were divorced in April 1925. Both remarried, but their fondness for
each other remained the rest of their lives.

One of Richard's boyhood friends was playwright and novelist
Kenyon Nicholson of Crawfordsville, Indiana. One of Nicholson's
plays, *The Barker*, was a wild and raw drama about carnival life that was
sprinkled with what was known then as "salty dialogue." Richard was
cast in the part of a carnival pitchman and relished the opportunity
to use this kind of language on the stage. During the run of *Barker*,
Richard heard that Morrison had married again. In spite of his amo-
rous derelictions, he still loved her dearly. Determined to show his
indifference, he married a society woman named Aimee Raisch Hastings on July 11, 1927. The marriage took place between a matinee and
an evening performance of *Barker* and lasted ten years.

After *Barker* closed in 1928, Richard began preparing for a new
production in New York called *Jarnegan*. Richard promised Joan, who
had just given birth to a baby and had divorced her alcoholic husband, the ingenue lead. *Jarnegan* opened on Broadway on September
24, 1928, and it gave Joan's career a jump start. He received nothing
but praise for his performance as a swearing, drinking, and lecherous
movie director. Richard loved being on stage with his daughter, and
his greatest pleasure was a father–daughter curtain call. His first talking motion picture was also released in 1928. He received top billing
for his role in *The Home Towners*.

In 1931 Richard, Constance, and Joan were all in Hollywood
making movies. When asked by a reporter what it felt like to be the
father of two celebrated daughters, Richard replied, "How the hell do
you think it feels? It feels just fine!" The first and only time Richard
played opposite his daughter Constance (other than when she was a
child) was in the 1931 film *Bought!* He played Constance's father. Of
the experience he said, "It seemed funny to be playing second fiddle
to one of my own kids, but I didn't resent the idea. It was rather stimulating." From 1931 to 1934, Richard played a variety of character
roles in films. In 1935 he made his last appearance on Broadway in
Maxwell Anderson's *Winterset*.

In June 1937 Richard returned to Logansport with his sister, Blanche. They had become traveling companions and had just
returned from a trip to South America. He stayed in Logansport for
several days, greeting old friends and visiting his childhood haunts.

He even went to the dingy third-floor room where as a youth he learned the tailor trade.

By the 1940s he was becoming better known as the father of actresses Constance and Joan than as a star in his own right. Although Richard's movie roles were not spectacular, he kept reasonably busy, and his opinion of the motion picture industry improved as more of his fellow stage actors went into the profession. His health began to deteriorate, but he refused to give up smoking cigars and hitting the bottle.

In 1942 Orson Welles, who had always been a fan of Richard, decided to cast him as Major Amberson in the film version of Hoosier Booth Tarkington's Pulitzer-prizewinning novel, *The Magnificent Ambersons.* Welles said of Bennett, "Dear man, I loved him so. I'd been such a breathless fan of his in the theater. He had the greatest lyric power of any actor I ever saw on the English-speaking stage. There is no way of describing the beauty of that man in the theater." Welles said he found Richard in a boardinghouse in Catalina, "totally forgotten by the world." Said Welles, "And think what it meant to him at the end of his life to be brought back and to suddenly play an important role! And to have people admire and respect him, as we did . . . as we all did." Welles said at that stage of his life Richard was incapable of memorizing dialogue, "so I spoke every line and he repeated it after me, and then we cut my voice from the sound track."

Welles treated Richard with the utmost deference and kindness, arranging shots in order to keep Richard from having to climb stairs. After he finished *Ambersons,* Richard wrote a letter of thanks to Welles, stating, "I feel sure you understand my gratitude . . . lifting as you did 'an old scow' from the mud banks and permitting it to see the sunshine once more." The following year Welles asked Richard to appear in *Journey into Fear,* in which the codirector was Richmond, Indiana, native Norman Foster. It was to be his last film.

In September 1944 Richard contracted his final illness, arteriosclerotic heart disease, and was sent to Good Samaritan Hospital in Los Angeles. He hated the confinement and sent ugly memorandums to his doctors and had his friends smuggle cigars to him. On October 22, 1944, he died of pulmonary edema. He was seventy-two. He was buried next to Mab in the Morrison family plot in Old Lyme, Connecticut.

Richard Bennett in *The Magnificent Ambersons* (1942).
©1942, RKO PICTURES INC.

BIBLIOGRAPHY

Bennett, Joan, and Lois Kibbee. *The Bennett Playbill.* New York: Holt, Rinehart and Winston, 1970.

Bennett, Richard. Interview. Margaret Herrick Library. Academy of Motion Picture Arts and Sciences, Beverly Hills, California.

Bogdanovich, Peter. *This Is Orson Welles.* New York: HarperCollins, 1992.

Brooks, Louise. *Lulu in Hollywood.* New York: Alfred A. Knopf, 1982.

Indiana Biographical Dictionary: People of All Times and All Places Who Have Been Important to the History of the State. 2nd ed. 2 vols. St. Clair Shores, Mich.: Somerset Publishers, 1999.

Indianapolis News, October 23, 1913, June 11, 1937.

Indianapolis Star, October 15, 1911, October 29, 1913.

The Internet Broadway Database. http://www.ibdb.com/.

HOOSIERS IN HOLLYWOOD

223
HOOSIERS IN HOLLYWOOD

Liebman, Roy. *From Silents to Sound: A Biographical Encyclopedia of Performers Who Made the Transition to Talking Pictures.* Jefferson, N.C.: McFarland and Company, 1998.

Parish, James Robert, and Don E. Stanke. *The Glamour Girls.* New Rochelle, N.Y.: Arlington House Publishers, 1975.

"Pauline Frederick." *Films in Review* (February 1965).

Tapert, Annette. *The Power of Glamour: The Women Who Defined the Magic of Stardom.* New York: Crown Publishers, 1998.

Young, William C. *Famous Actors and Actresses on the American Stage.* New York: R. R. Bowker Company, 1991.

Joan, Richard, and Constance (left to right) celebrate Richard's seventy-second birthday in 1944, the year he died.

THE LANE SISTERS
The Mullicans from Macy

The Lane sisters and their mother: Rosemary, Leota, and Priscilla (back row); Lola, Mrs. Cora Lane, and Martha (seated).

Lola Lane.

(Opposite page) Posed shot from *Four Daughters* (1938) showing the Lane sisters: Lola and Priscilla seated and Gale Page and Rosemary standing. Page was a contract player who was brought in to costar as the fourth sister.

©1938, VITAGRAPH INC.

D octor Lorenzo A. Mullican, a dentist, and his wife, Cora B. Hicks Mullican, were the parents of five very talented daughters, three of whom became well-known Hollywood stars. Lorenzo and Cora were married in Macy, Indiana, on December 24, 1902. Leota, Martha, and Dorothy (later called Lola) were all born in Macy. Leota was born in 1904, Martha in 1905, and Dorothy in 1906. In 1907 the family moved to Indianola, Iowa, a small college town south of Des Moines, where Mullican set up a dental practice. The Mullicans lived in a large house with twenty-two rooms, some of which they rented out to students attending nearby Simpson College. The last two daughters were born in Iowa—Rosemary in 1914 and Priscilla in 1915.

Cora was a reporter for the family-owned *Macy Monitor*, and she would have pursued an acting career had it not been for her Methodist parents' aversion for any form of public entertainment. Cora encouraged her daughters to sing and play musical instruments. All of the girls studied music at Simpson College. They sang at church and county fairs and had leads in plays put on by the town's small college.

The oldest daughter, Leota, showed an early interest in music and had a fine singing voice. She won a piano in a mail-order contest, and it was not long before the daughters started playing. Leota graduated from Simpson and went on to study at the Julliard School of Music in New York, winning an audition at the Metropolitan Opera. Meanwhile, Dorothy, at age twelve, was playing the piano accompanying silent films in the local theaters. She was considered the wild one of the five and once caused an uproar by dancing the Charleston in front of an Indianola church.

When Leota was signed by producer Gus Edwards to appear in one of his productions in New York City, Dorothy, who had been expelled from Simpson College for "disciplinary reasons," joined her sister there. Together they formed an act doing impressions of movie stars. The sisters toured with Edwards in his production of *Ritz Carlton Nights* and later toured with Lowe's and the Orpheum vaudeville circuits. In 1926 Edwards featured them in his *Greenwich Village Follies*. In 1928 Dorothy appeared opposite George Jessel in the Broadway stage production, *The War Song*. It was at this time that Edwards changed Dorothy's name to the more exotic-sounding "Lola Lane" to match her exotic looks.

A movie scout caught Lola's performance on stage and signed her to a contract with Fox Studios. For the next three and a half years the studio rushed her through such films as *Speakeasy* (1929), *The Girl from Havana* (1929), *Good News* (1930), *Hell Bound* (1931), and *Ex-Bad Boy* (1931).

Leota sang in operettas and in grand operas, including leading roles in *Tosca, La Boheme,* and *Mme. Butterfly.* During World War II she joined the WACS and sang in many wartime camp shows. She eventually gave up the New York stage and began to concentrate on voice lessons.

Back home in Indianola, Rosemary and Priscilla (or "Pat," as the family called her) were telling all their friends and neighbors that they were the proud sisters of Leota and Lola Lane. Rosemary and Priscilla harmonized very well and worked up a singing act. In 1932 Cora took her two youngest daughters to New York to visit their sisters. While in New York, Rosemary and Priscilla auditioned as vocalists with Fred Waring and his Pennsylvanians. Rosemary was hired and began singing duets with Tom Waring. A disappointed Priscilla was left behind because she was too young. It was at this time that Cora left her husband and Indianola, taking Priscilla with her. In New York, fourteen-year-old Priscilla joined Rosemary to form a duo for Waring, and they both changed their name to Lane, as did Cora. This turn of events was considered scandalous in Indianola, where there were no taverns and not a cigarette was sold in town. Martha was the only sister who did not go into show business. She was a talented writer and had some poetry published. She married an English instructor and settled down to being a housewife.

Lola continued to be very busy in films, appearing in three features and a serial in 1936. Her big break came in 1937 in *Marked Woman,* starring Bette Davis. When Warner Brothers saw her work during the first few days of shooting, they signed her to a seven-year contract. That year also saw Rosemary and Priscilla coming to the same studio with the Fred Waring Orchestra to make the musical, *Varsity Show.*

Rosemary and Priscilla's singing talents and sparkling personalities soon led to a Warner Brothers contract for each, and Cora bought a house in Van Nuys. Priscilla had six pictures released in one year (1938), and the studio, sensing a box office bonanza, searched for a vehicle to showcase all three sisters in the same film. The studio decided on a Fannie Hurst story, *Sister Act,* which had appeared in *Cosmopolitan* magazine. A screenplay was written based on the story, and Leota was brought in and tested to play the fourth sister in the film. She was deemed unsuitable for the screen in what the *Des Moines Tribune* in 1936 described as "an inclination toward operatic chubbiness." Warner Brothers engaged a contract player, Gale Page, to costar as the fourth sister in the film, *Four Daughters,* released in 1938. John Garfield made his film debut in this film. It was not much more than a glorified soap opera, but audiences loved it. Although Leota was not cast in the film, when *Lux Radio Theater* decided to produce a radio version of the film in 1939, Leota played the fourth sister.

Lorenzo died in January 1938, just a few months before *Four Daughters* was released. Martha was the only daughter to attend the funeral. A second film was rushed into production and released the same year. *Daughters Courageous* (1939) used the same cast, playing a new set of characters in a new story written by the famous Epstein brothers. Garfield was in this one, too, but played it in a lighter vein. Audiences flocked to theaters to see it. This led to a third film in the series, *Four Wives,* released in 1939. Finally, the formula began to wear thin, and the last film in the series, *Four Mothers,* was released in 1941.

Lola and Rosemary appeared in *Hollywood Hotel* in 1937 with Brazil, Indiana, native Johnnie "Scat" Davis. Lola again starred with Davis in *Mr. Chump* in 1938 and continued to make films at a steady rate, appearing in three films in 1937, four films in 1938, two films in 1939, and three films in 1940. The movie magazines were full of the Lanes—Priscilla's gleaming smile advertising tooth powder, Rosemary demonstrating how to "banish bulges," Lola looking sultry for Maybelline. However, by 1948 age and a string of less successful pictures had taken their toll, and their movie careers were over. In later years Rosemary went into real estate sales. Priscilla settled in New Hampshire, had four children, and chose to play down her Hollywood career in favor of becoming a housewife and mother. Leota died in 1963, Martha in 1972, Rosemary in 1981, and Priscilla in 1995.

Lola was married five times. In 1931 she married actor Lew Ayres, but the marriage lasted only two years. After Ayres came film director Al Hall, then businessman Henry Clay Dunham, then writer-director Roland West. West owned a nightclub with film star Thelma Todd. When he died, he willed his property to Lola. In addition to the nightclub, Lola received a circular-shaped home in which she resided with fifth husband, Robert Hanlon. The couple spent much time traveling, making many trips to Mexico. Lola's hobbies included making ceramics and macramé.

Lola had the longest career of the three sisters, enjoying the role of a Hollywood personality and playing it with stubborn dedication. She often played a girl reporter, and it was her portrayal of a reporter named Torchy Blane that inspired Jerry Siegel to create Lois Lane for the *Superman* comic strip. Although Siegel used a model for Lois Lane, he admitted she was not as voluptuous as he thought Lois Lane should be. It is easy to see the resemblance between the cartoon character and Lola.

Lola's real-life persona was much like that of her on-screen personality. She wore glamorous clothes, associated with well-known celebrities, and led a fast-paced life that resulted in much publicity and many husbands.

Lola retired from films in 1946. She was reluctant to see people and did not give interviews in her later years. She died in Santa Barbara, California, on June 22, 1981.

BIBLIOGRAPHY

Albert, Katherine. "Smart Baby." *Picture Play* (1939).

All Movie Guide. http://www.allmovie.com/.

Christian, Rebecca. "Star Struck." *The Simpson Magazine* (Winter 1998–99).

Daniels, Les. *Superman: The Complete History, the Life and Times of the Man of Steel.* San Francisco: Chronicle Books, 1998.

Felton, Mark. "The Lane Sisters in Hollywood." Simpson College Archives, Indianola, Iowa.

The Internet Broadway Database. http://www.ibdb.com/.

The Internet Movie Database. http://www.imdb.com/.

Roberts, Barrie. "Priscilla Lane: All American." *Classic Images* (February 1999).

Sennett, Ted. *Warner Brothers Presents: The Most Exciting Years—from* The Jazz Singer *to* White Heat. Secaucus, N.J.: Castle Books, 1971.

Stumpf, Charles K. "Down Memory Lane with the Lane Sisters." *The World of Yesterday* (July 1978).

———. Letter. June 11, 2001.

THE JACKSONS

An Entertainment Dynasty

Janet Jackson.

A crane operator in Gary, Indiana, used to spend hours playing guitar and writing songs. His wife, Katherine, sang country-western music with a touch of the blues. Joseph Jackson recalled how it all began: "When the kids were little, I played guitar with a group called the Falcons. We would rehearse at the house, and they would be around, lookin' up, you know. And from there they tried playing themselves. It wasn't hard to know they could go on to be professionals. They won practically all the talent shows and I wasn't surprised when they did make it. Because, you see, we were trying awful hard."

When it became apparent to Joe that he would never make it big as a musician, he decided that he would concentrate on developing musical talent in his children. When his five sons began demonstrating musical talent, Joe entered them in talent contests throughout Indiana. They traveled around in a Volkswagen bus and played weekends at colleges or in black theaters. In 1965 they won a talent contest at a Gary high school, performing their version of the Temptations' "My Girl."

When the mayor of Gary, Richard Hatcher, saw the boys perform, he arranged for them to meet Diana Ross, who was then the lead singer for the Supremes. Ross was impressed with the group and helped them get a Motown recording contract in 1969. Their success was almost instantaneous.

Their first million record seller was "I Want You Back" in 1970. They sang the national anthem at the opening game of the World Series in Cincinnati and began drawing sell-out crowds at their concerts. Before long, their recording of "I'll Be There" was the number one record in America. In an incredibly short time the Jackson Five became the fastest-selling recording group in Motown history, outselling such giants as the Temptations, the Supremes, Stevie Wonder, and The Four Tops. They had a succession of hits, including "ABC," "The Love You Save," "Mama's Pearl," and "Never Can Say Goodby."

By 1971 a Jackson Five cartoon aired weekly on ABC. Their live shows became a showcase for Michael's dancing skills as well as his singing prowess. Motown realized that Michael had star appeal, and he was the first member of the family to do a solo album. From "Got to Be There" in 1971 until the present, Michael's career has more than fulfilled that realization. He was so successful that the other brothers decided to follow his lead.

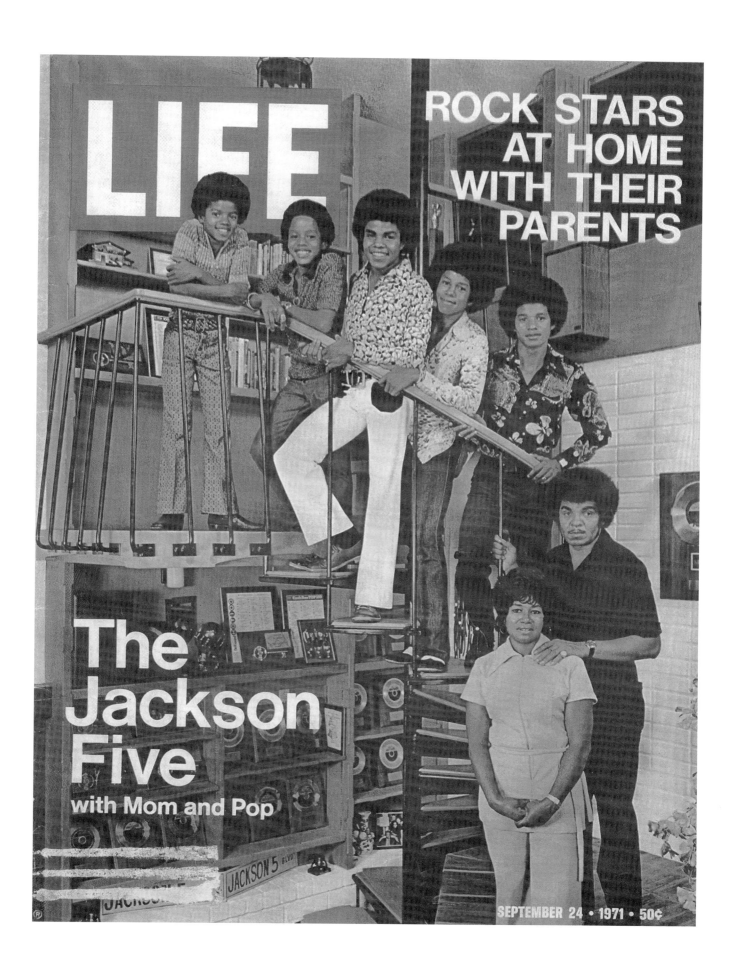

Michael is the youngest of the original group. The others who made up the Jackson Five are Marlon, Jermaine, Tito, and Jackie. The other Jackson children are Randy, Rebbie, LaToya, and Janet. Of the nine Jackson children, only Janet (the youngest of the siblings) has managed to come close to the success of Michael. Janet appeared briefly with her brothers during the early 1970s, but it was clear that she was determined to pursue her own path and signed with A&M in 1982. This relationship produced brilliant dance hits and beautiful ballads.

Through it all, Joe Jackson ruled with a firm hand. He served as their manager/promoter and made sure they were all properly educated. He said, "They go to school, do their chores, play ball. They have to maintain their personal lives, because if an entertainer doesn't, that's when he can get the big head." He enforced a strict curfew on the road and made sure they worked hard. He had a tutor and a physician with them when they toured. As the boys grew older and became more successful, Joe moved behind the scenes.

The influence of the Jackson family on the music of America is huge. They broke through and appealed to a rock audience that had previously seen little connection between black music and their own interests. Michael alone has used his writing and production skills to blaze a new trail in the world of rock music. His albums, *Off the Wall*, *Thriller*, *Bad*, *Dangerous*, and *HIStory* have changed the face of pop music. In October 2000 he was given the award for best-selling Male Pop Artist of the millennium at the World Music Awards.

The Jackson Five at the height of their popularity in the early 1970s.

BIBLIOGRAPHY

Indianapolis News, October 22, 1970.

"The Jackson Five." *Life*, September 24, 1971.

Meet the Family Online. http://meetthefamily.online.fr/j5bio.htm.

Michael Jackson Official Web Site. http://www.michaeljackson.com/.

Ostroff, Roberta. "The Jackson 5 (or 6)." *Indianapolis Star Magazine*, September 9, 1973.

CHAPTER 6

THE SUPPORTING PLAYERS

HOOSIERS WITH FACES MORE FAMILIAR THAN THEIR NAMES

One of the more important aspects of motion picture history has been the contribution of the supporting player or character actor. From the silent era to the present, these "little people" have played an important role in popularizing movies. While many moviegoers only have eyes for the big, glamorous stars, others have found that a supporting player's contributions frequently make a greater and more lasting impression.

The apex of the character actor was from 1930 to 1955. Every studio during those years had its own group of character actors under contract, and they were seen frequently in the company's products. Most character actors who were active during the golden age of movies came out of theater stock companies, where they were required to put on a new play every week or so with a small, versatile company of actors. With the advent of television, Hollywood changed, and as character actors began to retire, they were not replaced. Today their ranks are thin.

A great many Hoosiers enjoyed thriving careers as supporting players and/or character actors. Some became so prominent that they became marquee names. Marjorie Main, Claude Akins, Strother Martin, Beulah Bondi, and Scatman Crothers all were able to rise above the secondary status usually given to such actors. Conversely, some who were stars first survived by turning themselves into supporting actors later in their careers. Monte Blue, Richard Bennett, and Louise Dresser come to mind.

There were so many of these "little" players from Indiana that it is impossible to cover the careers of all of them. The people selected for biographies are those who are the most recognizable. Others will appear in the listing section of actors and actresses in this book.

CHARLES AIDMAN

Charles Aidman was born in Frankfort, Indiana, on January 31, 1925. In 1944 he was offered a football scholarship at Indiana University. A broken arm on the gridiron ended his football career, and he decided to concentrate on drama courses in order to compensate for his innate shyness. His education was interrupted when he joined the navy in 1946, earning the rank of lieutenant. He received his B.A. from IU in 1948. While at IU he performed in a variety of productions, including *Joan of Lorraine*, *The Barretts of Wimpole Street*, *Hotel Universe*, *I Remember Mama*, and *Ghosts*.

Aidman went to New York and began to appear in off-Broadway productions. He graduated from the Neighborhood Playhouse, where he studied with Sanford Meisner. Meisner also served as a mentor for Hoosiers Steve McQueen and Sydney Pollack. In 1956 he appeared in Joseph Papp's first production of *Julius Caesar*, performing as Marc Antony.

Aidman conceived, adapted, wrote the lyrics, directed, and performed in *Spoon River Anthology*. Aidman described it as "a play about 80 people . . . all dead, who are now talking to living people . . . the audience, telling them the thing in their lives that summed up everything more importantly than anything else." It was first produced at the UCLA Theater Group, and in 1969 it moved to Broadway, where it received unanimous acclaim. *Spoon River Anthology* was later aired as a CBS special, and Aidman received an Emmy nomination for his performance.

His stage career began in 1957, when he created the role of Sam Lawson in *Career*. In 1964 he was selected by Arthur Miller to play Quentin in the national tour of *After the Fall*. This role required him to be on stage the entire three hours of the production, and he was involved in every scene. The reviews were extremely complimentary. The *Saint Louis Post-Dispatch* said, "Aidman is magnificent!" The *San Francisco Examiner* said, "Aidman gives a moving, appealing superb portrayal," and *Variety* said, "Aidman is a forceful actor and shows dramatic power!" He began to work in films and appeared in major supporting roles in *Pork Chop Hill*, *Hour of the Gun*, *Kotch*, and *Twilight's Last Gleaming*.

Aidman also had a very prolific television career, starting in 1954 with a role on *The Web*. During the 1950s he worked on *Kraft Television Theater*, *Big Story*, *Matinee Theater*, *Have Gun-Will Travel*, and *Gunsmoke*. His later television appearances include *M*A*S*H*, *Lou Grant*, *Quincy*, *Eight Is Enough*, *Police Woman*, and *Kojak*, as well as the television specials *Amelia Earhart* and *The Red Badge of Courage*.

When Aidman moved to Hollywood, he helped found Theater West with Curt Conway and Joyce Van Patten. His versatility was legendary. He played every type of role, but the ones that suited him best were those requiring a quiet strength, sincerity, and humility. He was described as having an "everyman" personality. He was never a regular on any television series, although he did have a recurring role in *Wild, Wild West*, when he filled in while Ross Martin was recovering from a heart attack. In the 1985–86 season he was the narrator for the new *Twilight Zone*. He was in demand for his voice talent, narrating commercials for U.S. Air, Toyota, Minolta, American Airlines, and others.

In 1981 Aidman starred as George Shearer, the defense lawyer who fights for the freedom of several Chicanos unjustly accused of

Charles Aidman.

murder in the 1940s. The play was entitled *Zoot Suit* and opened on the Mark Taper Forum's Center Theater stage. It ran thirty-eight weeks in Los Angeles before going to Broadway. His costars in the play were Edward James Olmos and Tyne Daly. The play was filmed in 1981.

Aidman married actress/choreographer Betty Hyatt Linton on February 9, 1969. He said, "My wife, for me at least, is as tough a critic as I know." In person he was much like the roles he played. He was a soft-spoken man who felt that the most important part of being an actor was always working at it. While on stage, he had no problems with his early shyness: "When you are in character, you are no longer yourself so the shyness is gone." Aidman always enjoyed appearing on stage, saying, "I used to make it an absolute rule that I had to be on the stage at least once a year no matter what it cost me." He died in Beverly Hills of cancer on November 7, 1993. He was survived by his wife and stepson, Chuck.

BIBLIOGRAPHY

Los Angeles Herald Examiner, October 27, 1982.

Stages. (Fall/Winter 1994).

Variety. November 8, 1993.

Ward, Jack. *The Supporting Players of Television, 1959–1983.* Cleveland, Okla.: Lakeshore West Publishing Company, 1996.

"Zoot Suit." Press Release. Universal News, September 4, 1981. Academy of Motion Picture Arts and Sciences Library, Beverly Hills, California.

LEON AMES

The son of Russian immigrants Charles and Cora Waycoff, Leon Waycoff was born in Portland, Indiana, on January 20, 1902. A few years after his birth, his parents moved to Delphi, Indiana, where he finished school. He briefly attended Indiana University and worked at such diverse jobs as shoe salesman and barnstorming flyer. In 1925 he started to train as an actor with the Champlin Players, a repertory company in Langsford, Pennsylvania.

He was busy in theater from the beginning, appearing first in summer stock, then on the road with a number of plays. In 1931 he was given a screen test at Universal opposite a then-unknown Bette Davis. His debut film was *Quick Millions* in 1931. It was a small role, but his next film, *Murders in the Rue Morgue*, saw him as Pierre Dupin, Edgar Allan Poe's medical student/detective who solved the murders committed by the mad doctor (played by Bela Lugosi). In it he was billed as Leon Waycoff, and in fact he used his real name in all of his roles until 1935. After *Murders in the Rue Morgue*, his film career took off, and he appeared in ten films in 1932. Despite the fact he was now a busy film actor, he made his Broadway debut in 1933 with fellow Hoosier Martin Burton in *It Pays to Sin.* He appeared in eleven Broadway plays from 1933 to 1958, starring with such other Hoosiers as Richard Barbee and Will Geer.

Leon Ames.
METRO-GOLDWYN-MAYER

In 1938 Ames was chosen to play Louis Napoleon in *Suez*, a spectacular film starring Tyrone Power and Annabella. While working in this film, he met actress Christine Gossett. They were married on June 25, 1938. They had a daughter, Shelley, in 1941 and a son, Leon Jr., in 1944. By the late 1930s Ames was greatly in demand as a supporting actor, first as a dapper man-about-town and later as a good-natured father figure.

Although he was a busy actor most of the time, he later said he believed none of his films were very good. The one exception was *Meet Me in St. Louis* (1944), in which he played the father of a family that boasted Judy Garland, Lucille Bremer, Joan Carroll, and Margaret O'Brien as his daughters and Mary Astor as his wife. Fellow Hoosier Marjorie Main played the spinster maid. Ames was supposed to sing a duet with Astor in this film, but his voice was not deemed good enough. Arthur Freed, who cowrote the song ("You and I"), did the dubbing himself. Director Vincente Minnelli said, "I didn't want a pure singer's voice. I asked Arthur if he would dub the singing for Leon Ames. His sweet croak was perfect." Ames always said this film was his favorite.

In 1946 Ames was cast along with three other Hoosiers in *The Show-Off*. Red Skelton was the star and supporting him were Ames, Main, and Marilyn Maxwell. He appeared in two other Skelton films, *Merton of the Movies* in 1947 and *Watch the Birdie* in 1950. In all, he made more than 127 feature films from 1931 to 1986.

As his career began to wane, television was picking up steam. Ames starred in two series, *Life with Father* from 1953 to 1955, and *Father of the Bride* from 1961 to 1962. He also had a recurring role as the next-door neighbor on *Mr. Ed* from 1963 to 1965. Fellow Hoosier Allan "Rocky" Lane provided the voice of Mr. Ed.

He often stated that his real love was the New York stage. He was especially proud of playing with Henry Hull in *Tobacco Road*. His big Broadway hit was *The Male Animal*, in which he originated the role of the football hero. *Guest in the House* in 1942 was another of his Broadway successes. One of his biggest disappointments was when he had to turn down the role of Doc in the Broadway production of *Come Back Little Sheba*. His studio, MGM, refused to release him.

Ames was a founder of the Screen Actors Guild and served as its president for two terms in 1957 and 1958. He remained active in the organization as president emeritus. He also served as director of the Motion Picture Relief Fund. In addition to the two television shows in which he was a regular, he made frequent appearances on programs such as *The Beverly Hillbillies*, *The Andy Griffith Show*, *Bewitched*, and *Name of the Game*. In 1965 he took early retirement from films but came back in 1970 and remained active in his eighties. His last film was *Peggy Sue Got Married* in 1986, in which he played Kathleen Turner's grandfather and Maureen O'Sullivan played his wife.

Following retirement, Ames's income was supplemented by earnings from a Ford automobile dealership he had purchased during his movie years. He was known for his frugality and once said, "Don't lend your friends money, or they won't stay your friends. Unhappily we don't choose our relatives. So don't lend them money—they'll still be your relatives and if you're a celebrity, your friends and relatives will interpret the word 'loan' to mean 'give.'"

Leon Jr. runs an automobile agency in Abilene, Texas, and Shelley is an executive with Walt Disney Studios. Ames died of a stroke at age ninety-one on October 12, 1993, in Laguna Beach, California.

BIBLIOGRAPHY

Donnelly, Paul. *Fade to Black: A Book of Movie Obituaries.* London: Omnibus Press, 2000.

Fordin, Hugh. *The World of Entertainment! Hollywood's Greatest Musicals.* New York: Avon Books, 1975.

Indiana Biographical Dictionary: People of All Times and All Places Who Have Been Important to the History of the State. New York: Somerset, 1993.

The Internet Movie Database. http://www.imdb.com/.

Lamparski, Richard. *Whatever Became Of . . . ?* 8th ser. New York: Crown Publishers, 1982.

Minnelli, Vincente. *I Remember It Well.* Garden City, N.Y.: Doubleday, 1974.

Quinlan, David. *Quinlan's Illustrated Directory of Film Character Actors.* London: B. T. Batsford, 1995.

CHARLES ARNT

Charles Arnt was born in Michigan City, Indiana, on August 20, 1906. He was the son and grandson of bankers in his hometown. He finished high school in Indiana and enrolled

Carole Lombard (Fort Wayne), Charles Arnt, and Fred MacMurray in *Swing High, Swing Low* (1937).

at Princeton University, majoring in geological engineering. While at Princeton he became interested in the theater and was elected president of the Triangle Club.

Arnt's big break was a featured role on the New York stage opposite Walter Huston in *Knickerbocker Holiday*. His facial characteristics and his expertise in makeup gave him an opportunity to play older men and eccentrics, and he was usually cast as a reporter, train conductor, doctor, or mayor.

Arnt became a very busy character actor, appearing in more than one hundred films in a career running from 1933 to 1962, including a nice supporting role opposite fellow Hoosier Carole Lombard in 1937 in *Swing High, Swing Low*. With the advent of television, he played the same type of characters in such shows as *Maverick*, *The Rifleman*, and *Zane Grey Theater*. He died August 6, 1990, in Orcas Island, Washington.

BIBLIOGRAPHY

Chaneles, Sol, and Albert Wolsky, eds. *The Movie Makers*. Secaucus, N.J.: Derbibooks, 1974.

The Internet Movie Database. http://www.imdb.com/.

Manny, Carter. Interview with the author. March 30, 2003. Michigan City, Indiana.

Twomey, Alfred E., and Arthur F. McClure. *The Versatiles: A Study of Supporting Actors and Actresses in American Motion Pictures, 1930–1955*. New York: Castle Books, 1969.

JAMES BASKETT

James Baskett (sometimes credited as James Baskette or Jimmie Baskette) scored a lot of firsts as one of Hollywood's early prominent black actors. He was born in Indianapolis, Indiana, on February 16, 1904. He at first had ambitions to be a pharmacist, but as a teenager he was called upon to replace an ailing friend in a show. This show took him to Chicago, where he joined fellow Hoosiers Salem Tutt Whitney and J. Homer Tutt and began taking bit parts in anything available on the stage. He was in Connie's *Hot Chocolates* and Lew Leslie's *Blackbirds*. He joined the Lafayette Players Stock Company and went to New York City, where he became one of the featured performers in the company. Later he became a member of the Bill "Bojangles" Robinson troupe in New York.

In the 1920s and early 1930s Baskett was a very busy actor, appearing mostly in musicals and starring in black shows. He was in such productions as *Go Get 'Em* (1926), *Fancy Trimmings* (1928), *The Toy Boat* (1930), *Goin' to Town* (1934), and *Lucky Me* (1935). He was also in the New York stage production of *The Green Pastures* as The Lord, replacing Richard B. Harrison. During the 1930s he appeared as an actor in the following black films: *Harlem Is Heaven* (1932), with Bill Robinson and Eubie Blake; *Policy Man* (1938), featuring the Count Basie orchestra; *Straight to Heaven* (1939), with Nina Mae McKinney; *Gone Harlem* (1939), with Ethel Moss; and *Comes Midnight* (1940), with Eddie Green and Amanda

Glenn Leedy, James Baskett, and Bobby Driscoll (left to right) in *Song of the South* (1946).

Randolph. In 1943 he played Lazarus in the film *Revenge of the Zombies*, starring John Carradine and Gale Storm.

In 1944 Baskett was hired by Freeman Gosden and Charles Correll to play the fast-talking lawyer Gabby Gibson on the hit radio series *Amos 'n Andy*. Gosden and Correll, impressed with his talent and his virtuosity, asked him to play other parts on the show. He was the dignified Reverend Johnson and played supporting roles such as storekeepers and cops.

In a January 1946 episode, when Gosden was hospitalized with a sinus infection, Baskett had a very prominent role, as Gibson helped Andy search for "the missing Amos." Baskett also sang "Zip a Dee Doo Dah," from *Song of the South*, during this broadcast. He was a regular on the show from 1944 to 1948.

In 1945 Baskett answered an ad to provide a voice for a talking butterfly in *Song of the South*. After hearing his voice, Disney wanted to meet him personally. Not only did he get the part of the butterfly's voice but also the voice of Br'er Fox and the leading part of Uncle Remus. He was so versatile he even filled in for Johnny Lee, who was the voice of Br'er Rabbit in the "Laughing Place" sequence, when Lee was called away on a USO tour.

Gosden and Correll knew that Baskett was suffering from a severe form of heart disease and did not have long to live. They joined with

Disney to campaign for a special Oscar on his behalf. Baskett was given a special Oscar for his performance at the Academy ceremonies in April 1948. Jean Hersholt and Ingrid Bergman presented him with his statuette. The inscription read, "To James Baskett for his able and heart-warming characterization of Uncle Remus, friend and story teller to the children of the world, in Walt Disney's 'Song of the South.'"

Before Baskett was able to capitalize on his newfound fame, he died of a heart attack at his home in Hollywood on July 10, 1948, barely three months after receiving his Oscar. He was survived by his widow Margaret and his mother, Mrs. John Woolridge. He was cremated, and the ashes were buried in Crown Hill Cemetery in Indianapolis beside the body of his father.

BIBLIOGRAPHY

The African American Registry. http://www.aaregistry.com/.

Banta, Ray. *Indiana's Laughmakers: The Story of Over Four Hundred Hoosiers; Actors, Cartoonists, Writers, and Others.* Indianapolis: PennUltimate Press, 1990.

Bogle, Donald. *Blacks in American Films and Television: An Encyclopedia.* New York: Simon and Schuster, 1989.

Guerrero, Ed. *Framing Blackness: The African American Image in Film.* Philadelphia: Temple University Press, 1993.

Indianapolis Recorder, April 3, July 17, 1948.

The Internet Movie Database. http://www.imdb.com/.

New York Times, July 10, 1948.

Osborne, Robert. *Sixty Years of the Oscar: The Official History of the Academy Awards.* New York: Abbeville Press, 1989.

Sampson, Henry T. *Blacks in Black and White: A Source Book on Black Films.* 2nd ed. Metuchen, N.J.: Scarecrow Press, 1995.

———. *Blacks in Blackface: A Source Book on Early Black Musical Shows.* Metuchen, N.J.: Scarecrow Press, 1980.

Scene from *Fashions in Love* (1929) with (left to right) Adolphe Menjou, Miriam Seegar (Greentown), Russ Powell (Indianapolis), and Billie Bennett.
PHOTO BY PHILIP CAMMARATA, NEW YORK

BILLIE BENNETT

Billie Bennett was born Emily B. Mulhausen in Evansville, Indiana, on October 23, 1874. She began with small roles in films in 1914. One notable appearance was with Charlie Chaplin in 1914 in *Tillie's Punctured Romance.* Fellow Hoosier Charlie Murray was also in this film. In 1916 she began appearing in Mack Sennett's two-reel comedies. Her first two films with Sennett were *His Last Laugh* and *Hearts and Sparks.* She started making feature films in 1917 and made thirty-one films through 1930. She was a stage actress for years before she began to appear in motion pictures. She was forty-three years old when she made her first film, so it was only natural that she would be a character actress. Bennett played mostly mothers and, on a couple occasions, an aunt.

She appeared in at least ten Westerns, playing opposite such stars as Tom Tyler, Franklyn Farnum, and Blanche Sweet. One of Bennett's last films was *Fashions in Love* (1929), which starred Adolphe

Menjou and Greentown, Indiana, native Miriam Seegar. Bennett played the caretaker wife of J. Russell Powell, who was a native of Indianapolis.

She died May 19, 1951, in Los Angeles, California.

BIBLIOGRAPHY

The Internet Movie Database. http://www.imdb.com/.

Katchmer, George. "Forgotten Cowboys and Cowgirls." *Classic Images* 182 (August 1990).

JOHN BROMFIELD

John Bromfield in the television series *Sheriff of Cochise* (1956–58).

Shortly after the turn of the century, Cecil Brumfield and Martha Toner were married in Acton, Indiana, the hometown of the bride. The minister who performed the ceremony was the Reverend Samuel Joseph Tomlinson. One of those present at the ceremony was Tomlinson's daughter, Mary. Some time later Mary changed her name to Marjorie Main.

Many years later in California, Cecil and Martha's son, actor John Bromfield (somewhere along the way, the *u* in Brumfield was changed to an *o*), made an appearance in a parade and met Main, who was in the same parade. He told her that her father had married his parents and that she was present at the wedding. Bromfield said, "She told me she remembered that wedding. She got a big kick out of that."

Bromfield's father and mother set up housekeeping in Cecil's hometown of Pittsboro, Indiana. When Cecil had an opportunity to have his own grain elevator business in South Bend, the family moved there. Martha was an asthmatic, and shortly after the birth of their first son it was discovered that he also suffered from asthma. The asthmatic condition led to his death as a child. When their second son, Farron McClain Brumfield, was born in South Bend, Indiana, on June 11, 1922, Martha was determined not to let him suffer the same fate. She and two-year-old Farron moved to Venice, California. Her condition improved, and she enjoyed California so much she told her husband she was never coming back to Indiana. Cecil sold his business and joined his wife and son in California.

Farron grew up in Venice, playing beach football, swimming, body surfing, and fishing with his father. He graduated from Westminster Grammar School and entered Venice High School, where he was an All-Western end on the football team. He also boxed for the Venice Athletic Club. During summer vacations he worked on local commercial boats, hauling in tuna and mackerel nets.

Bromfield's prowess in football brought offers from several universities, and he finally chose St. Mary's College in Moraga, California. He wanted to be a coach and majored in physical education. By his sophomore year, he was the starting left end on the football team. He also joined the boxing team, on which he won a Golden Gloves Boxing Award. On summer vacations, he earned extra money fishing. He said, "My summer vacations were spent on tuna clippers on the deep Mexican waters out of San Diego. The work kept me in shape, and the pay was not bad!" He also found work fishing off the banks of Malibu for soupfin shark.

While in college he met and married his first wife, Grace Landes. After graduating from St. Mary's in 1944, his love of fishing led him to become a full-time fisherman. He said, "The sea was for me." One day in 1947 he was patching some shark gear on a pier when three men approached him about making a documentary film to be shot in the Bering Strait at Wales, Alaska. The men were producers and wanted him to live with Eskimos for five months while making a movie about whaling. He told them he would think about it and went home and told his parents. His father was involved as an actor in community theaters and encouraged his son to accept the offer. Bromfield went back to the men and signed a contract for the film.

While living with the Eskimos, Bromfield hand-harpooned two whales. The name of the documentary was *Harpoon*, and it was released in 1948. In 1972 Richard Paul, president of the New Bedford Port Society, told the *New York Times*, "He [Bromfield] is our only living member who has harpooned a whale by hand, and I would say that in all the world you'd have trouble finding more than a handful of men who have done so."

Bromfield had no intention of ever acting again, but producer Hal Wallis saw *Harpoon* and offered him a two-year contract. He was sent to the David Selznick Studio drama school. He changed his name to John and soon was cast in *Sorry, Wrong Number* (1948), starring Barbara Stanwyck. He appeared in two other films with Stanwyck, *The File on Thelma Jordon* (1950) and *The Furies* (1950). He endeared himself to science fiction fans by appearing in *Revenge of the Creature* (1955) and *Curucu, Beast of the Amazon* (1956).

Bromfield worked steadily through the 1950s in both feature films and television. In 1956 he signed with Desilu Productions to star in his own television series, *Sheriff of Cochise*. He made seventy-eight half-hour episodes between 1956 and 1958. When the series ended, he was asked to do another series, this time switching from Sheriff Frank Morgan to U.S. Marshal Frank Morgan. The series was called *U.S. Marshal*. During his film and television career, Bromfield had the opportunity to work with many other Hoosiers, including Beulah Bondi, James Best, Claude Akins, and Charles Aidman.

When *U.S. Marshal* ended, he went to the producer of the series, Lucille Ball, and told her he was going to quit the profession. Ball asked what he would do, and Bromfield replied, "I'm going back to the boats and be a fisherman again. That's what I want to do in life." Bromfield was never a dedicated actor. He said, "When I wasn't shooting, I was signing autographs, posing for pictures, or riding a horse in some damn rodeo. I had done very well financially and wanted some time for myself."

After divorcing his first wife, Bromfield married actress Corinne Calvet, then Larri Thomas. In 1963 he met a singer/dancer named Mary Ellen Tillotson, and she became his fourth wife in May of that year. They moved to Newport Beach, California, and lived there on the water, with John deep-sea fishing from his boat. After fourteen years, their land was sold to build condos, so they moved to Costa Mesa. Finally they decided they wanted back on the water again, and in 1992 they moved to Lake Havasu, Arizona. Bromfield was back in Indiana at least twice. In 1948 he visited relatives in South Bend. He went back to South Bend in the 1970s and then made a trip to Pittsboro to see the old homestead where his mother and father started housekeeping. He said, "It was still standing." He and Mary have been married more than forty years. In 2003 Bromfield was suffering from the early stages of Alzheimer's and Parkinson's diseases. He died September 18, 2005, in Palm Desert, California, of kidney failure.

BIBLIOGRAPHY

Bromfield, John and Mary. Telephone interview with the author. October 7, 2003.

The Internet Movie Database. http://www.imdb.com/.

Jessings, Jeff. "Between the Devil and the Deep: John Bromfield." *Scarlet Street* 46 (2002).

Lamparski, John. *Lamparski's Whatever Became of . . . ?* 1st ser. New York: Bantam Books, 1976.

AVERY BROOKS

"A brilliant actor, a magnificent singer, and a fiery political activist." This is a fitting description, not only for Avery Brooks, but also for the American icon he has portrayed in *Paul Robeson*, a biographical drama about the life of the great singer, actor, athlete, and social crusader.

Avery Franklin Brooks was born on October 2, 1949, in Evansville, Indiana. When he was eight, his family moved to Gary, where he grew up. He attended Oberlin College, Indiana University, and later, Rutgers University, where he was the first black MFA graduate in acting and directing. He has been a tenured professor of theater at Rutgers's Mason Gross School of the Arts for more than fifteen years.

Brooks comes from a musically talented family. His maternal grandfather, Samuel Travis Crawford, was a tenor who graduated from Tougaloo College in Mississippi in 1901. Crawford toured the country, singing with the Delta Rhythm Boys in the 1930s. Using the talent passed down to him, Brooks plays jazz piano and has sung in several major theatrical productions.

Brooks has been portraying Robeson since 1982, when he was first cast in the title role of the Phillip Hayes Dean play, *Paul Robeson*. This is a solo play with music. Brooks not only acts and delivers Robeson's most famous lines, from his portrayal of Othello to his political speeches, but he also sings several songs, including Robeson's signature "Ol' Man River." Brooks has subsequently appeared in this play at the Kennedy Center in Washington, D.C., and the Longacre Theater on Broadway. He also portrayed Robeson in *Are You Now or Have You Ever Been?* both on and off Broadway.

Brooks has played Shakespeare's Othello at the Folger Theater in Washington, D.C., and his role as Uncle Tom in Showtime's production of *Uncle Tom's Cabin* garnered him a cable Ace nomination. He has been the host of several documentaries, including *Marian Anderson* and *The Musical Legacy of Roland Hayes.*

Brooks was cast as Captain Benjamin Sisko, the Starfleet captain in charge of the space station in *Star Trek: Deep Space Nine.* He also served

Avery Brooks as Captain Benjamin Sisko in *Star Trek: Deep Space Nine* (1998). ©1998, PARAMOUNT PICTURES CORP.

as the director of several of the episodes. His voice is in great demand for narrative assignments. He was the narrator for such specials as *Africa's Elephant Kingdom* (1998), *Walking with Dinosaurs* (1999), and *Jesus, the Complete Story* (2001). He was one of the narrative voices in Ken Burns's documentary *Jazz* (2001).

In September 2000 Brooks returned to his native state, appearing in the Robeson play at the Walker Theater in Indianapolis. While in the city, he also made a guest appearance with jazz vocalist Mary Moss at the Walker Center's Jazz on the Avenue.

Brooks's awards and honors are many. He served as the National Black Arts Festival's artistic director throughout the 1990s in Atlanta, Georgia. He was given an honorary doctorate in fine arts from Oberlin College in 1996 and has received the NAACP Image Award.

About his work, Brooks has said, "If I were a carpenter, I'd find a way to empower using that skill. I'm using as much as God has given . . . my mind, my voice, my heart, my art forms. This is the highest form of expression on the planet from God, to me, to you."

BIBLIOGRAPHY

"Avery Brooks as Paul Robeson." *Indianapolis Monthly* (September 2000).

Indianapolis Star, September 17, 2000.

The Internet Movie Database. http://www.imdb.com/.

Star Trek: Deep Space Nine. http://www.startrek.com/startrek/view/series/DS9/cast/69054.htm.

The Sisko: The Unofficial Fan Page of Avery Brooks. http://www.geocities.com/Area51/Hollow/3259.

Kathleen Burke and Gary Cooper in *The Lives of a Bengal Lancer* (1935).
©1935, PARAMOUNT PICTURES CORP.

KATHLEEN BURKE

Kathleen Burke was the winner of a nationwide talent search by Paramount Studios, the likes of which was not seen again until David O. Selznick embarked upon his hunt for Scarlett O'Hara. The purpose of the contest was to find a young beauty to play the Panther Woman in the 1933 film version of the H. G. Wells novel *The Island of Dr. Moreau*. Burke won over sixty thousand other young women.

Burke was born in Hammond, Indiana, on September 5, 1913. She attended elementary school in Hammond and high school at Chicago's Waller High School. After high school, she was a copywriter for a Chicago advertising agency and a part-time model. She was working as a dentist's assistant when she heard about the contest and decided to enter.

Island of Lost Souls was a science-fiction tale that starred Charles Laughton as the sadistic Doctor Moreau and featured Richard Arlen and Bela Lugosi in supporting roles. Indianapolis native Monte Blue was also in this film, and Alan Ladd and Randolph Scott were unbilled extras. The film was a success thanks to Laughton's over-the-top portrayal of Moreau and the horrific makeup. Interestingly, the film was banned in Laughton's native country, England, as being "against the laws of nature." Burke gave a sensuous portrayal of a woman-beast hybrid. It was her best role.

After this film, Burke made only two major films. She was the top-billed woman in the 1935 film, *The Lives of a Bengal Lancer*, opposite Gary Cooper. Again Monte Blue had a featured role in this film. She played opposite Cary Grant in *The Last Outpost*, which was also released in 1935. Her last film was *Rascals*, released in 1938. Burke's movie career ended after only six years.

In 1965 she returned to Chicago, where she lived near the New Town area until her death on April 9, 1980. Her husband, Forrest Smith, survived her as did her daughter, Antonia Torres, and her mother, Eulalia.

BIBLIOGRAPHY

The Internet Movie Database. http://www.imdb.com/.

Jewell, James C. "Kathleen Burke: The Panther Woman." *The World of Yesterday* (February 1982).

LOIS BUTLER

Lois Butler was born in Indianapolis on February 13, 1931. When she was two and a half years old, she began taking dancing lessons from Jack Broderick in Indianapolis. When she was five years old, she sang in a recital at the Zaring Theater and "brought the house down." Broderick told Butler's mother, "If I were in your place, I'd take that child to Hollywood where she belongs, if I had to borrow the money to do it." That is exactly what happened. She borrowed money for train fare and headed to Los Angeles with five-year-old Lois in 1936.

Once in Hollywood, Lois and her mother rented a room, got a guidebook, and headed for the studios. She had no luck. She enrolled Lois in a talent school for children. In six weeks the money ran out. Lois's father, Fred J. Butler, was employment manager for P. R. Mallory Company until he became a building contractor. He decided to join his wife in Los Angeles and seek employment there as a builder. Shortly thereafter, they sent for their other children, who were staying with relatives in Indianapolis.

As their situation improved, the Butlers hired better voice and dancing coaches for Lois. They visited every studio dozens of times. Finally, they had a glimmer of hope when Lois was cast opposite Bobby Breen in a film called *Hawaii Calls*. Unfortunately, the picture was canceled. In 1939 Lois made her first film, *The Star Maker*, with Bing Crosby. She was part of a trio called The Sunbonnet Sue Trio, which appeared in the film. She was not able to get another film role for six more years, though Lois and her mother never wavered from her determination to get that "lucky break."

During the summer of 1946, the new Eagle-Lion Studio held a call for extras and bit players for a projected film, *Hollywood Hi*. Lois stood in line with one hundred other young hopefuls while director Benny Rubin looked them over. "We're going to have a school vaudeville show in the picture," Rubin said. "So if any of you have a

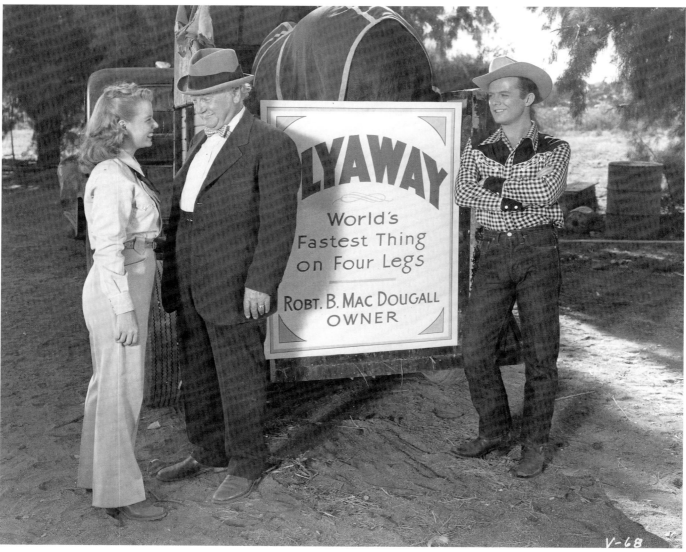

Lois Butler, George Cleveland (left), and Lon McAllister in *The Boy from Indiana* (1950).

NATIONAL SCREEN SERVICE CORP.

specialty, trot it out." After several young people displayed their "specialties," Lois asked, "May I sing?" She sang "If You Were the Only Boy in the World," and within half a minute there was no sound on the big stage except Lois's voice. In another minute, Rubin was on the phone talking with the head of the studio, saying, "There's an angel singing here on stage C. Come on over." Within hours, the wheels were put in motion to sign Lois to a contract.

Butler was now a fifteen-year-old high school sophomore. The contract stipulated she must maintain a B-plus grade average to maintain her $200 a week salary. She had additional perks in the contract that could raise her salary to $3,000 per week. The studio put her in training to be the lead in a film called *Mickey*. Coincidentally, the film was based on Bluffton, Indiana, native Peggy Goodin's novel, *Clementine*. Goodin was just twenty-two years old and had written the novel while a student at the University of Michigan.

Unfortunately, Butler's career did not take off after *Mickey*. She costarred with Lon McAllister in *The Boy from Indiana* in 1950 and was featured in *High Lonesome*, also in 1950. After three films, her career in movies was finished. She appeared in a television series, *The RCA Victor Show*, starring Ezio Pinza in 1951. She made appearances with Nelson Eddy, Perry Como, and the Los Angeles Philharmonic Orchestra, but she never made another motion picture.

Perhaps one of the reasons her career did not advance more was because she met producer/writer Hall Bartlett, and they were married in Brentwood on May 27, 1950. Bartlett's present to his eighteen-year-old wife was a new ranch home in Palisades, California.

BIBLIOGRAPHY

Indianapolis News, April 1, June 3, 1950.
Indianapolis Star, February 9, 1947, January 13, July 4, 1948.
The Internet Movie Database. http://www.imdb.com/.

CHARLES BUTTERWORTH

Charles Edward "Charlie" Butterworth started out to be a journalist, but like his friend and fellow Notre Dame student, Ralph Dumke, he turned to acting and became a successful comedian. He was born in South Bend, Indiana, on July 26, 1899, and graduated from law school there in 1924. He passed the bar soon after but decided he was not suited for the legal profession and took a job as a newspaper reporter with the *South Bend Times.* Things were moving slowly, so Butterworth decided he would do the paper a service by reporting the death of one of South Bend's leading citizens—a death based on a grossly exaggerated rumor. He was promptly terminated. He moved to New York and got into vaudeville while reporting for the *New York Times.*

Charles Butterworth.
PHOTO BY ELMER FRYER, HOLLYWOOD

While with the *Times*, he was drafted for a comedy role in a Press Club show. His "Luncheon Club Speech" was a hilarious satire of the average luncheon speaker. He sent the speech and some other humorous material he had written to J. P. McEvoy, who was working on a revue called *Americana.* It was one of the first *Little Show* revues. McEvoy put Butterworth in it, and his speech was the hit of the show.

This gave Butterworth name recognition and eventually propelled him into acting in other Broadway revues. He appeared in several Broadway musicals, including *Allez-oop*, *Good Boy*, and *Sweet Adeline.* In *Sweet Adeline*, a 1929 musical with Jerome Kern tunes, Butterworth costarred with Helen Morgan, who sang the memorable Kern tune, "Why Was I Born?" In 1932 he appeared with fellow Hoosier Clifton Webb in the hit *Flying Colors.*

When *Sweet Adeline* closed, Butterworth signed a contract with Warner Brothers. He quickly became known for a character he created—a man who could not make up his mind, the vacillating, indecisive sort of follower-of-the-crowd. Twittering timidity and a doleful look were his trademarks. His uniquely nervous manner and dubious expression complemented his stuttering voice delivery.

Butterworth never married. Of marriage he said, "The whole thing is done with cleverly-arranged mirrors." Once, when asked about his health, he said, "I feel terrible most of the time. I have spots before my eyes, but perhaps no one has noticed them. My heart pounds rather badly after running up twelve flights of stairs."

In 1934 Gilbert Seldes, the noted film historian, expressed his delight with Butterworth:

Charles Butterworth gets his name in lights, of course, but he is always in support. He began thinking of a nice ear of sweet corn in

the midst of a sentimental solo years ago, and to all intents and purposes, he does it still. In "Bulldog Drummond Strikes Back" he was
the abstracted husband who tried to sidestep Ronald Colman's activities so that he could, with all propriety, get to bed . . . it being his
wedding night. He did it well. It may be only a fancy of mine that he
could do other things also.

Butterworth returned to his home state in 1940 to appear in
Father's Day on the Lyric Theater stage in Indianapolis. In 1942 he took
part in the USO show, *Flying High*, at Fort Benjamin Harrison. He
remained a popular supporting player throughout his career until his
untimely death in an automobile accident on June 13, 1946. He made
more than forty-five films, appearing with such stars as Bob Hope,
Fred Astaire, and fellow Hoosiers Irene Dunne and Carole Lombard.
With his feigned distracted air, he was one of the screen's best zanies.

BIBLIOGRAPHY

Banta, Ray. *Indiana's Laughmakers: The Story of Over Four Hundred Hoosiers;
Actors, Cartoonists, Writers, and Others.* Indianapolis: PennUltimate Press,
1990.
Quinlan, David. *Quinlan's Illustrated Directory of Film Character Actors.*
London: B. T. Batsford, 1995.
Twomey, Alfred E., and Arthur F. McClure. *The Versatiles: A Study
of Supporting Character Actors and Actresses in the American Motion Picture, 1930–
1955.* New York: Castle Books, 1969.

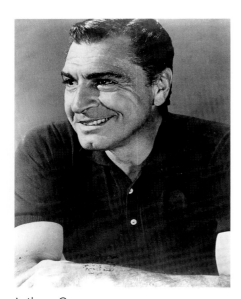

Anthony Caruso.

ANTHONY CARUSO

Born on April 7, 1916, in Frankfort, Indiana, Anthony Caruso
came from a large Italian family. He was the oldest of six children. His family moved to California when Anthony was ten
years old. He attended Long Beach Poly High School, where he first
met his good friend Robert Mitchum. After graduation from high
school in 1934, Caruso was a horseman and a boxer before he began
pursuing his ambition to become an actor. "It was just one of those
things I just had to do," he explained. "It wasn't even a matter of money
at the time, though we are talking about the Depression period. My
father worked in the produce business and always saw to it that we had
food on the table. So naturally he wanted me to follow him into the
same trade. However, when I told him I was going to be an actor, he
shook my hand and wished me, 'Good Luck.'"

Caruso's father even drove him to Pasadena to try out for the Pasadena Playhouse. While waiting his turn to perform, Caruso struck
up a conversation with the fellow next to him. When everyone broke
for lunch, Caruso invited the young man to come to lunch with them,
telling him, "My father will pay for it." Years passed, and Caruso was
doing a bit part in a film called *The Glass Key*. Unexpectedly, the star of
the film, Alan Ladd, called him into his dressing room. Ladd said,
"You don't know who I am do you?" Caruso said, "Sure, I do. You're
Alan Ladd, Paramount's new leading man." Ladd broke into a smile.

"I'm also the guy you and your father once treated to a lunch when I didn't know where my next meal was coming from." Ladd added, "If I can ever use you in any of my pictures, I will." Caruso said, "true to his word, he did . . . eleven more times."

Caruso won a scholarship to the Pasadena Playhouse and then went into stock playing juvenile leads. He then moved into radio and had a busy career there for several years. He had a nice voice and even considered a career as a singer. He made his movie debut in a supporting role in *Johnny Apollo* in 1940. Both he and Tyrone Power played gangsters. Power moved on to do a variety of other roles, but Caruso had found his niche, and he returned to that genre many times. He was much in demand starting in 1942, when he made five films. Throughout the 1940s, it was not unusual for Caruso to appear in five to eight films a year. He was under contract to Warner Brothers, but he was not happy, stating that, "Warners was notorious for signing people to long-term contracts and then refusing to raise their salaries." He decided to take a chance. "Finally I asked for my release . . . and got it. I didn't particularly want to return to free-lancing, but sometimes you get backed into a corner."

In 1951 Caruso appeared with his boyhood chum, Robert Mitchum, in *His Kind of Woman.* The script called for him to hit Mitchum in the stomach. Mitchum told him not to pull back and to make it look real. Caruso buried his fist in Mitchum's midriff, and everyone agreed it did indeed look real. Caruso's favorite film was *The Asphalt Jungle* (1950). He enjoyed working with John Huston on the film and suffered through several of Huston's practical jokes on the set.

In the 1950s Caruso began appearing in Westerns, playing mostly villains and Indians. Almost half of his films in that decade were Westerns. He worked with Ronald Reagan in *Tennessee's Partner* (1955) and *Cattle Queen of Montana* (1954). Caruso and his wife adopted two children and became active in working with adopted children. Because of his efforts with the Holy Family Adoption Services, he received a citation and a special letter from President Reagan.

In the 1960s and 1970s Caruso became actively involved in television and began making more television appearances than movies. When he was not acting, he enjoyed woodworking and carpentry projects of all kinds, and he built the house where he and his wife Tonia lived. Reflecting on his career, he said, "I've enjoyed my career in Hollywood and don't believe it was hindered by too many bad roles. People ask if I miss never having ended up with 'the girl.' Well, in the early days of playing gangsters, I had my gun molls and such. It's just that those relationships weren't very permanent. As a lawbreaker who has to pay for his misdeeds, I always got 'rubbed out' by the end of the last reel."

Caruso died in Brentwood, California, on April 4, 2003, after a long illness. He was survived by his wife of sixty-three years, former actress Tonia Valente, and their son, Tonio Caruso.

BIBLIOGRAPHY

Cullura, Joe. "Anthony Caruso, Hollywood Mobster." *Classic Images* 161 (November 1988).

Indianapolis Star, April 7, 2003.

Quinlan, David. *Quinlan's Illustrated Directory of Film Character Actors.* London: B. T. Batsford, 1985.

RUSSELL COLLINS

Scene from *Niagara* (1953) with (left to right) Russell Collins, Jean Peters, and Max Showalter.

Russell Collins was a very busy performer throughout his professional career, appearing in plays, films, and television productions. He was born in Indianapolis on October 11, 1897. He graduated from Manual Training High School, attended Indiana University, and then studied drama at Carnegie Tech in Pittsburgh. He studied voice with Glenn Friermood and at one time aspired to be a singer. He joined the Cleveland Playhouse in 1922 and became active in stock productions. In 1932 he joined the Group Theater in New York and made his Broadway debut that same year in *Success Story*.

In 1943 Collins returned to his hometown, appearing at the English Theater in *Tomorrow the World*. He made a return engagement at the English in 1950 in *The Ice Man Cometh*. He loved to return home to visit his relatives and visit his boyhood haunts.

Collins's mobile, pixielike face won him character roles in many major movies and kept him busy in television as well. He was a major player on the Broadway stage, appearing in forty roles, including that of the Starkeeper in *Carousel*. Other Broadway appearances included *The Ice Man Cometh*, *A View from the Bridge*, and *Sabrina Fair*. He also played Doc in the London production of *Mr. Roberts*, which starred Tyrone Power.

Collins was in twenty-two films from 1943 to 1965, usually playing crusty character parts. Notable films included *Raintree County*, *Bad Day at Black Rock*, *Niagara*, *Soldier of Fortune*, and *The Enemy Below*. In 1953 he won critical acclaim for his work in the role of the atheist in *The Chess Game*, an original teleplay for *Kraft Television Theater*. Referring to his many television appearances, he said, "I've played bums on Hitchcock's show so often, my friends don't recognize me with a shave." When asked about how a person can get into the movies, he said, "Young pretty girls always ask me if they could ever be in the movies. I tell them, 'You're pretty. Look at me. I'm ugly and I made it.'"

Collins died in West Hollywood on November 14, 1965.

BIBLIOGRAPHY

Indianapolis Star, October 21, 1943, February 24, 1953.
Indianapolis Times, May 27, 1957.
Jones, Ken D., Arthur McClure, and Alfred E. Twomey. *Character People*. South Brunswick, N.J.: A. S. Barnes, 1976.

JOE COOK

Joe Lopez Cook had a Spanish father and an Irish mother. Both parents were on the stage, but before Joe's birth, his father decided to take up portrait painting. He did it on a chain-store scale, with studios in Grand Rapids, Michigan, Chicago, and Pierceton, Indiana. Joe was born in Evansville on March 29, 1890. When he was just four years old, his father died in an accidental drowning. His mother went into shock and died shortly thereafter.

Joe and his brother were adopted by the Cook family in Evans-ville, who were distant relatives. Recalling his younger days in Evans-ville, he said, "We had the best back yard show in town then. Why we were charging them a nickel admission at a time when other kids in town were afraid to charge more than twelve pins. My foster father made me a pair of tights that I always wore under my clothes so that if the gang needed money I'd take off my outer garments and perform any place at all to pick up some change for the boys."

Cook made his first professional appearance when he was ten years old, receiving one dollar per night from Dr. Buckner's Corak Won-der Company's Show in Evansville. At the end of the summer, Doc still owed Cook two dollars, which he paid him in medication that was supposed to cure deafness. At age sixteen, Cook went to New York with his family and attended St. Francis Xavier Academy on Sixteenth Street. He had saved enough money to buy some Indian clubs and won an occasional five-dollar prize for his act with the clubs.

Finally, Cook got booked with The Juggling Barretts. Cook worked with his brother for a while, then decided to do a single in blackface. Cook also took up the ukulele, and in 1923 he attracted the attention of Earl Carroll, who featured him opposite Peggy Hopkins Joyce in the *Vanities*. Another edition of *Vanities* followed. It was a musi-cal comedy circus in which Cook played everything from ringmaster to a trained lion.

Joe Cook.
COURTESY OF THE ACADEMY OF MOTION PICTURE ARTS AND SCIENCES

About 1926 Marc Connelly, author of *The Green Pastures*, wrote a play called *How's the King?* It became Cook's first starring vehicle. Unfortu-nately, it never reached New York. However, in February 1928 Cook took New York by storm as the star of *Rain or Shine*, an uproariously funny musical comedy about circus life that ran for more than a year in New York. In 1930 *Rain or Shine* was transferred to the screen with Cook as the star. The film was directed by Frank Capra, and Cook's costar was Lafayette native, Louise Fazenda. He then went into the stage musical *Fine and Dandy* and followed that with another stage suc-cess, *Hold Your Horses*.

Cook was doing so well that he bought a large estate on Lake Hopatcong, a New Jersey vacation haven for burlesque performers. The summers there were happy ones, with cookouts almost every night and fishing and swimming during the day. Cook's dining room was like a Coney Island fun house, with chairs wired to give electric shocks and vents in the room to shoot jets of air up the women's skirts. He built a one-hole golf course that was designed so that anyone reach-ing the green would shoot a hole in one and owned one of the fast-est speedboats on the lake. He also displayed a collection of objects "smaller than a man's hand" hanging from the ceiling of his den.

Cook was a man of many talents. He could juggle in many ways, including foot juggling. He could do slack-wire walking, trapeze bal-ancing, and unsupported ladder antics, and he could propel a huge ball up a fifteen-foot incline with his foot and keep three hoops in motion atop a pole twenty feet in the air. He was a clog dancer, an acrobatic dancer, and an expert magician, and he could catch lighted candles with his mouth. He was known as "A One-Man Circus," with a stage persona once described as "contagious good-naturedness."

In 1930, while Cook was on Broadway with *Fine and Dandy*, he joined the Rudy Vallee radio program as a regular guest star. He continued to appear on the Vallee show through 1934. In 1930 he also started working with his announcer, John S. Young, as his straight man. He was the first Broadway comedian to use an announcer as his stooge. Cook was very busy in radio for several years. In 1934 and 1935 he was the headline star on the *Colgate House Party* on NBC, and in 1935 he headlined another radio series, *Circus Night in Silvertown*. From 1935 to 1937 he was a frequent guest star on the Al Jolson show, *Shell Chateau*, on the NBC Red network.

Unfortunately, Cook's success on the stage and in radio did not guarantee success in the movies. He did make some very good short subjects, especially those he made for Educational Pictures in the 1930s. Educational turned out a series of comedies featuring such stars as Milton Berle, Danny Kaye, and Buster Keaton. However, he made just two feature films: *Rain or Shine* (1930) and *Arizona Mahoney* (1936), in which he played the title role.

Cook's last stage appearance was in 1940 in *It Happened on Ice*. He was stricken with Parkinson's disease in 1942 and died on May 16, 1959, in Clinton Hollow, New York. His second wife, Alice Boulders Cook, survived him, as did four children by a previous marriage to Beatrice Helen Cook.

BIBLIOGRAPHY

Gilbert, Douglas. *American Vaudeville: Its Life and Times.* 1940. Reprint, New York: Dover Publications, 1968.

Indiana Biographical Dictionary: People of All Times and All Places Who Have Been Important to the History of the State. 2nd ed. 2 vols. St Clair Shores, Mich.: Somerset Publishers, 1999.

The Internet Movie Database. http://www.imdb.com/.

Joe Cook biography. Margaret Herrick Library. Academy of Motion Picture Arts and Sciences, Beverly Hills, Califronia.

Lackman, Ron. *The Encyclopedia of American Radio.* New York: Checkmark Books, 2000.

Lahr, John. *Notes on a Cowardly Lion: A Biography of Bert Lahr.* New York: Alfred A. Knopf, 1969.

Maltin, Leonard. *Selected Short Subjects: From Spanky to the Three Stooges.* 1972. Reprint, New York: Da Capo Press, 1983.

McLeod, Elizabeth. "Broadcast History Resources." http://www.midcoast.com/~lizmcl.

Annie Corley in *Free Willy 3: The Rescue* (1997).

©1997, WARNER BROS. PRODUCTIONS LIMITED, MONARCHY ENTERPRISES B. V. AND REGENCY ENTERTAINMENT U.S.A.

ANNIE CORLEY

Annie Corley was born and raised in Lafayette, Indiana. Her mother, Sarah Corley, is a native Hoosier, and her father was born in Illinois. Her parents divorced when she was very young, and her mother raised Annie and her brother, David. Annie graduated from McCutcheon High School in 1978. At McCutcheon she was very active in athletics and in speech, winning speech tournaments and traveling to the nationals twice.

Corley became interested in horses at an early age and won prizes for the horses she entered in Indiana State Fair contests. She wanted to be an actress, but her mother insisted she get a college education.

Corley was not too eager to go to college, but she came to love the experience. She obtained a scholarship to DePauw University, where she majored in speech communications and joined the Kappa Kappa Gamma sorority. Her work and her grades at DePauw helped her get a position as a "gopher" (or "slave," as she called it) at the Actors Studio in New York City. She was there one semester and then was invited back the following summer.

After receiving her degree cum laude from DePauw, Corley decided to move to New York. One of the few people she knew in New York who might help her was Dunreith, Indiana, native and fellow DePauw graduate, Gretchen Cryer, who is a successful actress and author. The two had dinner, and Cryer was extremely helpful in getting her started. Corley still found the going rough. She said, "This business is very hard. I spent a tough ten years working in restaurants and doing whatever theater I could get. But I held on and got lucky. I consider myself a workhorse actress."

Corley was in an off-Broadway play, and *New York* magazine gave the play and Corley a great review. This was the break that sent her to Los Angeles, where she became a busy television actress. In 1984 she made her first network television appearance in *Murder She Wrote*. She then began appearing on shows such as *L.A. Law*, *The Practice*, *NYPD Blue*, *Touched by an Angel*, and *The West Wing*. In 1992 she made her first feature film, *Malcolm X*, in which she played a television reporter.

Corley considers her biggest break to date as being cast by Clint Eastwood as Meryl Streep's daughter in *The Bridges of Madison County*. Since then, she says, she does "about two movies a year," along with television appearances. She played Coach Rivers in the basketball comedy *Juwanna Mann* in 2002, and she had a role in *Monster* in 2003.

Corley is still single and has finally been able to realize her dream, owning a house and land where she can have a horse. She moved to Norco, California, which is a "horse community." She said, "You can ride your horse everywhere, even to McDonald's. All the fast food places have corrals. I have five dogs, two cats, and a pregnant horse." Her love of horses worked very well for her when she landed the role of Mrs. Pollard in *Seabiscuit* (2003).

BIBLIOGRAPHY

Corley, Annie. Telephone interview with the author. September 29, 2003.

The Internet Movie Database. http://www.imdb.com/.

RICHARD CRANE

Richard Crane in *Wing and a Prayer* (1944).

Richard Crane, son of Otis O. and Edith Crane, was born in New Castle, Indiana, on June 6, 1918. He moved to California with his mother in the late 1930s. In 1940, while Crane was doing stock in Pasadena, director George Cukor spotted him and arranged a screen test. A week later the twenty-two year old landed his first role in a major MGM film, *Susan and God*. Fortunately, he had a nice part in the film that was directed by Cukor and starred Joan

Crawford, Fredric March, and Rita Hayworth. Crane's good looks and pleasant on-screen personality helped him keep busy in Hollywood during the war years, when most of Hollywood's leading men were in the service.

Although Crane worked at several studios, most of his career was spent at Twentieth Century Fox. He appeared in such features as *Bataan*, *Johnny Comes Flying Home*, *Eagle Squadron*, and *So Proudly We Hail!* The *Indianapolis Star* reported that he renewed his contract with Fox in 1944 at a substantial increase in salary. The renewal came as a result of his "excellent work in a forthcoming release, 'Wing and a Prayer,' starring Don Ameche."

After the war Crane's career began to wind down, and he began accepting parts in serials such as *Mysterious Island.* In 1953 he switched to television and was the star of a sci-fi television series, *Rocky Jones, Space Ranger. Rocky Jones* was a syndicated television series that took place one thousand years in the future. Crane flew through space in his "Orbit Jet" named The Silver Moon. His sidekick was former child star Scotty Beckett, and James Lydon was another regular on the series. A little more than thirty episodes were shot, and the series was off the air after just one season. Most early television series were shot live, and the only record of them is poor quality kinescope recordings. *Rocky Jones* was the first of its kind to be shot entirely on film. Today it enjoys a sort of cult status and is one of several early sci-fi series popular with a group calling themselves "The Space Rangers."

In 1961–62 Crane was Lieutenant Gene Plehan on television's *Surfside Six.* His face became very familiar to television viewers as he kept busy appearing on such shows as *77 Sunset Strip*, *Hawaiian Eye*, *Cheyenne*, *Perry Mason*, and *Maverick.* His last big-screen appearance was in *Surf Party* in 1964. Five years later he suffered a heart attack and died on March 9, 1969, at the age of fifty-one. He had appeared in more than fifty feature films and in countless television shows.

BIBLIOGRAPHY

All Movie Guide. http://www.allmovie.com/.

Henderson, Jan Alan. "United Planets Personnel." *Filmfax* 19 (March 1990).

Indianapolis Star, July 20, 1944.

The Internet Movie Database. http://www.imdb.com/.

The Space Patrol Web Site. http://www.solarguard.com/.

MARY JANE CROFT

Mary Jane Croft was born in Elwood, Indiana, in 1916 and first appeared on stage at Elwood High School. She received additional stage experience appearing in numerous Muncie Civic Theater productions and became very active in radio in the 1930s and 1940s. She appeared regularly on such network radio shows as *Blondie*, *The Mel Blanc Show*, *One Man's Family*, and *The Adventures of Ozzie and Harriet.* She began appearing on television in 1952 as Daisy Enright on *Our Miss Brooks.* She was also the voice of Cleo the basset hound on *The People's Choice* in 1955 and again when the show ran from 1956 to 1958.

When *The Adventures of Ozzie and Harriet* moved to television, Croft returned to her original radio role of Clara Randolph for the series, a role she played from 1956 to 1966. In 1956 she began appearing occasionally as Betty Ramsey in the original *I Love Lucy* series. One of the chief writers for the show was fellow Hoosier Madelyn Pugh Davis from Indianapolis. In May 1956 the *Lucy* episode, "Return Home from Europe," was aired. Croft appeared as a passenger sitting next to Lucy. She said, "It was not fun and games on the set. Lucy took her work very seriously. I had a hard time keeping a straight face, sitting next to her in the airplane set. When she took a swig of the baby formula, I had to look away. I really loved doing this episode."

Croft appeared semiregularly as Mary Jane Lewis in *The Lucy Show* from 1965 to 1974. In 1968, when the show switched titles and became *Here's Lucy*, Croft appeared again as the next door neighbor Mary Jane Lewis, which was her married name. She was married to Elliot Lewis, a mystery novelist, actor, and one of the show's producers. In this series she essentially took the place of Vivian Vance as Lucy's coconspirator. However, she did not appear regularly in this role until 1971. She said, "I don't know why they didn't use me more during the first couple of years after 'The Lucy Show' ended. I guess the writers just didn't think of me." The 1971 episode, "Lucy's Bonus Bounces," solidified her role as a regular. "From this point forward, I was asked to perform much more often," she recalled.

At the time of Croft's death, she was a widow. Her only child, Eric Zoller, was killed in the Vietnam War. She died on August 24, 1999.

Mary Jane Croft.

BIBLIOGRAPHY

Brooks, Tim, and Earle Marsh. *The Complete Directory of Prime Time Network TV Shows, 1946–Present.* 2nd rev. ed. New York: Ballantine Books, 1981.

Buxton, Frank, and Bill Owen. *The Big Broadcast, 1920–1950.* New York: Viking Press, 1972.

Fidelman, Geoffrey Mark. *The Lucy Book: A Complete Guide to Her Five Decades on Television.* Los Angeles: Renaissance Books, 1999.

What a Character! http://www.what-a-character.com/.

SCATMAN CROTHERS

Benjamin Sherman Crothers was born in Terre Haute, Indiana, on May 23, 1910. His father, also named Benjamin, operated a secondhand clothing store. After graduating from the eighth grade, Crothers entered Wiley High School.

Terre Haute was close enough to Indianapolis and Chicago to be on the major vaudeville circuits. Most of the big bands also came through Terre Haute to play. Those included Fletcher Henderson, Count Basie, and Duke Ellington.

Crothers began to entertain around town for the Elks, the Kiwanis, and other groups. Finally he was offered a job at a roadhouse in the red-light district. He played the drums and frequently would get up and sing and dance.

In 1929 Crothers left Terre Haute for Indianapolis. He could not find a job entertaining, so he took a job at Kingan's Packing Plant. After four or five months he headed for Chicago. The stock market had just crashed, and jobs were scarce. He came in contact with Montague's Kentucky Serenaders, a black band that had performed in Terre Haute. Montague hired him as an entertainer and director of the band. He also sang and acted as an emcee.

In 1931 Crothers went to Dayton, Ohio, where he was hired to do a fifteen-minute program five days a week. When asked what he wanted to be called, he said, "Call me Scat Man because I do quite a bit of scatting, what I call flirting with the melody." He later changed Scat Man to one word, Scatman. At age twenty-two, Crothers returned to Terre Haute and found that he was something of a celebrity. He was hired by WBOW radio and had his own program there for a while.

In 1936 Crothers met Helen Sullivan at a club in Canton, Ohio. They were married on July 15, 1937, in Cleveland. She was white. They had one child, Donna, born in 1948. Crothers used to say, "I did it before it was fashionable."

In 1948 Crothers was in Hollywood making the rounds of the clubs, and Eddie "Rochester" Anderson introduced him to Phil Harris of Linton, Indiana. As fellow Hoosiers, Harris and Crothers immediately had something in common. Harris recalled, "He was by himself, and he worked like a dog. He was doing scat songs and playing that little guitar of his, and he was very clever with it. He loved jokes, and everybody took to Scatman, everybody liked him."

In 1948 a friend called Harris and said he had written a song called "Chattanooga Shoe Shine Boy," and he wanted Harris and Crothers to record it. They agreed, and it was recorded by RCA Victor. Crothers provided the sound effects, popping the rag just as he had done to earn big tips in the old days. Harris and Crothers introduced the song on Harris's radio show, *The Phil Harris–Alice Faye Show.* Crothers began to get good notices. He also began to write original songs, which he performed.

The song with Harris and the appearance on radio brought increased bookings. In 1948 Crothers signed a contract with Capitol Records. He also began to make a few television appearances. His biggest break was an appearance on *The Colgate Comedy Hour* with Donald O'Connor. Crothers did so well that he became a regular on the show.

In 1951 Crothers was cast in a movie, *Yes Sir, Mr. Bones,* which led to his first feature role in a Hollywood film. The movie was *Meet Me at the Fair* (1953) and starred Dan Dailey, who had suggested Crothers for the role.

Early in 1974 Crothers auditioned for the role of Louie the garbageman in the television series, *Chico and the Man.* It was supposed to be just an occasional appearance, but he was so good that he became a regular. He wrote Louie's signature song himself. In 1979 Stanley Kubrick was casting the Stephen King thriller *The Shining.* Jack Nicholson was a good friend of Crothers, and he convinced Kubrick to give the part to Crothers. It was one of his best roles. After *The Shining* he make *Bronco Billy* (1980) with Clint Eastwood. It was one of his favorite roles.

In 1984 Crothers was featured on the *This Is Your Life* program hosted by Joseph Campanella. Terre Haute mayor Pete Chalos, high school teacher John Wesley Lyda, and old boyhood friend Demetrius Ewing were flown to Los Angeles for the show. Harris was also there, and

(Opposite page) Scatman Crothers.
©1978, COLUMBIA PICTURES INDUSTRIES, INC.

when he appeared Crothers and Harris broke into a duet of "Chattanooga Shoe Shine Boy."

In 1985 Crothers, a lifelong smoker, was diagnosed with lung cancer. The tumor was inoperable. When he was confined to a hospital, Harris visited. "I saw him when he was sick, when he went to the hospital, and then when he got out, I called him almost every day. He thought he was going to beat it, but it was in his throat." Crothers died on November 22, 1986. About three hundred mourners were at Forest Lawn Memorial Park the following Tuesday. Jack Nicholson recalled, "He had this saying: 'May you never die because I'm going to live forever.' He started today with his wish."

BIBLIOGRAPHY

Haskins, James, with Helen Crothers. *Scatman: An Authorized Biography of Scatman Crothers.* New York: William Morrow and Company, 1991.

The Internet Movie Database. http://www.imdb.com/.

Lucas, Bob. "Scatman Crothers: 56 Years of Show Biz, 44 Years of Marriage." *Jet*, June 11, 1981.

Quinlan, David. *Quinlan's Illustrated Directory of Film Character Actors.* London: B. T. Batsford, 1995.

JOHNNIE "SCAT" DAVIS

Johnnie Gustave "Scat" Davis did not have many options as far as a career was concerned. His grandfather was the director of the Royal British Navy Band and later was a pioneer director of the Brazil (Indiana) Concert Band, which was founded in 1863. His father, J. Gas Davis, who also led the Brazil Concert Band, could play all the instruments and was a gifted composer. An older brother, Nelson, was a trumpeter and the student leader of the Indiana University marching band, and his uncle, Charles Schmidt, was an accomplished pianist.

Davis was born in Brazil, Indiana, on May 11, 1910. He began cornet lessons at the age of three and a half and debuted at six, playing "America" with his grade school band. In 1924 he joined the Brazil Concert Band, and the next year his Uncle Charles helped him get a professional job with Jack O'Grady and the Varsity Entertainers at the Grand Opera House in Terre Haute, Indiana. Davis was too young to drive, so he arranged his schedule by taking morning classes at Brazil High School in order to make the bus to Terre Haute in the afternoon. He played for Paul Johnson's orchestra at the American Theater and for Len Baxter at the Liberty. Davis's younger brother, Art, also worked for Baxter.

When sound films became popular, Davis began playing one-night stands at the Trianon and Orpheum ballrooms in Terre Haute. He sometimes traveled to Greencastle, Bloomington, and Indianapolis. After graduation from Brazil High School in 1928, he joined Jimmy Joy's orchestra in Louisville, then played with Sammy Watkins's band in Cleveland and Austin Wilie's orchestra in New York. In New York he was reunited with his old Terre Haute chum Claude Thornhill.

In 1933 Red Nichols recruited Davis to join the Park Central Hotel orchestra. In the mid-1930s he joined the Fred Waring orchestra. Records cut by some of the bands Davis was with include such collectors' items as "Waiting for the Evening Mail," "Junk Man Blues," and "Let's All Sing Like the Birdies Sing," all featuring Davis's trumpet. Joining the Waring orchestra eventually took him to Hollywood. His first feature was *Varsity Show* in 1937. It had a distinct Hoosier flavor since, in addition to Davis, other cast members included Dick Powell and Priscilla and Rosemary Lane, who were singers with Waring. Powell spent a lot of time in Indiana with the Charlie Davis Band, and the Lane sisters' parents were Hoosiers. Of the five Lane sisters, only Priscilla and Rosemary were not born in Indiana. Warner Brothers was sufficiently impressed with Davis's performance in *Varsity Show* that it signed him to a contract. Priscilla and Rosemary were also offered film contracts. Davis's second film was *Over the Goal*, also in 1937. His next film, *Hollywood Hotel*, was his most notable. Released in 1937, Johnny Mercer and Dick Whiting specifically wrote the film's theme "Hooray for Hollywood" for Davis to sing in the opening scene. In addition to providing the signature vocal on the song that would become a theme song for Hollywood, he was featured as a trumpet player alongside Harry James in the Benny Goodman Orchestra in the film.

Davis continued making films for several years. His roles were those of a supporting player, with one exception: the leading role in *Mr. Chump* (1938). His costar was Lola Lane, a native of Macy, Indiana.

When Davis finally decided to form his own band, Art joined him as a trumpeter and principal arranger. During the 1950s and 1960s it was not unusual for Davis to return to the Wabash Valley to perform at nightclubs and showplaces such as the Flamingo Room or the Club Idaho. He also had his own television show from 1951 to 1952, emanating from WXYZ-TV in Detroit. On Friday evenings he was seen in a program called *Jazz Nocturne*. Until 1967 he played annual dates in Las Vegas, Reno, and Lake Tahoe.

When people used to ask Davis about his middle name, he would reply, "I know when they ask that they're awfully young. Anybody my age knows what scat is. It's a style of singing. I sing scat and play a little trumpet." He retired in the late 1960s and was living in Arlington, Texas, where he had settled with his wife and two daughters, when he died on November 28, 1983, while on a hunting trip in Pecos, Texas.

Johnny "Scat" Davis in *Mr. Chump* (1938).
©A WARNER BROS. PICTURE

BIBLIOGRAPHY

Alden, Ken. "Facing the Music." *Radio Mirror* (October 1937).

The American Big Bands Database. http://nfo.net/.

Lamparski, Richard. *Whatever Became Of . . . ?* 8th ser. New York: Crown Publishers, 1982.

McCormick, Mike. "Johnnie 'Scat' Davis." Wabash Valley Profiles. Vigo County Historical Society. http://web.indstate.edu/community/vchs/wvp.htm.

CHARLES DINGLE

Born in Wabash, Indiana, on December 28, 1887, Charles Dingle was a veteran of thirty-nine years in vaudeville and Broadway before making his debut in films at the age of fifty. He became one of the screen's busiest actors, playing mostly villainous roles. His parents, John Crockett and Bertie Hutton Dingle, moved to Kansas City when Charles was still a youngster.

One day Dingle answered an ad for a "talented young man to sing and play." He had been taking singing and piano lessons, and this preparation resulted in his being hired. He was just fourteen years old, and for the next few years he appeared in nearly every moderate-sized city in America in vaudeville singing Irish ballads. From musical shows, he gradually moved into stock. For the next twenty years he toured America in scores of plays. In 1928 he made his Broadway debut in *Killers.* He went on to appear in at least ten other Broadway productions. His last Broadway appearance was in 1954, when he appeared opposite Hoosier James Dean in *The Immoralist.*

Dingle began to work in radio in 1937. He played a recurring role on *The Road of Life* soap opera and was also heard on *The FBI in Peace and War, The March of Time, Pepper Young's Family, The O'Neill's,* and *Meet the Dixons.*

Dingle's biggest impression on Broadway was as Uncle Ben Hubbard in Lillian Hellman's *The Little Foxes,* opposite Tallulah Bankhead. In 1941, when MGM decided to film the stage play, Dingle repeated his role on the screen. His costar was Bette Davis. He quickly became known as one of Hollywood's leading character actors, and he followed up his breakthrough film with the role of A. Frazier Marco in *Johnny Eager,* Senator Jim Waters in *Tennessee Johnson,* and Mr. Prescott in *George Washington Slept Here,* all produced in 1942. In *The Song of Bernadette* (1943) he played Jacomet, the blustering police commissioner who tries to trick Bernadette into changing her story regarding the miracle at Lourdes. His performance in this role was hailed as a masterpiece of menace. In 1944 he was able to appear in a movie about his home state, *Home in Indiana,* and played opposite fellow Hoosier Red Skelton in *A Southern Yankee* in 1948. In his last two roles, Dingle played a senator in *Call Me Madam* in 1953 and *The Court-Martial of Billy Mitchell* in 1955.

During Dingle's career, he worked at nine different studios, indicating that he was a versatile actor who was much in demand. He was married in 1916 to Dorothy L. White, and they were the parents of two sons, Charles Dingle Jr. and John F. Dingle, both of whom had careers in the U.S. Navy.

Dingle died at Worcester, Massachusetts, on January 19, 1956.

BIBLIOGRAPHY

Biography of Charles Dingle. Margaret Herrick Library. Academy of Motion Picture Arts and Sciences, Beverly Hills, California.
The Internet Broadway Database. http://www.ibdb.com/.
The Internet Movie Database. http://www.imdb.com/.
New York Herald-Tribune, February 20, 1944.

Charles Dingle and Bette Davis (with two
actors in the background) in *The Little
Foxes* (1941).

ANDREW DUGGAN

In 1923 Edward Duggan was the football coach at Franklin College,
the school where actress Marjorie Main and director Robert Wise
were students. When Edward's son, Andrew, was born in Franklin
on December 28, 1923, Edward had no idea his son might follow in
the theatrical footsteps of those two famous alums.

After graduating from high school, Duggan enrolled at Indiana University, where he was given a scholarship as a theater major.
While at IU, he starred in Maxwell Anderson's *The Eve of St. Mark*,
which was being produced as a nonprofessional pre-Broadway tryout. On the basis of his performance, he was cast in the Chicago
company of the play. Unfortunately, his schooling and his theater
career were interrupted by service in the army in World War II. He
served in India, China, and Burma and was finally assigned to a
special services company led by actor Melvyn Douglas. Duggan and
Douglas became friends, and Douglas told Duggan that he should
look him up at the war's end.

Duggan did, and Douglas helped him land his first stage role, opposite Lucille Ball in *Dream Girl* at the Biltmore Bowl in Los Angeles. Between
engagements he worked at his uncle's Indiana farm, and he eventually

made his Broadway debut in 1951 in the long-running hit, *The Rose Tattoo.* He appeared on Broadway four more times, his last appearance being in 1958 in *Third Best Sport.*

While appearing in a stage production of *Paint Your Wagon,* Duggan met his wife, Elizabeth, who was a dancer. They had a son and two daughters. In addition to acting, Duggan was a writer for the CBS television series *Lux Video Theater,* which ran from 1950 to 1957. His first starring role was in 1959, when he was cast as Cal Calhoun in the television series *Bourbon Street Beat.* He also starred in the 1962 sitcom *Room for One More* and in 1964 was Brigadier General Ed Britt on the series *Twelve O'Clock High.* Duggan was Murdoch Lancer, the star of the television series *Lancer,* in 1968, and in 1971 he played John Walton in *The Homecoming: A Christmas Story,* which was the television pilot for *The Waltons.*

Perhaps because of his resemblance to Dwight D. Eisenhower, Duggan was frequently cast as generals and presidents. His last screen appearance was as Eisenhower in the 1987 television movie *J. Edgar Hoover.* He died in Westwood, California, of throat cancer on May 15, 1988.

BIBLIOGRAPHY

Erickson, Hal. "Andrew Duggan." All Movie Guide. http://www.allmovie.com/.

Quinlan, David. *Quinlan's Illustrated Directory of Film Character Actors.* New ed. London: B. T. Batsford, 1995.

What a Character. http://whatacharacter.com/.

Patricia Neal and Andrew Duggan in the television program *The Homecoming: A Christmas Story* (1974).
©CBS PHOTO DIVISION

RALPH DUMKE

In the early 1920s there were three students at the University of Notre Dame—Ralph Dumke, Charles Butterworth, and Charlie Davis—whose paths would intertwine over the years on the road to success in the world of entertainment. Dumke was born in South Bend on June 25, 1899, and chose Notre Dame because of its proximity. Dumke and Butterworth appeared together in campus shows at Notre Dame. Davis organized his own five-piece band while a student to help pay for his education.

After the three graduated, Davis hired Dumke to play banjo. A short while later he hired Bloomington native Ed East to play banjo as well. Both East and Dumke were very large men. The story goes that Davis "saw what he thought was a large sag in the tiny stage over the one-man banjo section. Something had to be done to balance the stage, so he hired Ed East as the second strummer." East and Dumke were versatile performers; East wrote funny songs, and Dumke sang. Dumke even tried light opera on the stage. Eventually, Dumke and East became a comedy team and decided to quit the Davis band and go into vaudeville with their own act.

Dumke and East went on the Keith-Orpheum circuit and later worked in radio on WGN in Chicago. They worked under various names, such as "The Fanny May Boys" and "The Want Ad Boys." Finally, they worked up an act making fun of the people who gave household hints. They called themselves "Sisters of the Skillet." It was a hit, and they were hired by NBC radio and went on the network on November 17, 1930. In May 1931 they moved to New York City and broadcast their show from there. *Sisters of the Skillet* ran on the NBC Blue network from 1930 to 1932 and was syndicated from 1932 to 1936. In 1936 they changed their act and became known as "The Quality Twins." This act involved improvisation and impersonations and was very successful.

The Quality Twins was on two networks; on Monday, Wednesday, and Friday they were on NBC Blue, and on Tuesday and Thursday they were on CBS. In 1937 they were dropped by NBC but stayed on CBS for that year. Unfortunately, no recording of these programs seems to have survived. During his years in radio, Dumke appeared in a number of other radio series as an actor or an emcee.

In the 1940s Dumke decided to move to Hollywood and try for a career in the movies. His first role was in the 1942 Alan Ladd film *Lucky Jordan*, playing a police sergeant. Fellow Hoosier Anthony Caruso was in the same film as a hired gun. Dumke became known as a "Sidney Greenstreet type" and had a career as a supporting actor, playing villains, entrepreneurs, and corrupt businessmen.

Dumke made more than thirty-five films from 1942 to 1961. Many of his roles were in major films such as *The War of the Worlds*, *All the King's Men*, *Daddy Long Legs*, *The Invasion of the Body Snatchers*, and *The Solid Gold Cadillac*. He also had an active television career, appearing on *The Andy Griffith Show* (playing Mayor Purdy), *Rawhide*, *Perry Mason*, and *I Love Lucy*. Adding to his busy schedule, he also appeared with the Los Angeles Civic Opera in productions of *The Chocolate Soldier*, *Merry Widow*, and *Rosalinda*. In 1946 he played Cap'n Andy in the Broadway revival of *Showboat*. His last film was *All in a Night's Work*, released in 1961. He died of a heart ailment on January 4, 1964, at his home in Sherman Oaks, California.

Scene from weekly television show, *December Bride* (December 3, 1954), with (left to right) Raymond Greenleaf, Dean Miller, Spring Byington, and Ralph Dumke.
AP NEWSFEATURES PHOTO

BIBLIOGRAPHY

Banta, Ray. *Indiana's Laughmakers: The Story of Over Four Hundred Hoosiers; Actors, Cartoonists, Writers, and Others.* Indianapolis: PennUltimate Press, 1990.

Buxton, Frank, and Bill Owen. *The Big Broadcast, 1920–1950.* New York: Viking Press, 1972.

Davis, Charlie. *That Band from Indiana.* Oswego, N.Y.: Mathom Publishing Company, 1982.

Dunning, John. *On the Air: The Encyclopedia of Old-Time Radio.* New York: Oxford University Press, 1998.

Indianapolis Star, February 7, 1937.

Lackman, Ron. *The Encyclopedia of American Radio.* New York: Checkmark Books, 2000.

Quinlan, David. *Quinlan's Illustrated Directory of Film Character Actors.* London: B. T. Batsford, 1985.

ED EAST

"Big Ed" East was born in Bloomington, Indiana, on April 4, 1894, and attended grade school in Bloomington with Hoagy Carmichael. At the age of fifteen, he ran away from home to become a barker for a carnival high-dive act. A year later he returned home and enrolled at Indiana University, where he wrote football songs and fraternity songs while working on a law degree. He received his law degree, was admitted to the bar, and entered law practice in Bloomington with his father. However, like fellow law graduate Carmichael, he did not find practicing law to his liking and abandoned his legal career to try his luck in show business.

After entertaining troops overseas during World War I, East returned to Indianapolis, where he opened a music shop on Illinois Street near Market Street. He became acquainted with local musicians and attracted the attention of Charlie Davis, the popular orchestra leader, and Davis hired him for a musical and comedy act. This act grew into a vaudeville and radio specialty with Ralph Dumke.

East provided countless "gag" songs for the Davis band during his stint with them as a banjo player and piano player. After he left the band to go into vaudeville with Dumke, East continued to write funny songs and humorous material for the team. At various times during their radio career, they were known as "Joey and Chuck," "Big Shot and Peewee," "The Fanny May Boys," and "The Antipest Clubbers."

Like his friend Dumke, East was successful in radio. In 1940 he was host of *The Ask-It Basket* on CBS. He also collaborated with orchestra leader Ted Lewis to write a song, "The Day Will Come," which was featured in the Broadway production, *The Passing Show*. From 1944 to 1950 East and his wife, Polly, were cohosts of a program called *Ladies Be Seated*, which ran on NBC Blue and later on ABC. For this series, Ed and Polly performed blindfold husband and wife gags, spaghetti eating contests, and other forms of audio slapstick. In the 1930s *Betty Crocker* (NBC) was one of radio's earliest recipe programs. Ed and Polly appeared on that show in a segment called "Kitchen Quiz." They also had their own show on NBC entitled *Fun and Folly with Ed East and Polly*. East also hosted *Meet the Missus*, which was similar to Art Linkletter's *House Party*.

Although East went to Hollywood, his movie career was not as successful as Dumke's. East appeared in just four movies, *Jackpot Jitters* (1949), *The Baron of Arizona* (1950), *Mrs. O'Malley and Mr. Malone* (1951), and *Stop That Cab* (1951).

Shortly after his last film, East suffered a heart attack and was forced into semiretirement. He continued to write jingles for radio and did some early television work. He died of a heart attack in New York City on January 18, 1952. He was survived by his wife, Polly; his mother, Mrs. Jimmie East; a brother, Judge Q. Austin East of Bloomington; a sister, Mrs. Reeves Burke of Philadelphia; and a daughter, Mrs. Wheeler Simmons of Chicago.

Ed East (left) and Ralph Dumke perform their "Sisters of the Skillet" radio act.

BIBLIOGRAPHY

Banta, Ray. *Indiana's Laughmakers: The Story of Over Four Hundred Hoosiers: Actors, Cartoonists, Writers, and Others*. Indianapolis: PennUltimate Press, 1990.

Buxton, Frank, and Bill Owen. *The Big Broadcast, 1920–1950.* New York: Viking, 1972.

Davis, Charlie. *That Band from Indiana.* Oswego, N.Y.: Mathom Publishing Company, 1982.

Dunning, John. *On the Air: The Encyclopedia of Old-Time Radio.* New York: Oxford University Press, 1998.

Indianapolis Star, February 7, 1937, February 21, 1952.

Lackman, Ron. *The Encyclopedia of American Radio.* New York: Checkmark Books, 2000.

ROBERT EMHARDT

Robert Christian Emhardt was born on July 14, 1914, in Indianapolis, the son of C. J. Emhardt, who was a lawyer, judge, and onetime mayor of the city. His early acting experience came at Butler University, and in 1937 he went to Europe to study for two years at the London Academy of Dramatic Art. He joined a repertoire company with London's British Broadcasting Corporation and enjoyed radio acting for a while. He returned to the United States and was on Broadway in 1940 in *Battle of Angels.* He became much in demand on Broadway and appeared in at least twelve other productions through 1959.

Emhardt also began appearing in summer stock and on television, eventually appearing in more than 150 television productions. His favorite role was that of the offbeat father in *The Group* in 1966. He married a well-known English actress, Silvia Sideli, and they had four children.

Emhardt died of heart failure in Ojai, California, on December 26, 1994.

Robert Emhardt (left) with his father Christian Emhardt.

Courtesy of David Emhardt

BIBLIOGRAPHY

Jones, Ken D., Arthur F. McClure, and Alfred E. Twomey. *Character People.* South Brunswick, N.J.: A. S. Barnes, 1976.

The Internet Movie Database. http://www.imdb.com/.

MIKE EPPS

The publicity kit for Mike Epps states he was born in Gary, Indiana, but his father, Tommy, says he was born in Wishard Hospital in Indianapolis. He grew up in Gary and Indianapolis in a large family, where he got a lot of encouragement for his natural comedic ability. Epps claims he was kicked out of every high school in Indianapolis: "OK, maybe it was only Manual, Decatur Central, and Tech." As a teenager in Indianapolis, he began performing standup comedy at a club called Seville's at Seventy-first Street and Michigan Road. "I rocked it," he said of his appearance. He left Indianapolis for Atlanta and worked at the Comedy Act Theater. When he was twenty-

Mike Epps in *Next Friday* (2000).
©1999, NEW LINE CINEMA INC.

one, he moved to New York, but found times were lean and hard. The Def Comedy Jam opened up a black comedy underground. He joined it in 1995 and was part of two HBO Def Comedy Jam shows.

Epps's first movie role came just two years later, when he starred in Vin Diesel's *Strays*, a dramatic portrayal of relationships and drugs. In 1999 he made an appearance on the HBO series, *The Sopranos.* He kept doing comedy, and soon his particular style of humor became similar to other African American artists in the same genre. He became friends with actor/performer Ice Cube and appeared in several films with him. Among those were *Next Friday* (2000) and *Friday After Next* (2002). In 2000 he was featured in *Bait*, and in 2001 he was in *Dr. Dolittle 2* with Eddie Murphy.

Indianapolis is still close to Epps. He has a daughter here, Bria, born in 1993. He also has a dream of opening a comedy club downtown, "And have it jumpin'."

BIBLIOGRAPHY

Indianapolis Star, January 12, 20, 2000.
The Internet Movie Database. http://www.imdb.com/.
Yahoo Movies. http://movies.yahoo.com/.

CHAD EVERETT

Raymond Lee Cramton was born on June 11, 1936, in South Bend, Indiana, the son of Mr. and Mrs. Harry Cramton. When he was five years old, his parents moved across the St. Joseph River to Dearborn, Michigan, where he grew up. He attended Fordson High School, where he was quarterback for the football team, and became interested in the stage while taking some dramatic classes. He said, "After three years of exposure on the stage, I was hooked." After high school, he decided to be an actor: "I'm a rarity. At 18 I decided to become an actor. And that's what I did."

Everett enrolled at Wayne State University as a theater major. His first job after college was working in a repertory company that toured India under the auspices of the U.S. State Department. He said, "That was a thrilling time for me. We carried our own complete package so we could perform anywhere." One night the power generator broke down, and Everett repaired it five minutes before the curtain went up. "I was playing Creon in 'Oedipus Rex' with greasy hands," he remembered.

Success did not come overnight. "I got jobs in the Lillian Bonstelle Playhouse productions in Dearborn. After I'd saved up $140, I headed out for Broadway," Everett said. When the going got rough, he took jobs modeling men's fashions and did television commercials. He went to Hollywood in 1960 and signed a contract with Warner Brothers for $250 a week. He made his film debut in a Warner picture, *Claudelle Inglish*, in 1961. In 1963 he landed a costarring role in the television series, *The Dakotas*, which was a Warner Brothers production. He was happy with his progress: "I'm under contract and I have to do what the studio says, but it's so much nicer to be working with good stuff than to be working with junk."

(*Opposite page*) *TV Guide* portrait of Chad Everett from *Medical Center* television series (1972).

Everett left Warner Brothers and signed with MGM the next year, making *Made in Paris* in 1964 and *The Singing Nun* in 1965. In 1969 he was cast in a television series that made him a household name. As Doctor Joe Gannon in *Medical Center*, he was nominated twice for a Golden Globe (1971 and 1973) for best television actor. The series ran until 1976.

Everett was now financially secure. He divided his time between theatrical movies and television movies, making for television *Hagen* in 1980, *The Rousters* in 1983, and *McKenna* in 1994. He has written, directed, and performed in many commercials and industrial films. He is also the author of a self-published book of romantic poetry dedicated to his wife, Shelby Grant, whom he married in 1965. They have two daughters.

Everett and Grant have been sponsors of Save the Children for eighteen years. He traveled to Ethiopia to see firsthand how Save the Children programs help overcome starvation and disease. He is also the national spokesperson for The Gift of Life, which assists children with failing hearts who live in poor nations.

BIBLIOGRAPHY

Indianapolis News, August 4, 1962.

Indianapolis Times, January 7, 1963.

Lewis, Richard Warren. "Thwack! There's Nothing Subtle about Chad Everett's Tennis Game . . . or His Life Style." *TV Guide*, March 8–14, 1975.

Entertainment MSN. http://entertainment.msn.com/celebs/celeb.aspx?mp=b&c=230762.

RICHARD "SKEETS" GALLAGHER

Few Hoosiers had a more enduring career in show business than Anthony Richard "Skeets" Gallagher. When asked why he chose a life in the theater, he replied, "It was easier than studying engineering at Rose Poly or pre-law at Indiana University." The theater "bug" may have come to him through his Aunt Margaret Gallagher, who appeared on the New York stage.

Gallagher was born in Terre Haute on July 28, 1891, to Anthony J. "Andy" and Sena Simmons Gallagher. Andy was a pioneer baseball player who was forced to go into the plumbing business because of the low salaries offered to professional athletes at that time. The Gallagher family resided at 604 S. Center Street in Terre Haute while Richard was attending St. Joseph's Academy at Fifth and Ohio streets. Because of his size and the fact he had the quickness of a mosquito, school chum Cliff Hammerstein started calling him Skeets. By the time he enrolled at Wiley High School, Skeets was his nickname.

Gallagher liked to entertain his friends and neighbors with soft-shoe routines. He made his official stage debut at Terre Haute's Lyric Theater in 1909. While attending IU, he formed a vaudeville duo

Norman Foster (Richmond), Richard "Skeets" Gallagher, and Carole Lombard (Fort Wayne) in *It Pays to Advertise* (1931).

COURTESY OF THE ACADEMY OF MOTION PICTURE ARTS AND SCIENCES

with singer Will K. Reardon of Montezuma. They joined the Keith vaudeville circuit, but Reardon abruptly decided to quit and manage an automobile agency in South Dakota.

Gallagher promptly formed a song-and-dance act with two chorus girls, Mary Ann Dentler and Anna Orr, and the act appeared in several New York vaudeville houses. The next year he teamed with dancer Irene Martin and began to successfully play the "two-a-day" circuit for five years. When his mother died on December 6, 1919, Gallagher was appearing at a vaudeville house in Vancouver, British Columbia.

On January 9, 1922, Gallagher made his Broadway debut as Richard Gallagher in *Above the Clouds*. The play toured the Midwest. He returned to New York to play the lead in *Up She Goes*, a musical comedy that opened on November 6, 1922, in the Forty-eighth Street Playhouse. It ran for 256 performances. He made his motion picture debut in 1923 in *The Daring Years*, a film that featured W. C. Fields.

Since Gallagher was a musical comedy performer, silent films were not really his cup of tea, but in 1927 he signed a contract with Paramount and appeared in his first talkie, *The Potters*. Coincidentally, this film also featured Fields. He made the headlines when the film premiered at the Indiana Theater on January 26, 1927. His first few films were, at best, mediocre. In 1928 he made *The Racket* and for the first time billed himself as Richard "Skeets" Gallagher. His performance generated excellent reviews, earning him top billing in two 1929 musical comedies, *Close Harmony* and *Pointed Heels*.

In the summer of 1929, Gallagher married actress Pauline Mason and moved into a home on Sunset Plaza in Los Angeles. The couple had two children, Richard Jr. and Pamela. Gallagher was much in demand in the 1930s, frequently making six or seven films a year. He made two films in 1931 with fellow Hoosiers Carole Lombard and Norman Foster—*It Pays to Advertise* and *Up Pops the Devil*. He was the White Rabbit in Paramount's star-studded production of *Alice in Wonderland* in 1933.

Before his father died in Terre Haute on September 13, 1936, Gallagher returned to the stage, appearing in *Good Night Ladies*, which ran for two years. While on stage he made at least one movie each year. In 1949 he retired after appearing in *Duke of Chicago*. However, at the request of Gloria Swanson, he came out of retirement to film *Three for Bedroom C* in 1952. He also appeared in several early television specials. He suffered a heart attack and died on May 22, 1955, in Santa Monica. He was buried at Holy Cross Cemetery in Hollywood.

BIBLIOGRAPHY

McCormick, Mike. "Richard 'Skeets' Gallagher." Wabash Valley Profiles. Vigo County Historical Society. http://web.indstate.edu/community/vchs/wvp.

Parish, James Robert, and William T. Leonard. *Hollywood Players: The Thirties.* New Rochelle, N.Y.: Arlington House, 1976.

WILL GEER

William Aughe Geer was born in New Hope, Indiana, a small community about four miles southeast of Colfax, on March 9, 1902. His parents were Roy and Catherine Ghere. His father came from a long line of Clinton County farmers, and his mother was a public school teacher whose family had lived in Frankfort for decades. While he was still a child, Geer's parents moved to Frankfort, Indiana.

Frankfort schoolteacher Flora Muller was the first to begin developing Geer's cultural interests. "She would bring us down to [James Whitcomb] Riley's over on Lockerbie and he'd recite a few of his poems for us," Geer told an interviewer in 1977. "Once I decided to be brave and join in so I stood up and did 'Out to Old Aunt Mary's' and I guess you could call that my debut."

Geer said of his Indiana roots: "My Indiana boyhood was right out of 'The Waltons.' Fishing in the summers. A Tom Sawyer time before the streams got all polluted. My grandfather had white hair and a white mustache. He'd been a 49er, made some gold money in California, and came back to Indiana to build the town's first opera house. We'd go for walks and he'd say hello to the trees by their Latin names." That is when young Geer decided he wanted to study botany. (He eventually earned a master's degree in botany from Columbia University.)

After his father left the family in 1911, his mother moved her brood to Chicago in search of a more lucrative teaching job. Geer entered Waller High School, where he made his first stage appearance in George Bernard Shaw's *You Never Can Tell*. In 1919 the family returned to Indiana, where Geer finished his high school education at Frankfort. After graduating from high school, he attended the University of Chicago but went off in a touring company after being bitten by the acting bug.

In 1920 Geer hitchhiked to Indianapolis from Frankfort and began his stage career, playing bit parts at the Murat Theater with the Stuart Walker Players. He gained additional experience in tent, repertory, and boat shows before making his Broadway debut in *The Merry Wives of Windsor*. He appeared in a number of plays on Broadway, including *Cradle Will Rock* and *Waiting for Lefty* and was a hit as Jeeter Lester in *Tobacco Road*. He played Lester for 623 consecutive performances until the play closed on May 31, 1941.

Geer also became a folksinger of some repute, and during the Depression years he toured the country with Woody Guthrie and Burl Ives, singing mostly at government work camps. Guthrie and Ives would remain his close friends throughout the years. Geer's movie career began in 1932 with *Misleading Lady*, and he appeared in at least sixty films from 1932 to 1978. He was versatile enough to play villains as well as comedy roles. He made many television appearances, but he is best remembered for his role as Grandpa Walton on *The Waltons*.

Geer's career was abruptly halted when he was put on the infamous McCarthy "Blacklist." He was proud of being a lifelong agitator: "A rebel is just against things for rebellion's sake. I'm a radical. Someone who goes to the roots, which is the Latin derivation of radical." Thanks to director/producer John Houseman, Geer was able to get back to

(*Opposite page*) Will Geer (top) on a *TV Guide* cover with Ralph Waite (left) and Richard Thomas (1974).
CHAS. P. MILLS & SONS

work. Houseman was the director of the American Shakespeare Theater in Stratford, Connecticut. Geer stayed with the company for five full seasons, even helping landscape the theater's grounds.

In 1951 Geer decided to combine his passion for acting and plants by forming a most unusual repertory theater situated in rustic Topanga Canyon in California's San Fernando Valley. He named it Theatricum Botanicum. Workshops were held for young actors, and Geer provided coaching and counsel. The sessions were not devoted just to the theater; philosophy and psychology were discussed as well. On Sundays folksinging lessons were held under the eucalyptus and oak trees.

Geer was always proud of his Hoosier background and consistently injected some Indiana flavor in almost every role he played. Columnist Earl Wilson said, "He is a tall amiable fellow with one of the really authentic Indiana accents this side of Abe Martin."

Geer was married three times and at the time of his death, on April 22, 1978, was survived by seven children, including actors Kate Linville and Ellen and Raleigh Geer and two grandchildren. At his bedside were family members singing "This Land Is Your Land" and reciting favorite poems from Robert Frost. Funeral services were at Theatricum Botanicum, and Geer was buried in a grove where he had often walked. His daughter, Ellen, said that when she thought of her father, "I think of love. He always made everyone feel at home and relaxed. He especially loved children. He was my favorite person in the whole world."

BIBLIOGRAPHY

Banta, Ray. *Indiana's Laughmakers: The Story of Over Four Hundred Hoosiers; Actors, Cartoonists, Writers, and Others.* Indianapolis: PennUltimate Press, 1990.

Finch, Evan. "Will Geer: Frankfort's Supporting Actor." *Traces of Indiana and Midwestern History* 10, no. 4 (Fall 1998).

Quinlan, David. *Quinlan's Illustrated Directory of Film Character Actors.* London: B. T. Batsford, 1985.

The Waltons Web Site. http://www.the-waltons.com/willsty.html.

RON GLASS

Ron Glass was born in Evansville, Indiana, on July 10, 1945. Following the divorce of his parents, he was raised by his mother, Lethia, who worked as a domestic to earn money to send Glass, his sisters, and his brothers to private school. He attended high school in Cincinnati but returned to his hometown to attend the University of Evansville, where he studied acting and literature. After graduation he joined Minneapolis's famed Tyrone Guthrie Theater. He spent four years there and then worked in several repertory companies before arriving in Los Angeles in 1972.

Glass had small parts in several television sitcoms, including *Sanford and Son*, *Good Times*, *The Bob Newhart Show*, and *All in the Family*, before he got his big break, the role of the wisecracking detective Ron Harris in the sitcom *Barney Miller*. Glass was part of the *Barney Miller* cast from 1975 to 1982. He also was in the short-lived *The New Odd Couple* as Felix Unger and is the voice of Mr. Carmichael on the *Rugrats* television series.

In 1983 Glass was named one of six distinguished Hoosiers honored by the Indiana Arts Commission for their contributions to the arts in Indiana and the nation. His latest role was that of Shepherd Book in the series *Firefly*, a futuristic sci-fi/western adventure set five hundred years in the future.

BIBLIOGRAPHY

Brooks, Tim, and Earle Marsh. *The Complete Directory to Prime Time Network TV Shows, 1946–Present.* 2nd ed. New York: Ballantine Books, 1981.

Hanafee, Susan. "A Glass Act." *Indianapolis Star Magazine*, March 20, 1983.

Indianapolis Star, August 19, 1979, April 27, 1982, July 24, 2002.

Ron Glass.

MAUDE TURNER GORDON

When she was growing up in Franklin, Indiana, Maude Turner Gordon was known as "Tanky Turner." The name Tanky came from the heroine of a book her mother read. Alexander Turner, Maude's father, could not be persuaded to accept that name, and he suggested they wait until the child was older and let her choose her own name. In the meantime, she would be called Tanky. Maude was born in Franklin on November 10, 1868. Her mother, Nancy Ann Wright Turner, died when Maude was seven years old. Not long afterwards, Tanky told her sister Emma that she wanted to be named Anna Maude, Anna in memory of her mother and Maude from the name of a song that appealed to her. She began appearing on stage in schools and churches in Franklin at age six. As she grew older, she became active in amateur school and college productions.

Maude met Major Jonathan W. Gordon, who was an attorney and a judge in Indianapolis, and the two eloped when Maude was still a student at Franklin College. The couple lived in Indianapolis and later moved to New York, where Maude realized her long-cherished ambition to appear on the legitimate stage. During her "trouping" days, she was seen in Indianapolis a number of times. One of her last appearances was in a touring company of *Glorious Betsy*, the musical in which she made her first Broadway appearance in 1908. She had a beautiful contralto voice and performed in sixteen Broadway productions from 1908 through 1925. One of her Broadway appearances was in a 1923 musical, *Elsie*, with music and lyrics by Indianapolis native Noble Sissle and his partner, Eubie Blake.

Eventually, the Gordons moved to California, where Jonathan became a postal inspector. Maude's prematurely gray hair and a regal bearing helped her gain entrance into the motion picture industry. Her first film was *The Idler* in 1914. She went on to have a formidable career in films, easily bridging the gap between silents and sound, and appeared in at least seventy-eight motion pictures from 1914 to 1938. She was always a supporting actress but appeared in such major films as *Sally* (1929), with fellow Hoosier Marilyn Miller; *Back Street* (1932), with Irene Dunne; *Flirtation Walk* (1934), with Fred Astaire and Ginger Rogers; and her last film, *Sweethearts* (1938), with Nelson Eddy and Jeanette MacDonald.

After her husband died, Maude moved to Oakland, California, and lived her remaining days with her sister, Emma. The Gordons adopted a daughter in 1907. Maude died on January 12, 1940.

Maude Turner Gordon (far right) in *The Glad Rag Doll* (1929).

BIBLIOGRAPHY

The Internet Broadway Database. http://www.ibdb.com/.
The Internet Movie Database. http://www.imdb.com/.

PHIL HARRIS

Clinton, Indiana's favorite son rose from his humble Greene County origins to become a nationally known multitalented entertainer. He was a drummer, bandleader, singer, recording artist, radio and television personality, sportsman, and, using his distinctive voice stylings, a voice-over artist for several Disney films.

Wonga Phil Harris was born in Linton on June 24, 1904, the son of Harry and Dollie Wright Harris. Dollie was a Linton native, and Harry was born in Kentucky. Harry was a musician in circus bands and tent shows and worked briefly as a coal miner. The couple traveled extensively, leaving young Phil with his maternal grandparents, the Allen "Sug" Wrights. The Wrights raised Phil along with help from various aunts and uncles who lived nearby. Phil became very close to his grandfather, a Civil War veteran who was a Linton policeman. He often described his grandfather as "more my father." Finally, his mother gave up show business and returned to Linton, where she worked in a clothing store and a millinery store.

Harris's Hoosier childhood helped him develop a love for the outdoors. His constant companion was Tom McQuade, and as Harris described it, "Tom and I were together every day. All we did was fish and hunt. We used to go to Haseman's Grove . . . used to be a great spot for rabbits . . . cotton-tail . . . and all around Linton. There were mostly rabbits in the wintertime, and then it could come hickory nut time, or black walnut time, or pawpaw time. We always had something to do."

Harris's formal schooling took place at the Linton-Stockton Elementary School and at the Northeast Ward, where students attended the upper elementary grades. He made good grades in school in Linton. At age ten, his parents moved to Nashville, Tennessee, where he finished elementary school and attended the Hume-Fogg High School for one year before dropping out to form a band.

Harris's musical career started at an early age, when he whittled out a pair of drumsticks. His father bought him a drum and taught him the fundamentals. At age nine, he began playing drums for silent movies at the Nicklo and Dreamland theaters in Linton. During summer vacations, he joined his parents on the road. A handbill from this era plugs the Harris trio: "Singles, Doubles, and Trios, An Act of High Class Harmony Singing That Always Pleases." On the handbill is a photo of Harry, Dollie, and a young Phil.

In Nashville, Harris's father found a steady job leading a band at the Knickerbocker Theater. Phil played drums in the band for a while, then left school to form The Dixie Syncopaters. He said, "It was a Dixieland band, but in those days you had to play everything . . . whatever they wanted . . . but basically we liked Dixieland." The band traveled and eventually wound up in Hawaii, where they helped open the Princess Theater. After a year in Hawaii, Harris left the band and headed for the West Coast, where he played drums in several bands, then went to Australia to help teach the Australians how to play swing music. While in Australia, he met Carol Lofner, and they formed the Lofner-Harris Band. The band returned to San Francisco and played a long engagement at the St. Francis Hotel. About this time, Harris started singing with the band. He was very successful and soon became the band vocalist.

In 1932 Harris formed his own band, settling in for a long stay at the Cocoanut Grove in Los Angeles. He became the hottest bandleader on the West Coast and the darling of the Hollywood set. Radio was very popular by now, and when Harris's orchestra was featured in a remote broadcast from the Cocoanut Grove, he became nationally known.

Phil Harris in *Buck Benny Rides Again* (1940).
©1940, PARAMOUNT PICTURES INC.

Phil Harris and wife Alice Faye.

Betty Grable and Phil Harris in *Wabash Avenue* (1950).

About 1933 Harris moved to the East and became as popular on that coast as he was on the West Coast. Bandleaders were becoming a hot property in films, and RKO director Mark Sandrich asked Harris to do a short film called *So This Is Harris!* It won an Academy Award for best short subject of 1934. The same year, Harris appeared in his first feature film, *Melody Cruise. Indianapolis Star* critic Corbin Patrick said, "He is what the flappers used to call a new kind of man, far removed from the crooners who have been all the rage. In appearance he might remind you slightly of Broadway's Harry Richman and he has the same easy-going good humored manner."

In 1936 Harris became a household name when he joined the Jack Benny radio show as a bandleader and character on the show. Harris noted that Benny was far from being cheap and often gave him unexpected raises. In 1941 Harris married actress Alice Faye, and in 1946 they started their own radio show based on their home life with their two daughters, who were played by child actresses. Their show was ranked among the top ten for most of the years it was aired until 1954, when television led to the demise of many radio shows.

Harris was a good actor as well as a comedian. Writer E. Jack Newman, who wrote for *Suspense* and *Lux Radio Theater*, said of him, "I always looked forward to getting comedians in different situations . . . like Phil Harris who was always drinking and clowning around and bragging. We did one [1951's *Death on My Hands*] where we had him whimpering and crying and begging. He was a brilliant actor. He could do it!" His acting abilities led to major roles in films such as *Wabash Avenue* (1950), with Betty Grable; *The High and the Mighty* (1954), with John Wayne; and *The Wheeler Dealers* (1963), with James Garner.

When Walt Disney asked Harris to record a test track for a bear (it was to be a cameo part) for *The Jungle Book* (1967), the animators wondered where "this old saloon singer" would fit into things. But Harris's warm, happy-go-lucky vocal quality and heartfelt improvisations inspired the animators. Frank Thomas, one of the chief animators, said, "Yeah, we knew we were in business. We had a character." After Disney saw Thomas's experimental animation using Harris's voice, he told his people that he wanted Baloo's role expanded. He said, "This bear is marvelous. We gotta keep him in the picture." "The Bear Necessities," sung by Harris in the movie, was nominated for an Oscar for best song. Disney later used Harris as the voice of Thomas O'Malley in *The Aristocrats* and Little John in *Robin Hood.*

His vocal stylings made him a best-selling recording artist with such novelty hits as "That's What I Like about the South" (which he wrote), "The Preacher and the Bear," "Darktown Poker Club," and "The Thing." In 1948 Eddie "Rochester" Anderson introduced Harris to Scatman Crothers, who was from Terre Haute, Indiana. The two Hoosiers became fast friends, recording "Chattanooga Shoe Shine Boy" together. Harris introduced the song on his radio show, and it launched Crothers into a show business career.

Harris made regular trips back to Linton, often sneaking into town unannounced to spend time with his boyhood friends and relatives. He enjoyed coming back to the Hoosier State and, as a good friend of Indianapolis Motor Speedway owner Tony Hulman, he inevitably was asked to sing the traditional "Back Home Again in Indiana" before the start of the Indianapolis 500.

In 1979 Harris originated the Annual Phil Harris Scholarship Festival in his hometown. Celebrities from all over the world trekked to Linton to play in Harris's golf tournament and perform or just attend his variety show in the Linton gymnasium. Some guests included Neil Armstrong, Buzz Aldrin, Roy Clark, Bobby Knight, Chris Schenkel, George Gobel, Pat Buttram, Claude Akins, Jimmy Dean, and several of the top golfing greats.

Harris once said, "I can't die until the government finds a safe place to bury my liver." He died of heart failure on August 11, 1995, in Rancho Mirage, California. He was survived by his wife, Alice, who died on May 9, 1998.

BIBLIOGRAPHY

Canemaker, John. *Walt Disney's Nine Old Men and the Art of Animation.* New York: Disney Editions, 2001.

Indianapolis Star, June 20, 1933.

Indianapolis Times, August 29, 1952.

Maltin, Leonard. *The Great American Broadcast: A Celebration of Radio's Golden Age.* New York: New American Library, 2000.

"That's What I Like about Indiana." *Indianapolis Star Magazine*, February 29, 1948.

LLOYD HAYNES

From 1969 to 1974 Lloyd Haynes was everybody's favorite high school history teacher. He starred as Pete Dixon, and Denise Nicholas was Haynes's girlfriend in the very popular television series, *Room 222*. The talented cast included Michael Constantine as the principal, Karen Valentine as a spunky student teacher, and a group of diverse students. It was an important series in the history of television in that it was one of the earliest attempts to deal with young black and white America coming of age during the politically restless 1960s. Haynes as a history teacher and Nicholas as the school guidance counselor had a position and manner distinct and new for blacks on television. The series received many awards and commendations from educational and civil rights groups.

Samuel Lloyd Haynes was born in South Bend, Indiana, on October 19, 1934, and graduated from South Bend Central High School. He served in the marines in the Korean War and a commander in the navy. After his service in the armed forces, he went to Hollywood to pursue an acting career. He held a job as an office assistant at Heatter-Quigley Productions and was a production assistant for a game show. He began appearing in many television shows, including two episodes of *Tarzan* in 1966, in which he and fellow Hoosier William Marshall played African tribesmen.

However, Haynes's film career was brief. In 1977 he had a small role in *The Greatest*, the story of Muhammad Ali, and was in the miniseries *Harold Robbins' 79 Park Avenue*. He was in *Good Guys Wear Black* in 1978. He also appeared in *The Fugitive*, *Star Trek*, *T. J. Hooker*, and other television shows. In 1981 he played a recurring role in *Dynasty*, appearing

Lloyd Haynes in the television series *Room 222* (1970).
ABC PHOTO

in four episodes as Judge Horatio Quinlan. His last role was that of Major Ken Morgan in the television series *General Hospital* from 1984 to 1986. He contracted lung cancer and died on December 31, 1986, at the age of fifty-two. He was buried at Eternal Hills Memorial Park, Oceanside, San Diego County, California. He was survived by a wife and one child.

BIBLIOGRAPHY

The African American Registry. http://www.aaregistry.com/.
The Internet Movie Database. http://www.imdb.com/.
MacDonald, J. Fred. *Blacks and White TV: African Americans in Television since 1948.* 2nd ed. Chicago: Nelson-Hall Publishers, 1992.

ANN HOVEY

Ann Hovey (1937).
© 1937, RKO RADIO PICTURES, INC. PHOTO BY ERNEST A. BACHRACH

Anna (she dropped the *a* when she went to Hollywood) Jacques Hovey was the great-granddaughter of former Indiana governor, Alvin Peterson Hovey. Hovey commanded the Indiana volunteers in the Civil War, was appointed minister to Peru, became a member of Congress, and was governor from 1888 to 1891.

Ann was the daughter of the governor's grandson, Dr. Alvin J. Hovey, a practicing dentist in Mount Vernon, and his wife. Ann had one sister, who married Colin Alexander and moved to Indianapolis while Ann took off for the West Coast. Ann was born in Mount Vernon, Indiana, on August 29, 1912. She graduated from Mount Vernon High School in 1929 and attended Evansville College briefly before going to Chicago to study drama, dance, and music.

Hovey was appearing in amateur theatricals when she heard that tests were being given on the West Coast for the Eddie Cantor musical, *The Kid from Spain* (1932). She went to California and was chosen to be part of the dancing troupe in the movie. This led to another test for a chorus girl/dancing part in a First National musical, *42nd Street.* According to publicity releases at the time, she was chosen from among five thousand applicants to be a part of this groundbreaking musical. Her work so pleased Warner Brothers officials that she was placed under contract. Her next film was another chorus girl part in *Gold Diggers of 1933.*

In 1934 Hovey was chosen as a Wampas Baby Star, announcing that she was on the way to stardom. Wampas, the Western Association of Motion Picture Advertisers, had been sponsoring the highly coveted award since 1920. She was only five feet three inches tall and weighed just ninety-eight pounds. As such, she was the "lightweight" of the thirteen women chosen. She had black hair and brown eyes. The promotion was discontinued after 1934.

Hovey appeared in at least sixteen movies from 1932 to 1938. However, the closest she came to leading-role status was the second feature lead in *Wild Boys of the Road* in 1933. Most of her parts were bits, and many were uncredited. She married press agent Robert Husey in 1933 and retired from the movies in 1934.

Scene from *Stepping Sisters* (1932) with (left to right) Louise Dresser (Evansville), Minna Gombel, and Jobyna Howland.

BIBLIOGRAPHY

Indianapolis News, December 8, 1932, March 29, 1934.

Indianapolis Star, March 16, 1934.

The Internet Movie Database. http://www.imdb.com/.

Liebman, Roy. *The Wampas Baby Stars: A Biographical Dictionary, 1922–1934.* Jefferson, N.C.: McFarland and Company, 2000.

Uselton, Roi A. "The Wampas Baby Stars." *Films in Review* (February 1970).

JOBYNA HOWLAND

By the time Jobyna Howland was twenty years old, she was already the toast of New York. The striking and statuesque young woman (she was six feet tall) came to the big city with an ambition to be a model, and she immediately attracted the attention of none other than Charles Dana Gibson. Although she became one of Gibson's favorite models, she also posed for such artists as Edwin Holand Blashfield and Thornoe Wenzel. When Gibson was commissioned to illustrate Anthony Hope's story, *The Prisoner of Zenda: Rupert of Hentzau*, he chose Howland to be his model for Queen Flavia.

Howland had performed in some society amateur performances but had no stage experience beyond that. Nevertheless, when theatrical producer Daniel Frohman began assembling a cast for production of *The Prisoner of Zenda*, he signed Howland for the role of Queen Flavia, and her acting career began. She made her Broadway debut in 1900 in *The Heather Field* and eventually appeared in eighteen Broadway productions through 1936.

Howland was born in Indianapolis on March 31, 1880. Her parents moved to Denver when she was a young girl, and it was there her brother, Olin Howland, was born in 1886. Jobyna and Olin both made their film debut in 1918. However, by the time Jobyna started appearing in films, she was thirty-eight years old. She was therefore usually cast as the mother of the star or a society matron. Olin became a major character actor, appearing in almost two hundred films during the 1940s, 1950s, and 1960s.

During her film career, Howland worked for such directors as George Stevens and George Cukor. Many of her films were comedies. She appeared in three films in 1930 with the zany duo of Bert Wheeler and Robert Woolsey and worked with Miriam Hopkins, Norma Talmadge, John Barrymore, Myrna Loy, and Joan Blondell. She played opposite fellow Hoosiers Richard "Skeets" Gallagher, Victor Potel, Louise Dresser, Lon Poff, Louise Fazenda, and Charlie Murray.

Howland was married to Arthur Stringer, but the marriage ended in a divorce. She died in Los Angeles on June 7, 1936.

BIBLIOGRAPHY

Indianapolis Press, May 17, 1900.
The Internet Broadway Database. http://www.ibdb.com/.
The Internet Movie Database. http://www.imdb.com/.

J. LOUIS JOHNSON

After a stage career spanning more than forty years and ranging from medicine shows to Florenz Ziegfeld productions, J. Louis Johnson at age sixty-four started a career in motion pictures. Johnson was born in Indianapolis on March 20, 1878. He attended public schools in Indiana and then entered the University of Kentucky, where he majored in commerce and music and set out to establish himself in a business career. However, he was exposed to show business after taking a job in the offices of the Lyceum vaudeville circuit in Chicago.

At age twenty-two, Johnson joined a medicine show. He left that show to become a member of the Georgia Minstrels troupe and began a long career in vaudeville. David Belasco introduced him to Broadway in his production of *Lulu Belle*. Johnson later appeared in *Blackbirds* and understudied both Jules Bledsoe and Paul Robeson in Ziegfeld's production of *Showboat*. When Bledsoe became ill and left the cast, Johnson stepped into the lead as Joe.

Johnson then joined the Orson Welles/John Houseman Federal Theater Project's production of *Macbeth* and was soon involved in other roles with the Welles-Houseman group. In 1940 Johnson joined Ethel Waters on Broadway in the cast of *Cabin in the Sky*. When the show went on national tour, he accepted a film role in *Syncopation* (1942). His next role, in that same year, was in the Welles film adaptation of Booth Tarkington's *The Magnificent Ambersons*, playing Sam, the butler. In 1946 Houseman called upon Johnson to appear in *Miss Susie Slagle's*. He played Hizer, a warm and genuine character who was a retainer at a boardinghouse for medical students.

Johnson died on April 29, 1954. His last role was as a butler in the Alfred Hitchcock thriller, *Strangers on a Train*, in 1951.

BIBLIOGRAPHY

"Biography of J. Louis Johnson." Paramount Pictures. Academy of Motion Picture Arts and Sciences, Beverly Hills, California.

The Internet Movie Database. http://www.imdb.com/.

ALEX KARRAS

Alex Karras and his wife Susan Clark in the ABC television series *Webster* (1985).
©1985, ABC, INC.

Alexander George Karras gained national prominence in two diverse careers. He was an outstanding college and professional football player and parlayed this notoriety into a successful motion picture career. He was born in Gary, Indiana, on July 15, 1935. He went to the University of Iowa on a football scholarship and played on the Hawkeyes' 1956 Rose Bowl championship team. In 1957 he was given the Outland Trophy, honoring the outstanding interior lineman in the nation, and was second in voting for the Heisman Trophy.

After being named a consensus all-American, Karras was drafted by the Detroit Lions, where he played as a tackle from 1958 to 1971. In 1968 he appeared as himself in the popular film *Paper Lion*. This led to more movie roles, starting with *Hardcase* (1971) and *The 500 Pound Jerk* (1972). He was a hit as Mongo in the Mel Brooks classic *Blazing Saddles* (1974). His successful transition to films led to a contract with ABC as a color commentator on *Monday Night Football* from 1974 to 1976.

In 1975 Karras played George Zaharias, the husband of Babe Zaharias, in the film biography *Babe*. In this film he met his future wife, Susan Clark, who played the title role. In 1975 he divorced his first wife, Joan Jurgeson, whom he had married in 1958, and married Clark in 1980. They became a team and appeared together in movies and television, including the hit television series *Webster*.

BIBLIOGRAPHY

Alex Karras biography. http://movies.yahoo.com/.

Karras, Alex. *Alex Karras: My Life in Football, Television, and Movies.* Garden City, N.Y.: Doubleday, 1979.

———, with Herb Glack. *Even Big Guys Cry.* New York: Holt, Rinehart and Winston, 1977.

Scene from *Daydreams* (1922) with (left to right) Buster Keaton, his father Joe Keaton, Eddie Cline, and Renee Adoree.

JOE KEATON

Terre Haute, Indiana, has the honor of being the city in which Buster Keaton made his first solo appearance on stage. His father, Joseph Hallie Keaton, was a Hoosier, born near Prairie Creek on July 6, 1867. Joe's family moved to Terre Haute in the late 1870s to allow him to attend Hook School. His parents, Joseph Z. and Libbie Keaton, managed the Henderson House, a small hotel at 209 S. Fourth Street.

As a teen, Keaton preferred billiard parlors to classrooms. He practiced flip-flops, the vaudeville term for backward somersaults, on the sawdust piles at Thomas John's Mill on North First Street. It was not long before he obtained a portable shoe-shine stand and located it in front of the Naylor Opera House at Fourth and Wabash. He used "acrobatic buffing" to become (in his words) "boss bootblack on Paul Dresser's Wabash Avenue."

Keaton heard about the land rush in Oklahoma and the investing in homestead claims. In 1889, at the age of twenty-two, he persuaded his father to loan him one hundred dollars, and he left Terre Haute and headed for the Cherokee Strip, located near Perry, Oklahoma. He was able to secure land in Perry and was waiting in line to clear his claim when a medicine show came through. He had always been intrigued with show business and became further infatuated when he met fifteen-year-old Myra Cutler, daughter of Frank Cutler, of the Cutler-Bryant Medicine Show. He joined the medicine show in 1892.

As Buster tells it, "As soon as he got his claim filed, he joined the show as a stagehand and worked his way up to playing bits in the show, and it was just automatically a natural thing for him. He was a natural dancer, a great pair of legs for eccentric work and high kicking, and a natural clown." Two years later, after Joe and Myra eloped, Frank fired Joe. The newlyweds, forced to make it on their own, joined the Mohawk Indian Medicine Show as "The Two Keatons." On October 4, 1895, Joseph Frank "Buster" Keaton was born while the act was playing in Piqua, Kansas. Buster said, "They left my mother there for two weeks, and then she rejoined the show with me." The family never returned to Piqua.

Buster recalled: "The show I was born with was called the Harry Houdini and Keaton Medicine Show Company. That was the great Harry Houdini, the handcuff king. That's how he started out. And he gave me the name of Buster. I was six months old, in a little hotel we were living at in some town. I crawled out of the room, crawled to the head of the stairs, and fell down the whole flight of stairs. When I lit at the bottom and they saw that I was all right, I wasn't hurt badly, Houdini said, 'It sure was a buster,' and the old man said, 'That's a good name for him.' I never lost the name."

In 1899 Keaton brought his athletic "Man with the Table" act to Terre Haute. They were on their way to New York City, where they would achieve much greater fame. During the two-week visit to Terre Haute, three-year-old Buster made his first solo appearance on stage. The act was now called "The Three Keatons," and Buster became known as "The Human Mop" when Joe threw him around the stage. Buster said, "we were the roughest knockabout act that ever was in the history of the theater, not only in the United States but all over Europe as well. We used to get arrested every other week . . . that is, the old man would get arrested."

Joe Keaton.

One of their routines involved Myra and her saxophone. During her syrupy, sad performance, Buster stretched a basketball to the end of a long elastic rope and let it go, bashing Joe's head into the mirror while he was shaving with a straight razor. Another was kind of a representation of the origin of all wars. As Buster swept a tabletop with a broom, he would pick up an imaginary object and move it to a different spot. Joe, interrupted in his declamation of some poem or song, would go over and replace the thing where it was before. Buster would take it away again, and Joe would grab it and put it back again. Soon they were "fighting wildly, blasting, kicking, punching, and throwing one another across the table and all over the stage." Routines like this, full of anger, danger, and suspense, were great crowd-pleasers on the vaudeville circuit. They also served to get Buster thoroughly in trim for the thrills and surprises that later would sell tickets in movie theaters.

The Keatons had two more children: Harry, named after Harry Houdini, and Louise Dresser, named for Joe's hometown idol. Keaton had offers to appear in motion pictures, but scoffed at them, preferring a live audience. In 1917, when Keaton's addiction to alcohol started to affect his timing on stage and made him difficult to live with, Myra forced the couple's separation.

Buster decided to go to New York to see what work he could find there. While appearing at Shubert's Winter Garden, he met Fatty Arbuckle. Arbuckle asked him if he had ever been in pictures. When Buster said no, Arbuckle invited him to do a bit with him. He did and began to find regular employment in the industry.

Buster perpetually credited Joe for his immense talent and cast him in thirteen of his films. Joe stayed married to Myra, whom he called "America's First Lady Saxophonist." On January 10, 1946, Keaton was struck and killed by an automobile. He was seventy-nine years old.

BIBLIOGRAPHY

"Buster Keaton." Columbia University Oral History Project, November 1958. Academy of Motion Picture Arts and Sciences, Beverly Hills, California.

MacCann, Richard Dyer, comp. *The Silent Comedians.* Metuchen, N.J.: Scarecrow Press, 1993.

Scene from *Written on the Wind* (1956) with (left to right) Rock Hudson, Robert Keith, and Grant Williams.

ROBERT KEITH

Robert Keith Richey was born on February 10, 1898 (some sources say 1896), in Fowler, Indiana. He began his career as a teenager in silent movie houses, where he sang illustrated songs to piano accompaniment. He later joined a stock company and began touring the country, appearing in dozens of plays.

Keith made his Broadway debut in 1921 in *Triumph of X.* He appeared in four more Broadway productions, including the lead in Eugene O'Neill's *Beyond the Horizon* in 1926. Richard Bennett, another Hoosier, had originated the role of Robert Mayo in the first production of this O'Neill play in 1920. In 1927 Keith wrote a play called *The Tightwad* that was produced on Broadway by Lee Shubert. The show did not have a long run, but it was well received by the critics. This brought him to the attention of Hollywood, and he started writing dialogue for Universal Studios in 1930. He managed to appear in bit parts in several movies during his stay at Universal.

Keith remained active on Broadway, appearing in nine productions in the 1930s. He had a daughter by his first wife, Laura Corinne Jackson, whom he had married in 1917. He had a son, Robert Keith Jr., by his second wife, actress Helen Shipman. He divorced Shipman in 1926 and in 1930 married Dorothy Tierney, who was his wife until his death. Robert Keith Jr. made his stage debut at age three with his father in 1924 in *The Pied Piper of Malone.* He also appeared in a number of films that featured his father. When Keith originated the role of Doc in *Mr. Roberts* on Broadway in 1951, Bob Jr. was listed as part of the ensemble. Robert Keith Richey Jr. eventually changed his name to Brian Keith and became a well-known motion picture and television actor.

Unfortunately, when *Mr. Roberts* was translated to film in 1955, many of the original Broadway actors were not used. William Harriman, who played the captain, was replaced by James Cagney. David

Wayne, who played Ensign Pulver, was replaced by Jack Lemmon, and Keith was replaced by William Powell as Doc. At least one Hoosier reversed this trend. Betsy Palmer of East Chicago, Indiana, replaced Jocelyn Brando as Lieutenant Ann Girard in the film version.

Keith died December 22, 1966, in Los Angeles.

BIBLIOGRAPHY

The Internet Broadway Database. http://www.ibdb.com/.

The Internet Movie Database. http://www.imdb.com/.

Twomey, Alfred E., and Arthur F. McClure. *The Versatiles: A Study of Supporting Character Actors and Actresses in the American Motion Picture, 1930–1955.* New York: Castle Books, 1969.

PRISCILLA SHORTRIDGE LAWSON

It was no coincidence that Priscilla Shortridge's last name was the same as her high school. The school was named after a relative, Abram Crum Shortridge, who was public schools superintendent in Indianapolis and later served as president of Purdue University. Some sources state that Abram was Priscilla's grandfather, but this information came from a studio publicity release and was not true. It is more likely he was a distant relative. The fact that her school was named after one of her relatives did not make Priscilla's lessons any easier. If anything, she recalled, the teachers were harder on her. Most of them knew her parents, so all the more reason for showing no favoritism. "At the time I hated them for it, but now I can't thank them enough for making me study. I was inclined to be lazy and, if they hadn't forced me to work, I never would have," said Shortridge.

Priscilla Lawson.

Priscilla was born in Indianapolis on March 8, 1914, the daughter of Elmer and Elizabeth "Minnie" Hess Shortridge. Her given name was Biscella, but she soon changed it to the more common Priscilla. She attended Eliza Blaker's kindergarten and continued through the grades, taking music lessons along the way. She always had a flair for the dramatic and liked to act out plays on the front steps with the neighbor children. She and her parents lived at 1112 Pleasant Street in Indianapolis.

John Thompson used to sit next to Priscilla in the history reference room at Shortridge High School. He said that it was not her last name that elicited excitement during those days. Groups of jealous girls and admiring boys gathered in the halls just to watch this tall, slender, Latin-type beauty walk by. Thompson said she was the prettiest girl in the school: "She allowed her coal black hair to grow long while most of the other girls bobbed and marcelled. With graceful carriage, erect head and shoulders, Priscilla was outstanding in the sea of excited, giddy school girls."

Priscilla's early role model was movie actress Priscilla Dean. However, she did not think she could become an actress and decided to try to become a jewelry designer. After her mother investigated this career and discovered there was only one jewelry designing school in the United States, she suggested that her daughter switch to designing clothes. Priscilla said of her mother's suggestion, "I have always thought she judged my ability, however, from the way I designed clothes for my dolls." She studied dress designing and art but did not take any dramatic classes. She said she read several plays a week and portrayed various roles in the privacy of her bedroom: "I was everything from a heroine to the villain those evenings. But there was no one there to laugh, boo or criticize me, so I slowly gained courage and self-assurance. But there was also no one to coach me and I acquired many bad acting habits which later required hours of practice to change."

After graduating from Shortridge, Priscilla got a job at the Charles Mayer and Company store in downtown Indianapolis and then was offered a modeling job at L. S. Ayres. When her mother decided she wanted to go to Miami for a rest, Priscilla left her Ayres job and headed for Miami in October 1934. There she swam, played tennis, and was hired by a large department store as a model. The following January, Priscilla was chosen to lead the annual fashion show at Burdine Department Store. After the show she began receiving other modeling offers, but she turned them all down because she had decided she wanted to go into commercial photography.

Priscilla Lawson and Buster Crabbe in *Flash Gordon* (1936).

In March 1935 she was walking along Miami Beach near Roman Pools when she met a friend who asked her why she was not in the bathing beauty contest that was being held at the beach. Priscilla said she did not know about it. She entered the contest just thirty minutes before it was to start, won first place, and was given the title "Miss Miami Beach." The judges were movie star George Bancroft, stage and screen star Harry Richman, and sportswriter Damon Runyan. Priscilla began to receive inquiries from stage and screen producers. A story in the *Indianapolis Star* about the contest refers to Priscilla as "Mrs. Priscilla Lawson." Apparently some time prior to 1935 she was married.

Lawson accepted an offer to become one of Earl Carroll's chorus girls in his famous Miami casino. After a brief stint at the casino, Lawson and her mother decided to move to New York in order to better pursue a modeling career. In New York she began modeling hats for Lili Dasche. A representative from Universal Studios saw her and told her he would like to test her for moving pictures. Lawson expressed interest, and the next day she was in front of cameras, posing for all kinds of shots. The next night she was asked to board the *Normandie*, which was in port. There she played her first screen role, a bit part in *Sweet Surrender* (1935), being partially shot on board the ship. Lawson appeared in an elaborate fashion show sequence. After this appearance, Universal announced she would next be seen in support of Jack Holt in *Captain Commanding*. Apparently, this film was never produced.

After her first film appearance, a surprised Lawson said, "Three days later we were on a plane bound for Los Angeles." When she arrived, she made a screen test and was given her first film credit—that of a maid in *The Great Impersonation* in 1935. She was in *His Night Out*, also in 1935, with fellow Hoosier Lola Lane. She was a saloon girl in a Buck Jones serial, *The Phantom Rider*, in 1936 and appeared in *Sutter's Gold*, codirected by Hoosier Howard Hawks the same year. Later that year she was cast in the role for which she will be most remembered.

Universal Studios was embarking on the production of a movie serial unlike any that had ever been made. It was the most expensive and perhaps most popular serial of all time. At first, Filmcraft Pictures titled the film *Rocket Ship* but later changed it to the name of the comic strip from which the plot and characters were taken—*Flash Gordon*. *Flash Gordon* cost a reputed $350,000 to produce, which was well over three times the cost of the average serial production. It boasted elaborate special effects, costumes, monsters, and weaponry. Out of approximately 220 talking serials made through the mid-1950s, this 1936 serial stands head and shoulders above the rest. Buster Crabbe was Flash Gordon, and Jean Rogers played Dale Arden. Lawson was chosen to play Princess Aura, daughter of Charles Middleton's Ming the Merciless. As Aura, Lawson falls in love with Flash and tries persistently to win him from Dale. There were thirteen episodes, but the serial proved so popular that a twelve-episode sequel was shot in 1940. Unfortunately, Lawson was replaced by Shirley Deane. Deane, however, was no match for the exotic beauty of Lawson.

Lawson had a one-year contract with Universal. It was not renewed, and she was picked up by Paramount but was only offered bit parts. When her Paramount contract ran out, she experienced several months of unemployment and decided to return to New York and resume her modeling career. However, before she left she was surprised by an offer from MGM. The studio offered her a contract and more substantial parts. She signed with MGM, and in October 1937 she met another MGM player, Alan Curtis. Both Lawson and Curtis had been models and came to Hollywood with no acting background. They hit it off and were married on November 14, 1937, in Las Vegas. Lawson was twenty-three, and Curtis was twenty-eight.

Shortly before her marriage Lawson was interviewed by Corbin Patrick, drama editor of the *Indianapolis Star*. Lawson talked of her new life in Hollywood: "I live in a small bungalow in Hollywood with my mother. [Her father stayed in Indianapolis.] I like the people here, the weather and the work, and I'll stay as long as Hollywood wants me." She told Patrick that she was currently playing the role of Myrna Loy's secretary in *Double Wedding*.

Lawson kept busy, appearing in four films in 1937 and nine films in 1938. Her last film was *Billy the Kid* (1941), where she was uncredited. She made at least twenty-nine films from 1935 to 1941. Most of her roles were small, and many were uncredited. As her career cooled down, so did her marriage to Curtis. They separated, and Curtis began dating Sonja Henie. Lawson left Los Angeles for an extended European trip, followed by a stay in New York. In early spring of 1941, Lawson's divorce became final. Shortly after, Curtis married actress Ilona Massey.

During World War II, Lawson joined the armed forces under her married name (Curtis's real name was Harry Ueberroth). The late Jean Rogers, who first met Lawson when they both had bit parts in *His Night Out* in 1935 and who costarred with Lawson in the *Flash Gordon* serial, stated in an interview that Lawson had lost a leg during the war, possibly in a jeep accident. This was not true, as photos of Lawson the year she died show her in shorts and both legs are intact. After the war, Lawson divorced Curtis and married Forest Jones, who was ten years younger than Lawson. The marriage did not last long. Jones left Lawson, and she never heard from him again. Due to his disappearance, Lawson never got a proper divorce. During her last years, she lived in her own home on Loma Avenue in Monrovia, California. She met a local carpenter named Richard Merchant, who became her common-law husband. She lived with him until her death in 1958. Merchant passed away in 1964.

Lawson never returned to the screen. She died in the Veterans Administration hospital at Wilshire and Sawtelle boulevards in West Los Angeles on August 27, 1958, at age forty-four. Her death certificate lists two last names—Jones and Ueberroth. The cause of death was listed as upper gastrointestinal bleeding due to a duodenal ulcer. She was buried in Live Oak Memorial Park in Monrovia, California.

BIBLIOGRAPHY

Bodenhamer, David J., and Robert G. Barrows, eds. *The Encyclopedia of Indianapolis.* Bloomington and Indianapolis: Indiana University Press, 1994.

Gordon, Jeff. "Flight to Nowhere: The Alan Curtis Story." *Films of the Golden Age* (Winter 2003/04).

The Internet Movie Database. http://www.imdb.com/.

Indianapolis Star, March 28, 1935, August 3, 1937.

Indianapolis Times, December 18, 1935.

Kinnard, Roy. "Priscilla Lawson: Mysterious Princess of Mongo." *Classic Images* 317 (November 2001).

Mast, Daniel. Interview with the author. August 27, 2002. Port Angeles, California.

Shortridge, Douglass. Interview with the author. December 7, 2001. Indianapolis.

Shortridge High School Yearbook, 1931.

Weiss, Ken, and Ed Goodgold. *To Be Continued . . . A Complete Guide to Motion Picture Serials.* New York: Crown Publishers, 1972.

Zinman, David H. *Fifty Classic Motion Pictures: The Stuff that Dreams Are Made Of.* New York: Crown Publishers, 1970.

BILLY LEE

When Billy Lee Schlensker was born on March 21, 1929, on a farm in Nelson, Indiana (near Terre Haute), there was little indication that this frail little boy would become a multitalented child movie star. Until he was two years old, Billy lived a quiet life on the family farm. In 1932 the Schlensker family moved to Los Angeles, California, in hopes of improving the health of Billy's asthmatic father.

After settling in Los Angeles, Billy's parents decided to give their son singing and dancing lessons. They enrolled him in the Meglin School for Stage Children, run by Ethel Meglin, who was a well-known music teacher and acting, dancing, and singing coach. Her former pupils included Shirley Temple, Judy Garland, Jane Withers, Ann Miller, June Lang, and Mickey Rooney. At one time her "Kiddies" were billed as "Ethel Meglin's Hollywood Wonder Kids." They appeared on film and stage and even did private parties.

(Opposite page) Billy Lee.

From the beginning, Meglin was delighted with Billy. He was a bright and cooperative child who was eager to learn and had a rare natural talent. Meglin became Billy's personal coach in voice, dance, and acting and also instructed him on a variety of musical instruments. Unfortunately, after only a few months of training, Billy's father discontinued his schooling, and the family returned to their farm in Indiana.

Meglin kept in touch with the parents and continued to show interest in Billy. The Schlenskers came to the conclusion that Billy did indeed have a great deal of natural talent, and they asked Billy if he wanted to return to his school in Hollywood. Billy readily agreed to return. In 1934 Billy was reenrolled at the Meglin School. Within two months, Meglin felt Billy was ready to handle his first film role. She learned that an *Our Gang* film was in need of some "outside kids." Billy was in a gang that was to compete with the Our Gang regulars in a radio contest. When Billy did a tap routine, Spanky threw up his hands and said, "Well! That's that!"

Beginning with this film experience at age four, Billy became Billy Lee. Meglin continued to work with Lee through the 1940s. Lee's next role was that of a small boy in *Wagon Wheels*, released in 1934 and starring Randolph Scott. His mother in the film was played by Gail Patrick. Lee sang the movie's theme song and went on to appear in more than forty films.

The film that ensured Lee an enduring legacy was the sleeper hit of 1940, *The Biscuit Eater*, the story of two little boys, one black and one white (Fred Toones was the black boy), who take an unwanted dog from a litter and name him "Promise." They enter a bird dog competition in which their fathers are also entered. The favorite to win is the dog belonging to the fathers. If the fathers do not win, they will lose their jobs. Although this was a B picture, some have called it the best film of 1940.

Lee's career ended in 1943 at the age of thirteen. His last film was *Eyes of the Underworld*, in which he played the son of Richard Dix, who was a chief of police. In later life, Lee said, "I missed out on a lot of things when I was a kid. But, on the other hand, I went places, saw things and knew people that a lot of kids only heard about." Lee's income went mostly to his parents. He said, "At age three my father quit working and he didn't work again the rest of his life. Please don't misunderstand. I think it's great when kids can help their parents. My point is, during 'my time' the kids had no protection. None of that went into effect until 1947. . . . I've always said that I raised [financially] two families."

Lee died on November 11, 1989, in Beaumont, California, of a sudden heart attack.

Billy Lee in a scene from *The Biscuit Eater* (1940).

© 1940, PARAMOUNT PICTURES INC.

BIBLIOGRAPHY

Best, Marc. *Those Endearing Young Charms: Child Performers of the Screen.* South Brunswick, N.J.: A. S. Barnes, 1971.

STROTHER MARTIN

The name Strother is derived from the German word for river. Perhaps Strother Martin's name was appropriate in that he would achieve his first claim to fame in the water. Martin was born in Kokomo, Indiana, on March 26, 1919. When he was five, his family moved to the countryside near Cloverdale, Indiana, where his father worked as a power company lineman. Later the family moved to Indianapolis, and Martin graduated from George Washington High School. He said he was reared in the "Hell's Kitchen" district of Indianapolis during the Great Depression. "I almost didn't graduate from high school, but when I did it was in shirtsleeves. We couldn't afford a suit," he said.

Martin then entered the University of Michigan, where he majored in theater arts and became the top diver on the school's championship swimming team, ultimately winning an NCAA diving championship. He finished third in the National Springboard Diving Championships, just missing a berth on the 1948 Olympic team. He once recalled, "The posturing and narcissism of diving might have influenced me to study drama. At any rate, it was the first course I got a B in, so I decided to major in it."

In his last year at Michigan, Martin joined the navy, rising to the rank of ensign. He was assigned to Pearl Harbor, where he taught sailors how to swim. After World War II he returned to Michigan, finished his degree, and headed for Hollywood. His first job was teaching swimming at an exclusive Santa Monica beach club. He began studying with Mikail Chekhov, and he recalled Chekhov giving him some advice that he never forgot: "I'm going to think of my part and let the characters come and play with me." Like many would-be actors, Martin struggled for years for recognition. He said, "I was thirty-five years old before I began to make a living. I have played many desperate persons and am well trained for it."

Strother Martin in Sssssss (1973).

Martin's first acting job was on television station KTLA's children's show, *Mable's Fables*. He played a leprechaun, for which he received five dollars per appearance. He finally landed his first movie role—a silent bit in *The Asphalt Jungle*. Then came steady employment in television. He made numerous appearances on *Gunsmoke* and *Have Gun, Will Travel*, and he eventually would make at least five hundred television appearances. About this heavy television exposure he said, "I worked so much in television, that one night I ran into Jack Oakie at a party and he yelled, 'Hey, I saw a TV show the other night and you weren't in it.'"

Martin starred with James Stewart in *Hawkins*, a short-lived television series, and toured the country with Henry Fonda in *The Time of Your Life*. He began to get some small movie parts and then came his big break. In 1967 he was cast as Captain in *Cool Hand Luke* after Telly Savalas was signed for the role but was dropped from the picture. In this film Martin uttered a phrase that has become one of the most memorable in all of motion pictures: "What we've got here is . . . failure to communicate." Reflecting on his being cast in *Luke*, he said, "Everything happened from *Luke*. Before then I was known mostly for TV. Directors don't count TV as film. You have to be a movie actor to work in the movies."

After *Luke*, Martin appeared in five more movies with Paul Newman. He was a favorite of Newman and directors Sam Peckinpah, George Roy Hill, and John Ford. He worked with Peckinpah in television and in 1969 was cast by Peckinpah in *The Wild Bunch*. Peckinpah described Martin as "one of the finest actors in the world." However, Martin's relationship with Peckinpah was tenuous. Martin did not like horses; Peckinpah knew this and purposely gave him the tallest horse and made him mount on a downhill grade. "He chewed my ass off every line, every, every one of them," Martin said. "I sensed that he liked me but I wasn't sure." Martin liked to impersonate Peckinpah, and he did a deadly accurate imitation of Peckinpah's whispery hissing voice. To add to the effect, he would put a pair of spoons over his eyes to mimic the way Peckinpah always wore mirrored sunglasses. "I could never tell if he was joking or serious," Martin said, "because his voice was completely devoid of emotion and you can't see his eyes because of those goddamned mirrored sunglasses."

Martin's versatility was amply demonstrated when he went from a memorable comic role in *True Grit* in 1969 (Colonel G. Stonehill) to a killer completely without conscience in *Hannie Caulder* in 1971. When he began to earn a decent living, he moved into then-rustic Laurel Canyon, saying, "I was born in the country. If I don't see the stars and the sunrise and sunset, I'm miserable. I like to see starlight zigzag in the water."

Martin said his three favorite movies were *Cool Hand Luke, The Wild Bunch*, and *Butch Cassidy and the Sundance Kid*. In most of his films, he was cast as a psychotic, a crooked frontier businessman, a not-too-bright bank robber, or something similar. He was called upon frequently to go psycho. He said, "Generally when I have that scene in a script, the director will take me aside and say 'Go ape.' I did that three times in one picture and got so tired of it."

Martin's celluloid viciousness paid off handsomely. He recalled, "Lee Marvin said to me once, 'We actors play all kinds . . . sex perverts, mother killers, deviates . . . and when we finish we laugh to ourselves and say 'What the heck, it's only a part,' but we're kidding ourselves. It's you, baby, it's you! What you do is take a fault in yourself and magnify it. You expose yourself; all art is confession. Like other actors I want to reveal more of myself, frightening as that may be."

Although Martin enjoyed his work as a character actor, deep down he had a yearning to play more sophisticated parts: "On the marquee they write my name down at the bottom. I'm very satisfied to keep it there. It's a nice spot . . . but I would look forward to a more complex role . . . and I would enjoy getting dressed up a bit more often and maybe one day playing a college graduate, because I am one and it was one tough struggle." He was delighted with his role in *Slap Shot*, another Newman movie, because he played the manager of a hockey team and he got to sit behind a desk in a suit, white shirt, and tie. "It's so nice to be off a horse," he said.

Martin's last film was *Hotwire* in 1980, playing a character called The Weasel. He enjoyed gardening, collecting antiques, and music. His home was elaborately rigged with an array of stereo equipment, and he usually studied his lines to a background of classical music.

Martin died on August 1, 1980, in Thousand Oaks, California, of a heart attack. He was survived by his wife, Helen, and a sister, Mrs. Durbin Williams of Indianapolis.

BIBLIOGRAPHY

Entertainment World, April 24, 1970.

Fine, Marshall. *Bloody Sam: The Life and Films of Sam Peckinpah*. New York: D. I. Fine, 1991.

Indianapolis Star, January 6, 1962, March 6, 1977.

Jones, Ken D., Arthur F. McClure, and Alfred E. Twomey. *Character People.* South Brunswick, N.J.: A. S. Barnes, 1976.

Los Angeles Herald-Examiner, March 30, 1970, March 14, 1977.

Quinlan, David. *Quinlan's Illustrated Directory of Film Character Actors.* London: B. T. Batsford, 1985.

Reed, John Shelton. "A Southerner Revisits *Cool Hand Luke*." AMC *Magazine* (November 2000).

MYRON McCORMICK

Myron McCormick was born in Albany, Indiana, on February 8, 1908. By the age of eleven he was touring with a medicine show, thanks to some Albany neighbors who operated one. Along with his duties as ticket taker, errand boy, and property man, he had several walk-on parts. He was stagestruck, and his future was settled. He attended New Mexico Military Institute and later went to Princeton, where he was the comedy star of one of the famous Triangle shows, *The Tiger Smiles.* The play was written by fellow student Josh Logan, who later served as coauthor and director of *South Pacific.* This fact helped McCormick land the plum role of Luther Billis in the original Broadway production.

In 1929 McCormick joined the University Players in Massachusetts, eventually sharing a New York City apartment with a trio of struggling performers: Henry Fonda, Logan, and James Stewart. Fonda and Stewart moved into motion pictures, but Logan and McCormick became closely associated with the New York stage. Other fellow University players were Jose Ferrer, Margaret Sullivan, and Bretaigne Windust.

Myron McCormick (1954).
©1954, COLUMBIA PICTURES CORP.

McCormick made his Broadway debut in 1932 in *Carrie Nation.* In 1935 he appeared in the brief Broadway run of a play, *On to Fortune*, which starred Robert T. Haines of Muncie, Indiana. An ingénue by the name of Martha Hodge was also in the cast. It was not long before she and McCormick were married. Hodge appeared in several more Broadway productions and even produced a play, *The Cat Screams*, in 1942.

While in New York, McCormick became a very busy radio actor, appearing in such soap operas as *Portia Faces Life* and *Joyce Jordan, Girl Intern.* He was in dramas such as *Mr. District Attorney*, *Inner Sanctum*, and *Gang Busters.* He made occasional movies, mostly when the entire Broadway cast was put in the film version. Maxwell Anderson's *Winterset* (1936) was one of these. Although he won a Tony award for best supporting actor as Luther Billis in *South Pacific*, the film role went to Ray Walston. When he created the role of the Sergeant in *No Time for Sergeants* in 1955, there was no one who could replace him and he was a big hit in the movie version.

McCormick began to appear in more films—*Jigsaw, Jolson Sings Again* (both 1949), *Not as a Stranger*, *Three for the Show* (both 1955), and *The Hustler* (1961). He said that stage, radio, and the screen performances have more in common than most people believe. "Although an actor can learn a great deal by working in all three mediums," he adds, "he should be able to succeed in all of them if he is able to make his mark in one of them." In 1962 he made his last film, *A Public Affair.* He died of cancer on July 30, 1962, in New York City.

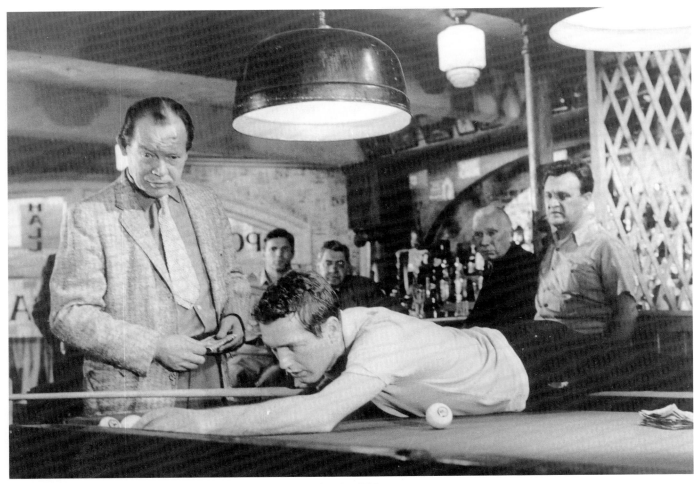

Scene from *The Hustler* (1964) showing
Paul Newman shooting pool as Myron
McCormick looks on.
©1964, TWENTIETH CENTURY-FOX FILM CORP.

BIBLIOGRAPHY

The Internet Broadway Database. http://www.ibdb.com/.
The Internet Movie Database. http://www.imdb.com/.
Jones, Ken D., Arthur F. McClure, and Alfred E. Twomey. *Char-
acter People.* South Brunswick, N.J.: A. S. Barnes, 1976.
Ross, John. "From Medicine Show to Broadway." *Indianapolis Star
Magazine*, December 1949.

PATRICK McVEY

Patrick McVey was born in Fort Wayne, Indiana, on March 17,
1910. After studying law at Indiana University, he practiced in
Fort Wayne. In 1938, after enrolling in the Pasadena Playhouse
in California, he left Indiana and headed west. After his training at the
Playhouse, he began getting bit parts in movies. To make ends meet,
he worked for a while in the classified ads department for the *Los Angeles Times.* He was uncredited in his first film in 1941, *They Died with Their
Boots On.* Indeed, his first few film appearances in 1941 and 1942 were
uncredited. However, he was appearing in some major films with major
stars, and this eventually led to larger roles and credited appearances.

McVey's big break came when he was cast as crusading newspaper editor Steve Wilson of *The Illustrated Press* in the television series *Big Town.* This
was in the early days of television, and he did one hundred *Big Town* programs—all live. The series ran from 1950 to 1954. In 1959 McVey again

had a regular role in a television series. This time he played a detective opposite Victor Jory in *Manhunt*. This series ran from 1959 to 1961.

McVey continued to perform in movies and, while seldom a leading man, kept busy with a variety of supporting roles. His Broadway career started in 1947, and he occasionally returned to the stage. He appeared in *Detective Story*, *Bus Stop*, and *The Subject Was Roses*. In 1970 he played Don Quixote in the revival of Tennessee Williams's *Camino Real*, and in 1972 he starred in *The Visitors*, a film by Chris Kazan, directed by Kazan's father, Elia Kazan. He was a member of the Actors Studio and The Players.

McVey died in New York City on July 7, 1973, and was survived by his widow, Courteen Landis McVey, and a brother.

BIBLIOGRAPHY

Ankenbruck, John. *Twentieth-Century History of Fort Wayne*. Fort Wayne, Ind.: Twentieth Century History of Fort Wayne, 1975.

The Internet Movie Database. http://www.imdb.com/.

Jones, Ken D., Arthur F. McClure, and Alfred E. Twomey. *Character People*. South Brunswick, N.J.: A. S. Barnes, 1976.

Los Angeles Times, July 7, 1973.

Patrick McVey and Mary K. Wells in the television series *Big Town* (1951).
©CBS PHOTO

MICHAEL MICHELE

Michael Michele was born in Evansville, Indiana, on August 20, 1966. She attended Howard Roosa Elementary School in Evansville and became a big basketball fan. She played basketball in high school, where her team made it to the state championships. She also participated in track and volleyball. She still is a committed runner and shoots baskets between takes when she is making a movie or a television show.

Michele moved to the East Coast to concentrate on an acting career in the late 1980s. In 1989, after a few minor television roles and some commercials, she got her big break when she was cast in Eddie Murphy's *Harlem Nights*. However, she was fired during the shooting and later filed a sexual harassment suit against Murphy. It was settled out of court.

Michele rebounded in 1991 with a good part in Mario Van Peeble's *New Jack City*. A year later she became a regular on the television series *Dangerous Curves*. Her performance in the miniseries *Trade Winds* (1993) gave her good notices and helped her land several roles. She was in *Homicide: Life on the Street* in 1998. A year later she moved in as a regular on *ER*, where from 1999 to 2002 she appeared as Dr. Cleo Finch. She has appeared in two major motion pictures, *Dark Blue* (2002) and *How to Lose a Guy in Ten Days* (2003).

Michele is a devoted jazz fan and actively works with underprivileged children.

Michael Michele.

BIBLIOGRAPHY

The Internet Movie Database. http://www.imdb.com/.

Yahoo! Biography. http://movies.yahoo.com/.

GENEVA MITCHELL

Born on February 3, 1908, in Medaryville, Indiana, and educated in Chicago, Geneva Mitchell went from the stage to the Ziegfeld Follies to a career in motion pictures. Studio publicity indicates that Mitchell was five feet five inches tall with brown hair and blue eyes. She was on stage for nine years, five of which were with the Follies. She played opposite Leon Errol on stage in *Louis the 14th* and then landed the role of the ingenue opposite fellow Hoosier Marilyn Miller in the Broadway hit musical *Sally.*

Unfortunately, when *Sally* was made into a film, Mitchell was not in the cast. However, she did enter films in 1929, making a few shorts until her feature debut in 1930 in *Son of the Gods*, which starred Richard Barthelmess and Constance Bennett.

Mitchell is fondly remembered by Western film buffs because of her four films with two of the most popular cowboys of the day. She costarred with fellow Hoosier Ken Maynard in three films—*Lawless Riders* and *Western Courage*, both in 1935, and *Cattle Thief* in 1936. She also played opposite Tim McCoy in *Fighting Shadows* in 1935.

Mitchell's movie career was certainly diverse. She was in *Morning Glory* with Katharine Hepburn in 1933, and near the end of her career she appeared in at least one Three Stooges short.

In 1938 Mitchell was arrested briefly when her agent, George H. Talbot, made a false report to the effect that Mitchell had been

Geneva Mitchell and Ken Maynard (Vevay) in *Cattle Thief* (1936).
COURTESY OF THE ACADEMY OF MOTION PICTURE ARTS AND SCIENCES

robbed of various personal effects, including a $250 platinum watch given to her by her late fiancé, director Lowell Sherman. Talbot said, "I did it against her wishes." The agent was fined, and Mitchell was exonerated.

Mitchell's last film in 1946 was a short starring comedian Andy Clyde. She died March 10, 1949.

BIBLIOGRAPHY

Los Angeles Examiner, September 24, 1935.

Truitt, Evelyn Mack. *Who Was Who on Screen.* New York: R. R. Bowker, 1984.

ALVY MOORE

Jack Alvin Moore was born to Roy and Elsie Moore in Vincennes, Indiana, on December 5, 1921. His family moved to Terre Haute, where his father operated the Liberty Meat Market on Wabash Avenue. Alvy attended elementary school, Sarah Scott Junior High, and Wiley High School. He also attended Indiana State University, known then as Indiana State Teachers College, and was active in bands and in theater classes.

Alvy Moore.

Moore was a skinny, crew-cut, fast-talking comedian during his most popular days in show business. His second cousin, Margaret Barksdale, and his boyhood pal, Dave Kirk, remember that he was good with voices and was one of the best stand-up comics. Kirk said, "He had an outstanding personality and was always quick with a joke. He was a mischievous rascal."

Before Moore's career really got started, he married Carolyn Mohr of Kokomo, Indiana. They were married forty-seven years and had three children, Barry, Janet, and Allyson. During World War II Moore served in the Marine Corps and fought in the battle of Iwo Jima. For a while in the 1950s he was a partner in a wrought iron foundry.

Moore managed to get on stage and got a big break when he replaced David Wayne as Ensign Pulver in *Mr. Roberts* on Broadway. Moore got his first movie role, a bit part in *Okinawa*, in 1952. He also had an uncredited part in the classic science fiction film, *The War of the Worlds*, in 1953. He was a busy actor in the 1950s, usually playing brash, bright young types, such as Mitzi Gaynor's boyfriend in *There's No Business Like Show Business* in 1954.

When television became widespread, Moore found even more opportunities to exploit his talent. He was Howie on *Pete and Gladys* in 1960, but in 1965 he landed the role that made him famous, appearing on *Green Acres* as Hank Kimball, the county agent. He was supposed to make just one appearance on the show but the response was so great, he became a regular. He and Arnold the pig received more fan mail than any of the other cast members. The series ran from 1965 to 1971, and Moore was one of the reasons for its success.

In the mid-1960s Moore became increasingly interested in production and formed a company with fellow character actor L. Q. Jones. Moore continued to act in comic roles and also acted as executive producer in many of his own "in-house" productions. He was a celebrity guest at West Coast golf tournaments and regularly returned to Indiana for the Phil Harris golf classic in Linton.

In 1997 Carolyn was visiting at a daughter's and called her husband, who was in their Pal Desert home. He told her he was not feeling well. The next morning, May 4, 1997, a friend found him dead. Death was caused by heart failure. He was seventy-five years old.

BIBLIOGRAPHY

McCormick, Mike. Wabash Valley Profiles. Terre Haute First National Bank.

Quinlan, David. *Quinlan's Illustrated Directory of Film Character Actors.* London: B. T. Batsford, 1985.

TOM NOLAN

Pia Zadora and Tom Nolan in *Voyage of the Rock Aliens* (1988).

The second oldest of eight children, Tom Nolan grew up in Indianapolis going to the theater with his famous grandmother, Jeannette Covert Nolan, who wrote biographies of famous people for juvenile readers. These trips with his grandmother created in him a love of the theater.

Nolan went to Harvard University to study law. However, after being cast in several school productions, his future was rewritten. He transferred to Cornell University and eventually received his master's degree in acting. After college, he moved to New York and performed in several off-Broadway productions. His first professional film job was in *Yanks*, which starred Richard Gere. He was an accomplished drummer, and his role in the film was that of a blonde GI drummer. The start of a film career meant moving to Hollywood, and soon he was in the NBC miniseries *Beggerman, Thief.* He then took a stage role in *Cause Celeb,* which starred fellow Hoosier Anne Baxter.

In 1979 Nolan and fellow Hoosier Sharon Gabet converted a former button factory into a theater in New York. They named it Tyson Studio. He has been in such feature films as *Up the Creek* (1984), starring Dudley Moore, and *The Falcon and the Snowman,* starring Sean Penn. Other films include *Pretty Woman* (1990), *Pacific Heights* (1990), *The Thing Called Love* (1993), and *White Man's Burden* (1995).

BIBLIOGRAPHY

The Internet Movie Database. http://www.imdb.com/.

Voyage of the Rock Aliens. Publicity Release, 1984. Academy of Motion Picture Arts and Sciences, Beverly Hills, California.

ROBERT PAIGE

John Arthur Paige was born in Indianapolis, Indiana, on December 2, 1910, to English parents. He attended West Point but left the academy to concentrate on a radio career. He went to the West Coast, where he became an usher for Fox West Coast theaters. He then found a singing job with Long Beach radio station KGER and next moved to Hollywood as an announcer/program director for KMTR. At this time he was using the name Dave Carlyle.

Paige got into pictures in a series of short subjects in 1931. By 1935 he began to appear in feature films. In 1936 he sang "I'll Sing You a Thousand Love Songs" to Marion Davies in *Cain and Mabel*. When he moved to Columbia Studios in 1937, he changed his name to Robert Paige and began appearing in lead roles in low-budget films and starred in several serials. In 1939 he moved to Paramount, where he again was cast as the lead in several B movies.

In 1940 Paige married Betty Henning and became the love interest in several Universal musicals. His first lead in a film musical was in the 1940 production *Dancing on a Dime*. For the next seven years Paige was cast in minor musicals and comedies at Universal Studios. He appeared with fellow Hoosier Ole Olsen in *Hellzapoppin* in 1941. Although he had a good singing voice and was certainly a decent actor, Paige seemed to be stuck in a number of repetitive, one-dimensional romantic leads. He costarred with such people as Dick Foran, Harriet Hilliard, Louise Allbritton, the Andrews Sisters, Donald O'Connor, and Jane Frazee. Finally, Paige was cast with the reigning queen of song at Universal, Deanna Durbin. The Durbin musicals were well produced and popular at the box office. He and Durbin provided some memorable duets, and he even had some nice solo numbers in these films.

Robert Paige and Deanna Durbin in *Can't Help Singing* (1944).
COURTESY OF THE ACADEMY OF MOTION PICTURE ARTS AND SCIENCES

Paige made his television debut in 1951 on *Bigelow Theater* and continued to appear on television for the next few years. In 1953 he appeared in a supporting role in Abbott and Costello films, *Pardon My Sarong* (1942) and *Abbott and Costello Go to Mars* (1953). In 1955 Paige won the Los Angeles Emmy Award as the "Most Outstanding Male Personality." Also in 1955 Paige was the host of *The Colgate Comedy Hour*. By 1957 he was hosting the afternoon network television show *Bride and Groom*. In 1962 he replaced Randy Merriman as the host of *The Big Payoff*. Paige was still doing movies in 1959 and 1960 while appearing in a number of television dramas. In 1960 he divorced his first wife and in 1961 married Joanne Ludden, who was a model in *The Big Payoff* series. With Ludden, he set up a television-sales promotion company, Paige-Ludden Enterprises. His last feature film was *Bye Bye Birdie* in 1963. In 1964 he became the father of a daughter, Colleen.

From 1966 to 1970 Paige was a successful newscaster for KABC-TV in Los Angeles. After his tenure as a newscaster, he became a deputy to Baxter Ward, Los Angeles County's somewhat controversial supervisor. Paige died of heart problems on December 21, 1987.

BIBLIOGRAPHY

Indiana Biographical Dictionary: People of All Times and All Places Who Have Been Important to the History of the State. New York: Somerset, 1993.

The Internet Movie Database. http://www.imdb.com/.

Lamparski, Richard. *Whatever Became Of . . . ?* New York: Bantam Books, 1976.

Parish, James Robert, and Lennard DeCarl. *Hollywood Players: The Forties.* New Rochelle, N.Y.: Arlington House, 1976.

JOHN PHILLIBER

John Philliber in *Ladies of Washington* (1944).

John Philliber was born in Elkhart, Indiana, in 1872. He entered motion pictures late in life, making his debut in 1943 at age seventy-one in *A Lady Takes a Chance*. He was in show business for fifty years and spent most of it on stage with touring companies. Most of his stage career was without much notice, until he finally landed on Broadway in 1942 in *Mr. Sycamore*. He followed this with parts in *The Star-Wagon*, *Two on an Island*, and *Winterset*. The latter also featured fellow Hoosier Richard Bennett. He received accolades from the New York critics for his performances, and this drew the attention of Hollywood.

In 1944 Philliber made his most memorable appearance on the screen, playing "Pop" Benson in United Artists' *It Happened Tomorrow*. The star of this film was an actor who had spent many years in Indianapolis, Dick Powell. Powell played a newspaper reporter who is given copies of the next day's paper for three successive days by Pop. It was a poignant role, and Philliber made the most of it. Suddenly, he became a busy actor. Although he only made a total of nine films, eight of them were made in one year (1944).

In March 1944 Philliber, who was known as Johnny to his Elkhart friends and relatives, returned to his hometown. He found that his friends did not believe he actually had an important role in a major motion picture. Philliber called the studio and asked it to ship him a print of *It Happened Tomorrow*. He screened the film in Elkhart on Wednesday, March 7, for a group of friends and relatives.

Philliber returned to Hollywood, but eight months after his personal "preview" in Elkhart, he returned to the place of his birth and died there on November 6, 1944.

BIBLIOGRAPHY

Indianapolis News, March 3, 1944.

The Internet Movie Database. http://www.imdb.com/.

SHARI SUE ROBINSON

Shari Sue Robinson started her theatrical career at an early age and disappeared from the screen at an early age. She was born in Indianapolis on November 5, 1938. Her mother enrolled her in the Arthur Jordan Conservatory to study dance. At age five she appeared on stage at Keith's Theater in downtown Indianapolis doing a hula. The *Indianapolis News* stated, "for one so young, little Shari has mastered a lot of hula technique." Her debut was marred by a drunk who climbed into the orchestra pit and loudly insisted that he be accompanied while singing "Paper Doll." Robinson ignored the confusion and impressed an appreciative audience who admired her poise.

As the newspaper reported, Robinson "won the weekly prize and then went on to win the contest finals." As a result of this triumph, she was engaged to play four days with a professional vaudeville group. She "stopped the show cold" every time she went into her hula act. The theater was swamped with calls following her appearances. This favorable reaction prompted Robinson and her parents to set their sights on the film industry.

The family decided to spend the family vacation in 1946 investigating possibilities in the film capital. They stayed at a trailer camp, and Robinson took acting and singing lessons six days a week. They soon discovered there were no welcome mats out for them. After a brief stay, they returned to Indianapolis, and Robinson began appearing at private parties and recitals. Her mother decided they would try Hollywood again, only this time they would "camp on the film maker's doorsteps." Robinson's first break came in 1948, when she was cast as an extra and bit player in *The Boy with Green Hair*, which starred Dean Stockwell, Pat O'Brien, and fellow Hoosier Charles Arnt. Her next appearance in that same year was another bit in *Kiss the Blood Off My Hands*, which starred Burt Lancaster and Joan Fontaine and was directed by Richmond, Indiana, native Norman Foster.

Shari Sue Robinson with (left to right) Anne Revere, Dan Dailey, and Anne Baxter (Michigan City) in *You're My Everything* (1949).

One day in 1949, a friend living in the same trailer camp, who was a matron at Twentieth Century Fox, told Robinson of the studio's search for a successor to Shirley Temple. The studio was auditioning youngsters for a major role in *You're My Everything*. Robinson was at the casting office in a half hour and ultimately won the part over almost one hundred competitors. The stars were Dan Dailey and Michigan City native Anne Baxter. Robinson played Dailey's daughter. Her hair was curled to resemble Temple's, and she even sang "On the Good Ship Lollipop." Although Robinson did a commendable job in the film, shortly after its completion she turned twelve and entered the dreaded "awkward stage," though she managed to be cast in one more film, *The Goldbergs* (1950), as Nomi.

Robinson was now too old to be a "moppet" and too young for teenage work. She did manage to get into a stage revue titled *This Is It*. She toured the West Coast with the show that was cast mostly with "home guarders" (people who are so eager for movie work and so certain their big break will come, they refuse to leave Hollywood).

Robinson's mother brought her back to Indiana at Christmastime in 1950 to visit her grandparents, Mr. and Mrs. Harvey Prentiss, in Madison. She stated at that time that Robinson had no immediate hopes in film but was going to stick around for a while anyway to see if something would come her way. Nothing ever did, and she retired from films.

BIBLIOGRAPHY

Indianapolis News, December 3, 1943.
Indianapolis Star, October 31, 1948, August 31, 1949.

Indianapolis Times, October 8, 1950.
The Internet Movie Database. http://www.imdb.com/.

IVAN ROGERS

Ivan Rogers.

Born in Indianapolis on September 20, 1954, Ivan Rogers was one of three sons born to Paul B. Rogers, a building contractor, and his wife Ola. He attended Pike High School and graduated in 1972. He won a music scholarship to Ball State University and began study as a percussion major. While at Ball State, he began taking karate lessons. This eventually earned him a 2nd degree black belt. He tired of college and decided to go on the road with a music group. It was not long before he tired of touring. He decided to resume his training in karate and became a world-rated light heavyweight.

Rogers was approached to make a video about karate. He took up the challenge and wrote, produced, and starred in the video. It was commercially successful. This led him seriously to consider writing, producing, and directing. He began reading everything he could find on writing for feature films. While preparing himself for a film career, he moved to the island of Maui in Hawaii. There he managed a youth center and taught karate.

In 1984 Rogers finished his first feature script, *The Pivot*. He entered his script in an international script writing contest and placed in the winner's category. Since this did not trigger any immediate offers, he took up kick-boxing on the islands. A health club owner saw him perform and asked him to train some fighters at his health facility. Rogers eventually became part owner of the club and was instrumental in making the Atlantic Health and Fitness Center into the largest fitness and karate center in the Pacific.

Rogers met Maui native Mike Stone, who had made movies for Cannon Films and for the NBC Movie of the Week. Stone urged Rogers to move back to Los Angeles. He did, and the two collaborated on a film entitled *The Angkor Rescue* (later re-titled *Tiger Shark*). He met another Hollywood veteran who helped him hone his skills as a writer. Upon his own reflection, and the advice of others, he realized he had to produce films on his own. Producer Bob Waters helped further educate Rogers in the business of moviemaking. This resulted in a script entitled *No Way Out* (later changed to *One Way Out*).

Rogers then met fellow Hoosier Fred Williamson, who was from Gary. Williamson had worn many hats in his productions, frequently producing, writing, and starring. Williams told Rogers he could do the same thing, but should not take on too much. Upon Williamson's advice, Rogers wrote and produced his next film, but did not direct it. *No Way Out* was shot in Rogers's hometown of Indianapolis. He said he received tremendous help and cooperation from the city. The film was screened at the Cannes Film Festival, received a favorable review from *Variety*, and was a commercial success.

Rogers kept busy turning out such films as *Two Wrongs Make a Right* (1987), *Slow Burn* (1989), and *Laserhawk* (1997). He returned to his hometown to shoot most of *Caged Women II* (1996). His old friend, Fred Williamson, cast him in his film, *Down n' Dirty*, in 2000. *Forgive*

Me Father (2001) saw him return to wearing many hats as he produced, directed, and starred in it.

Rogers is still active today, producing, acting, and distributing feature films.

BIBLIOGRAPHY

The Internet Movie Database. http://www.imdb.com/.
Ivan Rogers official Web site. http://www.ivanrogers.com/.

FORREST TUCKER

Forrest Meredith Tucker was born in Plainfield, Indiana, on February 12, 1919, the son of Forrest and D. D. (Doris) Herringlake Tucker. Forrest's father died when he was five years old. At the age of eight, his mother took Forrest and his sister, Betty, to Des Moines, Iowa, where they lived with her parents. Forrest attended school at Casady Elementary and North High School in Iowa. During his brief stay at North High School, he got his first taste of show business, accompanying his mother, who began touring the Midwest in an attempt to establish a career as a singer.

After his mother's attempt at a singing career, she moved the family back to Indiana, and Forrest attended Plainfield High School, which he left at age sixteen. On a visit to Indianapolis in 1960, he said, "I was brought up on a farm and did all things that boys in rural areas do . . . sold lemonade, hauled coal from Brazil (Indiana), played basketball and tackle in football at Plainfield high."

When Tucker was fourteen years old, he went to Chicago to see fellow Hoosier Phil Harris perform on stage between a program of feature films and shorts. Inspired by Harris, Tucker got his first job in show business at the Gayety Burlesque Theater in Washington, D.C., but was forced to leave after it was found he was underage. Taking advantage of his older looks, he lied about his age and joined the army. He was accepted and served two years with the Third Cavalry stationed in Arlington, Virginia. When he was again discovered as underage, he was abruptly dismissed. After leaving the army, he decided he would finish high school, enrolling at Washington–Lee High School in Arlington. He lettered in football, basketball, and track, became a class officer, and had the starring role in the senior class production of *The Whole Town's Talking*.

During his last days in high school, Tucker returned to the Gayety and performed there in the evenings. He owed his trip to Hollywood to hot weather. He said, "It was hot weather that led me into movies. Back in my burlesque days, the burlesque houses were never air-conditioned, so in the summer they closed. One summer, I decided to visit Hollywood and came up with a seven-year contract. I stayed twenty-one years and made ninety-one pictures."

Tucker arrived in Hollywood in 1939, when he was barely twenty years old. Herman Sartorius, a wealthy friend of Tucker's mother who had bankrolled several Broadway plays, took Tucker under his wing and helped him get started in Hollywood. Tucker's first film was an

Forrest Tucker.

Lupe Velez and Forrest Tucker in *Honolulu Lu* (1941).
PHOTO BY WHITEY SCHAFER

auspicious one. He was twenty-one, and Dana Andrews was twenty-nine, when they each made their film debut in *The Westerner* in 1940. In his first movie, Tucker was given the opportunity to do something he would do many times over: he engaged the hero (Gary Cooper) in a rousing fistfight.

Tucker's size (a solidly built six feet five inches) and blustering personality continued to give him roles as a nasty, brutal heavy in many Westerns and action films. His good friend, John Wayne, called him "Taller than Most." Tucker was one full inch taller than Wayne. "Duke doesn't mind though. Whenever we've been in a brawl together, on screen that is, he always wins and that makes him look mighty good," Tucker recalled.

When World War II broke out, Tucker enlisted as a private. He was discharged in 1946 as a second lieutenant and returned to filmmaking. He had four films released in 1942. One of his most memorable roles was the marine who squared off with Wayne in *Sands of Iwo Jima* (1949). Most of his films were made through two studios, Columbia and Republic.

When the era of big men began to disappear with the deaths of Victor McLaglen, Cooper, and Ward Bond, Tucker tried something new. After twenty years of playing cowboys and cavalry soldiers, his good friend, Rosalind Russell, asked him to try his hand at comedy in the movie version of *Auntie Mame*. He took the gamble, playing the gentle millionaire Beauregard Burnside to Russell's indefatigable Mame. He transformed himself into a soft-spoken, bighearted, lovable leading man.

The same year that *Auntie Mame* was released (1958), Tucker was offered the role of Professor Harold Hill in the touring company of *The Music Man*. He said, "I had never done any real singing before, except at parties and occasionally at clubs where I knew they wouldn't throw me out. And for years I wanted to give it a try. It was a long wait, but it was worth it." In 1960 Tucker was still touring with the show when it came to the Murat Theater in Indianapolis. In an interview with the *Indianapolis News*, he said he did eight performances a week with travel on Sunday. "But the show doesn't tire me," Tucker said. "After all, acting is a profession. A dentist doesn't get bored with the 1,200th tooth and an actor can't afford to be bored with the 1,200th performance."

Tucker had appeared on television as early as 1956 in a series called *Crunch and Des*. Other shows in which he had a role included *Dusty's Trail*, *The Ghost Busters*, and *The Rebels*. Although he had a flair for comedy, it was seldom realized on the big screen. He was given a chance to showcase his comedic talents in 1965 when he was signed to play Sergeant Morgan O'Rourke in television's *F Troop*. The series was a hit and ran for two years. After *F Troop*, Tucker went to Chicago and became an associate producer at Chicago's Drury Lane Theater.

In 1970 Tucker went on stage to play Father Day in *Life with Father*. The play opened in Chicago, and *Variety* said, "An indestructible star and an indestructible vehicle are well met in Evergreen Park, where doughty Forrest Tucker is playing the pompous pater-familias in the classic 'Life with Father.' Tucker stated that he waited for years to grow old enough for this role."

Tucker continued his career in films, appearing in *Chisum* with Wayne in 1970. Although they were both up in years at the time, they staged a very realistic fistfight without using any stunt doubles. Tucker's last film was *Thunder Run* in 1986. He was last seen in public on August 21, 1986, at the unveiling of his star on the Hollywood Walk of Fame. He collapsed moments before the ceremony and was taken to a hospital by ambulance. The unveiling continued with his sister, Betty Hitchcock, and his daughter, Cindy Tucker, accepting the honor on his behalf. He was placed in the Motion Picture Country Home and Hospital in Woodland Hills, California. On October 25, 1986, his wife, Sheila, visited him. Five minutes after she left, he died. The cause of death was attributed to throat cancer.

Tucker was married four times, to Sandra Jolley, Marilyn Johnson, Marilyn Fisk, and Sheila Forbes. All four wives were dancers. He had three children: Pam (by Sandra Jolley), Cindy (adopted with Marilyn Fisk), and Sean (by Marilyn Fisk).

Forrest Tucker as Sergeant Morgan O'Rourke in *F Troop* (1965–67).

BIBLIOGRAPHY

Chicago Tribune, April 8, 1962, May 29, 1970.

Indiana Biographical Dictionary: People of All Times and All Places Who Have Been Important to the History of the State. New York: Somerset, 1993.

Indianapolis News, November 21, 1960, July 9, 1962, October 27, 1986.

The Internet Movie Database. http://www.imdb.com/.

Ritter, Henry. "Tuck, the Life and Career of Forrest Tucker." *Classic Images* 345 (April 2003).

LURENE TUTTLE

Author James Hilton once said of Lurene Tuttle, "The way Lurene can take a bad line and make it sound good is almost dangerous." Tuttle was one of the most versatile actresses ever to grace the silver screen. She was never out of work from the moment she went into show business, and her career included all the media—stage, radio, motion pictures, and television. Tuttle was born on August 29, 1906, in Pleasant Lake, Indiana. At an early age her parents moved to a ranch in Arizona.

As a child, Tuttle displayed an interest in acting, and her father took her into Phoenix for acting lessons. She began her career in Burbank, California, as a child actress in *Murphy's Comedians.* She graduated into ingenue roles with a stock company in San Antonio. Returning to Los Angeles, she was featured in Henry Duffey's productions and followed this playing stock in Salt Lake City, San Francisco, Los Angeles, and Portland.

Tuttle described how she moved from stock to radio: "I had been doing a play at the Hollywood Playhouse, which is now the El Capitan Theater on Vine Street. Someone told me about a radio show going on. Auditions were down at the Fiquero Playhouse. I went down there. I didn't have an agent with me. I just went by myself. So the director had me do something in his office. He said, 'I like this. Go out to the microphone.' And because of my stage training, I knew how to modulate my voice, and to do what he wanted." As a result of that audition, Tuttle was cast opposite Dick Powell in a program called *Hollywood Hotel.*

Tuttle subsequently played Effie, the secretary to Sam Spade, played by Howard Duff. She went on to do radio with Orson Welles and Dick Haymes and was a mainstay on such popular programs as *Ozzie and Harriet, Duffy's Tavern, Dr. Christian, The Great Gildersleeve,* and *One Man's Family.* She played in numerous *Lux Radio Theater* shows opposite such stars as Paul Muni, Gary Cooper, Cary Grant, James Stewart, Joan Crawford, and Leslie Howard. She said the big stars would get five thousand dollars and she would get fifty-five dollars. She said, "They'd get somebody who could hold up her end of the acting with a big star, and it would be all right. So that's how I got so many leads opposite stars, because I didn't charge too much." About appearing with big stars on radio, Tuttle recalled, "I could play opposite Jimmy Stewart or Fredric March or Cary Grant or Gary Cooper or Leslie Howard, and on the air I would be the most glamorous, gorgeous, tall, black-haired female you've ever seen in your life. Whatever I wished to be, I could be with my voice, which was the thrilling part for me." Speaking of her talent, she said, "My imagination has always been strong, from the time I was able to talk."

Tuttle also played opposite many Hoosiers on radio. Among those she worked with were Mary Jane Croft, Forrest Lewis, and Red Skelton. She worked on the Red Skelton radio show for many years, playing the mother of Skelton's Mean Widdle Kid. Working with Skelton was one of the highlights of her career. She said, "He was the funniest, dearest man. We used to have a Thursday night preview, and then we had a Friday show. On the Thursday night preview he was allowed to say anything he wanted to say, you know. Of course, some of it got very

A young Lurene Tuttle.
©CBS, PHOTO BY BEN POLIN

(*Opposite page*) Lurene Tuttle as Ma Barker in *Ma Barker's Killer Brood* (1960).

blue. We laughed so hard. And my face would hurt. He would wander from the script. He goes on and on about something, but he always comes back to the cue, so that you know where you are. He always did his ad-libbing very cleverly, and he used to love it when anybody on the show would get into a mix-up about something. Some comedians are tough. Some comedians are very cross with you. But he never was. Oh no. And he was so generous at Christmas time. He gave me a sable stole one time. Real sable stole for Christmas."

Another Hoosier Tuttle worked with on radio was James Dean. In 1951, when Dean was a struggling unknown, he appeared with Tuttle on the radio program *Alias Jane Doe*. After Dean's death, she was named to the board of trustees of the James Dean Foundation.

Tuttle began her career in motion pictures as a stenographer in Shirley Temple's 1934 film, *Stand Up and Cheer!* and made at least fifty-nine films. Her last film was released in 1987, the year after she died. Her roles in motion pictures and television were as diverse as her radio roles. She played everything from one of the witches in Orson Welles's 1948 production of *Macbeth* to the notorious Ma Barker in *Ma Barker's Killer Brood* in 1960.

She was married to Mel Ruick and the mother of actress Barbara Ruick. Barbara appeared in fourteen motion pictures and married composer John Williams, with whom she had two sons. Joseph Williams was the lead singer of the rock group Toto and the singing voice of the adult Simba in Disney's *The Lion King*. Mark Towner Williams is a recording artist and music producer. Ruick died in 1974 after suffering a cerebral hemorrhage.

Tuttle died May 28, 1986. Duff, her costar on the *Sam Spade* radio series, said of her: "She could just take hold of a part and do something with it. As I said in her eulogy, I think she never met a part she didn't like. She just loved to work; she loved to act. She's a woman who was born to do what she was doing and loved every minute of it, I guess."

BIBLIOGRAPHY

Buxton, Frank, and Bill Owen. *The Big Broadcast, 1920–1950.* New York: Viking Press, 1972.

Dunning, John. Radio interview. KNUS, Denver, Colorado. National Public Radio Broadcasting Archives. Library of American Broadcasting, College Park, Maryland.

The Internet Movie Database. http://www.imdb.com/.

Maltin, Leonard. *The Great American Broadcast: A Celebration of Radio's Golden Age.* New York: Dutton, 1997.

Twomey, Alfred E., and Arthur F. McClure. *The Versatiles: A Study of Supporting Character Actors and Actresses in the American Motion Picture, 1930–1955.* New York: Castle Books, 1969.

HARRY VON ZELL

Harry von Zell was born in Indianapolis on July 11, 1906. At a young age, his family moved to the West Coast and he enrolled at the University of California at Los Angeles, where he became involved in music and drama. After leaving the university, he worked as a bank messenger and a payroll clerk, but all the while he was yearning to get into show business.

While visiting a rehearsal for a radio program, some friends jokingly decided to announce that von Zell would be singing on the program. He took up the challenge and ultimately received offers from small radio stations in the area. His first job in radio was in 1922. At first, he was a volunteer, but then he began to get paid. He received twenty-five dollars a week for a weekly half-hour show on KNX radio, where he performed as a singer. In 1925 he married Minerva McGarvey, and they had one son. In 1926 KMIC in Inglewood, California, hired him as a singer-announcer. He moved to KMTR as a sports announcer and then went to San Diego's KGB as its program director.

Bandleader Paul Whiteman began a series of shows on radio, and von Zell auditioned to be his announcer. He was chosen from 250 candidates to be the announcer and to read commercials on the show. When the series ended in May 1930, he went to New York and became a CBS staff announcer. He then decided he wanted to branch out into comedy and was soon doing small character parts with Fred Allen and Colonel Stoopnagel. In a little over a year, he began to work with most of the big names in radio, including Will Rogers, Phil Baker, Ed Wynn, and Eddy Duchin. He was a familiar voice on such shows as *Vick's Open House*, *We the People*, and *The Aldrich Family*. He also announced more serious programs such as *The March of Time* and *Newspaper of the Air*. Von Zell worked with Eddie Cantor on the *Time to Smile* program and also announced the radio version of *Truth or Consequences* for a short time.

Harry Von Zell, circa 1930.

In 1931 von Zell made the blooper that was to become the most famous announcer error in broadcast history. While von Zell was working at CBS, the network did a birthday tribute to President Herbert Hoover, arranging an evening's entertainment featuring many of the big radio stars of that time. Von Zell was still very young, and he said he did not expect to get the assignment to announce this very prestigious program. When he learned he had been chosen, he was very nervous. However, the program went very well, and he said he must have mentioned Hoover's name twenty times during the program. Finally, at the end of the program, he said something like—"We hope we have conveyed the enormous respect and esteem we have for our President on his birthday. Happy birthday to our President, HOOBERT HEEVER." Von Zell said, "If the windows on the twenty-third floor of CBS had not been fixed, I would have jumped." He thought his career in radio was finished. To his surprise, everyone was very kind. The chairman of CBS, William S. Paley, came to him and said, "Son, you did a beautiful job. You needn't worry because it's understandable how you could have been so emotionally moved that you had this slip of the tongue."

Von Zell's career began to blossom after this mishap. He announced big band shows for people such as Ozzie Nelson, Glen Gray, and Tommy and Jimmy Dorsey. He introduced a number of famous people on their first radio appearance—the Boswell Sisters, the Mills Brothers, and Stoopnagel and Bud. About 1927 von Zell saw a stage show, *Flying High*, which featured a singer/tap dancer named Kate Smith. He told Freddie Rich, a producer at CBS, that he should

Scene from *Dear Wife* (1949) with Harry Von Zell standing at the microphone and Mona Freeman seated.

catch Smith's act because she had a wonderful singing voice for radio. Rich went to see her and immediately hired her. Von Zell was the announcer on her first radio show.

Beginning in 1945, von Zell began to carve out a niche for himself in the film industry. He worked in such films as *Till the End of Time* (1946), *Where the Sidewalk Ends* (1950), and *Son of Paleface* (1952). In 1950 he worked with Hoosier director Robert Wise in *Two Flags West.* With the advent of television, he moved into roles on such programs as *Wagon Train* and *Perry Mason.*

Von Zell was the announcer of *The George Burns and Gracie Allen Show* television series from 1951 to 1958 and a regular performer on *The George Gobel Show* from 1959 to 1960. He stayed active in radio and television, doing mostly commercials, until he contracted cancer. He died in Woodland Hills, California, on November 21, 1981.

BIBLIOGRAPHY

Indiana Biographical Dictionary: People of All Times and All Places Who Have Been Important to the History of the State. New York: Somerset, 1993.

The Internet Movie Database. http://www.imdb.com/.

Von Zell, Harry. Audiotape interview with Chuck Schaden. February 19, 1975. Author's collection.

RAYMOND WALBURN

Raymond Walburn was the epitome of the cheeky braggart, the bumbling con man, and the pompous politician. He was a favorite of audiences and directors throughout the 1930s and 1940s. His busy screen career totaled at least eighty-five films from 1916 to 1955.

Walburn was born in Plymouth, Indiana, on September 9, 1887. His actress-mother decided to move to Oakland, California, when Walburn was about sixteen years old. At age eighteen, he made his stage debut in *Macbeth* for five dollars a week. The following year, his stage performance in San Francisco was interrupted by the 1906 earthquake. In 1911 he made his Broadway debut in *Greyhound.* It was a flop, but five years later he was cast in the long-running *Out of the Kitchen.*

Walburn made his screen debut in a serial, *The Scarlet Runner,* in 1916. Shortly after that he served in World War I. He resumed his career after returning from the service, appearing alternately on stage and in silent films. He starred in the original production of George Kelly's *The Show Off* on Broadway. His film portrayal of Colonel Pettigrew, a racetrack con man, in *Broadway Bill* in 1934 earned him kudos and probably typecast him for the rest of his career. Frank Capra directed *Broadway Bill* and used Walburn extensively in other films, even having him reprise his Colonel Pettigrew role in *Riding High* in 1950.

Walburn was able to break free of the role of a blustering, unctuous windbag at least a couple of times. In 1934 he played a treacherous villain in *The Count of Monte Cristo* and was the villain in *Mills of the Gods.* He also appeared many times opposite fellow Hoosiers. In 1934 he played the press agent for fan dancer Carole Lombard in *Lady by Choice.* In 1937 he played Irene Dunne's father in *High, Wide, and Handsome* and Frances Farmer's father in *Flowing Gold* (1940), and in 1951 he was the mayor in the Red Skelton film *Excuse My Dust.*

Raymond Walburn.

In 1949 Walburn starred in a series of comedies about a man named Henry. They were inexpensive films made by Monogram. However, he was delighted to be the star of the series and to have the opportunity to work with his lifelong pal, actor/comedian Walter Catlett.

Walburn retired after appearing in *The Spoilers* in 1955 with fellow Hoosiers Anne Baxter and Forrest Lewis. He revived his Broadway career in 1962, at the age of seventy-five, when he was persuaded by producer Harold Prince to play Erronious in *A Funny Thing Happened on the Way to the Forum.* He appeared in one more Broadway play, *A Very Rich Woman,* with Ruth Gordon in 1965.

Walburn married Gertrude Steinman and after her death married Jane Davis in the mid-1950s. His portrayals of lovable, bumbling, and pompous rogues remain among the highlights of the films of Hollywood's golden age. He died at age eighty-one in New York City on July 28, 1969.

BIBLIOGRAPHY

All Movie Guide. http://www.allmovie.com/.
The Internet Movie Database. http://www.imdb.com/.

WILLIAM (BILL) WALKER

William Franklin Walker had a sixty-five-year film career in which he appeared in more than one hundred films. He was not only a star of stage and screen, but he was also an early civil rights activist. He worked in almost every phase of the theater— actor, director, and writer. Perhaps his most memorable film appearance was as the Reverend Sykes in the 1962 film *To Kill a Mockingbird.*

Walker was born on July 1, 1896, in Pendleton, Indiana. He grew up in Pendleton and graduated from Pendleton High School in 1915. He was the first black graduate of that school. His grandfather had fought for the Union in the Civil War and then settled in Indiana. His parents were Robert and Carrie Walker. Shortly after graduation from high school, he enlisted in the U.S. Army and fought with the Ninety-second Division in World War I. Returning from the service, he moved to Chicago and then Detroit, where he worked for the U.S. Post Office. He played in a small band in his spare time, and during one of his performances, a scout from the Morrison Agency handed him a card and told Walker to call him.

Walker did not think much about it and continued to work at the post office. One day he said he got up and did not feel like going to work. He remembered the card and decided to visit the agency. The receptionist told him she was sorry but he had no appointment. As he started to leave, the agent came out of his office and said, "I've wondered why you never came to see me." Walker said in that split second his lifestyle and career changed. He signed a contract and began working as a band musician in the famous Zelli's Night Club in Paris.

When Walker returned to the United States, he began appearing in stock, and in 1945 he traveled to Hollywood to play his first screen role with Burt Lancaster in *The Killers.* Walker returned to Detroit, but Hollywood kept calling him back for more roles, and he finally decided to make a permanent move to California.

In 1960 Walker married Peggy Cartwright, who was one of the original *Our Gang* cast members. It was one of the earliest interracial marriages in Hollywood. They were married for thirty-two years until Walker's death. He was a very busy screen actor from the late 1940s to the early 1970s. He made the transition into television and kept busy there, appearing on such shows as *Perry Mason, Dr. Kildare, Marcus Welby, M.D., Ironside,* and *Hunter.*

Walker was an early activist for civil rights and a member of the board of directors of the Screen Actors Guild. When he died in Woodland Hills, California, on January 17, 1992, the Screen Actors Guild arranged a special tribute to him in June of that year. His old friend from *To Kill a Mockingbird,* Gregory Peck, was the honorary chairman for the event. Walker's wife said, "He was not a star . . . not one of those people whose face was blazed all around, but one who was remembered by the people who saw his face flashed around their living room." She also recalled, "He was very proud of his ancestry . . . and very proud of being from Indiana."

BIBLIOGRAPHY

Anderson Bulletin, June 22, 1972, January 30, February 8, 1992.
The Internet Movie Database. http://www.imdb.com/.

MICHAEL WARREN

Michael Warren was born in South Bend, Indiana, on March 5, 1946. He said he was blessed with a great family. "Mom and Dad, who were married some 50-odd years until my father passed away, were still as lovey-dovey in their 70s as one could imagine. They provided me with a great environment to grow up in."

Warren's biggest regret is that he never won the Indiana state high school basketball championship while playing at South Bend Central. He did score twenty-two points in the 1963 state finals loss to Muncie Central. He went on from there to go to UCLA unrecruited, making the team, playing for fellow Hoosier John Wooden, and becoming an All-American. He was on the same team as Lew Alcindor (later known as Kareem Abdul-Jabbar), which won two national championships. Still, he said he would trade one of his college championships for a win at the state level.

After graduation from UCLA, Warren gave up a career in professional sports to try acting. He was lucky. He landed the role of Officer Bobby Hill in NBC's Emmy award-winning series *Hill Street Blues*. The show ran successfully from 1981 to 1987. However, when it ended, he said, "Having done 'Hill Street Blues,' I knew that I had the kind of look that appeals to television and commercials, this clean-cut kind of guy. But when it was all said and done, I looked across the horizon and I saw everybody on 'Hill Street' having done, or at least turned down, commercials and movies of the week. Myself and Taurean Blacque (the show's two main black actors) were the only ones who didn't get any offers. It was pretty eye-opening, to say the least."

The subsequent thirteen years were tough ones. Warren worked intermittently on unspectacular productions, waiting for another great role. He finally got his opportunity in the 2000 television season. Steven Bochco, his old boss on *Hill Street*, cast him as Ron Harris, the man who runs Angels of Mercy hospital in inner-city Los Angeles. The series was entitled *City of Angels*. Warren's costar was Vivica Fox from Indianapolis.

City of Angels had a good run and received positive critical notices. Unfortunately, it fell victim to the ratings game and was canceled. Warren is again waiting for another great role.

Michael Warren.

BIBLIOGRAPHY

Indianapolis Star, February 1, 2000.
The Internet Broadway Database. http://www.ibdb.com/.
The Internet Movie Database. http://www.imdb.com/.

ISABEL WITHERS

Isabella Irene Withers was born on January 20, 1896, in Frankton, Indiana, and was the daughter of Edward H. and Minnie Snow Withers. Her father was a photographer who was well known and respected in the Moweaqua-Macon area of Illinois. He married

Isabel Withers in *A Sporting Chance* (1945).

Minnie in Moweaqua, and in October 1894 they moved to Frankton, where Edward had accepted a position in a glass factory. After Isabella was born, the couple moved back to Moweaqua for a while and then, in 1901, returned to Frankton.

When Edward got a job in a glass factory in Coffeyville, Kansas, the young family moved there in 1903. It was here that Isabella, called Isabel for short, attended school and graduated from Field Kindley High School in 1914. By this time she had decided to become an actress. Although her family was against her entering such a profession, a cousin offered to pay her tuition to the Georgia Brown Dramatic School in Kansas City. She began to appear in stage productions and in 1916 had her first chance to be in the movies. She played the Sunflower Princess in a film shot on location in Kansas City for the Pageant Film Company. It was her only silent film.

After finishing drama school in 1917, Withers joined a chautauqua company in Kansas City. The company was directed by William Keighley, who later became a noted film director. She was given the lead in *The Melting Pot*. She toured with this play and wound up in New York, where she began working as a model and taking bit parts in several stage productions.

Withers's big break came when she joined Alice Brady in the original stage production of *Little Women*. She then began receiving better roles and kept busy in a number of productions. Her reputation was such that she was hired by George M. Cohan to play opposite Lowell Sherman in the Chicago production of *The Tavern*. She did so well that Cohan asked her to come to Broadway and play opposite him in the same play.

Withers was now an established stage actress and toured unceasingly in many productions. In the late 1920s sound came to motion pictures, and stage actors were suddenly much in demand in Hollywood. Withers made her sound film debut in 1930 opposite Joan Crawford in *Paid*. She followed this with films opposite Frank McHugh, Joe E. Brown, Barbara Stanwyck, and George Brent. As well, she was still busy on the stage between movie roles. She opened on Broadway opposite the prestigious stage star Pauline Frederick in *Her Majesty the Widow* in 1934.

Withers also began doing radio work and worked with people such as Walter Huston, Claudette Colbert, and Richmond, Indiana, native Norman Foster. In the next decade she would make more than three dozen motion pictures. She was an accomplished actress who was much in demand by the studios. Among her films during this period were *George Washington Slept Here* (1942), *Lady of Burlesque* (1943), *Mr. Belvedere Goes to College* (1949), *The Fountainhead* (1949), *Monkey Business* (1952), and even a Ma and Pa Kettle film with fellow Hoosier Marjorie Main.

Withers lived in a small cottage near Hollywood Hills, where she enjoyed cooking and sewing and had a large collection of antiques. Her mother moved in with her in the 1940s and stayed until her death in 1948. Her close friends were Pat Buttram and his wife, actress Sheila Ryan; Marsha Hunt; and Otto Kruger and his wife. When television came along, Withers began to appear in such programs as *Lassie*, *San Francisco Beat*, *Jane Wyman Theater*, and *Love That Bob* with Bob Cummings. She also had a recurring role in *The Life of Riley* with William Bendix.

Withers's last film was *Tonight We Sing* in 1953, but she kept active in television until at least 1960. In 1968 she was injured in a fall in her home and, being in frail health, she never recovered and died on September 3 of that year. Her ashes were returned to Moweaqua, where she was buried beside her parents and her brother. Although she spent only a few of her young years in Madison County, she often spoke of the hot summer days in Indiana that were some of her most treasured memories.

BIBLIOGRAPHY

Anderson Herald, June 22 1975.

Martin, Mike. "Character Actress Isabel Withers." *Classic Images* 122 (August 17, 1985).

JO ANNE WORLEY

Jo Anne Worley.

Of her background, Jo Anne Worley once said, "I'm from Lowell, the home of Bobo Rockefeller. My grandpa was a fundamentalist minister heavy with the threat of brimstone, and death on drinking, necking and the movies. He finally got a TV only to see me on the *Merv Griffin Show*." Worley was born in Lowell, Indiana, on September 6, 1937. She was one of five children raised on a farm in this small town near Gary. She said, "I was the middle child. I probably started being funny in self-defense . . . a bid for attention." She attended a two-room country school for eight years and then, as an honor-roll student at Lowell High School, her talent began to win her recognition. She was voted school comedienne as a freshman, and the drama award at Lowell High is now called the Jo Anne Worley Award.

After graduation, Worley went to work as a waitress at Roberts Café, a truck stop on U.S. 41. With the money she saved, she went to Blauvelt, New York, to join the Pickwick Players. There she did so well that she was awarded a drama scholarship to Midwestern University in Wichita Falls, Texas. She studied there from 1955 to 1957 and then took a long bus ride to Los Angeles, where she attended Los Angeles City College and the Pasadena Playhouse. Her first professional stage role at Pasadena Playhouse was as the Talking Lady in the revue, *Laff Capades of 1959*. Of her stay at the Pasadena Playhouse, Worley said, "I crept out of there . . . they kept it like a girl's dormitory . . . and went out for a night on the Strip. But they caught me crawling in again and I was expelled. That's when I came to New York."

Worley auditioned for and was cast in her first musical as Ruth in *Wonderful Town* and began formal singing lessons, discovering that she had a three-octave range. Her first real break came when she did a nonmusical pantomime that so charmed Billy Barnes he signed her for his musical revue, *The Billy Barnes People*. This gave Worley her Broadway debut when it had a very brief run in 1961.

Worley maintains she is actually a shy person. When she first arrived in Hollywood, her shyness was a problem, but she overcame it by appearing to be an out-and-out extrovert. She admits it was not hard: "I have a big mouth, and I'm sorry to say I've always had one. When I was young, in church, I never sang with everybody else. I only mouthed the hymns, so I wouldn't drown everyone out."

While playing in a musical in Hollywood in 1959, Worley went to see *Mr. Roberts.* In the cast was Roger Perry. She said he not only lit up the stage, he lit up her heart. However, Perry was married at the time, so nothing came of Worley's infatuation. She went back to work but never forgot Perry.

During the 1960s she appeared in stock plays such as *Gentlemen Prefer Blondes*, *Naughty Marietta*, and *The Student Prince.* On Broadway, she was the understudy for Kaye Ballard in *Carnival* and for Carol Channing in *Hello Dolly!* While understudying for Channing, she was moonlighting in other shows such as *The Second City Revue* off Broadway.

Worley was also a regular on the *Las Vegas Show* series in 1966. While in Las Vegas she again met Perry, who had just broken up with his wife. He and Worley started dating. She began making guest appearances on such television shows as *The Dobie Gillis Show* and *This Is Tom Jones.* In 1968 she was cast in a television show that changed her life and brought her national fame. She was in Hollywood doing *The Mad Show* when Perry came to see her. She let him look at the script for a television special she was going to do called *Rowan and Martin's Laugh-In.* Perry glanced at it and said, "It'll never work."

The special was such a big hit that NBC decided to make it a series. Worley was one of the regulars, along with a friend from Indiana, Dave Madden. When producer George Schlatter cast her as a regular on the show, he did so without even requiring an audition. All he did was chat with her in his office. Her zany sense of humor and raucous laughter won him over.

Worley did one of her few serious roles in the 1971 television movie, *The Feminist and the Fuzz.* Perry was also in the cast, and finally in 1975 they were married. She was a panelist on *Hollywood Squares* and had roles in such television series as *Caroline in the City*, *Mad about You*, and *Sabrina, the Teenage Witch.*

Worley appeared on Broadway in 1989 in *Prince of Central Park* and was in *Grease* as Miss Lynch. She continues to take roles in television and on the dinner circuit. Thanks to her unique voice, she is in demand for cartoon voices and was the Wardrobe in *Beauty and the Beast*, Miss Maples in *A Goofy Movie*, and Mrs. Buzzard in *The Elf and the Magic Key.*

In recent years Worley has starred in such national road productions as *Gypsy* (as Mama Rose), *The Wizard of Oz* (as the Wicked Witch of the West), *Annie*, and *A Funny Thing Happened on the Way to the Forum.* Although she was divorced from Perry in 2000, she is still very close to her two stepchildren. She is vice president of Actors and Others for Animals and carries her four-pound Yorkshire terrier around in her handbag and dotes on it like a child. "If you're a dog lover, you understand," says Worley.

BIBLIOGRAPHY

Holland, Jack. "I Fell in Love with a Married Man." *TV Mirror* (February 1970).

Indiana Biographical Dictionary: People of All Times and All Places Who Have Been Important to the History of the State. New York: Somerset, 1993.

The Internet Broadway Database. http://www.ibdb.com/.

The Internet Movie Database. http://www.imdb.com/.

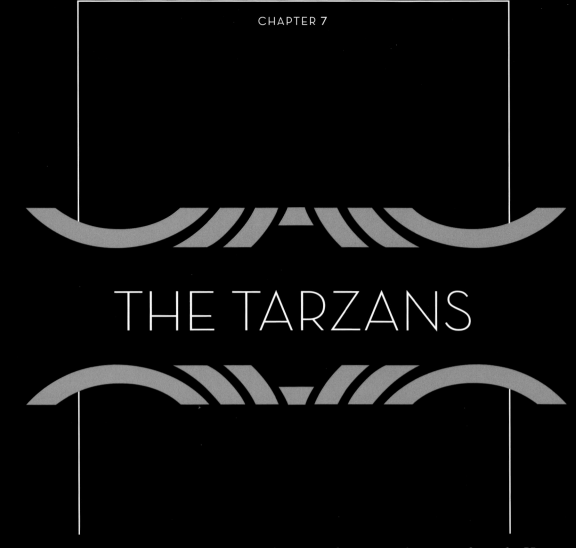

CHAPTER 7

THE TARZANS

Indiana has given birth to more movie Tarzans than any other state. Three men from the Hoosier State have played Tarzan. Elmo Lincoln from Rochester, Indiana, starred in the first Tarzan film, *Tarzan of the Apes*, in 1918. James Pierce of Franklin, Indiana, starred in the last silent Tarzan film, *Tarzan and the Golden Lion* in 1927; and Denny Miller of Bloomington, Indiana, starred in *Tarzan, the Ape Man* in 1959.

ELMO LINCOLN

Elmo Lincoln.

Otto Elmo Linkenhelt was born in Rochester, Indiana, on February 6, 1889, at 129 West Jefferson Street, to Louis R. and Eldora Hunter Linkenhelt. According to Eldora, he was named after a book she read, "I named him after 'St. Elmo.' I thought it was the most wonderful story I had ever read." *St. Elmo*, written by Augusta J. Evans, was extremely popular following the Civil War and into the 1920s. Elmo had one brother, Don, and two half brothers, Harry and Fred. All of the men in the family were known for their large, muscular stature.

Elmo attended Lincoln School in Rochester, where his schoolmates remember him as being the biggest kid in their class. His father was a veterinarian, and for a while he studied medicine under his father. He gained enough knowledge to be declared a "first-aid" man. He and his brother Don also became barbers. This skill helped him travel across the country with his friend Eddie Reimer, barbering as he went. Their journey would eventually take them to California. He said, "I left Rochester when I was in my teens. I tried everything . . . but I'd never thought of being an actor. I wanted to be an engineer on the railroad." He went into railroading for a few years and then was "just a passenger . . . riding the rails." He worked as a dock hand, sailor, boxer, and in later years, as a miner.

Shortly before he left home, Elmo had a romantic liaison with a young woman in Rochester named Della Morris Rosebrock. When he came back from California two years later, he discovered that Della had given birth to a son. Della and Elmo were never married, but he told her to use his name to raise the child. Maurice Linkenhelt stayed in Rochester and raised his own family there.

Linkenhelt was married three times, first to Sadie Whited, second to Edith Coules, and third to Ida Lee Tanchuck, whom he married in 1935. This union produced a child, Marci'a Eldora (pronounced Mar-she-ah).

In 1912 Linkenhelt was working in an Arkansas sawmill when a flood washed it away. He returned to California, where D. W. Griffith was looking for some extras for a two-reel film, *The Battle at Elderbush Gulch*. He was given a part, and on a break between scenes he decided to remove his shirt for relief from the hot sun. Griffith was nearby and inquired, "How big is your chest?" He replied, "About 44 inches." Griffith asked, "How much expansion have you?" He answered, "Any amount you want." Linkenhelt later recalled, "I didn't explain that it

Elmo Lincoln in *Tarzan of the Apes* (1918).

really isn't an expansion. Doctors who have looked me over say I'm 'double-ribbed.' Not that I have two sets of ribs, but my diaphragm is unusually developed and my chest and rib bones are pretty big and heavy. I can put my chest way out and leave it there all morning . . . breathing doesn't affect it."

Griffith was so impressed with Linkenhelt's physique that he put him in his next production, *Judith of Bethulia*, portraying a warrior and a torturer. He changed his last name to Lincoln, and in 1915, when Griffith made *Birth of a Nation*, Lincoln was cast as an African American blacksmith who has a terrific fight with Wallace Reid. He also played other bit parts in the film, including the role of a black "mammy." Two Hoosiers were involved in the making of this landmark film, as Monte Blue from Indianapolis was a stuntman and an extra.

Lincoln and Blue were together again in Griffith's *Intolerance.* Lincoln's role in *Intolerance* was that of The Mighty Man of Valor. He went on to act in similar brute-strength roles in *Hearts of the World, Man of Genesis,* and *The Kaiser, the Beast of Berlin,* and he played the genie in *Aladdin and the Wonderful Lamp* in 1917. However, his greatest role and the one that gave him movie immortality came his way in 1918.

In 1912 *Tarzan of the Apes* appeared in *All-Story* magazine. Author Edgar Rice Burroughs had created a pop icon that was to last for generations. He tried to peddle his Tarzan stories to the movies for several years, but producers turned him down, feeling it was too ambitious a project for a film venture. Finally, in 1916, Burroughs signed a personal contract with Bill Parsons, a Chicago life insurance salesman. The contract gave Parsons the movie rights to *Tarzan of the Apes*. Parsons started a film corporation and began to sell stock to raise the money to produce the picture. Burroughs received five thousand dollars and fifty thousand dollars worth of capital stock in the new company, which was called National Film Corporation of America.

Parsons filmed the story near Morgan City, Louisiana, incorporating some background footage that was shot in Brazil. Ten-year-old Gordon Griffith was hired to portray Tarzan as a boy, and Winslow Wilson, a stocky New York actor and ukulele player, was signed for the lead. However, before filming began, the money ran out, and production was stopped.

About this same time World War I broke out, and Wilson joined the army. A frantic search began for a replacement. Director Scott Sidney saw Lincoln in a movie fight and asked him to do a screen test for the Tarzan role. "The test," Lincoln recalled, "consisted of my going up a telephone pole guy-wire hand over hand and keeping my chest out. When I came down we talked salary. They wanted to pay me $75.00 a week and I asked for $100.00." The twenty-eight-year-old Lincoln got the $100 a week salary.

The first actress to play Jane was Enid Markey, whose shy portrayal contrasted greatly with Lincoln's vitality. He was a huge man for that day and age—almost six feet tall, weighing more than two hundred pounds. Burroughs was on hand during the filming to make sure

Elmo Lincoln in *The Adventures of Tarzan* (1918).

his novel was not distorted. The film was remarkably faithful to the book.

One of the most notorious scenes in the film was one in which Lincoln was supposed to kill a lion. He said, "The only animal we had in the whole picture was 'Old Charlie,' a lion, and I killed him." The lion was supposed to crawl through a window and attempt to devour Markey. Lincoln said, "The lion was doped and tied up. I was supposed to jump on his back and stab him with a knife, but they gave me an old butcher knife to use and the damn thing broke when I tried to stab it. That's when I started using a bayonet. It was too long, so I had to file it down."

The next day the tough-hided old lion was doped again, and they did a retake. This time he was successful in getting through the lion's hide with the bayonet. Lincoln said, "When the lion jumped me, I stabbed him and he died. After a stunned moment, we continued shooting and I stepped on him to beat my chest. As my foot pressed on him, the remaining air in his lungs escaped with a loud 'woosh.' I thought old Charlie was still alive. I set a new record for the broad jump trying to get away."

There is some question as to whether or not Lincoln was really supposed to kill the lion. One story states he stabbed the lion on the spur of the moment when the lion jumped at him. At any rate, it is obvious that the ASPCA or the equivalent had not yet been established to protect animals from this sort of treatment.

The eight-reel film opened at the Broadway Theater in New York on January 27, 1918. It was a critical and financial smash. *Tarzan of the Apes* was one of the first half dozen silent films to gross more than a million dollars. Parsons became a wealthy man, and plans were immediately made for a sequel. Burroughs objected, but Parsons pointed out that he had purchased the screen rights to the novel, and if he chose to film the book in two parts, Burroughs could do nothing about it.

Lincoln and Markey starred in the sequel, *The Romance of Tarzan*, which opened in September 1918. It did not receive the same raves as the original, probably because it was not as painstakingly produced. Another problem was that the sequel had Tarzan in civilized clothing for part of the film. The *New York Times* said, "as the uncivilized ape man, Elmo is splendid, but as Tarzan in a dress suit . . . that is different."

Two years later Parsons reissued the two films on a double bill, and they played to sold-out houses. Burroughs received no more than his advance money and got no more even after he sued Parsons for royalties, making Burroughs very leery of future film deals.

Competition now began for the rights to a third Tarzan film. Burroughs was determined not to let Parsons get another nickel out of his hero, and he sold the rights to the Great Western Producing Company. When Lincoln was contacted to star in another film as the "Lord of the Jungle," he declined, saying he was "already committed to do a number of serials for Universal." The company replied that it was just as well, since they needed a man who looked equally good in a tuxedo and lion skins, and Lincoln did not.

In 1918 Lincoln appeared in *The Greatest Thing in Life*, playing opposite one of the biggest stars in movies at that time, Lillian Gish. (The Rochester, Indiana, paper played up this combination in its "Coming Attractions" in August 1919. It gave top billing in bold face to Lincoln and secondary billing in standard type to Gish.

Lincoln made three successful serials in 1920—*Flaming Disk*, *Elmo, the Mighty*, and *Elmo the Fearless*. After other actors were unsuccessful in duplicating the success of the Lincoln Tarzan films, he was persuaded to come back as Tarzan in a serial. Sixteen-year-old Louise Lorraine, who had costarred with Lincoln in two of his serials, was recruited to play Jane. *The Adventures of Tarzan* was shot in fifteen episodes, and Lincoln was prominently billed as "The Tarzan of Tarzans." The series was so successful that *The Adventures of Tarzan* was one of the top four attractions of 1921, equal to Rudolph Valentino's *The Four Horsemen of the Apocalypse*, Charlie Chaplin's *The Kid*, and Pola Negri's *Passion*.

The Adventures of Tarzan was Lincoln's last appearance as Tarzan. He began to find it difficult to land other roles since he was now typecast as Tarzan. He did manage to get a part in *Quincy Adams Sawyer* (1922), a movie that also featured Hoosiers Louise Fazenda, John Bowers, and Victor Potel.

In 1927 Lincoln made a cheap serial entitled *King of the Jungle*, in which one of Lincoln's good friends, Gordon Standing, was attacked and killed by a lion during a jungle scene. Lincoln said, "We didn't use as much caution then as they do now. The incident made me want to get away from the business for awhile, so I went to Mexico to check up on some mining investment." He had mining holdings in Mexico and Arizona, and although the mines were not very successful, he managed to hold on and actively operate them until the crash of 1929.

After Lincoln lost his mines, he went to Salt Lake City, Utah, and operated a junkyard business until he returned to pictures in 1938. He got a small part in *The Hunchback of Notre Dame* (1939), which starred Charles Laughton. After being cast in the film, Lincoln said, "I'm glad to get a part in 'The Hunchback.' I think Charles Laughton is one of the best in the business. But it's the size of these sets that gets me. They're bigger than we had for 'Intolerance,' and that was a sight-seeing center for years after the picture was made."

Lincoln continued to play bit parts in movies and even did a brief stint in the Seals Brothers Circus, where he was billed as "The Original Tarzan." He contacted Burroughs to make sure he could use that title, and Burroughs gave him permission. Lincoln also got bit parts in two Tarzan films, *Tarzan's New York Adventure* (1942) and *Tarzan's Magic Fountain* (1949). His final screen appearance was in *Carrie* (1952), which starred Laurence Olivier. He was pleased to have a few scenes with Olivier, whom he admired greatly.

Lincoln was always a man to speak his mind. When he was presented with a plaque from the Hollywood Chamber of Commerce in 1951, "For your outstanding contribution to the art and science of Motion Pictures . . . For the pleasure you have brought to millions the world over . . . For your help in making Hollywood the film capital of the world," Lincoln quickly realized the whole affair was not much more than exploitation for a movie—*The Hollywood Story*. When Lincoln was handed the plaque, he said, "Can I eat this?" He went on to say, "I've had all the honors. I'm not asking for charity, or to be a big star again, or even for feature parts. Just an opportunity to work."

Lincoln suggested that Hollywood take care of its old-timers by putting them in a "revolving stock company." He said, "The major studios could pay us steady salaries, and we wouldn't expect big ones. Then they could use us in small character parts whenever they wanted

to. We'd earn our keep." Lincoln's statements embarrassed the Hollywood moguls, but his suggestion was ignored.

In his last years, Lincoln made several television appearances on such shows as Art Linkletter and *You Asked for It*. On June 27, 1952, Lincoln suffered a fatal heart attack. His mother had moved to California in 1949 and was living with him. She stated, "He went with a sudden heart seizure very suddenly on the 27th." The news was reported in the Rochester, Indiana, newspaper, which stated, "During his career in the picture industry, Lincoln often came to Rochester to visit his mother who resided here." His brother Don and his two half brothers preceded him in death.

Shirley Willard, Fulton County historian and president of the Fulton County Historical Society, knew Lincoln had a daughter and wanted to contact her to invite her back to Rochester to meet Lincoln's relatives and see the place of his birth. Her search for Marci'a encompassed a frustrating seventeen years. "We knew she existed but we didn't even have her married name," Willard said. She discovered that the Hollywood Memorial Cemetery, where Lincoln was buried, had no marker on his grave. He was in a community niche. Through the cemetery office, she was able to locate Marci'a. In July 1991 Willard met Marci'a Rudolph in Santa Monica. They drove to Lincoln's grave together and placed a marker on his grave that reads, "Elmo Lincoln, the First Tarzan."

Willard found that Rudolph believed she was an only child. She was not aware of her half brother in Rochester nor the fact she had many cousins there. On September 20, 1991, Rudolph came to Rochester for her first visit to her father's hometown. More than one hundred people attended a reception at the Fulton County Museum for Rudolph and her daughter Chrisse Burdick. Her half brother had passed away but she met her nephew, Jay Linkenhelt, and his son, Jeff Linkenhelt, and many other Linkenhelts from Rochester and Kokomo.

Rudolph was asked if her father had retired from acting before his death. She replied, "I don't think so. An actor never retires. He's always waiting for that phone call."

BIBLIOGRAPHY

Chicago Tribune, September 22, 1991.

Essoe, Gabe. *Tarzan of the Movies: A Pictorial History of More Than Fifty Years of Edgar Rice Burroughs's Legendary Hero.* New York: Cadillac Publishing Company, 1968.

Indianapolis News, September 17, 1991.

Los Angeles Daily News, May 7, 1951.

Los Angeles Examiner, June 28, 1952.

New York Times, June 28, 1952.

Rudolph, Marci'a Lincoln. *My Father Elmo Lincoln: The Original Tarzan.* Studio City, Calif.: Empire, 2001.

Walton, Lloyd B. "Me, Tarzan!" *Indianapolis Star Magazine*, December 6, 1970.

JAMES PIERCE

James Pierce and Joan Burroughs Pierce as Jane in *Tarzan and the Golden Lion* (1927).

James Pierce made more than forty-two films from 1926 to 1951, but he will be remembered most for a film he made in 1927, *Tarzan and the Golden Lion.* It was the last silent Tarzan film. Pierce was born in Franklin, Indiana, on August 8, 1900. He was the son of Mr. and Mrs. James Pierce. The senior Pierce was an agent for the Pennsylvania Railroad. The young Pierce was an all-American center for the Indiana University football team, where he centered the ball to fullback Kermit Maynard who followed his brother Ken to Hollywood, where he also became a film cowboy. Pierce was known to his classmates as "Babe" Pierce.

After graduation from IU in 1921, Pierce went to Arizona to coach football. It was there he began to do some amateur acting and decided to move to Hollywood in 1923. He was coaching football at Glendale High School when he was invited to a party at Edgar Rice Burroughs's Tarzana ranch. "There's Tarzan!" yelled Burroughs when he saw Pierce. "And then he proceeded to talk me into playing the Apeman," recalled Pierce. "He said I looked just like what he had always had in mind." Pierce took the role for seventy-five dollars a week, giving up a small role in a picture called *Wings.* That role eventually went to then-unknown Gary Cooper.

Pierce played Tarzan exactly as Burroughs described him in forty novels, and until the day he died Burroughs maintained that Pierce's characterization was the only accurate one. The Ape Man could not only speak and read English but also was supposed to be fluent in French. Halfway through the film, Pierce began to wonder if he had made the right decision. In one scene where he was chased by a lion, he had to climb hand-over-hand along a rope vine stretched thirty feet across a sixty-foot-deep ravine. The studio applied moss on the vine, which nearly caused him to lose his grip. Pierce later recalled, "The whole thing was as much fun as running barefoot over rough, rocky ground can be." He finally resorted to wearing tennis shoes in some of the outdoor scenes because his feet had been cut rather severely.

Tarzan and the Golden Lion was made by FBO, a studio controlled by Joseph P. Kennedy (father of President John F. Kennedy). Costarring with Pierce were Dorothy Dunbar as Jane and Boris Karloff. Before the premiere Burroughs exclaimed, "I have seen some of the work during the making and also some of the rushes, and am convinced that it is going to be the greatest Tarzan picture ever made. We have found a man who really is Tarzan, and whom I believe will be raised to the heights of stardom." Unfortunately, the critics did not share

Scene from *Flash Gordon* (1936) with (left to right) James Pierce, Buster Crabbe, Priscilla Lawson (Indianapolis), and Frank Shannon.

Burroughs's opinion. Although the film did well at the box office, it was not a critical success.

Pierce said, "Because of poor direction, terrible story treatment and putrid acting, the opus was a stinkeroo. I emerged with nothing to show for my strenuous effort except being typecast as Tarzan. I was out of a job." Pierce returned to coaching high school football teams and playing bit parts as they were offered. Pierce and Burroughs's daughter Joan had become very close during the film's production, and on August 8, 1928, they were married. As a wedding present, Burroughs gave Pierce the screen rights to an unpublished Tarzan manuscript.

When Burroughs decided to do a radio series, he cast his son-in-law and his daughter as Tarzan and Jane. The first program was introduced from the stage of the Fox Pantages Theater on September 10, 1932, two days before its designated premiere on radio. This first episode was played over the sound system, and the entire cast appeared on stage.

The series ran from 1932 to 1934. It was transcribed by the American Radio Syndicate and made its debut on WOR in New York. Three hundred sixty-four fifteen-minute episodes were recorded, running three times a week. It was sponsored by the Signal Oil Company. This original Tarzan radio adaptation has come to be regarded as the first major syndicated radio serial. It was well received across the nation, but Burroughs declined to renew it because he felt the syndicator had strayed from his story line. Pierce said, "In the long run, I made more money on radio than I would have in a movie. It was one of the first recorded shows, so I never felt tied down."

In 1927 Pierce played Frank James in the Fred Thompson film *Jesse James.* He began to specialize in playing heavies and appeared in many films with his friend, Richard Dix. Some may remember Pierce as one of the villainous football players in the Marx Brothers feature *Horse Feathers* in 1932, and in 1936 he was King Thun, the Lion Man in Universal's much acclaimed serial *Flash Gordon.* The film starred two other Hoosiers, Priscilla Lawson from Indianapolis, who played Princess Aura, and Lon Poff of Bedford, who played The First High Priest. Flash Gordon was Buster Crabbe, who played Tarzan in 1933. Pierce also made a Republic serial, *Zorro's Fighting Legion*, in 1939. He began to appear in Westerns, supporting such cowboy stars as Tex Ritter, Tim McCoy, and Bob Livingston.

In the 1940s Pierce decided to devote more time to his booming real estate agency in the San Fernando Valley, but while in real estate, he also was writing, directing, and producing radio programs. In 1954 he came to Indianapolis for the premiere of his new radio series, *Sky Gypsies*, on WFBM.

Pierce was an excellent pilot and was very active during World War II, helping form the National Airmen's Reserve Inc. at the Metropolitan Airport in Van Nuys, California. The reserve group was the foundation for today's Air National Guard.

The Pierces had two children, Joan and Michael, and seven grandchildren. Pierce and his wife bought a large home in Apple Valley, California, and filled it with Burroughs memorabilia. Pierce once said, "Anybody can act in a movie. Very few people are lucky enough to remain very happily married for almost half a century. That, to my way of thinking, is glamorous."

Joan Burroughs Pierce died on New Year's Eve, 1972. James Pierce died on December 11, 1983, in Apple Valley.

Scene from *The Mike Douglas Show* on which Douglas welcomed six Tarzans as his guests. (Left to right): Johnny Weismuller, Mike Douglas, Gordon Scott, Totie Fields, Jock Mahoney, Buster Crabbe, Denny Miller, and James Pierce.

BIBLIOGRAPHY

Dunning, John. *On the Air: The Encyclopedia of Old-Time Radio.* New York: Oxford University Press, 1998.

Essoe, Gabe. *Tarzan of the Movies: A Pictorial History of More Than Fifty Years of Edgar Rice Burroughs's Legendary Hero.* New York: Cadillac Publishing Company, 1968.

Indianapolis Star, September 8, 1954.

The Internet Movie Database. http://www.imdb.com/.

"James Pierce." *Screen Thrills Illustrated* (April 1963).

Lamparski, Richard. *Lamparski's Whatever Became Of . . . ?* New York: Bantam Books, 1977.

Weiss, Ken, and Ed Goodgold. *To Be Continued . . . .* New York: Crown Publishers, 1972.

DENNY MILLER

Watching movies on a whitewashed outside wall in Bourbon, Indiana, for sixteen summers, Denny Miller had no dreams of being an actor. Basketball filled his dreams, and athletes were his heroes. His father, Ben W. Miller, was a physical education instructor at Indiana University and a former member of the Waldron High School basketball team that had made it to the "Sweet Sixteen" in the 1920s. Ben met his wife, Martha Alice Linn, a native of Bourbon, Indiana, at IU. Denny was born in Bloomington on April 25, 1934, and he and his brother Kent started playing basketball almost from the day they were born.

The Miller family left Bloomington when Denny was in the fourth grade. He and his brother played basketball in Silver Springs, Maryland, and Baldwin, Long Island, before the family moved to Los Angeles. It was in Los Angeles at University High School in Westwood that Denny and Kent came to the attention of Hoosier John Wooden. Denny said, "Kent was the best. He earned All-City honors in both basketball and track. Coach Wooden recruited both of us and we got full-ride scholarships." The Miller brothers played together for UCLA for one year, and Ben joined the faculty at UCLA.

While Miller was at UCLA studying to be a coach, he also worked at a summer job moving furniture. While loading a truck with office furniture in Hollywood, he heard someone yell at him. He saw a man leaning out the window of a car. The man said, "Come here and let me see your hair line." Miller said, "I thought the guy was loony tunes so I brushed the hair out of my face, and said, 'How's that?' and turned to go back to work. Over my shoulder I heard, 'Here's my card, call me at my office.' The card said, 'talent agent.'"

This encounter led to an interview, and after a screen test directed by the famed George Cukor, Miller was signed to an MGM contract. His first role was a bit part in *Some Came Running*, which was filmed in Madison, Indiana. He said, "I was the only one who came running. I came running to tell Dean Martin that somebody was in town to shoot him!" He stayed in Madison two weeks: "We worked nights at a Carnival and ate in the high school gym. Dean Martin used to kid me and say that they named the movie after my one line in the film."

With this minimal experience and his six foot four inch, 212-pound frame, and blonde good looks, Miller was signed by MGM to a seven-year contract at $180.00 per week. His budding career was interrupted

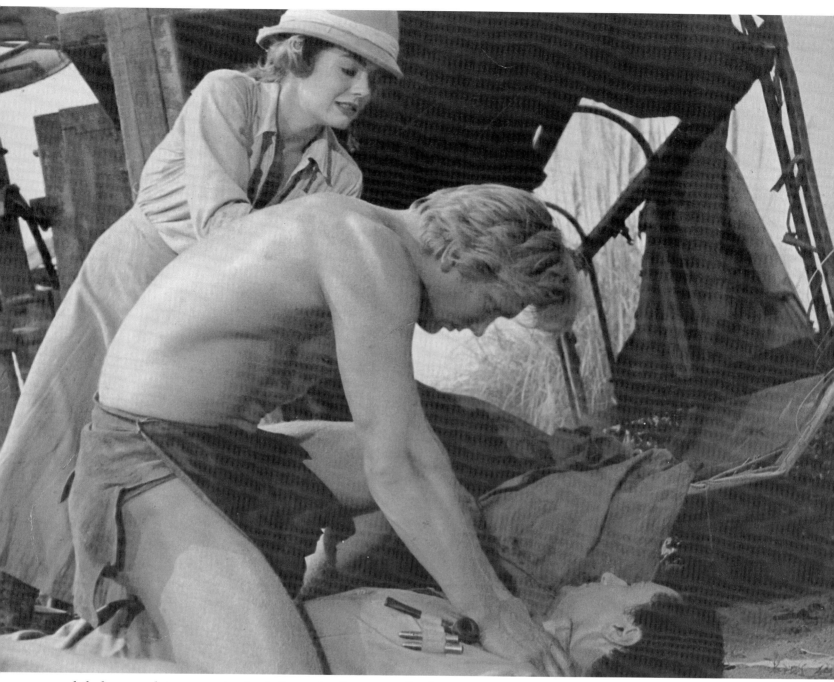

Denny Miller and Joanna Barnes in *Tarzan, the Ape Man* (1959).
©1959, LOEW'S INC.

while he served two years in the infantry in Germany. On his return, he made his first television appearance on *The Life of Riley*, in which he played an athlete. He appeared in the movie *Northwest Passage* and then was called to audition for Tarzan. Sy Weintraub had just taken over the Tarzan series from longtime producer Sol Lesser and had launched a talent hunt for a new Tarzan to replace Gordon Scott.

Miller said the Tarzan role was a lucky break—he was there, he was already on the MGM payroll, and he was "cheaper than some of the elephants." The 1959 movie *Tarzan, the Ape Man* was a remake of the 1932 movie that starred Johnny Weissmuller and Maureen O'Sullivan. Joanna Barnes played Jane. In spite of MGM's publicity touting the film as a "big budget" extravaganza, large chunks of the 1932 film were inserted and tinted in an attempt to match the color of the new film. Costumes from *King Solomon's Mines* were used, and an old mechanical crocodile showed up for Miller to wrestle.

Once Miller was free from his MGM contract, he started doing television shows such as *Riverboat*, *General Electric Theatre*, and *Laramie*. The producer of *Wagon Train* wanted him but asked him to change his name to Scott Miller. The intent was to build up Miller's part so that he eventually could replace Robert Horton. After Horton departed, Miller took over the role of Duke Shannon and became the costar with John McIntire, who stepped in after the death of Ward Bond. Miller was a regular on the show from 1961 to 1964.

In the 1965–66 television season, Miller was in a new series, *Mona McCluskey*, as the husband of Juliet Prowse. For this series he changed his name back to Denny Miller. He has done innumerable guest shots on such television shows as *Gilligan's Island*, *I Spy*, and *Dr. Quinn, Medicine Woman*, and he played Sheriff Owen Kearney in *Lonesome Dove*. He has appeared in at least 138 commercials, 234 television episodes, and 20 feature films. He was the Brawny Paper Towel giant for about twelve years and the Gorton's Fisherman for more than fourteen years. He hosted a special thirty-year retrospective of *Wagon Train* that featured clips from the eight years the series ran.

Miller's degree from UCLA is in physical education, and he has taught fitness at health spas and been a personal trainer. He wrote and directed, as well as hosted, a video on relaxation called *Homestretch*.

Over the years, Miller has worked with several Hoosiers, including director Sydney Pollack. Pollack's career was just beginning when he directed Miller in an episode of *Wagon Train*.

Miller now lives in Las Vegas, Nevada. In September 2003 he decided to return to Bloomington after attending a Tarzan

©1959, LOEW'S INC.

"Look out! Here comes Tarzan, the Ape Man!" (Denny Miller)

M-G-M Presents "TARZAN, THE APE MAN" in TECHNICOLOR

8

59-272

convention in Louisville, Kentucky. He took photos of the town and the university.

Miller's biography, published in 2004, is entitled *Didn't You Used to Be What's His Name?*

BIBLIOGRAPHY

The Astounding B Monster Web Site. http://www.bmonster.com/.

The Denny Miller Web Site. http://www.denny-miller.com/.

Essoe, Gabe. *Tarzan of the Movies: A Pictorial History of More Than Fifty Years of Edgar Rice Burroughs's Legendary Hero.* New York: Cadillac Publishing Company, 1968.

The Fifties Web Site. http://www.fiftiesweb.com/.

McWhorter, George T. Telephone interview with the author. February 5, 2004. University of Louisville.

Miller, Dennis. E-mail to the author. September 26, 2003.

———. Telephone interview with the author. February 14, 2004. Las Vegas, Nevada.

Denny Miller as backwoodsman Noah McBride in the television series *Dr. Quinn, Medicine Woman* (1996).

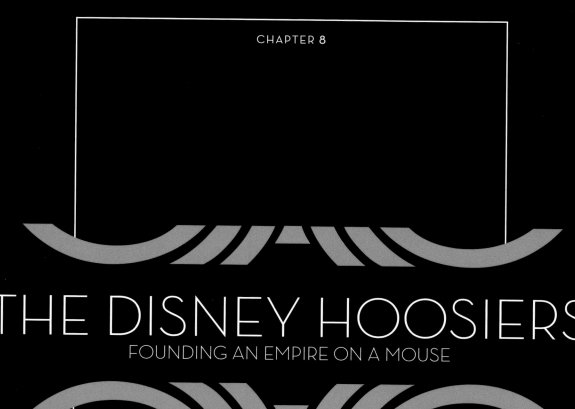

CHAPTER 8

THE DISNEY HOOSIERS

FOUNDING AN EMPIRE ON A MOUSE

It could be said that without the help of certain Indiana artists, the Walt Disney empire would not have been the success it is today. Several Hoosiers played critical roles in the success of the fledgling Walt Disney Studios. They joined the studios as early as 1929, when Disney had barely started on his road to fame and fortune. At least nine Hoosiers made the trek from Indiana to Hollywood to become part of those early years of animation, and most were trained at the John Herron Art Institute in Indianapolis. Most had grown up familiar with Hoosier folklore, which contributed to their ability to picture and sketch the songs, habits, and day-by-day struggles of the average American. In addition to the early animators, Indiana provided actors, directors, and voice-over artists for a multitude of Disney productions.

BILL PEET

Bill Peet achieved the greatest stature of all the Disney Hoosiers. He was a multitalented artist, animator, writer, and producer. He was born William Bartlett Peed on January 29, 1915, in Grandview, Indiana. (In 1945 he legally changed his last name to Peet.) He was three years old when his father, Orion Hopkins Peed, was drafted into the army. After his father left, Bill's mother, Emma Thorpe Peed, found a job teaching handwriting in Indianapolis, where Bill and his two brothers went to live with their widowed grandmother. When World War I ended in 1918, his father never came home. Whenever anyone asked about him, Peet's mother always explained, "he's a traveling salesman out on the road somewhere."

Life became better when Peet's grandmother used her life's savings to buy a house on the east side of Indianapolis. The house at 518 North Riley was at that time just a ten-minute trot to the open countryside. Peet recalls that those years in the house on Riley were the happiest of his boyhood. His favorite room in the winter was the warm attic, where he filled fat five-cent tablets with drawings of monsters.

One day Peet's father showed up unexpectedly. He had run out of money and decided to live with them. Peet's mother accepted him, but his grandmother did not. After several arguments and some abusive behavior, his father left once more. Shortly before he started attending high school, his grandmother died, and they were forced to sell the Riley house and divide the proceeds among the heirs. The family then moved into rented quarters.

Peet went to high school at Arsenal Technical, one of the largest schools in the nation. Tech had several buildings on a large campus, and Peet recalled that it was like being lost in a big city and he was miserable. He did not do well in high school until a friend suggested he take more art courses. The art courses proved to be easy and inspirational for him, and his art teachers, Roberta Stewart and Sara Bard, recognized his talent and encouraged him. This helped him handle his other classes, and he managed to graduate. One of the accomplishments of which Peet was most proud was getting one of his sketches in the 1933 Tech yearbook along with photos of the football team. It was a pen drawing of a football pileup just above the picture of the varsity team.

Although Peet's mother was unsupportive and even dismissive of his work, he received encouragement from Margaret Brunst of Ladoga, Indiana, whom he met on the first day of art school at John Herron in Indianapolis. He dedicated his autobiography to "The Girl I Met in Art School." While a scholarship student at Herron from 1933 to 1936, he won several prizes for his work, including the Thomas Meeks Butler and Culver Military Academy awards and the J. I. Holcomb award.

After leaving Herron, he started painting. His first painting was of his great-uncle Eli, an old farmer who lived in Kentucky. Peet entered the painting, along with a few others, in the art exhibition at the Indiana State Fair. This was 1934, and no artist could pass up a chance to win a cash prize, but he knew the competition would be tough. When he went to the fair to see his picture, he discovered a red ribbon attached to the frame. He said it was an overwhelming moment and

Bill Peet.
© Peet Family

remained one of the biggest thrills in his memory. He was stunned to see that all of his pictures had been put up for display. The money he won at the fair and subsequent cash prizes were not enough to live on, however, so he started designing department store ads.

One day Peet dropped by Herron for a visit, and the director of the school handed him a brochure from Disney soliciting artists. He filled out the form and sent in a variety of action sketches as required. He had always enjoyed the Disney films but "was never interested in any kind of cartooning." A form letter arrived offering him a tryout. He managed to get to Los Angeles for twenty dollars by sharing the driving time with a friend Brunst knew. He went to the Disney studio on Hyperion Avenue on September 9, 1937. He was one of three of the original fifteen to apply who were hired.

Peet hated his work but diligently drew Donald Ducks and Mickey Mouses and even some of the Dwarfs for *Snow White and the Seven Dwarfs*, working five and a half days a week for twenty-two dollars a week. Brunst came to Los Angeles, and they were married on November 30, 1937. His brother George also came and worked as a story sketch man.

One day Peet got so fed up with his work he went up and down the halls shouting, "No more ducks! No more lousy ducks!" He fully expected to be fired, but the next day he found a bonus check for twenty-five dollars in his mailbox. He had submitted drawings of several zany monsters for the bogey land sequence in Disney's new film, *Pinocchio*. They were well received and earned him the bonus in the nick of time.

Then came years of frustration as he became an assistant to the storymen. During this time Peet did not receive screen credits for anything he did. He drew for *Fantasia* and *Peter Pan*, and he did get to develop a story on his own for *Dumbo*. His first son Bill Jr. had recently been born, and Peet modeled the baby elephant after him. Another version of the creation of *Dumbo* came from Peet's mother, Emma. She said he conceived the idea from the fact that his teachers at school called him "dumb," and she jokingly referred to him as an elephant when he was at the awkward boy stage. The fact is Peet was very familiar with elephants because every time a circus would come to Indianapolis, he was always on hand. He even carried water for the elephants and other animals to pay for his admission.

Disney finally began to notice his work and became enthusiastic about his talent. Peet worked on *Victory through Air Power* and then was chosen to develop characters for *Song of the South* (1946), which starred fellow Hoosier James Baskett as Uncle Remus. In 1948 he was put in charge of the cartoon-story treatment for *So Dear to My Heart*, a live action film with animated sequences. This film was based on Sterling North's reminiscent book (*Midnight and Jeremiah*) about growing up in Pike County, Indiana. No filming took place in Indiana, but because of its Indiana setting the film was premiered in Indianapolis on January 19, 1948. At the time of the premiere, some of Peet's animation was put on display at the John Herron Art Museum.

Peet then worked on *Cinderella* (1950), designing the mice and the cat. On *Alice in Wonderland* (1951) he designed the Mad Tea Party and the Walrus and the Carpenter. He won more and more respect as an effective writer who was, unlike many of his colleagues in the story department, also a gifted cartoonist; it was easy to envision his drawings as animated cartoons.

Disney began to be envious of Peet's talents, and it was not long before the two men had a major argument. Disney wanted some changes made in *Sleeping Beauty* (1959), and Peet refused to make them. As a result, Peet was banished to working on commercials and short subjects. It was during this time that he decided he needed some kind of a backup in case he lost his job. He started writing and illustrating children's books. His first was *Hubert's Hair-Raising Adventure* (1959). He told friends that he "imagined this big rabbit as living in southern Indiana, somewhere near Hazelton where I spent a few vacations as a boy." His second book in 1961 was *Huge Harold*, about the further adventures of the large rabbit.

One Hundred and One Dalmatians (1961) finally got Peet out of Disney's doghouse. Disney was busy with his theme parks, and he knew he needed someone with a strong story presence to run things in his absence. He began to see Peet as his equal in this regard and entrusted him to adapt *One Hundred and One Dalmatians.* Peet drew all the storyboards and even cast the voices and supervised the recording. Disney agreed with Peet on everything.

Peet again went solo doing *The Sword in the Stone* (1963). He modeled Merlin after Disney—"cantankerous, argumentative. He can't be wrong." Peet now had five children's books published and decided he would retire after his next film, *The Jungle Book* (1967). The show-stopping song and sequence, "The Bare Necessities," sung by fellow Hoosier Phil Harris, was a hit with Disney. Before *The Jungle Book* was finished, however, Peet and Disney got into another argument over the voice of the leopard in the story. The disagreement came on Peet's birthday, January 29, 1964. Peet left the studio and never returned.

Peet began writing and illustrating children's books in a studio over his garage. In 1967 he was named outstanding Hoosier author of children's literature. He won the Box Office Magazine Blue Ribbon Award for best screenplay in 1961 and 1964. He won the Indiana University Writers Conference award for the most distinguished work in children's literature in 1966 for *Cappyboppy*, and he was given the Southern California Council on Literature of Children and Young People Award in 1967 for *Farewell to Shady Glade.*

In 1975 tragedy struck. Peet's youngest son, Steve, committed suicide over an unhappy marriage. Two years later Peet had a heart attack and triple-bypass surgery. In 1989 he had another bypass. In 1991 he suffered a stroke, which left him unable to draw. He was working on two books in his studio but was unable to finish them. He died on May 11, 2002, in Studio City, California.

BIBLIOGRAPHY

Barrier, J. Michael. *Hollywood Cartoons: American Animation in Its Golden Age.* New York: Oxford University Press, 1999.

"Brush Strokes to Fame." *Indianapolis Star Magazine*, April 4, 1954.

Canemaker, John. *Paper Dreams: The Art and Artists of Disney Storyboards.* New York: Hyperion, 1999.

Indianapolis News, July 19, 1941, April 16, 1945.

Indianapolis Star, April 16, 1942, July 1, 1961.

Indianapolis Times, December 25, 1948.

Peet, Bill. *Bill Peet: An Autobiography.* Boston: Houghton Mifflin, 1989.

GEORGE PEED

George Peed attended Arsenal Technical High School and Herron Art School and then followed his brother, Bill, to Hollywood, becoming a story sketch man for Disney. George was hired March 3, 1938, at the company's New York office. He left August 22, 1938, and was rehired on March 30, 1959, staying until January 1, 1960. He joined the army during the Second World War and became assistant manager of the film training production laboratory, a unit of the Army Signal Corps at Fort Monmouth, New Jersey. He later became a commercial artist in New York City.

BIBLIOGRAPHY

Banta, Ray. *Indiana's Laughmakers: The Story of Over Four Hundred Hoosiers; Actors, Cartoonists, Writers, and Others.* Indianapolis: PennUltimate Press, 1990.

Indianapolis News, January 7, 1942.

WILLIAM COTTRELL

William (Bill) Cottrell was another Herron Art School gift to the Walt Disney Studios. Cottrell was born in South Bend, Indiana, on November 19, 1906. He studied four years at Herron. However, Cottrell did not use his pencil as much as he used a typewriter. After arriving at Disney, Cottrell was partnered with Richard Huemer and Joe Grant. Erudite and sophisticated, the trio was interested in the fine arts, literature, history, theater, classical music, opera, and film. Cottrell and his partners brought wit, a light touch, a fondness for wordplay, and, in general, a more literate approach to cartoon comedy and drama than did the slapstick gagsters.

Cottrell came to Disney in 1929 at age twenty-three. Six years before, his father had brought the Cottrell family to Los Angeles from South Bend on an oil business venture. The Great Depression came early for the family when the deal did not materialize and, as Cottrell recalled, the family found itself "in tough straits." He found work as a sportswriter/cartoonist on the *Orange County Plain Dealer* and submitted some continuity dialog and ideas to George Herriman for his *Krazy Kat* comic strip.

As luck would have it, Cottrell's sister worked in a bank where Roy Disney did business. "He knew my sister, knew me," said Cottrell, "so I applied at the Studio because of Roy. I met Walt, he saw my drawings which were not too great." In fact, the only thing in the portfolio that impressed Disney were the full pages of *Krazy Kat* on which Herriman thanked Cottrell for writing the continuity. "I think that had an influence on Walt. He saw me as a gagman," said Cottrell.

At first he was given the menial task of inking and painting cels. The studio had released only six Mickey Mouse shorts and the first *Silly Symphony*, and there were "only about a dozen people working at Disney at that time, including the front office and the legal department and everything," recalled Cottrell. Within a few weeks the studio's lone cameraman needed help, and Cottrell began to photograph shorts frame by frame and to cut foreign versions of them. "Eventually it got so that you had departments to do all this stuff because it got to be a big business, but in that time they couldn't afford a lot of people so one person did it all," he said. Cottrell found his apprenticeship as an inker/painter/cameraman/cutter "very helpful" when he moved into story. "I knew how to do it mechanically . . . it could give you ideas of how to accomplish something that you wouldn't think of doing before without the knowledge," said Cottrell.

While working at Disney, Cottrell met Hazel Bounds, who was a secretary and the sister of Walt Disney's wife, Lillian. They were married, and it was not long before Cottrell, in addition to becoming one of the studio's most talented story men, also became Disney's lifelong friend, traveling companion, and trusted confidant. He even was recruited by Disney to be a member of the Disney polo team, which played against such famous people as Will Rogers, Darryl F. Zanuck, Spencer Tracy, and James Gleason.

After a period in the story department contributing detailed typewritten gags and story continuity ideas to various films, including *Three Little Pigs*, Cottrell was paired with Grant, a newspaper cartoonist. Grant recalls he and Cottrell had a "wonderful rapport," and their working partnership was "probably one of the most enjoyable times I had." They shared "an intellectual bond," and the twenty-seven-year-old Cottrell showed the twenty-five-year-old newcomer the ropes. Their work on *Three Orphan Kittens* (1935) helped win Disney a fourth Academy Award. *Pluto's Judgement Day* (1935), *Who Killed Cock Robin?* (1935), and *Three Little Wolves* (1936) were also superior shorts because of their contributions.

"Cottrell was very intelligent in his approach to things," said Grant. In *Cock Robin*, Cottrell suggested Gilbert and Sullivan rhymes to move the play along and clever cinematic transitions, such as dissolving a policeman whacking a prisoner's head in rhythm to a judge's pounding of a gavel for order in the court. Grant caricatured Mae West as a pouter pigeon and found Cottrell's "little touches all through" to be "a great inspiration." Ideas for new films flew out of the team, pleasing Disney.

Cottrell and Grant were assigned as story developers for all the Queen and Witch sequences in *Snow White and the Seven Dwarfs*. He was credited as a sequence director. "Maybe we just had a flair for an interest in the melodramatic," said Cottrell. The transformation scene, in which the queen uses a potion to turn herself into a hag, was inspired "a bit by the three witches scene in Macbeth Act IV," Cottrell recalled. "Round about the cauldron go," which concludes "Something wicked this way comes."

After *Snow White* opened in 1937, Disney split up Cottrell and Grant. Disney had a way of breaking up teams if they became too close or too successful. In 1952 Disney set up WED Enterprises, an organization to plan and design the first Disney theme park. Cottrell was one of several artists and writers recruited from the studio. Recalling his time at WED, Cottrell stated, "We all did a lot of things. It was the same formula as the early days in the studio. And I think this was part of the great pleasure of WED. We began all over again doing anything and everything that was needed to be done. And so you worked on concepts of rides . . . you wrote dialogue for spiels . . . copy for signs, nomenclature, and all of these things developed. . . . It was sort of starting all over again."

Cottrell was president of the Disney Family company, Retlaw, until his retirement in 1982. He died on December 22, 1995, in Burbank, California.

BIBLIOGRAPHY

Banta, Ray. *Indiana's Laughmakers: The Story of Over Four Hundred Hoosiers; Actors, Cartoonists, Writers, and Others.* Indianapolis: PennUltimate Press, 1990.

Canemaker, John. *Paper Dreams: The Art and Artists of Disney Storyboards.* New York: Hyperion, 1999.

Eliot, Marc. *Walt Disney: Hollywood's Dark Prince.* Secaucus, N.J.: Carol Publishing Group, 1993.

The Internet Movie Database. http://www.imdb.com/.

Maltin, Leonard. *The Disney Films.* 3rd ed. New York: Hyperion, 1995.

EARL FREEMAN

Earl Freeman graduated from the John Herron School of Art and was a friend of Bill Peet (Peed) and George Peed. Through his connection with Bill and George, Freeman was hired at Disney. He first joined Disney in 1939 as a messenger. He served in the armed forces from 1941 to 1945. After returning to Disney he served as a layout artist from 1945 to 1947. However, his stay there appears to have been brief, and not much is known about Freeman's work.

BIBLIOGRAPHY

Banta, Ray. *Indiana's Laughmakers: The Story of over Four Hundred Hoosiers; Actors, Cartoonists, Writers, and Others.* Indianapolis: PennUltimate Press, 1990.

Indianapolis News, April 16, 1945.

BILL JUSTICE

Bill Justice was born in Dayton, Ohio, and grew up in Greenfield and Indianapolis. Justice got his early art training at Arsenal Technical High School in Indianapolis. In addition to his artistic talent, he was also an athlete, playing center on the football team. After graduation from Tech in 1931, he attended the John Herron Art Institute.

Justice began work as a commercial artist for the Eiteljorg-Menke advertising agency and later with the Polar Ice and Fuel Company. Shortly after his graduation from Herron in 1936, he said, "at the time Walt Disney was making its first full length cartoon, 'Snow White,' and they advertised in a magazine for artists. After I wrote them, they sent me a questionnaire and drawings for me to interpret. Another letter asked me to come to Hollywood for a tryout, so I joined 30 other hopefuls for a month's work at $12.50 a week. Twelve of us got jobs. I think our salaries went up to about $25 a week."

Justice went to Hollywood in 1937 in answer to the same ad that attracted Bill Peet, Victor Haboush, and Cornett Wood. Justice helped complete the animation for *Snow White and the Seven Dwarfs*. He received film credit as an animator for *Fantasia* (1940), *Bambi* (1942), *Alice in Wonderland* (1951), *Peter Pan* (1953), and others. He was responsible for developing such memorable characters as Thumper and Chip and Dale. He also directed short subjects such as *Jack and Old Mac* (1956), *Noah's Ark* (1959), and *A Symposium on Popular Songs* (1962). Two of his shorts were Academy Award nominees—*The Truth about Mother Goose* (1957) and *A Cowboy Needs a Horse* (1956).

In 1965 Disney moved Justice to WED Enterprises, where he programmed audio-animatronics figures for Great Moments with Mr. Lincoln, Pirates of the Caribbean, The Haunted Mansion, The Country Bear Jamboree, The Hall of Presidents, and others. He designed many of the character costumes for Disneyland parades, including the Main Street Electrical Parade. He retired in 1979 and has written an autobiography entitled *Justice for Disney*. He is married to the former Dorothy Eakin of Indianapolis and was named a Disney Legend in 1996.

BIBLIOGRAPHY

Banta, Ray. *Indiana's Laughmakers: The Story of Over Four Hundred Hoosiers; Actors, Cartoonists, Writers, and Others.* Indianapolis: PennUltimate Press, 1990.

"Brushstrokes to Fame." *Indianapolis Star Magazine*, April 4, 1954.

Indianapolis News, January 6, 1943, October 10, 1958.

Maltin, Leonard. *The Disney Films.* 3rd ed. New York: Hyperion, 1995.

Smith, Dave. *Disney A to Z: The Updated Official Encyclopedia.* New York: Hyperion, 1998.

VICTOR HABOUSH

Victor Haboush began his art training at the John Herron Art Institute in 1942. His work on *Song of the South* (1946) and a number of Donald Duck shorts was uncredited. He received credit as an animator for *Lady and the Tramp* (1955). He did layout for *Sleeping Beauty* (1959) and also did layout work for *One Hundred and One Dalmatians* (1961).

BIBLIOGRAPHY

"Brushstrokes to Fame." *Indianapolis Star Magazine*, April 4, 1954.

Maltin, Leonard. *The Disney Films.* 3rd ed. New York: Hyperion, 1995.

HARRY REEVES

Harry Reeves was one of the first artists to work for Walt Disney. He joined Disney in 1930, long before Disney thought about producing a feature-length cartoon. Reeves was born in Terre Haute, Indiana, in 1906. As a bored teen, he "bummed his way out" to California and "fell in love with it," but returned to his Hoosier hometown to finish high school.

Not wanting to be a meat salesman like his father, Reeves studied art at the John Herron Art Institute in Indianapolis, but ran away just a few days before receiving his diploma. When asked why he left, he replied, "I couldn't stand it any longer. I was so undernourished." He "bummed" his way to New York, where he found it much easier to get night work, which allowed him to attend the National Academy of Design and a year at Columbia University. When he saw the first Mickey Mouse short, he knew he wanted to be an animator and make people laugh.

Fascinated by show business, and in order to keep body and soul together, Reeves took a job at a Broadway movie palace as a doorman and barker who stood in front of a theater trying to entice people to come inside. His experience as a loud, hard-sell pitchman helped him later as a story man for Disney. One day at the theater, during a promotion for a *Tarzan* movie, a live monkey got loose. As Reeves scrambled up onto the marquee to capture the monkey, three animators from the nearby Felix the Cat studio asked when the cartoon would be shown. The excitable Reeves let the monkey go and talked himself into a job: "Hey, are you fellas in the cartoon game? I wanna be a cartoonist, too. How do I get a job? Where's the studio? Can I follow you fellas back? I got a lotta ideas, an' maybe I can do gags! Let's go!" At the studio, under Otto Messmer's tutelage, Reeves quickly learned the ropes and became a Felix the Cat animator. Within a year he moved to Los Angeles to animate at Disney. "Dear Walt: Can Pay My Own Expenses If You Can Use Me Answer Yes or No Collect Can Leave Saturday," Reeves wired Disney on November 13, 1930. By December 1 he had a contract as an "assistant cartoon animator" at sixty dollars a week.

In 1934 Reeves's revised contract stated his duties as "animator and apprentice story writer and gagman." By 1937 he became a story director on a number of Donald Duck shorts, including *Good Scouts* (1938), *Donald's Lucky Day* (1939), and *The Autograph Hound* (1939).

A photo of a young, wavy-haired Reeves sticking his fingers in his ears and mugging in front of a Donald Duck storyboard, to the amusement of several story men, became an oft-seen image of the "fun" atmosphere of the Disney factory. In reality, the pressure in the story department was intense, and Reeves had a very volatile personality. A coworker remembered, "Harry got mad real quick. He was red-faced to begin with and always pulling at his shirt collar continually. He'd get beet-red arguing with everybody." Even as a young man he was named "Old Man Reeves" because of his temper tantrums.

At Disney, Reeves was usually partnered on stories with fun-loving Homer Brightman. They got along well and became lifelong friends. Brightman and Reeves were notorious for their loud, fast, and furiously energetic storyboard pitches. According to Bill Peet,

"Homer and Harry oversold and that would bug the hell out of Walt, who would often say, 'I'm not laughing at the board, I'm laughing at you.'" They were among the initial storyboarders on the first version of *Pinocchio* that was halted and revised.

They worked on versions of *Peter Pan* and *Alice in Wonderland*, but those versions were postponed. During the Second World War the team worked on *Saludos Amigos* (1942) and *The Three Caballeros*, then the postwar films *Make Mine Music* (1946), *Melody Time* (1948), *Fun and Fancy Free* (1947), and *The Adventures of Ichabod and Mr. Toad* (1949).

After writing a script (with Ted Sears) for *Cinderella* (1950), Brightman and Reeves prepared initial boards for the film that attempted to appeal to Disney by drawing seven mice who were "seven Mickey Mice." Disney did not like the idea and took them off the film and gave Peet the key sequences with the cat and mice. When Reeves protested, Disney became angry, and Reeves was "released" by the studio in August 1948. He left the animation business altogether and became a San Fernando Valley real estate developer. "He bought forever, he sold forever," says his daughter Joan Reeves Gelms.

When he died at age sixty-five of cardiac arrest after a 1971 earthquake, he was a millionaire.

BIBLIOGRAPHY

"Brushstrokes to Fame." *Indianapolis Star Magazine*, April 4, 1954.

Canemaker, John. *Paper Dreams: The Art and Artists of Disney Storyboards.* New York: Hyperion, 1999.

Indianapolis News, July 19, 1941.

Maltin, Leonard. *The Disney Films.* 3rd ed. New York: Hyperion, 1995.

CORNETT WOOD

Cornett Wood was another Disney artist who was trained at the John Herron Art Institute. Like many of the other Disney artists, Wood's work went uncredited for a number of years. He did get credit for his work on *Fantasia* (1940). Specifically, he was an animator on the *Toccata and Fugue in D Minor* and *The Sorcerer's Apprentice*. Wood worked as a special effects animator at Disney from March 7, 1938, to September 12, 1941.

BIBLIOGRAPHY

Banta, Ray. *Hoosier Laughmakers: The Story of Over Four Hundred Hoosiers; Actors, Cartoonists, Writers, and Others.* Indianapolis: PennUltimate, 1990.

"Brushstrokes to Fame." *Indianapolis Star Magazine*, April 4, 1954.

Maltin, Leonard. *The Disney Films.* 3rd ed. New York: Hyperion, 1995.

JOHN SIBLEY

John Sibley joined Disney a little later than most of the other Hoosiers mentioned above. He was born and raised in South Bend, Indiana, and headed for Hollywood in the 1930s, becoming an animator. He was with Disney from 1938 to 1965. One of his best jobs was creating the wild chase of Ichabod and his horse, with Ichabod and the horse reacting as one entity, for the 1949 release, *The Adventures of Ichabod and Mr. Toad.* Sibley also was an animator in many of the delightful Goofy cartoon shorts.

BIBLIOGRAPHY

The Internet Movie Database. http://www.imdb.com/.

Special thanks to Margaret Adamic and DISNEY Publishing Worldwide for editing and providing additional information for this chapter.

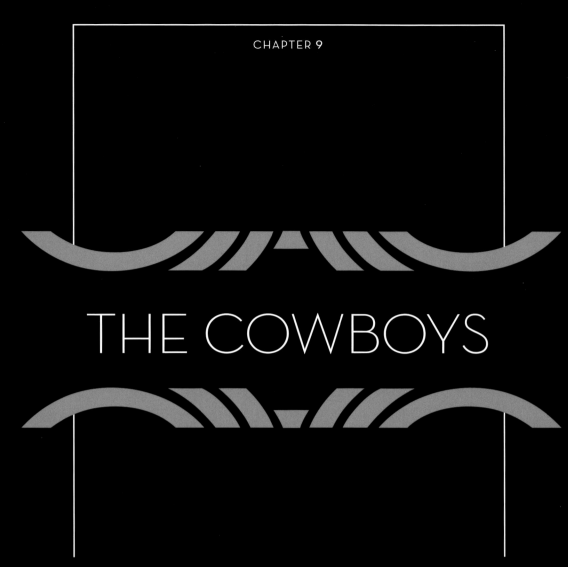

CHAPTER 9

THE COWBOYS

The lifespan of the B Western was only about fifty years. It began in 1903 when Edison released *The Great Train Robbery*. One of the players in that film, Gilbert M. Anderson, soon made another Western in which he played a character named Bronco Billy. The name caught on, and Anderson made hundreds of one- and two-reel Westerns based on the Bronco Billy character and became the first Western hero. Like thousands of youngsters across the nation, two young boys in Indiana, one in Vincennes and another in Columbus, were dreaming about becoming cowboys just like Bronco Billy.

Unlike most other youngsters, Charles Gebhart and Kenneth Maynard not only realized their dreams, they became cowboy heroes of such stature they dwarfed the popularity of Bronco Billy. While Anderson had to be taught to ride a horse, Gebhart and Maynard were expert horsemen before they ever made their first film appearances. They were skilled rodeo performers and could outride and out trick most of the real cowboys.

The days of the B Western are over, but Westerns are still being made, and Hoosiers are still portraying cowboys. Hoosiers Steve McQueen, Forrest Tucker, Denny Miller, Will Geer, Strother Martin, and David Canary have all saddled up and ridden across the silver screen. But there was a time when an actor was known as a cowboy and rarely, if ever, did he venture out of that category.

Indiana produced several of the greatest and most beloved screen cowboys. Charles Gebhart became Buck Jones, a name that still conjures up an image of the best of the old "straight-shootin'" cowboys. Kenneth Maynard rode his famous horse Tarzan into screen immortality as Ken Maynard. The third in a trio of Western stars from Indiana was Allan "Rocky" Lane, who came along later and was the last of the great B Western cowboys.

BUCK JONES

"He Was the Real Thing"

Buck Jones.
©1939, PARAMOUNT PICTURES INC.

Tony Thomas, Canadian broadcaster and movie historian, said about Buck Jones, "he had an air of authority and dignity as well as being tough. He was the real thing."

Jones was the most beloved and idolized of the Western stars after Tom Mix. While Mix had an adventure-filled real life before his screen career, he chose to adopt costumes that were fancy and full of frills, similar to those of Gene Autry and Roy Rogers in years to come. Although he was a good rider, many of the tricks he performed on and off his horse were created by special effects.

Jones's screen persona was more or less a combination of Mix, William S. Hart, and Ken Maynard. Hart portrayed the West as a very nonglamorous place, where there were no superheroes in ten-gallon hats. Mix and Maynard were at the other extreme, using trick riding and roping, great-looking costumes, and beautiful and well-trained horses. Jones was always well attired but not flashy. He named his horse Silver long before the Lone Ranger came into being. He underplayed his parts, allowing a certain form of sincerity to come through. Perhaps it was his real personality people saw. He was a warm, generous, and kind individual who worked hard to make his films the best product possible.

Charles Frederick Gebhart, who later was known as Charles "Buck" Jones and finally Buck Jones, was born on December 12, 1891, in Vincennes, Indiana. He was the son of Charles and Evelyn Showers Gebhart. Shortly after his birth, his parents were divorced, and his mother remarried. Jones was unhappy with his mother's second marriage and went to live with a couple in Vincennes who had a little general store. Jones loved these people. He worked in the store, took care of the horse, and delivered groceries. When learning to ride, he acquired the nickname Buckaroo. This was shortened to Buck, which would remain his nickname his entire life.

Jones's stepfather, Ernest McCammon, was in the hardware business. When he had the opportunity to move to Indianapolis, he took it. Jones and his sister Ada moved to Indianapolis as well. They grew up in the area of North and Alabama streets in Indianapolis. Some accounts state that Jones left school at age twelve, but his sister said he attended high school in Indianapolis until age sixteen. The *Indianapolis News* featured a brief biography of Jones on March 29, 1932, and stated that his sister Ada, who was then Mrs. Walter Mendell, still lived in Indianapolis at 127 E. St. Joseph Street. Some reports state the family moved to Oklahoma when Jones was about twelve years old, but there is no evidence to support this.

On January 5, 1907, Jones enlisted in the army in Indianapolis. Although some sources state his name was Gebhardt, he signed his name on his enlistment papers as "Charles F. Gebhart." He listed his occupation at that time as tin worker and his residence as 25 W. Walnut Street. His mother, Mrs. Eva McCammon, signed a consent form certifying he was eighteen years old, although he was only sixteen. He was assigned to Troop G, Sixth Regiment United States Cavalry. He arrived in the Philippine Islands on October 9, 1907, and came back to the United States on December 14, 1909. He was honorably discharged as a private on December 20, 1909, at Fort McDowell, California.

After his discharge, Jones came back to Indianapolis. Here he developed an affection for motor cars and tinkered with cars for the rest of his life, making two movies in which he portrayed a race-car driver. Due to his love of cars, he became acquainted with race driver Harry Stillman. According to Indianapolis Motor Speedway historian Donald Davidson, Stillman never drove in the famous 500-mile race but did drive in other races held at the track in 1909 and 1910. Through his friendship with Stillman, Jones was given a job with the Marmon Motor Company in Indianapolis. The Indianapolis Motor Speedway opened in 1909, though the 500-mile race did not start until 1911. Jones test-drove Marmon cars around the Indianapolis oval before the 500-mile race was conceived and became an international event.

After a short stay in Indianapolis, Jones became restless again and rejoined the army on October 12, 1910, in Indianapolis and served as a sergeant in the Sixth Cavalry at Fort Des Moines, Iowa. On March 19, 1913, he requested a transfer to the Signal Corps Aviation Squad. He was transferred, but as a private, and ordered to be assigned duty with the First Aero Squadron, Signal Corps. His reason for the transfer was that he wanted to learn to fly, but unfortunately, he found that only officers could become pilots. He was discharged from his last hitch in the armed forces on October 23, 1913, in Texas City, Texas.

After his discharge, Jones discovered that the 101 Ranch Wild West Show was appearing in Galveston. He got in touch with Joe Miller and joined the famous Miller Brothers 101 Ranch that was headquartered near Bliss, Oklahoma. Jones did not know much about being a cowboy, but he knew horses and he could ride well, thanks to his two hitches in the cavalry. When he tried out for the Miller Wild West show, Jones said, "I put resin on my chaps to help me hold the saddle and drove horseshoe nails into the heels of my boots to keep my spurs on." According to a history of the 101 Ranch by Collins and England, "He was given the only opening . . . the task of currying horses for the cowboys. Soon an opening occurred in the cowboy 'string,' and Jones was given an outfit and a horse. He made a splendid arena performer."

While the show was appearing in New York, a beautiful equestrienne named Odille Dorothy Osborne, affectionately known as Dell, joined the show. In 1915 she left the show to join the Julia Allen Wild West Show. Jones followed her and got a job with the same show. Several months later they decided to get married, but they had no money for a wedding. The owners of the show told them they would foot the bill if they would get married during an actual performance. Jones and Osborne agreed. The wedding march was played by the show band, and the bride, groom, and minister were all on horseback. It was a spectacular wedding. Jones later said, "It took, and that's the main thing."

Times were rough for the couple. They once sat up all night playing cards because the room was too cold to sleep, and they once ate for more than a month on ten dollars, sharing their rations with a pet bulldog.

When World War I started, the Allies needed horses, and top-notch horse breakers were urgently needed to break and tame the half-wild creatures from the Southwest and West. Jones went to work in the Chicago stockyards, where he was employed by Chicago horse dealers Ellworth and McNair. Because of his talent as a horse breaker, Jones was considered essential to the war effort and stayed with the job until 1916, when his job was eliminated.

The couple formed their own "one man–one woman" riding expedition circus and toured many towns in the West and then joined the Ringling Brothers Circus. The circus played in Los Angeles, shortly before the couple's first and only child, Maxine, was born. Jones decided it was time to settle down and began to pursue a job with the Hollywood studios. In 1918 Universal hired him as a bit player and stuntman for five dollars a day. After a short stay at Universal, Jones moved to Canyon Pictures to support Western star Franklyn Farnum, making shorts (two-reelers) and worked steadily. When his Canyon contract expired, he found work at Fox as a stuntman for forty dollars a week. In this capacity he appeared in several Tom Mix and William

WILLIAM FOX
Presents

CHARLES JONES

IN

BIG DAN

STORY BY
FREDERICK AND FANNY
HATTON

DIRECTED BY
WILLIAM WELLMAN

Farnum films. Osborne found work as a stuntwoman and appeared in several Mix and William S. Hart films.

When Jones's salary rose to $150 a week, Osborne's show business career ended. About this same time, studio head William Fox was looking for a backup to Mix, who was demanding a salary increase. According to Osborne, her husband changed his name when he signed with Fox: "He signed in 1919, and that was so fresh after the war that putting a German name like Gebhart on a marquee might have kept people away. They made a long list of names and Buck Jones just seemed to happen to gibe. After a few years, we changed it legally." (It was legally changed in 1937.)

Jones's appearance changed rather dramatically while at Fox. He was given specific instructions about his grooming. His hair was to be neatly combed, cut, washed, and oiled once a week. His teeth were capped, and he was told to "open your mouth a little wider when you smile so that your teeth are seen more." Other details, such as clipping and cleaning his fingernails and special attention to his clothing, were among a list of requirements the studio thought was needed to establish a star. Audiences responded favorably, and Fox was elated.

As Jones's pictures for Fox continued to be well received, his salary soared to $3,500 a week. Mix was not happy with Jones's new stardom. Osborne said, "Oh, he was so nasty! But after a few years, when Buck made it, he admitted there was no way you could keep him out. So then they became good friends." During their competitive years, Jones and Mix remained best friends, and each respected the other's talents. When Mix died in an automobile accident in 1940, the *San Francisco Examiner* ran a photo of the mourners. In the front row, Jones is standing a few feet from fellow Hoosier Monte Blue, who delivered the Masonic funeral rites.

Jones made at least sixty silent films for Fox, working with many directors, including fellow Hoosier Lambert Hillyer (South Bend, Indiana), who also wrote screenplays for several of Jones's films. Jones could ride and fight with the best and seldom used a double. Because he had developed into such a good actor, he was given the opportunity to appear in several non-Westerns. Film historian William K. Everson says of Jones's acting ability, "he was a serious actor, one of the best among Western stars." In fact, Jones's histrionic ability was taken so seriously that he was one of the front-runners for the role of Ben-Hur in the 1925 production. Undoubtedly, his muscular good looks and his ability to "drive a wicked chariot" were factors in his being considered for the role. However, the part was eventually given to Ramón Novarro.

Jones even had a flair for comedy and preferred to do the comic relief himself. His was a folksy humor, unstressed and similar to that of Will Rogers. Other than Hoot Gibson, Jones was the only Western star to really stress comedy featuring himself rather than the comic sidekick that seemed to be mandatory in so many B Westerns.

In 1925 Jones made three films with seventeen-year-old Carol Lombard (at that time she had not added the *e* to Carol). Lombard, the former Jane Peters from Fort Wayne, had bit parts in *Gold and the Girl* (1925) and *Durand of the Badlands* (1925) (the latter written by Logansport native Maibelle Heikes Justice), but was given her first leading lady role in *Hearts and Spurs* (1925). In this film Jones plays an honest cowboy who saves Lombard's life and then falls in love with her.

Jones and Lombard were part of an Indiana Colony in Hollywood

Buck Jones and Carole Lombard in *Hearts and Spurs* (1925).

in the 1920s and 1930s. The list included John Bowers, Howard Hawks, Monte Blue, Skeets Gallagher, Charles Butterworth, Raymond Walburn, Ken and Kermit Maynard, and Carmelita Geraghty. They frequently helped each other move ahead in the competitive world that was Hollywood.

By 1928 things were going so well that Jones decided to leave Fox and form his own production company. His first film was *The Big Hop*. In it he played a cowboy who was also an airplane pilot. It was released as a silent film, but sound was catching on so fast that he had to hurriedly add sound to it, although it had no spoken dialog. The film was not received well. On top of that, Jones lost a lot of money in the stock market crash of 1929. His venture into independent film making was a disaster.

Following the failure of his first independent film, Jones decided to try to form his own Wild West show. It was a huge show, transported by a fifteen-car train. Jones performed on Silver, Osborne performed on her horse, Bumper, and eleven-year-old Maxine rode her pony in the show. For a variety of reasons, including financial mismanagement by the man Jones hired to run the show, the tour lasted only two months. He lost more than $300,000. Jones said, "It was pretty tough. Especially hard on Mrs. Jones and our daughter, Maxine. They knew I didn't have a dollar . . . or a contract. It was right in the middle of the depression. I went to my creditors and asked them to give me a chance. They promised not to force me into bankruptcy . . . and I promised to pay back every nickel. Later, slowly but surely, I made good that promise." Jones would never again form his own road show.

Jones went back to the studios and a changed medium. Sound had changed the film industry and had affected many careers. William S.

Buck Jones and Loretta Sayers in *The Fighting Sheriff* (1931).

Hart retired in 1925 before sound was even a factor. Fred Thompson died in 1928, and Mix retired but tried to make a comeback in 1929. New cowboy stars were coming on strong. Tim McCoy, Bob Steele, Tom Tyler, and the next big Western star, Hoosier Ken Maynard, all easily made the transition to sound. Jones's first talkie was *The Lone Rider* for Columbia in 1930. He moved to Universal in 1934 to take over for Maynard, who had quit Universal when he regularly went over budget on his films. Jones's first Universal film, *Rocky Rhodes*, was actually written and tailored for Maynard.

Jones easily established himself as a star of the talkies because he already had a huge following, his voice was pleasant and natural, and he was greatly respected in the industry. Many times he made a film without the benefit of a signed contract; everyone knew his word could be trusted. He was a professional on the set and a gentleman off the set, a devoted family man who adored his wife and daughter.

He remained a big cowboy star through the 1930s, until Gene Autry came along.

In the 1930s radio was well established, and programs with cowboy stars became an important part of radio's golden age. Gene Autry, Roy Rogers, Johnny Mack Brown, and Tom Mix all had radio programs. (Mix, however, did not actually do his own radio programs. His part was taken by various actors.) In 1937 Jones started a short-lived radio series called *Hoofbeats*. There were only thirty-nine episodes, each fifteen minutes in length, sponsored by Grape Nuts Flakes. The series aired from June 25, 1937, to March 18, 1938, and was transcribed and syndicated. A character named the Old Wrangler narrated stories about Jones and his horse Silver. At the end of the show, Jones pitched The Buck Jones Club, which included a free membership badge (for a Grape Nuts box top) along with information on prizes such as a hat and chaps.

Jones was now at the point in his career where he could write his own stories for his films. Universal paid him an additional ten thousand dollars for each original story. Some were his ideas, and some were based on pulp novels. In 1936 he wrote the story for two films, *Ride 'Em Cowboy* and *The Cowboy and the Kid*. From 1934 to 1937 he also served as producer for at least twenty-two of his films. He and his wife had improved their standard of living considerably. They now owned a large Spanish hacienda ranch home in the San Fernando Valley, with a swimming pool, stables for six horses, and peach orchards. They bought an eighty-six-foot yacht in 1937 and named it *The Sartartia*.

Buck Jones on his yacht *The Sartartia*.
PHOTOPLAY. PHOTO BY ROY D. MACLEAN

Jones left Universal in 1937 for several reasons but mostly because he was upset that William Boyd (Hopalong Cassidy), who cared nothing about being a cowboy and still had trouble riding, was making more money per film than he was. Exhibitor polls at that time showed Jones was the most popular screen cowboy. His fan club, Buck Jones Rangers, had a membership of more than four million. *Sudden Bill Dorn* (1937) was his last starring film at Universal.

Jones was not too happy with the advent of the singing cowboy. A United Press article in 1940 stated that Jones was taking up the career of a villain. "A mandolin did it," Jones said. "All these years I've been an actor. I've ridden my horse myself, without doubles, and I've fought my own fights—at least twice in every picture—and now look what's happened to horse operas. They've turned into musical comedies—with chaps. And I can't croon. I can't strum a mandolin and I don't intend to learn. From now on I'm a heavy." Perhaps this comment was instigated by the fact that he had played a crooked sheriff in *Wagons Westward* in 1939. Legions of Buck Jones fans protested. They refused to accept this change in his image, and Jones's career as a villain came to an abrupt end.

In 1941 Jones joined Tim McCoy and Raymond Hatton and did eight pictures for Monogram in which the three were called the Rough Riders. It was hoped this teaming would become as popular as the Three Mesquiteers for Republic. Several combinations of actors portrayed the Three Mesquiteers; the most popular of these featured Bob Livingston, Ray "Crash" Corrigan, and Hoosier Max Terhune. *The Rough Riders* was a successful and popular series, but McCoy did not enjoy being a second banana to Jones, and he rejoined the service.

After World War II began, Jones went on several war-bond tours. In

Buck Jones in *Hoofbeats* radio series, sponsored by Grape Nuts (1937).

November 1942 Jones went to Boston for an appearance at the Buddies Club (a sort of USO) to meet with servicemen for a couple of hours. While in Boston he attended the Holy Cross-Boston College football game. After the game he called Osborne and told her he had caught a bad cold and begged off the Buddies Club engagement. However, he felt obligated to attend a testimonial dinner for him that same evening at the Cocoanut Grove. Shortly past 10 p.m., a sixteen-year-old busboy at the club tried to replace a light bulb that had been removed by merrymaking patrons. He lit a match and perched himself precariously on a chair. The match ignited an artificial palm tree, and the highly flammable decor in the club quickly became an inferno. Four hundred eighty-seven people, including Jones, died in the twelve-minute tragedy.

There was some confusion over Jones's last actions, and some question as to whether he was ever able to get out of the club. Osborne gives this account: "Buck was dancing with one of the wives of a theatre owner when the fire started. They were near a door and got pushed out. Two soldiers testified at the trial they saw Buck outside and then watched as he climbed over people to get back in." It was thought he was under the impression his agent, Scott Dunlap, was still inside. However, Dunlap managed to escape and was lying under a fire truck waiting to be taken to a hospital. Some feel that Jones never got out of the club because he was found close to the table he occupied, badly burned.

After Jones was examined by hospital officials, all hope for his recovery was abandoned. He died two days later on November 30, 1942. He was fifty-one years old. His ashes were spread in the ocean near Catalina Island off the Southern California coast.

Jones's sister, Ada Mendell, who was living in Indianapolis at the

Buck Jones with wife Dell and daughter Maxine.

Buck Jones (right) and John Wayne
(middle) in *Range Feud* (1931).

time of his death, went to Los Angeles for his services. He was also
survived by his wife, mother, daughter Maxine Beery (she was the wife
of actor Noah Beery Jr.), and a granddaughter.

Jones is fondly remembered as one of the most well-liked cowboy stars. He was a kind and sincere person off camera. His cooperation and attitude toward his fellow actors and production people was
unparalleled, and most of the cast and crew freely cried when they
viewed the final cut of his last film, shortly after his death.

What would have happened to Jones's career if his life had not
ended so soon? John Wayne, who appeared in several Jones films
in the 1930s, appearing as a guest on the *Dick Cavett* television show,
reiterated that Jones was his favorite and said that if he had lived, he
would have made an excellent character actor after his starring days
ended.

BIBLIOGRAPHY

Barbour, Alan G. *The Thrill of It All.* New York: Macmillan, 1971.

Brownlow, Kevin. *The Parade's Gone By.* Berkeley: University of California Press, 1968.

———. *The War, the West, and the Wilderness.* New York: Alfred A. Knopf,
1979.

Buxton, Frank, and Bill Owen. *The Big Broadcast, 1920–1950.* New
York: Viking Press, 1972.

Corneau, Ernest N. *The Hall of Fame of Western Film Stars.* North
Quincy, Mass.: Christopher Publishing House, 1969.

Davidson, Donald. Interview with the author. February 20, 2000.

Indianapolis, Indiana.

DeMarco, Mario. *Photostory of Buck Jones.* Worcester, Mass.: M. De Marco, [197?].

Dunning, John. *On the Air: The Encyclopedia of Old-Time Radio.* New York: Oxford University Press, 1998.

Everson, William K. *A Pictorial History of the Western.* Secaucus, N.J.: Citadel Press, 1969.

Fenin, George N., and William K. Everson. *The Western: From Silents to Cinerama.* New York: Bonanza Books, 1962.

Holland, Ted. *B Western Actors Encyclopedia: Facts, Photos, and Filmographies of More Than 250 Familiar Faces.* Jefferson, N.C.: McFarland and Company, 1997.

Indianapolis News, March 29, 1932, April 24, 1940, December 1, 1942.

Indianapolis Star, December 1, 2, 1942, November 8, 1982.

Indianapolis Times, December 1, 1942.

The Internet Movie Database. http://www.imdb.com/.

Jones, Dell. Letter to the author. November 27, 1983.

Jordan, Joan. "A Rodeo Romeo." *Photoplay* (October 1921).

Los Angeles Examiner, October 17, 1940.

Markey, Dow. "Keeping Up with the Joneses." *Motion Picture* (January 1938).

New York Times, November 31, 1942.

The Old Corral. http://www.surfnetinc.com/chuck/trio.htm.

Parish, James Robert, and Michael R. Pitts. *The Great Western Pictures II.* Metuchen, N.J.: Scarecrow Press, 1988.

Rainey, Buck. *The Life and Films of Buck Jones.* Vol. 1, *The Silent Era.* Waynesville, N.C.: The World of Yesterday, 1988.

———. *The Saga of Buck Jones.* [Nashville, Tenn.]: Western Film Collector Press, 1975.

———, and Les Adams. *Shoot-em-ups: The Complete Reference Guide to Westerns of the Sound Era.* New Rochelle, N.Y.: Arlington House, 1978.

Reinhart, Ted. "The Day I Lost Buck Jones." *Western Trials* (September–October 1975).

Tinseltown: Wild Westerns. Tony Thomas Productions. The Discovery Channel. 1987.

Tuska, Jon. *The Filming of the West.* Garden City, N.Y.: Doubleday, 1976.

KEN MAYNARD

The Best Athlete of Them All

Ken Maynard circa 1930s.

On screen, Ken Maynard was as dashing and daring as Buck Jones. He was a little more flamboyant than Jones and in many respects resembled Tom Mix in style. His principal strengths were his athleticism and his wonder horse, Tarzan, which he had trained to do a series of spectacular stunts. In fact, many reviews praised Tarzan more than Maynard.

Off screen, Maynard was the antithesis of Jones. Maynard was not much of an actor. He had a short temper and antagonized most of those he worked with as well as friends and relatives. His alcoholism contributed to the dissolution of two of his marriages, and he often fell into drunken rages and viciously beat some of Tarzan's stunt doubles.

In spite of all this, Maynard rose to Western stardom faster than either Mix or Jones. Although he was a complex and difficult person to understand, it was obvious he had talent, determination, and a desire to succeed and become a star. He accomplished his goal and holds a firm place in the development of the Western genre.

Kenneth Olin Maynard, the son of William H. and Emma May Maynard, was born on July 21, 1895, in Vevay, Indiana. He was the oldest of five children. He had three sisters, Trixie, Willa, and Bessie, and one brother, Kermit, who also became a Western star.

Wayne Guthrie, a columnist for the *Indianapolis News*, lived about a block from the Maynards in Columbus, Indiana. Guthrie and Maynard were good friends, and in a 1964 article Guthrie recalled sitting on a vacant lot next to the Maynard home as Ken tried to learn to be a cowboy. "I watched with envy and awe as he learned the hard way—by experience—and trained himself to become one of the greatest trick and fancy riders and ropers and crack rifle shots of that halcyon era of the old-time cowboy." Guthrie had it right when he said, "By sheer determination and effort he rose to place his name alongside other great cowboy movie stars."

Many years later Maynard gave out his birthplace as Mission, Texas, and many sources on Maynard still list him and his brother as being born in Mission. According to Kermit, "Ken gave his birthplace as Mission, Texas, or Sherman, Texas, as motion picture cowboys were supposed to come from the West." Kermit also added they could never admit to being married because "that was supposed to remove all the romance."

Maynard was an adventurous youth and was an early daredevil. On one occasion when a circus came to Columbus, its owners offered twenty-five dollars to anyone who could ride a steer around the ring

KEN MAYNARD in

A First National Picture The CANYON of ADVENTURE

Ken Maynard and Carmelita Geraghty (Rushville) with two men looking on in *The Canyon of Adventure* (1928).

three times without falling. Maynard stayed on the steer two times around. This experience and others like it probably got him to thinking he could make it as a circus or Wild West performer. At the age of twelve he ran away with Doc Clayton's medicine show. His father tracked him down in Kentucky and brought him back to Columbus.

In the summer of 1911, when Maynard reached the age of sixteen, his parents gave their consent and permitted him to join a traveling carnival. During the next five years he worked with Buffalo Bill's Wild West Show, Kit Carson's Buffalo Ranch Wild West Show, and the Hagenbeck-Wallace Circus. He also perfected his roping technique under the tutelage of Oro Peso, a Mexican rope artist. When World War I broke out, he put aside his professional life and joined the army in 1917, serving as an engineer at Fort Knox, Kentucky, where it was purported that he married a young Kentucky "mountain girl." However, when he left the army and Kentucky at the end of the war, he left without a wife.

In 1920 Maynard became a member of Pawnee Bill's (Major Gordon Lillie, born in Bloomington, Indiana) troupe. Pawnee Bill was a buffalo trapper who worked with the Buffalo Bill Wild West Show before he started his own troupe. One of the highlights of this association was that Maynard was assigned to ride in the Rose Bowl Parade dressed as Buffalo Bill. After a short stay with Pawnee Bill, Maynard rejoined the Hagenbeck-Wallace Circus.

In 1921 Maynard was hired by Ringling Brothers' Barnum and Bailey Circus as the star attraction in their Wild West show. While with Ringling in Newhall, California, Maynard bought a three-year-old golden palomino for fifty dollars. He named him Tarzan after the Edgar Rice Burroughs jungle hero. Tarzan became the most exceptional horse in the movies and was almost as big a box-office draw as Maynard. Maynard stayed with the circus until it arrived in Los Angeles in 1922, when he decided to give movies a try.

While working in these early Westerns (at a substantially lower salary than he made at the circus), Maynard met Jeanne Knudsen. They were married on February 14, 1923. The marriage lasted less than a year. In 1925 he received his first recognition as a film actor when *Variety* gave him a positive review for his portrayal of Paul Revere in *Janice Meredith*. He was selected for the role because of his riding ability. It would be one of the few non-Westerns in which he appeared.

After Maynard appeared in a series of low-budget Westerns, produced by the independent Davis film production company, it quickly became apparent that he had the potential to be a major star. The next step was a contract with First National, a major studio. Under that contract, he rapidly became a top cowboy star, rivaling Tom Mix and Buck Jones.

In 1926, shortly before Maynard signed his contract with First National, he married Mary Leeper from South Bend, Indiana, on the set of *North Star*, a film he was shooting at the time. The marriage was a stormy one because of Maynard's alcoholism. He often carried live ammunition in his gun and would go on a spree of destruction, riding his horse and shooting out streetlights, while on location for a film.

There is no question Maynard was one of the most daring and accomplished Western stunt artists of the 1920s. Much of this was due to his remarkable horse, Tarzan, who could do a wide variety of stunts from rolling over and playing dead to dancing. Their work together revealed a special relationship. Maynard also assembled an entire string of palomino horses to support Tarzan. One would buck or rear, one would run up to a certain mark and stop cold, and one was good at pulling and tugging at objects like jail bars. Faithful fans would always look for the identifying black birthmark on Tarzan's rear flank and thereby could tell if it was the original or the double. Maynard loved Tarzan deeply, perhaps more than he was ever able to love a human being.

Maynard's riding expertise was well known among his peers. In the 1940s writer/cartoonist Mario DeMarco was in Hollywood talking to three character actors who had worked with most of the big cowboy stars. Hank Bell, Charles "Slim" Whitaker, and Fred Burns once were asked who they thought was the best rider among the Western stars. Bell said, "I've seen a lot of real good riders in my years in this business, but I'll have to give the nod to Ken Maynard. That fella could do anything on top, sideways and under a hoss and at full gallop!" Burns said, "Mix and Jones were real good as riders, but Ken was a real dare-

A young Ken Maynard.

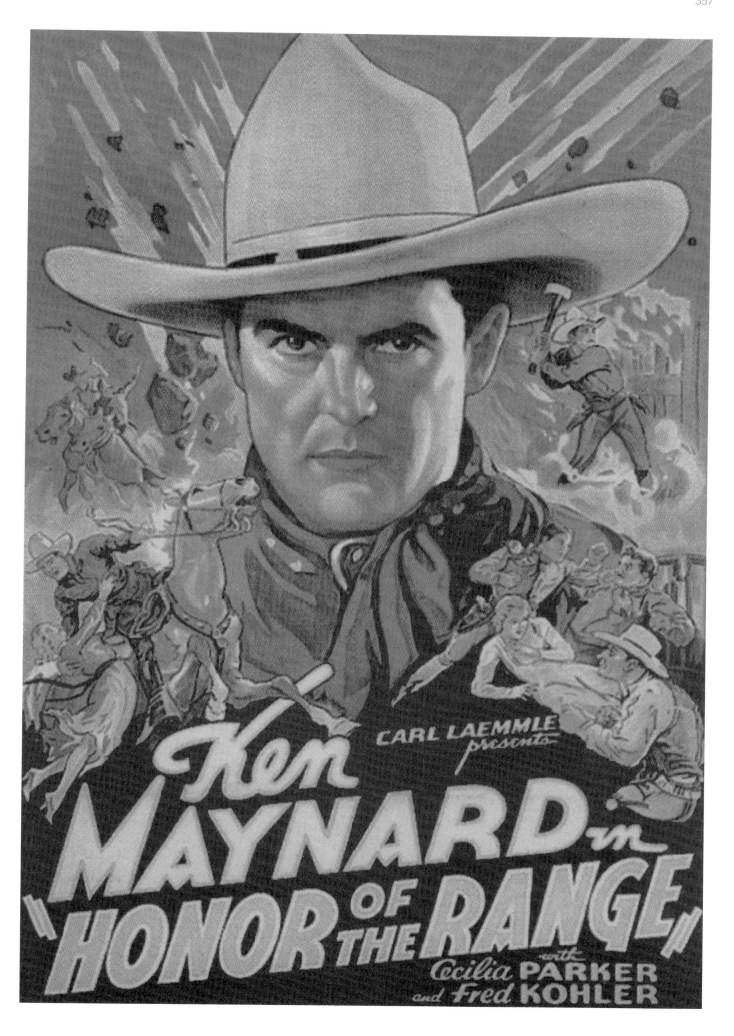

devil, a damn good roper and a real good athlete to boot!" Whittaker said, "About the only one as good as Ken was his brother Kermit."

In a 1928 interview in the magazine *Motion Picture Classic*, Maynard spoke of his expertise on a horse: "I am the greatest rider in the world. I can do tricks no one else can do. Nobody can come anywhere's near 'em. I can climb from the saddle and ride under my hoss's belly. I can climb under his belly, go back through his hind legs and do a crupper somersault back in the saddle. I can stand on my head on the saddle while my hoss is runnin'. I can stand on his neck on one shoulder. I can pick a handkerchief off the ground while I'm upside down. Or even pick up a dime."

The films Maynard made at First National were by no means the typical B Western. They were seven-reel spectaculars. One film in particular, *Señor Daredevil* (1926), inspired this review from *Harrison's Reports*: "If the subsequent Westerns which First National has announced with this star will contain only one-half the entertainment that 'Senor Daredevil' possesses, those who buy them will have nothing to worry about . . . it is an exceptionally good Western. . . . Mr. Maynard is a wonderful rider who displays his horsemanship frequently."

Señor Daredevil's spectacular climax had Maynard racing a food convoy of wagons to a town starved and besieged by villains. One or two critics compared this sequence with the chariot race in *Ben-Hur* for the excitement it generated. Unfortunately, this film has disappeared and is not available for reappraisal. Other First National films that still exist, particularly *The Red Raiders* (1927), confirm that the praise for *Señor Daredevil* was probably more than justified. A sequence in *Red Raiders* shows a wounded man being dragged in the dust by his galloping horse. Maynard, riding at full gallop and hanging precariously backwards out of his own saddle, swoops the man up to safety.

In 1929 Warner Brothers bought First National and phased out all Western films. Maynard then did several films for Tiffany and KBS World Wide before signing an eight-picture contract with Universal. By this time Maynard was a big star, and his contract gave him control over his films. His years with Universal were his most creative and financially successful.

Despite Maynard's problems with alcohol, he continued to work hard at Universal as a producer, director, scriptwriter, and actor. He had his own ideas about how his movies should be made, and he regularly went over his budget, causing a lot of problems with the Universal executives. Finally, after one particularly strong argument, he quit Universal and joined Mascot Pictures.

Nat Levine, the head of Mascot, felt audiences were getting bored with "shoot-em-ups." Levine saw a twenty-seven-year-old cowboy singer on the *National Barn Dance* on WLS radio. He called him to Hollywood in 1934 and asked Maynard to introduce him to the public in *In Old Santa Fe.* The credits read, "Introducing Gene Autry."

Although Autry was known as "the singing cowboy," Maynard had already produced several films in which he not only sang the theme songs but also wrote the music as well. He was a self-taught musician and played at least four instruments. He wrote Western music and even recorded several Western songs for Columbia Records. A good case could be made for the fact that Maynard was the original singing cowboy. Maynard introduced *In Old Santa Fe* with one of his own compositions. The lyrics dealt with "married strife" and how he liked his

Ken Maynard and his horse Tarzan.

dog better than women and the fact that "my own boss is my Tarzan hoss." Levine did not think much of Maynard's voice, and Bob Nolan of The Sons of the Pioneers dubbed Maynard's voice for this opening song. These musical innovations and the introduction of Autry started a trend that became a standard for future B Westerns.

Autry idolized Maynard and modeled himself on the way Maynard appeared on screen. Maynard followed *In Old Santa Fe* with *Mystery Mountain*, also released in 1934. Autry visited the set and watched all of Maynard's scenes during the filming. When Autry started gaining notoriety as a cowboy star and began turning out his own films, he maintained his relationship with Maynard. When he was not working in one of his own pictures, he would visit the Maynard set and sit quietly on the sidelines watching Maynard work.

However, Maynard was not happy at Mascot. It was evident that the studio was a step or two lower than Universal. Levine was considering Maynard for *The Phantom Empire*, but he was fed up with Maynard's drinking, tantrums, and inability to bring his films in on budget and decided not to take any more chances with him. Maynard next signed a contract to make eight films for Columbia. Like Buck Jones, Maynard was partial to people from his native state. He was particularly fond of Geneva Mitchell from Medaryville, Indiana. She was his leading lady in three films at Columbia, *Lawless Riders* and *Western Courage* in 1935 and *Cattle Thief* in 1936. He had already used Carmelita Geraghty from Rushville as his leading lady in *Fighting Thru* in 1930.

Ken Maynard and his wife Mary Leeper (South Bend) sail for England on the liner *Berengaria* from New York City on March 22, 1934.
ASSOCIATED PRESS PHOTO

Maynard's marriage to Leeper began to crumble, and they were divorced in 1939. He put together a big Wild West show in 1936, but it did not make a profit, and he was forced to disband the company at a great loss. In 1937 he joined the Cole Brothers Circus, and in January of that year he returned to his home in Columbus, Indiana, to visit his parents. The *Indianapolis News* stated that "Maynard is working on the script of a new serial picture, 'Ghost Mountains' which is to be produced shortly. The serial will be produced in eight sections under his own direction, with his own company."

According to the *Columbus Republic* Maynard "regularly made trips back to Columbus to visit his parents and cousin. At times the visits were like a one-man circus—Maynard walking down the main streets of Columbus, children of the city close on the cowboy star's heels. He knew people here by their first names and would walk from store to store and say hello." After Maynard's father died in 1945, his mother moved to California and lived there until her death in the late 1960s.

In 1937, 1938, and 1939 Maynard appeared with the Cole Brothers Circus with Tarzan. He married Bertha Rowland Denham, a high-wire artist, in 1940. He was still making pictures, this time with Grand National. However, he injured his foot, and his increased weight made it doubly difficult for him to perform as a "dashing daredevil."

When Tarzan died in 1940, Maynard could no longer do the stunts that made him famous. He made several films for different studios until 1944, when he made *Harmony Trail* with Eddie Dean and fellow Hoosier Max Terhune. It was his last cowboy picture. He then was relegated to making personal appearances in circuses and rodeos.

In the 1950s Maynard was offered his own radio show on the regional Liberty radio network. It was called *Tales of the Diamond K*. It was a fifteen-minute show, simply produced. There were no other actors, music, or sound effects, except for a recorded whinny from his horse, Tarzan, at the opening and close. Maynard told stories about the Old West and about his own experiences exploring the Yucatan jungles.

In 1968 Denham, Maynard's wife of twenty-eight years, died. He continued his heavy drinking. He became involved with Marilyn Ann Murray, who used the stage name Marilyn Marlowe. She used him to promote her own career, claiming they were married. She advertised and sold most of his movie memorabilia. Her son, Ken Murray, called Maynard "Grandpa," and Maynard referred to him as "Grandson" in several letters.

In 1970 Maynard was given a chance to appear in a small role in *Bigfoot*. He relished the opportunity and even managed to get Murray in the film. Time went by, and no other films were offered to him. In the early 1970s Maynard was booked to appear on *The Merv Griffin Show*. He came on the show drunk and walked off before it was over. He lived alone in a trailer and drank heavily until his health deteriorated. In 1973 he was placed in the Motion Picture Country Home, where he died on March 23 of stomach cancer.

Maynard was survived by his three sisters; Kermit died in 1971. The *Columbus Republic* quotes Trixie Strange, who lived in Memphis, Indiana, at the time, as saying the burial would be in Forest Lawn Memorial Gardens in California, but she was too ill to attend. The other two sisters, Bessie Maynard and Willa Stetler, were living in Louisville at the time of Maynard's death. His funeral was not a big affair, but several television stations covered it, including one owned by Gene Autry. A telegram sent by President Richard M. Nixon praised Maynard as among the first to bring the American West to the motion picture screen.

Ken Maynard.

BIBLIOGRAPHY

Columbus Evening Republican, October 23, 1940, March 24, 1973.

DeMarco, Mario. *Ken Maynard: The Fiddling Buckaroo.* [California ?: s.n., 1979?].

Fenin, George N., and William K. Everson. *The Western: From Silents to Cinerama.* New York: Bonanza Books, 1962.

Harmon, Jim. *Radio and TV Premiums: A Guide to the History and Value of Radio and TV Premiums.* Iola, Wis.: Krause Publications, 1997.

Holland, Ted. *B Western Actors Encyclopedia: Facts, Photos, and Filmographies for More Than 250 Familiar Faces.* Jefferson, N.C.: McFarland and Company, 1997.

Indianapolis News, January 30, 1937, September 23, 1943, September 29, 1949, August 4, 1964.

Indianapolis Star, September 23, 1946, February 6, 1983.

The Internet Movie Database. http://www.imdb.com/.

Katchmer, George A. *Eighty Silent Screen Stars: Biographies and Filmographies of the Obscure to the Well Known.* Jefferson, N.C.: McFarland and Company, 1991.

McClure, Arthur F., and Ken D. Jones. *Heroes, Heavies, and Sagebrush: A Pictorial History of the "B" Western Players.* South Brunswick, N.J.: A. S. Barnes, 1972.

McDonald, Archie P., ed. *Shooting Stars: Heroes and Heroines of Western Film.* Bloomington: Indiana University Press, 1987.

The Old Corral. http://www.surfnetinc.com/chuck/trio.htm.

Rainey, Buck, and Les Adams, *Shoot-em-ups: The Complete Reference Guide to Westerns of the Sound Era.* New Rochelle, N.Y.: Arlington House, 1978.

Tuska, Jon. *The Filming of the West.* Garden City, N.Y.: Doubleday, 1976.

———. *The Vanishing Legion: A History of Mascot Pictures, 1927–1935.* Jefferson, N.C.: McFarland and Company, 1982.

Woodridge, Dorothy. "A Big Lot of Whoopee." *Motion Picture Classic* (May 1928).

KERMIT MAYNARD

Kermit Maynard.

K ermit Maynard was as good or better an athlete and stuntman than his brother. He certainly was a better actor, and he did not smoke or drink. Of the many who worked with both actors, Buster Crabbe summed up the difference between the brothers when he said, "The difference between Ken and Kermit was like comparing night to day. Kermit, always the gentleman, excellent horseman and a real pleasure to work with. Never an unkind word for anyone and above all, my friend." Although Kermit never achieved the stardom of his older brother, he was still able to earn a reputation as a performer who made a string of highly popular and highly entertaining Western films.

Kermit Roosevelt Maynard was born in Vevay, Indiana, on September 20, 1897. At Columbus High School Maynard became involved in baseball, basketball, and football. However, as a result of a fatality during a football game, all athletics at the school were suspended. Kermit then joined the Columbus Commercials, an amateur basketball team that played on the second floor of City Hall. When Kermit went to Indiana University, he played on the varsity teams in the same three sports. As a fullback, Kermit took snaps from center Jim Pierce, who later went on to a movie career of his own, including one film in which he portrayed Tarzan. Wayne Guthrie, Kermit's roommate at IU and reporter for the *Indianapolis News*, recalled that Kermit was a "splendid athlete" at IU, winning letters three years straight in three sports. Unfortunately, he left the university before receiving his degree.

Kermit went to work for the Hormel Meat Packing Company in Minneapolis shortly after marrying his wife, Edith. In 1927, after receiving several letters from Ken asking the couple to come to Hollywood, Kermit and Edith decided to take the plunge. His first appearance in a film was a football story, *Wild Bull of the Campus*. He acted in the film and served as a stunt double. He did the stunt work so well that he began doing stunts for others, including doubling for his brother. Edith was hired at Fox, where she eventually became head of the Fox script department.

The brothers did not get along well. Kermit objected to Ken's drinking and behavior, and they frequently argued. Ruth Hall, a contract player for Universal, was in at least three of Ken's pictures at a time when Kermit was doubling for his brother. She said, "Kermit was a pillar of strength and encouragement to me. I will never cease to

Kermit Maynard aiming gun at villain John Elliott while Fuzzy Knight and Billie Seward look on in *Trails of the Wild* (1935).

be grateful to him for his understanding and kindness. He seemed to have more control over Ken than anyone else. If he had to be spoken to, it was Kermit who approached him."

After two years of stunt work, Kermit began to appear in a few features billed as "Tex" Maynard. By 1930 he had graduated to leading roles in a series for the Rayart Film Company. During these early years, he spent many hours at the Fat Jones Stables in Hollywood, learning and practicing trick riding skills. He mastered most of the riding skills, and in 1933 he decided to follow his brother's example and enter a rodeo competition. He won the title of World's Champion Trick and Fancy Rider at a national rodeo in Salinas, California. This enhanced his value at the box office.

Maurice Conn, an independent producer of quickie-action films, came up with the idea of doing a series based on the Royal Canadian Mounted Police as depicted in the writings of James Oliver Curwood. Conn approached Kermit about starring in the series. A three-year association began with Kermit starring in eighteen films, ten of which were Mountie stories. These were cheaply assembled films but nevertheless very entertaining and displayed Kermit's breezy, naturalistic acting style and talents as a stuntman and expert rider.

Kermit was more than capable of handling any and all action that came his way. He frequently included scenes in his films where he was involved in a thrilling rooftop chase, hopping from building to building. Like most other Western stars, Kermit was careful to feature his horse, Rocky, in all his films. Kermit was an accomplished musician. In *Galloping Dynamite* (1937), he was given a chance to sing, accompanying himself on the banjo and harmonica.

Westerns were becoming big business, and when studios such as Republic and Paramount got serious about Westerns, Conn was forced to shut down his company. Kermit moved into supporting roles in serials and Western features. He frequently did character parts and even played villains opposite Gene Autry, Bob Livingston, Johnny Mack Brown, and others. During the early to mid-1940s, Kermit was very busy. He appeared in more than 150 films in his career, making his last film, *Taras Bulba*, in 1962.

The Maynards settled in the San Fernando Valley. In 1943 their son, William, was born. Kermit became a representative for the Screen Extras Guild, which later merged with SAG (the Screen Actors Guild). In this capacity, he was able to initiate several improvements for stuntmen who filmed dangerous action sequences. He retired from that job in 1969. That same year he returned to IU, where he received a fifty-year award from the school's athletic department between halves at the annual homecoming football game.

Kermit died of a heart attack in his home in North Hollywood on January 16, 1971. After his death, his widow received many letters from fans throughout the world, all expressing deep sorrow at his passing.

Kermit Maynard (left) and Buster Crabbe, circa 1942-43.

BIBLIOGRAPHY

Barbour, Alan G. *The Thrill of It All.* New York: Macmillan, 1971.

Corneau, Ernest N. *The Hall of Fame of Western Film Stars.* North Quincy, Mass.: Christopher Publishing House, 1969.

DeMarco, Mario. *Ken Maynard: The Fiddling Buckaroo.* [California?: s.n., 1979?].

Everson, William K. *A Pictorial History of the Western.* Secaucus, N.J.: Citadel Press, 1969.

Indianapolis News, May 6, August 4, 1964, October 26, 1966, April 20, 1971.

McClure, Arthur F., and Ken D. Jones. *Heroes, Heavies, and Sagebrush: A Pictorial History of the "B" Western Players.* South Brunswick, N.J.: A. S. Barnes, 1972.

Parish, James Robert, and Michael R. Pitts. *The Great Western Pictures II.* Metuchen, N.J.: Scarecrow Press, 1988.

Tuska, Jon. *The Vanishing Legion: A History of Mascot Pictures, 1927–1935.* Jefferson, N.C.: McFarland and Company, 1982.

ALLAN "ROCKY" LANE
The Last of the Great B Western Stars

Allan "Rocky" Lane.

After Buck Jones and Ken Maynard, Allan "Rocky" Lane was the best-known Hoosier cowboy. Lane, whose real name was Harry Leonard Albershart, was born in Mishawaka, Indiana, on September 22, 1909. He grew up idolizing Tom Mix and fellow Hoosier Ken Maynard. Harry worked on the family farm, and an *Indianapolis Star* story on Lane in 1948 said, "Working on the farm as a youngster gave him both a profound respect for harvesting and enough spending money to go to town on Saturday and marvel over the escapades of Tom Mix and Tony and William S. Hart and his great horse."

The Albersharts moved to Grand Rapids, Michigan, and Harry finished high school there. He made claims that he attended the University of Notre Dame and excelled in several sports there. However, the school's records show no Harry Albershart was ever enrolled at the school.

Lane became interested in commercial photography shortly after high school and started his own company. Lucky Strike Cigarettes and the Ford Motor Company were among his clients. He also became interested in acting and began appearing in amateur theatrical productions. He landed the lead in *Hit the Deck* and toured with that show. For several years he divided his time between acting and his photography business.

Allan Lane was his stage name. Although he was not the athlete he claimed to be, he nevertheless was an imposing figure. He was 6'2" tall and weighed 190 pounds. He had a marvelous speaking voice and was very handsome.

In 1929 Lane came to the attention of Winfield Sheehan, president of Fox Pictures, and was cast in *Not Quite Decent*. He was given another small part that same year in a film called *The Forward Pass*. He subsequently appeared in at least sixteen feature films and a number of short subjects over the next three years, none of which were Westerns.

In 1932 Lane was still getting bit parts and decided to quit the movies and go back to the stage. He also wanted to see if he could reestablish his photography business. He did not appear in any films between 1932 and 1936, when he was cast in a Shirley Temple movie, *Stowaway*. He landed an even bigger part in the 1937 production, *Charlie Chan at the Olympics*. In 1937 he also appeared in his first film for the newly formed Republic Pictures. He played a boxer in *The Duke Comes*

Back. He was so impressive that RKO signed him to a contract. Unfortunately, Lane was relegated to a series of minor roles in B films. However, in 1938 he got a break that would lead him to stardom in the Western genre. He appeared in a Harry Carey Western entitled *The Law West of Tombstone.* He must have looked good on a horse because Republic's serial producer, Hiram S. Brown, saw him and decided to test him for the lead as Sergeant King of the Royal Canadian Mounted Police. Lane won the role and not only did that serial, but also starred in three other serials for Republic.

Lane now had made a name for himself with the Saturday matinee crowd, and for the next thirteen years he was at the top of the industry as the star of a number of very popular serials. About 1944 Republic decided to promote Western star Don "Red" Barry to leading-man status, leaving a vacancy that Lane was more than ready to fill. He eagerly stepped into the roles meant for Barry and improved on them by adding more action. His pictures were popular. Lane said about their appeal, "I believe the folks like the pictures because they're in the old Mix and Hart tradition. Full of action, fights and chases." Arthur F. McClure and Ken D. Jones, authors of *Heroes, Heavies, and Sagebrush: A Pictorial History of the "B" Western Players,* called Lane "the hardest hitting of the two-fisted cowboys, and he made better use of the excellent Republic stunt team than did anyone else. Every Lane adventure had at least one well-staged jaw rattling brawl in a saloon, jail, café or stage depot; sometimes all of the above."

Allan Lane and Frances Mercer in *Crime Ring* (1938).

In 1948 Lane owned a small ranch in the San Fernando Valley, where he kept eighteen head of registered stock. His horse, Black Jack, was his pride and joy. When someone asked what the horse was worth, Lane replied, "You might as well ask me the value of my sister." Black Jack was insured for twenty thousand dollars. Lane said that was more insurance than he carried on himself. Lane spent his time between films training his horses, making public appearances, speaking to youth groups, and conferring with publishers about his Allan "Rocky" Lane comics and with manufacturers about products that he endorsed. His parents eventually moved to California, and Lane always found time to spend with them.

When "Wild Bill" Elliott dropped out of the *Red Ryder* film series, Lane again was ready and willing to fill that vacancy. He played the Red Ryder character during the 1946–47 season, making seven excellent action-packed films. After the *Red Ryder* films were discontinued, Lane launched into a phase of his career that would make him a cowboy legend. From 1947 to 1953 he made a series of B Westerns that included some of the finest of that genre.

Lane was a complex individual. He was difficult to know and to understand, and he made many enemies. Actress Kay Aldridge described him as "the most conceited human being I've ever met." His frequent costar, Peggy Stewart, said, "I don't mean to be unkind, but he was the dullest man I ever met. Truly I think the main problem with Allan is that he had absolutely no sense of humor . . . none at all." Actor Tris Coffin, who played the heavy in some of Lane's films, said, "He was a practically impossible kind of a guy. He was so egotistic, so impressed with himself, and he gave the impression that nobody else had any ability or any talent."

Lane worked with several sidekicks, including fellow Hoosier Chubby Johnson, who was with him in three films. Also working with

Lane in several films were Hoosiers Kenneth MacDonald, Kermit Maynard, Max Terhune, and Steve Clark. He also used Helene Stanley of Gary as his leading lady in *Bandit King of Texas* (1949).

Allan "Rocky" Lane and Claudia Barrett in *Night Riders of Montana* (1951).
©REPUBLIC PICTURES CORP.

Several events appeared on the scene in the mid-1950s that led to the demise of the B Western. First and foremost was the advent of television. Production costs were rising, and the public began to demand more sophisticated fare. Lane was one of the last of the B Western stars to give up on the genre. Other Western stars such as Gene Autry, Roy Rogers, and William Boyd made a successful transition to television. For whatever reason, Lane was not able to make this move. He appeared in several shows such as *Gunsmoke* and even made a pilot for a Red Ryder television series, but it was not to be. Lane thus found himself in unfamiliar territory. He was out of work. To support himself he became a Los Angeles car salesman. Then suddenly and unexpectedly he was cast as the voice of the television talking horse Mr. Ed. Lester Hilton, the well-known animal trainer, brought his horse to the stables. Lane had fallen on such hard times that he was staying at the stables, sleeping on Hilton's couch. Two of the producers of the television show, Al Simon and Arthur Lubin, had been searching for an appropriate voice for Mr. Ed. As Alan Young, the star of the series, tells it, "Ed's voice was found one afternoon when Al and Arthur were visiting Lester. Lester was painstakingly getting Ed to pose properly as Al and Arthur looked on. Suddenly a drawling Midwestern voice boomed out from the little ranch house. 'Hey, Lester, where d'yuh keep the cawfee?' Al's eyes popped. 'That's him!' he gasped. The voice belonged to Allan 'Rocky' Lane."

The movie series *Francis the Talking Mule* was the inspiration for Mr. Ed. Chill Wills provided the voice of the mule on the big screen, but Wills was busy making movies and could not do the voice for the television series. Lane needed work and was in no position to turn down this offer. However, he insisted that his name not be listed in the credits and no one was to let it be known that he was doing the voice. The producers agreed. When the series became a hit, Lane had second thoughts and asked that he be given screen credit. By that time the show's credits read that Mr. Ed played himself. Lane was offered more money in lieu of screen credit, and he took it. With his new money he bought a racehorse. He loved the track, and his favorite preoccupation was going to the early morning workouts. Everyone thought he was crazy for buying a horse, but miraculously the horse won her first race. From the beginning, his little mare did beautifully, and Lane made a very nice profit.

Lane had trouble getting along with his fellow workers and might have been fired had his voice not become an invaluable ingredient in the series. Young managed to get along with Lane. In fact, Lane defended Young when a producer suggested that this series would make Young a star. Lane told Young he should take the producer to task because Young was already a star. Lane also taught Young how to ride a horse. Young said during one shot he was hanging onto the horse's mane and the saddle horn and bouncing all over the place. Lane was watching. He walked over to Young and asked, "You haven't ridden long, have you?" Young said, "Not long." "How long?" "For about twenty seconds. Just now." Lane whispered gruffly, "If you keep your toes pointed down in the stirrup the way you're doing, you're gonna sail over the jump better than any stunt man. Only you're not gonna land so good. Keep your heels down, toes up, press down on the stirrup, pinch your knees, lean back, and relax." After Lane's instruction, they did the shot in one take.

The television series ran for five years and provided Lane with a comfortable retirement. After the *Mr. Ed* series ended, Lane did some work in rodeos and a circus before finally retiring in 1966. He left the screen knowing he had made his mark as one of the best B movie cowboys in a career that spanned seventeen years and more than 125 films. His private life was comparatively uneventful. He was married twice and divorced twice. His first wife was the former Gladys Leslie, and his second wife was actress Sheila Ryan. When he died from bone cancer on October 27, 1973, his obituary listed his mother as his sole survivor.

Allan "Rocky" Lane and Chubby Johnson (Terre Haute) in *Wells Fargo Gunmaster* (1951). Lane is holding Johnson's arm with gun in hand.

BIBLIOGRAPHY

The Internet Movie Database. http://www.imdb.com/.

Kinnard, Roy. *Fifty Years of Serial Thrills.* Metuchen, N.J.: Scarecrow Press, 1983.

McClure, Arthur F., and Ken D. Jones. *Heroes, Heavies, and Sagebrush: A Pictorial History of the "B" Western Players.* South Brunswick, N.J.: A. S. Barnes, 1972.

The Old Corral. http://www.surfnetinc.com/chuck/trio.htm.

Ragan, David. "Rocky's Road to Fame." *Indianapolis Star Magazine,* November 21, 1948.

Thornton, Chuck, and David Rothel. *Allan "Rocky" Lane: Republic's Action Ace.* Madison, N.C.: Empire Publishing, 1990.

Young, Alan, with Bill Burt. *Mister Ed and Me.* New York: St. Martin's, 1994.

MAX TERHUNE

Of all the sidekicks who rode across the silver screen, Max Terhune was certainly the most versatile. He was a master showman whose talents included feats of magic, card manipulation, juggling, impersonations, whistling, and ventriloquism. In addition to these skills, he was also an accomplished athlete.

Robert Max Terhune was born in a log cabin in Amity, Indiana, just south of Franklin on February 12, 1891. He was the son of Garrat and Mary Sawins Terhune. He spent most of his first thirty years in the Hoosier State. He was a toolmaker for Remy Tools in Anderson in the 1920s and in 1922 married Maude Cassidy of New Castle, Indiana. They had three children, Maxine, Robert Max Jr., and Donald Roltaire.

Max Terhune.

Terhune played baseball for the Morgantown Blues in 1911. While working at Remy, he joined its baseball team as a pitcher. He would later have a fling at professional baseball, joining a team in Minnesota as a pitcher, but a wrist injury ended his career.

Terhune learned to imitate barnyard sounds while growing up on a farm and became proficient in doing bird calls and whistling. When he was about twenty-three years old he accompanied his uncle, who was a fiddler, to Shelbyville, Indiana, where he entered a whistling contest. He won the championship. He began honing his skills in other areas, and in 1924 he made his first appearance in vaudeville as a one-man show. He was an instant success.

Terhune was an active performer in vaudeville during the 1920s and early 1930s. When the Great Depression hit, he lost his job at Remy and went into vaudeville full time, touring the Orpheum circuit with the Weaver Brothers and the Arkansas Travellers. He also started working on his ventriloquism skills. He said, "I learned ventriloquism by reading a book and practicing. I learned distance ventriloquism before I used a puppet." He bought a dummy and named him Skully Null. He later changed the dummy's name to Elmer when a film director did not like the name Skully.

Terhune began appearing with a group that eventually became the Hoosier Hot Shots. When Terhune joined them, they were known as Ezra Buzzington and His All Rube Band. Mark Schaefer was Ezra Buzzington. Terhune got a nice write-up in *Billboard* magazine and sent it to George McBiggers of WLS radio. McBiggers auditioned him, and Terhune was hired in 1933. Terhune made his national debut that year on the WLS *Barn Dance.* This gave him the opportunity to meet some of the well-known performers such as Curt Massey, Pat Buttram, Red Foley, George Gobel, Lullabelle and Scotty, and Gene Autry. Terhune and Autry became good friends. In 1934 Terhune and Autry were in Aurora, Illinois, when a telegram arrived asking Autry to come to Hollywood to appear in the Ken Maynard film *In Old Santa Fe.* Autry told Terhune, "You're the one I want to go with me," but Terhune did not go with him immediately. As Terhune tells it, "He wanted me to go out there in 1934. He asked again in 1935 but I put him off. In 1936 he was getting popular, and he asked again and I went."

Terhune made his film debut in 1936 with Autry in *Ride Ranger Ride.* According to Terhune, he became friends with another Hoosier who appeared in that film: Monte Blue. Terhune must have impressed the people at Republic Pictures because he was immediately signed to a three-year contract. Terhune moved his family to California and quickly made another picture with Autry, *The Big Show* (1936).

Terhune's film appearances with Autry were brief. Autry was soon joined with another sidekick, Lester Allen "Smiley" Burnette. Terhune told how Autry discovered Burnette: "Gene went to this little town in Illinois where Smiley was on the program. Smiley was doing everything. He was even the Master of Ceremonies. He was making $17.00 a week, and Gene offered him $35.00 a week to join him."

In 1936 Republic released a picture entitled *The Three Mesquiteers*, starring Ray "Crash" Corrigan, Bob Livingston, and comic Sid Saylor. Terhune replaced Saylor for the second film in the series, *Ghost-Town Gold* (1936). This move made Terhune a well-known star. His characterization of "Lullaby" Joslin was a hit. Fifty-one *Mesquiteers* films were made, and a variety of actors portrayed the Mesquiteers over those years, but the most memorable grouping was that of Corrigan, Livingston, and Terhune. When Livingston dropped out, a young John Wayne replaced him, and Terhune costarred with Wayne in eight Mesquiteer films. Terhune said of Wayne, "He was a wonderful actor and a great guy."

Max Terhune as a very young man in vaudeville.

Terhune provided the comic relief in the series. He put his ventriloquism skill to good use by using his dummy, now called Elmer Sneezeweed, in the films. He was the first ventriloquist to appear as a major character in the movies. Terhune had the privilege of working with a number of actors in addition to Wayne who went on to bigger and better things. Rita Cansino (later Rita Hayworth), Phyllis Isley (later Jennifer Jones), Carole Landis, and Louise Brooks all appeared in films with Terhune.

While making the Mesquiteer series, Terhune began to appear in some non-Westerns. In one of these, *Hit Parade of 1937*, he received such good notices that the studio gave him a raise. Taking note of his ability to do impersonations, Disney Studios called on him to do voices for its cartoons. In one cartoon, Terhune did all the voices with the exception of the lead character, Donald Duck. Terhune was listed in the *Motion Picture Herald* as one of the top ten moneymaking Western film stars in 1937, 1938, and 1939.

Terhune left Republic in 1940 after running into contract difficulties. Shortly after he left, Terhune was followed by his friend and costar, Corrigan. Terhune and Corrigan went to Monogram Studios and began a new series of Westerns called Range Busters. They were joined by John "Dusty" King, and the trio made twenty-four features before Monogram stopped production. For this series Terhune changed his on-screen name from "Lullaby" to "Alibi."

In 1944 and 1945 Terhune played sidekick to two fellow Hoosiers. In 1944 he appeared as Third Grade Simms with Allan "Rocky" Lane in *Sheriff of Sundown.* In 1944 Terhune joined Ken Maynard in *Harmony Trail*, appearing as a featured player. Terhune and Maynard both had once lived in Columbus, Indiana. After *Harmony Trail* was finished, Johnny Mack Brown needed a sidekick, and Terhune made a series of films with him over the next two years at Monogram. Terhune called him "a powerful man, a football player . . . a very handsome fella."

In 1949 Terhune went to PRC (Producers Releasing Corporation) films and made a few Westerns before retiring in 1950. In addi-

Max Terhune, John Wayne, and Ray "Crash" Corrigan in one of the *Three Mesquiteers* films.

tion to B Westerns, he made several appearances in some big-budget movies. He was in *Rawhide* (1951) and *The King and Four Queens* (1956), in which he was a double for Clark Gable's hands for a close-up in a card scene. His last film was *Giant* (1956), which was also fellow Hoosier James Dean's final film.

After retirement, Terhune made a number of personal appearances at Corrigan's Corriganville Movie Ranch in Simi Valley. Terhune also made several stage appearances with Bob Steele and Jack O'Shea. He had his own television show, *Alibi's Tent Show*, on KNXT in Los Angeles in the 1950s. He made appearances on several other shows, including *I Love Lucy* and *Ramar of the Jungle*. He even recorded some of his imitations and whistling for Decca, London, and Capitol recording studios.

In 1968 Terhune retired to Cottonwood, Arizona, where he lived surrounded by three generations of Terhunes. He was the only member of the family who resisted the move. He felt at home in California, and all his friends were there. But he realized California had changed considerably from that day in 1936 when he made the move at Gene Autry's request. He did not enjoy the pollution and the congested highways and later said he was glad he made the move to Arizona.

Terhune's son, Bob, became a stuntman and a sometime actor, doing stunts for John Wayne and Hoosier Forrest Tucker, among others. Terhune's other son, Donald Roltaire Terhune, died in 1958 as a result of an auto accident, and his wife Maude died in 1966. After her death, Terhune wrote to his grandson, Gary, who was in the army at the time, "I really loved her . . . and I know I'll never be the same."

Terhune remained active into his eighties, making personal appearances at benefits, magicians' conventions, and Western film conventions. His last visit to Anderson was in July 1972, where he performed for a General Motors retiree picnic at Killbuck Park.

In 1973 Terhune had a heart attack, and, after being admitted to the hospital, had a stroke. He was put in intensive care, and family members conducted a round-the-clock vigil at his bedside. He died on June 5, 1973, and was buried in Clarksdale, Arizona.

In 1984 Anderson College in Anderson, Indiana, where Terhune labored as a toolmaker, was raising funds for its new $5.5 million auditorium. One of the donors was Gene Autry, who gave a sizable sum in memory of his old stage and screen partner.

BIBLIOGRAPHY

Anderson Daily Bulletin, June 6, 1973.

Barbour, Alan G. *The Thrill of It All.* New York: Macmillan, 1971.

Corneau, Ernest N. *The Hall of Fame of Western Film Stars.* North Quincy, Mass.: Christopher Publishing House, 1969.

Indianapolis News, June 6, 1973.

Maltin, Leonard. *The Real Stars Number Two.* New York: Curtis Books, 1973.

McClure, Arthur F., and Ken D. Jones. *Heroes, Heavies, and Sage-brush: A Pictorial History of "B" Western Players.* South Brunswick, N.J.: A. S. Barnes, 1972.

Taylor, Robert M. Jr., Errol Stevens, Mary Ann Ponder, and Paul Brockman, eds. *Indiana: A New Historical Guide.* Indianapolis: Indiana Historical Society Press, 1989.

Tuska, Jon. *The Filming of the West.* Garden City, N.Y.: Doubleday, 1976.

Max Terhune with dummy Elmer and Lynn Roberts in *Heart of the Rockies* (1937).

CHUBBY JOHNSON

Charles Randolph Johnson appeared in more than one hundred feature films and three hundred television shows from 1950 to 1969—not bad for a person who did not embark on a movie career until he was almost fifty years old. Johnson's first career was that of a journalist, a profession to which he would return after his acting career ended.

Johnson was born in Terre Haute, Indiana, in 1902 (some sources say 1903). After working for the local paper a few years, he decided to go to California and try to become an actor. He joined the Harvey Hart Players in Pasadena, and it was not long before he realized that he could not make a living as an actor. He took time off from acting to learn the butcher business, which would later provide him with a livelihood during the lean seasons in show business.

Johnson moved to Nevada in the 1930s and became active in Nevada politics. He did radio shows and wrote a newspaper column in Las Vegas. He credited the start of his motion picture career to May Mann, a magazine writer, and her husband Buddy Baer. The Baers were visiting Las Vegas and heard Johnson's *Old Timer* radio show. They got in touch with him and introduced him to an agent.

Johnson made his film debut in 1950 in *Rocky Mountain*. It was an auspicious debut because it was a big-budget Western starring Errol Flynn and Patrice Wymore. Johnson played a stagecoach driver who is taken prisoner by marauding Confederates. During the filming he endeared himself to members of the cast and crew by showing up on the set every day or two with a fresh supply of good steaks, cut to his own specifications. His next film, also in 1950, was one in which he became a sidekick to Allan "Rocky" Lane. The film was *Night Riders of Montana*, and Johnson played Sheriff Skeeter Davis.

Johnson apparently did well in the role because he reprised the character in two more films, *Fort Dodge Stampede* and *Wells Fargo Gunmaster*, both released in 1951. Another film made by Lane in 1951 again featured Sheriff Skeeter Davis, but this time veteran actor Irving Bacon played the part. Johnson did not need to remain Lane's sidekick because he had developed into a very good character actor and began appearing not only in B Westerns but in big-budget films as well. He appeared in such films as *Bend of the River* (1952) with James Stewart, *Calamity Jane* (1953) with Doris Day, *The Far Country* (1954) again with Stewart, and *Twilight of Honor* (1963) with Richard Chamberlain. His last films were *Sam Whiskey* and *Support Your Local Sheriff!* (both 1969).

Johnson also had an active television career that ran from 1954 to 1965. He made at least three hundred television appearances, including *The Wild, Wild West*, *Gunsmoke*, *The Andy Griffith Show*, *Maverick*, and *Bonanza*. In 1963 he landed a regular role as Concho in *Temple Houston*, an NBC series starring Jeffrey Hunter.

After Johnson's career in movies started to wind down, he coached drama classes in Los Angeles and then went back to his first love, journalism. He became a syndicated columnist and was active in that profession until he suffered a leg infection that eventually caused his death on October 31, 1974. He was survived by two sons and two daughters.

Chubby Johnson and (left to right) Jimmy Stewart, Arthur Kennedy, and at the far right Stepin Fetchit in *Bend of the River* (1952).

Chubby Johnson and Ozzie Nelson in *Here Come the Nelsons* (1952).
©1951, UNIVERSAL PICTURES CO., INC.

BIBLIOGRAPHY

All Movie Guide. http://www.allmovie.com/.
Hollywood News, October 2, 1950.
The Internet Movie Database. http://www.imdb.com/.
McClure, Arthur F., and Ken G. Jones. *Heroes, Heavies, and Sagebrush: A Pictorial History of "B" Western Players.* South Brunswick, N.J.: A. S. Barnes, 1972.
Terre Haute Star, November 2, 1974.
Truitt, Evelyn Mack. *Who Was Who on Screen.* New York: R. R. Bowker, 1984.
Variety, November 4, 1974.

STEVE CLARK

Steve Clark was probably the most prolific Hoosier Western actor of all, at least in roles in which he could be easily identified. He has been identified in at least 270 feature films in a career that spanned twenty years from the 1930s through the early 1950s. Only six of his films were non-Westerns.

Elmer Stephen Clark was born on a farm north of Washington, Indiana, known as The Marsh, on February 26, 1891. His parents were Wesley Richard Clark and Nancy Eloise Cross. Before breaking into films, he was a stage actor, a director, and a talent manager. He never was a leading man, but he was very much in evidence in many films during the B Western heyday in Hollywood. He usually played kindly ranchers, heroines' fathers, judges, and sheriffs. Frequently he survived only until the second reel, when the villain put a bullet through his heart.

Steve Clark (right) and Kenneth MacDonald (Portland) (second from right) in *The Durango Kid* (1940), directed by Hoosier Lambert Hillyer.

Clark was never without work, and his film credits show he worked for almost every studio in Hollywood that produced Westerns. He stayed with Republic Studios for at least thirty films, working with such stars as Johnny Mack Brown and Bob Steele.

Clark's first film appearance was in 1933. At that time he was already forty-two years old, an age when most leading men would be considered over the hill. He settled into character roles and was busy year after year. He seldom made less than five or six films a year. In 1938 he was in at least fifteen films.

With this many Westerns to his credit, Clark was bound to appear in some films that featured other Indiana cowboys. He appeared in at least four films with Allan "Rocky" Lane, two with Buck Jones, two with Ken Maynard, and other appearances with Max Terhune, Kermit Maynard, and Kenneth MacDonald. He also worked with at least two Hoosier directors, the prolific Lambert Hillyer and Mack Wright.

Clark's last feature appearance was in *Security Risk* in 1954. However, he is also credited with an appearance in *Ghost of Zorro*, which was released in 1959. Since he died on June 29, 1954, it appears the feature that was released in 1959 was a compilation of the 1949 *Zorro* serial episodes in which he played the feature role of Jonathan White. Near the end of his career, he was just about as busy in television as he was in motion pictures. He appeared in such programs as *Alfred Hitchcock Presents*, *The Cisco Kid*, *The Gene Autry Show*, *The Adventures of Wild Bill Hickok*, and *The Lone Ranger*.

BIBLIOGRAPHY

All Movie Guide. http://www.allmovie.com/.

Census Records, 1900. Elmore Township. Daviess County, Indiana.

The Internet Movie Database. http://www.imdb.com/.

McClure, Arthur F., and Ken G. Jones. *Heroes, Heavies, and Sagebrush: A Pictorial History of "B" Western Players*. South Brunswick, N.J.: A. S. Barnes, 1972.

The Old Corral. http://www.surfnetinc.com/chuck/trio.htm.

KENNETH MACDONALD

Tom Santschi of Kokomo might have set the stage as the first recognizable cowboy villain, but a number of years after Santschi disappeared from the screen, Indiana provided another cowboy villain in the person of Kenneth MacDonald. While Santschi's career was mostly in silent films, MacDonald did most of his work in sound film and even had a nice career in television. Some sources list his last name as McDonald, but neither was his birth name. He was born Kenneth Dollins on September 8, 1901, in Portland, Indiana. He officially changed his name to MacDonald in 1930. He grew up in Richmond, Indiana, where he earned seven letters at Richmond High School as a member of its football, basketball, and track squads. He was also the first president of the Richmond Athletic Association.

MacDonald went on stage in the 1920s, but when he decided to try to break into the movies, he found the going rough. He wrote and published a pamphlet that he entitled *The Case for Kenneth MacDonald.* This self-promoting booklet was distributed to all the studios and finally caught the attention of studio executives. His first feature was a Western, *Slow as Lightning*, in 1923. He worked steadily throughout the 1930s, portraying a mustachioed villain in Westerns and other films and appearing in short subjects made by the Three Stooges and Hugh Herbert.

MacDonald became a regular fixture at Columbia Studios, portraying villains in cowboy star Charles Starrett's series of Westerns. With his suave demeanor and excellent rich, booming voice, he played con men, crooked lawyers, and gang leaders. During MacDonald's career he appeared in several major movies, including *The Caine Mutiny* (1954), *The Ten Commandments* (1956), and *Return to Peyton Place* (1961). He made his last film, an Audie Murphy Western, *40 Guns to Apache Pass*, in 1967. MacDonald made at least 150 films during his career; at least forty were Westerns. He played with such Western stars as Buster Crabbe, Jock Mahoney, Rod Cameron, and Randolph Scott, and fellow Hoosiers Allan "Rocky" Lane, Chubby Johnson, Steve Clark, and Forrest Tucker.

MacDonald went into semiretirement in 1955. Television was just coming on strong, and thanks to his work in the Three Stooges shorts, he landed a recurring role as a judge in the popular *Perry Mason* series. Sam White, whose brother Jules was in charge of many of the Stooges films, was a member of the *Perry Mason* production team. He remembered MacDonald and suggested him for the role of the judge. The series ran initially from 1957 to 1966, and MacDonald was part of it for most of that run. It is this role for which he will be most remembered.

MacDonald was married to LaMee Nave MacDonald. He died in the Motion Picture and Television Hospital in Woodland Hills, California, on May 8, 1972.

Kenneth MacDonald.

BIBLIOGRAPHY

All Movie Guide. http://www.allmovie.com/.

Barbour, Alan G. *The Thrill of It All.* New York: Macmillan, 1971.

Brooks, Tim, and Earl Marsh. *The Complete Directory to Prime Time Net-*

work TV Shows, 1946–Present. 2nd rev. ed. New York: Ballantine Books, 1981.

Holland, Ted. *B Western Actors Encyclopedia: Facts, Photos, and Filmographies for More Than 250 Familiar Faces.* Jefferson, N.C.: McFarland and Company, 1997.

Indianapolis Star, May 8, 1972.

The Internet Movie Database. http://www.imdb.com/.

"Kenneth McDonald." *Classic Images* 200 (February 1992).

The Old Corral. http://www.surfnetinc.com/chuck/trio.htm.

TEX TERRY

Tex Terry was born Edward E. Terry on August 22, 1902, in Coxville, Indiana. He appeared in several hundred films between the early 1920s and the late 1950s. Terry's screen credits were mostly in B Westerns, and he supported such stars as Gene Autry, "Wild Bill" Elliott, and Sunset Carson. Terry also was quite active in television, making a number of appearances on Westerns, including *Gunsmoke.* He usually played heavies since he was a big man with a well-worn, chiseled face. He got his taste for Westerns and horses from serving in the U.S. Cavalry from 1919 to 1922. He later served as a private in the army in World War II.

He died on May 18, 1985, and was buried in his hometown at the Coxville Cemetery in Coxville, Indiana. He had spent fifty years in film and television.

BIBLIOGRAPHY

All Movie Guide. http://www.allmovie.com/.

Find a Grave. http://www.findagrave.com/.

Indianapolis News, October 6, 1967.

FREDERICK GAMBLE

Frederick Alvin Gambold was born in Indianapolis on October 26, 1868. He started his career in vaudeville at age fifteen and eventually became a member of a singing group named Queen City Four. He was one of the founders of The Troupers and moved to Hollywood in 1906, before the film industry started.

Gamble joined the American Film Company in 1912. His first movie was a thousand-foot comedy short titled *Oh, Daddy!* His first feature film was *The Girl from His Town* (1915) with Margarita Fisher. He began appearing in a number of the American Film Company's early social comedy dramas in 1914. He continued to make many short films in the 1910s while making about one feature film a year.

In 1920 Gamble made his first Western, *Bullet Proof,* with Harry Carey and was in at least eight other Westerns through 1928. In the 1920s he went by the names of Fred Gamble and Fred Gambold. He was relegated to character roles when movies hit their stride in the 1910s and 1920s. He was stocky in appearance and can be seen as the hotel proprietor in *Tumbleweeds* (1925) and Yakima Canutt's sidekick in *The Fighting Stallion* (1926). His roles ran the gamut of character parts: priest, guardian, theatrical manager, country bumpkin, hotel proprietor, butler, bartender, ranch owner, and innkeeper.

Gamble was in a fifteen-chapter serial, *The Screaming Shadow*, in 1920. His career apparently ended with the advent of sound. He died in Hollywood on February 17, 1939.

BIBLIOGRAPHY

All Movie Guide. http://www.allmovie.com/.
"Forgotten Cowboys." *Classic Images* 191 (May 1990).
The Internet Movie Database. http://www.imdb.com/.
Variety, February 22, 1939.

THOMAS LINGHAM

Thomas Lingham was born in Indianapolis on April 7, 1874. He made his stage debut as an actor at age twenty-one and performed all over the country for eighteen years. In 1914 he made his film debut in *The Boer War*. In 1914 he was in *Shannon of the Sixth* for Kalem Pictures, playing Shah, the king of Delphi. He began appearing regularly in a variety of films and then settled down into Westerns. In 1916 he played the sheriff in *Whispering Smith*. He made several silent serials; the first, also in 1916, was *The Lass of the Lumberlands,* which was fifteen chapters and starred Helen Holmes, who had spent much of her young life in South Bend, Indiana. In 1917 he made another fifteen-chapter serial, *The Railroad Raiders*, again starring Holmes. The Holmes serials became very popular, so much so that Holmes was the chief rival to Pearl White. In another serial, *The Lost Express* (1917), Lingham was again featured with Holmes. Other serials in which Lingham appeared were *The Lion's Claws* (1918), *The Red Glove* (1919), *Ruth of the Rockies* (1920), and *The Vanishing Dagger* (1920). He appeared in more than forty Western feature films with such stars as Bob Steele, Jack Hoxie, Art Acord, Tom Mix, Hoot Gibson, and Harry Carey. He died on February 19, 1950, in Woodland Hills, California.

BIBLIOGRAPHY

The Internet Movie Database. http://www.imdb.com/.
"Tom Lingham." *Classic Images* 176 (February 1990).

MAJOR GORDON "PAWNEE BILL" LILLIE

"Pawnee Bill" was never a Western movie star but was probably closer to a real cowboy than most of those who portrayed them on film. Gordon W. Lillie was born in Bloomington, Indiana, on February 14, 1860. His father was a miller in Bloomington until the mill burned down. He salvaged what he could of the equipment and moved his family to Wellington, Kansas, when Gordon was about ten years old.

A miller's existence was too tame for young Lillie, and he joined an outfit run by Trapper Tom Evans, who was killing buffalo for their hides and trapping other animals. After a year of the trapper's life, a narrow escape from a band of Comanche Indians, and another escape from a stampeding buffalo herd, Lillie entered the government's Indian Service at Pawnee, Oklahoma, in 1882, becoming an interpreter. In 1888 Lillie took up the fight to open up the Oklahoma Territory for settlement. The territory was then occupied by cattle barons who resisted the efforts of any farmers to enter. Lillie organized the Oklahoma Boomers and entered Oklahoma with them on April 22, 1889, known now as the birthday of the state.

Lillie's wife, May, was known for her skill with a rifle and was an expert equestrienne. Together they joined William F. "Buffalo Bill" Cody's Wild West Show. Lillie and Cody represented the last phase of the frontier era. He was a colorful showman, and his partnership with Cody made him a comfortable fortune. He appeared as himself in two films, *Buffalo Bill's Wild West and Pawnee Bill's Far East* (1910) and *In the Days of the Thundering Herd* (1914).

After Cody died, Lillie retired to his ranch on the outskirts of Pawnee, where he accumulated one of the largest privately owned buffalo herds in the country. As a financier, he became active in a number of business enterprises in his hometown of Pawnee. On February 4, 1942, as the town's residents were preparing to celebrate his eighty-second birthday, his heart failed and he died. He had been in ill health since being injured in an automobile accident that killed his wife.

BIBLIOGRAPHY

New York Times, February 4, 1942.
Variety, February 11, 1942.

Many well-known actresses got their start in Westerns. Among them were Rita Cansino (Rita Hayworth), Phyllis Isley (Jennifer Jones), Louise Brooks, Ann Sheridan, Carole Landis, and Indiana's Miriam Seegar (chapter 5), Geneva Mitchell (chapter 6), Carmelita Geraghty (chapter 5), and Jane Peters (Carole Lombard [chapter 4]). Other Hoosier actresses who appeared occasionally in Westerns were Helene Stanley, Jan Wiley, and Lydia Knott.

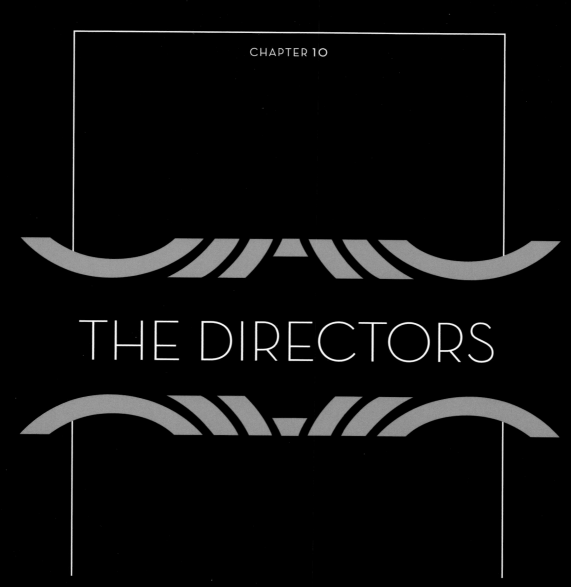

CHAPTER 10

THE DIRECTORS

Of the ten major directors in this chapter, seven were born in the nineteenth century, thus virtually assuring their careers would begin with silent films. The senior director in this compilation is Lambert Hillyer, while the youngest is Sydney Pollack. There are younger Hoosier directors of note, such as Tommy O'Haver and David Anspaugh. This chapter will be devoted to ten directors whose body of work and contribution to the industry has already given them a firm place in film history.

AL AND RAY ROCKETT

Feature Photodramas

Al Rockett.

Ray Rockett.

Two sets of Indiana brothers in the early days of Hollywood became director/producers. Howard and Kenneth Hawks of Goshen are better known, but Al and Ray Rockett from Vincennes preceded the Hawks and were considered outstanding director/producers in the early 1920s.

In the early days of motion pictures, there were no producers. The term "supervisor" was used during most of the silent era. The early supervisors were not considered important to the making of motion pictures and were frequently called snoopervisors. Humorist Irvin S. Cobb said, "They're like goldfish. They can swim around with their eyes open and still be asleep." However, at the end of the era, producers were firmly entrenched and became a vital part of the industry. Some of the early producers were such men as David O. Selznick, Irving Thalberg, and Al and Ray Rockett. Selznick, Thalberg, and the Rocketts gave the term "producer" a new dignity.

Albert was the better known of the two brothers. Albert L. Rockett was born in Vincennes, Indiana, on September 24, 1889. At an early age he became a proficient pianist and played at nickelodeons for five years before deciding in 1914 that he wanted to produce motion pictures. Before long, Al apparently felt he had gained enough experience to start his own company. It is not known whether Ray was already in California or if Al convinced him to join him. At any rate, the brothers formed their own company, the Rockett Film Corporation, in 1921, with offices on Hollywood Boulevard. An advertisement in the 1921 *Film Daily Yearbook* read: "Our first production . . . The Truant Husband."

In 1923 the brothers produced the tremendously successful *The Dramatic Life of Abraham Lincoln.* It was released in 1924 and starred George A. Billings as Lincoln. In the cast as "Sally, a country girl," was Hoosier Louise Fazenda. The scenario writer was Frances Marion, who was to become one of the most respected screenwriters of the twentieth century. She won two Oscars for writing in a long and illustrious career, and her script for the Rockett brothers' *The Dramatic Life of Abraham Lincoln* was one of her first major triumphs.

After *The Dramatic Life of Abraham Lincoln*, the brothers went their separate ways. Ray set up his own production company, Ray Rockett Productions, and began to produce films in conjunction with director Joseph Henabery, who was an assistant director with D. W. Griffith. Ray did not work on any films after 1930, and his life and career after that is unknown.

Al became head of production at First National Pictures. In 1928 he produced Crawfordsville native Kenyon Nicholson's *The Barker*, starring Douglas Fairbanks Jr. By 1930 he was with the William Fox Studios as a producer. The first film he produced at Fox was *Such Men Are Dangerous* (1930), directed by Goshen native Kenneth Hawks. Hawks died that same year in an airplane crash while shooting a movie. In 1942 Al moved to Famous Artists, where he alternated between being a producer and an associate producer. He was instrumental in the discovery of such actresses as Ann Blyth, Dana Wynter, and Joan Collins. Al died on August 30, 1960, in Hollywood after a long illness. He was survived by his wife, Laura (Lottie), and son, Norman.

BIBLIOGRAPHY

Brownlow, Kevin. *The Parade's Gone By*. Berkeley: University of California Press, 1968.

The Internet Movie Database. http://www.imdb.com/.

Ramsaye, Terry. *A Million and One Nights: A History of the Motion Picture*. 1926. Reprint, New York: Simon and Schuster, 1964.

Variety, September 7, 1960.

Wid's Year Book 1920–21. New York: Arno Press, 1971.

Wid's Year Book 1921–22. New York: Arno Press, 1971.

LAMBERT HILLYER
Buck Jones's Favorite

Lambert Hillyer.

ambert Hillyer was one of the American cinema's most prolific and least pretentious directors. Born in South Bend, Indiana, on July 8, 1889, he directed countless low-budget Hollywood productions for more than three decades, many from his own scripts. He wrote stories and scenarios for at least forty-eight Western films. He directed more than 150 films, the vast majority of which were Westerns. In one year alone, 1941, he directed thirteen films.

Hillyer's mother was actress Lydia Knott, a Tyner, Indiana, native. She made more than eighty films from 1919 through 1937. Her son directed her in two of those films, *The Super Sex* in 1922 and *The Defense Rests* in 1934. Like her son, she did most of her work in Westerns, playing fellow Hoosier Buck Jones's mother in two of his films.

Hillyer started his career as a newspaperman and short-story writer. Most likely influenced by his actress mother, he moved into summer stock and vaudeville. He worked as a grip, gofer, stage manager, actor, director, and writer and finally got into films in 1914 as a writer for D. W. Griffith. He probably did some uncredited directing for Griffith. He joined the Thomas Ince company, where he received his most important training as a director. In 1917 he joined Triangle. It was here that he directed his first picture, *An Even Break* (1917). He moved to Artcraft Pictures and directed fourteen films through 1921. He became much in demand as an efficient, fast-working, freelance director. He directed films at Goldwyn, Paramount, Universal, First National, American Releasing, FBO, Fox, and Principal.

Hillyer formed an association with the first great Western star, William S. Hart, in 1917, writing the screenplay for *The Desert Man.* After completing a couple films, he received sole credit for directing. When Hart left Triangle films in late 1917 and moved to Paramount, Hillyer directed twenty-five out of the twenty-seven films Hart made for Paramount. He also wrote at least five scripts for Hart's films. Sometimes Hart would come up with the story line, and Hillyer would write the script from Hart's outline. When his association with Hart ended in 1922, Hart's films were never as good as when he worked with Hillyer.

Hillyer also directed three films for Tom Mix and several for Johnny Mack Brown. He worked with many Hoosiers. For example, Steve Clark from Washington, Indiana, was a regular in Hillyer's films, appearing in at least twenty-five of them. Hillyer also worked with Max Terhune, Kermit Maynard, Charlie Murray, Louise Fazenda, Kenneth MacDonald, and Tom Santschi.

In 1926 Hillyer started a collaboration with fellow Hoosier Buck Jones. This became an informal partnership in which Hillyer would direct and frequently pen the script for both Fox and Columbia. From 1926 to 1933 he directed fifteen films that starred Jones. Of those fifteen, Hillyer wrote the screenplay for nine of them.

While the vast majority of Hillyer's films were Westerns, he showed his versatility by directing a number of dramas with established stars such as Blanche Sweet, Florence Vidor, and Lon Chaney. With the coming of sound, he became entrenched in doing low-budget second features. However, the small budgets did not prevent him from producing above-average product. In 1936 he joined Universal Studios, where he directed such B movie horror hits as *Dracula's Daughter* (1936) and *The Invisible Ray* (1936). The latter starred the dynamic duo of Boris Karloff and Bela Lugosi.

In 1943 Hillyer directed the first big screen treatment of the famous Batman cartoon strip. The strip's creator, Bob Kane, wrote the screenplay for the serial, titled *The Batman*. Lewis Wilson starred as Batman and Douglas Croft as Robin. When television began, Hillyer moved effortlessly into that medium, directing countless television Westerns, most notably many episodes of *The Cisco Kid* between 1951 and 1955.

Hillyer's direction of Westerns was much in the manner of John Ford. Unlike Ford, Hillyer's films were made hastily and inexpensively, but to his credit, they did not look cheap. It may be that Hillyer became too proficient in completing films on time and on budget. Studios tended to assume that if a director could do ten features a year and never go over budget or schedule, he could do eleven. Thus, he may have been a victim of his own professionalism.

Hillyer's last film was *Haunted Trails*, released in 1949. The star was "Whip" Wilson, and in the cast was Steve Clark. Hillyer died in Woodland Hills, California, on July 5, 1969.

BIBLIOGRAPHY

Brownlow, Kevin. *The War, the West, and the Wilderness*. New York: Alfred A. Knopf, 1979.

Dixon, Wheeler W. *The "B" Directors: A Biographical Directory*. Metuchen, N.J.: Scarecrow Press, 1985.

Everson, William K. *A Pictorial History of the Western*. Secaucus, N.J.: Citadel Press, 1969.

Fenin, George N., and William K. Everson. *The Western: From Silents to Cinerama*. New York: Bonanza Books, 1962.

Fraser, Harry. *I Went That-a-Way: The Memoirs of a Western Film Director*. Metuchen, N.J.: Scarecrow Press, 1990.

The Internet Movie Database. http://www.imdb.com/.

Katz, Ephraim. *The Film Encyclopedia*. New York: Perigee Books, 1979.

Monaco, James, ed. *The Encyclopedia of Film*. New York: Perigee Books, 1991.

Quinlan, David. *Quinlan's Film Directors*. London: B. T. Batsford, 1999.

Wid's Year Book. 3 vols. New York: Arno Press, 1971.

TIM WHELAN

Harold Lloyd to The Thief of Bagdad

A young Tim Whelan.

Vivien Leigh, Maureen O'Hara, and Geraldine Fitzgerald might never have been American movie stars had it not been for Indiana's Tim Whelan. He also helped Frank Sinatra get his film career started by directing two of his early films, *Step Lively* (1944) and *Higher and Higher* (1943). Whelan was always able to spot talent, and these are only a few of the screen stars he helped along the road to success.

Whelan was born on November 2, 1893, in Cannelton, Indiana. After finishing high school, he moved to Denver, Colorado, to study law, but he became interested in the theater and gave up his law studies to seek a career on the stage. From 1910 to 1920 he appeared on the legitimate stage and in vaudeville as an actor, writer, and producer.

In 1920 Whelan went to Hollywood and secured a job as a gag writer. In this capacity he became a major contributor to the success of two of the greatest comedians of the silent era. He joined Harold Lloyd as a collaborating writer from 1921 to 1925 and helped write some of Lloyd's most successful films. These included *Safety Last!* and *Why Worry?* (1923), *Girl Shy* and *Hot Water* (1924), and *The Freshman* (1925). Lloyd encouraged Whelan to turn his talents to direction. Whelan took his advice and left to pursue a directing job. After Whelan left, Lloyd suffered a decline in popularity from which he never recovered.

After leaving Lloyd, Whelan began work with a young director named Frank Capra. Capra thought an unknown comedian by the name of Harry Langdon had possibilities if he could find the right material for him, and Capra knew he was fortunate to get Whelan to help him with his first feature-length comedy. Whelan wrote many of the gags that gave Langdon his two biggest comedy hits, *Tramp, Tramp, Tramp* and *The Strong Man*, both released in 1926. Today, *The Strong Man* is considered one of the classic silent comedy features, ranked with the best of Charlie Chaplin, Buster Keaton, and Lloyd. During the making of the two films, Whelan and Capra formed a strong and lasting friendship.

In 1927 Whelan was one of the writers for Mary Pickford's last silent film, *My Best Girl*. There were three Hoosiers in this film: Carmelita Geraghty of Rushville, Sunshine Hart of Indianapolis, and Carole Lombard of Fort Wayne. Late in 1927 Whelan went to England to work for British International Films Corporation. It was a move that finally gave him an opportunity to direct. However, it caused him

to be identified with British films more than American films, and his magnificent sense of comedy was little used thereafter. Between pictures Whelan came back to America and in 1931 married Greentown, Indiana, native and film actress Miriam Seegar, whom he met in London in 1929 while directing her in *When Knights Were Bold*. The couple had two children, Tim Jr. and Michael.

After his marriage, Whelan returned to England, this time staying for seven years. In 1938 he directed Vivien Leigh and Charles Laughton in *Sidewalks of London* (a.k.a. *St. Martin's Lane*). Leigh's portrayal of a willful, over-ambitious leading lady led to her selection as Scarlett O'Hara in *Gone with the Wind*. A year later Whelan gave a screen test to a young girl who had come to London from Dublin seeking an acting career. Whelan gave the test to Laughton, who was so impressed that he made his partner, Erich Pommer, look at it. The partners signed Maureen O'Hara to a seven-year contract, and Laughton immediately cast her in *Jamaica Inn* (1939). Laughton's next project was *The Hunchback of Notre Dame* (1939), which was to be shot in the United States. Laughton thought O'Hara would be perfect for the role of Esmeralda, and she accompanied him to Hollywood, where her screen career took off.

In 1938 Whelan was selected by Alexander Korda to direct a Technicolor comedy, *The Divorce of Lady X*, starring Merle Oberon, Laurence Olivier, and Ralph Richardson. Presumably he was chosen because of his flair for comedy and his work with Lloyd and Capra. The *New York Times* praised the film, noting that "a screen that had grown sad from Hollywood's neglect is being delightfully watered by a gay and urbane comedy." The next year Korda called on Whelan to direct Olivier and Richardson in *Q Planes*, a film about "a plane that went up and never came down." Whelan was unhappy with Brock Williams's script and rewrote it as the film was being shot. Apparently much of the dialogue was made up by Whelan, Olivier, and Richardson on the spot. It was obvious the actors and Whelan had a lot of fun with the film, and it was a hit.

In 1940 Whelan was one of a team of directors who shared the credit for directing Alexander and Zoltan Korda's *The Thief of Bagdad*. It was a strikingly handsome picture and one of the great Technicolor screen classics. Eventually five directors had a hand in making the film. Whelan, who by now had earned the respect of the Kordas, was an important part of the team, directing many of the action sequences. Shooting began at the Denham Studios in London and in Morocco, but after World War II engulfed Europe, the film was finished on the soundstages in Hollywood and on location in the Mojave Desert and the Grand Canyon. *The Thief of Bagdad* became one of the most popular and enduring screen fantasies of all time. It has had a seminal influence on many modern filmmakers, including Martin Scorsese and Francis Ford Coppola. It won four Oscars in 1940.

Whelan returned to the United States and worked for RKO from 1942 to 1947. It was during this time he worked with Sinatra on *Step Lively* and *Higher and Higher*. The ending shot in *Higher and Higher*, showing Sinatra standing without visible support among the clouds and swelling from a pinpoint to a giant, was "a stroke of simple genius on the part of director Tim Whelan," according to Sinatra biographer Arnold Shaw. Sinatra's career exploded in like fashion shortly thereafter.

Tim Whelan.

(*Opposite page*) Tim Whelan (right) directs Basil Rathbone and Ellen Drew in *The Mad Doctor* (1941).
PARAMOUNT PHOTO BY TALMAGE MORRISON.

In 1945 Whelan wrote and directed a Christmas comedy, *Dinner for Three*, which opened in Philadelphia and starred his wife, Miriam. In the cast were such familiar names as Les Tremayne and Marjorie Lord. It never made it to Broadway.

Many of Whelan's postwar films were minor musicals and Westerns unworthy of his talent. His two best postwar films were *This Was a Woman* (1948) and *Rage at Dawn* (1955).

Whelan died of lung cancer on August 11, 1957, in his home in Beverly Hills.

BIBLIOGRAPHY

Capra, Frank. *The Name above the Title: An Autobiography.* New York: Macmillan, 1971.

Dardis, Tom. *Harold Lloyd: The Man on the Clock.* New York: Penguin Books, 1983.

Higham, Charles. *Charles Laughton: An Intimate Biography.* Garden City, N.Y.: Doubleday, 1976.

The Internet Movie Database. http://www.imdb.com/.

Lieber, Perry. "Tim Whelan, RKO Radio Director Biography." RKO Studios, February 15, 1946. Margaret Herrick Library. Academy of Motion Picture Arts and Sciences, Beverly Hills, California.

Los Angeles Examiner, August 12, 1957.

Los Angeles Times, August 12, 1957.

McBride, Joseph. *Frank Capra: The Catastrophe of Success.* New York: Simon and Schuster, 1992.

Osborne, Robert. *60 Years of the Oscar: The Official History of the Academy Awards.* New York: Abbeville Press, 1989.

Paramount Pictures Publicity, February 7, 1940. Margaret Herrick Library. Academy of Motion Picture Arts and Sciences, Beverly Hills, California.

Quinlan, David. *Quinlan's Film Directors.* London: B. T. Batsford, 1999.

Shaw, Arnold. *Sinatra: Twentieth-Century Romantic.* New York: Holt, Rinehart and Winston, 1968.

Stockham, Martin. *The Korda Collection: Alexander Korda's Film Classics.* London: Boxtree, 1992.

Whelan, Miriam Seegar. Interview with the author. December 12, 16, 2001. Pasadena, California.

CLIFFORD SMITH

With William S. Hart and Tom Mix

Clifford Smith was born in Richmond, Indiana, on August 22, 1894. He worked as a newspaperman, a short-story writer, and a cowboy before becoming an actor. His film career began in 1915, when he appeared in *The Disciple* for Triangle Films. He became a leading director of silent Westerns, working with such stars as William S. Hart, Tom Mix, Art Acord, Yakima Canutt, Hoot Gibson, and Jack Hoxie. According to his own account in 1921, he worked on forty-five Hart pictures before moving on to direct other leading Western stars.

Hart had been signed by Thomas Ince as a director/actor, and during his first film as a director, *The Passing of Two-Gun Hicks*, in 1914, he realized he needed Smith's immense experience in order for the film to be successful. In 1915 Hart's film, *The Taking of Luke McVane*, was not only codirected by Smith but also featured Smith in a leading role. In 1916 Hart produced an elaborate five-reel Western, which cost eight thousand dollars to shoot. Smith was assistant director and was paid thirty dollars a week. Although Hart was always in control of his films, he was so dependent on Smith that he asked Ince to promote Smith to codirector of his films.

Smith acted in and scripted some of the films he directed and later became a producer. He started his own production company in the early 1920s, but when sound came in, he found it difficult to gain employment. He freelanced at Goldwyn, Paramount, Universal, First National, American Releasing, FBO, Fox, Associated, and Principal before finally finding a semipermanent home at Columbia in 1931.

Smith turned to acting for a while and appeared in the 1935 version of *Les Miserables*. He finally became a director of serials for Universal Pictures in 1936. One of the serials he directed, *The Adventures of Frank Merriwell* (1936), was written by Rushville native Maurice Geraghty, and another, *Secret Agent X-9,* starred Indianapolis native Monte Blue. Smith was preparing to codirect *Tim Tyler's Luck* when he died in Los Angeles on September 17, 1937, of a ruptured appendix. He was survived by his widow and one child.

BIBLIOGRAPHY

Brownlow, Kevin. *The War, the West, and the Wilderness.* New York: Alfred A. Knopf, 1979.

Dixon, Wheeler W. *The "B" Directors: A Biographical Directory.* Metuchen, N.J.: Scarecrow Press, 1985.

Everson, William K. A *Pictorial History of the Western.* Secaucus, N.J.: Citadel Press, 1969.

Fenin, George N., and William K. Everson. *The Western: From Silents to Cinerama.* New York: Bonanza Books, 1962.

Katz, Ephraim. *The Film Encyclopedia.* New York: Perigee Books, 1979.

Variety, September 15, 1937.

MACK V. WRIGHT

Stuntman, Action Star, and Director

M ack Wright's career was primarily confined to Westerns. In 1963 Wright talked about his career:

> I was born in Princeton, Indiana, in 1895 and later moved to New Albany. I graduated from Brown's Business College in Centralia, Indiana, and came to California in 1915. My first job there was at the Fifth Street Store, which is now known as the May Company. I called upon J. Warren Kerrigan and his brother, Wallace, at their home. They were both from New Albany, and J. Warren was a Western star at Universal Studios, while Wally was in charge of the Universal ranch. Wally offered me a job on the ranch and I accepted. The next day I reported to the ranch and was made up as an Indian in the morning, and then I would perform as a cowboy or soldier in the afternoon. The salary was eighteen dollars per month, and I found it kept me from telling him I had never ridden a horse, let alone riding Indian-bareback style. The cowboys in those days were real, they wore big hats, high boots and carried all their possessions in a gunny sack with their saddles. I worked hard, learned to ride, and made friends who helped me to get ahead. When it was necessary to fall off a horse as a stunt, we received fifty cents extra. So, in my spare time I would hide out and practice.

Wright became an expert stuntman, then was promoted to assistant property man, then assistant director. Three years after he saw his first camera, he had become a respected director of Western films.

While pursuing his career as a director, Wright still appeared frequently as an actor. He was cast primarily as a villain because of his rough looks and black mustache. In 1918 he enlisted in the army, but when he returned to Universal, the studio refused to pay him what he thought he was worth, so he quit. However, he found it difficult to get another job as a director and returned to being an actor, stuntman, and assistant director.

In 1919 Wright played the villain in a fifteen-chapter serial, *The Lion Man.* However, he also was the assistant director and stuntman. This serial was tops in its day and drew thousands of moviegoers week after week to see the death-defying cliff-hangers that Wright helped fashion.

In 1920 Wright directed seven two-reelers, starring Hoot Gibson. Wright wrote the screenplay for one of those films, *Wolf Tracks* (1920). He developed a close friendship with actor/director J. P. McGowan and worked on a number of McGowan productions as assistant director. In 1927 he was assistant director on *Tarzan and the Golden Lion*, starring Franklin, Indiana, native James Pierce as Tarzan.

Wright wrote two other screenplays in 1928 and appeared in both of them as an actor. It is not clear why he did not star in more films since he was a handsome, well-built man and a good actor. Apparently it was thought his appearance made him more believable as a villain. He usually was a well-dressed villain, playing a crooked banker or the rival for the girl.

In addition to the Kerrigan brothers and Pierce, Wright worked with fellow Hoosiers Buck Jones, Max Terhune, Monte Blue, and Maurice Geraghty. He worked on four films in the Mesquiteers series and four Gene Autry films. His handling of actors, action, and camera work made those films outstanding directorial achievements and contributed to the success of the films.

In 1938 the Wright talent delivered a smash serial to Columbia, *The Great Adventures of Wild Bill Hickok*, featuring "Wild Bill" Elliott in his first starring Western. Wright kept busy in films until television provided more work for him in the 1950s. His last work as an assistant director was with the television series *Sea Hunt* in 1958.

Wright retired and moved to Boulder City, Nevada, in 1960. Summarizing his career, he said, "I will say that the first six months of my career were hectic, but I couldn't let the Kerrigans down, being a 'Hoosier.'"

Wright died in Boulder City on August 14, 1965. He was survived by his wife Geraldine, a former script supervisor.

BIBLIOGRAPHY

Katchmer, George. "Forgotten Cowboys and Cowgirls." *Classic Images* 177 (March 1990).

The Internet Movie Database. http://www.imdb.com/.

"Serial, Stunts and Six-Guns." *Screen Thrills Illustrated* (February 1963).

Variety, August 25, 1965.

RAY ENRIGHT

Solid as a "Brick"

Ray Enright was born in Anderson, Indiana, on March 25, 1896. He began his film career in 1914 as a cutter (film editor) on some of the early Charlie Chaplin comedies. When World War I broke out, he saw service in France, returning to work for the Thomas Ince Studio. He moved to the Mack Sennett Studios, where he worked for seven years, rising from gagman to editor in chief of comedies. He eventually moved to Warner Brothers, where he was given his first chance to direct. After directing two shorts in 1921, *Verse and Worse* and *His Unlucky Job*, he made his debut as a feature director in 1927, directing fellow Hoosier Tom Santschi in a Rin Tin Tin film, *Tracked by the Police*. Thereafter, he was steadily employed as a director through the end of his career, directing several Joe E. Brown comedies as well as several Dick Powell musicals, including *Dames* and *Twenty Million Sweethearts* (both 1934). While he was not primarily a director of Westerns, he turned out quite a few. He apparently was Randolph Scott's favorite and directed Scott in a number of films through the 1940s. Most of these were Westerns, including the highly rated *The Spoilers* (1942), which paired Scott with John Wayne and Marlene Dietrich. His ventures outside of Westerns included the Humphrey Bogart films *The Wagons Roll at Night* (1941) and *China Clipper* (1936).

In addition to Santschi, Enright worked with other Hoosiers such as Monte Blue, Forrest Tucker, Julanne Johnston, Louise Fazenda, John Bowers, and Norman Foster. He also was a writer and wrote at least four screenplays. He was a workhorse in the Warner Brothers' stable, cranking out fifty-three pictures for the studio and sixty-nine total during a twenty-seven-year directing career. His dependability and work ethic gave him the nickname by which he was known throughout the industry—"Brick Enright."

Enright was one of the founders of The Masquers Club (1925), which played a role in the founding of the Screen Actors Guild (1933). He retired from the screen in 1953 and died of a heart attack in Hollywood on April 3, 1965. He was survived by his wife, Vern.

BIBLIOGRAPHY

The Internet Movie Database. http://www.imdb.com/.

Katz, Ephraim. *The Film Encyclopedia*. New York: Perigee Books, 1979.

Roberts, John. "Ray Enright, Workhorse Director." *Classic Images* 171 (September 1989).

Schuster, Mel. *Motion Picture Directors: A Bibliography of Magazine and Periodical Articles, 1900–1972*. Metuchen, N.J.: Scarecrow Press, 1973.

Variety, April 7, 1965.

HOWARD AND KENNETH HAWKS

Silents to Sound the "Hawksian" Way

The Hawks brothers became directors in the waning years of silent film. Howard went on to become one of the most respected directors in the history of films in a remarkable and diverse career that lasted more than fifty years. He was a commercial director, an efficient maker of hits who made films in all genres. Despite his protestations that he was not an artist, he is today regarded as one of the greatest of American film artists. His brother Kenneth was on his way to becoming a successful director when he was killed in an aviation accident just as his career was beginning.

Howard Winchester Hawks was born in Goshen, Indiana, on May 30, 1896, to Frank Winchester and Helen Howard Hawks. Frank was born in Goshen, but Helen was a native of Neenah, Wisconsin. At the time of Howard's birth, the family lived in Goshen on South Fifth Street in a home on the present Masonic Temple site.

The Hawks family can be traced back to the founding of Boston. In the 1830s Howard's grandfather started a mill in Waterford, Indiana, later moving it to Goshen. By the middle of the nineteenth century, the Hawks family practically owned Goshen. There was Hawks Electric, Hawks Hardware, Hawks Furniture, and the biggest company in town, Hawks Mill.

In 1898 a second son, Kenneth Neil, was born. Frank and Helen began to find they were more comfortable in Helen's hometown, and Frank's brothers resented the fact he was not totally committed to the family business. So with two-year-old Howard and infant Kenneth, Frank and Helen moved to Neenah, where Frank became secretary-treasurer of the Howard Paper Company.

From the beginning, the Hawks boys were pampered. They wore the finest clothes, and the Howard grandparents lavished toys on them. Three other children were born while the family was in Neenah. In 1902 a third son, William Bellinger Hawks, arrived. In 1903 a fourth child, Grace Louise, was born. By the time a fifth child, Helen Bernice, was born in 1906, Helen was not in good health. The doctor advised her to spend the winter of 1906–07 in Pasadena, California. In 1910 the family moved permanently to California. Frank became vice president of a hotel chain, and the family lived in Glendora and Pasadena. When Helen's father, C. W. Howard, died in 1916, the Hawks family benefited from his will.

Howard was enrolled at Phillips Exeter Academy, but he failed to make good enough grades to finish and went back to Pasadena High

Howard Hawks (right) directing *The Road to Glory* (1936).

School and graduated. He was accepted at Cornell University and studied engineering. When World War I broke out, he was called into military service and had to forego his senior year at Cornell. However, in a patriotic gesture, Cornell decided to award degrees to the entire class of 1918.

After the war Hawks developed an interest in the movie industry. He was a good athlete and managed to play tennis with Douglas Fairbanks. This led to a friendship with Fairbanks, who at that time was romancing Mary Pickford. Fairbanks convinced Pickford to hire Hawks as a property man, and he eventually became an assistant director. One day during the shooting of *The Little Princess*, the director came to work drunk. Pickford asked Hawks if he could do a few scenes. She liked his work, and it was then that Hawks decided to become a director. He began to see as many movies as he could, often two or three a day. When he saw a picture he liked, he would sit through it a second time to study the director's technique. He particularly admired John Ford.

Hawks was also writing scripts at this time and came up with a story for a modern Western called *Quicksands* (1923). He decided to produce it, using his own money. (Hawks's father died when Hawks was in his teens, and he and his siblings inherited a fortune.) He hired Jack Conway to direct it, and Richard Dix and Helene Chadwick were the stars. He cut corners and paid his people next to nothing, bringing in the film for $18,000. The film got good reviews but did only fair business.

Finally, in 1925 Hawks was signed by Fox Studios. His brother Kenneth, an assistant director at Paramount, joined Howard at Fox and quickly became a top production supervisor.

The deal with Fox was that Howard was to write as well as direct. His first writing project was *The Road to Glory*. The film was released in 1926 and received good reviews, although Howard later said, "It didn't have any fun in it. It was pretty bad." He decided his films from that time on would be entertaining and commercial. Howard was now directing three films a year and writing at least one a year. However, writing during the silent era did not require anything more than a brief scenario.

In 1927 one of Howard's best friends, Victor Fleming, was dating actress Norma Shearer. Fleming arranged for Howard to meet Norma's sister, Athole Shearer Ward. It was love at first sight. Athole was married with a young son but was separated from her husband. During this same year, Kenneth was introduced to a twenty-year-old actress. Mary Astor was immediately attracted to Kenneth, recalling, "He had prematurely gray hair, very twinkling blue eyes behind horn-rimmed glasses, and a grin a mile wide."

Kenneth and Mary were married on February 24, 1928. Howard and Athole were supposed to be married on February 8 of that year, but Athole suffered a severe bout of depression. Howard did not know it, but Athole had a history of mental illness. The Shearers successfully kept the truth from Howard by telling him she had a bad attack of the flu. The wedding date was reset for May 8, 1928.

Howard had always had an interest in racing cars, motorcycles, anything associated with speed. He said, "I started racing because my grandfather gave me a car that was the best car of that era . . . a little Mercer racer. And having the best car, I was able to win quite a few races." As an adult, Howard competed in a number of road races in the Los Angeles area. He said, "Later I drove the car that won Indianapolis. I raced for two or three years professionally and had the fastest speedboat."

Kenneth Hawks and Mary Astor on their wedding day, February 24, 1928.

In 1932 he directed *The Crowd Roars*, a film about racing, with much of it centered on the Indianapolis 500-Mile Race. The film was shot entirely in Hollywood, but Howard cast a number of racing veterans in the film. He called the film "the first picture that I made where I did something that was fun." He cast Billy Arnold, Fred Frame, Ralph Hepburn, Wilbur Shaw, Shorty Cantlon, Mel Keneally, and Stubby Stubblefield in the film. They all played themselves. The stars were James Cagney and Joan Blondell. The film was so successful that it was remade in 1939 as *Indianapolis Speedway* with Pat O'Brien and Ann Sheridan. Howard's younger brother, William, was a writer for this 1939 film.

On January 2, 1930, Kenneth went to Santa Monica's Clover Field to shoot some scenes for a film he was directing, *Such Men Are Dangerous*. He had asked Howard, who was a more experienced pilot, to come to the airport to help check things out and watch the stunt they planned to film just off the coast. Howard, however, was busy at home with his wife and three-month-old son. The scene involved a parachute jump. Two planes carrying the camera crews would fly close together, one slightly above the other. One would film closeups, the other long shots.

Kenneth had been an aviator in World War I and according to Astor, "He loved flying. On the bedside table in our room, there are books about flying . . . 'Above the Blue Sky' and five or six others."

Howard had his own ideas about Kenneth's flying skill: "Ken wasn't much of a flyer, and I said, 'You'd better look out, you're liable to run into one another. Take care about it, and especially if the man you're flying with isn't much good.'"

The two planes collided in clear weather during a test run over Santa Monica Bay. All ten people on the two planes were killed. Lieutenant Colonel Roscoe Turner, who lived in Indianapolis a good part of his life, was the pilot on the lead plane that had the parachutist. Turner did not see the crash, but a member of his crew did and told Turner, "Look, they've hit each other." Turner said, "I winged over and turned around to get a look at them. They were tangled together, both afire, and plunging toward the ocean. Just as they were about to hit, two or three of the men either jumped or were thrown out of the burning planes. . . . I don't know how it could have happened unless the sun got in the eyes of the other two pilots. They were probably jockeying to get in position and one swung into the glare of the sun, hitting the other head on before he knew it."

After the accident Astor discovered that she was destitute. Kenneth lost all his money in the stock market crash and did not tell his wife that he was behind on their mortgage payments and had been forced to discontinue his life insurance policy. The sale of their home barely paid the back taxes. Astor participated in damage suits against Fox and the airplane company with the widows of the men killed in the disaster. The court found that Fox was not negligent in the accident. The *New Movie Magazine* reported that Astor "won" her suit against the airplane company in January 1932.

Howard was unquestionably affected by his brother's death. However, he never spoke publicly about the incident until years later, when he was interviewed by Kevin Brownlow: "I thought he had a good deal of promise. He had a great deal of warmth, much more than I have. I don't think he knew as much about story as I do but he had his own little way, he had a very good sense of humor and he showed that in his first picture and they definitely thought he had talent."

In 1934 Hawks cast his second cousin, Carole Lombard, opposite John Barrymore in *Twentieth Century*. He coached her into becoming one of the finest screwball comediennes in Hollywood. In 1938 he directed Cary Grant and Katharine Hepburn in *Bringing Up Baby*. Two years later he made *His Girl Friday* and became the premiere director of screwball comedies. In 1944 he cast another young star with a veteran actor with much of the same success he achieved in *Twentieth Century*. Lauren Bacall started her career opposite Humphrey Bogart in Hawks's *To Have and Have Not*. Hawks wrote her famous line, "If you want anything, just whistle. You know how to whistle don't you? Just put your lips together and blow." He directed Bogart and Bacall again in 1946 in Raymond Chandler's *The Big Sleep*. Hawks said of the film, "I never figured out what was going on, but I thought that the basic thing had great scenes in it and it was good entertainment."

In 1936 Hawks directed *Come and Get It*, starring Frances Farmer and Edward Arnold. The film was based on an Edna Ferber novel that was partially inspired by the life of Hawks's grandfather. Near the end of the filming, Hawks clashed with Samuel Goldwyn and was fired. The picture was completed by William Wyler, who received codirector credit. Hawks said of Goldwyn, "He didn't think a director should write."

Carole Lombard, Howard Hawks, and John Barrymore in *Twentieth Century* (1934).

Howard Hawks directs John Wayne and James Caan in *El Dorado* (1966).

Hawks himself was not a sentimental man, and probably for this reason his characters lack sentimentality. They face the world squarely and refuse to be controlled by external forces or influences. In his Westerns, Hawks's heroes varied from men who found fulfillment in male camaraderie and female companionship to men who were increasingly isolated and alone. He said: "I decide to make a film whenever the subject interests me. It may be auto racing or on aviation: it may be a Western or a comedy: but the major drama for me is the one which has as its subject a man in danger . . . when I made 'Red River' I thought that it might be possible to make an adult Western, for and about mature people, and not one of those about mediocre cowboys."

Hawks never won an Oscar and received only one nomination, in 1941, for *Sergeant York.* In 1974 the Academy of Motion Picture Arts and Sciences gave him a special Oscar for his work as "a master American film-maker whose creative efforts hold a distinguished place in world cinema." In 1956, in an interview for *Cahiers du Cinema,* he was asked to list his three favorite films. They were *The Dawn Patrol* (1930), *Scarface* (1932), and *Twentieth Century* (1934).

Hawks died on December 27, 1977, from complications from a fall in his home. He was married three times: to Athole Shearer Ward from 1928 to 1940, to Nancy "Slim" Gross from 1941 to 1948, and to Dee Hartford from 1953 to 1959. All three marriages ended in divorce. He was survived by four children—sons David and Gregg, daughters Barbara Campbell and Kitty Tanen, and an adopted son,

Peter Ward. At the time of his death Hawks had been making plans to return to moviemaking with a Western.

BIBLIOGRAPHY

Astor, Mary. *A Life on Film.* New York: Delacorte Press, 1967.

"Bravo Profiles Howard Hawks." A BFI production for BBC, 1997.

Calhoun, Dorothy. "Man Size." *Motion Picture* (April 1930).

Cook, Ted. "Hollywood Scandals." *New Movie Magazine* (January 1932).

Donnelly, Paul. *Fade to Black: A Book of Movie Obituaries.* London: Omnibus Press, 2000.

Goshen News, December 28, 1977.

Indianapolis News, December 28, 1977.

McCarthy, Todd. *Howard Hawks: The Grey Fox of Hollywood.* New York: Grove Press, 1997.

Meyer, William R. *Warner Brothers Directors: The Hard-boiled, the Comic, and the Weepers.* New Rochelle, N.Y.: Arlington House, 1978.

Sarris, Andrew, ed. *Interviews with Film Directors.* New York: Discus Books, 1969.

Schickel, Richard. *The Men Who Made the Movies: Interviews with Frank Capra, George Cukor, Howard Hawks, Alfred Hitchcock, Vincente Minnelli, King Victor, Raoul Walsh, and William A. Wellman.* New York: Atheneum, 1975.

Truffaut, François, and Jacques Rivette. *Cahiers du Cinema* (February 1956).

Tuska, Jon. *The American West in Film: Critical Approaches to the Western.* Westport, Conn.: Greenwood Press, 1985.

Variety, December 28, 1977.

GEORGE SEATON

From the Lone Ranger to Double Oscars

George Seaton was born on April 17, 1911, in South Bend, Indiana. He decided at an early age that he wanted to become an actor, and when his family moved to Detroit, he got a jump start on his career, joining the Jessie Bonstelle stock company. In early 1933 he heard about an audition at WXYZ in Detroit, one of the nation's premiere radio stations. The station's owner, George W. Trendle, had come up with an idea for a new radio hero—the Lone Ranger.

Seaton said, "I auditioned. I was known by those who were working in the local entertainment field. Consequently I was contacted among many others to try out for the role." Seaton won the audition and became the first voice of the Lone Ranger. Seaton also had his sights set on a writing career. He had written a play, *Together We Two*, and had given it to his agent. In July 1933 he heard that there was interest in his play as a Broadway production. Seaton immediately gave up his role as the Lone Ranger. His replacement was Earle W. Graser. When Graser was killed in an automobile accident in 1941, Brace Beemer became the Lone Ranger. Beemer began his radio career in Indianapolis in 1922.

Shortly before he left for New York, Seaton discovered that his play would not be produced. Fortunately, the head of the MGM story department read the play, and Seaton was offered a contract to write for MGM under the personal supervision of Irving Thalberg. On August 23, 1933, he left for Hollywood, beginning a writing and directing career that made him one of the most polished and professional directors in America.

One of the first productions Seaton wrote for was *Student Tour* (1934), which featured two fellow Hoosiers, Charles Butterworth and Monte Blue. In 1937 he was one of the writers for *A Day at the Races*, one of the Marx Brothers' funniest films. He moved to Columbia Studios in 1940, where he was one of three writers for *The Doctor Takes a Wife*. The producer of the film was William Perlberg. The two men decided to form a partnership, writing and producing films. This partnership lasted twenty-five years.

After a brief stay at Columbia, the partners moved to Twentieth Century Fox. At this time Fox was into musicals, and Seaton found himself writing for several of the top Fox musicals of the 1940s. These included *That Night in Rio* (1941), *Moon over Miami* (1941), *Coney Island* (1943), *Diamond Horseshoe* (1945), and *The Shocking Miss Pilgrim* (1947). He

George Seaton directing Bing Crosby, Grace Kelly, and William Holden (back to camera) in *The Country Girl* (1954).

shared directing credit with Edmund Goulding for *The Shocking Miss Pilgrim*, but received sole directing credit for *Diamond Horseshoe*. *Diamond Horseshoe* was based on Crawfordsville native Kenyon Nicholson's play, *The Barker*. Seaton rewrote it for the screen and directed it.

In 1947 Seaton wrote and directed *Miracle on 34th Street*. The original screenplay, about a department store Santa Claus who had to prove to a disbelieving little girl that he was real, was a turning point in Seaton's career. It was his best effort to date, and he was given an Academy Award for the screenplay. At age seventy-one, Edmund Gwenn also won an Oscar for his performance in the film. Seaton and Gwenn were close personal friends, and the following year Seaton adapted a novel for another film for Gwenn, *Apartment for Peggy*, which was warmly received.

Seaton was now a force in Hollywood, and he could write and direct almost anything he wished. In 1950 he adapted a play for the screen entitled *For Heaven's Sake*, working with two fellow Hoosiers, Clifton Webb and Harry Von Zell. After doing one more film for Twentieth Century Fox, he left for Paramount Studios.

Seaton's first film with Paramount was *Little Boy Lost* (1953). He was impressed with Bing Crosby's acting ability, and the next year he adapted Clifford Odet's play *The Country Girl* for the screen. Crosby was cast as an aging alcoholic actor, and Grace Kelly starred as his long-suffering wife. Crosby, Kelly, and Seaton were nominated for Oscars. Seaton won his second Oscar for writing, and Kelly won her only Oscar.

Seaton had a few successes after *The Country Girl*, notably *Teacher's Pet* (1958), which he directed but did not write, and *Airport* (1970). *Airport* was a monstrous success and started a trend for disaster films. Seaton was again nominated for an Oscar for best writing. Helen Hayes won a best supporting actress Oscar for this film.

Seaton was president of the Academy of Motion Picture Arts and Sciences from 1955 to 1957 and president of the Screen Writers Guild from 1948 to 1949. He was married to Phyllis Loughton from 1936 until his death in Beverly Hills on July 28, 1979, from cancer.

BIBLIOGRAPHY

The Internet Movie Database. http://www.imdb.com/.

Quinlan, David. *Quinlan's Film Directors.* London: B. T. Batsford, 1999.

Rothel, David. *Who Was That Masked Man? The Story of the Lone Ranger.* Rev. ed. San Diego, Calif.: A. S. Barnes, 1981.

Sennett, Ted. *Great Movie Directors.* New York: Abrams, 1986.

ROBERT WISE

The Consummate Craftsman

Robert Wise.

Who would have thought that a shy little boy born September 10, 1914, in Winchester, Indiana, who grew up in the midst of the Great Depression, would someday go to London to give a command performance for Queen Elizabeth, win four Academy Awards and the prestigious Irving Thalberg award, and become president of the Academy of Motion Picture Arts and Sciences? Robert Wise would have been the last to predict achievements such as these.

Robert Wise Jr. was the son of Robert Sr. and Olive Longenecker Wise. His family moved to Connersville when he was in junior high school. In a 1978 interview he recalled, "I worked on the high school paper in Connersville. That's where I went to school from the eighth grade on through high school. I worked on the school paper as a sports writer and I got kind of hooked on the whole journalism thing. I wanted to get into something like that. I'd worked for my father first in his meat packing plant and then in his store, and I decided right then I didn't want to get into anything where I had to deal one-on-one with the public." As his father's business began to falter during the Great Depression, Wise's hopes for a college education dimmed. However, he was able to attend Franklin College for one year on a scholarship.

At the end of his freshman year, Wise went home to Connersville, where his brother, Dave, was visiting. Dave had worked his way up at RKO, and he was in the accounting department at the studio. Dave felt he could get his brother a job if he would return with him to Hollywood.

Wise, remembering how the decision was made that brought him to Hollywood, stated, "It was decided at our family conclave that since I hadn't the money to go back for another year of college . . . there were no jobs to be had in Franklin and Dad's business was really on the rocks . . . that I should go to Los Angeles to try to earn my living."

In August 1933 Wise left Connersville for Hollywood, where Dave got him a job at RKO as a film porter. Wise gradually worked into other jobs, becoming an apprentice sound effects editor and doing some music editing. Finally, he was able to convince his superiors to let him try his hand at cutting pictures, or film editing.

Wise's first screen credit came in 1935, when he was paired with veteran sound effects editor T. K. Woods to create a ten-minute film on the South Seas out of some extra footage. He earned a $500 bonus in addition to the screen credit for *A Trip through Fijiland*. He decided he would rather work on the picture-side than the sound-side of films. He went to his boss and asked if he could become an assistant film editor. He became an assistant editor at RKO and worked on several Ginger Rogers-Fred Astaire films and on the highly acclaimed *Hunchback of Notre Dame* (1939), achieving a reputation as a very good film editor. His newly earned reputation served him well when a boy wonder named Orson Welles arrived in Hollywood. Welles was looking for a good film editor and according to Wise, "They sent me down to the old RKO Pathe studios in Culver City to meet Orson and talk to him. I did and it seemed to work because the next thing I knew I was assigned."

Thus it was that Wise became the editor of what many consider to be the greatest motion picture ever made, *Citizen Kane*. In 1941 Wise received his first Oscar nomination for film editing, but *Citizen Kane* won only one Oscar, original screenplay. After *Citizen Kane*, Welles asked Wise to edit his next film, an adaptation of Hoosier Booth Tarkington's Pulitzer Prize–winning novel, *The Magnificent Ambersons*. This landmark film involved three Hoosiers in important roles. Wise was the editor, and Richard Bennett and Anne Baxter had significant roles in the film. After the principal photography was finished, Welles left for Brazil to work on a semidocumentary and was not available for the final cut. Wise was not only given the opportunity to edit the film after it got bad reaction from preview audiences, but also was assigned to direct a few new scenes. The most substantial scene Wise directed was the death of Major Amberson. Wise now had a firm place in motion picture history, having played a crucial role on two of the most innovative films ever made.

Shortly before the release of *Citizen Kane*, Wise was sent to New York to let the RKO lawyers look at the film and suggest possible changes to lessen the chance of a lawsuit from William Randolph Hearst. *Citizen Kane* turned out to be a thinly disguised biography of the famous publisher. After the changes were made, Wise decided to stop off in Indiana on his way back to the West Coast. This was in 1940, and he had not been back to Indiana since he left in the midst of the Depression in 1933. He said:

> I had a favorite Aunt and Uncle who lived in Union City, Indiana, and that was about ten miles from Winchester where I was born. So I stopped there to visit my Aunt Dessa and Uncle Bob. I took the occasion to borrow my uncle's car and drive down to Connersville to see if I could find any of my old chums. I'll never forget, I was trying to find the president of my senior class. His family ran a tire store in Connersville, and I finally found him there, grumpy and dirty, changing a tire. He was very down-in-the-mouth, not happy with what he was doing. I had arrived in Connersville at dusk. It was midwinter and dirty and sooty and very unattractive. I didn't have much luck in finding anyone else, so I got out of town in about an hour and a half. I did enjoy visiting my relatives, but by that time California was for me.

Eventually the whole Wise family made the move to California.

It was not until 1943 that Wise was given his first chance to direct a film. *The Curse of the Cat People* had fallen behind schedule, and Wise was assigned to take over as director. He completed the film in ten days.

It was a critical and box office success. He directed two more films for producer Val Lewton at RKO and then was given the chance to direct his breakthrough film. *The Set-Up* (1949) has been called the best film about boxing ever made.

Before long, Wise gained recognition as one of the top half dozen directors in Hollywood. His 1951 science-fiction thriller, *The Day the Earth Stood Still*, is regarded as a classic in its genre. Other distinguished films followed, including *Executive Suite* (1954), *Tribute to a Bad Man* (1956), *Somebody Up There Likes Me* (1956), and *I Want to Live!* (1958). In 1959 he became a producer and director with the release of *Odds Against Tomorrow* and continued in this capacity with *West Side Story* (1961) and *The Sound of Music* (1965). He won dual Oscars (best picture and best director) for these two films. *The Sound of Music* was so successful that the industry dubbed it "The Sound of Money." *West Side Story* garnered ten Oscars.

Wise states that one of his favorite films was *The Sand Pebbles* (1966), starring Beech Grove native Steve McQueen. McQueen received his only Oscar nomination for his performance in the film. Wise came to Indiana in 1967 for the premiere of *The Sand Pebbles* at the Lyric Theater. Governor Roger Branigin proclaimed March 1, 1967, as Robert Wise Day, and Wise was named a Sagamore of the Wabash.

Wise returned the next year, 1968, to receive an honorary degree from Franklin College. He came back again in 1970 for his first Trustee in Residence Series at Franklin College and attended the Franklin College board meetings. In 1981 Wise and Indianapolis attorney Eugene Henderson were named to head a campaign to raise $10 million for Franklin College.

In 1966 Wise received the Irving G. Thalberg Memorial Award for consistently high quality of production. He has been president of the Directors Guild of America, chairman of the American Film Institute Center for Advanced Film Studies, and has received the National Medal of the Arts from the president of the United States. He was named president of the Academy of Motion Picture Arts and Sciences, serving from 1985 to 1988. Following his tenure as president, he produced several of the television productions of the award ceremonies for the Academy. In 1979, when he was honored for his body of work at the Telluride Film Festival, film historian William K. Everson remarked, "Robert Wise's well-deserved tribute brought out the point that while there are many 'artists' at work in film today, there are relatively few 'craftsmen' . . . and that Wise . . . is a master craftsman in every sense of the word."

Star Trek: The Motion Picture (1979) was the last major film Robert Wise directed. At the age of eighty-six he directed a Showtime cable television movie, *A Storm in Summer* (2000), starring Peter Falk, which aired in the spring of 2001. After he retired from directing, he was still sought out as a lecturer, adviser, and consultant. Wise died of heart failure on September 14, 2005, in Los Angeles. His place in the history of motion pictures is a secure and prominent one.

Wise returned to Connersville in 1990, when the Robert Wise Performing Arts Center at the school was named after him. In his hometown of Winchester, he is depicted in a mural of famous Randolph County natives that adorns a wall of the courthouse.

Perhaps the contribution of Wise was best summed up at the ceremony at Franklin College when he received his honorary degree of Doctor of Fine Arts: "As director-producer of some of the world's most dynamic movies, and for his versatility throughout the whole spectrum of the movie industry, Robert Wise has few peers. Hollywood's stars may catch the public's attention, but there are few persons more active, versatile, and important to the film industry than this son of Hoosier soil."

Until his death on September 14, 2005, Wise remained the unassuming Hoosier he was when he left Indiana for Hollywood. One of his fellow movie colony workers said of him, "For all his genius and success, Bob's a very shy man. Sometimes that's the way it is with giants."

BIBLIOGRAPHY

Emery, Robert J., comp. *The Directors: Take One.* New York: TV Books, 1999.

Films in Review 16 (August 1966).

Gittelson, Natalie. "Robert Wise: Mythmaker." *Harper's Bazaar* (May 1971).

Indianapolis News, February 4, 1981.

Indianapolis Star, February 5, 1981.

The Internet Movie Database. http://www.imdb.com/.

Kantor, Bernard R., Irwin R. Blacker, and Anne Kramer, eds. *Directors at Work: Interviews with American Film-makers.* New York: Funk and Wagnalls, 1970.

Leemann, Sergio. *Robert Wise on His Films: From Editing Room to Director's Chair.* Los Angeles, Calif.: Silman-James Press, 1995.

Louisville Courier-Journal, October 17, 1978.

Muncie Star Press, March 26, 2001.

Powers, James. "Dialogue on Film: Robert Wise." *American Film* (November 1975).

Sennett, Ted. *Great Movie Directors.* New York: Abrams, 1986.

Smith, David. "The New Voyage of the Starship Enterprise." *Saturday Evening Post* (June 1979).

———. "Robert Wise: A Star Trek Which Led to Star Trek." *Indianapolis Star Magazine*, February 4, 1979.

Variety, September 11, 1979.

Wakeman, John, ed. *World Film Directory.* 2 vols. New York: H. W. Wilson, 1987–88.

David and Lucy Smith with Robert Wise at Franklin College, circa 1985.

SYDNEY POLLACK
Drama Instructor, Actor, Oscar-winning Director

Sydney Pollack.

Both Lafayette and South Bend like to claim Sydney Pollack. He was born in Lafayette on July 1, 1934, the eldest son of David and Rebecca Miller Pollack. He was in elementary school when his parents moved to South Bend. He recalled his first exposure to theater was in the fifth or sixth grade in South Bend: "I remember a man who worked for the school system coming around who put on plays. I remember him being very amusing. We were gonna make up a play and put it on, and he made each one of us get up and act out something. I remember being absolutely terrified and forcing myself to sort of dive into doing this the way you would dive into the deep end of a pool or something. I also remember the exhilaration I felt from forcing myself to do it, and I think that's sort of my first memory of acting."

The theater from that point on became increasingly appealing to Pollack. His father was a pharmacist and wanted Pollack to become a dentist. He prepared to go to college to pursue that vocation, but at the last minute he convinced his father to let him study acting for two years.

Pollack went to New York and enrolled at the Neighborhood Playhouse and studied fencing, mime, dancing with Martha Graham, and acting with Sanford Meisner. Meisner shaped the careers of many well-known actors, including Hoosier Steve McQueen. The seventeen-year-old Pollack studied at the playhouse for two years, then embarked on an acting career. He was barely making a living in live television when Meisner asked him to come back to the school as a teacher. Pollack said he did it because he was in awe of the man and wanted to be close to him to observe him. For a while he balanced two careers, teaching and acting.

Through his teaching, Pollack began to get jobs as an acting coach. His big break came when John Frankenheimer asked him to coach two children for a *Playhouse 90* production of *The Turn of the Screw*, starring Ingrid Bergman. Pollack took the job with the production, and Frankenheimer called him again to work on his film *The Young Savages* (1961), which starred Burt Lancaster. Pollack and Lancaster became friends, and Lancaster was responsible for Pollack becoming a director.

Pollack said, "I had never thought about being a director. I didn't particularly want to be a director, to be honest with you. But Burt Lancaster said I should be a director. He said I should be telling people what to do, not having people tell me what to do." Lancaster set

Sydney Pollack and Dustin Hoffman in
Tootsie (1982).
©1982, COLUMBIA PICTURES INDUSTRIES, INC.

up an interview for Pollack with Lou Wasserman, who was head of the giant MCA and one of the most powerful men in the business. After the interview, Wasserman asked, "Can you move to California?" Pollack replied he could. Wasserman asked how much he would need to live on. Pollack said, "like a dope I said seventy-five dollars a week."

Pollack and his wife moved to California, where he was put under the wing of Dick Irving, a television producer. Pollack watched and learned for several months. Then he was given the opportunity to direct his first television show, *Shotgun Slade*, which had already been canceled. He proved to be a fast learner and soon was directing episodes of *Ben Casey*, *The Alfred Hitchcock Hour*, and *The Fugitive*.

By the mid-1960s Pollack had earned a reputation in television and was nominated for several Emmys. A *Ben Casey* episode was nominated for five Emmys, including best director. He was part of what he called "the second wave of directors." Robert Altman, Richard Donner, and Mark Rydell were fellow television directors at that time. Pollack's first feature film was *The Slender Thread* (1965), with Elizabeth Ashley, Sidney Poitier, and Anne Bancroft.

In 1966 Pollack directed *This Property Is Condemned* with Natalie Wood and Robert Redford. Pollack and Redford met each other while appearing in *War Hunt* (1962). They became friends and have made several films together. Pollack received his first Oscar nomination for

They Shoot Horses, Don't They? in 1969. It was the first serious role for Jane Fonda, and she was also nominated for an Oscar. The film was an international success and brought Pollack worldwide recognition.

In 1982 Pollack made a film that some say was an odd choice for him. He had always been associated with straight drama and never considered himself a comedy director. Dustin Hoffman and Larry Gelbart had a script called *Tootsie*, and they wanted Pollack to direct. Pollack did not like the script, however, so the three of them reworked it. It was not an easy film to make, and Pollack and Hoffman argued a lot, but they turned out a very entertaining film. *Tootsie* brought Pollack his second Oscar nomination for best director.

In 1985 *Out of Africa* won Pollack his first Oscar. In 1995 he did a remake of *Sabrina* because he wanted to work with Harrison Ford. He also cast Greg Kinnear of Logansport, Indiana, in his first big film role.

Most of Pollack's work highlights social and political issues, including discrimination (*The Scalphunters*, 1968), the Great Depression (*They Shoot Horses, Don't They?* 1969), Hollywood blacklisting (*The Way We Were*, 1973), commercial exploitation (*The Electric Horseman*, 1979), media exploitation (*Absence of Malice*, 1981), and feminism (*Tootsie*, 1982).

Today Pollack has his own company, Mirage, allowing him to produce films without the responsibility of directing. Some of his Mirage films are *The Fabulous Baker Boys* (1989), *Searching for Bobby Fischer* (1993), and *Sense and Sensibility* (1995). In April 2003 he acted as a host on cable television station TCM for a series of classic movies labeled *The Essentials*. He still likes to act, showing up occasionally in the NBC sitcom *Will and Grace* as Will's philandering father.

Pollack is married to the former Claire Griswold, who was once one of his acting students. They have a son and two daughters. He is a camera and hi-fi fan, collects jazz recordings, and builds his own equipment to play them on. He likes sports cars and is a licensed pilot.

BIBLIOGRAPHY

Emery, Robert J., comp. *The Directors: Take One*. New York: TV Books, 1999.

Indianapolis Star, March 28, 2003.

Sarris, Andrew, ed. *The St. James Film Directors Encyclopedia*. Detroit: Visible Ink Press, 1998.

Sennett, Ted. *Great Movie Directors*. New York: Abrams, 1986.

Wakeman, John, ed. *World Film Directors*. 2 vols. New York: H. W. Wilson, 1987–88.

CHAPTER 11

SCREENWRITERS AND NOVELISTS

As the motion picture industry grew, so did the number of nationally recognized authors in Indiana. The golden age of Indiana literature ran from the late 1880s through 1920. During that time, many Hoosier authors such as George Ade, Charles Major, George Barr McCutcheon, Meredith Nicholson, James Whitcomb Riley, Gene Stratton-Porter, Lew Wallace, and Booth Tarkington had their works made into movies.

Tarkington, born in Indianapolis (1869–1946), was so popular with the movie colony that for a while nearly everything he wrote was bought and filmed. More than fifty films have been based on Tarkington's works. His work began to appear in films as early as 1914, when he was a rising star as a popular story writer. One of his earliest film successes was *The Gentleman from Indiana* (1915), starring Dustin Farnum.

Some of Tarkington's stories were filmed two and three times. The two works of fiction for which he won the Pulitzer Prize were each filmed twice: *The Magnificent Ambersons*, 1925 and 1941, and *Alice Adams*, 1923 and 1935. The second screening of both, helped by the advent of sound, resulted in a definitive film of rare charm and taste. George Stevens directed Katharine Hepburn and Fred MacMurray in the 1935 version of *Alice Adams*, and Orson Welles directed Joseph Cotton and Hoosiers Anne Baxter and Richard Bennett in the 1941 version of *The Magnificent Ambersons*.

Tarkington liked the film medium, and almost everything he wrote for publication or for the theater proved to be easily translated to film. During the 1920s there were at least nineteen Tarkington films and one series of twelve two-reelers that Goldwyn produced based on *The Adventures and Emotions of Edgar Pomeroy*. Tarkington's Penrod and Sam stories were neatly adaptable to film, and at least four films were based on them. In 1924, when his short story, *Uncle Jack*, was about to be filmed under the title of *Pied Piper Malone*, Tarkington joined Thomas Jefferson Geraghty (who wrote the screenplay) to write subtitles so he could be on the set and around the studio during production. Tarkington and Geraghty were not strangers. Geraghty, a native of Rushville, had interviewed Tarkington and most of the golden age authors while he was editor of the *Rushville Daily Republican*.

In the August 1924 issue of *Motion Picture* magazine, there is a photo of Tarkington talking with film star Thomas Meigham. The caption states, "It is becoming more and more usual for authors and actors to meet and discuss characterizations. The photograph to the right was taken when Booth Tarkington and Thomas Meigham met to talk over the portrayal in Tarkington's 'Whispering Men,' upon which Tommy was about to begin work."

Also in 1924 Tarkington's *Monsieur Beaucaire*, which had been highly successful as a play, became a film vehicle for Rudolph Valentino. It remains one of Valentino's best films. Bob Hope was in a remake of *Beaucaire* in 1946, but it was given a campy, highly stylized treatment.

In 1943 Tarkington's novel, *Presenting Lily Mars*, was made into a very effective movie starring Judy Garland as the stagestruck heroine. *On Moonlight Bay* (1951), starring Doris Day and Gordon MacRae, and *By the Light of the Silvery Moon* (1953), again starring Doris Day were suggested by the Penrod stories.

Though not as prolific as Tarkington, Lew Wallace, born in Brookville (1827–1905), provided motion pictures with one of the most lavish and most successful movies ever made. *Ben-Hur* was first translated from the novel to a stage play starring William S. Hart. It became a silent movie blockbuster in 1925 and an Oscar-winning megahit in 1959.

Alan LeMay of Indianapolis (1899–1964) became a writer of Westerns in the late 1920s. Several of his Western stories were made into films. His *The Searchers*, filmed by John Ford in 1956, has been called "the most influential film in motion picture history" and has been consistently ranked by critics in the top twenty films of all time.

The works of Indiana writers were not confined in appeal to their home state. Their material proved popular to readers across the nation. A 1947 study by John H. Moriarty, a Purdue University librarian, found that Hoosier authors ranked second to New Yorkers in the number of best sellers produced in the previous forty years. When the golden age of Indiana literature began to fade, it was not long before new Hoosier writers appeared. Some were novelists, while others entered a new world of writing called scenario writing or screenwriting.

Following is an alphabetical listing of other Hoosiers who became screenwriters and those whose novels and/or other works have been converted to film.

CHARLES GRAHAM BAKER, *Evansville (1893-1950)*

A prolific screenwriter, Charles Graham Baker (sometimes writing under the name Leslie S. Barrows) wrote almost one hundred screenplays from 1917 until 1950. He started as a newspaper reporter and moved to Brooklyn and Manhattan before entering films as a screenwriter. He wrote a number of screenplays for early film comedian John Bunny and worked for many studios, including Fox, Universal, and Warner Brothers. In 1923 he wrote the screen adaptation of Hoosier George Barr McCutcheon's novel *The Man from Brodney's*, which starred another Hoosier, J. Warren Kerrigan. Baker produced *The Swiss Family Robinson*, *Little Men*, and *Tom Brown's School Days* in 1940 and *Valley of the Sun* in 1942.

GRETCHEN CRYER, *Indianapolis (b. 1935)*

A playwright/actress, Gretchen Cryer graduated from Spiceland High School and DePauw University. In collaboration with DePauw classmate Nancy Ford, who wrote the music, Cryer wrote the book and lyrics for a number of successful plays based on her experiences growing up in Henry County. Her most personal work is *I'm Getting My Act Together and Taking It on the Road*. Other works written with Ford include *Now Is the Time for All Good Men*, *The Last Sweet Days of Isaac*, and *Shelter*. Her son, Jon Cryer, appears on television's *Two and a Half Men*. Her daughter, Robin, has appeared with her mother in cabaret shows, and her youngest daughter, Shelley, works in theater makeup.

JIM DAVIS, *Marion (b. 1945)*

Jim Davis grew up on a small farm near Fairmount, Indiana, with his brother Dave, and twenty-five cats. He was stricken with asthma when he was four months old and spent much of his childhood and youth fighting for air. "I was thankful to survive my childhood. The only way I could get out of the house was in my imagination," he said. With little more than a pencil, paper, and his imagination, he began to create pictures, which he soon discovered were more fun when accompanied by words.

Davis was a painfully shy youngster until he discovered drama class at Fairmount High School. His drama teacher was Adeline Nall, who also taught fellow Marion native James Dean. Nall said of Davis, "He was a bit shy, but he was always smiling that precious smile." Davis managed to graduate from Ball State University with what he says was "the lowest accumulative grade point ratio in the history of the University." Nevertheless, he was president of his fraternity and a member of the student senate.

After leaving Ball State, Davis worked for a while for a Muncie advertising agency. He had always been interested in cartooning and decided to approach Muncie resident Tom Ryan, creator of *Tumbleweeds*, for a job. Davis served as Ryan's assistant from 1969 to 1978, drawing borders, thought balloons, and backgrounds, and sweeping up the office.

This experience helped Davis to understand what it took to maintain a syndicated feature. "I got more confidence," he said. "I knew I had a good enough sense of humor and a good enough hand." He decided to create his own cartoon strip. His first idea was a bug called Gnorm Gnat. Syndicators liked his drawings but informed him that bugs just weren't funny. He noticed the comic strips were full of dogs—Marmaduke, Snoopy, Fred Bassett—but no cats. He created a bumbling bachelor named Jon Arbuckle who owned a cat named Garfield.

Gretchen Cryer.

Jim Davis.

(On page 411) (Standing) James Whitcomb Riley and Meredith Nicholson; (front row) George Ade and Booth Tarkington.

(On page 411) Booth Tarkington.

(Opposite page) Lew Wallace in his study in Crawfordsville, Indiana.

Davis described the strip in the following manner: "Garfield is strictly an entertainment strip built around the strong personality of a fat, lazy, cynical cat. Garfield consciously avoids any social or political comment. My grasp of the world situation isn't that firm anyway. For years I thought OPEC was a denture adhesive."

In 1981 Davis formed PAWS Inc., the company that handles art for Garfield merchandise. Garfield products are sold worldwide. In 1982 Davis became the sixth cartoonist to have one thousand newspapers carry the strip. Today the number is more than two thousand. He has had fifteen books on the *New York Times* bestseller list, received three Emmy awards, and has served as a writer, producer, and executive producer for his television shows as well as the Garfield feature movies.

Davis lives in Albany, Indiana, where he owns five hundred acres filled with ponds, a large greenhouse, and flower-lined paths that provide pleasant walks between the buildings that house more than thirty-five employees of PAWS Inc.

BIBLIOGRAPHY

Indianapolis News, May 17, 1988.
The Internet Movie Database. http://www.imdb.com/.
Jim Davis biography, PAWS Inc.
Kaelble, Steve. "Funny Business." *Indiana Business Magazine* (June 1993).

MADELYN PUGH DAVIS, *Indianapolis (b. 1921)*

When Madelyn Pugh was growing up in Indianapolis, the couple who lived down the street had names that intrigued her. She never forgot

Madelyn Pugh with Lucille Ball and Desi Arnaz.
INDIANAPOLIS STAR, PHOTO BY TOMMY WADELTON

them, and when she and Bob Carroll Jr. were creating the *I Love Lucy* television series, she used the names of her old Indianapolis neighbors Dr. and Mrs Mertz. Pugh and Carroll made up the names Ethel and Fred.

Pugh graduated from Shortridge High School, then studied journalism at Indiana University, graduating in 1942. She applied for a job at all three of Indianapolis's daily newspapers but was not hired. She became a writer for radio station WIRE. She eventually left that job to move to Los Angeles to join her sister, who resided there. She got a staff job at CBS and met Carroll and Lucille Ball.

In 1948 Pugh began writing for Ball's radio series, *My Favorite Husband*. In 1951 Pugh and Carroll wrote the first episode of *I Love Lucy*, and Pugh continued her association with the various Lucy shows for the next twenty years. *I Love Lucy* won two Emmys for best situation comedy in 1953 and 1954, and Pugh was nominated for an Emmy in 1956 for best comedy writing. She also cowrote the screenplay for Ball's film, *Yours, Mine, and Ours* (1968).

When the television series *Alice* was floundering, the producers asked Pugh and Carroll to come in and try to save the show. Carroll jokingly said what resulted was an "attack of the Hoosiers." Pugh surrounded herself with Hoosiers. Michael Ballard from Indianapolis played a regular customer, Dave Madden from Terre Haute was Flo's boyfriend, Duane Campbell from Evansville was cast as Chuck, and Mark Berko Sommers was the warm-up announcer for the studio audience. Pugh also signed fellow Hoosier Forrest Tucker as a guest on the show.

Pugh married television producer Quinn Martin and then Richard Davis, a general surgeon. Her son is a television producer.

ISABEL DAWN, *Evansville (1905-1966)*

Isabel Dawn was a busy screenwriter from 1932 to 1954. Her works included *Lady for a Night* (1942), *Ice-Capades* (1941), *A Man Betrayed* (1941), and *The French Line* (1954).

THOMAS JEFFERSON GERAGHTY, *Rushville (1883-1945)*

A very busy screenwriter from 1917 to 1937, Thomas Jefferson Geraghty was the father of writers Maurice and Gerald Geraghty and actress Carmelita Geraghty, all born in Rushville. He was a newspaperman in Rushville. He later moved to New York City to work for the *New York Herald* and then the *New York Tribune*.

Geraghty began writing screenplays and became a friend of Douglas Fairbanks. He wrote several Fairbanks films, as well as films for W. C. Fields, Joe E. Brown, and other stars of the day. Maurice and Gerald were active screenwriters from the 1930s through the 1950s. Maurice wrote eight films in *The Falcon* mystery series, as well as several Westerns. Gerald was mostly a Western writer.

GROVER JONES, *Terre Haute (1883-1940)*

In Grover Jones's brief biography, he rather succinctly relates how he got to Hollywood: "I ran away from home in 1913, because I wanted to get into the motion picture business. I was eighteen. A banker gave me both the idea and the money. He said there was no future for a prospective writer in any small Indiana town. I went away, overlooking the fact that George Ade and Booth Tarkington were doing quite well."

Thomas Jefferson Geraghty.

Jones eventually did quite well in Hollywood, where he was a busy screenwriter from 1922 until his death in 1940. He was a close friend of fellow Hoosier screenwriter Thomas Jefferson Geraghty. He wrote the screenplay for the sophisticated romantic comedy *Trouble in Paradise* (1932) for director Ernst Lubitsch. Many consider it to be Lubitsch's greatest film. Other screenplays by Jones include *The Plainsman* (1936), *Trail of the Lonesome Pine* (1936), and *Abe Lincoln in Illinois* (1940). *The Kid from Brooklyn* (1946) was based on his screenplay, *The Milky Way* (1940). He wrote original screenplays and adapted existing works for at least eighty-eight films.

MAIBELLE HEIKES JUSTICE, *Logansport (1871–1926)*

A novelist and screenwriter, Maibelle Heikes Justice wrote several screenplays for early film stars Mary Miles Minter and Kathlyn Williams. Hoosier Edna Goodrich starred in her screenplay, *Her Husband's Honor*, in 1918. Another Hoosier, Tom Santschi, appeared in two of her screenplays, and her novel, *Durand of the Bad Lands*, was filmed twice—in 1917 with Dustin Farnum and in 1925 starring two Hoosiers, Buck Jones and Carole Lombard.

LARRY KARASZEWSKI, *South Bend (dates unknown)*

Larry Karaszewski started writing comedy sketches at the age of fourteen for a Junior Achievement television show, *Beyond Our Control*, aired on WNDU-TV in South Bend. One episode included a fake newscast reporting that the University of Notre Dame's famed Golden Dome had been stolen and a cheap replacement left behind. Calls flooded the station's switchboard.

Karaszewski later said, "I don't really feel like I went to high school. . . . I went to WNDU TV." Other *Beyond Our Control* alumni included writers Chris Webb, who wrote the screenplay for *Toy Story 2*

(1999), and Dan Waters, who wrote *Batman Returns* (1992) and *Hudson Hawk* (1991). After high school, Karaszewski worked as a cameraman for WNDU-TV and did movie reviews.

Karaszewski worked his way through college. After graduation from USC, he and his college roommate, Scott Alexander, sold their first script. He and Alexander have a number of excellent writing credits. Among them are *The People vs. Larry Flint* (1996), *Ed Wood* (1994), *That Darn Cat* (1997), *Man on the Moon* (1999), *Screwed* (also known as *Pittsburgh*) (2000), and *Agent Cody Banks* (2003). Karaszewski, his wife, and two children always try to make it home to South Bend for Christmas.

JOHN W. KRAFFT, *Indianapolis (1888-1958)*

A 1907 graduate of Manual Training High School, John W. Krafft wrote and produced the senior-class play there. He worked for the *Indianapolis News* as an editorial writer and stage and movie reviewer. Krafft began his film career at Universal, writing titles for silent films, and began contributing to magazines such as *Puck*, *Life*, *Film Fun*, and *Judge*. He moved into being a "film doctor" and scenario writer, and in 1928 he signed a contract with Cecil B. DeMille. He was with DeMille at Pathe for four years before becoming a freelancer, working on pictures for Paramount, First National, Universal, and the old Goldwyn Associated Distributors. He wrote such films as *Strange Cargo* (1929) and *Deerslayer* (1943). His last writing assignment was with *The Cisco Kid* television series in 1950. He married Emma Noble of Pendleton, Indiana, and they had two sons and a daughter. He died in Los Angeles.

BARTLETT McCORMACK, *Hammond (1898-1942)*

A writer at the beginning of sound film, Bartlett McCormack wrote at least twenty-three films from 1928 to 1951. His play, *The Racket*, was filmed twice (1928 and 1951).

JOHN McGREEVEY, *Muncie (b. 1923)*

John McGreevey is a well-traveled Hoosier. He was born in Muncie and lived in Tipton, Logansport, Bloomington, and Evansville. He attended St. Vincent Catholic School in Logansport, where he skipped from the third grade to the fifth grade. At the age of seven he wrote his first play, *The Easter Rabbit*, forcing his two sisters to perform in it with him. He graduated from Logansport High School, where he was on the debate squad, and wrote, directed, and starred in *The Debate Squad Follies of 1938*.

At Indiana University, McGreevey majored in English and dabbled in theater and radio. In his senior year, two of his plays, *Angels Alone* and *But Is It Art?* were presented by the drama department. After graduation, he found work at radio station WGBF in Evansville. He then moved to KTAR in Phoenix, where he worked for nine years as a script writer and occasionally, a reluctant announcer.

In 1952, after selling a half dozen television scripts, McGreevey realized he could move to Hollywood or New York. He chose New York City and worked as a writer during television's golden age. He wrote for such shows as *The Web*, *Suspense*, *Circle Theatre*, *Philco Television Playhouse*, and *Studio One*. By 1955 live television was fading, and he moved to Hollywood. Since then he has written more than four hundred shows for such programs as *Wagon Train*, *Laredo*, *Zane Grey Theater*, *My Three Sons*, *Family Affair*, and others.

In the 1970s McGreevey began writing specials. He wrote *The Woman I Love*, about the abdication of King Edward VIII, and *A Man Whose Name Was John*, based on the life of Pope John XXIII. He began to write for *The Waltons* television series and won an Emmy for the episode "The Easter Story." He received his widest acclaim for *Judge Horton and the Scottsboro Boys*, the story of the wrongful conviction of a group of black men for the rape of two white women in Alabama in the 1930s. The show won four Christopher awards, the Silver Gavel from the American Bar Association, the Peabody award, and an Emmy, Writers Guild, and NAACP Image nominations.

"Today," McGreevey says, "it's getting harder and harder to get good things on." He has concentrated lately on docudramas, including *Ruby and Oswald* (1978), which he wrote with his son, Michael, an actor/writer. *The Disappearance of Aimee* (1976) starred Faye Dunaway and Bette Davis, and *Little Mo* (1978) was the story of tennis great Maureen Connolly. *Roots: The Next Generation* (1979), *Murder in Texas* (1981), and *Charles & Diana: A Royal Love Story* (1982) are a few of his better-known efforts.

DALE MESSICK, *South Bend (1906–2005)*

Dale (Dalia) Messick was neither a novelist nor a screenwriter, but her work served as the basis for several screenplays. She holds the distinction of being America's first woman syndicated comic strip writer/artist. She has been called "the most important woman cartoonist of the 20th century." She changed her name from Dalia to Dale because she said, "If I sent in my stuff and they knew I was a woman they wouldn't even look at it." After many tries, she finally created a winner. She based the character, Brenda Starr, on her favorite actress, Rita Hayworth: "Like Hayworth, she was feisty, dauntless, unabashedly sexy, and had this gorgeous red hair that could go through any sort of adventure and look great." The strip drew readership from both sexes and became very popular. The movie industry took notice, and at least three films were based on her creation. In 1945 a thirteen-episode serial based on the character was released. In 1976 a television movie was produced, starring Jill St. John as Brenda. In 1989 Brooke Shields had the title role in a feature film based on the character. In 2004 the Brenda Starr strip was sixty-three years old, and Dale Messick was ninety-eight. Messick died on May 4, 2005.

PAUL OSBORN, *Evansville (1901–1988)*

Much in demand as a screenwriter, Paul Osborn also was a playwright. His play, *On Borrowed Time* (1939), became a successful movie starring Lionel Barrymore. While writing the screenplay for *East of Eden* (1955), he suggested that director Elia Kazan take a look at a promising young actor he had just seen in a play. Kazan went to see the actor, and James Dean was given his first major screen role. Osborn also wrote screenplays for such hit movies as *Sayonara* (1957) and *The World of Suzie Wong* (1960).

ANGELO PIZZO, *Bloomington (b. 1948)*

An Indiana University graduate, Angelo Pizzo writes mostly in conjunction with fellow Hoosier director David Anspaugh. Their collaboration produced such films as *Hoosiers* (1986) and *Rudy* (1993). In 2004 they teamed up again for *The Game of Their Lives*, a film about the 1950 United States soccer team, a group of underdogs.

RAYMOND SCHROCK, *Goshen (1892–1945)*

An early screenwriter, Raymond Schrock wrote for 121 films from 1915 to 1950. He was one of several writers credited with writing Lon Chaney's *Phantom of the Opera* (1925). He wrote many of the better B movies, such as *Crime Doctor's Gamble* (1947) and *The Secret of the Whistler* (1946).

ROBERT H. SHANKS, *Lebanon (b. 1932)*

A 1954 Indiana University theater graduate, Robert H. Shanks won three Emmys and was an executive with all three of the major networks. He created *Good Morning America*, *20-20*, and *The Great American Dream Machine*. He has written three books, as well as plays for television and the movies.

JERI SUER TAYLOR, *Evansville (b. 1938)*

Jeri Suer Taylor lived in several Indiana towns before moving to Wilmington, Ohio, where she went to Wilmington High School, graduating in 1955 as valedictorian of her class.

Taylor's mother taught mathematics at Indiana University–Purdue University at Indianapolis for many years. It was only natural then that Taylor should enroll at Indiana University. Taylor was the cocreator and executive producer of *Star Trek: The Next Generation* and *Star Trek: Voyager*. While a student in 1959, she met and married sports announcer Dick Enberg. They were divorced in 1973. She is the mother of Alexander Enberg, an actor and producer.

Jeri Suer Taylor.

STEVE TESICH, *Yugoslavia (1942–1996)*

Born in Yugoslavia, but raised in Bloomington, Steve Tesich wrote the screenplay for *Breaking Away* (1979). This led to a successful career in screenwriting, and he wrote such films as *Eyewitness* (1981), *The World According to Garp* (1982), *Four Friends* (1981), and *American Flyers* (1985).

DANIEL WATERS, *Cleveland, Ohio (b. 1963)*

With Larry Karaszewski and Chris Webb, Daniel Waters started out writing for a Junior Achievement television show, *Beyond Our Control*, on WNDU-TV in South Bend. All three went on to be very successful writers. He has written for such films as *Heathers* (1989), *Hudson Hawk* (1991), *Batman Returns* (1992), *Demolition Man* (1993), and *Happy Campers* (2001).

CHRIS WEBB, *South Bend (dates unknown)*

A high school friend of Larry Karaszewski and Daniel Waters, Chris Webb was part of a triumvirate who went on to become successful screenwriters. He wrote the screenplays for *Toy Story 2* (1999) and the television series *Duckman* (1994).

Steve Tesich.
©TWENTIETH CENTURY-FOX FILM CORP.

WILLIAM H. WRIGHT, *Lawrenceburg (1902–1980)*

An Indiana University graduate, William H. Wright began his career in silent films. He started as a reporter for the *Cincinnati Post* and then worked for the *Indianapolis Star*. He became an exploitation man for Paramount Pictures and began to aid in the production of such films as *Anna Karenina*, *A Tale of Two Cities* (both 1935), *The Prisoner of Zenda* (1937), *The Young in Heart* (1938), and *The Adventures of Tom Sawyer* (1938). He began freelance writing and was elevated to producer for such films as *The Bride Goes Wild* (1948), *Stars in My Crown* (1950), *The People Against O'Hara* (1951), and fellow Hoosier Red Skelton's *The Clown* (1953). In the 1960s Wright became involved with television and wrote and produced many of *The Dick Powell Theatre* shows.

GEORGE ADE, Kentland (1866–1944)

George Ade was known as "The Aesop of Indiana," and his *Fables in Slang* became a popular source for early films. More than ninety short films were based on his fables. Sixteen of his plays were produced on Broadway, and at least fourteen feature films were based on his writings. He even served as the director for five of his films in 1914 and 1915.

Ade was the youngest of seven children born to John and Adaline Bush Ade. He was an avid reader and did not care for the work on his parents' farm. He entered Purdue University in 1887, where he became a lifelong friend of Hoosier cartoonist John T. McCutcheon. After graduation, Ade became a reporter for the *Lafayette Call* and then moved to the *Chicago Morning News*, where he started a column, "Stories of the Streets and of the Town," illustrated by McCutcheon. This series became the basis for *Fables in Slang*, which was published in 1899 and became an immediate hit. Ade wrote such Broadway hits as *The Sultan of Sulu* (1902–3), *Peggy from Paris* (1903), and *The College Widow* (1904). The latter play was set in Crawfordsville on the Wabash College campus. He was also a composer and lyricist, as witnessed by at least one play for which he wrote the music, lyrics, and the book. *The Night of the Fourth* premiered on Broadway in 1901. He wrote the lyrics and book for three other Broadway musicals and wrote the libretto for *The Sho-Gun* (1904).

As Ade became financially secure, he built a large home near Brook, Indiana, which he named Hazelden. Ade hosted many celebrities at Hazelden. It was a campaign stop in 1908 for William Howard Taft. He was a generous supporter of Purdue University, and his gifts resulted in the building of the Ross-Ade football stadium. He died in Brook on May 16, 1944.

George Ade.
INDIANA HISTORICAL SOCIETY

JAMES SOLOMON BARCUS, Sullivan County (1863–1920)

An author and publisher, James Solomon Barcus was a fervent Republican. He was elected to the state senate in 1902 and in 1896 wrote *The Boomerang*, a satirical analysis of William Jennings Bryan. He bought the *Terre Haute Gazette* in 1904 and merged it with the *Tribune*. He devised Publisher's Clearing House to allow institutions to buy book sets on the installment plan. On April 13, 1914, *The Governor's Boss*, an original play by Barcus, opened on Broadway. It was made into a movie in 1915 with Terre Haute native Edward Roseman as one of the stars.

GENE BREWER, Muncie (b. 1937)

A native of Muncie and a graduate of DePauw University, Gene Brewer studied DNA replication and cell division at several major universities. His 1995 novel *K-PAX* was transferred to the screen in 2001 and starred Kevin Spacey and Jeff Bridges. Brewer served as associate producer on the film. The novel's sequel, *On a Beam of Light*, was published in March 2001. It takes place five years after Robert Porter went into a catatonic state. He awakens to find himself Prot again. The third and last of the trilogy, *K-PAX III: The Worlds of Prot*, was published in 2002.

MEGGIN PATRICIA CABOT, Bloomington (b. 1966)

While a student at Bloomington High School South, Meg Cabot used to escape to the Monroe County Library, where she would read historical novels. She went to the library because the family home on

Meggin Patricia Cabot.

Ballantine Road was not air conditioned. "I did tons of reading there. We used to go every day or every other day. We were the nerds at the library."

After years of rejection notices, Cabot finally broke into the publishing world when St. Martin's Press published her steamy romance novel, *Where Roses Grow Wild* (1998). Since then she has written more than twenty-five books under several different names, but it was her *Princess Diaries* series that brought her success. After the success of the first *Princess Diaries* book, Disney offered Cabot an amount in the mid-six figure range for the film rights to her story about a city teenager who learns she is the heir to the throne of a small country.

The film, starring Anne Hathaway and Julie Andrews, brought in more than $22 million its first week in theaters in 2001. *Princess Diaries 2: Royal Engagement* was released in 2004.

ELMER HOLMES DAVIS, *Aurora (1890–1958)*

During his lifetime Elmer Holmes Davis was showered with awards, including three honorary doctorates. He was president of the Authors League of America, one of the founders of Americans for Democratic Action, and was appointed by President Franklin D. Roosevelt to head the Office of War Information. He wrote nineteen books, both fiction and nonfiction. He was an internationally known radio commentator who was every bit as influential as his colleagues H. V. Kaltenborn, Raymond Gram Swing, Gabriel Heatter, Fulton Lewis Jr., and Edward R. Murrow.

Davis was the only child of Elam Davis, a bank cashier, and his second wife, Louise, a teacher at Aurora High School and later its principal. Davis excelled in school, and at sixteen he entered Franklin College, graduating magna cum laude and winning a Rhodes scholarship to Oxford University. During his days at Oxford, he traveled extensively throughout Europe. While in Paris he met another American student, Florence MacMillan. They discovered they shared the same birthday, January 13, and so began a four-year courtship, during which Davis always sent MacMillan thirteen roses on her birthday.

Davis returned to Indiana in 1913, when he was informed his father was seriously ill. However, his father died before he arrived. He took his widowed mother and moved to New York City, where he got a job on the editorial staff of *Adventure* magazine. In 1914 he became a reporter for the *New York Times.*

Davis turned out several best-selling novels, four of which became motion pictures. *Times Have Changed* was brought to the screen in 1923. In 1925 his novel, *I'll Show You the Town*, was filmed. Raymond Schrock from Goshen, Indiana, was the screenwriter on the latter film. In 1934 his 1925 novel, *Friends of Mr. Sweeney*, was filmed, and *My American Wife* became a film in 1936.

Elmer Holmes Davis.

LLOYD C. DOUGLAS, *Columbia City (1877–1951)*

Lloyd C. Douglas had an amazing literary career. For more than twenty years his novels appeared regularly on best-seller lists. He not only proved himself a master of the entertaining and thrilling narrative, but gave readers something worthwhile to think about.

The son of a country parson, Douglas emulated his father and became a clergyman. He was a solemn, moody, and lonely child, and it was his mother who pointed him in the direction of becoming a

Theodore Dreiser.

minister. After attending schools in towns that his father served, he worked his way through Wittenberg College and Seminary in Spring-field, Ohio. Following his ordination as a Lutheran minister, he married Bessie Porch in 1904. They had two daughters.

From 1903 to 1911 Douglas filled Lutheran pastorates in Indi-ana, Ohio, and Washington, D.C. He served as director of religious work at the University of Illinois for four years. From 1915 to 1933 he officiated at Congregational churches in Ann Arbor, Michigan; Los Angeles; and Montreal, Canada. He never stated why he changed denominations. His sermons were marked by a lively narrative style and found their way into print as a collection of religious essays. While working on another such volume, he decided to incorporate his ideas into fiction in the hope of reaching a larger audience. His first novel,

Magnificent Obsession, is the story of a rich playboy whose life is saved at the cost of another's. The hero undergoes a spiritual transformation that occurs in virtually all of Douglas's stories.

Magnificent Obsession was rejected by two major houses, but was published in 1929 by Willett, Clark and Colby, a small firm that specialized in religious writings. It grew slowly and finally in 1932 it became a best seller. It eventually sold three million copies and was filmed in 1935, starring Irene Dunne and Robert Taylor. It was remade in 1954 starring Rock Hudson and Jane Wyman. Douglas quit the ministry to become a full-time writer. Willett sold the rights to the book to Houghton Mifflin, which published all of Douglas's subsequent works.

Douglas's next two works, *Forgive Us Our Trespasses* (1932) and *Precious Jeopardy* (1933), sold well, and his fourth, *Green Light*, was the top-selling novel of 1935. He was now the most popular novelist in America. He wrote *White Banners* in 1936, *Home for Christmas* in 1937, and *Doctor Hudson's Secret Journal* and *Disputed Passage* in 1939. The climax of Douglas's literary career was *The Robe*, which was on the best-seller lists from 1942 through 1945, selling more than 3,300,000 copies.

The film of *The Robe* was released in 1953 with Jean Simmons, Richard Burton, and Victor Mature. Other films based on Douglas's works include *The Green Light* (1937), starring Errol Flynn and Anita Louise; *White Banners* (1938), starring Claude Rains and Fay Bainter; *The Big Fisherman* (1959), starring Howard Keel and Susan Kohner; and *Demetrius and the Gladiators* (1954), a sequel based on *The Robe*. He also wrote the story for *Disputed Passage* (1939), starring Dorothy Lamour and Akim Tamiroff. *Dr. Hudson's Secret Journal* (1956) was a television series based on his work.

On June 18, 1938, Douglas returned to his birthplace for the movie premiere of *White Banners*. Columbia City welcomed its distinguished son with a parade through Main Street. Douglas visited the house where he was born and the church where his father preached. He autographed books and posed for pictures with the townspeople. His mother, who was ninety at that time, was present for the festivities. She was still writing a weekly column for the *Monroeville Breeze*.

Douglas died on February 13, 1951, in Los Angeles.

THEODORE DREISER, *Terre Haute (1871–1945)*

As a novelist and journalist, Theodore Dreiser had a major impact on American society in the 1920s and 1930s. Beyond this, he had an interest in contributing to another area of American popular culture—the motion picture. In 1914 he tried to sell a screenplay entitled *The Born Thief* to Pathe. In September 1915 he considered the possibility of becoming a "scenario director" for a new company, Mirror Films Inc.

On November 14, 1919, Dreiser visited the Famous Players-Lasky Studios in Hollywood but was refused admission. He went back on December 30 and met with Jesse L. Lasky, who rejected Dreiser's ideas for scenarios. It is no wonder that after this series of events, Dreiser developed a critical stance toward the motion picture industry.

Herman Theodore Dreiser was the second youngest of thirteen children. One of his brothers, Paul, changed his name to Dresser and became a very successful composer of popular songs. In the mid-1890s Dreiser moved to New York, and with Dresser's help got a job as the editor of *Ev'ry Month*, a magazine that promoted songs by a company partially owned by Dresser.

Marilyn Durham.
INDIANA PICTURE COLLECTION, MANUSCRIPT SECTION,
INDIANA STATE LIBRARY

On one of his visits to Hollywood in 1919, Dreiser met Helen Richardson, who was a bit player and an extra in films, mostly comedies. She had been formerly married to an actor named Frank Richardson. Dreiser had married Sara White in 1899 but stopped living with her in 1914. Richardson and Dreiser started living together in 1939. They finally married in 1944 after Dreiser's wife's death.

In 1926 Paramount Pictures paid Dreiser eighty thousand dollars for the rights to film *An American Tragedy*, but it was not until 1930 that they became serious about filming the novel. The first attempt to film *An American Tragedy* was as a sixteen-reel silent film directed by Russian director Sergei Eisenstein. It would be Eisenstein's first American film. The Paramount moguls, however, found the script to be a "monstrous challenge" and dropped the project. When the project was revived as a talkie with Joseph von Sternberg as the director, Dreiser collected a further $55,000 for the sound rights. A new script was written, which did not please Dreiser. He felt it mistakenly portrayed the killer as a "sex-starved idle loafer." Dreiser traveled to Hollywood, met with von Sternberg, made some script alterations, and left. The film was made, and Dreiser loathed it. He tried to stop its distribution and took Paramount to court, but the judge ruled in favor of the studio.

Dreiser's works were translated to the screen seven times from 1931 to 1959. In 1951 *An American Tragedy* was remade as *A Place in the Sun*. The film won two Oscars, one for George Stevens as director and one for best screenplay.

However, Dreiser did not get to see this last version of his novel. He died of a heart attack on December 28, 1945, and was interred at Forest Lawn in Glendale, California.

MARILYN DURHAM, *Evansville (b. 1930)*

Marilyn Wall was the daughter of Russell and Stacy Birdsall Wall, she attended Evansville College (now the University of Evansville), and married Kilburn Durham in 1950. One night she announced to her husband that she could write a better book than some of those she had been spending her time reading, and she wrote *The Man Who Loved Cat Dancing*. It was published in 1972 and became a best seller, winning the Fiction Award from the Society of Midland Authors. In 1973 it became a movie, starring Burt Reynolds and Sarah Miles. Durham has written two other novels, *Dutch Uncle* (1973) and *Flambard's Confession* (1982).

EDWARD EGGLESTON, *Vevay (1837–1902)*

Edward Eggleston's book *The Hoosier Schoolmaster* was made into a film three times: 1914, 1924, and 1935. *The Hoosier Schoolboy* was filmed in 1937.

PEGGY GOODIN, *Bluffton (b. 1923)*

Two of Peggy Goodin's novels were made into films. *Mickey* (1948) starred Hoosier Lois Butler, and *Take Care of My Little Girl* (1951) starred Jeanne Crain.

GORDON GORDON, *Anderson (1912–2004)*

With his wife, Mildred, Gordon Gordon wrote *The Undercover Cat*, which was filmed in 1965 as *That Darn Cat*. At least five films have been based on their writings.

Edward Eggleston.
INDIANA HISTORICAL SOCIETY, C6254

ALFRED BERTRAM GUTHRIE JR., *Bedford (1901–1991)*

Alfred Bertram Guthrie Jr.'s first novel, *The Big Sky* (1947), was an immediate success. His next book, *The Way West*, won a Pulitzer Prize for fiction. In 1953 he wrote the screenplay for *Shane*. This movie garnered him an Oscar nomination for best screenplay. He also wrote the screenplay for *The Kentuckian* (1955).

BERTITA HARDING, *Nuremburg, Germany (1902–1971)*

Bertita Carla Camille Leonarz came to Indianapolis in 1926 and was married to Jack Ellison de Harding the same year. When Harding died in 1954, she married Count Josef Radetsky Von Radetz, but later divorced him. In addition to authoring novels, she was a pianist and a lecturer. She lived in Indianapolis from 1926 to 1954.

Harding's novel *The Phantom Crown: The Story of Maximilian and Carlota of Mexico* was filmed in 1939 under the title *Juarez*. It starred Paul Muni, Bette Davis, Brian Aherne, and Claude Rains. Her novel *Magic Fire* was filmed in 1956. It starred Yvonne De Carlo and Rita Gam. Harding was cowriter of the screenplays for both films.

JOSEPH HAYES, *Indianapolis (b. 1918)*

At Arsenal Technical High School in Indianapolis, Joseph Hayes got his writing start and met his wife Marrijane Johnston. In 1941 he and Johnston moved to New York City, where he became an assistant editor for Samuel French, publisher of plays. He and Johnston were inspired and began to write plays, turning out some vehicles for amateur and stock productions. They were so successful that they decided to go freelance in 1943.

In the years that followed, Hayes wrote stories that were published in *Colliers*, *Woman's Home Companion*, and *Redbook*. He also wrote for radio and television. In 1948 he won first prize in the Charles H. Sengel play contest for *Leaf and Bough*. It later was produced on Broadway.

When their son became ill, the couple decided to spend the winter in Florida. While there Hayes killed time writing what was to be his first novel. The title of the novel was his wife's suggestion—*The Desperate Hours*. The setting for the novel was Kessler Boulevard in Indianapolis. It became a best seller, and Hayes converted it to a play. It was a Broadway hit, winning the 1955 Tony for best drama. In 1955 he wrote a screenplay of the novel, and it was released that year with an all-star cast that included Humphrey Bogart, Frederic March, Martha Scott, and Arthur Kennedy. It was directed by the legendary William Wellman.

Hayes was now a well-known writer. He had several other novels converted to the screen. *Bon Voyage* and *Terror after Midnight* both became films in 1962. *The Third Day* was a film in 1965, and *The Desperate Hours* was remade in 1990, starring Mickey Rourke, Anthony Hopkins, and Mimi Rogers.

ANNIE FELLOWS JOHNSTON, *Evansville (1863–1931)*

After the death of her husband, the Reverend Albion Fellows, a Methodist minister, Mary Erskine Fellows took her three daughters to her father's farm in McCutchanville, Indiana, near Evansville. They grew up on that farm with ten cousins all living nearby. Annie Fellows remembered her mother saying, "I have always wanted to write a book, but the leisure has come too late. You must do it for me."

Book cover for Annie Fellows Johnston's *Mary Ware's Promised Land.*

Emily Kimbrough.
THE INNOCENTS FROM INDIANA (N.Y.: HARPER, 1950)

Ross Lockridge Jr. At the top of the photo, peering at Lockridge, is the author, David L. Smith, when he was a teenage employee at L. S. Ayres & Co.
INDIANAPOLIS STAR

Charles Major.
INDIANA HISTORICAL SOCIETY, C191

When Annie was sixteen and her sister Albion was fourteen, they had poems published in a publication called *Gems of Poetry*. Annie's poem, "Apple Blossoms," won seventy-five cents, her first payment for her work. She was soon contributing to *Harper's Weekly* and other magazines of the day. She attended the University of Iowa for one year (1881–82). She married her mother's cousin, Will Johnston, and when he died after three years of marriage, she supported herself and her three stepchildren with her writing. In 1893 she published her first book, *Big Brother*, based on her experience one summer in Iowa with her sister. Her second book, *Joel*, won a prize of one thousand dollars.

While visiting with her stepchildren in Pewee Valley, Kentucky, she was inspired by its antebellum atmosphere and the relationship between an old colonel and his ill-tempered granddaughter. Johnston's *Little Colonel* series sold more than a million copies. In 1935 her heroine came to life in the person of child actress Shirley Temple, who at that time was at the peak of her career. In addition to Temple, *The Little Colonel* series starred Lionel Barrymore, Evelyn Venable, and Bill Robinson.

EMILY KIMBROUGH, *Muncie (1899–1989)*

When Emily Kimbrough graduated from Bryn Mawr College, she embarked on a voyage to England and France with her best friend, Cornelia Otis Skinner. Upon their return, they wrote about their adventures in a novel entitled *Our Hearts Were Young and Gay*. In 1944 their novel became a film with Diana Lynn as Kimbrough and Gail Russell as Otis Skinner. A 1946 sequel, *Our Hearts Were Growing Up*, also featuring Lynn and Russell, was written by studio writers but retained the Kimbrough and Otis Skinner characters. In 1959 a television series, *The Girls*, was based on the two movies. Kimbrough also wrote *How Dear to My Heart* about her childhood in Muncie.

FREDERICK LANDIS, *Logansport (dates unknown)*

Frederick Landis was a lawyer and an ex-congressman. He wrote *The Glory of His Country*, which was made into a film in 1920 under the title *The Copperhead*, starring Lionel Barrymore.

ROSS LOCKRIDGE JR., *Bloomington (1914–1948)*

The son of a historian father and a psychologist mother, Ross Lockridge Jr. began writing a novel in 1941 based in part on his mother's side of the family. *Raintree County* was published in 1948 and became a big-budget movie in 1957, starring Montgomery Clift and Elizabeth Taylor. Lockridge committed suicide on March 6, 1948, one day before his novel was announced the number-one best seller.

CHARLES MAJOR, *Shelbyville (1856–1913)*

Charles Major's novel *When Knighthood Was in Flower* was filmed three times in 1908, 1922, and 1953 (which was re-titled *The Sword and the Rose*). His novel *Sweet Alyssum*, a story of Indiana oil fields, was filmed in 1915 and starred Tyrone Power Sr. and Kathlyn Williams. *Yolanda* was filmed in 1924 with Marion Davies.

GEORGE BARR McCUTCHEON, *Lafayette (1866–1928)*

Twenty-six films have been based on George Barr McCutcheon's work. He appears to be second only to Booth Tarkington in the number of films made from his works. *Brewster's Millions* has been made into a motion picture six times, 1914, 1921, 1926, 1945, 1961, and 1985. McCutcheon's novel *Graustark* was filmed in 1915 and 1925. In 1926 *Beverly of Graustark* was filmed, starring Marion Davies and Antonio Moreno.

RUTH McKENNEY, *Mishawaka (1911–1972)*

Ruth McKenney's short stories in *The New Yorker* were the basis for the film *My Sister Eileen* (1942). It was filmed again in 1955. Three other stories by McKenney that were made into films were *San Diego I Love You* (1944), *Margie* (1946), and *Song of Surrender* (1949).

CHARLES BRUCE MILLHOLLAND, *Economy (1903–1991)*

Charles Bruce Millholland wrote a play based on his experiences on the Twentieth Century Limited train. He called it *Napoleon of Broadway.* Charles MacArthur and Ben Hecht liked the script, reworked it, and retitled it *Twentieth Century.* It was made into the 1934 classic film with Carole Lombard and John Barrymore, directed by Hoosier Howard Hawks. It has been on Broadway at least three times and has been rewritten as a musical. Indiana University graduate Kevin Kline won a Tony for best featured actor in a musical for his role in *On the Twentieth Century* in 1978.

KENYON NICHOLSON, *Crawfordsville (1894–1986)*

Kenyon Nicholson was a novelist, playwright, and screenwriter. He was the son of Thomas Brown and Anne Kenyon Nicholson. He graduated from Wabash College in 1917 and served in Europe during World War I. He worked as a press agent in Indianapolis and taught dramatic composition at the extension division of Columbia University. In 1924 he married Lucile Nikolas. By the middle of the 1920s he was actively writing and producing plays.

Nicholson's first work to be filmed was an adaptation of his novel *The Barker* in 1928. This proved to be his most successful work. It became a long-running stage play and was made into a film three times. It was entitled *Hoop-La* in 1933 and *Diamond Horseshoe* in 1945.

Nicholson wrote eighteen plays and saw his work transferred to film twenty times from 1928 to 1952.

MEREDITH M. NICHOLSON, *Crawfordsville (1866–1947)*

Meredith Nicholson was a prominent author and diplomat near the turn of the twentieth century. He was born in Crawfordsville, and his family moved to Indianapolis when he was six years old. Except for a few years in Denver, he lived in Indianapolis the rest of his life. In 1901 he became a full-time writer, and between 1903 and 1925 he turned out an average of one book each year. He also wrote essays, poetry, and one play.

The first film based on a Nicholson novel was *The Port of Missing Men* in 1914. His novel *The House of a Thousand Candles* was filmed three times. It was filmed first in 1915 as a silent film and again as a silent in 1919 under the title *Haunting Shadows.* In 1936 a sound version was made starring Phillips Holmes and Mae Clarke. *Langdon's Legacy* (1916) starred New Albany, Indiana, native J. Warren Kerrigan. Nine feature films were made based on Nicholson's novels and writings.

George Barr McCutcheon.
INDIANA PICTURE COLLECTION, MANUSCRIPT SECTION, INDIANA STATE LIBRARY

Meredith Nicholson.
INDIANA PICTURE COLLECTION, MANUSCRIPT SECTION, INDIANA STATE LIBRARY

Jeannette Covert Nolan.
GATHER YE ROSEBUDS (N.Y.: APPLETON-CENTURY CO., 1946

David Graham Phillips.
INDIANA PICTURE COLLECTION, MANUSCRIPT SECTION,
INDIANA STATE LIBRARY

Ernie Pyle.
INDIANA HISTORICAL SOCIETY PRESS

JEANNETTE COVERT NOLAN, *Evansville (1897–1974)*

One of Indiana's most prolific authors, Jeannette Covert Nolan wrote biographies of famous people, mostly for juvenile audiences. In 1946 she wrote a novel that focused on Evansville in 1910 titled *Gather Ye Rosebuds*. It was filmed under the title *Isn't It Romantic?* in 1948, starring Veronica Lake, Mona Freeman, and Patrick Knowles. Unfortunately, Nolan's story was barely recognizable. Nolan's son, Tom, is an actor in Hollywood.

DAVID GRAHAM PHILLIPS *(pen name: John Graham), Madison (1867–1911)*

David Graham Phillips was educated in the public schools in Madison. He attended Asbury College (present-day DePauw University), but left without graduating and entered Princeton University. He graduated from Princeton with a degree in journalism and quickly rose to the top in New York City's competitive newspaper industry.

Phillips's stories were published by the *Saturday Evening Post* and other important publications. However, he yearned to be a novelist. His first novel was *The Great God Success*, published in 1901. Other novels included *The Cost*, *The Plum Tree*, *The Second Generation*, and *The Husband's Story*.

Phillips's novels were mostly about society's ills and political corruption. Late in the summer of 1910 he received anonymous threatening letters condemning him for his cynical depiction of American society women. The author of the letters was Fitzhugh Colye Goldsborough, a member of an old and well-known Washington family, who imagined that the leading character in Phillips's novel, *The Fashionable Adventures of Joshua Craig*, was a caricature of his sister. Phillips, however, had never heard of the Goldsborough family.

On the afternoon of January 23, 1911, Goldsborough accosted Phillips as he took his customary walk through Gramercy Park and shot him five times and then shot himself. Phillips died the next night. His novel *Susan Lenox: Her Rise and Fall* was published posthumously in 1917 and opened on Broadway as a play in 1920. Hoosier Robert T. Haines was the leading man. In 1931 it was made into a film starring Greta Garbo and Clark Gable.

ERNIE PYLE, *Dana (1900–1945)*

Adela Rogers St. John said of Ernie Pyle, "'Unpack your heart,' Ernie Pyle said, and so no other newspaperman or broadcaster of our generation has come anywhere near him in readership and influence. We must not forget. They had to give him the Pulitzer Prize, practically by public demand."

Pyle attended Indiana University, studying journalism, and then became a newspaper reporter and a war correspondent. He wrote several books about World War II. The film *Story of G.I. Joe* (1945) was based on several of his writings. He was killed in action in the Pacific near the end of the war.

JEAN SHEPHERD, *Chicago (1921–1999)*

Jean Shepherd's family moved to Hammond, Indiana, when he was an infant. He grew up there, and his most famous work, *A Christmas Story* (1983), was a theatrical film based on recollections of his childhood in Hammond. A sequel to *A Christmas Story* was made into a theatrical film in 1994. It was titled *It Runs in the Family*. Shepherd wrote other feature-length productions that were made for television, including *The Star-Crossed Romance of Josephine Cosnowski* (1983), *The Phantom of the Open Hearth* (1976), *The Great American Fourth of July and Other Disasters* (1982), and *Ollie Hoopnoodle's Haven of Bliss* (1988).

FRED MUSTARD STEWART, *Anderson (b. 1932)*

Four of Fred Mustard Stewart's novels have been made into movies. *Ellis Island* was a 1984 miniseries based on his novel. *Six Weeks* in 1982 starred Dudley Moore and Mary Tyler Moore. *The Norliss Tapes* was a 1973 television movie starring Hoosier Claude Akins, Roy Thinnes, and Angie Dickenson. *The Mephisto Waltz* (1971) starred Alan Alda. Stewart is also a composer. He composed several pieces for *Ellis Island*.

REX STOUT, *Noblesville (1886–1975)*

Creator of detective Nero Wolfe, Rex Stout's novels have been made into at least nine movies and/or television shows. The movie that introduced Wolfe was *Meet Nero Wolfe* in 1936. Edward Arnold played Wolfe, and Lionel Stander played Archie. In 1969 an Italian television series was based on the character. Hoosier Anne Baxter was in a 1977 *Nero Wolfe* television movie. In 2000 *The Golden Spiders: A Nero Wolfe Mystery* was shot for television starring Maury Chaykin as Wolfe and Timothy Hutton as Archie. It later became a series.

GENE STRATTON-PORTER, *Wabash (1863–1924)*

Geneva Grace Stratton was the youngest of twelve children. Hollywood's first film of her work was a screenplay adaptation of *Freckles* in 1917, starring Jack Pickford. *Freckles* was so popular it was made into a movie four times—1928, 1935, 1960, and 1942, called *Freckles Comes Home*.

Several of Stratton-Porter's works were made into films more than once. *The Harvester* and *Keeper of the Bees* had two film treatments. *Laddie* was filmed three times. Other works made into films include *A Girl of the Limberlost*, *Michael O'Halloran*, and *The Magic Garden*. Stratton-Porter moved to Los Angeles, where she became very involved with the motion picture industry. Her daughter, Jeanette Porter Meehan, became a screenwriter. James Leo Meehan, Jeanette's husband, directed at least seven of Stratton-Porter's films, and Stratton-Porter appeared as an actress in three of her films.

Stratton-Porter died as a result of an automobile accident in Los Angeles in 1924 at the age of sixty-one.

JAMES ALEXANDER THOM, *Gosport (b. 1933)*

James Alexander Thom's novel *Follow the River* was made into a television movie in 1995 starring Ellen Burstyn. *Panther in the Sky* was made into a television movie in 1995 with the title *Tecumseh: The Last Warrior*. It was produced by Francis Ford Coppola.

KURT VONNEGUT, *Indianapolis (b. 1922)*

A graduate of Orchard School and Shortridge High School in Indianapolis, Kurt Vonnegut comes from an old Indianapolis family. His father, Kurt Vonnegut, and his mother, Mary Lieber, were both from prominent families. Vonnegut began writing at Shortridge,

Jean Shepherd.
THE AMERICA OF GEORGE ADE, 1866-1944: FABLES, SHORT STORIES, ESSAYS (N.Y.: PUTNAM, 1961)

Rex Stout at age eighty-nine.
INDIANA HISTORICAL SOCIETY CLIPPING FILE

Gene Stratton-Porter.
INDIANA HISTORICAL SOCIETY PRESS

James Alexander Thom.
INDIANA PICTURE COLLECTION, MANUSCRIPT SECTION,
INDIANA STATE LIBRARY, PHOTO BY DAVE REPP

Kurt Vonnegut.
INDIANAPOLIS STAR

Jessamyn West.
INDIANA PICTURE COLLECTION, MANUSCRIPT SECTION,
INDIANA STATE LIBRARY

serving as a reporter, columnist, and editor for the school paper, *The Daily Echo.*

Upon graduation from Shortridge, Vonnegut enrolled at Cornell University as a biochemistry major and contributed to the *Cornell Sun* as managing editor and columnist. In 1943 he enlisted in the United States Army and was sent to Carnegie Institute and the University of Tennessee for training in mechanical engineering. In 1944 his mother committed suicide, and he was captured in the Battle of the Bulge. In 1945 he was in Dresden, Germany, when it was bombed.

Vonnegut was freed in 1945 and awarded the Purple Heart. The same year he married his high school sweetheart, Jane Marie Cox. He worked steadily the next few years, publishing *The Sirens of Titan, Mother Night, Cat's Cradle,* and *God Bless You, Mr. Rosewater.* In 1967 he was awarded a Guggenheim Fellowship to go to Dresden to research *Slaughterhouse-Five.* It was published in 1969 and hit number one on the *New York Times* best-seller list, catapulting Vonnegut to national prominence.

Vonnegut began writing for television, and then his novels started to become movies. His play *Happy Birthday, Wanda June* was made into a movie in 1971. This was followed by *Slaughterhouse-Five* in 1972. Subsequently, films have been made of many of his other works, including *Slapstick* (1982), *Mother Night* (1996), and *Breakfast of Champions* (1999).

DAN WAKEFIELD, *Indianapolis (b. 1932)*

Dan Wakefield is the son of Ben H. and Brucie Ridge Wakefield and earned an A.B. degree from Columbia College in 1955. He became a news editor for the *Princeton Packet* in New Jersey and then a staff writer for *The Nation* from 1956 to 1959. He became a freelance writer in 1959.

Wakefield was a staff member of the Bread Loaf Writers Conference in 1964 and 1966 and received a short story prize from the National Council of the Arts in 1968. His novel *James at 15* was made into a television movie in 1977. His first theatrical film was of his novel *Starting Over* in 1979, starring Burt Reynolds and Jill Clayburgh. He adapted Mark Twain's *The Innocents Abroad* for television in 1983. His novel *Going All the Way* was filmed in 1997 and starred Ben Affleck, Jill Clayburgh, and Lesley Ann Warren. Wakefield also wrote the screenplay for this film.

In 2001 Wakefield's book *New York in the Fifties* was filmed as a documentary and featured the likes of Jack Kerouac, James Baldwin, and William F. Buckley. Wakefield also appeared in this film.

MARY JANE WARD, *Fairmount (1905-1966)*

Mary Jane Ward is best known for her novel *The Snake Pit.* Two years after its publication in 1946, Olivia De Havilland starred in the film version. It received six Oscar nominations. It won one for best sound recording. Among Ward's other works was *A Little Night Music,* published in 1951.

JESSAMYN WEST, *North Vernon (1902-1984)*

Much of Jessamyn West's writings used her Indiana background. The film *Friendly Persuasion* (1956) was based on her first book. West went to Hollywood and wrote the screenplay from her novel. The film, directed by William Wyler and starring Gary Cooper, was a box-office success. Acton native Marjorie Main had a major role in the film. Other screenplays by West include *The Big Country* (1958) and *Stolen Hours* (1963).

BIBLIOGRAPHY

Annie Fellows Johnson: A Short Biography. http://www.littlecolonel.com/bio.htm.

"Drama TV Highlight Alumni Day." *Indiana University Alumni Magazine* (1983).

Fang, Irving E. *Those Radio Commentators.* Ames: Iowa State University Press, 1977.

Hamilton, Ian. *Writers in Hollywood, 1915–1951.* New York: Harper and Row, 1990.

Indiana Authors and Their Books. 3 vols. Crawfordsville, Ind.: Wabash College, 1949–81.

Indianapolis News, October 8, 1978; December 1, 1983.

Indianapolis Star, April 29, 1979; February 16, 2003.

The Internet Movie Database. http://www.imdb.com/.

Kurt Vonnegut Chronology—The Vonnegut Web. http://www.duke.edu/~chr4/vonnegut/vonnrgutia/chronology.html.

La Porte Bulletin, January 26, 1911.

Leger, Jackie. "Dale Messick: A Comic Strip Life." *Animation World Magazine* (July 2000).

Lockridge, Larry. "A Brief Synopsis on Ross Lockridge, Jr." http://raintreecounty.com/synopsis.html.

Madison Courier, April 7, 1930.

Mann, Dorothea Lawrance. "The Author of the Little Colonel Series." *Publishers Weekly*, October 2, 1931.

Marilyn Durham. http://www.bsu.edu/csh/english/events/iwp/IndianaAuthors/Pages/Durham%20Marlyn.html.

Morrow, Barbara Olenyik. *From Ben-Hur to Sister Carrie: Remembering the Lives and Works of Five Indiana Authors.* Indianapolis: Guild Press of Indiana, 1995.

Munster Times, October 21, 2001.

Slide, Anthony, comp. *"They Also Wrote for the Fan Magazines": Film Articles by Literary Giants from E. E. Cummings to Eleanor Roosevelt, 1920–1939.* Jefferson, N.C.: McFarland and Company, 1992.

Terre Haute Tribune-Star, April 14, 2002.

CHAPTER 12

MUSICIANS AND COMPOSERS

Note: Some musicians became actors, thus people such as Phil Harris and Johnnie "Scat" Davis will be listed in "The Supporting Players" chapter in this book. The Jackson family can be found in "The Families" chapter.

The motion picture has occupied the center stage of our cultural imagination since its inception, and music has always served as a prime expression of our dreams and aspirations. It was no surprise then when movies began to talk, they also began to sing and dance.

The early talkies owed much to the Broadway stage, but it was not long before a unique form of entertainment emerged. Musical numbers on film began to appear that could never have been produced on a stage. Composers were in great demand to provide the music that generations would hum, sing, dance to, and be romanced to.

Hoosier composers Cole Porter, Hoagy Carmichael, and George Duning provided music for a host of films in the 1930s and 1940s. Johnnie "Scat" Davis, Phil Harris, Eddie Condon, and Claude Thornhill entertained through the 1950s and beyond. Michael Jackson, Axl Rose, Kenneth "Baby-face" Edmonds, and John Mellencamp have become icons in the world of modern music.

Some Hoosiers provided scores for films, while others wrote songs. There will always be memories associated with music from the movies. The medium has been a strong and continuing influence in popularizing music. Here are some of the Hoosiers who, through their unique musical gifts, have made significant contributions in composing and performing music for the movies.

ROSS EDWIN BARBOUR, *Burnsville (b. 1928)*

In 1947 Hal Kratzsch convinced brothers Ross and Don Barbour, along with Marvin Pruitt, to form a barbershop quartet. The four young Hoosiers were freshmen at the Arthur Jordan Conservatory of Music, which was a division of Butler University. They called themselves Hal's Harmonizers and the Toppers before eventually becoming the Four Freshmen. Ross recalled that one of their regular jobs was singing at the LVL Club three nights a week. He said, "The LVL Club was 'The Liberal View League' and they had gambling in a back room. It was raided once in awhile. It was on highway 37 on the way to Bloomington."

At the end of his freshman year, Pruitt went home to Rensselaer, Indiana, got married, and settled down. He was replaced by the Barbours' cousin, Bob Flanigan, who had just returned from army duty in Germany, and the group went on the road seeking fame and fortune. The group was one of the few vocal acts to provide its own accompaniment, and Ross served as the group's master of ceremonies, a position that he held for almost twenty-nine years.

Their first professional booking was on September 20, 1948, at the 113 Club in Fort Wayne. (At this time they were still the Toppers.) In 1950 the Four Freshmen were playing at the Esquire Lounge in Dayton, Ohio, when someone told Stan Kenton to catch the

The original Four Freshmen: Don Barbour (with guitar), Ross Barbour (left), Hal Kratzsch (right), and Bob Flanigan (top).

act. Kenton thought these four guys sounded like five-or-six-part harmony, and at the same time, they were playing a dozen instruments. Kenton was so impressed that he persuaded Capitol Records to give the group a contract in 1950.

The Freshmen's first two singles did not do well, and Capitol was considering dropping them without releasing the third single. The group managed to get a copy of the third single and asked several Detroit disc jockeys to promote a Freshmen engagement at a bowling alley called The Crest. Within a week, "Blue World" was a hit. By the fall of 1952 the Freshmen sound was known all over the world. "Mood Indigo" and "Graduation Day" were released in 1956. "Graduation Day" was later recorded in similar style by the Beach Boys. The group made more than thirty albums during the 1950s and 1960s and represented a modernizing force in close harmony quartet in American popular music, influencing many groups that followed them. The Beach Boys, the Lettermen, and the Mamas and the Papas all emulated the Four Freshmen.

The Four Freshmen recorded several tunes by fellow Hoosier Hoagy Carmichael—"Old Buttermilk Sky," "I Get Along without You Very Well," "The Nearness of You," and "The Baltimore Oriole." They appeared as themselves in *Rich, Young and Pretty* (1951) and sang "How Can I Tell Her?" on the soundtrack of *Lucy Gallant* (1955). They also made a few short films with people such as Jerry Gray and David Rose. Today they are recognized as one of the best vocal groups of their generation.

Ross Barbour said, "'The Freshmen' have earned a paycheck every week for 56 years now. There have been more than 20 young men playing and singing as 'Freshmen,' and the group is still doing what we did in 1948 . . . affecting history."

BIBLIOGRAPHY

Barbour, Ross. Interview on Hoagy Carmichael. http://www.indiana.edu/~wfiu/ross_barbour.htm.
——. Letter to the author. January 6, 2005.
——. *Now You Know: The Story of the Four Freshmen*. Lake Geneva, Wis.: Balboa Books, 1995.
——. Telephone interview with the author. January 17, 2005.
The Four Freshmen. http://www.musicweb-international.com/encyclopaedia/f/F68.HTM.
The Four Freshmen. http://www.vocalhalloffame.com/.
The Internet Movie Database. http://www.imdb.com/.
Laing, Dave. "Ross Edwin Barbour: The Four Freshman." Grove Music Online. http://www.grovemusic.com/.
Mainly A Capella . . . The Four Freshmen. http://www.a-capella.com/catalog/jazz/cat_four-freshmen.html.

JOSHUA BELL, *Bloomington (b. 1967)*

At age three, Joshua Bell tried to make music by stretching rubber bands around the handles of a dresser drawer and attempting to pluck out melodies he heard his mother playing on the piano. He said, "By opening the drawers to different degrees, I could make them play at different pitches." When he was five, his parents gave him a violin. Today he plays a $3 million Stradivarius made in 1713.

When Bell was twelve, renowned violinist Josef Gingold, a faculty member at the Indiana University School of Music, heard Bell play and

HOOSIERS IN HOLLYWOOD

decided to take him on as a pupil. At age fourteen, he won a *Seventeen* magazine/General Motors competition and attracted national attention. He made his solo debut with the Philadelphia Orchestra and began his international career as a soloist. He soon made the first of many recordings. In 2001 he won a Grammy Award for his performance of Nicholas Maw's *Violin Concerto*, a piece written for him. His performance of Leonard Bernstein's *West Side Story Suite*, for which he wrote the second cadenza, won a Grammy for best-engineered performance.

In 1998 he performed the Oscar-winning music from the motion picture *The Red Violin*. He even served as a body double—playing the violin while a naked Greta Scacchi seduced her fiddler lover. Asked how he felt, Bell blushes saying, "I don't know how to describe the scenes, but it was fun. It was a totally different experience." His album covers capitalize on his movie-star looks. *West Side Story Suite* shows Bell on a fire escape, clad in leather and jeans, his hair windblown, looking a lot like Tony thinking about Maria.

In 2004 Bell again was the featured violinist in a major feature film, *Ladies in Lavender*, which was set in 1936. Filmed in the United Kingdom, the film concerns two older women (played by Judi Dench and Maggie Smith), who find a young man washed up on the beach. They nurse him back to health and discover he is a gifted Polish violinist who is unable to speak English. Bell plays all of the violin music in the film.

Bell's personality and magnetic performance have earned him acclaim far beyond the concert hall. *People* magazine named him one of the fifty most beautiful people in the world. He has appeared on *The Tonight Show*, *Late Night with Conan O'Brien*, *The Charlie Rose Show*, CNN, CBS *This Morning*, and in his home state on the Indy 500 victory celebration on ESPN. He has appeared on *Sesame Street* and was included on a program on Mozart in the A & E *Biography* series.

A multifaceted artist, he has appeared with such musicians as James Taylor, Chick Corea, and Bobby McFerrin. Bell plays 100 to 150 concerts a year.

BIBLIOGRAPHY

Brown, Jeremy K. "Joshua Bell." *Current Biography*. Vol. 61, no. 7. July 2000.

Campbell, Margaret. "Joshua Bell." Grove Music Online. http://www.grovemusic.com/.

Indianapolis Star, July 8, 2001, November 19, 2002.

Joshua Bell Web Site. http://www.joshuabell.com/.

WALTER BULLOCK, *Shelburn (1907-1953)*

During the late 1920s and early 1930s, two young brothers, Jim and Walter Bullock, hosted a popular radio show over WFBM in Indianapolis, billing themselves as a "harmony duo." Jim was blind, a handicap he easily surmounted with his good humor and quick wit. Walter, a graduate of DePauw University, was very active in Indianapolis Civic Theater productions and was an advertising copywriter at the radio station.

The brothers left for Hollywood in 1933. In Hollywood, Walter became a continuity writer for comedian Ben Bernie. He began writing lyrics, and his first movie credit was in 1935 in the film *Coronado*, which starred singer Johnny Downs. He wrote the lyrics for one song in the movie, "I've Got Some New Shoes." His next assignment was his big break. He wrote the lyrics for the title song of *Rhythm on the Range* (1936), starring Bing Crosby and Frances Farmer. The music was composed by Richard Whiting. Bullock also wrote "Hang Up My Saddle" for the same movie with Whiting. In addition to Whiting, he also collaborated with Jule Styne and Alfred Newman.

His collaboration with Whiting resulted in an Oscar nomination for best song in 1936 for "When Did You Leave Heaven?" from *Sing, Baby, Sing.* Tony Martin sang Bullock's lyrics in the movie. Bullock was very busy in 1936, writing the lyrics for "Magnolias in the Moonlight: Who Minds about Me?" for the movie *Follow Your Heart,* starring Nelson Eddy and Jeanette McDonald. Bullock continued to write lyrics for songs featured in such films as *52nd Street* (1937), *Happy Landing* (1938), and *Sally, Irene and Mary* (1938).

In 1938 he was given the opportunity to write lyrics for a movie starring the biggest box-office attraction of the thirties, Shirley Temple. He wrote the lyrics for a song featured in *Little Miss Broadway* and sung by Jimmy Durante, "Thank You for the Use of the Hall." Temple made *Just around the Corner* in 1938, and this time Bullock wrote the score for the film along with Harold Spina.

In 1940 Bullock received another Oscar nomination for best song, "Who Am I?" from the film *Hit Parade of 1941,* which starred Frances Langford and Kenny Baker. In addition to "Who Am I?," Bullock collaborated with Jule Styne on three other songs featured in the movie: "Swing Low Sweet Rhythm," "Make Yourself at Home," and "In the Cool of the Evening."

Bullock's "In the Cool of the Evening" was also featured in 1943 in the film *Is Everybody Happy?* In 1940 he again worked on a Shirley Temple film, *The Blue Bird.* This time he was not a lyricist but a dialogue writer for the Maurice Maeterlinck play from which the film was adapted.

In the early 1940s Bullock turned to screenwriting and wrote screenplays for such popular Fox musicals as *Springtime in the Rockies* (1942), *The Gang's All Here* (1943), and "The Gift of the Magi" sequence in *O. Henry's Full House* (1952). In 1944 Bullock received his last film credit for a song in the film *Music for Millions.* The song, written especially for Jimmy Durante, was "Toscanini, Iturbi and Me."

No information could be found on the career of Walter Bullock's brother Jim, other than the fact they went to California together.

BIBLIOGRAPHY

All Movie Guide. http://www.allmovie.com/.
The ASCAP Biographical Dictionary of Composers, Authors, and Publishers. 3rd ed. New York: ASCAP, 1966.
Friedersdorf, Burk. *From Crystal to Color: WFBM.* Indianapolis: WFBM, 1964.
Hirschhorn, Clive. *The Hollywood Musical.* New York: Crown Publishing, 1981.
The Internet Movie Database. http://www.imdb.com/.

GARY BURTON, *Anderson (b. 1943)*

A self-taught vibraphonist, bandleader, and writer of music, Gary Burton made his first recording with RCA at age seventeen. He studied for two years at Berklee College of Music in Boston and joined

George Shearing's quintet in 1963. He rose to prominence as a member of Stan Getz's quartet from 1964 to 1966 and then broke away to form his own group.

In the early 1970s Burton toured Europe, Japan, and Australia. He performed duos, most notably with Chick Corea. He became a teacher on the staff of Berklee in 1971, and by the 1990s he had become dean of the curriculum there. He has published method books and *A Musician's Guide to the Road* (1981).

Burton is considered a virtuoso vibraphonist with an original style of improvisation. He has won five Grammy awards. In 1997 he played the vibes in the movie *Afterglow,* which starred Nick Nolte and Julie Christie.

BIBLIOGRAPHY

Grammy Awards. http://www.grammy.com/awards.

Gridley, Mark C. "Gary Burton." Grove Music Online. http://www.grovemusic.com/.

The Internet Movie Database. http://www.imdb.com/.

J. WILL CALLAHAN, *Columbus (1874-1946)*

J. Will Callahan wrote the words for a song that was immensely popular from 1918 through the 1950s. The popularity of the song, "Smiles," was largely the result of its introduction by a young lady who was to have distinctly Hoosier ties. Helene Davis had been a performer since age six. When General John J. Pershing asked for performers to go to Europe to entertain American troops, Davis volunteered. She was quickly accepted and began to look for appropriate songs to perform. One of her selections was an unpublished song, "Smiles," composed by Lee S. Roberts with words by Callahan. The song was a hit, and for the rest of her life she was known as "Smiles" Davis. It was easy to see how the song could appeal to soldiers overseas. Here are Callahan's words for the refrain:

> There are smiles that make us happy,
> There are smiles that make us blue,
> There are smiles that steal away the tear drops,
> As the sunbeams steal away the dew,
> There are smiles that have a tender meaning,
> That the eyes of love alone may see,
> And the smiles that fill my life with sunshine
> Are the smiles that you give to me.

Callahan's "Smiles" has been sung in at least eleven motion pictures. The first film it was featured in was *Applause* (1929) with Helen Morgan, just two years after sound was introduced. Other films in which it was heard were *Stella Dallas* (1937), *Tin Pan Alley* (1940), *Smilin' Through* (1941), *Waterloo Bridge* (1940), *For Me and My Gal* (1942), and *Somebody Loves Me* (1952).

After "Smiles," "Tell Me (Why Nights Are Lonely)," composed by Max Kortlander, was Callahan's biggest hit. In the movie *For Me and My Gal,* Judy Garland sang "Smiles," and "Tell Me" was sung by Marta (Martha) Eggerth. "Tell Me" was also featured in the film *On Moonlight Bay* (1951) and was sung by Doris Day.

BIBLIOGRAPHY

The ASCAP Biographical Dictionary of Composers, Authors, and Publishers. 3rd ed. New York: ASCAP, 1966.

Hirschhorn, Clive. *The Hollywood Musical.* New York: Crown Publishing, 1981.

The Internet Movie Database. http://www.imdb.com/.

SECONDO (CONTE) CONDOLI, *Mishawaka (1927–2001)*
PETE CONDOLI, *Mishawaka (b. 1923)*

Conte and Pete Condoli started performing together as teens in Indiana. Conte performed for a while with the Woody Herman orchestra. The brothers joined *The Tonight Show* band on NBC in the 1970s and continued with it until Johnny Carson's retirement in 1992.

Both appeared in the movie, *Bell, Book and Candle* (1958), and Pete played trumpet in *West Side Story* (1961). Conte appeared as a trumpet player in David Lynch's film, *Mulholland Drive* (2001).

BIBLIOGRAPHY

Conte Candoli obituary. *Classic Images.*

The Internet Movie Database. http://www.imdb.com/.

HOAGLAND HOWARD "HOAGY" CARMICHAEL, *Bloomington (1899–1981)*

One of the master songwriters of the twentieth century, Hoagy Carmichael has been called the most talented, inventive, sophisticated, and jazz-oriented of all the great craftsmen. His chosen lyrics and his regional songwriting frequently celebrated his small-town upbringing in Bloomington, Indiana.

Hoagland Howard Carmichael was the son of Howard Clyde and Lida Mary Robinson Carmichael. His mother was a trained pianist and acquainted her son with the rudiments of the keyboard. As a tiny child, she would take him with her to silent movies where she played the accompanying piano music. It was not long before "The Piano had me body and soul," Carmichael said. A chance meeting with black pianist Reginald Du Valle provided Carmichael with a teacher who was known as "the elder statesman of Indiana jazz." Carmichael made many trips to Du Valle's house in Indianapolis trying to figure out what he was doing. "Reggie had the new black music tricks and he made ragtime sound old hat," Carmichael recalled. "With his head hanging to one side, as if overcome with ecstasy, he'd play and play . . . and grin. 'Are you listening boy?' I would sit, absorbed, watching the movements of those crazy hands."

Although music was becoming his master, Carmichael did not ignore his education, eventually earning a law degree in 1926 from Indiana University. He left Bloomington and headed for West Palm Beach, Florida, to pursue a career as a lawyer. While there, he heard a recording of a song he wrote while a student at IU. It was called "Washboard Blues," and it was played by Red Nichols. Carmichael decided to abandon law and try his hand as a musician and songwriter. He returned to Bloomington where, on a stroll across the campus in 1927, a tune came to him. The tune was "Star Dust" (later it became one word, "Stardust"). It was recorded several

Scene from *Young Man with a Horn* (1950) with Hoagy Carmichael at the piano and Kirk Douglas playing the trumpet.

times with no lyrics. It was an unusual melody at the time because of its unconventional structure and unusual key changes. It originally was a jazz tune, but in 1929 Mitchell Parrish wrote lyrics for it, and it was introduced at the Cotton Club in Harlem. Today, it has become one of the most recorded songs in the history of music.

In 1928 Carmichael moved to Hollywood to work in motion pictures. He could find no work there, so he went to New York where he became a song plugger. The early 1930s were his most productive years. During the decade he wrote "Rockin' Chair," "Georgia on My Mind," "Lazy River," Little Old Lady," "Small Fry," "Two Sleepy People," "Heart and Soul," "I Get Along without You Very Well," "Blue Orchids," and "Hong Kong Blues." He also made a series of recordings for RCA Victor, organizing an ensemble that included the Dorsey brothers, Jack Teagarden, Gene Krupa, Benny Goodman, Joe Venuti, and Bix Beiderbecke.

Carmichael was now accepted in Hollywood and made his debut as an actor in a small cameo in *Topper* (1937). Carmichael and fellow Hoosier Howard Hawks became friends, and Hawks tapped Carmichael for the role of Cricket in *To Have and Have Not* (1944). Two of

Carmichael's songs appeared in this film, "Hong Kong Blues" and "How Little We Know." Lauren Bacall sang "How Little We Know" with Carmichael at the piano. (Contrary to popular legend, her voice was not dubbed by Andy Williams.) This role established Carmichael as a supporting actor. He went on to play similar roles in nine films.

Two Carmichael songs received Oscar nominations. In 1947 the nomination was for "Old Buttermilk Sky." It did not win. In 1952 he finally won, but it came about in a rather circuitous way. Carmichael and Johnny Mercer once wrote a complete show and film score together. It was a musical biography of silent comedy mogul Mack Sennett. The show was called *Keystone Girl*, but it was never produced. In 1951 Paramount filmed *Here Comes the Groom*, starring Bing Crosby and Jane Wyman. One of the songs from the unproduced Carmichael/Mercer show was put into the film. "In the Cool, Cool, Cool of the Evening" was sung by Crosby and Wyman, and Carmichael finally won his Oscar for best song.

BIBLIOGRAPHY

Brown, Jeremy K., ed. *Current Biography*. New York: H. W. Wilson and Company, 2000.

Friedwald, Will, and Paul Grein. *The Envelope Please . . . Academy Award Winning Songs: 1934–1993*. Rhino Records Inc., 1995.

Grove Music Online. http://www.grovemusic.com/.

Indianapolis News, February 4, 1942.

McCarthy, Todd. *Howard Hawks: The Grey Fox of Hollywood*. New York: Grove Press, 1997.

Sudhalter, Richard M. *Stardust Melody: The Life and Music of Hoagy Carmichael*. New York: Oxford University Press in association with the Indiana Historical Society, 2002.

ALBERT EDWIN "EDDIE" CONDON, *Goodland (1904–1973)*

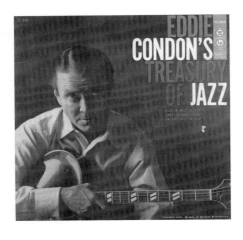

A multifaceted musician who was a jazz guitarist, composer, promoter, and bandleader, Eddie Condon first played the ukulele, then the tenor banjo, tenor lute, and four-string guitar. Condon left Goodland when his family moved to Chicago Heights, Illinois, where he began his first year at Bloom Township High School. He left school at age fifteen, after getting his musician's card. He joined Homer Peavey's Jazz Bandits and began his career as a highly respected jazz guitarist.

Condon worked with the Austin High School Gang in Chicago, promoting and organizing many sessions. He arrived in New York in 1928 and began playing with the Bobby Hackett and the Artie Shaw orchestras. He formed his own band in the 1930s and hired such people as Gene Krupa and Hackett. Condon became a jazz promoter in the 1940s, presenting Fats Waller at Carnegie Hall and working on the first televised jazz concert in 1942. In 1945 he opened Eddie Condon's, a nightclub in Greenwich Village.

Condon's television series, *The Eddie Condon Floor Show* (1948), featured such artists as Louis Armstrong, Billie Holiday, Jack Teagarden, and many other jazz greats. He was the coauthor of three valuable sourcebooks on jazz: *We Called It Music*, *Generation of Jazz*, and *The Eddie Condon Scrapbook of Jazz*.

BIBLIOGRAPHY

Grove Music Online. http://www.grovemusic.com/.

Indiana Biographical Dictionary: People of All Times and All Places Who Have Been Important to the State. New York: Somerset, 1993.

The Internet Movie Database. http://www.imdb.com/.

PAUL DRESSER (JOHANN PAUL DREISER JR.),
Terre Haute (1858–1906)

A songwriter, lyricist, publisher, and performer, Paul Dresser learned to play the guitar and piano as a boy in Terre Haute. He attended St. Bonaventure Lyceum in Terre Haute and then St. Meinrad's Academy. He ran away from St. Meinrad's at age sixteen to join a medicine show. By 1885 he was performing with Billy Rose Minstrels and had begun to compose sentimental songs. After his first successful songs, "The Letter That Never Came" (1886) and "The Outcast Unknown" (1887), he became one of the first American performers to enter music publishing as a staff composer for Willis Woodward

Paul Dresser.
INDIANA HISTORICAL SOCIETY, MARTIN COLLECTION, 18990

Company. In 1895 he introduced one of his most popular songs, "Just Tell Them That You Saw Me."

Dresser wrote "On the Banks of the Wabash, Far Away," in 1897. It became the Indiana state song in 1913. A protégée, Louise Kerlin, took his surname and introduced many of his works on the vaudeville stage. As Louise Dresser she later became a very successful Hollywood actress. During the Gay Nineties Dresser was the nation's most celebrated and affluent composer. No songwriter, other than Stephen Foster, had a greater impact on American popular music of that era. After 1902 Dresser's popularity diminished, and his publishing company failed, despite the success of his last and best-known song, "My Gal Sal." The song was dedicated to Annie Brace, better known as Sallie Walker, an Evansville brothel madame.

Dresser died in 1906, just before "My Gal Sal" became his biggest seller ever. In 1942 a film biography, *My Gal Sal*, loosely based on brother Theodore Dreiser's memoir, *My Brother, Paul*, starred Victor Mature and Rita Hayworth.

In 1963 Dresser's childhood home was moved to Fairbanks Park in Terre Haute. Restoration began that year, with the Vigo County Historical Society attempting to match a photo taken in 1906. In May 2004 the home was opened to the public.

BIBLIOGRAPHY

Grove Music Online. http://www.grovemusic.com/.

Hardy, Phil, and Dave Laing. *The Faber Companion to 20th-Century Popular Music.* Boston: Faber and Faber, 1990.

Indianapolis Star, May 8, 2004.

Henderson, Clayton W. *On the Banks of the Wabash: The Life and Music of Paul Dresser.* Indianapolis: Indiana Historical Society, 2003.

McCormick, Mike. "Paul Dresser." Wabash Valley Profiles. Vigo County Historical Society. http://web.indstate.edu/community/vchs/wvp.htm.

GEORGE WILLIAM DUNING, *Richmond (1908–2000)*

George Duning is one of the least-known but most respected composers in the history of sound film. Duning earned five Oscar nominations for his film music. The list is impressive—*Jolson Sings Again* (1949), *No Sad Songs for Me* (1950), *From Here to Eternity* (1953), *Picnic* (1955), and *The Eddy Duchin Story* (1956).

Duning grew up in a musical family in Richmond. His father was a concert singer and his mother a piano and organ teacher. He began playing the piano before he was five years old. In his early teens he took up the trumpet, and by age fifteen he was leading his own dance band. He also studied at the Cincinnati Conservatory of Music. He went to New York City and joined NBC radio, where he was assigned to work with bandleader Kay Kyser. Kyser and Duning created the hit radio series *Kay Kyser's Kollege of Musical Knowledge* in 1935.

Kyser made a number of short films in Hollywood and brought Duning along as his chief arranger and orchestrator. World War II interrupted his career. After a three-year hitch in the navy, he was hired at Columbia Studios in 1946. Over the next fifteen years, Duning scored an average of seven films a year from B movies and Three Stooges films to pictures such as *Bell, Book and Candle* (1958) and *That Touch of Mink* (1962).

Duning began writing for television in the mid-1950s and contributed scores to such programs as *Naked City*, *Big Valley*, *Farmer's Daughter*, and *Star Trek*. He was on the board of ASCAP and was vice president of ASCAP in 1978–79. He also served on the board of the Academy of Motion Picture Arts and Sciences.

Duning visited Indianapolis from November 5 to 7, 1993, for the Second Annual Festival of Indiana Music, which was held in the Indiana War Memorial auditorium. A complete performance of one of his film scores was featured as well as the first performance of his "Clarifications" for clarinet and chamber ensemble.

BIBLIOGRAPHY

Indianapolis News, September 28, 1993.
The Internet Movie Database. http://www.imdb.com/.
Space Age Pop. http://www.spaceagepop.com/duning.htm.

KENNETH "BABYFACE" EDMONDS, *Indianapolis* (b. 1958)

In December 2002 Kenneth "Babyface" Edmonds spoke to the National Black Caucus of State Legislators at the Westin Hotel in Indianapolis. "Don't tell me what I can't do," he said. He repeated this phrase throughout his speech, which drew heavily from his childhood in Indianapolis. Edmonds drew inspiration from those who tried to discourage him. He maintains that a defiant will has allowed him to become a success in the highly competitive field of popular music.

At age thirteen Edmonds started his own band, Tarnished Silver. Immediately after graduating from North Central High School, he joined the R & B band Manchild as a guitarist. The group hit the singles chart in 1977 with "Especially for You." He then formed his own band that he called April for the month in which he was born. This band included his brother Devon. After leaving April, Edmonds joined the Ohio-based band The Deele in 1983. The Deele had several top-ten singles. His first album was *Street Beat* in 1984. It was at this time that bass player Bootsy Collins gave him the name "Babyface."

In 1987 Edmonds began collaborating with Antonio "L. A." Reid, a relationship that endures to this day. They cofounded LaFace Records in 1989 and launched platinum careers for many performers. Edmonds has written songs for a wide range of artists, including Celine Dion, Mary J. Blige, Whitney Houston, Mariah Carey, Boyz II Men, Dru Hill, and Madonna. In 1996 he wrote "Power of the Dream," which was the anthem for the Summer Olympic Games. In 1997 *Time* magazine named him one of the twenty-five most influential people in America. In 1988 he formed a company to produce independent films. Edmonds was executive producer and wrote the soundtrack for *Soul Food* (1997), starring fellow Indianapolis native Vivica Fox.

Edmonds donated $60,000 to establish a "Save the Music" chapter in Indianapolis in 1999. That same year he also gave $50,000 to Black Expo Youth Video Institute. In 2000 he was nominated for a Golden Globe for "How Can I Not Love You?" from *Anna and the King*. He has collected ten Grammy awards. A seventeen-mile stretch of I-65 running through Indianapolis is named the Kenneth "Babyface" Edmonds Memorial Highway.

Edmonds and his wife Tracey have two sons, Brandon and Dylan.

BIBLIOGRAPHY

Babyface Official Web Site. http://www.babyfacemusic.com/.
Indianapolis Star, October 31, 2000, September 12, 2002.
The Internet Movie Database. http://www.imdb.com/.

JANIE FRICKE (FRICKIE), *South Whitley (b. 1947)*

Janie Fricke was raised on a four hundred-acre farm in Indiana where her father taught her how to play guitar. Her mother was a piano teacher and organist. She began singing at age ten in a "little church up the road" where her mother played piano. She performed at county fairs, high school events, and coffeehouses. She sang commercial jingles to help pay her way through Indiana University, where she earned a degree in elementary education.

Instead of becoming a teacher, Fricke chose a music career. Believing she could get work as a sessions singer, she moved to Los Angeles and became one of the marketing industry's most successful jingle singers. This success led her to Nashville and singing sessions for country artists such as Loretta Lynn, Eddie Rabbitt, Crystal Gayle, Ronnie Milsap, and Barbara Mandrell. She also sang on albums for Charlie Rich and Elvis Presley.

Finally, one line in a song brought Fricke to the attention of the public. She recorded a single with Johnny Duncan ("Stranger") in which she sang the line, "Shut out the light and lead me." As a result she began singing duets with Mel Tillis, Merle Haggard, Moe Bandy, and others. This led to her first major recording contract and such smash hits as "Don't Worry 'Bout Me Baby" and "It Ain't Easy Bein' Easy." She was named Country Music Female Vocalist of the Year in 1982 and 1983. She was chosen to be on the Country Hall of Fame Walkway of Stars and was twice nominated for the Grammy Award. She has released twenty-three albums and thirty-six hit singles and has appeared on such television shows as *The Dukes of Hazzard*, *Austin City Limits*, and *The Tonight Show*.

Twenty-five years ago she moved to a ranch in Dallas, which she dubbed Texana, a combination of Texas and Indiana. With her husband, Jeff, she spends time taking care of her animals and attending a church near her home. She still records in her home studio with Jeff handling the production and all the engineering. She believes that the values she learned growing up in Indiana have helped her become the woman she is today.

BIBLIOGRAPHY

Janie Fricke Biography. http://www.keepmedia/Muze/.
Janie Fricke Guest Starring Roles. http://www.tvtome.com/.
Janie Fricke Official Site. http://www.janiefricke.com/.
Paxman, Bob. "Catching Up with Janie Fricke." http://www.countryweekly.com/stories/feature/60624.

IRVING "IZZY" FRIEDMAN, *Linton (1898–1981)*

Izzy Friedman began his musical career as a clarinetist and a saxophonist working in a theater orchestra in Terre Haute. In 1923 he moved to Chicago, where he studied with the principal clarinetist of the Chicago Symphony Orchestra and played at the Moulin Rouge Café.

The following year he went to New York and worked as a freelance musician, while also studying composition and conducting.

Friedman played with several bands, including Vincent Lopez (1925–26), and made recordings with Bix Beiderbecke, Eddie Lange, Frankie Trumbauer, and Joe Venuti. After appearing with Paul Whiteman in the film *The King of Jazz* in 1930, he settled in Hollywood, working as a studio musician until his retirement in 1963. He was music director for almost fifty films, including *The Big Cat* (1949), *Tulsa* (1949), and *Adventures of Casanova* (1948), written by Shelburn, Indiana, native Walter Bullock. He worked for Warner Brothers (1932–43), MGM (1943–45), and Eagle-Lion (1945–49). Friedman composed music for television shows in the fifties, including *Dennis the Menace*, *The Donna Reed Show*, *Father Knows Best*, and others.

BIBLIOGRAPHY

Grove Music Online. http://www.grovemusic.com/.
The Internet Movie Database. http://www.imdb.com/.

DOLORES (EBLE) FULLER, *South Bend (b. 1923)*

When she was eleven years old Dolores Fuller appeared in the famous motel scene in Frank Capra's Oscar-winning film *It Happened One Night* (1934). She acted in school plays, modeled, and landed a few jobs in television in the 1950s. She became the "Gustinette Girl" on *Queen for a Day*, advertising marabou slippers. She also worked as a model for such clients as Westwood Knitting Mills, Evans/Picone, and others. She became a regular on NBC's *Dinah Shore Chevrolet Show* and managed to appear in a few movies.

One day Fuller and fellow actress Mona McKinnon went on a casting call where they met director Edward Wood. Fuller became Wood's girlfriend. In 1953 she appeared in Wood's production of *Glen or Glenda*, in which Wood played a cross-dresser and Fuller was his girlfriend. Costar Bela Lugosi died before the film was finished, but Wood managed to complete the film using a double for Lugosi. Fuller appeared in several more Wood films until his drinking caused them to split up.

Fuller turned into a songwriter and cowrote songs with Nelson Riddle, Peggy Lee, Duane Eddy, and others. She also cowrote at least twenty songs for Elvis Presley's 1960s features, including songs for *Spinout* (1966), *Clambake* (1967), *Blue Hawaii* (1961), and *Kid Galahad* (1962). She founded her own record company, Dee Dee Records, and became a talent manager, launching the careers of Tanya Tucker and Johnny Rivers.

In 1994 a biographical film, *Ed Wood*, directed by Tim Burton and starring Johnny Depp as Wood and Sarah Jessica Parker as Fuller, was released. Fuller has been vocal about her dislike of the way she was portrayed by Parker in the film. Today, Fuller lives in Las Vegas with her husband, Philip Chamberlin. She remains active in show business, always on the lookout for new talent.

Bela Lugosi and Dolores Fuller (right).
©1994 WADE WILLIAMS PRODUCTIONS

BIBLIOGRAPHY

Dolores Fuller. http://www.briansdriveintheater.com/dolores fuller.html.
The Internet Movie Database. http://www.imdb.com/.

JAMES FREDERICK HANLEY, *Rensselaer (1892–1942)*

Composer/lyricist James Hanley is best known in the Hoosier State for composing a song that rivals the official state song. "Back Home Again in Indiana" was written by Hanley in 1917. The state song (so designated in 1913) is "On the Banks of the Wabash, Far Away" by Terre Haute's Paul Dresser. The lyrics of the two songs are similar. They both speak of the Wabash River and a candlelight gleaming through the sycamores. More often than not, Hanley's "Back Home Again in Indiana" is sung at functions such as the start of the Indianapolis 500-Mile Race, while the state song is ignored.

Hanley left Indiana to attend Champion College and the Chicago Musical College. In 1914 he joined the army and served during World War I in the Eighty-second Division. While overseas, he wrote and produced an army show, *Toot Sweet.*

After the war, Hanley found work as an accompanist for vaudeville shows. Soon thereafter, he began work on a succession of Broadway stage scores, including *Jim Jam Jems* (1921), *Spice of 1922*, *Big Boy* (1925), *Honeymoon Lane* (1926), and *Sidewalks of New York* (1927). He worked with such collaborators as B. G. DeSylva, Eddie Dowling, Theodore Morse, and Ballard McDonald.

Hanley's hits included "The Little White House (At the End of Honeymoon Lane)," "Gee, But I Hate to Go Home Alone," "Just a Cottage Small by a Waterfall," "Zing! Went the Strings of My Heart," "Dig a Little Deeper," and "Dreams for Sale." He was a composer for the Ziegfeld Follies in the early 1920s, working on "Rose of Washington Square" for a Ziegfeld production. In 1939 it was sung on the screen in a film of the same name by Alice Faye. The song also appeared in the 1967 film *Thoroughly Modern Millie.* It was sung by Ann Dee. Hanley wrote the music for "Second Hand Rose" for Fanny Brice for the Ziegfeld Follies of 1921. It was later a featured number in *Funny Girl* (1968) and was sung by Barbra Streisand.

Hanley was employed by Twentieth Century Fox from 1931 to 1934. Just before his death, he completed (with Vernon Crane) the score for a new show, *The Band Plays On.* He died at age forty-nine of a heart attack, brought on by a blood clot. He was survived by his widow and five children.

BIBLIOGRAPHY

The Internet Movies Database. http://www.imdb.com/.

The Songwriters Hall of Fame. http://www.songwritershallof fame.org/.

Variety, February 11, 1942.

BOBBY HELMS, *Bloomington (1933–1997)*

Bobby Helms started singing with his father and brother while in grade school. When he was nine years old he was singing on WTTS Radio in Bloomington twice a day. For a while, he toured regionally with his brother as the Helms Brothers. He became a fixture on Bob Hardy's *Hayloft Frolic* show on WTTV in Bloomington, where he performed for five years.

Helms was invited to perform on Ernest Tubb's Record Shop *Midnight Jamboree* in Nashville, Tennessee. After hearing Helms sing, Tubb arranged for Helms to audition for producer Paul Cohen.

Cohen immediately signed Helms to the national recording label of Decca Records. He made his debut on *Grand Ole Opry* in 1950.

In January 1957 Cohen released a song called "Fraulein." Helms recorded it, and it reached number sixteen on the pop charts. Before "Fraulein" left the country charts, Decca released "My Special Angel." Then with "Fraulein" still on the charts after nearly a year and with "My Special Angel" making its way toward number one, Cohen decided Helms should be the first to put a "little rock" in Christmas with the release of "Jingle Bell Rock." All three songs were on the Billboard charts at Christmas, setting a record for one artist having the number one, two, and seven hits at the same time. He was given the Cashbox Male Vocalist of the Year Award in 1957.

Helms moved with Cohen to Kapp Records in 1957 where he had several charted records. He then signed with Little Darlin' Records, where he had three top-twenty songs. In 1958 he was a regular on the *Ranch Party* television series with Johnny Cash, Smiley Burnette, Ray Price, and Tex Ritter. In 1960 Helms had a hit with "Jacquelin" from the movie *The Case against Brooklyn* (1958), in which he appeared as himself. In 1970 he joined Centron Records where "Mary Goes Round" reached number thirteen. In 1974 he began touring with the Bobby Helms Show. He bought several nightclubs, sponsored an annual music festival, and performed more than 150 tour dates each year. In 1989 he released *Greatest Hits and More*, a ten-song videotape.

Helms's songs have appeared in several movies. "Jingle Bell Rock" was on the soundtrack of *Lethal Weapon* (1987), *Casual Sex?* (1988), and *Vanilla Sky* (2001). "My Special Angel" was in *Strange Invaders* (1983), and "Fraulein" was in *Country* (1984).

BIBLIOGRAPHY

Bobby Helms Biography. http://www.oldies.com/.
Bobby Helms Biography. http://www.cmt.com/.
The Internet Movie Database. http://www.imdb.com/.

HOOSIER HOT SHOTS

Charles Otto "Gabe" Ward, Knightstown (1904–1992)
Kenneth Henry Trietsch, Arcadia (1903–1987)
Paul Edward "Hezzie" Trietsch, Arcadia (1905–1980)
Frank Delaney Kettering, Monmouth, Illinois (1909–1973)

For three decades one of the coolest phrases bandied about by the preboomer generation was "Are you ready, Hezzie?" This was the opening question Ken Trietsch asked his brother Hezzie before they began to wreak musical mayhem on stage, screen, and radio.

The Trietsch brothers grew up on a farm seven miles south of Muncie on State Road 3. Their grandfather had a piano, a banjo, and a horn. Their family recreation was music, and they made many of their instruments or used what was available—a washboard, a pair of spoons, a couple of sticks, a cornstalk whistle, or a kazoo. They began working with their three other brothers as entertainers in 1922. The five brothers worked mostly around the state of Indiana until they joined a group called Ezra Buzzington's Rube Band. Fellow Hoosier Mark Schaefer was Ezra Buzzington. In 1927 he hired all five of the brothers as well as Hezzie's wife Bessie. For years they traveled all over

To Jessie - our little "night" at the Barn Dance very Best wishes

The "Hoosier Hot Shots" NBC.

The original Hoosier Hot Shots.

the United States and Canada before the Great Depression caused them to stop.

Ken and Hezzie teamed with Gabe Ward, who also had been with the Buzzington group, and did a charity show for flood victims that brought them to the attention of WOWO in Fort Wayne. They began to do a fifteen-minute daily show on the station without receiving any pay. They had to join the musicians' union, but Hezzie could not join because he did not play a recognized instrument. Hezzie played the washboard, pie tins, wood blocks, bicycle horns, and garbage can lids. Ken played the guitar, tuba, bass fiddle, and banjo. Ward played a variety of instruments but was best known for his clarinet. In 1934 they hired Frank Kettering, who played the organ, piano, flute, guitar, banjo, and bass fiddle and could also read music. Kettering taught Ken how to read and write music, enabling him to compose such hits as "From the Indies to the Andes in My Undies," "I Like Bananas Because They Have No Bones," "When There's Tears in the Eyes of the Potato," "Meet Me by the Ice House Lizzie," and "Blues My Naughty Sweetie Gives to Me."

As their tunes began to be published and their performances increased, they were able to quit their jobs and devote their full time to their music. When they auditioned for the *National Barn Dance* in Chicago, WLS did not know what to do with them. The Hot Shots did not play country, did not play popular music, and did not yodel or fiddle. They were finally allowed a spot on a Michigan State Fair show. They were met with astounding enthusiasm and were immediately signed by WLS to become regulars on the *National Barn Dance*. They bought homes in Chicago and raised their children there. They began to make records that sold very well.

Gene Autry, who was a regular on the *National Barn Dance*, asked the Hot Shots to come to Hollywood to make a movie with him. They eventually quit the *National Barn Dance* and moved to Hollywood. While in Hollywood, they made at least twenty-one movies, most of which were Westerns. In 1944 Kettering left the group to serve in the armed forces, and Gil Taylor took his place. The Hot Shots did USO tours and went to North Africa and Italy to entertain the troops. Taylor quit the group in the 1960s, and Nate Harrison and Keith Milheim took his place over the years.

When a young man named Spike Jones wanted to join the group, Ken told him, "We're ready to retire and enjoy our homes and families. Go ahead and use any of our ideas you want." Jones went on to create his own group, Spike Jones and the City Slickers. Jones billed himself as "The Man Who Murdered Music." If Jones was the man who murdered music, the Hoosier Hot Shots first beat the victim to a pulp, making it easier for Jones to deliver the lethal blow.

BIBLIOGRAPHY

Daniels, Wayne. "Are You Ready Hezzie?" *The Nostalgia Digest* (1996).
The Internet Movie Database. http://www.imdb.com/.
Memories of the Hoosier Hot Shots. http://www.hoosierhotshots.com/.

FREDERICK "FREDDIE" DEWAYNE HUBBARD, *Indianapolis (b. 1938)*

Freddie Hubbard received his first professional training at the Jordan Conservatory of Music in Indianapolis, working with the principal trumpeter of the Indianapolis Symphony Orchestra. As a teenager, he worked with Wes and Monk Montgomery and eventually formed his own band, the Jazz Contemporaries.

Hubbard moved to New York in 1958 at age twenty and began to astonish fans and critics with the depth and maturity of his playing. He worked with several veteran jazz artists, including Philly Joe Jones, Sonny Rollins, Slide Hampton, and fellow Hoosier J. J. Johnson. In 1960 he toured Europe with Quincy Jones. Hubbard recorded *Open Sesame*, his solo debut, in June 1960, at the age of twenty-two. Within ten months, he recorded his second album, *Goin' Up*. In August 1961 he recorded what many consider his masterpiece, *Ready for Freddie*. He joined Art Blakey's Jazz Messengers and quickly established himself as an important new voice in jazz. He won *Down Beat*'s New Star Award on trumpet.

Hubbard left Blakey in 1966 to form his own small group. Through the years he played in bands led by others. He achieved his greatest success in the 1970s with a series of crossover albums for CTI Records. One of those, *First Light* (1972), received a Grammy. In the 1980s he was again leading his own jazz group touring the United States and Europe. In 1986 he played trumpet for the movie *Round Midnight*. He is an exceptionally talented and virtuoso performer, achieving notoriety as one of the best hard-bop as well as jazz-rock trumpeters.

BIBLIOGRAPHY

Indianapolis News, September 29, 2003.

The Internet Movie Database. http://www.imdb.com/.

Jazz Trumpet Solos. http://www.jazztrumpetsolos.com/Hubbard .htm.

SYLVIA KIRBY HUTTON, *Kokomo (b. 1956)*

Sylvia Kirby Hutton has managed to parlay her interests in art and country music into a career. During her high school years, she traveled frequently to Nashville, Indiana, where she could hear the singers she loved at the Little Nashville Opry. She began drawing portraits of her favorite country stars. Dolly Parton was so impressed with her drawing skills that she invited the aspiring singer on her bus. Inspired by Parton's encouragement, Hutton set her sights on Nashville, Tennessee, after her graduation from high school.

Hutton made a demo tape, and her rendition of Patsy Cline's "Crazy" caught the attention of publisher and producer Tom Collins. Although he could not offer anything at that time, he told her to keep in touch. She returned to Indiana, but four months later she was back in Nashville as a secretary answering phones and typing letters. She learned more about the music business by spending time in the studio with Collins when he was producing Barbara Mandrell. This led to

Sylvia Kirby Hutton.

her first singing job doing background vocals for Mandrell. Mandrell invited Hutton to sing backup in a series of concerts in Las Vegas.

Hutton came to the attention of Jerry Bradley of RCA when she auditioned for the group Dave and Sugar. She was signed to the RCA label and made her debut single, "You Don't Miss a Thing," in 1979. The following year she had a top forty hit with "It Don't Hurt to Dream." She had more top forty successes in the early 1980s. Then came the biggest song of her career. "Nobody" shot to number one on the country charts and crossed over to number fifteen on the pop chart. BMI named it "The Most Performed Song of the Year." Hutton then teamed with Irish flutist James Galway for reprise of the old hit, "The Wayward Wind," which went to the top sixty.

Hutton had several other top forty hits until 1987 when she grew weary of touring and decided to concentrate on songwriting. She married psychologist Roy Hutton in 1991. She began writing music for children and did limited television performing in the Nashville area. She had her own cooking show, *Holiday Gourmet*, in 1992.

Hutton has sold more than four million records and scored several number-one hits. Her many television appearances include *Austin City Limits*, *The Country Music Awards*, *The Grammy Awards*, and the *Academy of Country Music Awards*. The Bluebird Café in Nashville is her home base, where she performs with her band.

In 1999 a single copy of Hutton's 1983 CD *Snapshot* was sold on eBay for $280.00. When she heard about the sale, she replied, "You know, I think it's really sweet. I'm trying to think of who I would spend $280 on a CD for, and I can't think of anyone."

When asked if she had made any movies, Hutton replied, "I played the title role of 'Petronella' (1986) for a Disney Channel movie. Jimmy Osmond of the Osmond Brothers produced this children's story. But, that is the only movie I've ever done. Singing is more my forte."

BIBLIOGRAPHY

Hutton, Sylvia. Interview with the author. March 3, 2001.

Movies—Petronella. http://www.vh1.com/movies/movie/26846/castcrew.jhtml.

Nashville Tennessean, April 19, 1997, June 19, 1999.

http://www.countrycharts.com/.

http://www.countryworks.com/.

INK SPOTS

Orville "Hoppy" Jones, Chicago (1902–1944)
Ivory "Deek" Watson, Mounds, Illinois (1909–1969)
Charlie Fuqua, New Haven, Connecticut (1910–1971)
Jerry Daniels, Indianapolis (1915–1995)

Information on the Ink Spots's origins is limited and somewhat contradictory. Details relating to the various pre-Ink Spots groups are sketchy.

For the most part, the origins of this popular and influential group were in Indianapolis. In 1928 Mifflin "Miff" Campbell was working in a candy store in Indianapolis when he met Orville "Hoppy" Jones, who delivered ice cream to the store. They formed a dance duo called Jones and Campbell and performed in vaudeville, carnivals, and small clubs in the Indianapolis area.

Ivory "Deek" Watson was performing at this time in a coffeepot band in Indianapolis with a group called the Percolating Puppies. The band played a small teapot, a medium coffeepot, a very large coffeepot, and guitars. Charlie Fuqua was a member of an Indianapolis group called the Patent Leather Kids. Fuqua left this group to join Jerry Daniels and Bernie Mackey to form another coffeepot band.

Daniels and Fuqua left Mackey (who later returned as a member of the Ink Spots to fill in when Fuqua was in the armed forces) to form a duet, Jerry and Charlie. They appeared in vaudeville and were heard regularly on WKBF Radio in Indianapolis. In 1931 Jones and Campbell added Leonard Reed and became a trio called the Peanut Boys, performing on WFBE in Cincinnati. In 1932 Reed left the Peanut Boys, and Watson joined the group along with Oliver "Slim" Green and the name was changed to the Four Riff Brothers. In February 1933 the Four Riff Brothers succeeded the Mills Brothers on WLW in Cincinnati. They had their own fifteen-minute show and appeared regularly on a show called *The Rhythm Club.*

In September 1933 the Riff Brothers broke up when Watson and Green left to become solo artists. However, in October 1933 Fuqua, Daniels, and Watson were together as King, Jack, and Jester. They were featured three times a week on WHK in Cleveland and later on WLW in Cincinnati. In July 1934 "Hoppy" Jones joined the group, and they became King, Jack, and Jesters. Shortly thereafter they went to New York and met Paul Whiteman, who was interested in featuring the group. Whiteman, however, already had a group called the Jesters, so he asked them to change their name. They became the Four Ink Spots.

The Ink Spots.

The first known appearance of the Four Ink Spots was at the Apollo Theater in New York City. (Also on the bill that day was another Indianapolis native, James "Jimmie" Baskett.) The original Ink Spots included Ivory "Deek" Watson (second tenor, guitar), Jerry Daniels (lead tenor, guitar, ukulele), Charlie Fuqua (baritone, guitar, ukulele), and Orville "Hoppy" Jones (bass, string bass, and a cello strung as a bass). They started out singing "jump" tunes, and their early recordings for RCA and Decca reflected this style.

In early 1936 Daniels left the group, and Bill Kenny, a non-Hoosier, became his replacement. Shortly afterwards, the group changed to a ballad style that featured Kenny's high tenor and Jones's deep "talking" chorus. On November 6, 1936, they performed on the first "live" demonstration of television at NBC in New York, becoming the first black performers to appear on television and indeed the earliest of any performers to appear on television.

On January 12, 1939, the Ink Spots recorded "If I Didn't Care," receiving $37.50 for the recording session. When the sales on the single reached 200,000, Decca paid the group an additional $3,750.00. They were now nationally known. In August 1939 they recorded "Address Unknown." It went to number one on the pop charts and stayed there for nine weeks. The next month they recorded "My Prayer," which hit number three on the pop charts. The Ink Spots sang with many of the popular big bands of the day, including Woody Herman, Glenn Miller, Bob Crosby, Glen Gray, and Harry James.

During World War II they entertained servicemen at home and in Europe. They also appeared in films, including *The Great American Broadcast* (1941), in which they sang "If I Didn't Care," and *Pardon My Sarong* (1942), in which they sang "Do I Worry?" Jones collapsed on stage and died October 18, 1944, and was replaced by Herb Kenny, Bill's brother. From 1933 to the early 1950s there were two quartets calling themselves the Ink Spots. After 1953 Kenny decided to embark on a solo career. He called his act Bill Kenny and the Ink Spots. However, no other members of the group sang. Others took over the Ink Spots name, and Deek Watson was forced to change his split-off group to the Brown Dots. Groups bearing the Ink Spots' name continued to appear and make records.

BIBLIOGRAPHY

Hardy, Phil, and Dave Laing. *The Faber Companion to 20th-Century Popular Music.* Boston: Faber and Faber, 1990.

The Ink Spots. http://www.theinkspots.com/.

JAMES LOUIS "J. J." JOHNSON, *Indianapolis (1924-2001)*

James Louis Johnson studied piano in Indianapolis between the ages of nine and eleven. He switched to trombone at age fourteen, partly because he found it challenging, but mostly because his band needed a trombone player. "I never had any formal training on this instrument, other than in school and spending Sunday afternoons, after church, with a tutor, who happened to play trombone with the local YMCA band. He was a marvelous person with a BIG sound. Therefore, early on, I became very preoccupied with sound, more so than technique," said Johnson.

In 1941 and 1942 Johnson toured with bands led by Clarence Love and Isaac Snookum Russell, whose trumpeter Fats Navarro had a strong impact on Johnson's playing. He joined Benny Carter's orchestra, playing with them until 1945. His earliest recorded solo was on "Love for Sale" in 1943 for Capitol Records. He appeared in the first Jazz at the Philharmonic concert in 1944.

By May 1945 Johnson was with the Count Basie orchestra, playing mostly in New York. For several years he played with small jazz groups at various clubs and became increasingly absorbed with the new bop style. He toured with Miles Davis until his financial situation forced him to retire from music in 1952. He worked as a blueprint inspector and performed only sporadically until August 1944, when he formed a highly successful trombone duo with Kai Winding. Their group, Jay and Kai, remained intact until 1956. His "Poem for Brass," recorded for Columbia in 1956, drew attention to his talents as a jazz composer.

After disbanding Jay and Kai, Johnson led his own quintet until the summer of 1960, touring Europe and composing large-scale works such as "El Camino Real" and "Sketch for Trombone and Band." He taught at the Lenox School of Jazz and in 1961 wrote a new major work, "Perceptions," for Dizzy Gillespie. Johnson continued his career as a performer and composer throughout the 1960s. He played with Miles Davis's group, led a sextet, and in 1967 became a staff composer and conductor for MBA Music in New York. In 1970 he moved to Hollywood where he began composing scores for television and films. Some films for which he composed scores were *Shaft*

(1971), *Top of the Heap* (1972), *Cleopatra Jones* (1973), and *Willie Dynamite* (1974). His television scores were used on *Mod Squad*, *Barefoot in the Park*, and *The Six Million Dollar Man*.

BIBLIOGRAPHY

Grove Music Online. http://www.grovemusic.com/.
The Internet Movie Database. http://www.imdb.com/.
J. J. Johnson. http://www.jazzbrat.com/.

JOHN MELLENCAMP, *Seymour (b. 1951)*

Raised in a strict fundamentalist household, John Mellencamp religiously ignored its injunctions against drinking, smoking, dancing, and fooling around. "The guy who used to go out and get drunk and beat up people and get beat up and drive down Indiana roads at 100 miles an hour with beer spilling all over the car . . . that was me. I don't do that any more," said Mellencamp.

As a child, Mellencamp suffered from spinal bifida and had a troubled youth marked by several brushes with the law. He eloped with his pregnant girlfriend at seventeen and began performing in a band at eighteen. At twenty-four he was determined to break into the music business and moved to New York. His teenage idol looks brought him to the attention of David Bowie's manager who signed him with MCA. His first album, *Chestnut Street Incident*, was released under the name Johnny Cougar. Mellencamp maintains that his agent gave him this name without his knowledge or consent. The album was a failure, and he lost his contract with MCA Records.

Mellencamp signed with tiny Riva Records and recorded *A Biography* in 1978. It was not a hit in the United States but did well in Australia. His next album, *Johnny Cougar* (1979), was a minor success. After one more album with Riva, he signed with Mercury Records and released his breakthrough album, *American Fool*, in 1982. The singles "Hurt So Good" and "Jack and Diane," which were given nice exposure on the new MTV channel, sent the album to the top of the charts. He sang "Hurt So Good" in the 1984 movie hit *Footloose*. Now, with a major hit under his belt, he changed his name to John Cougar Mellencamp.

In 1985 Mellencamp released *Scarecrow*, which focused on the plight of the American family farmer. He and Willie Nelson organized Farm Aid in which they played benefit concerts supporting American farmers. It was at this time he changed his name to John Mellencamp and refused to allow alcohol or tobacco companies to sponsor his tours. He had a hit in 1987 with "The Lonesome Jubilee." In 1988 he sang "Rave On" for the sound track of the movie *Cocktail*. In 1992 he sang "Jailhouse Rock" for the sound track of *Honeymoon in Vegas*. He then decided to take a turn at acting and enlisted the help of *Lonesome Dove* author Larry McMurtry to write a script called *Falling from Grace* (1992). Mellencamp directed the film himself. By 1993, with the release of *Human Wheels*, his critical reception was solid. His *Dance Naked* in 1993 was his biggest hit in years. However, his frantic pace led to a heart attack in 1994.

Mellencamp left Mercury Records in 1994 and in 1998 released an album, *John Mellencamp*, through Columbia Records. It included the songs "Your Life Is Now" and "I'm Not Running Anymore."

(Opposite page) John Mellencamp and Mariel Hemingway star in *Falling from Grace* (1992).

He appeared in more movies, *After Image* (2001) and *Lone Star State of Mind* (2002). In the early twenty-first century, he began teaming with other artists in a more laid-back style. Mellencamp's sound has been a major influence on such artists as Sheryl Crow, Garth Brooks, Joan Osborne, and Kid Rock.

BIBLIOGRAPHY

Hardy, Phil, and Dave Laing. *The Faber Companion to 20th-Century Popular Music.* Boston: Faber and Faber, 1990.

Indianapolis Star, August 22, 1982.

The Internet Movie Database. http://www.imdb.com/.

John Mellencamp. http://en.wikipedia.org/wiki/John_Cougar_Mellencamp/.

JOHN LESLIE "WES" MONTGOMERY, *Indianapolis* (1923-1968)

Wes Montgomery.
INDIANA HISTORICAL SOCIETY, *INDIANAPOLIS RECORDER* COLLECTION, PO303, BOX 92, FOLDER 20

Wes Montgomery, a self-taught musician, became one of the most influential jazz guitarists of all time. When he was twelve years old, his brother bought him a four-string guitar. At nineteen he happened to hear jazz guitarist Charlie Christian. He said later, "I didn't know what to think. I'd never heard anything like that." He liked Christian's sound so much he went out and bought a brand-new guitar and amplifier. He found learning to play it was more difficult than he imagined. "That was more trouble than I'd ever had in my life! I didn't want to face that. It let me know where I really was," Montgomery recalled.

Fortunately, Montgomery did not give up. He said, "With a little drive within myself, I stayed on the inspiring side." His practicing with an amplifier brought complaints from his wife and the neighbors. He recalled, "So I laid my pick down on the amplifier and just fiddled around with my thumb." When he got a pick he found that he liked the different sound using just his thumb." Montgomery and his brothers, Buddy and Monk, started jamming around the end of World War II.

Montgomery's lifestyle at this time was extremely rigorous. He worked as a welder from 7 a.m. to 3 p.m., then played a gig at a bar from 9 p.m. to 2 a.m. Afterwards, he played a club called the Missile Room from 2:30 a.m. to 5 a.m. One night jazz pianist Don Wilhite heard the Montgomery brothers and approached them about playing jingles in a band he had for his musical advertising business. Wilhite discovered that although the Montgomery brothers could not read music, they could immediately play back anything they heard. He said, "I would play a flashy run, perhaps two times, and they would play it back with perfection and remember it when they came into the studio in a brand new context. It was really amazing!"

Montgomery's big break came when jazz saxophonist Cannonball Adderly heard him play in an Indianapolis nightclub in 1959. Adderly was astounded by what he heard and arranged Montgomery's first album as a solo performer, *The Wes Montgomery Trio: A Dynamic Sound.* A series of pathbreaking albums followed. He partnered with George Shearing and Nat Adderly on a couple of albums. He moved to Verve where he was given strings and choruses. He later recorded for A&M, scoring a hit with "Windy" (1967) and *A Day in the Life* (1967). The latter was his most successful recording.

Montgomery died suddenly of a heart attack in 1968 at age forty-five. In 1970 the movie *Maidstone* was released, featuring music composed and performed by Montgomery and Isaac Hayes. Montgomery was inducted into the Big Band and Jazz Hall of Fame in 1983. He was featured in a television special, *A Celebration of America's Music*, in 1998.

BIBLIOGRAPHY

Hardy, Phil, and Dave Laing. *The Faber Companion to 20th-Century Popular Music.* Boston: Faber and Faber, 1990.

The Internet Movie Database. http://www.imdb.com/.

Mills, Andrew M. "'Probably a Thousand Cats Are Using Their Thumbs:' A Brief Biographical Sketch of Wes Montgomery." *Black History News & Notes* 86 (November 2001).

COLE ALBERT PORTER, Peru (1891–1964)

Cole Porter is an example of a comparative rarity among songwriters. He was born with a silver spoon in his mouth, without a need to rise from rags to riches. In another departure from the norm, he became internationally acknowledged as the king of sophistication through his music, lyrics, and lifestyle despite his upbringing in a small, rural Indiana community. Porter confided to Richard Rodgers that the secret to his hit songs was that he learned to write Jewish or eastern Mediterranean tunes. Rodgers observed later, "It is ironic that the one who has written the most enduring Jewish music was an Episcopalian millionaire from Indiana."

Growing up in Peru, Indiana, Porter lived a less than idyllic family life. His mother, Kate Cole, apparently inherited the strong will of her father, J. O. Cole, who was a self-made millionaire. Porter's father, Samuel Fenwick Porter, was thoroughly dominated by his wife and his father-in-law. After losing two children, Kate made Cole the center of her life as soon as he was born. There were no other children, so Cole was the recipient of his mother's full attention.

Kate did not allow Cole to play ball or roughhouse. Instead, she bought him a pony, taught him to ride, and gave him piano and dance lessons. Porter also studied the violin, traveling to the Marion, Indiana, Conservatory of Music for lessons. Because it was about a thirty-mile trip, Porter took the train to Marion. His lessons finished around noon, but there was no train back to Peru until evening. He began to spend his time reading penny dreadfuls he picked up at a shop in Marion. Later he said, "I suppose some of my lyrics owe a debt to those naughty books."

At age eleven, Porter composed a song he called "The Bobolink Waltz." Kate paid one hundred dollars to have it published. She distributed one hundred copies to friends and relatives. At the age of thirteen, Kate sent Cole to the Worcester Academy in Massachusetts. J. O. wanted the boy to stay in Indiana and to learn farming, hunting, and business pursuits. There was an argument between the two, and Kate and her father did not speak to each other for two years. Cole did not return to Indiana for three years.

In 1908 Porter took the preliminary entrance exams for Yale and, at the urging of his grandfather, came home to Peru. He proceeded to spend as much time as possible at Lake Maxinkuckee, playing the piano on the lake's excursion boat. Race car driver Ralph De Palma remembers Porter playing with a heavy foot to overcome the noise of

Cole Porter, circa 1930s.

the boat's engines. At the finish of one number De Palma said, "If he could drive an automobile with the same heavy foot he plays the piano, what a race driver he'd be."

Porter attended Yale University, studying law. However, his musical talent led him to sing with and conduct the university glee club and to compose songs such as "Bingo, Eli Yale" and "Bulldog." "Bulldog" is still sung at Yale today. Porter graduated from Yale in spite of the fact he had failed a number of courses during his four years. Because he was so involved in extracurricular activities, the university advanced him credits for his work, which made it possible for him to graduate. Upon the insistence of his grandfather, Porter entered Harvard Law School in the fall of 1913. After his freshman year, the dean of the law school happened to witness an impromptu entertainment at which Porter performed. What he heard reinforced his conviction that Porter was in the wrong school. The dean arranged for a transfer, much to Porter's delight, to the school of music.

Porter kept composing, and in 1915 two of his songs were performed on Broadway. In 1916 he had his first Broadway show, *See America First*. Fellow Hoosier Clifton Webb delighted the audience with his dancing, but the show was not successful. Porter moved to Paris in 1917, where he met Linda Lee Thomas. Thomas was a very rich and beautiful divorcée, eight years older than Porter. Her roots were in Louisville, Kentucky, but she was widely regarded as one of the most beautiful women in the world. Porter thought she was the ideal, the perfect thing—amusing, sensitive, and endowed with absolute taste. They were married in 1919.

Also in 1919, Porter enjoyed his first hit, a song written for the Broadway show, *Hitchy-Koo of 1919*, entitled "Old-Fashioned Garden." The Porters spent most of the 1920s in Europe, where he experienced a relatively inactive musical lull. He and Linda were having too much fun. There was little time to compose music. In 1928 a song he had written in 1924 was inserted into a Broadway musical, *Wake Up and Dream*. It was "I'm in Love Again," and it became a hit.

Porter felt he needed a show of his own. He got it in 1928 with *Paris*, which starred Irene Bordoni. It produced the song "Let's Do It (Let's Fall in Love)." The following year *Fifty Million Frenchmen* became a hit, featuring as part of the score, "You Do Something to Me." A fellow Peru native, Ole Olson, who knew Porter as a boy, was in the show. In 1932 *The Gay Divorce* opened on Broadway starring Fred Astaire. *Anything Goes*, which perhaps had the best score of any Porter musical, opened in 1934. In 1935 came *Jubilee*, which contained "Begin the Beguine." The song did not attract much attention until a young clarinetist named Artie Shaw recorded it. In 1936 there was *Red, Hot and Blue!* followed in 1938 by *You Never Know*. Porter's old friend from Indiana, Webb, was the star.

Hollywood called, and Porter answered. Unfortunately, many of Porter's Broadway hits, when transferred to the screen, were virtually unrecognizable. He began to write songs to be used in films, notably *Born to Dance* (1936) and *Rosalie* (1937). He was nominated four times for an Oscar for best song but never won. In 1937 Porter was injured in a riding accident on Long Island that cost him the use of his legs and caused him constant pain for the rest of his life. Eventually, one leg had to be amputated. Despite this tragedy, he continued to write and in 1948 produced what many consider to be his masterpiece, *Kiss Me, Kate*. Of his later musicals, only *Can-Can* (1953) was successful. His last hit was in 1956 when he wrote "True Love" for the film *High Society*. After Linda died in 1954, he became a recluse in New York. Two films were based on his life, *Night and Day* in 1946 and *De-Lovely* in 2004.

Porter died in 1964 and was buried in Peru, Indiana, between the bodies of his mother and his wife. As a composer/lyricist, he created some of the most elegant, sophisticated, and musically complex songs of American twentieth-century popular music.

BIBLIOGRAPHY

Eells, George. *The Life That Late He Led: A Biography of Cole Porter.* New York: G. P. Putnam's Sons, 1967.

Grove Music Online. http://www.grovemusic.com/.

Hardy, Phil, and Dave Laing. *The Faber Companion to 20th-Century Popular Music.* Boston: Faber and Faber, 1990.

The Indiana Biographical Dictionary: People of All Times and All Places Who Have Been Important to the State. New York: Somerset, 1993.

Mayhill, Tom. "Cole Porter: Composer." *Indianapolis Monthly* (February 1984).

J. RUSSEL ROBINSON, *Indianapolis (1892-1963)*

While still a teenager at Shortridge High School, J. Russel Robinson started playing piano in the Star Theater on West Washington

Street in Indianapolis. He sometimes played nine to ten hours a day. He and his brother, Johnny, who played drums, were very conscientious about their work "cueing pictures" as it was called. They billed themselves as the Famous Robinson Brothers and began playing in New Orleans, Birmingham, Memphis, and other cities. J. Russel decided he had to break up the act and go to New York. Once he arrived, he said he "literally fell into a job as pianist with the famous Dixieland Five."

Robinson went to England with the group during World War I. When he came back to the states, he began touring in vaudeville as an accompanist to singer Marion Harris. He began writing lyrics, helped by his wife who was his high school sweetheart. In 1920 he wrote the lyrics to his most famous song, "Margie," in collaboration with Con Conrad and Benny Davis. In his autobiography, Eddie Cantor said, "Con Conrad wrote 'Margie' with Benny Davis and J. Russel Robinson and the minute they finished it they brought it over to 'plug' it to me because I had a daughter named Marjorie." Other compositions include "Mary Lou" and "Blue-Eyed Sally."

Robinson's music has been featured in many films, starting with *Good News* (1930), *Frankie and Johnnie* (1936), *Stella Dallas* (1937), *Margie* (1946), and *Mary Lou* (1948). In 2001 Peter Bogdanovich directed *The Cat's Meow*, and "Margie" was a featured song in the movie.

BIBLIOGRAPHY

Cantor, Eddie, with Jane Kesner Ardmore. *Take My Life.* Garden City, N.Y.: Doubleday and Company, 1957.

Indianapolis News, February 4, 1942.

The Internet Movie Database. http://www.imdb.com/.

KNOWLES FRED ROSE, *Evansville (1897–1954)*

Born in Evansville, Fred Rose was raised by relatives in Saint Louis. He attended Saint Louis schools and played the piano for tips in various saloons in the area as a boy. In his teens, he moved to Chicago where he became a singer and songwriter. His first success was "Red Hot Mama," which he wrote for Sophie Tucker. Rose moved to Nashville where he had a fifteen-minute radio show called *Freddie Rose's Song Shop.* The program did not last long, and he moved to New York to try his luck on Tin Pan Alley.

In the 1930s Rose was introduced to Gene Autry. Rose and Autry began collaborating on songs, and some of the hits they produced included "Be Honest with Me" and "Tears on My Pillow." This collaboration led to a number of songs by Rose appearing in movies. His musical contribution to motion pictures includes more than forty films from 1937 to 1953. His songs still find their way into motion pictures to this day.

In 1942 Rose joined with Grand Ole Opry star Roy Acuff to set up a music publishing company in Nashville. Acuff-Rose Publications published and promoted the songs of several country music legends, including Hank Williams. As a songwriter, Rose collaborated with various composers and lyricists and was a composer of pop tunes as well as country tunes. His best-known pop tune was "Deed I Do." Songs he wrote for Williams include "Kaw-Liga" and "A Mansion on the Hill," the latter written with Williams. Ray Charles had a hit with

Rose's "Take These Chains from My Heart" in 1963. In 1975 Willie Nelson revived Rose's "Blue Eyes Crying in the Rain."

Rose was inducted into the Country Music Hall of Fame in 1961.

BIBLIOGRAPHY

Hardy, Phil, and Dave Laing. *The Faber Companion to 20th-Century Popular Music.* Boston: Faber and Faber, 1990.

The Internet Movie Database. http://www.imdb.com/.

The Songwriters Hall of Fame. http://www.songwritershallof fame.org/.

W. AXL ROSE (WILLIAM BRUCE ROSE), *Lafayette (b. 1962)*

Axl Rose.

Shortly after his birth, William Rose's mother divorced his father and remarried. William Rose became William Bailey. At age seventeen he boarded a Greyhound bus for Los Angeles. A little later his longtime friend Jeff Isbell (also from Lafayette) joined him. After auditioning for a number of punk bands, they joined the rock band L. A. Guns. It was not long before Rose formed Guns and Roses. He changed his name to W. Axl Rose, and Isbell changed his name to Izzy Stradlin. Rose's wailing voice was impressive in its range and rhetorical punch. Heavily influenced by Aerosmith, the group was popular with heavy metal fans; however, its music had a blues influence and lacked the features of classical music that typified heavy metal at that time.

Guns and Roses released several successful albums, but it was a tender rock ballad, "Sweet Child O'Mine," that established its stardom. *Appetite for Destruction* has remained the best-selling debut album to date. Drug problems disrupted the group's momentum, and the declining popularity of rock star excesses diminished its appeal. Their music has been featured in a number of films, including *State of Grace* (1990), *Terminator 2: Judgment Day* (1991), *Selena* (1997), and *End of Days* (1999).

BIBLIOGRAPHY

The Internet Movie Database. http://www.imdb.com/.

Grove Music Online. http://www.grovemusic.com/.

DAVID LEE ROTH, *Bloomington (b. 1954)*

David Lee Roth.

At an early age David Roth's father introduced him to the music of Al Jolson, Ray Charles, Frank Sinatra, and Louis Prima. Roth's family moved to California when he was a teenager, and by the early 1970s Roth was singing in local bands, including the Red Ball Jets, who played shows with another rising band from Pasadena, Mammoth. Roth became friends with the members of Mammoth, which included brothers Eddie and Alex Van Halen. In the mid-1970s Roth joined them, and they began performing as Van Halen. Van Halen signed with Warner Brothers and in 1978 released its landmark self-titled debut album mixing heavy metal with punk's fury. The band created a whole new sound, and it issued a string of classic megaselling albums. In 1985 Roth left Van Halen and embarked on a solo career. He had several hits, had a sold-out tour, and did some hilarious and highly original music videos.

In 1996 Roth had a short-lived reunion with Van Halen. In 1997 Roth's tell-all biography *Crazy from the Heat* was published. Roth has composed music for at least fourteen films, including *Airheads* (1994), *Private Parts* (1997) and *Mission to Mars* (2000), and the video game *Grand Theft Auto:Vice City* (2002). He has appeared on numerous television programs and specials, including an appearance on the popular *Sopranos* television series.

BIBLIOGRAPHY

David Lee Roth. http://www.VH1.com/artists/az/roth_david_lee/bio.jhtml.

Hardy, Phil, and Dave Laing. *The Faber Companion to 20th-Century Popular Music.* Boston: Faber and Faber, 1990.

The Internet Movie Database. http://www.imdb.com/.

BOBBY SHERWOOD (ROBERT J. SHERWOOD JR.), Indianapolis (1914-1981)

Bobby Sherwood first appeared on stage while still a child in his parents' vaudeville act. He learned to play guitar, trumpet, trombone, and piano. In 1933 he replaced Eddie Lange as Bing Crosby's guitar accompanist and for the next nine years lived in Hollywood, where he was a studio musician for MGM. He also was the bandleader for Eddie Cantor's radio show and briefly played with Artie Shaw in 1940.

Sherwood married Judy Garland's sister, Dorothy Gumm, and fronted studio bands on several of Garland's Decca recordings. In the film *Andy Hardy Meets Debutante* (1940), Sherwood's orchestra accompanied Garland singing "I'm Nobody's Baby." In the spring of 1942 Sherwood formed his first big band, working in the Los Angeles area. It was quickly signed to a recording contract by Capitol Records. The band's first session produced "Elk's Parade," which became a million seller. (Kitty Kallen sang "Moonlight Becomes You" at this session but left the band soon after.) The success of this recording session led to a cross-country tour.

In October 1946 Sherwood appeared on the Broadway stage in *Hear that Trumpet.* He returned to Los Angeles and his band in early 1947 for a three-month engagement at the Casion Gardens. He released two records in 1950 with Mercury and two records in 1954 with Coral Records, and then spent the remainder of his career as a deejay. He had a featured role in *Campus Sleuth* (1948), and his last film role was in *Pal Joey* (1957). He was a regular on *The Red Buttons Show* (1955) and was a game show host for *Quick as a Flash* (1953). He was a panelist on *Masquerade Party* from 1954 to 1957.

BIBLIOGRAPHY

American Big Bands Database. http://nfo.net/usa/s2.html.

The Internet Movie Database. http://www.imdb.com/.

Whitburn, Joel. *Joel Whitburn's Pop Memories, 1890–1954: A History of Popular Music.* Menomonee Falls, Wis.: Record Research, 1986.

NOBLE SISSLE, Indianapolis (1889-1975)

Noble Sissle changed the face of musical theater. He was a producer, director, lyricist, singer, and actor. The shows of this multitalented Hoosier launched the careers of Josephine Baker, Lena Horne, Adelaide Hall, and Paul Robeson. His Broadway hit, *Shuffle*

Along, cowritten with Eubie Blake, legitimatized the black musical and was a critical turn away from the minstrel tradition. Sissle's lyrics with Blake's tunes are still performed today.

Sissle was also a pioneer in motion pictures. He and Blake made a landmark film on April 15, 1923. It was a short sound film showcasing their vaudeville act, *Noble Sissle and Eubie Blake Sing Snappy Songs.* This film was produced and directed by Lee DeForest using the Phonovision system that he invented in 1920. The film was shown at the Rivoli Theater in New York City. Others who appeared in the film with Sissle and Blake were Phil Baker, Eddie Cantor, Eva Puck, Sammy White, and Conchita Piquer. Most film historians list 1927 as the beginning of sound motion pictures when *The Jazz Singer* was premiered. However, Sissle and Blake's sound debut was four years earlier.

Noble Lee Sissle was born on July 10, 1889, in Indianapolis. His father was a schoolteacher who turned to the ministry. Reverend George A. Sissle traveled between Kentucky, Indiana, and Ohio serving various congregations. Sissle said, "My father hoped I would go into the ministry and follow in his footsteps. I used to get a great thrill when my father or some member of the congregation would lead us in a hymn, reading off the lyrics ahead of us. Then everyone would join in and every foot would keep time, and soon the whole church would be swaying in rhythm or patting their hands and feet. Whenever I sing a rhythm song, even today, I still pat my foot the same way." His mother, Martha Angeline Sissle (who was also a schoolteacher), had six children to care for, three boys and three girls, and she stressed the importance of good diction and skill in declamation.

Noble Sissle.

Sissle attended Shortridge High School until his family moved to Cleveland, Ohio, in 1906. He completed his secondary education at Central High School, where out of fifteen hundred students, only six were black. All students were given an equal opportunity to participate in school activities. Sissle was on the baseball and football teams. After he was injured in football, he became the yell master. He was a tenor in the glee club and soon was a featured vocalist. With Edward Thomas's Male Quartet, he played the chautauqua circuit throughout the Midwest while still in high school. After graduation he joined Hann's Jubilee Singers and toured extensively.

Sissle's family returned to Indianapolis in 1913 after the death of George Sissle. Noble went to Chicago, where he hoped to get a job on the Pullman cars, but he had no luck. He even tried vaudeville, but flopped. Finally, his mother sent him a telegram telling him she had a playground job for him for the summer. The job paved the way for him to go to college, and in the fall of 1913 Sissle enrolled at DePauw University in Greencastle, Indiana. After one semester, he transferred to Butler University in Indianapolis to study for the ministry. While at Butler, he wrote parodies and yells for the football games, including "Butler Will Shine Tonight," and sang, with a megaphone, in a local movie house frequented by Butler students. He left school in order to help support his family.

Early in 1915 Sissle was waiting tables at the Severin Hotel in Indianapolis when the manager told him he had just returned from New York, where black musicians were playing and entertaining in every café. The manager asked Sissle to organize an orchestra, and Sissle began to play regularly there. After a number of other engagements in Indianapolis, he was hired as a vocalist for Joe Porter's Serenaders at River View Park in Baltimore, Maryland. In Baltimore Sissle met pianist and composer Blake and they formed a songwriting partnership that became the famous team of Sissle and Blake, entertainers, composers, and theatrical entrepreneurs. They had immediate success with "It's All Your Fault," performed by Sophie Tucker.

Sissle and Blake went to New York and joined James Reese Europe's Society Orchestra. Europe was a New York impresario and boss of the Clef Club. In December 1916 Sissle joined the U.S. Army, serving as a lieutenant in the 369th Division Band. After his discharge, he rejoined Europe's outfit. Sissle was the drum major for Europe's regimental band and took over the band after the leader's death in 1919. He now had his own orchestra and toured Europe.

Noble Sissle and Russell Smith in the early 1920s.
DUNCAN SCHIEDT COLLECTION

After the tour, Sissle reunited with Blake, playing vaudeville together as the Dixie Duo. They are credited with being the first black team to play in tuxedos and without burnt cork on their faces. They played on stage with only a piano as their prop. One of the many hit songs they produced for their vaudeville show was "Gee; I'm Glad I'm from Dixie."

In 1921 Sissle, Blake, Flournoy Miller, and Aubrey Lyles wrote and produced *Shuffle Along*. This marked the revival of African American folk humor, jazz dance, and ragtime. The show opened at the 63rd Street Theater in New York. This theater was off the beaten path and was somewhat dilapidated. Blake said, "It was really off-Broadway, but we caused it to be Broadway." *Shuffle Along* ran for more than five hundred performances and then went on tour. It served as a launching pad for the careers of many black performers, including Josephine Baker.

When *Shuffle Along* was staging tryouts for the show in Philadelphia, a very young Josephine Baker auditioned. Sissle recalled his first impression of her: "Josephine was a nervous little girl with big brown eyes like saucers. She stood shivering in the doorway in the cold March rain that was coming in torrents outside." Miller, a partner in the show, took Sissle aside, saying, "That kid looks awfully young to me." "I'm fifteen," Baker said. Sissle patted her on the back. "There's a New York law prohibiting the use of chorus girls under sixteen years of age. Sorry." Sissle said, "Big tears filled her eyes, and with drooping head looking like a wilted flower she slowly turned, half stumbling down the steps leading to the stage door exit. We stood there watching her as she walked down the alleyway bursting forth in a flood of grief."

Noble Sissle with Lena Horne.
DUNCAN SCHIEDT COLLECTION

Baker could not get *Shuffle Along* out of her mind and popped up again and again for tryouts. Finally, when she turned sixteen, she was cast in a road company of the show but quickly transferred to the Broadway production. The public loved her, and eventually she was put in the touring company of *Shuffle Along*, which played in Boston, Milwaukee, Des Moines, Saint Louis, and in Sissle's hometown, Indianapolis.

Shuffle Along introduced jazz dancing to Broadway, leaving an indelible impression on the Broadway musical, and helped stimulate the black cultural renaissance of the 1920s. It also was the first black musical to play all-white theaters across the country. Some of the Sissle and Blake songs in *Shuffle Along* were "Everything Reminds Me of You," "If You've Never Been Vamped by a Brownskin," "I'm Just Wild about Harry," and "Love Will Find a Way." Florenz Ziegfeld and George

White were so impressed by the dancing in *Shuffle Along* that they hired women from its cast to teach dance steps to the white women in their all-white productions.

The song "I'm Just Wild about Harry" not only became President Harry Truman's theme song in 1948 but also was featured in at least six motion pictures from 1939 to 1949. Judy Garland sang it in *Babes in Arms* (1939). Other memorable songs by Sissle and Blake include "In Honeysuckle Time," "Gypsy Blues," "Hello, Sweetheart, Hello," "Goodnight Angeline," "Slave of Love," "Lowdown Blues," "Characteristic Blues," "Okey Doke," "Yeah Man," and "You Were Meant for Me." (The latter title was used for two different songs. In 1929 Arthur Freed and Nacio Herb Brown wrote "You Were Meant for Me" for the film musical *The Broadway Melody*. The Freed/Brown tune was used in many more movie musicals over the years.)

Sissle and Blake wrote for the musical *London Calling*. With C. W. Bell, Sissle wrote twelve songs for *Elsie* in 1923. Just as Sissle collaborated with other composers, Blake worked with other lyricists over the years, but the show that recalls most vividly the style and music of the 1920s era was *Shuffle Along*. Many of Blake and Sissle's songs were also featured in the 1978 hit Broadway show *Eubie!*, which ran a year on Broadway and then successfully toured the country.

In 1924 Sissle and Blake wrote some special material for Baker in their new all-black Broadway show, *The Chocolate Dandies*. The show opened at the New Colonial Theater in New York. Although Baker was a hit, she was far from the chic European figure she would later become. In the mid-1930s Sissle hired a girl singer named Lena Horne for his band, fresh from the chorus line at the Cotton Club. In December 1932 *Shuffle Along* had a successful rebirth. This time it was called *Shuffle Along of 1933*.

Sissle and his band played in several black-cast movies in the late 1930s and early 1940s. One outstanding film was a short musical called *That's the Spirit*, released in 1933. Some have declared this to be "one of the greatest jazz shorts ever made." Featured on the film is Sissle's band playing "Tiger Rag" and "St. Louis Blues." The great clarinetist Buster Bailey is featured in the band, and the brilliant Harlem singer and dancer Cora La Redd gives a memorable performance.

During the 1930s Sissle periodically returned to Indianapolis with his orchestra for engagements at the Indiana Roof Ballroom. It was during this time that his orchestra featured the great jazzman Sidney Bechet. In 1931 Sissle and his orchestra recorded "Got the Bench, Got the Park," featuring Bechet on the clarinet and soprano sax. It was recorded by Brunswick. Sensing a need for an organization for black entertainers, Sissle organized and was first president of the Negro Actors Guild. At one time he was known as the unofficial mayor of Harlem.

In 1938 Sissle began a twelve-year span working as a bandleader at Billy Rose's Diamond Horseshoe in New York. In his spare time he toured the United States and overseas for the USO during World War II. In the 1960s he managed his own publishing company and eventually had his own nightclub, Noble's.

In 1941 Sissle appeared in *Murder with Music*, a fifty-nine-minute film that featured Nellie Hill and Bob Howard. In 1947 he was in *Junction 88* with Howard and Pigmeat Markham. It was just sixty minutes long. In 1943 the great all-black musical *Stormy Weather* premiered. It starred Bill Robinson and Lena Horne, and Ernest Whitman played

Jim Europe. This film was loosely based on the careers of Sissle, Europe, and Adelaide Hall.

Sissle wrote historical pieces for several magazines and was in the process of writing a book on the history of black music in the United States when he died in Tampa, Florida, on December 17, 1975.

BIBLIOGRAPHY

The ASCAP Biographical Dictionary of Composers, Authors, and Publishers. 3rd ed. New York: ASCAP, 1966.

Bodenhamer, David J., and Robert G. Barrows, eds. *The Encyclopedia of Indianapolis.* Bloomington and Indianapolis: Indiana University Press, 1994.

Bogle, Donald. *Blacks in American Films and Television: An Encyclopedia.* New York: Simon and Schuster, 1989.

———. *Brown Sugar: Eighty Years of America's Black Female Superstars.* New York: Harmony Books, 1980.

Green, Abel, and Joe Laurie Jr. *Show Biz: From Vaude to Video.* New York: Holt, 1951.

Haney, Lynn. *Naked at the Feast: A Biography of Josephine Baker.* New York: Dodd, Mead, 1981.

Indiana Biographical Dictionary: People of All Times and All Places Who Have Been Important to the History of the State. 2nd ed. 2 vols. St. Clair Shores, Mich.: Somerset Publishers, 1999.

Indianapolis Star, February 10, 1980.

Krasner, David. *A Beautiful Pageant: African American Theatre, Drama, and Performance in the Harlem Renaissance, 1910–1927.* New York: Palgrave Macmillan, 2002.

Kimball, Robert, and William Bolcom. *Reminiscing with Sissle and Blake.* New York: Viking Press, 1973.

New York Times, December 18, 1975.

Sampson, Henry T. *Blacks in Black and White: A Source Book on Black Films.* 2nd ed. Metuchen, N.J.: Scarecrow Press, 1995.

———. *Blacks in Blackface: A Source Book on Early Black Musical Shows.* Metuchen, N.J.: Scarecrow Press, 1980.

Whitburn, Joel. *Joel Whitburn's Pop Memories, 1890–1954: The History of American Popular Music.* Menomonee Falls, Wis.: Record Research, 1986.

Wool, Allen L. *Black Musical Theatre: From Coontown to Dreamgirls.* Baton Rouge: Louisiana State University Press, 1989.

CONNIE SMITH (CONSTANCE JUNE MEADOR), *Elkhart (b. 1941)*

Country singer Dolly Parton once said, "There are only three great singers, Connie Smith, Barbra Streisand and Linda Ronstadt. The rest of us are just pretending." Smith has few peers when it comes to plumbing a heartache, and no one has ever matched her for sheer emotional power.

Smith was one of fourteen children born into a poor family. Her father was an abusive alcoholic, and the family moved often. She grew up in West Virginia and Ohio. She married young and was starting a family when she won a talent contest in 1963 that brought her to the attention of singer/songwriter Bill Anderson. Anderson persuaded her to come to Nashville, and she signed a contract with RCA Records the following year.

Smith cut several songs in her first RCA sessions, and among them was Anderson's "Once a Day." It entered Billboard's charts in 1964 and went on to hit the number one spot, remaining there for eight consecutive weeks.

Smith became a fixture on the Grand Ole Opry and was on the country charts through the 1970s. Smith had a clause inserted in her contract that permitted her to record at least one gospel album a year. Although she abandoned her career in the 1980s to raise her five children, she is at peace with her decision stating, "I've got the five greatest kids in the world, and three grandbabies. I wouldn't trade any of those years. I feel confident I would have been more popular, but to me, the price would have been too high."

Smith's movie appearances include *The Las Vegas Hillbillys* (1966), *Second Fiddle to a Steel Guitar* (1966), *The Road to Nashville* (1967), and *The Hi-Lo Country* (1998).

BIBLIOGRAPHY

Connie Smith Biography. http://www.cmt.com/artists/az/smith_connie/bio.jhtml.

The Internet Movie Database. http://www.imdb.com/.

Nashville Scene, October 19, 1998.

THE VON TILZERS

Harry Gumm (Gumbinsky), Detroit (1872–1946)
Albert Gumm (Gumbinsky), Indianapolis (1878–1956)

Harry Von Tilzer was born Harry Gumm (shortened from Gumbinsky) in Detroit, Michigan. He was one of five children. The family moved to Indianapolis when Harry was still a youngster. Harry was initiated to the theater by a stock company that gave performances in the loft above his father's shoe store. He fell in love with show business and began attending burlesque shows, minstrel shows, and any other form of entertainment available in Indianapolis. He would sit for hours in the lobby of the English Hotel waiting to catch a glimpse of some of the performers.

Harry ran away from home at age fourteen, joining the Cole Brothers Circus with whom he did a tumbling act. After a year he moved on to a traveling repertory troupe where his varied tasks included playing the piano (which he learned without any formal instruction), writing songs, and performing juvenile roles. Harry changed his name to Von Tilzer (Tilzer was his mother's maiden name). He thought Von added class and began performing with a burlesque company touring the Midwest.

While living in Chicago he composed "I Love You Both." It was published in 1892, marking his first appearance in sheet music. Encouraged by this success, he began to write in earnest. It was soon apparent that if Von Tilzer wanted a lucrative career as a songwriter he would have to leave Chicago. He moved to New York City and found a cheap room and a job as a saloon pianist. He completed more than one hundred songs during his first years in New York. Some he sold outright for two dollars each. A handful got published.

But before the 1890s were over Harry had two smash hits. First came "My Old New Hampshire Home," which he wrote with lyricist

Harry Von Tilzer.

Albert Von Tilzer.
INDIANA HISTORICAL SOCIETY, HERBERT LONDON
COLLECTION, M0747

Andrew B. Sterling. The second was "I'd Leave My Happy Home for You." "My Old New Hampshire Home" became a feature of silver-toned tenors in vaudeville. The sheet music sold handsomely, and he became a recognized songwriter.

Harry soon became versatile enough to be successful in almost all song styles. He became a partner in Shapiro, Bernstein and Von Tilzer and wrote one of the most successful ballads of the entire era, "A Bird in a Gilded Cage," with lyrics by Arthur J. Lamb. Harry left Shapiro and Bernstein to form his own music company in a shop on Twenty-eighth Street—a street soon to be known as Tin Pan Alley. Harry soon became king of Tin Pan Alley with four songs whose sheet-music sales exceeded five million copies.

In 1900 Harry's brother, Albert, adopted the name Von Tilzer and joined Harry's publishing house as an arranger. In 1903 Albert formed the York Music Company with another brother, Jack Von Tilzer. Albert began to write some of the most popular songs of the early twentieth century, including "Teasing," "Take Me Out to the Ball Game," and "I'll Be with You in Apple Blossom Time."

Meanwhile, Harry was busy writing his own hit songs. He wrote a ragtime number, "Good-bye, Eliza Jane," and "What You Goin' to Do When the Rent Comes Around?" In 1905 he produced another million-copy ballad, "Wait 'Til the Sun Shines Nellie." A "mother" song that is still remembered is "I Want a Girl Just Like the Girl That Married Dear Old Dad." Harry was the first to write a telephone song, "Hello Central, Give Me 603," the first to write rural-type songs, "Down on the Farm," and the first to write a hit song inspired by a popular dance, "The Cubanola Glide."

The Von Tilzers were probably the most prolific composers Tin Pan Alley ever produced. Harry insisted that he had written 8,000 songs, 2,000 of which were published. He also insisted that the total sales of his songs went into hundreds of millions. His last hit was "Just Around the Corner," popularized by Ted Lewis. Harry's songs were in twenty-four films between 1925 and 1948.

Albert's songs have been heard in thirty films, and he also wrote works for Broadway, including popular musical comedies *Honey Girl* (1920) and *The Gingham Girl* (1922).

BIBLIOGRAPHY

Ewen, David. *Great Men of the American Popular Song: The History of the American Popular Song Told through the Lives, Careers, Achievements, and Personalities of Its Foremost Composers and Lyricists—From William Billings of the Revolutionary War through Bob Dylan, Johnny Cash, Burt Bacharach.* Englewood Cliffs, N.J.: Prentice-Hall, 1972.

———. *The Life and Death of Tin Pan Alley: The Golden Age of American Popular Music.* New York: Funk and Wagnalls, 1964.

Grove Music Online. http://www.grovemusic.com/.

SALEM TUTT WHITNEY, *Logansport (d. 1934)*
J. HOMER TUTT, *Logansport*

In the early twentieth century two brothers from Logansport, Indiana, Salem Tutt Whitney and J. Homer Tutt, were the leading impresarios of black theater in America. An article in the *New York*

Messenger in 1925 stated that "two-thirds of our leading theatrical artists of the present day received their initial training with Whitney and
Tutt. These two producers have always maintained a very high standard of show and a high standard of conduct for the people with their
shows." Their careers would intertwine with at least two other black
Hoosier performers, James Baskett and Noble Sissle.

Both brothers were born in Logansport. At age five, J. Homer
became a cow dogger, which was a shepherd charged with a herd of
cows. He was paid five cents a head. He went to Indianapolis and
attended Manual Training High School, where he was a champion
sprinter and broad jumper. Salem Tutt Whitney studied for the ministry before embarking on an acting career. In 1904 the brothers
began their theatrical career with S. H. Dudley's Smart Set Company.
They were successful and remained with the company through the
1906 season. After gaining experience with the Smart Set Company,
Salem formed the Baynard and Whitney Troubadours.

In the 1908–09 seasons the brothers organized a No. 2 Smart Set
Company and were very successful. They began to write and produce
musical comedies and presented them all over the United States and
into Canada. In 1916 they took full charge of the Smart Set Company
and renamed it the Smarter Set.

On February 5, 1910, Elwood Knox, the publisher of the *Indianapolis Freeman*, wrote a review of the Whitney and Tutt musical *The Ruler
of the Town*. He recalled Salem as "the most natural born comedian I
had ever seen."

Homer wrote comedy lyrics for Salem and composed several popular songs, including "Struttin' Sam," "Smile on Sue," and "Dream
and Glide." Apparently the show was a hit, as witnessed by this notice
on February 22, 1919, in the *Chicago Defender*, "Salem Tutt Whitney and
J. Homer Tutt's 'Smarter Set' is cleaning up at the Grand Theatre in
Cleveland this week."

One of Whitney and Tutt's most successful shows was *Oh! Joy!* Ethel
Waters, who had just made some hit recordings, appeared as the lead
in the show, the first in which she was a name performer. The Boston
run of the show was a hit, even weathering the touring production of
their fellow Hoosier Noble Sissle and Eubie Blake's *Shuffle Along*. Whitney and Tutt wanted to book *Oh! Joy!* in New York, but they could not
find a theater. Whitney and Tutt overcame the problem by converting
the Van-Kelton tennis stadium into a theater. They rented a tent,
built a stage, and placed cushions on the bleachers. However, Waters
refused to perform in the tent.

Faced with criticism that Broadway musicals were exploiting
"Negro primitivism" and that the "stricter theatre arts" should be
followed in a similar urge for expression, Salem wrote the following
essay in 1920:

> We are necessarily breadwinners, we must produce and sell
> according to demand, and just now there is not sufficient
> demand or a large enough market for the Negro Drama to
> make its productions a paying proposition. . . . Managers of
> white theatres would not be induced to play a Negro drama as a
> regular attraction, and a four or eight weeks' season would not
> prove alluring to the players. . . . Managers of colored shows
> are now dependent upon white managers of white theatres for

most of their bookings . . . naturally the white companies get the preference and the colored companies must take what is left wherever and whenever they can get it. . . . Now is the time for colored capitalists to act. . . . Give us theatres and we will give you the shows. Not only the first-class vaudeville and high-class musical comedy, but the legitimate Negro drama.

Finally, Salem and Homer decided that instead of competing with Sissle and Blake's immensely successful all-black *Shuffle Along*, they would join the cast. In 1922 a touring company of the show opened at Harlem's Lafayette Theater. The starring roles were taken by Salem and Homer. The show enjoyed standing-room-only crowds that were "almost six deep."

In 1930 Homer was on Broadway in the cast of *The Green Pastures*, where he became known for his versatility. Both brothers appeared in films directed by the great black filmmaker Oscar Micheaux. They were together in Micheaux's *Birthright* in 1924. Salem was in *Marcus Garland*, a 1925 Micheaux film, and Homer appeared in Micheaux's *The Broken Violin* in 1927.

Salem was the more prolific writer and wrote many sketches for leading vaudeville artists, writing twenty-five musical comedies, fifty tabloids, one hundred sketches, three hundred poems, and fifty songs. His best-known shows were *The Mayor of Newtown*, *George Washington Bullion Abroad*, *My People*, *Darkest Americans*, *Children of the Sun*, *Bamboola*, *Up and Down*, *Oh! Joy!*, *North Ain't South*, and *Yellow Mustings*. Salem died in 1934 at the age of sixty-five.

BIBLIOGRAPHY

Chicago Defender, February 22, 1919.

Krasner, David. *A Beautiful Pageant: African American Theatre, Drama, and Performance in the Harlem Renaissance, 1910–1927*. New York: Palgrave Macmillan, 2002.

Sampson, Henry T. *Blacks in Blackface: A Source Book on Early Black Musical Shows*. Metuchen, N.J.: Scarecrow Press, 1980.

———. *The Ghost Who Walks: A Chronological History of Blacks in Show Business, 1865–1910*. Metuchen, N.J.: Scarecrow Press, 1988.

Waters, Ethel, with Charles Samuels. *His Eye on the Sparrow: An Autobiography by Ethel Waters*. Garden City, N.Y.: Doubleday, 1951.

DENIECE WILLIAMS, *York, Pennsylvania (b. 1951)*

Deniece Williams grew up in Gary, Indiana, singing gospel music in a Pentecostal church. After high school, her family moved to Chicago. Although she had no serious ambitions to become a singer, she listened with great interest to her favorites, Carmen McCrae and Nancy Wilson.

However, when it was apparent that college was not a possibility, she decided to pursue a singing career. A cousin, John Harris, was Stevie Wonder's valet and arranged for Williams to meet Wonder backstage at a concert. Six months later, Williams auditioned for Wonder and was selected as one of Wonder's three backup singers. The three were known as Wonderlove.

She toured with Wonder until 1975 when she teamed with producer Maurice White, the leader of Earth, Wind & Fire. Under

White's direction, Williams learned the music business. Her first album, *This Is Niecy*, was released in 1976 and featured several hit songs, including "Free" and "That's What Friends Are For."

In 1977, her second album, *Songbird*, was released featuring "Baby, Baby, All for You." It became the number-thirteen single of that year. The following year she recorded her first number-one song, "Too Much, Too Little, Too Late," which was a duet with Johnny Mathis. Its success led to a follow-up single with Mathis, "You're All I Need to Get By." She moved to the American Recording Company, where she composed and recorded "Silly," which became a smash hit. In 1982 she had a number one single with "Its Gonna Take a Miracle."

Williams was now writing her songs. "Do What You Feel" was a top-ten single, and in 1984 she recorded "Let's Hear It for the Boy," which was featured on the soundtrack of the hit movie *Footloose*. That same year she recorded "Black Butterfly," which served as a prelude to her return to gospel music. She recorded an album for Sparrow Records, featuring the Grammy award—winning single, "They Say." That same year she also won a Grammy for "I Surrender" and in 1987 won another for "I Believe in You."

Williams's television and movie credits include singing the theme for the *Family Ties* television series and appearing in *The Hunting of the Snark*, a film based on a Lewis Carroll nonsense poem. The film also featured Julian Lennon and Art Garfunkel and was produced in England. While in England she appeared on BBC Radio 2 with her own program, *The Deniece Williams Show*.

Williams still enjoys singing, but she also enjoys her family (four boys) and her home. Today she is basically a homebody who occasionally performs or makes a personal appearance.

BIBLIOGRAPHY

Deniece Williams. http://www.soulwalking.co.uk/Deniece%20williams.html.

Deniece Williams Biography. http://www.vh1.com/artists/az/williams_deniece/bio.jhtml.

The Internet Movie Database. http://www.imdb.com/.

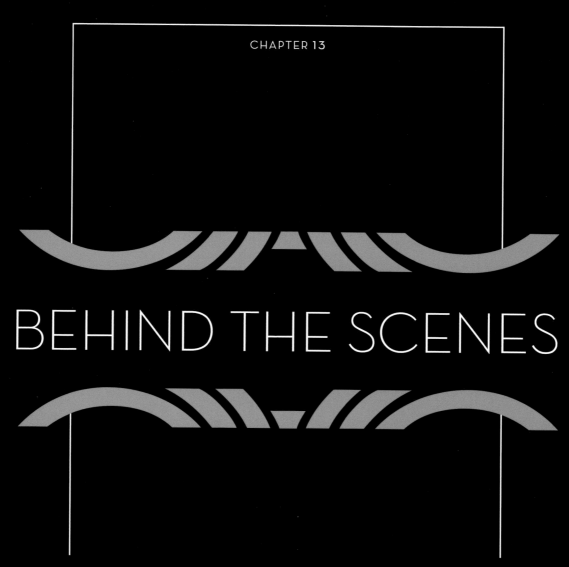

CHAPTER 13

BEHIND THE SCENES

Many Hoosiers have labored behind the scenes in a variety of capacities. Despite the fact that motion pictures have been categorized as a medium in which the director is solely responsible for the end result, most industry observers know that the making of movies is a team effort. No matter how talented the director is, behind-the-scenes people can make or break a motion picture.

Cinematographers, costume designers, special effects people, stuntmen and stuntwomen, assistants or second-unit directors, and even animal trainers are critical to the success of a film. Many Hoosiers labored in these areas with little notice other than their name being mentioned in the end credits. Following are some of the Hoosiers who contributed to the art of motion pictures from behind the camera.

LOUIS DA PRON, *Herman (1913–1987)*
Choreographer

Louis Da Pron's career as a choreographer/actor ran from 1936 to 1953. During that time he appeared in at least nineteen films as an actor and choreographed at least twenty-four motion pictures. He was the favorite choreographer for Donald O'Connor, choreographing no less than seven films featuring O'Connor. Da Pron worked as a choreographer for a number of other stars, including Jack Oakie and Gloria Jean.

Da Pron worked with fellow Hoosier Ole Olsen in *Ghost Catchers* (1944). After choreographing *Walking My Baby Back Home* in 1953, he retired. However, in 1975 Ben Vereen persuaded him to come back to choreograph his televisions series, *Ben Vereen: Comin' at Ya.* This marked Da Pron's last work as a choreographer. He made an appearance in the part of a choreographer in *Funny Lady* (1975).

BIBLIOGRAPHY

The Internet Movie Database. http://www.imdb.com/.

SID GRAUMAN, *Indianapolis (1879–1950)*
Movie Exhibitor

Sid Grauman was not an actor, director, or producer, but his name will forever be associated with most of the legendary names in Hollywood. He was a close friend to almost every big name in the industry and was a superb promoter and entrepreneur who helped create the glamour and the glory that was Hollywood.

At the age of thirteen Grauman left Indianapolis with his father, D. J., for the Alaskan gold rush. They did not find much gold and moved to San Francisco, where his father managed to put enough money together to build the St. Francis Theater. Unfortunately, shortly after the theater opened, the San Francisco earthquake destroyed the building. With all the city's theaters destroyed, the Graumans got a big show tent and with some church pews opened another showplace with the slogan, "Nothing to fall on you except canvas."

Grauman purchased a theater in Los Angeles, beginning a cycle of building, selling, and building again. This eventually led him to build four famous theaters—the Million Dollar (1918), the Egyptian (1922), the Metropolitan (1923), and finally, the famed Chinese (1926). He built the Chinese Theater in honor of his many Chinese friends in Los Angeles and San Francisco.

Grauman was the first to conceive the idea of a premiere and was one of the thirty-six founders of the Academy of Motion Picture Arts and Sciences. One day in 1927, as he was laying concrete between his Chinese Theater and the sidewalk, he got an idea. "All that wet concrete set the wheels in my head to turning," he recalled. "I ran to the phone, called my friends, Douglas Fairbanks, Mary Pickford, and Norma Talmadge, and asked them to hurry down. I didn't give them any explanation. When they got there, they thought I was crazy, but they were game. They were the first."

The honor of being selected to place a permanent autograph in the cement at the Chinese Theater became almost as tantamount as receiving an Academy Award. Today, the sets and prints in concrete attract thousands of people from all over the world. There are foot-

prints, handprints, and brief handwritten messages all addressed, "To Sid." In 1949, a year before his death, he was given an honorary Academy Award for "raising the standard for film exhibition."

Sid Grauman (standing) with (left to right) Henry Fonda, Charles Boyer, Rita Hayworth, Charles Laughton, and E. G. Robinson.

BIBLIOGRAPHY

Beardsley, Charles. *Hollywood's Master Showman: The Legendary Sid Grauman.* New York: Cornwall Books, 1983.

Endres, Stacey, and Robert Cushman. *Hollywood at Your Feet: The Story of the World-Famous Chinese Theatre.* Los Angeles: Pomegranate Press, 1992.

Ragan, David. "Sid's Sidewalk." *Indianapolis Star Magazine,* October 9, 1949.

GLORIA GRESHAM, *Indianapolis (b. 1945)*
Costume Designer

Gloria Gresham is the daughter of Mr. and Mrs. Stokes Gresham. Her father was chief engineer for WISH-Radio and WISH-TV in Indianapolis in the 1950s and 1960s. Her interest in costuming began at North Central High School. This led to a scholarship in costume design at Indiana University. Shortly after graduation, she moved to

New York City, where she and three other Hoosiers became involved in the CBS television series *Beacon Hill*. Brian Davies (Indianapolis) was an actor in the series, Jeffry Mont (Greencastle) worked with the Stigwood Group that was producing the series, and Gresham and Marcia Eck (Noblesville) were costumers. Eck and Gresham had been friends at Indiana University. *Beacon Hill*, a lavish soap opera set in the 1920s, ran for thirteen episodes on CBS.

After *Beacon Hill* Gresham began assisting some of New York's most famous theatrical costume designers. One of her first breaks was assisting Broadway costumer Tony Walton for the screen version of *The Wiz* in 1978. She worked alone for the first time on *Urban Cowboy*, also in 1980.

Gresham specializes in contemporary apparel, although her only Oscar nomination was for costumes created for a period film, *Avalon* (1990), directed by Barry Levinson. She and Levinson have worked on many films: *Diner* (1982), *The Natural* (1984), *Tin Men* (1987), *Sleepers* (1996), *Sphere* (1998), *Bandits* (2001), and *Envy* (2004). She also has been a favorite with directors Rob Reiner (*When Harry Met Sally*, 1989), Arthur Hiller (*Outrageous Fortune*, 1987, with fellow Hoosier Shelley Long), and William Friedkin (*Rules of Engagement*, 2000, and *The Hunted*, 2003).

Gloria Gresham with director Barry Levinson on the set of *Bandits*, starring Bruce Willis.

COURTESY OF GLORIA GRESHAM

BIBLIOGRAPHY

Indianapolis News, September 3, 1975.

The Internet Movie Database. http://www.imdb.com/.

Author's notes from conversation with Stokes Gresham, Gloria's father.

W. DONN HAYES, Brookston (1893–1973)
Film Editor

In a career that started near the beginning of motion pictures in 1916, W. Donn Hayes edited motion pictures and then television shows for more than fifty years.

Hayes was educated at the University of Wyoming after his parents moved to Laramie. After college he went into vaudeville, and in 1916 he became an assistant editor at Universal Studios. He began to master his trade and eventually became one of Hollywood's premiere editors.

Hayes edited the 1921 version of *Peck's Bad Boy*, starring Jackie Coogan, and *The Girl of the Golden West* (1938), starring Jeanette MacDonald and Nelson Eddy. In 1939 he was one of the primary editors for the Oscar-winning Alfred Hitchcock thriller *Rebecca*.

Hayes was one of the founding members of the American Cinema Editors and was responsible for the acronym ACE. In 1949 he began working in television, editing such shows as *The Life of Riley*, for which he won an Emmy as supervising editor and codirector.

Hayes was a leader in the fight to bring the art of film editing to the forefront of the Hollywood scene.

W. Donn Hayes and Frances Langford in an editing room.

BIBLIOGRAPHY

ACE Web page. http.//www.ace-filmeditors.org/history.htm.

Cinema Editors Magazine (1971).

Hayes, Donn Jr. Interview with the author. January 12, 2004. Grinnell, Iowa.

WILL H. HAYS, *Sullivan (1879-1954)*
Censorship Czar

Will H. Hays was once described by his good friend Meredith Nicholson in this fashion: "Bill is a jolt of lightning in fragile platinum setting. He presents as many different pictures as an old-fashioned kaleidoscope. He can be an 18th century gallant, a 20th century high-pressure executive, an exuberant playboy or a bashful country bumpkin. He can impersonate the impersonal." After graduation from Wabash College, Hays began a career in politics, moving up the ranks to the chairmanship of the Republican National Committee from 1918 to 1921.

Hays became campaign chairman for Warren G. Harding, and when Harding was elected, he appointed Hays postmaster general. Hays used the office to campaign against sending obscene material in the mail. When the Fatty Arbuckle and Wallace Reid scandals rocked Hollywood in the 1920s, the studio moguls had to do something to prevent government regulation of the industry. Will Hays, who did not smoke, drink, or swear, was the perfect choice to serve as the studios' "movie czar."

Hays took the job in 1922 for the enormous sum of $100,000 a year. He hired Indianapolis native Charles C. Pettijohn, who got his start in the industry as an attorney for Frank Rembush, an Indiana exhibitor. In 1918 Pettijohn moved to Hollywood, where he served as an attorney for the Mutual Film Company and the Selznick organization. Hays appointed Pettijohn general counsel for the Motion Picture Producers and Distributors of America Inc. Thus it was that two Hoosiers were anointed as guardians of the public morality.

Carl Sandburg (right), noted American poet, and Will H. Hays.

The famous Hays Code came into full force in 1934. At the height of Hays's power virtually every movie turned out by Hollywood had to have his stamp of approval. In 1939, when David O. Selznick went to Hays about Clark Gable's last line in *Gone with the Wind*, Hays said it would be ridiculous for Gable to say, "Frankly my dear, I don't give a durn."

By the late 1940s Hays's power began to slip as the Supreme Court verified the fact that the movie industry was protected by the first amendment. After Hays left the office, his successors, Joseph Breen, Eric Johnson, and Jack Valenti, never had the power Hays wielded. In 1967 Valenti scrapped the last vestiges of the Hays Code and instituted the present-day rating system.

BIBLIOGRAPHY

Gardner, Gerald C. *The Censorship Papers: Movie Censorship from the Hays Office, 1934–1968.* New York: Dodd, Mead, 1987.

McIntyre, O. O. "The Truth about the Czar of the Movies." *New Movie Magazine* (March 1931).

Ramsaye, Terry. *A Million and One Nights: A History of the Motion Picture.* 1926. Reprint, New York: Simon and Schuster, 1964.

Thorp, Margaret Farrand. *America at the Movies.* New Haven, Conn.: Yale University Press, 1939.

FRANK INN, *Mooresville (1916–2002)*
Animal Trainer

Frank Inn was born Frank Freeman, the son of Ernest, a Quaker minister, and Ada Mae Freeman. Unhappy at being a preacher's kid, Frank joined the Civilian Conservation Corps (CCC) and then began train hopping, hoping to wind up in California. His first attempt to reach California was aborted when he was arrested by police who were searching for the killer of a railroad brakeman. Not wanting to be sent home, he refused to give his name to authorities and was imprisoned. He served on a chain gang for several months until he and eleven others escaped. He returned to Indiana with a new made-up name, Inn, but he soon hit the road again. This time he made it to Los Angeles.

Inn's first job in the movie industry was with MGM, tearing down old sets. His career as an animal trainer began serendipitously. While Inn was undergoing physical therapy for a back injury, a friend gave him a puppy to cheer him up. Inn named the puppy Jeep and taught him a few tricks. Sometime after his recovery, he and Jeep dropped by the MGM set, where Myrna Loy and William Powell were filming *The Thin Man* (1934). The animal trainer was having difficulty getting a dog to perform a stunt. When Jeep performed the stunt perfectly, Inn was hired to be an assistant to the trainer.

Inn became one of the best-known animal trainers in movie history and had more than one thousand animals and thirty trainers working for him. He worked with Daisy on the *Blondie* series and with Lassie. He supplied animals for six television shows, including Cleo on *The People's Choice*, Tramp on *My Three Sons*, Bullet on the *Roy Rogers Show*, and Arnold the pig on *Green Acres*.

In 1960 Inn rescued a puppy from an animal shelter and named him Higgins. Higgins was seen in the series *Petticoat Junction*. After seven years on the show, Higgins retired at age thirteen. Producer/director Joe Camp was looking for a dog to star in a movie told from a dog's point of view, and Camp convinced Inn that old Higgins would be perfect for the part. The movie was *Benji*, and Inn gained his greatest fame as the trainer of "America's huggable hero" in that 1974 film. Three years later a sequel was made, but Higgins (now called Benji) was too old. Benji's daughter starred in many of the sequels. The original Benji died in 1978.

Inn also trained cats, including one named Orangey. Orangey was Audrey Hepburn's cat in *Breakfast at Tiffany's* (1961). Inn was the recipient of numerous Patsy Awards and more than forty awards from the American Humane Association during his career.

BIBLIOGRAPHY

"Frank Inn." *Classic Images* (September 2002).
Indianapolis Star, March 11, 1990, August 30, 2003.

JOHN LEROY JOHNSTON, *Bloomfield (1896–1946)*
Movie Executive

Hoosiers Carmelita Geraghty, Ann Christy, Julanne Johnston, and Ann Hovey all were WAMPAS baby stars. WAMPAS was the Western Associated Motion Picture Advertisers. From 1922 to 1934 this organization selected a group of actresses each year who were supposed to be star material. It was quite an honor to be named a WAMPAS baby star. John L. Johnston was president of WAMPAS in 1931. This title was one of only a few he held during his career in the motion picture industry. After a brief newspaper career, he was offered a job in New York in the publicity department of Paramount Pictures. Then came an offer to become the editor of press material for First National. When he joined MGM, he was charged with discovering new talent. He discovered Phillips Holmes and had much to do with the careers of Clara Bow, Corinne Griffith, Billie Dove, Dolores Del Rio, Lew Ayres, Boris Karloff, and Sidney Fox.

BIBLIOGRAPHY

Indianapolis News, March 25, 1932.
The Internet Movie Database. http://www.imdb.com/.
Liebman, Roy. *The Wampas Baby Stars: A Biographical Dictionary, 1922–1934.* Jefferson, North Carolina, and London: McFarland and Co. Inc., 2000/.

ROBERT AND HERMAN LIEBER, *Indianapolis* (1870–1929; d. 1939)
Motion Picture Entrepreneurs and Executives

Robert and Herman were the sons of Herman and Mary Metzger Lieber and members of the Lieber family, who were influential businessmen and art patrons in Indianapolis in the early twentieth century. Robert and his brother Herman, along with A. L. Block, organized a group to build the Circle Theater and invested $500,000 in the project. The Circle, which opened on August 30, 1916, was the first building constructed in Indianapolis expressly for the presentation of feature-length motion pictures and was one of the first movie "palaces" in the Midwest. The Circle was so successful that the group built an even larger theater in downtown Indianapolis in 1927. It was a magnificent building with a Moroccan facade, a huge stage, and seating for 3,200. In the building were a luncheonette, soda fountain, barbershop, and a ballroom on the top floor. It was called the Indiana Theater and was the largest cinema ever built in Indianapolis. Herman contributed to the success of the Indiana Theater by booking the Charlie Davis orchestra as the stage band. Davis brought along his popular featured vocalist, Dick Powell.

Robert was vice president of the H. Lieber Company, art dealers, a director of the Citizens Gas Company, and a vice president of the Tower Realty Company. As the manager of the photographic department of the H. Lieber Company, Robert believed that the film industry would offer a new channel of distribution for the company and positioned the company to become an important factor in the distribution of films throughout the state. The Lieber company became affiliated with the General Film Company, and Robert became Indiana manager. His organization of the Circle Theater Company in 1915 gave him national status in the industry.

Robert became the president of First National Pictures, a motion picture production and distribution company formed in 1917 by a group of exhibitors who were upset by the block-booking practices of Famous Players-Lasky. Rather than be forced to buy a package of routine films in order to get one important production with a name star, such as Mary Pickford, the exhibitors decided to make their own films and set out to lure stars to the newly formed company. Under Robert's leadership, First National came to be one of the conspicuous stabilizing factors in the film industry.

After it was formed, First National quickly signed up stars of the magnitude of Charlie Chaplin and Pickford and became an important factor in the industry. Robert steadied everyone's nerves when sound pictures arrived, and the company successfully made the transition. Shortly after the advent of sound, First National was absorbed by Warner Brothers.

BIBLIOGRAPHY

Bodenhamer, David J., and Robert G. Barrows, eds. *The Encyclopedia of Indianapolis.* Bloomington and Indianapolis: Indiana University Press, 1994.

Davis, Charlie. *That Band from Indiana.* Oswego, N.Y.: Mathom Publishing Company, 1982.

Indianapolis Star, September 23, 1929.

Katz, Ephraim. *The Film Encyclopedia.* New York: Perigee Books, 1979.

Moore, Colleen. *Silent Star.* Garden City, N.Y.: Doubleday and Company, 1968.

Ramsaye, Terry. *A Million and One Nights: A History of the Motion Picture.* 1926. Reprint, New York: Simon and Schuster, 1964.

THAMER (Ted) D. McCORD, Sullivan County (1898-1976)
Cinematographer

Ted McCord's fifty-year cinematography career spanned many film genres. His work can be seen in more than 130 motion pictures dating from 1921 to 1966. He worked with fellow Hoosiers Robert Wise (*The Sound of Music*, 1965), James Dean (*East of Eden*, 1955), and Hoagy Carmichael (*Young Man with a Horn*, 1950). He also became good friends with two Hoosier cowboys, Buck Jones and Ken Maynard, shooting more than twenty of Maynard's films and at least eight Buck Jones films.

McCord's love of the outdoors was instilled in him during his boyhood in Indiana, and his film work became notable for his use of outdoor locations. He started in film in 1917, and at age nineteen he was an assistant to cinematographer James Van Trees. By the early 1920s McCord was on his own, filming a number of comedies for First National starring Colleen Moore.

By 1936 McCord had settled at Warner Brothers, where he spent most of the next two decades shooting inexpensive B films until the World War II years. He finally moved up to A films with the Humphrey Bogart film *Action in the North Atlantic* (1943). His career was interrupted by military service, where he rose to the rank of captain in the military's photographic division. He was one of the first Americans to enter Berlin, photographing scenes in Hitler's chancellery.

McCord's best known and most prestigious films came after the war. *Johnny Belinda* (1948) won him his first Oscar nomination. *East of Eden* allowed him to use his skill shooting outdoor scenes. Westerns never left his repertory, and one of his best was *The Hanging Tree* (1959). He received his second Oscar nomination for *Two for the Seesaw* (1962), and Robert Wise chose him to shoot the breathtaking mountain vistas in the Oscar-winning film *The Sound of Music*. This film gave McCord his third Oscar nomination. McCord's last film was *A Fine Madness* (1966).

BIBLIOGRAPHY

Hoffman, Henryk. *"A" Western Filmmakers: A Biographical Dictionary of Writers, Directors, Cinematographers, Composers, Actors, and Actresses.* Jefferson, North Carolina, and London: McFarland and Co. Inc., 2000.

The Internet Movie Database. http://www.imdb.com/.

McCord, Ted. Biography.

Monaco, James, ed. *The Encyclopedia of Film.* New York: Perigee Books, 1991.

BERNIE POLLACK *(birth date unknown)*
Costume Designer

Bernie Pollack, whose older brother is Sydney Pollack, was interested in acting, but his career veered off that path into something behind the scenes. He became interested in costume design and in 1965 worked as an apprentice costumer on a film entitled *This Property Is Condemned*, starring Natalie Wood and Robert Redford. This was a fortuitous circumstance for Bernie because he developed a relationship with Redford that continued for two decades. Sydney also became associated with Redford, and the three worked together on some high-profile pictures. Bernie earned his first costume credit for the 1979 Redford film *The Electric Horseman*. He had earlier worked with costumes on *The Sting* (1973), *The Great Gatsby* (1974), *All the President's Men* (1976), and *The Way We Were* (1973). Pollack worked with fellow Hoosier Gloria Gresham on *The Natural* (1984), where they shared credit for costume design.

Pollack also developed a rewarding relationship with Dustin Hoffman, costuming films such as *Tootsie* (1982), *Marathon Man* (1976), and *Rain Man* (1988). In 1989 he designed a new look for Sylvester Stallone in *Tango and Cash*.

Pollack will occasionally take an acting role. He had small parts in *Bobby Deerfield* (1977), *Tootsie*, and *Havana* (1990).

BIBLIOGRAPHY

The Internet Movie Database. http://www.imdb.com/.
Rio's Attic. http.//www.river-phoenix.org/.

PHILIP PROCTOR, Goshen (b. 1940)
Voice-over Specialist

Several Hoosiers who started out to be actors carved out a nice career niche using their special voice talents. Julie McWhirter Dees, Jo Ann Worley, Phil Harris, and Bill Thompson all were in demand for voice-over work. Philip Proctor is one of the busiest of this group. In 1972 he started this unique line of work doing voices for Martians in *Martian Space Party*. He has been busy ever since, more recently with voices for *Aladdin* (1992), *Toy Story* (1995), and *Hercules* (1997). He was the voice of the drunken monkey in *Doctor Dolittle* (1998) and Howard DeVille in *The Rugrats Movie* (1998).

BIBLIOGRAPHY

The Internet Movie Database. http://www.imdb.com/.

CHARLES SCHULTHIES, Ferdinand (b. 1922)
Special Effects

Charles Schulthies has made his mark in the field of special effects and production design. The first film for which he received credit was *Ambush Bay* (1966), starring Hugh O'Brian. His two most notable films were *Diner* (1982) and *Westworld* (1973). *Westworld* was the first theatrical feature directed by author Michael Crichton; Schulthies created the brutal Old West theme park of the future that was the site for the film. Schulthies was also the special effects/production designer for the television series *How the West Was Won* in 1977–78.

BIBLIOGRAPHY

The Internet Movie Database. http://www.imdb.com/.
Turner Classic Movies. http://www.alt.tcm.turner.com/.

MELVIN SIMON (b. 1926)
Producer/Executive

Melvin Simon started his career as an owner of malls by working at one of the first malls in Indianapolis, Eastgate Shopping Center. His company is now the largest owner of malls in the United States.

In 1967 Simon founded a joint venture and independent motion picture and television company, AVCO Embassy Pictures, as a sister company to Columbia. He was the head producer and president for AVCO Embassy and produced fourteen films from 1978 to 1983. Notable films include *The Stunt Man* (1980), *Chu Chu and the Philly Flash* (1981), and *Porky's* (1982). When AVCO Embassy Pictures collapsed in 1982, Simon sold it to television executive Norman Lear, who changed the name to Embassy Entertainment.

BIBLIOGRAPHY

The Internet Movie Database. http://www.imdb.com/.

JULES STEIN, *South Bend (1896-1981)*
Talent Agent

When Jules Stein was a teenager in South Bend, he gave himself a middle name, Caesar. A little more than two decades later, he established a company that became one of the most powerful in show business and that eventually made him a virtual "Caesar" in Hollywood.

Louis and Rosa Stein were Lithuanian immigrants. Louis was an itinerant peddler who eventually settled in South Bend and opened a dry-goods store. Orthodox Jews, Louis and Rosa's was an arranged marriage. The Steins had five children and lived in a two-story house, adjoining the store.

Although Louis was a hard worker, the family remained poor. Jules decided he would be different. He enrolled in summer school at Winona Lake Academy in order to finish high school early. It was his first time away from home, and he became very homesick, but stuck it out. He started promoting Saturday dances for students at his school and also at Indiana University. He found a dance hall at Warsaw and arranged for a streetcar line to run a special car from Warsaw back to Winona at midnight. He graduated from high school at sixteen and negotiated a deal with the University of West Virginia to play in the school band in exchange for tuition. He graduated at age eighteen. He went to Chicago and took a year of postgraduate study.

Stein soon realized he could make more money booking bands than playing in them. Thanks to his band booking, he was able to put himself through medical school in Chicago. He later spent a year in eye research at the University of Vienna. By 1924 he had completed his studies and was working for a Chicago ophthalmologist. That same year, with $3,000 in capital, Stein started a band-booking agency that he called the Music Corporation of America (MCA).

From a tiny two-room office in Chicago, MCA became a giant in the music and entertainment industry. Stein successfully rebuffed Al Capone and other gangsters in Chicago who wanted a piece of his business. He opened an MCA office in New York in 1927, followed by offices in Los Angeles, Dallas, and Cleveland. He began offering radio sponsors package deals, booking not just orchestras but comedy writers, singers, producers, and even guest stars.

In 1936 Stein shifted the major focus of his talent agency (as it was now known) to the movie industry. In 1939 MCA signed Bette Davis to the agency. Others began to follow her lead, and by 1945 MCA was the most important and largest agency in the world and the most powerful organization in the motion picture business. It was eventually purchased by Universal Studios.

BIBLIOGRAPHY

Bruck, Connie. *When Hollywood Had a King: The Reign of Lew Wasserman, Who Leveraged Talent into Power and Influence.* New York: Random House, 2003.
The Internet Movie Database. http.//www.imdb.com/.

Twyla Tharp.
INDIANA PICTURE COLLECTION, MANUSCRIPT SECTION,
INDIANA STATE LIBRARY

TWYLA THARP, *Portland (b. 1941)*
Choreographer

One of the most innovative choreographers in contemporary dance, Twyla Tharp began taking dance lessons at age four. She later took lessons in ballet, acrobatics, baton, and musical instruments, including violin and viola. She attended Barnard College in New York City from 1960 to 1964, majoring in art history. While in college, she studied modern dance at both the Martha Graham and Merce Cunningham studios, classical ballet at the American Ballet Theater, and jazz with Luigi. She considered Cunningham her master teacher. She also joined the Paul Taylor Dance Company but left after one year to form her own company.

By the fall of 1965 Tharp had choreographed *Stride,* a quartet in five sections designed for film. In January 1971 she premiered *Eight Jelly Rolls* at Oberlin College and then presented it in Central Park in New York City. Set to the jazz music of Jelly Roll Morton, it was declared to be an astounding masterpiece. Another of her jazz or pop ballets was *The Bix Pieces,* danced to the music of Bix Beiderbecke, played by Paul Whiteman's orchestra. She has created more than fifty works. She was the choreographer on such motion pictures as *Hair* (1979), *Ragtime* (1981), *Amadeus* (1984), and *White Nights* (1985).

BIBLIOGRAPHY

The Internet Movie Database. http://www.imdb.com/.
New York Times, February 22, 2001.
Robinson, Alice M., Vera Mowry Roberts, and Milly S. Barranger. *Notable Women in the American Theatre: A Biographical Dictionary.* New York: Greenwood Press, 1989.

BILL THOMPSON, *Terre Haute (1913–1971)*
Voice-over specialist

A Hoosier from Terre Haute is credited with introducing the word "wimp" to the English language. Bill Thompson created the character of Wallace Wimple on the popular *Fibber McGee and Molly* radio show. Wimple was a hen-pecked husband, and Fibber always greeted him with "Hello Wimp!" Thompson was a multitalented performer who created many unforgettable characters in a career that spanned vaudeville, radio, motion pictures, and television.

Thompson was born on July 8, 1913, at 2001 N. Second Street (now Woodlawn Avenue) in Terre Haute. He got his start in show business as a tap dancer when he was two years old. By the time he was five he was touring the Midwest in vaudeville with his show business parents. He was billed as "Jackie Coogan's Double." He worked on the vaudeville circuit until he was twelve. At that time the family settled for a while in Chicago, and he finished high school there.

Thompson credits veteran vaudevillian Arthur Donaldson with helping him perfect his multifaceted style using tongue and mouth contortions. In 1933, at age nineteen, Thompson appeared on *Saturday Jamboree* and *Don McNeill's Breakfast Club* radio shows. The next year he won a talent contest at Chicago's Century of Progress Exposition by using ten different dialects. This earned him a contract with the NBC radio network. He debuted on the *Fibber McGee and Molly Show* on NBC in 1935.

Thompson soon was doing six distinct characters on the radio show. In addition to Wallace Wimple, he was Widdicomb Blotto, a character that was later renamed Horatio K. Boomer (a W. C. Fields type), Greek restaurateur Nick Depopoulous, the Old Timer, who upstaged Fibber's tall tales with, "That's purty good, Johnny, but that ain't the way I heered it." Other characters he created were Vodka and Uncle Dennis.

Jim and Marian Jordan, who played Fibber McGee and Molly, made just five movies, and Thompson was in two of them. In the first, *Look Who's Laughing* (1941), he played Wallace Wimple. In *Here We Go Again* (1942) he played a veteran.

When Thompson joined the Navy shortly after Pearl Harbor, the McGee show lost a whole cast of characters. The Navy used him to promote savings bonds and on its *Meet the Navy* radio show. He came back to the Terre Haute area in 1945 to visit his maternal grandfather, John Mushett, who lived in Clinton.

After the war Thompson returned to the *Fibber McGee and Molly* radio show and also embarked on a career as a voice-over actor in motion pictures. He was particularly busy at the Disney studios, where he provided the voices for Jock, Bull, Dachsie, and Joe in *Lady and the Tramp*. He was Mr. Smee in *Peter Pan*, the White Rabbit in *Alice in Wonderland*, and King Herbert in *Sleeping Beauty*. He also was the voice of park ranger J. Audobon Woodlore in several Donald Duck features. MGM used him for the voice of Droopy, a police dog, and Spike, the bulldog, in the *Counterfeit Cat* cartoons.

In 1956 Thompson was an occasional television guest on *The NBC Comedy Hour*. With the total demise of radio as he had known it, Thompson moved into another profession. In 1957 he became an executive with the Union Oil Company. In 1970 he provided the voice of Uncle Waldo in Disney's *The Aristocats*, which also featured the voices of fellow Hoosiers Phil Harris (Thomas O'Malley) and Scatman Crothers (Scat Cat). This was his last motion picture. He died in Los Angeles on July 15, 1971.

Bill Thompson.

BIBLIOGRAPHY

Banta, Ray. *Indiana's Laughmakers*. PennUltimate Press, 1990.

Dunning, John. *The Encyclopedia of Old-Time Radio*. Oxford University Press, 1998.

McCormick, Mike. "Wabash Valley Profiles: Bill Thompson." 1985.

The Internet Movie Database. http://www.imdb.com/.

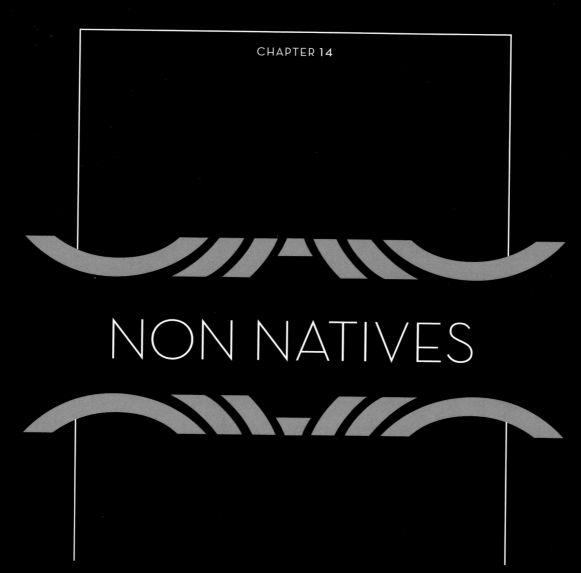

CHAPTER 14

NON NATIVES

Many people who went to Hollywood from Indiana were not native Hoosiers. Irene Dunne, Karl Malden, Beulah Bondi, and Herb Shriner spent more time in Indiana than natives Brendan Fraser, Clifton Webb, Marilyn Miller, and Steve McQueen. In spite of this disparity, we attach the name Hoosier to people in both of these groups.

Clifton Webb, born in Indianapolis, did not wish to be considered a product of the Midwest, in spite of the fact his Hoosier ancestry was quite extensive. Steve McQueen's youthful days in Indianapolis were too painful for him to recall, and he seldom talked about them. Marilyn Miller, who was born in Evansville primarily because her mother was fleeing from yellow fever in Memphis, loved to be called a Hoosier, even though she left Indiana at an early age. Herb Shriner moved to Indiana from Ohio as a youngster and became one of the best-known Hoosiers in show business.

Many nonnative Hoosiers contributed greatly to the art of motion pictures. This chapter will cover only a few who spent significant time in the state.

CLAUDE AKINS (Claude Marion Akins)
Nelson, Georgia (1926-1994)

The Akins family moved to Bedford, Indiana, when Claude Akins was a youngster. After graduating from high school in Bedford, he enrolled at Indiana University but left and enrolled at Northwestern University, where he graduated with a major in theater.

Akins went back to Bedford and worked as a salesman for a limestone firm. The president of the firm was a theater fan and helped him get a job with the Barter Theater in Abingdon, Virginia. After one season he moved to Broadway in 1951, where he won a part in *The Rose Tattoo.* His next step was Hollywood, and he landed a role in a major hit movie, *From Here to Eternity* (1953). He began to get steady work, making six films in 1954. While some of the films were notable, his roles were not. He played roles such as Big Soldier and Truck Driver.

Akins realized he would forever be typed as a character actor because of his size and his looks, saying, "A guy who looks like Robert Redford will most often be cast as a hero. A guy like me or Ernie Borgnine plays a lot of heavies. If you're big, they think you're tough. And if you're tough, they think you're dumb." He built a solid career as either a good old boy or a rugged, mean villain. He said, "For some reason, Hollywood's mainstream has eluded me." Nevertheless, he managed to keep busy in the industry, making more than eighty-five films and appearing in almost one hundred television shows.

Claude Akins.

In 1974 Akins costarred with Frank Converse in the NBC television series *Movin' On*. The show was a hit and ran for two years. After *Movin' On* had run its course, Akins was cast as Sheriff Lobo in the series *B. J. and the Bear* (1978). It was moderately successful, but Fred Silverman, president of NBC, liked Akins's portrayal and decided to change the show and the title. In 1979 it became *The Misadventures of Sheriff Lobo* (1979–81). Akins had now graduated from the scowling villains he used to play and began to play more sympathetic roles, showing his cheerful grin. After the last adventure of Sheriff Lobo, Akins returned to character acting and began doing television commercials. His biggest commercial job was as a spokesperson for AAMCO transmissions. His last television appearance was in *Seasons of the Heart* in 1993.

BIBLIOGRAPHY

Indiana Biographical Dictionary: People of All Times and All Places Who Have Been Important to the State. 2nd ed. 2 vols. St. Clair Shoes, Mich.: Somerset Publishers, 1999.

Indianapolis Star, July 5, 1979.

The Internet Movie Database. http://www.imdb.com/.

Los Angeles Times, January 28, 1994.

Quinlan, David. *Quinlan's Illustrated History of Film Character Actors*. London: B. T. Batsford, 1995.

POLLY BERGEN (NELLIE PAULINA BURGIN)
Knoxville, Tennessee (b. 1930)

In July 1953 a crowd gathered around the railroad station in Richmond, Indiana, waiting for a former resident to arrive. Many remembered her as a little red-headed girl who used to sing over the local radio station. Others remembered her as an enthusiastic high school basketball fan. Some remembered singing with her in the high school choral group. They knew her then as Nellie Burgin, but she was now movie star Polly Bergen.

Bergen's family moved from Knoxville to Richmond when she was in elementary school, and she finished junior high and one year of high school there before moving with her parents to Compton, California.

After moving to California, Bergen worked as a drugstore clerk, carhop, and linotype operator. She eventually became the featured soloist with several big bands and made a hit record with a country tune, "Honky Tonkin'." Shortly after that release, the movies became interested in her. Her popularity increased after she appeared in *That's My Boy* (1951) and *The Stooge* (1953), starring Dean Martin and Jerry Lewis. She began to appear on television and served as a panelist on *To Tell the Truth* from 1956 to 1961. She also had her own show, *The Polly Bergen Show*, from 1957 to 1958. She got a big break with a role as Gregory Peck's wife in *Cape Fear* in 1962. She was a busy actress through the 1960s and 1970s, appearing in feature films and on television. She was nominated for three Emmys for *Playhouse 90* ("The Helen Morgan Story") (1957), *The Winds of War* (1983), and *War and Remembrance* (1988).

Bergen returned to singing, and in 2001 she was nominated for a Tony as best featured actress in the Broadway revival of Stephen Sondheim's *Follies*. In March 2002 she played Fraulein Schneider in the long-running revival of *Cabaret* at Studio 54 in New York. In October 2003 she opened on Broadway opposite Mark Hamill in a two-actor

Polly Bergen.

comedy, *Six Dance Lessons in Six Weeks*, playing a formidable Florida retiree who hires an acerbic dance instructor (Hamill).

BIBLIOGRAPHY

Indianapolis Star, November 2, 2003.
The Internet Movie Database. http://www.imdb.com/.
"Polly Comes Home." *Indianapolis Star Magazine*, July 26, 1953.

JAMES BEST (JULES GUY)
Powderly, Kentucky (b. 1926)

James Best.

James Best was adopted at age four by a family in Corydon, Indiana, where he spent the rest of his youth. He left Corydon in 1943 to enlist in the U.S. Air Force. He has appeared in more than six hundred television shows and has made eighty-three feature films, working with many of Hollywood's most prominent stars. He was a very busy actor in the 1950s and 1960s, playing a wide range of roles, from villains to country bumpkins. He moved into script writing and producing, including work on three Burt Reynolds films, *Gator* (1976), *The End* (1978), and *Hooper* (1978). He also became active in Reynolds's Jupiter Theater in Florida, directing and starring in several productions.

In the early 1970s Best went into semiretirement, becoming an artist in residence at the University of Mississippi for two years. He returned to California under contract to Warner Brothers in 1979, appearing as Sheriff Roscoe P. Coltrane on *The Dukes of Hazzard*. The series ran for seven and a half years and enjoyed a long run in syndication.

Best eventually moved to Florida, where he taught at the University of Central Florida. He is an accomplished painter and songwriter and devoted fisherman. He and his wife, Dorothy, formed their own independent film company called Best Friend Films. Their first feature production was entitled *Death Mask* (1998), which Best wrote and for which his wife and daughter Janeen served as executive producers.

BIBLIOGRAPHY

Best, James. E-mail interview with the author. December 3, 2000.
The James Best Web Site. http://www.jamesbest.com/.

KAREN BLACK (KAREN BLANCHE ZIEGLER)
Park Ridge, Illinois (b. 1939)

Karen Black grew up in Lafayette, Indiana, and became interested in drama at Lafayette Jefferson High School. After graduation, she enrolled as a theater major at Northwestern University and then moved to New York City and began to appear in a few revues and was accepted into the famed Actors Studio, studying under Lee Strasberg. Black began appearing in off-Broadway productions and made her first film, *The Prime Time*, in 1960.

In 1965 Black made her Broadway debut in *The Playroom*. It ran only a month, but she was nominated for a New York Critic's Circle award for her performance. In 1966 she appeared in Francis Ford Coppola's *You're a Big Boy Now*. She did not become well known, however, until she was cast as a spaced-out, LSD-taking hooker in the box-office sleeper *Easy Rider* in 1969. The following year she appeared as a small-town waitress who falls for upper-class drifter Jack Nicholson in *Five Easy Pieces*, garnering a Golden Globe, New York Film Critics award, and an Oscar nomination.

After this impressive beginning, Black became a busy actress, appearing in many major films through the 1970s. She was in Nicholson's directing debut, *Drive, He Said*, in 1971. She won a Golden Globe for best supporting actress in *The Great Gatsby* (1974) and was nominated for another Golden Globe for *Day of the Locust* in 1975. In Robert Altman's *Nashville* (1975) she was given the opportunity to show off her singing ability. She also ventured into the horror genre when she played four roles in the television thriller *Trilogy of Terror* (1975). The movie became a cult classic and launched Black into a twenty-year run in such horror films as *Burnt Offerings* (1976), *Savage Dawn* (1985), *It's Alive III: Island of the Alive* (1987), *Mirror, Mirror* (1990), *Children of the Night* (1991), and *Children of the Corn IV: The Gathering* (1996). In 1982 Robert Altman cast Black as a transsexual in *Come Back to the Five and Dime, Jimmy Dean, Jimmy Dean*, which also starred Cher and Sandy Dennis.

While some actresses are highly selective about which roles they take, Black decided to pursue parts that many others would not even consider. She said her working life has been "very circumstantial, very happenstantial, which is no way to run anything." A turbulent third marriage and the need to be an attentive mother sidetracked her career in studio pictures at its apex in the mid-1970s. She has maintained a busy film career, but the films and roles have lacked quality.

Summing up her career, Black said that if she obeyed the conventions of mainstream Hollywood, she would have quit making movies a long time ago. "In the end, I sidestepped the business in order to keep on working," she said. Black is married to writer Kit Carson. Their son, Hunter Carson, is an actor.

Karen Black.

BIBLIOGRAPHY

The Internet Movie Database. http://www.imdb.com/.
MSN entertainment. http://movies.msn.com/celebs/.
Wall Street Journal, June 26, 2000.

BUDD BOETTICHER (OSCAR BOETTICHER JR.)
Chicago (1916–2001)

Budd Boetticher was the adopted son of a hardware retailer in Evansville, Indiana. He was raised in Evansville and attended Culver Military Academy in northern Indiana. He then went to Ohio State University, where he ran track, became an intercollegiate boxing champ, and played football.

During a trip to Mexico in 1928, Boetticher saw his first bullfight and became entranced. He studied and became a professional matador. Through his college chum, Hal Roach Jr., he got his first job in films as technical adviser to Rouben Mamoulian for his film *Blood and Sand* (1941). Boetticher worked in apprentice jobs at the Hal Roach Studios for several years until he was hired as a director at Columbia Studios.

Boetticher began to grind out a number of formula films. He wrote the screenplay for and directed *Bullfighter and the Lady* (1951), which was an account of his experiences in Mexico. He was nominated for an Oscar for best original story. John Ford took over and, without Boetticher's approval, cut the film from 129 minutes to 87.

Boetticher directed a number of Randolph Scott films, making these B Westerns seem like A films. He considered his two best films *Bullfighter and the Lady* and *Seven Men from Now* (1956). In 1960 he began a seven-year odyssey, attempting to film a documentary on the life of famed matador Carlos Arruza. This project bankrupted him, cost him his marriage, and almost killed him when he contracted a near-fatal illness. Arruza died in an automobile accident during the filming. Although the film, *Arruza*, was released in 1972, it was not the film Boetticher had hoped it would be.

Boetticher was married to Emily Erskine Cook from 1946 to 1959, actress Debra Paget from 1960 to 1961, and Mary Chelde from 1971 until his death in Ramona, California, on November 29, 2001. Boetticher had two daughters, Georgia and Helen.

BIBLIOGRAPHY

Chute, David. "Man of the West." *LA Weekly* (July 28–August 3, 2000).

The Internet Movie Database. http://www.imdb.com/.

Maltin, Leonard. *Leonard Maltin's Movie Encyclopedia.* New York: Penguin Putnam, 1994.

Sherman, Eric. *The Director's Event: Interviews with Five American Film Makers.* New York: Atheneum, 1970.

BEULAH BONDI (BEULAH BONDY), *Chicago (1888–1981)*

As a child, Beulah Bondi moved with her family to Valparaiso, Indiana, where she made her stage debut at age nine in a production of *Little Lord Fauntleroy* at the Memorial Opera House. She was the daughter of Abraham and Eva Marble Bondy. Abraham was a realtor, merchant, and businessman. (A Bondy business building still stands in Valparaiso.)

Bondi enrolled at Valparaiso University and was chosen class poet in the 1916 university *Record.* While attending Valparaiso, she was in several stage productions. After graduation, she went to Indianapolis, where she was signed by Stuart Walker, head of one of the foremost repertory companies in the country. She made her professional debut in Indianapolis at the English Theater. Near the end of her life she recalled, "Mr. Walker was very severe that first summer in Indianapolis. He told me years later, he knew I had talent, and that the theater was a hard life. He was either going to make me or break me; he was very hard on me, but would always give me a pat on the back when I did things right."

Bondi moved to New York City and appeared in *Wild Birds.* While job hunting in New York, she ran into Melville Burke, one of Walker's directors, who was starting a new play and needed someone to play an eighty-year-old woman. Bondi recalled, "That's luck! You come out of the subway, meet your former director, and he's starting a play, and he takes you over and fights the battle for you." Thus came about her Broadway debut in 1925 in *One of the Family.* It was at this time she replaced the *y* in her name with an *i*.

Within weeks of the opening of this production, Bondi was cast in Guthrie McClintic's *Saturday's Children,* playing an unpleasant, tight-lipped landlady. McClintic liked her so much that he immediately cast her in *Mariners.* Bondi found herself in the unique position of appear-

A rare photo of the producer (John Wayne), the star (Randolph Scott), and the director (Budd Boetticher) on location for the filming of Warner Brothers' *Seven Men from Now* (1956).

Beulah Bondi.

ing in two Broadway shows at the same time. McClintic kept Bondi busy, putting her in two more of his Broadway productions.

Then, in 1929, Bondi was given the breakthrough role that led to a long and distinguished motion picture career. She was cast as Emma, a malicious gossip, in the Elmer Rice play, *Street Scene*. "Mr. Rice had written the part for me," Bondi said. In 1931, when *Street Scene* was translated to the screen, King Vidor brought her to Hollywood to re-create her role. Her performance was hailed by the critics, but when Sam Goldwyn offered her a seven-year contract guaranteeing her five hundred dollars a week, she tore it up. She was so confident in her ability as an actress that she knew she did not need a contract.

Bondi was right. In 1931 she was in *Arrowsmith*, playing Helen Hayes's mother, and was the self-righteous wife of Walter Huston in the 1932 production of *Rain*. In 1933 she was in two films with John Barrymore, *The Stranger's Return* and *Christopher Bean*.

Bondi once said that Leo McCarey's *Make Way for Tomorrow* (1937) was her favorite role. Her greatest disappointment, however, was losing the role of Ma Joad in John Ford's *The Grapes of Wrath*. She later recalled, "I was told I was the only one being considered. I went up to Bakersfield and visited and talked with migrant workers. I went to five different Okie camps. I dressed in old clothes; no one recognized me. I was all prepared to do the film. When I came back, I did two tests. The man playing my husband spilled the beans. He said, 'I'm just an extra, but of the five actresses I've played opposite against in this part, you're the best.' John Ford was pleased with the tests, but Mr. Zanuck said I was not the type. They ended up casting Jane Darwell. She was a fine actress, no jealousy there, but the thing was, they lied to me."

Bondi was nominated for Oscars twice—*The Gorgeous Hussy* (1936) and *Of Human Hearts* (1938). She played Jimmy Stewart's mother in five films, the most notable being *It's a Wonderful Life* (1946). She said, "I didn't feel like he was Jimmy Stewart . . . he was my son. And they were all different sons."

Although Bondi was a very busy film actress, making sixty-five movies in a film career that spanned forty years, she never deserted the stage. She appeared on Broadway in *Hilda Crane* in 1950, and in 1953 she re-created her 1939 film role as Granny opposite Victor Moore's Gramps in Hoosier Paul Osborn's *On Borrowed Time*. When her film roles began to diminish, she started doing television work. At age eighty-eight, her portrayal of Aunt Martha on "The Pony Cart" episode of *The Waltons* late in 1976 won her an Emmy. Appropriately, it was her last dramatic role.

BIBLIOGRAPHY

"Alumna Actress Breaks Ribs; Dies in Los Angeles Hospital." *Alumni News* (Valparaiso University) (January 1981).

Doyle, Billy H. *The Ultimate Directory of Silent and Sound Era Performers: A Necrology of Actors and Actresses.* Lanham, Md.: Scarecrow Press, 1999.

Indiana Biographical Dictionary: People of All Times and All Places Who Have Been Important to the History of the State. 2nd ed. 2 vols. St. Clair Shores, Mich.: Somerset Publishers, 1999.

The Internet Movie Database. http://www.imdb.com/.

Jewell, James. "Beulah Bondi." *The World of Yesterday* 42 (August 1983).

Quinlan, David. *Quinlan's Illustrated Directory of Film Character Actors.* London: B. T. Batsford, 1995.

Valparaiso Messenger, January 12, 1981.

Young, Jordan. *Reel Characters: Great Movie Character Actors.* Beverley Hills, Calif.: Moonstone Press, 1986.

JOYCE DEWITT, *Wheeling, West Virginia (b. 1949)*

Joyce DeWitt.

As a youngster, Joyce DeWitt came to Speedway, Indiana, with her parents Paul and Norma DeWitt. She knew she wanted to be an actress from the time she was three years old, and she performed in her first play at Speedway High School at age fourteen. She studied theater at Ball State University and was part of a comedy troupe, which also featured David Letterman, that played various clubs in Muncie.

DeWitt received a Clifton Webb scholarship to UCLA and earned a master of fine arts degree from that university. She did secretarial work to pay the rent and took any acting job that came her way. She landed a part in a B movie and made one-time-only appearances on television shows such as *Baretta*, *The Tony Randall Show*, and *Manhunter*. She also appeared on game shows and talk shows, including those of Merv Griffin, Mike Douglas, and Dinah Shore.

Finally, in 1978 DeWitt was cast with two other unknowns, John Ritter and Suzanne Somers, in the television series *Three's Company*. It was an instant hit, and the three performers became overnight stars. Of her sudden fame she said, "I couldn't have anticipated any of this . . . the excitement, the national attention, people recognizing me and asking for autographs. . . . I hadn't intended to have this sort of career."

It was obvious DeWitt did not enjoy her celebrity status as much as Ritter and Somers. "I'm pleased not to be as visible as John and Suzanne. I think it's great for them and they enjoy it all. We just think differently about our careers." DeWitt hoped that her role in the hit series would lead to other opportunities in the acting field. Unfortunately, not much materialized. She resolved not to take just anything that came along.

In 1981 the former office clerk for the Indianapolis Motor Speedway was invited back to Indianapolis to serve as grand marshal for the 500 Festival Parade. After *Three's Company* ended in 1984, she said her passion for acting, which had consumed her from childhood, was gone. She retired from show business and moved to Santa Fe, New Mexico.

After twelve years of very little theatrical activity, she decided to resume her career, starring in a number of theatrical productions, including the American rock musical *Leader of the Pack*; *Noises Off*, a revival of fellow Hoosier Cole Porter's *Anything Goes*; and the musical *Olympus on My Mind*.

BIBLIOGRAPHY

Banta, Ray. *Indiana's Laughmakers: The Story of Over Four Hundred Hoosiers; Actors, Cartoonists, Writers, and Others.* Indianapolis: PennUltimate Press, 1990.

"From Muncie to L.A. Joyce DeWitt's Name Shines with Stars." *The Ball State Alumnus* (November 1977).

Indianapolis Star, May 4, 1980, May 23, 1981.

Jackson, Paula. "Joyce DeWitt: From Teen-aged Thespian to TV Star." *Indianapolis Magazine* (September 1977).

IRENE DUNNE (IRENE MARIE DUNN)
Louisville, Kentucky (1898–1990)

Like her good friend Carole Lombard, Irene Dunn added an *e* to her name. Carole added the *e* to her first name and Irene to her last name. These two Hoosiers had a special friendship and, after Lombard's tragic death, Dunne was asked to christen the Liberty Ship S.S. *Carole Lombard.*

Born in Louisville, Dunne was the daughter of Joseph John Dunn, who was chief engineer on a number of riverboats. Her mother was Adelaide Antoinette Henry Dunn, an accomplished musician who had studied at the Cincinnati Conservatory and hailed from Newport, Kentucky.

Dunne spent her early childhood in Louisville and Saint Louis, where her father was transferred. She was educated by the Sisters of Loretto at Saint Benedict's Academy in Louisville and the Loretto Convent in Saint Louis. Dunne's father died of a kidney ailment when she was eleven, and her mother moved the family to Madison, Indiana. Dunne's grandfather operated the boiler works that constructed and installed boilers in riverboats traveling the Ohio and Mississippi rivers.

Dunne graduated from the eighth grade at Madison Grammar School. She made her stage debut that same year in a school production of *A Midsummer Night's Dream.* Adelaide Dunn encouraged her daughter's talents, giving her voice and piano lessons. She was awarded a scholarship to the Oliver Willard Pierce Academy of Fine Arts in Indianapolis. She graduated from Madison High School in 1916.

Dunne earned her teacher's certificate and was on her way to Gary to accept a position as an art instructor. She decided to stop off at Chicago to visit relatives, and while there she entered a voice contest and won a scholarship to the Chicago Musical College. She won another scholarship and returned to the college for the 1919–20 school year. Her career goal was no longer teaching; it was to sing with the Metropolitan Opera.

Dunne made her first trip to New York in the summer of 1920. The *Madison Herald*, as well as *Modern Screen Magazine*, reported that upon arriving in New York, she joined a friend, Rosemary Pfaff, who was also pursuing a musical career. Dunne accompanied Pfaff and her mother to an audition for the touring company of the musical *Irene*. Pfaff was turned down because of her height, but Pfaff's mother suggested Dunne for the role. After hearing Dunne sing, the business manager gave her a script and asked her to read the lines of the first act with him the next day. She memorized the script and astounded the manager with an excellent reading.

However, Dunne almost lost the job because of her lack of dance training. The company told her to study with its choreographer, and she was eventually cast in the touring company without any previous professional experience. Programs of the show list Helen Shipman as the lead and do not even list Dunne in the cast. It is likely Dunne was in the chorus and left the production in 1921.

In 1922 Dunne appeared on Broadway in a very small role in *The Clinging Vine.* She was hired several times as an understudy, and in 1926 she replaced the lead in the musical *Sweetheart Time* on Broadway. She began getting good notices and came to the attention of Jerome Kern, Richard Rodgers, and Lorenz Hart. The year 1928 was a good one for Dunne. She appeared in two Broadway shows. She was with fel-

Irene Dunne.

Irene Dunne and Forrest Lewis (Knightstown) in *It Grows on Trees* (1952).
©1952 UNIVERSAL PICTURES COMPANY, INC.

low Hoosier Clifton Webb in *She's My Baby*, and she finally originated
a lead with *Luckee Girl.* That same year she married Francis "Frank" D.
Griffin, a New York dentist, who was twelve years her senior. At first
Dunne planned to give up her career. Griffin, however, encouraged
her to continue, saying, "If she didn't have talent, I would have asked
her to drop her career." The marriage was one of the happiest in show
business and lasted until his death in 1965.

One of Dunne's biggest breaks was when she was hired to replace
the leading lady in the touring company of *Showboat*, touring for seventy-two weeks as Magnolia. RKO took notice and offered her a contract. She accepted and headed for Hollywood. When Fay Bainter had
a disagreement with the producer of *Cimarron*, Richard Dix (who had
seen Dunne perform on the stage in New York) suggested Dunne
for Bainter's replacement. *Cimarron* premiered on January 26, 1931,
and was considered one of the best Westerns ever made. It won three
Oscars. (Until *Dances with Wolves* in 1991, it was the only Western to win
an Oscar for best picture.) Dunne also received her first Oscar nomination for this film.

After Dunne concluded her RKO contract, she freelanced, working for Columbia, Paramount, Universal, Warner Brothers, Twentieth

Century Fox, and RKO. Her other Oscar nominations were for *Theodora Goes Wild* (1936), *The Awful Truth* (1937), *Love Affair* (1939), and *I Remember Mama* (1948). She is not as well remembered as she should be, as many of her films were held out of release to television, and many were remade. *Love Affair* was remade twice under the titles *An Affair to Remember* (1957), and, using much of the same plot, *Sleepless in Seattle* (1993).

Dunne's forty-first and last movie was *It Grows on Trees* (1952), in which she costarred with another Hoosier, Dean Jagger. Also in the cast was Forrest Lewis (Knightstown). She was one of a five-member U.S. delegation to the United Nations Twelfth General Assembly, where she served along with delegate Herman B Wells of Indiana University. She was finally recognized for her lifetime achievement by the American Film Institute in 1985 but was too ill to attend the ceremonies.

Dunne died of heart failure at the age of ninety-two in her Holmby Hills home. She was survived by her daughter, Mary Frances Gage, grandchildren Ann and Mark Shinnick, a great-granddaughter, and a niece.

BIBLIOGRAPHY

Ellrod, J. G. *The Stars of Hollywood Remembered: Career Biographies of Eighty-two Actors and Actresses of the Golden Era, 1920s–1950s.* Jefferson, N.C.: McFarland and Company, 1997.

The Indiana Alumni Mini Magazine. (Spring 2000).

Indianapolis Star, October 24, 1930.

Schultz, Margie. *Irene Dunne: A Bio-Bibliography.* New York: Greenwood Press, 1991.

Thomson, David. *The New Biographical Dictionary of Film.* 4th ed. New York: Knopf, 2002.

JOHNNY GRUELLE, *Arcola, Illinois (1880–1938)*

John Barton Gruelle was an author, composer, and artist. His family moved to Indianapolis when he was two years old. His father was R. B. Gruelle, who became one of the Hoosier Group of impressionist artists. By the time John reached his teens, he knew he wanted to be a cartoonist.

Gruelle hopped a train to Cleveland in 1894 and tried to get a job with a local newspaper. He did not stay in Cleveland long, and by 1901 he was working in Indianapolis at a tabloid called *People*. The same year he married Myrtle Swann, with whom he had three children. He worked for the *Indianapolis Sun* until 1903 when he was hired by the *Indianapolis Star* to be the paper's first assistant illustrator. In 1905 Gruelle accepted a job with World Color Printing Company in Saint Louis to produce four-color Sunday comics. A year later he was in Cleveland doing the same work for the *Cleveland Press* and the Newspaper Enterprise Association.

By 1908 Gruelle began to aim his cartooning toward children. One of his most popular cartoons was *Mr. Twee Deedle*, which appeared in the Sunday comics. *Mr. Twee Deedle* was a success, and Gruelle began attracting offers from a number of monthly and weekly magazines. In 1917 he served as director/cartoonist/writer for six animated *Quacky Doodles* short films.

Sometime in the early 1900s Gruelle found an old doll in the attic of his parents' Indianapolis home and created a character he named Raggedy Ann to entertain his daughter, Marcella, who had just come down with a mysterious illness. He patented Raggedy Ann in 1915. P. F. Voland, a juvenile publisher in Chicago, published the Raggedy Ann Stories in 1918. The stories were immediately popular, and Gruelle introduced a matching male doll, Raggedy Andy.

In 1922 Gruelle's *Adventures of Raggedy Ann and Andy* stories were published in serialized form in papers all over the country. He also illustrated other juvenile features. In 1929 he introduced a Sunday comic named Brutus. It ran for nine years. By 1934 his *Raggedy Ann* proverbs were in national syndication.

By the time of Gruelle's death in 1938, the dolls and books were popular worldwide. In 1941 Gruelle's son, Worth Gruelle (born in Indianapolis), wrote the screenplay for a two-reel Raggedy Ann and Andy short. It had considerable charm, and many critics lamented the fact it was not a feature-length film. The ingredients were all there, including the imaginative setting in Ragland, with its echoes of Oz. In addition, the songs and score were very good.

In 1944 the movie *Heavenly Days*, starring Fibber McGee and Molly, was released. In it Marion Jordan, who played Molly, sang a Johnny Gruelle song, "Raggedy Ann." In 1977 Raggedy Ann and Andy finally appeared in a full-length feature. At least twenty animators from all over the world were gathered to work on the film. It had a $4 million budget, an excellent director in Richard Williams, and *Sesame Street* composer Joe Raposo.

In 2000 United Media, toy maker Hasbro, and Simon and Schuster began a Raggedy Ann mass-market campaign. The companies published the books, created clothes for children, created collectible figurines, and, of course, the ever-popular stuffed dolls. Raggedy Ann celebrated her nintieth birthday in May 2005.

BIBLIOGRAPHY

Hall, Patricia. "Johnny Gruelle." *Traces of Indiana and Midwestern History* 2, no. 4 (Fall 1990).

Indianapolis Star, January 29, 2000; May 9, 2001.

The Internet Movie Database. http://www.imdb.com/.

Maltin, Leonard. *Of Mice and Magic: A History of American Animated Cartoons.* New York: New American Library, 1980.

Peary, Danny, and Gerald Peary. *The American Animated Cartoon: A Critical Anthology.* New York: Dutton, 1980.

Jean Hagen.

JEAN HAGEN (JEAN SHIRLEY VERHAGEN), *Chicago (1923–1977)*

Leonard Maltin said, "If she had never played anyone other than the squeaky-voiced Lina Lamont, the hopelessly vain silent-screen star of 'Singin' in the Rain' (1952, for which she was Oscar-nominated), this attractive, talented blond actress would still rate a place in Hollywood history."

Jean Hagen moved to Elkhart, Indiana, when she was twelve years old. About her years in Indiana, she said, "People are generous and thoughtful because they want to be. Not because the book says it is right." She remembered the Mennonite people coming into Elkhart on Saturdays to sell pastry, butter, cheese, and bread.

"Bills! Bills! Bills! I'm going to sell the house and move back to the city!" Ben (Red Skelton) threatens his wife (Jean Hagen).

M-G-M's "HALF A HERO"

right 1953 Loew's Incorporated   Country of Origin U. S. A.   2   Property of National Screen Service Corp. Licensed for display only in connection with the exhibition of this picture at your theatre. Must be returned immediately thereafter.   53/499

After graduation from high school in Elkhart, Hagen enrolled at Northwestern University, majoring in drama and music. After graduation, she headed for New York City, where she worked as an usherette during the day and acted in radio dramas in the evening. Her film debut was in *Adam's Rib* in 1949 as a femme fatale who comes between Judy Holliday and Tom Ewell. This led to an MGM contract and another good role in *The Asphalt Jungle* (1950). In 1952 she was cast in her best screen role, that of Lina Lamont in *Singin' in the Rain.* She was nominated for an Oscar for best supporting actress, but the award went to Gloria Grahame, who won for *The Bad and the Beautiful.*

In 1953 Hagen joined the cast of the television series *Make Room for Daddy* as the wife of Danny Thomas. She left the show in 1957 and was replaced by Marjorie Lord. Hagen also had good roles in *The Shaggy Dog* (1959) and *Sunrise at Campobello* (1960), but after that her career began to wind down.

Hagen said she was always amazed at the number of people she met in Hollywood whom she liked immediately and then found out they were Hoosiers, in particular Leon Ames, Marjorie Main, Anne Baxter, and William H. Wright. She met a young man named Tom Seidel in New York while working on Broadway. He was a Hoosier, born in Indianapolis. They had two daughters before their divorce in 1965.

BIBLIOGRAPHY

The Internet Movie Database. http://www.imdb.com/.
Maltin, Leonard, ed. *Leonard Maltin's Movie Encyclopedia.* New York: Penguin Putnam, 1994.
Yahoo Movies. http://movies.yahoo.com/.

HELEN HOLMES, *Chicago (1893–1950)*

One of the most popular forms of entertainment in the early days of silent movies was the serial, or cliff-hanger. Most were thrilling epics dominated by beautiful women, and one of these early serial queens was Helen Holmes, an athletic young lady from South Bend, Indiana. She was born in Chicago but grew up in South Bend. The family later moved to California's Death Valley, where Holmes prospected for gold and lived among the Indians. She moved to New York in 1910 and began appearing on stage. She became friends with Mabel Normand and was invited to come to Hollywood. She began modeling and doing bit parts in movies.

By 1913 Holmes was starring in her own films. She married J. P. McGowan, a director at Kalem Studios. In 1914 she began starring in a serial *The Hazards of Helen.* Later that same year Pathe released *The Perils of Pauline*, starring Pearl White. White became better known than Holmes, but *The Hazards of Helen* was so popular Kalem produced forty-two chapters, an all-time record. Most stories in those days were twelve to fifteen chapters.

Holmes was a very good athlete and did most of her own stunts, leaping from burning buildings, chasing villains atop moving trains, and leaping from horseback to a runaway boxcar. She did other successful serials, including *The Girl and the Game* (1915), *The Lass of the Lumberlands* (1916), *The Lost Express* (1917), and *The Railroad Raiders* (1917). When Mutual Films, which was the distributor for Holmes's series, folded, she was forced into independent production. Without budgetary support from Mutual, she could no longer make elaborate railroad serials, and by the late 1920s she was reduced to supporting roles. In the early 1930s she retired and opened an antique shop in Burbank, California. She died of a heart attack on July 9, 1950, just two days after her fifty-seventh birthday.

Helen Holmes.

BIBLIOGRAPHY

Indianapolis Star, August 12, 1973.
The Internet Movie Database. http://www.imdb.com/.

BURL IVES, *Hunt, Illinois (1909–1995)*

Burl Ives attended Eastern Illinois University for a couple of years, then in the late 1930s he went to Terre Haute to attend Indiana State University. While a student there, he started singing on radio station WBOW. He also sang at the Washington Avenue Presbyterian Church in Terre Haute.

Ives credits Madame Clara Lyon, who gave him his first singing lesson in Terre Haute, for turning his life around. She gave Ives books to read and was the person he says who had more to do with his education than anyone else. She urged him to go to New York to pursue a singing career. He took her advice and left Terre Haute.

Burl Ives in *Smoky* (1946).

BIBLIOGRAPHY

Ives, Burl. *Wayfaring Stranger.* New York: Whittlesey House, 1948.

DEAN JAGGER (IRA DEAN JAGGER)
Columbus Grove, Ohio (1903–1991)

In 1985 representatives of United Telephone from Whitley County wrote to Dean Jagger to see if he would allow his face to grace that year's telephone book. They received a letter from Jagger's wife, Etta, who said, "He would be delighted to participate since he still calls Indiana his home."

Jagger was born in Ohio, but when he was five, his father Albert Jagger, a farmer, moved the family to a farm near Larwill, Indiana (not far from Fort Wayne). While a student at Whitley County's Larwill High School, Jagger entered a speech contest sponsored by the Woman's Christian Temperance Union. He found he liked to speak in public. "I discovered right then that that was for me," he said. But he had already decided to become a schoolteacher. He attended a normal school for ten weeks and got his first teaching job in a one-room school in Troy Township in Whitley County. After one school term he enrolled in Wabash College in the fall of 1922 but left without graduating. He went to Chicago and enrolled at the Elias Day Lyceum Arts Conservatory.

Jagger graduated from the conservatory and went on the chautauqua circuit, but he was not able to make enough money to sustain himself. He was forced to labor in a biscuit factory and as a bouncer in a dance hall and continued to act as much as he could. In 1929 he appeared opposite rising starlet Mary Astor in the film *The Woman from Hell.* He moved to Hollywood and was signed to a contract at Paramount Studios. However, he was disappointed when he began to be cast in a number of low-budget productions. In 1933 he was delighted to be given the chance to appear in the Broadway production of Erskine Caldwell's *Tobacco Road*, which starred Henry Hull.

Jagger continued to make films but became bored with the string of inferior movies in which Paramount cast him. When he had the opportunity to return to Broadway, he jumped at the chance. His second Broadway appearance was in the 1938 production *Missouri Legend.* He fondly remembered this play because he portrayed Jesse James, and it was the first time his name was put up in lights on Broadway. "I sat and cried for a few moments," he said. In addition to Jagger, the following Hoosiers were in the cast: Russell Collins (Indianapolis), Karl Malden (Gary), and John Philliber (Elkhart). Jagger appeared in seven Broadway productions from 1933 to 1948.

In 1940 Jagger was selected to play the title role in *Brigham Young— Frontiersman* for Twentieth Century Fox. It was a big-budget film, and he did well in the role. In 1949 he won an Oscar for best supporting actor in *Twelve O'Clock High.* He was much in demand as a film actor, but with the advent of television he moved into that medium as well. In 1963 he was a regular on the *Mr. Novak* series and also appeared on such shows as *The Loretta Young Show*, *The Fugitive*, *Bonanza*, *Columbo*, *Playhouse 90*, and *Medical Center.*

In 1974 Jagger's fraternity at Wabash College honored him with its Life Achievement award in a ceremony held on the Crawfordsville campus. In addition to his Oscar, he won many other awards during his career, including a Peabody and an Emmy.

Dean Jagger and Irene Dunne in *It Grows on Trees* (1952).
©1952 UNIVERSAL PICTURES COMPANY, INC.

Jagger married three times: Antoinette Lawrence (1935–43); Gloria Ling (1947–67), with whom he had a daughter; and Etta Norton (1968 until his death).

Jagger had a film career spanning fifty-eight years in which he made ninety-seven feature films. Leonard Maltin said he "always gave an intelligent characterization and delivered smooth performances."

BIBLIOGRAPHY

Columbia City Post and Mail, June 26, 1985.

"Dean Jagger." *Indianapolis Star Magazine*, April 24, 1950.

The Internet Broadway Database. http://www.ibdb.com/.

The Internet Movie Database. http://www.imdb.com/.

Jarboe, Evelyn. Letter. December 4, 1985. Larwill, Indiana. (Courtesy of Robert Schreiber).

Maltin, Leonard, ed. *Leonard Maltin's Movie Encyclopedia.* New York: Penguin Putnam. 1994.

KEVIN KLINE, *Saint Louis (b. 1947)*

Kevin Kline's father owned a music store and then a toy store in Saint Louis. Kline learned to play the piano at an early age and went to Indiana University as a music major. He decided to switch majors, becoming a theater major, saying, "They were auditioning 'the Scottish play.' I went to watch, and the director saw me and said, 'You haven't auditioned' and that I hadn't filled out the cards. The whole drama school was there, like 200 kids in the classroom, I got up and read some part in the deepest voice I could muster. I had no clue to what I was saying. I read the part, and I got a little part in 'Macbeth' and it was fun." Kline's first role was the bleeding soldier in *Macbeth*, directed by William Kinzer.

Kline had the lead in *Prometheus Unbound*, directed by Richard Scammon. He was part of the acting ensemble for the IU Showboat Majestic and was in *Waltz of the Toreadors* in 1969 at the Brown County Playhouse in Nashville, Indiana. While in Bloomington, he and several fellow actors formed a troupe called the Vest Pocket Players. They presented weekly topical satirical revues at a local coffeehouse. After graduating from IU, he headed for the Juilliard School in New York, where he was chosen by John Houseman to be a member of the John Houseman Acting Company. He toured with the Houseman troupe for four years.

Kline landed a regular role in the television soap opera *Search for Tomorrow* playing the role of Woody Reed. He made his stage debut in New York in *The Robber Bridegroom* and his Broadway debut in 1978 in *On the Twentieth Century*. He has won two Tony awards and one Oscar. The Tonys were for *On the Twentieth Century* (1978) and *The Pirates of Penzance* (1981).

In 1985 Kline was in *Silverado* with fellow actor John Cleese. He mentioned to Cleese that he had settled into a pattern of low-key roles, such as *The Big Chill* (1983) and *Violets Are Blue* (1986), and he was eager to break out. Cleese was eager to let him do it. He was cast as a bumbling demonic jewel thief in a story Cleese had written: *A Fish Called Wanda* (1988). His character was loud, mean, and out of control. "It was great to break all the rules I had made for myself in the films before," he said. His performance won him an Oscar for best supporting actor.

Kline married actress Phoebe Cates on October 14, 1991. They have a son, Owen, and a daughter, Greta.

(Opposite page) Kevin Kline in *The Pirates of Penzance* (1983).

The Pirates of Penzance...

A hundred and two and still kicking
by Alan Arnold

In 1880 the U.S.A. had less than fifty million inhabitants, pioneers were still opening up the Golden West and Hollywood was a place where lemons grew. An enterprising Mr. F.W. Woolworth had opened some five- and ten-cent stores, the telephone had just been invented, so too the talking machine, and in New York theatregoers were flocking to *The Pirates of Penzance*, a musical by two Englishmen, lyrics by William Schwenck Gilbert, music by Arthur Seymour Sullivan.

The play had opened on New Year's Eve, 1879, Sullivan having finished the score just two days earlier. He had forgotten to pack his original outline of the last act when leaving London, a two-week voyage away; so he had been working under pressure and from memory. But invariably he produced his best work when faced with an urgent deadline, unlike Gilbert who always had book and lyrics completed well in advance.

This leaving things to the last minute

BIBLIOGRAPHY

Indianapolis News, January 24, 1992.

Kevin Kline Online. http://dramafan.tripod.com/kevinkline/notes.html.

KARL MALDEN (MLADEN SEKULOVICH), *Chicago (b. 1914)*

Karl Malden.

Karl Malden moved with his family to Gary, Indiana, when he was four years old. Recalling his youth in Indiana, he said, "My father went to work in the steel mills there. I have early memories of the movies from then. Gary, Indiana had a theater called the Family Theater. I think they charged ten cents. It was nothing but a store with benches. And I think they could only seat 150 people. A store with a screen on the end and a guy on a platform in the back projecting pictures." It was there he laughed at the antics of Charlie Chaplin and memorized many of his comic routines.

Malden's father was involved in an amateur Serbian theater in Gary and started putting his sons in plays at an early age. Malden was interested in the theater, but he eventually went into the steel mills. He was a "cinder snapper." He said, "I worked in the steel mills in Gary for three years. And I knew I had to get out of that some way. I didn't want to spend my whole life there. And the Goodman Theater in Chicago used to admit one person every year in Gary, for the winner of a one-act contest. And that's how I got into acting. I really thought I was going to go there and be a stagehand." He went to the head of the Goodman Theatre and found it cost nine hundred dollars to get in. He only had three hundred dollars, so he made a deal. He would be allowed to stay for three months and after that, if his instructors thought he belonged there, he would be given a full scholarship. He stayed three years.

After Goodman, Malden chose New York over Hollywood because he wanted to be on the stage. He changed his name when he joined the Group Theatre in New York, rearranging Mladen to become Malden and taking his first name, Karl, from his mother's side of the family. He spent twenty years in New York, appearing in twenty-four plays. His film debut was with fellow Hoosier Carole Lombard in *They Knew What They Wanted* (1940). In 1947 he had his big break on Broadway with *A Streetcar Named Desire*, directed by Elia Kazan. His costar was Marlon Brando, and he enjoyed and respected Brando, saying, "I've always said, when you work with a genius, you know you can't be as great as a genius, but you certainly are going to try to push him around."

Malden won an Oscar for best supporting actor for the film version of *Streetcar* in 1951. He was again nominated in 1955 for *On the Waterfront* but did not win. (Although he never won another Oscar, he was nominated five times for an Emmy and won once for *Fatal Vision* in 1984.) He signed a contract with Warner Brothers and was with that studio for nine years.

Although Malden was considered a top actor and was well known, he said he never made much money until 1972 when producer Quinn Martin came to him with a proposal for a television series. Martin said, "I want you in this, because you've never been in a TV show, and I think you can do it." Malden took the series and was teamed with a young unknown actor named Michael Douglas. The name of the series was *The Streets of San Francisco*. Malden said, "For the first time in my life, I made some money. In all those movies, I never made big money. If I hadn't gotten 'Streets of San Francisco,' and if I hadn't gotten the American Express commercials, I would still have to be working."

In 1998 Malden received the Crystal Heart Career Achievement Award at the Heartland Film Festival at the Indiana Convention Center. Actress Carroll Baker, who appeared with Malden in *Baby Doll* (1956), presented the award to him. Commenting on today's films, Malden said, "I see bad pictures being made, and I see people who don't show up on time or come to work unprepared. Believe me, with Spencer Tracy and Clark Gable and Jimmy Cagney and Humphrey Bogart, it wasn't glamour, it was a job. You were the pro in this job, and boy, you stayed a pro. Now it's all different. It's a different world."

Malden married Mona Graham in 1938, and they have two daughters. In 1988 he was elected president of the Academy of Motion Picture Arts and Sciences, a title he held for five years.

BIBLIOGRAPHY

Indianapolis Star, December 31, 1980, October 18, 1998.

The Internet Movie Database. http://www.imdb.com/.

Maltin, Leonard, ed. *Leonard Maltin's Movie Encyclopedia*. New York: Penguin Putnam, 1994.

Zollo, Paul. *Hollywood Remembered: An Oral History of Its Golden Age*. New York: Cooper Square Press, 2002.

MARILYN MAXWELL (MARVEL MARILYN MAXWELL)
Clarinda, Iowa (1921–1972)

Marilyn Maxwell.

Marilyn Maxwell apparently got her talent from her mother, who was a piano accompanist for dancer Ruth St. Denis. Maxwell traveled with her mother as a child and at age three made her first stage appearance in a dance number. Her mother settled in Fort Wayne, Indiana, where Maxwell began to take singing lessons. She dropped out of high school after her sophomore year and began working as an usher at the Rialto Theater in Fort Wayne.

In the summer of 1936, at age fifteen, Maxwell joined the Amos Ostot band at Lake Manitou and then moved to Indianapolis with the band. Robert Young, who was Maxwell's boyfriend in Fort Wayne, and who subsequently moved to Indianapolis, became her friend again when she came to Indianapolis. She sang at the Columbia Club and lived in a rented room in Indianapolis. Young took her to visit Arsenal Technical High School, where he thought she might finish her education. She met Principal Hanson H. Anderson, who encouraged her to enroll, but the call to show business was too strong, and she stayed with the Ostot band until she received a better offer from the Buddy Rogers band.

Rogers, however, fired Maxwell after she and Rogers were in a car accident and Rogers's wife, Mary Pickford, did not like the fact the two of them were together. She then joined the Ted Weems orchestra. She left the band when it reached California and enrolled in the Pasadena Playhouse to train for a stage career.

In 1942 MGM signed Maxwell as a contract player. Louis B. Mayer insisted she drop Marvel and use her middle name as her first name. Her first film was Booth Tarkington's *Presenting Lily Mars* (1943), starring

Judy Garland. Cannelton, Indiana, native Tom Whelan directed her in *Swing Fever* (1943), in which she played a torch singer for Kay Kyser. She was Hoosier Red Skelton's girlfriend in *The Show-Off* (1946), which also featured Hoosiers Marjorie Main and Patrick McVey. She was Kirk Douglas's girlfriend in *Champion* (1949), and she helped introduce a wonderful new Christmas carol when she sang "Silver Bells" with Bob Hope in *The Lemon Drop Kid* (1951).

During World War II and the Korean War, Maxwell entertained American servicemen all over the world. When her work in films began to taper off in the mid-1950s, she started performing in top nightclubs and appeared in several stock stage productions. In 1952 she returned to Fort Wayne with Bob Hope to dedicate the Allen County War Memorial Coliseum.

Maxwell became a close friend to actor Rock Hudson, helping to closet his homosexuality by making frequent appearances with him and teasing reporters about how their relationship was "only a friendship." She was married three times. She had a son, Matthew, by her third husband, Jerry Davis (whom she divorced in 1960). In 1972 her son found her dead in the bathroom of their home, the victim of high blood pressure and a pulmonary ailment.

BIBLIOGRAPHY

The Internet Movie Database. http://www.imdb.com/.
Yahoo Movies. http://movies.yahoo.com/.
Young, Robert. Interview with the author. February 16, 2001.

DICK POWELL (RICHARD EWING POWELL)
Mountain View, Arkansas (1904-1963)

In the late 1920s, Indianapolis bandleader Charlie Davis was looking for a good singer. Word had come to him that a young former choir boy from Arkansas, singing with Dick Kent's band in Louisville, was very good. When Davis heard Kent's band was running out of engagements and was about to break up, he quickly offered the job to Dick Powell. Powell's first song with the Davis band was "I Can't Give You Anything but Love, Baby." It was the only time in the band's experience that a singer sang an encore of the same song. Davis immediately resolved not to place too much dependence upon Powell because Indianapolis would only be one rung in his climb to success.

Powell attended Little Rock College and began his career as a singer in 1921. After singing with an assortment of bands and occasionally acting as a master of ceremonies, he began singing with Kent's band. When Powell joined the Davis band, he had only the sketchiest knowledge of instrumental music. However, he had a burning desire to play the banjo. In three weeks Powell had learned to play all the chords on a banjo and took his place on the bandstand with the other instrumentalists. Davis worked with Powell on his stage presence. In Davis's words, "His gestures were godawful." He was told to casually lean on the piano and try not to move his hands. The spotlight man was instructed to light his head and shoulders only.

The Davis band played at several venues around Indianapolis, including the new Columbia Club, the Ohio Theater, and the Circle Theater. After Powell improved and was doing very well with the band, he left for a fling in vaudeville. In 1927 the Circle Theater Company, which had much success with its theater, started to build a real movie palace on West Washington Street. It was to be called the Indiana Theater. One of the principals in the company, Herman Lieber, approached Davis about serving as the stage band with Davis as the emcee. Davis accepted, and as fortune would have it, shortly thereafter he received word that Powell was not doing well with his vaudeville act and wanted to rejoin the Davis band.

Powell stayed with Davis two more years, then left when he was offered his own band as well as the emcee job at the Circle. In 1930 he began to make recordings and had a hit with *Beloved*. This brought him to the attention of Warner Brothers, who were considering making a return to musicals. He was given a screen test and was cast in his first film, *Blessed Event*, in 1932. He wrote a letter to Carl Niesse, the Indiana Theater manager, saying, "Hello everybody in Indianapolis. Here I am in Hollywood, the dreamland of every performer . . . and I owe it all to good old Indianapolis. When I stepped off the train, I was unusually frightened. If I ever needed my Hoosier friends it was then . . . with you out there to give me encouragement, which you gave me back in my pioneering days, I have felt quite secure." He told of his first meeting with his future wife. "The day I met Joan Blondell I was so nervous I could hardly talk to her. I just stood there and stuttered and stammered."

In 1933 Powell made his first film with Ruby Keeler, *42nd Street*, which broke new ground for musicals and established Powell as a star. He expressed dissatisfaction with the type of singing roles he had been getting and was determined to change his image. The turning point came in 1944, when he played hard-boiled private detective Philip Marlowe in *Murder, My Sweet*. He then set his sights on directing and directed several films, including *The Conqueror* (1956), which starred John Wayne, Susan Hayward, Pedro Amendáriz, and Agnes Moorehead. (It was shot in Utah near an atomic test site. Most of the cast and many of the crew members later were stricken with cancer.)

Powell formed an independent telefilm production company with actors David Niven and Charles Boyer. It was called Four Star Productions, and its first project was a television series, *Four Star Playhouse*. The stars rotated appearing in the series with a weekly guest star. In its second season, Ida Lupino became one of the partners. Four Star became a powerhouse in the television industry with Powell at the helm. It produced such series as *The Rifleman*, *Zane Grey Theatre*, *Alcoa Theatre*, *Johnny Ringo*, and the series that gave fellow Hoosier Steve McQueen his start, *Wanted: Dead or Alive*.

In early 1961 Powell reduced his involvement in the overall productions at Four Star and focused on *The Dick Powell Show*, a star-studded anthology. This series yielded a number of pilots that became hit television shows, among them the highly successful *Burke's Law*. He was married three times: Mildred Maund (1925–32); Joan Blondell (1936–44); and June Allyson from 1954 to his death. He was survived by a son, Norman, and a daughter, Ellen, from his marriage to Blondell, and two children, Pamela and Richard Jr., from his marriage to Allyson. After his death, Four Star was never as successful as it was when Powell was running it. It was sold in 1967.

Dick Powell, Norman Scott Barnes Powell (Powell's adopted son), and Joan Blondell (Powell's second wife).
ACME PHOTO

BIBLIOGRAPHY

Davis, Charlie. *That Band from Indiana.* Oswego, N.Y.: Mathom Publishing Company, 1982.

Dick Powell. http://www.museum.tv/archives/etv/P/htmlP/powell dick/powelldick.htm.

Indianapolis News, April 29, September 10, 1932, February 9, 1940.

Indianapolis Star, February 10, 1940.

Wilkinson, Harry. "Looking Hollywood Way." *Good Old Days* (August 1997).

HERB SHRINER (HERBERT ARTHUR SHRINER)
Toledo, Ohio (1918–1970)

Born in Toledo, Herb Shriner once said, "I moved to Indiana as soon as I heard about it." Nonnative Shriner probably became the best-known Hoosier in show business. He started out playing the harmonica "as soon as I was able to defend myself." As a schoolboy in Fort Wayne, he formed a harmonica quintet and began playing at dances, small theaters, and on local radio stations.

One night Shriner's lips gave out and, to cover his embarrassment, he started talking. He found his audience was more anxious to hear his droll, extemporaneous humor than to hear him play the harmonica. He got a solo spot at the Oriental Theater in Chicago and was a big hit.

Shriner made several appearances on network radio shows and then was drafted in World War II. While overseas, he developed a monologue reflecting gripes of his fellow soldiers. This made him well known nationally. In 1949 he married Eileen McDermott. They had three children: a daughter, Indy (named for Indiana), and twin boys Wil and Kin.

In 1948 Shriner was the star of *Herb Shriner Time* on CBS radio. Durward Kirby (who got some of his early radio training in Indianapolis) was his announcer. On November 7, 1949, he debuted *The Herb Shriner Show* on CBS television. It ran until December 4, 1956.

Herb Shriner and Mary Murphy appeared in *Main Street to Broadway* in 1953.

In 1952 comedian Fred Allen was scheduled to host a new game show. He became ill, and Shriner was called in to take his place. The show was *Two for the Money*. When Shriner took over the show, he requested that the theme song for the show be "Back Home Again in Indiana." He left the show in 1956. He appeared in one movie, *Main Street to Broadway*, in 1953.

Shriner moved his family from New York to Fort Lauderdale, Florida, because he wanted his children to be brought up in a small-city environment. Summer vacations were spent in Angola, Indiana. In April 1970 Shriner and his wife were killed in an automobile accident in Delray Beach, Florida. Their children were raised by their grandparents. Wil Shriner followed in his father's footsteps. He has been the host of many television series and had his own nationally syndicated talk show, *The Wil Shriner Show*, which was nominated for three Emmy Awards. Twin brother Kin is an actor who portrayed Scott Baldwin on ABC's daytime drama, *General Hospital*.

"The Herb Shriner Hoosier Boy" harmonica is still in great demand for those who love to play the mouth organ.

BIBLIOGRAPHY

The Herb Shriner Story. http://www.spah.org/shriner.htm.

Patterson and Associates Bios. http://www.pattersonandassociates.com/bios/Wil_Shriner/index.html.

MICHAEL E. USLAN, *Jersey City, New Jersey (b. 1951)*

Michael Uslan has been a collector of comic books since the seventh grade. Little did he know this hobby would help pay his way through college and lead to a career in motion pictures. He decided to enroll at Indiana University based on several recommendations, including a number of cousins who were alums.

Uslan lived in Bloomington eight years and received three degrees, the last being a JD in 1976. In 1971 he decided he would try to teach a course on comic book history. Shortly after he won acceptance from the dean's office to teach the course, he picked up a phone and called United Press International. When he was connected to a reporter on the education beat, he started screaming, "I don't know what the hell is going on in this state, but it's the end of civilization as we know it! I hear there's a course on comic books at IU, those damn hippies. I'm a taxpayer, and they're ruining our educational system!" He then hung up.

The result was a wire story picked up by newspapers throughout the country. NBC's nightly news carried the story. This led to a call from Stan Lee, the co-creator of *Spider-Man*, *The Hulk*, and other Marvel Comics characters. It wasn't long before the president of DC Comics called. Soon Uslan was on a plane to New York to accept a job with DC. He began writing comics by night while completing his master's and a law degree from IU.

After receiving his law degree, Uslan moved to New York City to accept a job as an entertainment lawyer at United Artists. He said, "It was there I learned the ins and outs of financing movies." In 1979, after working three years as an entertainment lawyer on such films as *Rocky II* (1979), *The Black Stallion* (1979), and *Raging Bull* (1980), he optioned the feature rights for Batman from DC Comics. The result was the movie *Batman*, released in 1989 and starring Michael Keaton,

Michael E. Uslan.

Jack Nicholson, and Kim Basinger. It was directed by Tim Burton, and Uslan served as executive producer.

Uslan has been the executive producer on every *Batman* film since.

BIBLIOGRAPHY

Author's phone interview with Michael Uslan, July 28, 2004.

Branded Entertainment Press Releases. http://www.brandedentertainment.com/pressreleases.html.

Crawford, Andrea. "The Secret Life of Comic Books." *Indiana Alumni Magazine* (January/February 2004).

Harris, Dana. "Uslan Ushers in Branded Consultancy." *Variety*, October 3, 2001.

Indiana University Alumni Association.

The Internet Movie Database. http://www.imdb.com/.

Kanfer, Stefan. *Ball of Fire: The Tumultuous Life and Comic Art of Lucille Ball.* New York: Alfred A. Knopf, 2003.

HERB VIGRAN (HERBURT VIGRAN), *Cincinnati, Ohio (1910–1986)*

Herb Vigran (on ladder) with Burt Lancaster and Dorothy McGuire in *Mister 880* (1950).

Herburt Vigran's family moved to Fort Wayne, Indiana, when he was a youngster. He attended school there and always thought of Fort Wayne as his hometown. He enrolled at Indiana University and received a law degree in 1933. Shortly afterward he decided he would rather be an actor than a lawyer.

Vigran moved to Hollywood and in short order appeared in his first film, *Happy Landing*, in 1934. However, film work was not easy to find, and he switched to radio. In 1949 he became a regular on the *Father Knows Best* radio series as the next-door neighbor. Unfortunately, when the series was transferred to television, Vigran was not included in the cast.

Vigran remained active in radio, appearing on such shows as *The Ed Wynn Show* and *The Adventures of Superman*. He frequently played villains. Shortly after returning from service in World War II, he was cast as *The Sad Sack*, a radio version of the comic strip. The series began in June 1946 and ran for thirteen episodes. He began getting bit roles in movies and got stage work in New York on the basis of a portfolio of photos showing him sharing scenes with several well-known actors. (There was no mention that most of the film roles were bit parts.)

Vigran eventually appeared in more than 150 films. His favorite role was that of a rumpled private eye in the 1954 comedy *Susan Slept Here*. He is also remembered for his role that same year as the all-too-affable mobile home salesman who sold Lucille Ball and Desi Arnaz *The Long, Long Trailer*. He was quite busy on television, appearing in a recurring role as Judge Brooker on *Gunsmoke*. He also did voice-over work for commercials and animated films. He was the voice of Lurvy in *Charlotte's Web* and played several characters in the series *Top Cat*. When he died in 1986, he was survived by his wife, Belle, and two sons, Richard and Robert, both of Pasadena. He had two sisters, Florence Shapera of Portland, Oregon, and Juell Laub of Los Angeles.

BIBLIOGRAPHY

The Indiana University Alumni Association, Bloomington, Indiana.

The Internet Movie Database. http://www.imdb.com/.

APPENDIXES

Oscar Winners and Nominees
Soap Hoosiers
Movies Shot in or about Indiana
Hoosiers on the Hollywood Walk of Fame
Other Players
County by County List

The Academy Award ceremony was held in Hoosier Sid Grauman's (Indianapolis) Chinese Theater in 1944, 1945, and 1946. Three Hoosiers have been Academy presidents: George Seaton (South Bend) from 1955 to 1957; Robert Wise (Winchester) from 1985 to 1988; and Karl Malden, born in Chicago but grew up in Gary, from 1988 to 1993.

JAMES BASKETT, *Indianapolis (1904-1948)*

Received a special Oscar for "his able and heart-warming characterization of Uncle Remus, friend and storyteller to the children of the world," in *Song of the South* (1946).

ANNE BAXTER, *Michigan City (1923-1985)*

Best Actress in a Supporting Role for *The Razor's Edge* (1946).

Nominated for Best Actress for *All About Eve* (1950).

KAREN BLACK (KAREN BLANCHE ZIEGLER), *Park Ridge, Illinois, grew up in Lafayette (b. 1939)*

Nominated for Best Actress in a Supporting Role for *Five Easy Pieces* (1970).

BUDD BOETTICHER (OSCAR BOETTICHER JR.), *Chicago, raised in Evansville (1916-2001)*

Nominated for Best Writing (Motion Picture Story) for *Bullfighter and the Lady* (1951).

BEULAH BONDI, *Chicago, grew up in Valparaiso (1889-1981)*

Nominated for Best Actress in a Supporting Role for *The Gorgeous Hussy* (1936) and *Of Human Hearts* (1938).

WALTER BULLOCK, *Shelburn (1907-1953)*

Nominated for Best Music (Song) for "When Did You Leave Heaven?" from *Sing, Baby, Sing* (1936) (shared with Richard A. Whiting) and "Who Am I?" from *Hit Parade of 1941* (shared with Jule Styne).

HOAGY CARMICHAEL, *Bloomington (1899-1981)*

Best Music (Song) for "In the Cool, Cool, Cool of the Evening" from *Here Comes the Groom* (1951) (shared with Johnny Mercer).

Nominated for Best Music (Song) for "Old Buttermilk Sky" from *Canyon Passage* (1946).

JAMES DEAN, *Marion (1931-1955)*

Nominated for Best Actor for *East of Eden* (1955) and *Giant* (1956).

GEORGE W. DAVIS, *Kokomo (1914-1993)*

Best Art Decoration—Set Decoration (Color) for *The Robe* (1953).

Nominated for Best Art Direction—Set Decoration (Black and White) for *All About Eve* (1950), *The Diary of Anne Frank* (1959), *Period of Adjustment* (1962), *Twilight of Honor* (1963), *The Americanization of Emily* (1964), *A Patch of Blue* (1965), and *Mister Buddwing* (1966).

Nominated for Best Art Decoration—Set Decoration (Color) for *David and Bathsheba* (1951), *Love Is a Many-Splendored Thing* (1955), *Funny Face* (1957), *Cimarron* (1960), *The Wonderful World of the Brothers Grimm* (1962), *Mutiny on the Bounty* (1962), *How the West Was Won* (1962), *The Unsinkable Molly Brown* (1964), and *The Shoes of the Fisherman* (1968).

LOUISE DRESSER, *Evansville (1878-1965)*

Nominated for Best Actress for *A Ship Comes In* (1928).

GEORGE DUNING, *Richmond (1908-2000)*

Nominated for Best Music (Scoring of a Musical Picture) for *Jolson Sings Again* (1949) and *The Eddy Duchin Story* (1956).

Nominated for Best Music (Music Score of a Dramatic or Comedy Picture) for *No Sad Songs for Me* (1950), *From Here to Eternity* (1953), and *Picnic* (1955).

IRENE DUNNE, *Louisville, raised in Madison (1898-1990)*

Nominated for Best Actress for *Cimarron* (1931), *Theodora Goes Wild* (1936), *The Awful Truth* (1937), *Love Affair* (1939), and *I Remember Mama* (1948).

GLORIA GRESHAM, *Indianapolis (b. 1945)*

Nominated for Best Costume Design for *Avalon* (1990).

SID GRAUMAN, *Indianapolis (1879-1950)*

Awarded an honorary Oscar in 1949 for being a "master showman who raised the standard of exhibition of motion pictures."

A. B. GUTHRIE JR., *Bedford (1901-1991)*

Nominated for Best Writing (Screenplay) for *Shane* (1953).

JEAN HAGEN, *Chicago, lived in Elkhart (1923-1977)*

Nominated for Best Actress in a Supporting Role for *Singin' in the Rain* (1952).

PHIL HARRIS, *Linton (1904-1995)*

Starred in *So This Is Harris* (1933), which received the award for Best Documentary (Short Subject).

As Baloo the Bear, sang "The Bare Necessities" from *The Jungle Book* (1967), which was nominated for best song.

HOWARD HAWKS, *Goshen (1896–1977)*

Nominated for Best Directing for *Sergeant York* (1941).

Awarded an honorary Oscar in 1974 for being "a master American filmmaker whose creative efforts holds a distinguished place in world cinema."

DEAN JAGGER, *Columbus Grove, Ohio, grew up in Larwill (1903–1991)*

Best Actor in a Supporting Role for *Twelve O'Clock High* (1949).

GROVER JONES, *Terre Haute (1893–1940)*

Nominated for Best Writing (Original Story) for *Lady and Gent* (1932).

Nominated for Best Writing (Screenplay) for *The Lives of a Bengal Lancer* (1935).

GREG KINNEAR, *Logansport (b. 1973)*

Nominated for Best Actor in a Supporting Role for *As Good As It Gets* (1997).

KEVIN KLINE, *St. Louis (b. 1947), graduated from Indiana University*

Best Actor in a Supporting Role for *A Fish Called Wanda* (1988).

JOHN KORTY, *Lafayette (b. 1936)*

Best Documentary (Feature) for *Who Are the DeBolts? And Where Did They Get Nineteen Kids?* (1977).

Nominated for Best Documentary (Short Subject) for *Breaking the Habit* (1964).

CAROLE LOMBARD (JANE ALICE PETERS), *Fort Wayne (1908–1942)*

Nominated for Best Actress for *My Man Godfrey* (1936).

MARJORIE MAIN (MARY TOMLINSON), *Acton (1890–1975)*

Nominated for Best Actress in a Supporting Role for *The Egg and I* (1947).

KARL MALDEN (MLADEN SEKULOVIC), *Chicago, raised in Gary (b. 1914)*

Best Actor in a Supporting Role for *A Streetcar Named Desire* (1951).

Nominated for Best Actor in a Supporting Role for *On the Waterfront* (1954).

THAMER (TED) D. MCCORD, *Sullivan County (1900–1976)*

Nominated for Best Cinematography (Black and White) for *Johnny Belinda* (1948) and *Two for the Seesaw* (1962).

Nominated for Best Cinematography (Color) for *The Sound of Music* (1965).

STEVE MCQUEEN, *Beech Grove (1930–1980)*

Nominated for Best Actor for *The Sand Pebbles* (1966).

PAUL OSBORN, *Evansville (1901–1988)*

Nominated for Best Writing (Screenplay) for *East of Eden* (1955).

Nominated for Best Writing (Screenplay—Based on Material from Another Medium) for *Sayonara* (1957).

SYDNEY POLLACK, *Lafayette (b. 1934)*

Best Directing for *Out of Africa* (1985) (the film also won Best Picture).

Nominated for Best Directing for *They Shoot Horses, Don't They?* (1969) and *Tootsie* (1982) (which won Best Picture).

COLE PORTER, *Peru (1891–1964)*

Nominated for Best Music (Song) for "I've Got You Under My Skin" from *Born to Dance* (1936), "Since I Kissed My Baby Goodbye" from *You'll Never Get Rich* (1941), "You'd Be So Nice to Come Home To" from *Something to Shout About* (1943), and "True Love" from *High Society* (1956).

GEORGE SEATON (GEORGE STENIUS), *South Bend (1911–1979)*

Best Writing (Screenplay) for *Miracle on 34th Street* (1947) and *The Country Girl* (1954).

Best Directing for *The Country Girl* (1954).

Nominated for Best Writing (Screenplay) for *The Song of Bernadette* (1943).

Nominated for Best Writing (Screenplay—Based on Material from Another Medium) for *Airport* (1970).

Received the Jean Hersholt Humanitarian Award in 1961.

CLIFTON WEBB (WEBB PARMELEE HOLLENBECK), *Indianapolis (1889-1966)*

Nominated for Best Actor for *Sitting Pretty* (1948).

Nominated for Best Actor in a Supporting Role for *Laura* (1944) and *The Razor's Edge* (1946).

ROBERT WISE, *Winchester (1914-2005)*

Best Directing for *West Side Story* (1961) and *The Sound of Music* (1965) (both films also won Best Picture awards).

Nominated for Best Directing for *I Want to Live!* (1958).

Nominated for Best Film Editing for *Citizen Kane* (1941).

Directed *The Sand Pebbles* (1966), which was nominated for Best Picture.

Received the Irving G. Thalberg Memorial Award in 1966.

The first soap opera was probably *The Arabian Nights*. This format proved to be so popular it was used by many giants of literature. Charles Dickens and Arthur Conan Doyle made good use of it by publishing their novels in installments. When motion pictures began, one of the most popular attractions was the serial. The serial form reached radio in the 1920s. However, newspapers and magazines were locked in print. Movie serials were action thrillers ending with a cliff-hanger every week. The radio serial was about family life, love and romance and, until recently, featured little thrilling action.

In the late 1920s and early 1930s, soap product manufacturers took over the radio serials. Because these dramas featured all the elements of grand opera, they were dubbed soap operas. American soap operas soon became a unique dramatic art form. In addition to providing the housewife release from her workaday world, they contributed to the entertainment genre in several ways. Most important, perhaps, was the training ground they provided for aspiring actors, directors, and writers.

In earlier days, vaudeville artists migrated into radio, and radio artists migrated into television. Today, there is no vaudeville or radio to provide up-and-coming actors with experience. There is no subsidized national theater in every great American city, and the studio system in Hollywood is long gone. But there are soap operas, which easily made the transition from radio to television. Today, they serve as an opportune training ground for many young actors. Conversely, they frequently provide work for those actors whose careers are winding down.

When radio was in its heyday in the 1930s and 1940s, many Hoosiers were very busy radio actors, and many went on to successful movie careers. Mary Jane Croft, Forrest Lewis, and Lurene Tuttle all were part of *One Man's Family*. Lewis played several different roles on *Joyce Jordan, Girl Intern* and *Portia Faces Life*. Will Geer was a regular on *Bright Horizon*. Fran Carlon was in several radio soap operas, and when television took over the soaps she was a regular on *As the World Turns*. Don Hancock was the announcer for *The Romance of Helen Trent* and *Life Can Be Beautiful*.

Most soap operas today still move amazingly slow. However, actors change with frequency. Many go on to bigger and better things. Some move from one soap to another, and a few make a whole career out of their tenure in the soaps. Following are some Hoosiers who have achieved prominence in soap operas.

JULIA BARR, Fort Wayne (b. 1949)

Julia Barr began acting as a youngster in Fort Wayne, acting, singing, and dancing in almost every local production between the Fort Wayne Community Theater, Civic Theater, Wagon Wheel Playhouse, and Enchanted Hills Playhouse. She followed with several Purdue University productions, including such plays as *A Streetcar Named Desire*, *Our Town*, and *The Killing of Sister George*. She joined Buffalo's Studio Arena Theater, where she earned her equity card starring in *Scapino* and *A Girl in My Soup*. When she moved to New York City, her first job was with the New York City telephone service. She got her first professional break in NBC's *A Gathering of One*. In 1976 she began portraying Brooke English on *All My Children* and has played it ever since. Her work on *All My Children* has earned her eight Emmy nominations, winning twice in 1998 and 2001 for outstanding supporting actress. Other television credits include *The Adams Chronicles* and *Ryan's Hope* (1975–76). Her film credits include *I, the Jury* (1982). She has been married to Dr. Richard Hirschlag for more than twenty years, and they have a daughter, Allison. Allison played Lizzie Spaulding on the daytime soap *The Guiding Light* until February 2003.

ABRAHAM BENRUBI, Indianapolis (b. 1969)

The son of Asher ("Atom Smasher"), a former disc jockey at WNAP in Indianapolis, Abraham Rubin Hercules Benrubi began taking acting lessons while in elementary school. He was an only child whose parents divorced when he was six years old. His mother, Patricia, encouraged his acting ambitions through grade school and Broad Ripple High School. He began appearing in local theater productions, and shortly after his graduation from high school he got his big break. He landed a small role in a movie that was being shot in Indianapolis called *Diving In* (1990). Soon after his film debut, he moved to Los Angeles and six months later was cast as a regular on a new television series, *Parker Lewis Can't Lose* (1990). He has been working steadily ever since.

Benrubi made several movies in the early 1990s and then was cast as Jerry Markovic on *ER* (1994–99, 2002–). He has remained a regular on the show while doing movies and other television appearances. He has guest starred on *Buffy the Vampire Slayer*, *Wings*, *Roseanne*, and *Married with Children*. His film credits include *George of the Jungle* (1997), with fellow Hoosier Brendan Fraser; the Coen Brothers' *The Man Who Wasn't There* (2001); *ZigZag* (2002), with Wesley Snipes; and *Open Range* (2003), with Kevin Costner.

STEVE BURTON, *Indianapolis (b. 1970)*

Born in Indianapolis and raised in Cleveland, Ohio, Steve Burton moved to California with his father in time to graduate from Beverly Hills High School. The school gave him the opportunity to study drama and join its acclaimed "Theatre 40." He began his career by doing commercials. His first regular television role was as Chris Fuller in the syndicated comedy series, *Out of This World* (1987). His first daytime soap opera role was in 1988 as Harris Michaels in *Days of Our Lives*. His big break was being cast as Jason Quartermaine in *General Hospital* in 1991. Burton was also cast as Jason Morgan, a leader of organized crime. Morgan was actually Quartermaine who had a memory loss. Burton won an Emmy in 1988 for outstanding supporting actor in a drama series. Burton left the soaps in 2000 for films. In 2001 he was cast with Robert Redford in *The Last Castle* and starred in *Taken* (2002), a twenty-hour miniseries on the Sci-Fi Channel.

Burton reprised his role as Jason Quartermaine and signed a long-term contract in May 2002 to return to *General Hospital*. He is hoping someday to produce and direct. He married Sheree Gustin in 1999, and they had their first child in August 2003.

DAVID CANARY, *Elwood (b. 1938)*

As a youngster, David Canary's family moved to Massillon, Ohio, where he grew up. He went to the University of Cincinnati on a football scholarship and graduated with a degree in music, specializing in voice. He made his Broadway debut in 1961 in *The Happiest Girl in the World*. The next year he was on Broadway with Colleen Dewhurst in *Great Day in the Morning*. Over the years he has also appeared in films, theater, and television. He was drafted into the army, where he won an all-army entertainment contest for best popular singer. When he left the service, he starred in a West Coast production of *The Fantasticks* in San Francisco.

His first big break in television was being cast as Candy in *Bonanza* (replacing Pernell Roberts) in 1969–70 and 1972–73. Canary was Russ Gehring in *Peyton Place* from 1965 to 1966. His first daytime soap opera job was playing Steven Frame in *Another World* from 1981 to 1983.

In 1980 he returned to Broadway in Tennessee Williams's *Clothes for a Summer Hotel*, opposite Geraldine Page. He became a regular on *All My Children* in 1983. He has won four Emmys for his work on *All My Children*, playing the dual roles of Adam and Stuart Chandler. He writes plays and works closely with Robert Lupone's Manhattan Classic Company. He keeps busy in stock theater, playing a variety of roles.

DRAKE HOGESTYN, *Fort Wayne (b. 1953)*

Drake Hogestyn grew up in Fort Wayne and attended the University of Florida on a baseball scholarship, majoring in premed dentistry. After graduation he was drafted by the St. Louis Cardinals and the New York Yankees. He chose the Yankees' farm team, where he played third base until he suffered a career-ending injury in 1978. It was then that he decided to try an acting career. He was one of seventy-five thousand applicants in a talent search conducted by Columbia Pictures. He went to Los Angeles, where he participated in an intensive four-month acting workshop. He was selected to play a starring role in the prime-time television series, *Seven Brides for Seven Brothers* (1982).

In 1986 he joined the cast of *Days of Our Lives*, which is a Columbia Pictures property. His role of The Pawn, John Black, gave him instant soap stardom. He received best actor awards from as far away as Australia, South Africa, and Germany. He also received five consecutive wins from *Soap Opera Update*, was named Hottest Male Star at the Soap Opera Digest Awards for two straight years, and received more number-one rankings than any actor in the history of soap operas from the *Daytime TV* Readers Poll.

In 1998 he was asked by fellow Fort Wayne native Shelley Long to play her husband on a new sitcom, *Kelly Kelly*. Hogestyn tried to arrange it so he could continue in *Days* and do the sitcom as well. Unfortunately, his schedule would not permit it, and the part went to Robert Hays. He married his childhood sweetheart, Victoria, and they have three daughters and one son.

PETER RECKELL, *Elkhart (b. 1955)*

Peter Reckell was born in Elkhart, but grew up on a farm in Michigan. He was the second oldest of six children. While in junior high, he built theater sets, sang in the chorus, and became a technical director. He appeared in several plays in high school and then attended the prestigious Boston Conservatory, where he received a bachelor of fine arts degree in theater with minors in music and dance.

After receiving his degree, Reckell headed for New York, where he landed a job in the longest-running musical in the world, *The Fantasticks*. He then moved into television, playing Eric Hollister on *As the World Turns* (1980–82). In 1983 he joined the *Days of Our Lives* cast as Bo Brady, a bearded, long-haired, tattooed motorcyclist who wore an earring. Audiences went wild. The producers were happy but surprised since this was during the Reagan administration when things were getting more conservative.

Reckell climbed to the top of the daytime polls and then left *Days of Our Lives* to join *Knots Landing* (1988–89). In 1995 he returned to *Days of Our Lives*, resuming his role of Bo Brady.

Reckell has made several movies and has interest in doing a sitcom. He has published a self-titled country rock album with the help of his wife, singer/ songwriter Kelly Moneymaker.

KRISTINA WAGNER, *Indianapolis (b. 1963)*

The youngest of three children, Kristina Crump Wagner started her career dancing and acting in high school in Indianapolis. She enrolled at Indiana Central University (now University of Indianapolis), where she majored in drama, then transferred to Indiana University–Purdue University in Indianapolis, earning a degree in theater. After graduation, Wagner worked doing commercials for local companies while performing with the University Theater Group. Her brother suggested that she send a picture and résumé to a modeling agency. That led to auditions for roles on *All My Children*, *Ryan's Hope*, and eventually *General Hospital*. She joined *General Hospital* in 1984 in the role of Felicia Cummings Jones. At that time she was known as Kristina Malandro. She married actor/singer Jack Wagner, who played her on-screen husband, Frisco Jones. They have two sons, Peter and Harrison. "My first love is motherhood. There just isn't anything better. I love nesting, being domestic at home on our ranch with our two sons."

Hoosiers have been appearing in daytime television soap operas from the 1950s to the present. Following is a listing of actors from Indiana who have contributed to this unique form of drama.

ALL MY CHILDREN
Julia Barr (Fort Wayne): Brooke English, 1976–81, 1982–present
David Canary (Elwood): Stuart and Adam Chandler, 1983–present
Greta Lind (Goshen): Kate Kenicott, 1990–91

ANOTHER WORLD
David Canary (Elwood): Steve Frame, 1981–83
Sharon Gabet (Fort Wayne): Brittany Peterson, 1984–85

AS THE WORLD TURNS
Fran Carlon (Indianapolis): Julia Burke, 1968–75
Terri Conn (Bloomington): Katie Peretti, 1998–present

Terry Lester (Indianapolis): Royce Keller, 1992–94
Neil Maffin (Indiana): Beau Farrell, 1988–89
Betsy Palmer (East Chicago): Suz Becker, 1981
James Rebhorn (Anderson): Henry Lange, 1988–91
Peter Reckell (Elkhart): Eric Hollister, 1980–82
Kin Shriner (Herb Shriner's son): Keith Morrisey, 2004–present

DAYS OF OUR LIVES
Vivica Fox (Indianapolis): Carmen Silva, 1988
Drake Hogestyn (Fort Wayne): John Black aka Roman Brady, 1986–present
Peter Reckell (Elkhart): Bo Brady, 1983–87, 1990–92, 1995–present

THE EDGE OF NIGHT
Jayne Bentzen (Evansville): Nicole Travis Drake, 1978–81
Sharon Gabet (Fort Wayne): Raven Alexander, 1977–84
Philip Proctor (Goshen): Julie (Julian) Kurtz (1962)

GENERAL HOSPITAL
Steve Burton (Indianapolis): Jason Quartermaine, 1991–present
Lloyd Haynes (South Bend): Ken Morgan, 1984–86
Kin Shriner: Scotty Baldwin, 1977–80, 1981–84, 1988–93, 2000–2003
Melanie Vincz (Indianapolis): Corinne, 1981
Hunter Von Leer (Terre Haute): Larry Joe Baker, 1977
Kristina Wagner (Indianapolis): Felicia Cummings Jones, 1984–present

GENERATIONS
Vivica Fox (Indianapolis): Maia, 1989–91

THE GUIDING LIGHT
James Rebhorn (Anderson): Bradley Raines, 1983–85, 1989

MISS SUSAN
Betsy Palmer (East Chicago), 1951

ONE LIFE TO LIVE
Claude Akins (Bedford): Marcus, 1992
Braden Danner (Indianapolis): Buddy McGillis, 1988
Sharon Gabet (Fort Wayne): Melinda Cramer, 1987–89

PASSIONS
Brook Kerr (Indianapolis): Whitney Russell, 1999–present

PORT CHARLES
Carly Schroeder (Valparaiso): Serena Baldwin, 1997–2003
Kin Shriner: Scotty Baldwin, 1997–2000, 2001
Barbara Stock (Indianapolis): Nicole Devlin, 1997

RYAN'S HOPE
Julia Barr (Fort Wayne): Reenie Szabo, 1976

SANTA BARBARA
Terry Lester (Indianapolis): Mason Capwell, 1989–90

SEARCH FOR TOMORROW
David Canary (Elwood): Arthur Benson (1978)
Ken Kercheval (Wolcottville): Nick Hunter, 1965–67, 1972–73
Kevin Kline (IU graduate): Woody Reed, 1976

THE SECRET STORM
Ken Kercheval (Wolcottville): Archie Borman, 1968

TEXAS
James Rebhorn (Anderson): John Brady, 1981–82
Kin Shriner: Jeb Hampton, 1980–81

THE YOUNG AND THE RESTLESS
Vivica Fox (Indianapolis): Stephanie Simmons, 1995
Terry Lester (Indianapolis): Jack Abbott, 1980–89

BIBLIOGRAPHY

Julia Barr Biography. http://www.juliarosebarr.com/bio.htm.
Steve Burton Biography. http://abc.go.com/daytime/general hospital/bios/Steve_Burton2.html.
Groves, Seli. *The Ultimate Soap Opera Guide*. Detroit: Visible Ink Press, 1995.
Drake Hogestyn Web site. www.drakehogestynonline.com/about.htm.
The Internet Movie Database. http://www.imdb.com/.
Peter Reckell Biography. http://daysofourlives.about.com/library/biography/blbio reckell.htm.
Wagget, Gerard J. *The Soap Opera Encyclopedia.* New York: HarperPaperbacks, 1997.
Kristina Wagner Biography. http://abc.go.com/daytime/generalhospital/bios/Kristina_Wagner2.html.

The Internet Movie Database lists more than two hundred movies that have been fully or partially shot in Indiana. Following is a representative sampling of some of the more notable films shot in the Hoosier state.

Speedway (1929). Part of this silent film was shot on location. Costarring were William Haines, Ernest Torrence, John Miljan, and Karl Dane.

To Please a Lady (1950). Shot at Indianapolis Motor Speedway. Clark Gable, Barbara Stanwyck, and Hoosier Will Geer.

Johnny Holiday (1949). Shot in Plainfield. William Bendix, Hoosier Hoagy Carmichael.

Some Came Running (1958). Shot in Madison. Frank Sinatra, Shirley MacLaine, and a cast of Hoosier extras.

Winning (1969). Shot at Indianapolis Motor Speedway. Paul Newman, Joanne Woodward, Richard Thomas, Robert Wagner, and a host of Hoosier extras.

Brian's Song (1971). Much of this film was shot in Rensselaer.

A Girl Named Sooner (1975). Shot in Vevay. Lee Remick, Richard Crenna, Don Murray, and Hoosier Susan Deer.

Breaking Away (1979). Shot in Bloomington. John Cusack, Steve Gutenberg, and scenes from "The Little 500" at Indiana University.

Four Friends (1981). Shot partially in East Chicago. Written by Steve Tesich, born in Yugoslavia but raised in East Chicago and a graduate of Indiana University.

The Escapist (1983). Local radio owner Bill Shirk starred in this film originally entitled *Modern Day Houdini*. It was shot in Indianapolis with mostly local actors except for *Mission: Impossible* star Peter Lupus.

Hoosiers (1986). Shot in various Indiana locations. Gene Hackman, Barbara Hershey, and Dennis Hopper with a cast of Hoosier extras.

Pushed Too Far (1986). Shot in Greenfield. Star is Hoosier Claude Akins.

Eight Men Out (1988). Shot in Indianapolis and Evansville. Charlie Sheen, John Cusack, and a cast of Hoosier extras.

Viper (1988). Shot in Indianapolis and Bloomington. Linda Purl.

Terror Squad (1987). Shot in Kokomo, starring Chuck Connors.

Rain Man (1988). Shot partially in Franklin County. Tom Cruise, Dustin Hoffman, with costumes by Indianapolis native Gloria Gresham.

Prancer (1989). Filmed at director John D. Hancock's childhood home, the Hancock Fruit Farm in La Porte. Hancock was born in Kansas City, Missouri, but grew up in Indiana.

A League of Their Own (1992). Shot in Evansville and Huntingburg. Tom Hanks, Geena Davis, Madonna, and a host of Hoosier extras.

Falling from Grace (1992). John Mellencamp. Shot in various locations in Indiana.

Freeze Frame (1992). Shot in Indianapolis, starring Shannen Doherty and directed by Hoosier William Bindley.

Rudy (1993). Shot mostly in South Bend at the University of Notre Dame. Directed by Hoosier David Anspaugh and written by fellow Hoosier Angelo Pizzo.

Blue Chips (1994). Nick Nolte, Shaquille O'Neal, Reggie Miller, Bobby Knight, and others. Segments were shot in Indiana.

Natural Born Killers (1994). The courtroom scenes in which Woody Harrelson is tried as a serial killer were filmed at the Hammond City Court.

Going All the Way (1997). Based on the novel by Hoosier author Dan Wakefield. Much of the film was shot in Indianapolis.

In the Company of Men (1997). Primarily shot in Fort Wayne.

Best Man in Grass Creek (1999). Written, directed, and starring Hoosier John Newcombe. Shot in Grass Creek.

A Piece of Eden (2000). Shot mostly in the La Porte County area. Directed by John D. Hancock, who grew up in La Porte.

Madison (2001). Starring Hoosier Jake Lloyd. Directed by Hoosier William Bindley and written by Bindley and his brother, Scott. Shot mostly in Madison.

MOVIES ABOUT INDIANA BUT NOT SHOT IN INDIANA

The Hoosier Schoolmaster (1914), (1924), and (1935). Based on the novel by Hoosier author Edward Eggleston. Made three times but never shot in Indiana. The 1935 version starred Richmond native Norman Foster in the leading role.

The Gentleman from Indiana (1915). Written by Booth Tarkington (Indianapolis). Dustin Farnum was the star. Tarkington's writings were translated into at least fifty-nine motion pictures.

Indiana (1916). This was a docudrama about the birth of the state. It was directed by Frank Beal and written by Gilson Willets, neither of whom were Hoosiers. The Indiana Historical Society reportedly worked with the producer/director. The film was produced by Selig Polyscope Company. It was also known as *The Birth of Indiana* and *Historic Indiana*. According to an article in *Photoplay* magazine in June 1916, the film was seven reels and was to be "a visualized state history."

A Hoosier Romance (1918). Based on James Whitcomb Riley's poem, "A Hoosier Romance," starring Colleen Moore.

Little Orphant Annie (1918). Starring Colleen Moore and Hoosier Tom Santschi (Kokomo). Based loosely on James Whitcomb Riley's poem.

On the Banks of the Wabash (1923). Starring Madge Evans and Terre Haute native Edward Roseman.

The College Widow (1927). Based on George Ade's (Kentland) play, this comedy about college life and football was set on Crawfordsville's Wabash College campus. It starred Dolores Costello and William Collier Jr. There were more than one hundred movies made based on George Ade's writings, including *The County Chairman*, starring Will Rogers and Hoosier Louise Dresser.

The Crowd Roars (1932). Directed by Hoosier Howard Hawks, the film featured Indy 500 drivers Wilbur Shaw, Billy Arnold, Fred Frame, Ralph Hepburn, Shorty Cantlon, Mel Keneally, and Stubby Stubblefield.

Hoosier Schoolboy (1937). Based on Hoosier Edward Eggleston's book and starring Mickey Rooney.

Road Demon (1938). Set against a background of the Indianapolis Motor Speedway and using much stock footage, this movie deals with racketeers trying to dominate the business. The film is interesting in that Bill (Bojangles) Robinson appears as a junkyard owner and does a little tap dancing. Lon Chaney Jr. appears as a "race racketeer."

Indianapolis Speedway (1939). Starring Pat O'Brien and Ann Sheridan with a screenplay written by Hoosier Howard Hawks. This was a remake of a Hawks 1932 film, *The Crowd Roars*.

My Gal Sal (1942). Highly fictionalized biography of Hoosier composer Paul Dresser (Terre Haute). Victor Mature and Rita Hayworth.

The Magnificent Ambersons (1942). Written by Hoosier author Booth Tarkington, the plot was set in Indianapolis. Hoosier stars in this film were Anne Baxter (Michigan City) and Richard Bennett (Bennett's Switch, Indiana) as Major Amberson.

Hoosier Holiday (1943). Dale Evans and The Hoosier Hot Shots.

Home in Indiana (1944). Lon McAllister, Jeanne Crain, and Hoosier actors Charles Dingle (Wabash) and Noble "Kid" Chissell (Indianapolis). Another Hoosier, Hector Kirk, was the race announcer in the film.

Night and Day (1946). A highly fictionalized biography of Hoosier composer Cole Porter. Cary Grant and Alexis Smith. Some scenes portrayed Porter's home in Peru, Indiana.

Isn't It Romantic? (1948). Veronica Lake, Mona Freeman, Billy DeWolfe, and Pearl Bailey. Written by Hoosier Jeannette Covert Nolan, this was supposed to be set in Evansville in 1910. However, the movie hardly resembled the book.

So Dear to My Heart (1949). Written by Sterling North, who was inspired by tales his mother told him of her native Indiana. Burl Ives, Beulah Bondi, and Bobby Driscoll. Pike County is the setting for this film.

On Moonlight Bay (1951). Based on Booth Tarkington's "Penrod" stories. Starred Doris Day and Gordon MacRae.

By the Light of the Silvery Moon (1953). Again starring Doris Day and again based on Booth Tarkington's "Penrod" stories.

The Desperate Hours (1955). Written by Hoosier Joseph Hayes, it was supposed to take place in Indianapolis. The first version starred Humphrey Bogart. In 1990 a second version of this story was made starring Anthony Hopkins.

Raintree County (1956). Written by Indiana University professor, Ross Lockridge Jr., the story takes place in southern Indiana. However, most of the film was shot in Danville, Kentucky.

Friendly Persuasion (1956). Gary Cooper, Dorothy McGuire, Anthony Perkins, and Hoosier Marjorie Main (Acton). Based on the writings of Hoosier Jessamyn West (Vernon), this film takes place in Jennings County during the Civil War when Morgan's Raiders came into southern Indiana and gave the state its only taste of any kind of skirmish.

The Man Who Knew Too Much (1956). Doris Day and James Stewart star as a vacationing couple from Indianapolis.

All the Young Men (1960). Alan Ladd and Sidney Poitier star in a film about a soldier from Muncie.

Bon Voyage (1962). A Disney film written by Hoosiers Joseph and Marrijane Hayes (Indianapolis), starring Fred MacMurray and Jane Wyman as The Willards from Terre Haute.

Close Encounters of the Third Kind (1977). Richard Dreyfuss was supposed to be living in Muncie and even wore a Ball State University T-shirt, but nothing was filmed in Indiana, an obvious fact if you observed the mountains in the background.

A Christmas Story (1983). Jean Shepherd's recollections of his boyhood growing up in Hammond, this film has become a Christmas classic. A sequel was filmed in 1994, *My Summer Story* aka *It Runs in the Family*.

The Hudsucker Proxy (1994). Produced by the Coen brothers and starring Tim Robbins, Jennifer Jason Leigh, and Paul Newman, this film has many references to Muncie.

In and Out (1997). Kevin Kline, Joan Cusack, and Tom Selleck. The setting for this film is in the fictional town of Greenleaf, Indiana.

Say It Isn't So (2001). Starts out and ends in Muncie but was shot mostly in Pomona, California. Stars Muncie native Ezra Buzzington (Jonathan Harris), Heather Graham, Sally Field, Chris Klein, and Ileanna Douglas.

The Hollywood Walk of Fame was started in 1960 with 2,500 blank stars. Only a few hundred are left at this date. The walk lines both sides of Hollywood Boulevard from Gower to La Brea and both sides of Vine Street from Yucca to Sunset.

The selection process is confusing. Names on the walk include Thomas Edison, Big Bird, Snow White, and Lassie. Major names with no stars include Clint Eastwood, Robert Redford, Mel Gibson, and Hoosier Sidney Pollack. Kevin Kline, who spent a number of formative years in Indiana, was awarded a star in 2005.

There are five categories, and many people were awarded stars in more than one category. The categories are: Motion Pictures, Television, Radio, Recording, and Live Theater.

HOLLYWOOD BOULEVARD STARS

Anne Baxter 6741
Monte Blue 6290
Charles Butterworth 7036
Scatman Crothers 6712
Louise Dresser 6538
Irene Dunne 6440*
Dick Enberg 6752*
Chad Everett 6922
Louise Fazenda 6801
Sid Grauman 6379
Phil Harris 6651 (Radio) and 6508 (Recording)
Will H. Hays 6116
Florence Henderson 7070
Michael Jackson 6927
Buck Jones 6834
Kevin Kline 7000*
Elmo Lincoln 7042
Carole Lombard 6930
Karl Malden 6231*
Ken Maynard 6751
Steve McQueen 6834
Marilyn Miller 6301
Dick Powell 6915 (Motion Pictures)
    and 6745 (Television)
Red Skelton 6763 (Radio) and 6650
    (Television)
Jules Stein 6821
Alice Terry 6626
Bill Thompson 7021
Forrest Tucker 6385
Lurene Tuttle 7011
Harry Von Zell 6521
Clifton Webb 6850
Robert Wise 6340

VINE STREET STARS

John Bowers 1709
Beulah Bondi 1718*
Hoagy Carmichael 1720
James Dean 1719
Jean Hagen 1560*
Howard Hawks 1708
Janet Jackson 1500
Michael Jackson 1541
The Jacksons 1500
Dean Jagger 1623*
Dick Powell 1560 (Radio)*
George Seaton 1752
Lurene Tuttle 1760 (Radio)

*Nonnatives
This information comes from the Web site for the Hollywood Chamber of Commerce. http://www.hollywoodchamber.net/.

THE SILENT ERA

C. Graham Baker
Evansville, 1888–1950

V. L. Barnes
Indiana, 1870–1949

Carlton Brickert (aka Carl Brickert)
Martinsville, 1890–1943

Frederick Burton
Indianapolis, 1871–1957

Pomeroy Cannon
New Albany, 1870–1928

James Carew
Goshen, 1876–1938

Marjorie Benton Cooke
Richmond, 1876–1920

Curtis Cooksey
Indiana, 1891–1962

Marie Crisp (Hazel Stark)
Terre Haute, dates unknown

Jack Draper (Lauren Draper)
Spencer, 1892–1962

Tex Driscoll (John W. Morris)
Indiana, 1889–1970

Fred Eric
Peru, 1874–1935

Mattie Ferguson
Indianapolis, 1862–1929

Al W. Filson
Bluffton, 1857–1925

David S. Garber
Floyd Knobs, 1898–1984

James Gibson
Putnam County, 1865–1938

Harry Griffith
Indiana, 1866–1926

Rhea Haines
Indiana, 1894–1964

Robert T. Haines
Muncie, 1868–1943

Michael E. Hanley
Fort Wayne, 1858–1942

Hope Harriman
Fort Wayne, dates unknown

Grace Hayward
Terre Haute, 1868–1959

Maud Hosford
Terre Haute, dates unknown

Harry Keenan
Richmond, 1867–1944

Clara Knott
Indiana, 1871–1926

Edward T. Langford
Indiana, d. 1926

Ned Mann
Redkey, 1893–1967

Maurine Powers (aka Maureen Powers)
Terre Haute, b. 1907?

Edward Roseman
Terre Haute, 1875–1957

John P. Wade (John Patrick Wade)
Indiana, 1876–1949

May Wallace (May Maddox)
Russiaville, 1877–1938

George Webb (George Webb Frey)
Indianapolis, 1887–1943

Helen Weir
Anderson, b. 1898

Bessie (Emerick) Wharton
Rochester, 1875–1939

Olive White (Olive Celeste Moore White)
Indianapolis, 1889–1960

Walker Whiteside
Logansport, 1869–1942

THE SOUND ERA

The following list consists of actresses and actors
whose careers were primarily in sound films.
For Hoosier silent film actors, see above.

ACTRESSES

Lillian Albertson
Noblesville, 1881–1962

Betty Alden
Indianapolis, 1891–1948

Jane Allen
Lafayette, 1916–1970

Theresa Allen
Indianapolis, 1908–1997

Wendy Baker
Indianapolis, dates unknown

Arija Bareikis
Bloomington, b. 1966

Amy Bebout (Amy Michelle Bebout)
Crawfordsville, b. 1983

Sue Bennett (Sue Benjamin)
Indianapolis, 1928–2001

Candi Brough
Indiana, dates unknown

Randi Brough
Indiana, dates unknown

Pamela Jane Bryant
Indianapolis, b. 1959

Claudia Craddock
Warsaw, 1889–1945

Catherine Craig
Bloomington, b. 1917

Susan Deer
Indianapolis, dates unknown

Jenniphr and Greer Goodman
Indiana, dates unknown

Sunshine Hart (Lucia Hart)
Indianapolis, 1886–1930

Anissa Jones
West Lafayette, 1958–1976

Lenore Keefe
Indianapolis, b. 1918

E. (Elaine) Katherine Kerr
Indianapolis, b. 1937

Greta Lind
Goshen, b. 1968

Patsy May (sometimes known as "Baby" Patsy May)
Gosport, dates unknown

Margaret McConnell
Kewanna, dates unknown

Julie McWhirter (sometimes credited as Julie Dees)
Indianapolis, dates unknown

Carolyn Monroe
Bloomington, b. 1968

Irene Purcell
Hammond, 1901–1972

June Purcell
Indianapolis, b. 1903

Ellen Ross
Muncie, dates unknown

Jeanne Snow (Jeanne Jones Snow)
Middleton, dates unknown

Liz Stauber (Elizabeth Stauber)
Indianapolis, b. 1979

Irene Vernon (Irene Vergauwen)
Mishawaka, 1922–1998

Jan Wiley
Marion, 1916–1993

ACTORS

Jim Aleck
Indiana, dates unknown

James (Jimmy) Alexander
Indiana, 1914–1961

Richard Barbee
Lafayette, 1885–1965

Richard Bergman
Plymouth, dates unknown

Lee Bonnell (aka Terry Melmont)
Royal Center, 1918–1986

Frederick Burton
Indianapolis, 1871–1957

Martin Burton
Mitchell, 1904–1976

Dan Butler
Fort Wayne, b. 1954

Walter T. Butterworth
Indiana, 1892–1962

Ezra Buzzington (Jonathan Harris)
Muncie, dates unknown

John Calvert (sometimes credited as John Trevlac)
New Trenton, b. 1911

Sean Cameron
Kokomo, b. 1970

James Carew
Goshen, 1876–1938

Sidney Catlett (also known as "Big Sid" Catlett)
Evansville, 1910–1951

Michael Champion (Michael Campbell Champion)
Anderson, dates unknown

Noble "Kid" Chissell
Indianapolis, 1905–1987

Steve Clark (Elmer Stephen Clark)
Daviess County, 1891–1954

John Clarke
South Bend, b. 1932

Curtis Cooksey
Indiana, 1891–1962

John Craig (Joe E. Cline)
Indianapolis, 1928–1999

Dick Curtis
Indianapolis, b. 1928

Braden Danner
Indianapolis, b. 1975

Brian Davies
Indianapolis, dates unknown

Frank Dietl
Lakeville, 1875–1923

Tex Driscoll (John W. Morris)
Indiana, 1889–1970

Michael Duane (Duane McKinney)
Dunkirk, b. 1914

Andy Edwards
Muncie, b. 1962

Corey Edwards
Anderson, b. 1968

David Emge
Evansville, dates unknown

Albert Fields (Albert Jean Pierre Fields)
Gary, b. 1975

Med Flory
Logansport, b. 1926

Jared Fogle
Indiana, b. 1978

Jim Gaffigan
Chesterton, b. 1966

William M. Griffith
Indiana, 1897–1960

Tim Grimm
Columbus, dates unknown

Jess Hahn
Terre Haute, 1921–1998

Tom Harmon
Rensselaer, 1919–1990

George D. Hay
Attica, 1895–1968

Robert T. Haines
Muncie, 1868–1943

Kevin Hershberger
Indianapolis, b. 1973

Joe Higgins
Logansport, 1925–1998

James Hill
Jeffersonville, 1916–2001

Ken Hixon
Indianapolis, dates unknown

Bruce Hubbard
Indianapolis, d. 1991

Scott Andrew Hutchins
Indianapolis, 1976

Bill Hutton
Evansville, b. 1950

William L. Johnson
Gary, dates unknown

Jeremy Jordan (Donald Henson)
Hammond, b. 1973

William Jordan
Milan, dates unknown

Adam Kennedy
Otterbein, 1922–1997

Ken Kercheval
Wolcottville, b. 1935

Art LaFleur
Gary, b. 1943

Forrest Landis
Oaklandon, b. 1994

David Letterman
Indianapolis, b. 1947

Forrest Lewis
Knightstown, 1899–1977

Ralph Littlefield
Gary, 1901–1977

Robert Long
Indiana, 1894–1972

Peter Lupus (sometimes credited as Rock Stevens)
Indianapolis, b. 1932

Neil Maffin
Indiana, b. 1959

Earl McCarthy
Fort Wayne, 1906–1933

Billy McClain
Indiana, 1857–1959

Charles McMurphy
North Vernon, 1892–1969

Roger Mobley
Evansville, b. 1949

Anthony Montgomery
Indianapolis, b. 1971

Greg Neff
Elwood, b. 1955

Thomas (Tom) R. S. Noel
Fortville, 1911–1986

Richard (Rich) Oliver
Indianapolis, b. 1930

Jeff Osterhage
Columbus, b. 1953

George Paulsin
Hammond, dates unknown

Corey Pearson
Indianapolis, b. 1974

Lon Poff
Bedford, 1870–1952

Ed Porter (Edward D. Porter)
Columbus, 1881–1939

Drew Powell
Noblesville, b. 1976

J. Russell Powell (sometimes credited as
    Russ Powell or Russell Powell)
Indianapolis, 1875–1950

Philip Proctor (actor, writer, producer, director,
    voice specialist)
Goshen, b. 1940

Billy Record
Willow Branch, dates unknown

Churchill Ross (Ross Weigle)
Lafayette, 1901–1962

Harlan Sanders
Henryville, 1890–1980

Chris Schenkel
Bippus, 1924–2005

Paul Scherrer (Paul Scherier Jr.)
Rochester, b. 1968

Tom Seidel (Emil Seidel)
Indianapolis, 1917–1992

Bill Shirk (William Poorman)
Muncie, b. 1945

Bill Shirley
Indianapolis, 1921–1989

James J. Sloyan
Indianapolis, b. 1940

Sam Smiley
Columbus, b. 1931

T. J. Storm
Indiana, dates unknown

Marc Summers (Marc Berkowitz)
Indianapolis, b. 1950

Ernest Thomas
Gary, b. 1950

Randy Thompson
Fort Wayne, b. 1954

Donald Torres
Santa Barbara, California, 1936–1986

Jon Van Ness (Jon Van Ness Philip)
Summitville, dates unknown

Vincent Ventresca
Indianapolis, b. 1965

Andy Voils
Brown County, b. 1980

Hunter von Leer (Paul Hunter Von Leer)
Riley, b. 1944

John P. Wade (John Patrick Wade)
Indiana, 1876–1949

DIRECTORS

David Anspaugh
Decatur, b. 1946

Glenn Belt
Macy, 1890–1940

Eddie Beverly Jr.
Indiana, dates unknown

William Bindley
Indianapolis, dates unknown

George Daugherty
Pendleton, b. 1955

Herschel Daugherty
Clark's Hill, 1910–1993

Frank T. Davis
Richmond, b. 1890

Nathan Gotsch
Fort Wayne, b. 1983

Mark W. Gray Jr.
Indianapolis, dates unknown

Christopher Gregory
Albany, dates unknown

Joan Grossman
Indianapolis, dates unknown

John Guedel
Portland, 1913–2001

Dan T. Hall
Indianapolis, dates unknown

Howell Hansel
Indiana, 1860–1917

John Korty
Lafayette, b. 1936

Jack McKeown
Indiana, 1891–1967

Tom Moore (Thomas R. Moore)
Lafayette, dates unknown

Tommy O'Haver
Indianapolis, b. 1967

James B. Rogers
Indianapolis, dates unknown

William D. Russell
Indianapolis, 1908–1968

Stephen Scaia
Indianapolis, b. 1976

Tracey Trench
Terre Haute, dates unknown

Matt Williams
Evansville, dates unknown

Unless otherwise indicated, persons listed
are actors/actresses. The author could not find
persons in counties not included in this appendix.

ADAMS
Decatur
> David Anspaugh (director)

ALLEN
Fort Wayne
> Julia Barr
> Dan Butler
> Sharon Gabet
> Nathan Gotsch (director)
> Michael E. Hanley
> Hope Harriman
> Drake Hogestyn
> Stephen King (author)*
> Jim Leonard (writer)
> Carole Lombard
> Shelley Long
> Marilyn Maxwell*
> Earl McCarthy
> Patrick McVey
> Herb Shriner*
> Lyn (Jaqueline) Thomas
> Randy Thompson
> Herb Vigran*
> Virginia Philley Withey (writer/actress)
> Dick York

BARTHOLOMEW
Burnsville
> Ross Edwin Barbour (singing group,
> "The Four Freshmen")
> Don Barbour ("The Four Freshmen")

Columbus
> J. Will Callahan (composer)
> Tim Grimm
> Jeff Osterhage
> Ed Porter
> Sam Smiley

BENTON
Fowler
> Robert Keith

Otterbein
> Adam Kennedy

BOONE
Lebanon
> Bob Shanks (producer/writer)

BROWN
> Andy Voils

CASS
Herman (Anoka)
> Louis Da Pron (choreographer)

Logansport
> Ann Christy
> Med Flory
> Edna Goodrich
> Joe Higgins
> Maibelle Heikes Justice (author)
> Greg Kinnear
> Frederick Landis (author)
> J. Homer Tutt (writer/composer/actor)
> Walker Whiteside
> Salem Tutt Whitney (actor/composer/writer)

CLARK
Jeffersonville
> James Hill (producer)

CLAY
Brazil
> Johnnie "Scat" Davis

CLINTON
Frankfort
> Charles Aidman
> Anthony Caruso

DAVIESS
Odon
> Autumn Sims (actress/dancer)

Washington
> Steve Clark

DEARBORN
Aurora
> Elmer Holmes Davis (author/radio news)

Lawrenceburg
> William H. Wright (writer/producer)

DEKALB
Garrett
> John Bowers

DELAWARE
Albany
> Christopher Gregory (director)

Muncie
Gene Brewer (author)
Ezra Buzzington (Jonathan Harris)
Andy Edwards
James Edwards
Jami Ferrell
Robert T. Haines
Emily Kimbrough (author)
John McGreevey (author)
Ellen Ross
Bill Shirk
Robert C. Smith (screenwriter/actor)

DUBOIS
Ferdinand
Charles Schulthies (special effects)

ELKHART
Elkhart
Jean Hagen*
John Philliber
Peter Reckell
Connie Smith (singer/composer)

Goshen
James Carew
Howard Hawks (director)
Kenneth Hawks (director)
Greta Lind
Philip Proctor (voice-over specialist)
Raymond L. Schrock (screenwriter)

FLOYD
Floyds Knobs
David S. Garber (art director)

New Albany
Pomeroy Cannon
J. Warren Kerrigan
Kathleen Kerrigan*
Wallace Kerrigan (studio manager/costumer)

FOUNTAIN
Attica
George D. Hay

FRANKLIN
Brookville
Lew Wallace (author)

Laurel
Charlie Murray

New Trenton
John Calvert

FULTON
Kewanna
Margaret McConnell

Rochester
Elmo Lincoln
Bessie Emerick Wharton

GIBSON
Owensville
Valeska Suratt
Princeton
Mack V. Wright (director/actor)

GRANT
Fairmount
Jim Davis (cartoonist/writer)
Phil Jones
Mary Jane Ward (author)

Marion
James Dean
Rusty Gorman (writer/director)
Emma-Lindsay Squier (author)
Jan Wiley

GREENE
Bloomfield
John Leroy Johnston (movie executive)

Linton
Irving (Izzy) Friedman (composer/musical director)
Phil Harris

HAMILTON
Noblesville
Lillian Albertson
Marcia Eck (costume designer)
Drew Powell
Rex Stout (author)
Steve Wariner

Arcadia
Hezzie Trietsch ("Hoosier Hot Shots")
Ken Trietsch ("Hoosier Hot Shots")

HANCOCK
Fortville
Thomas R. S. Noel

Greenfield
Charlie Davis (composer/musician)
Kevin McClarnon
James Whitcomb Riley (author)

HENDRICKS
Plainfield
Forrest Tucker

HENRY
Dunreith
Gretchen Cryer (actress/writer)

Knightstown
Forrest Lewis

Middletown
Jeanne Jones Snow (dancer)

New Castle
Richard Crane

HOWARD
Greentown
Miriam Seegar
Sara Seegar

Kokomo
Sean Cameron
Sylvia Hutton (singer)
Strother Martin
Tom Santschi
Tavis Smiley

Russiaville
May Wallace

HUNTINGTON
Bippus
Chris Schenkel

JACKSON
Seymour
John Mellencamp (singer/composer/actor)

JASPER
Rensselear
James F. Hanley (composer)
Tom Harmon
JAY
Dunkirk
Michael Duane
Donn Gift*

Portland
Leon Ames
John Guedel (director/producer)
Kenneth MacDonald
Twyla Tharp (choreographer)

Redkey
Ned Mann (special effects)

JEFFERSON
Madison
Irene Dunne*
David Graham Phillips (author)

JENNINGS
North Vernon
Jessamyn West (author/screenwriter)

JOHNSON
Franklin
Andrew Duggan
Maude Turner Gordon
James Pierce
Max Terhune

KNOX
Vincennes
Buck Jones (Charles Gebhart)
Alvy Moore
Al Rockett (producer)
Ray Rockett (producer) (sometimes known as
R. R. Rockett)
Red Skelton
Alice Terry

KOSCIUSKO
Warsaw
Claudia Craddock
Rick Fox*
Hal Kratzsch ("The Four Freshmen")

LAKE
East Chicago
Betsy Palmer

Gary
Bill Cable
Albert Fields
The Jackson Five
Janet Jackson
Michael Jackson
William L. Johnson
Alex Karras
Art LaFleur
Ralph Littlefield
Karl Malden*
William Marshall
Ernest Thomas
Deniece Williams*
Fred Williamson

Hammond

Kathleen Burke
Bianca Ferguson
Jeremy Jordan
Bartlett McCormack (author)
George Paulsin
Irene Purcell
Jean Shepherd (author)*

Lowell

Jo Ann Worley

LA PORTE
Michigan City

Charles Arndt
Anne Baxter
Dick Cathcart

LAWRENCE
Bedford

Claude Akins*
Alfred Bertram Guthrie Jr. (author)
Lon Poff

Mitchell

Martin Burton

MADISON
Alexandria

Gabe Ward ("The Hoosier Hot Shots")

Anderson

Gary Burton (musician)
Michael Champion
Corey Edwards
Ray Enright (director)
Gordon Gordon (screenwriter)
James Rebhorn*
Fred Mustard Stewart (author)
Helen Weir

Elwood

David Canary
Mary Jane Croft
Greg Neff

Frankton

Isabel Withers

Pendleton

George Daugherty (director)
William Walker

MARION
Acton

Marjorie Main

Beech Grove

Steve McQueen

Indianapolis

Betty Alden
Theresa Allen
Wendy Baker
James Baskett
Sue Bennett (Benjamin)
Abraham Benrubi
Scott Bindley (writer)
William Bindley (director)
Monte Blue
Pamela Jane Bryant
Frederick Burton
Steve Burton
Lois Butler
Fran Carlon
Noble "Kid" Chissell
Russell Collins
John Craig (Joe E. Cline)
Dick Curtis
Braden Danner
Brian Davies
Madelyn Pugh Davis (writer)
Susan Deer
Julie McWhirter Dees
Kenneth "Babyface" Edmonds (composer/musician)
Robert Emhardt
Mike Epps
Frances Farmer*
Mattie Ferguson
Hugh Fink (writer)
Vivica Fox
Brendan Fraser
Fred Gamble
Sid Grauman
Mark Gray (director)
Gloria Gresham (costume designer)
Joan Grossman (writer/director)
Johnny Gruelle (cartoonist/writer)*
Walter Gumm (lyricist)
Dan T. Hall (producer/director)
Michael R. Hanley
Bertita Harding (author)*
Sunshine Hart
Joseph Hayes (author/playwright)
Kevin Hershberger
John Hiatt

Ken Hixon (actor/screenwriter)
Jobyna Howland
Bruce Hubbard (singer)
Freddie Hubbard (musician)
Scott Hutchins
James Louis "J. J." Johnson (musician)
Julanne Johnston
Bill Justice (Disney director)
Lenore Keefe
Brook Kerr
E. Katherine Kerr
John W. Krafft (writer/editor)
Forrest Landis
Priscilla Lawson
Alan Le May (author)
Terry Lester
David Letterman
Herman Lieber (movie exhibitor)
Robert Lieber (movie executive)
Thomas G. Lingham
Peter Lupus
L. E. McCullough (composer/musician)
Anthony Montgomery
Wes Montgomery (musician)
Margo Moore*
Ryan Murphy (director)
Tom Nolan
Tommy O' Haver (director)
Robert Paige
Corey Pearson
Dick Powell*
J. Russell "Russ" Powell
June Purcell
J. Russel Robinson (composer)
Shari Robinson
Ivan Rogers (director/actor)
James B. Rogers (director)
William Russell (director)
Chris Rutkowski (composer/arranger)
Stephen Scaia (director)
Wade Schenck
Paul Scherrer
Tom Seidel
Bobby Sherwood
Bill Shirley
Noble Sissle (lyricist/actor/producer)
James Sloyan
Liz Stauber
Barbara Stock*
Mark Summers
Booth Tarkington (author)
Donald Torres
Vincent Ventresca
Melody Vincz
Kurt Vonnegut (author)

Albert Von Tilzer (composer)
Harry Von Tilzer (composer)*
Harry Von Zell
Kristina Wagner
Dan Wakefield (author)
Ivory "Deek" Watson (The Inkspots)
Clifton Webb
George Webb
Olive White
Roger E. Young (director/writer)*

Speedway
  Joyce DeWitt*

MARSHALL
Plymouth
  Richard Bergman
  Raymond Walburn

Tyner
  Lydia Knott

MIAMI
Deacon's Mills (Bennett's Switch)
  Richard Bennett

Macy
  Glenn Belt (director)
  Lola Lane (Dorothy Mullican)
  Leota Lane (Leota Mullican)
  Martha Mullican

Peru
  Fred Eric
  Ole Olsen
  Cole Porter (composer/playwright)

MONROE
Bloomington
  Arija Bareikis
  Joshua Bell (musician)
  Meg Cabot (author)
  Hoagy Carmichael (composer/actor)
  Terri Conn
  Catherine Craig
  Ed East
  Bobby Helms (singer)
  Kevin Kline*
  Pawnee Bill Lillie
  Ross Lockridge Jr. (author)
  Denny Miller
  Carolyn Monroe
  David Lee Roth (musician)
  Michael Uslan (producer)*

MONTGOMERY
Crawfordsville
Amy Bebout
Kenyon Nicholson (author/playwright)
Meredith Nicholson (author)

MORGAN
Martinsville
Carlton Brickert

Mooresville
Frank Inn (Freeman) (animal trainer)

NEWTON
Kentland
George Ade (author/playwright)

Goodland
Albert Edwin (Eddie) Condon (musician)

NOBLE
Wolcottville
Ken Kercheval

OWEN
Gosport
Patsy May ("Baby" Patsy May)
James Alexander Thom (author)

Spencer
Jack Draper (cinematographer/editor/director)
William Vaughn Moody (author)

PERRY
Cannelton
Tim Whelan (director)

PORTER
Chesterton
Harry Mark Petrakis (screenwriter)*

Dune Acres
Jim Gaffigan

Valparaiso
Harry Benham
Beulah Bondi*
Carly Schroeder

POSEY
Mt. Vernon
Ann Hovey

PULASKI
Medaryville
Geneva Mitchell

PUTNAM
Greencastle
Bob Flanigan ("The Four Freshmen")
Jeffry Mont (producer)

Jefferson
James Gibson

RANDOLPH
Winchester
Robert Wise (director)

RIPLEY
Milan
William Jordan

RUSH
Rushville
Carmelita Geraghty
Thomas Geraghty (screenwriter)
Maurice Geraghty (screenwriter)
Gerald Geraghty (screenwriter)
Norman Selby ("Kid McCoy")

ST. JOSEPH
Mishawaka
Conte and Pete Condoli (musicians)
Allan "Rocky" Lane
Ruth McKenney (author)

South Bend
John Bromfield
Charles Butterworth
John Clarke
William Cottrell (Disney animator)
Ralph Dumke
Chad Everett
Dolores Fuller (actress/composer)
Lloyd Haynes
Lambert Hillyer (director)
Helen Holmes*
Larry Karaszewski (screenwriter)
Dale Messick (cartoonist/writer)
George Seaton (producer/director/writer)
John Sibley (Disney animator)
Jules Stein (talent agent)
Irene Vernon (Irene Vergauwen)
Michael Warren
Daniel Waters (screenwriter)*
Mark Waters (director/writer)
Chris Webb (screenwriter)

SHELBY
Shelbyville
  Tasha Louise Danner
  Charles Major (author)

SPENCER
Dale
  Florence Henderson

Grandview
  Bill Peet (Peed) (Disney artist/writer/director)
  George Peed (Disney animator)

STEUBEN
Pleasant Lake
  Lurene Tuttle

SULLIVAN
Shelburn
  Walter Bullock (composer/screenwriter)

Sullivan
  James S. Barcus (author)
  Will H. Hays (film czar)
  Thamer (Ted) D. McCord (cinematographer)

SWITTZERLAND
Vevay
  Edward Eggleston (author)
  Ken Maynard
  Kermit Maynard

TIPPECANOE
Clarks Hill
  Herschel Daugherty (director)

Lafayette
  Jane Allen
  Richard Barbee
  Karen Black (Ziegler)*
  Annie Corley
  John Korty (director)
  Brian Lamb
  George Barr McCutcheon (author)
  Tom Moore (director)
  Bernie Pollack (costume designer)
  Sydney Pollack (director)
  Victor Potel
  W. Axl Rose (musician)
  Churchill Ross

West Lafayette
  Louise Fazenda
  Anissa Jones

VANDERBURGH
Evansville
  Charles Graham Baker (author)
  Billie Bennett
  Jayne Bentzen
  James Best*
  Budd Boetticher (director/writer)*
  Avery Brooks
  Sid Catlett
  Joe Cook
  Isabel Dawn (screenwriter)
  Louise Dresser
  Marilyn Durham (author)
  David Emge
  Ron Glass
  Bill Hutton
  Annie Fellows Johnston (author)
  Michael Michele
  Marilyn Miller
  Roger Mobley
  Jeannette Covert Nolan (author)
  Paul Osborn (screenwriter)
  Fred Rose (composer)
  Jeri Taylor (writer/producer/director)
  Matt Williams (director)

VERMILLION
Clinton
  Eddie Polo (musician)*
  Robert M. Rogers

Dana
  Ernie Pyle (author)

VIGO
Terre Haute
  Joseph Benti*
  Marie Crisp (Hazel Stark)
  Scatman Crothers
  Theodore Dreiser (author)
  Paul Dresser (composer)
  Ross Ford
  Richard "Skeets" Gallagher
  Jess Hahn
  Grace Hayward
  Maud Hosford
  Burl Ives*
  Orin Jackson
  Chubby Johnson
  Grover Jones (screenwriter)
  Joe Keaton
  Billy Lee
  Dave Madden*
  Mick Mars (musician/producer)

Rose Melville
Maurine Powers
Harry Reeves (Disney writer/animator)
Edward Roseman
Bill Thompson (voice specialist)
Claude Thornhill (bandleader)
Tracy Trench (director/producer)
Hunter Von Leer
Rob Youngblood

WABASH
Wabash
Charles Dingle
Crystal Gayle* (singer)
Gene Stratton-Porter (author)

WARRICK
Boonville
Monte Katterjohn (screenwriter)

WASHINGTON

WAYNE
Economy
Charles Bruce Millholland (playwright)

Richmond
Polly Bergen (Nellie Burgin)*
Larry Blanford (cinematographer)
Marjorie Benton Cooke (author)
Frank T. Davis (director)
George W. Duning (composer for the screen)
Harry Keenan
Clifford Smith (director)

Spring Grove
Ned Rorem (composer)

WELLS
Bluffton
Al W. Filson
Peggy Goodin (author)

WHITE
Brookston
W. Donn Hayes (film editor)

WHITLEY
Columbia City
Lloyd C. Douglas (author)

Larwill
Dean Jagger*

South Whitley
Janie Fricke (Frickie) (country singer/actress)

*nonnative

Illustrations are indicated in bold. All film titles are listed with year of release.

A & M Records, 458

Abbott and Costello, 297

Abbott and Costello Go to Mars (1953), 297

ABC (network), 188, 189, 201, 228, 262, 263, 279

Abdul-Jabbar, Kareem (Lew Alcindor), 311

Abe Lincoln in Illinois (1940), 416

Abie's Irish Rose, 29

Aborn Opera Company, 74

About Town, 141

Above the Clouds, 267

Absence of Malice (1981), 410

Academy of Motion Picture Arts and Sciences, 142, 209, 399, 403, 404, 406, 445, 476, 507

Acord, Art, 378, 391

Action in the North Atlantic (1943), 483

Actors and Others for Animals, 314

Actors Studio, 104, 112, 251, 293, 492

Acuff, Roy, 462

Acuff-Rose Publications, 462

Adams, Neile, **103**, 104, 105, 106, 107

Adams Chronicles, The (television), 518

Adam's Rib (1949), 501

Adderly, Cannonball, 458

Adderly, Nat, 458

Ade, Adeline Bush, 420

Ade, George, xiii, 142, 202, 205, 206, 411, **411**, 415, 420, **420**, 523, 537

Ade, John, 420

Adoree, Renee, **280**

Adventure (magazine), 421

Adventures and Emotions of Edgar Pomeroy, The (1920/21), 412

Adventures of Casanova (1948), 447

Adventures of Frank Merriwell, The (1936), 391

Adventures of Kathlyn, The (1913), 36

Adventures of Ichabod and Mr. Toad, The (1949), 340, 341

Adventures of Ozzie and Harriet, The: radio, 252, 304; television, 253

Adventures of Raggedy Ann and Andy, 500

Adventures of Robin Hood, The (1938), 59

Adventures of Superman, The (radio), 512

Adventures of Tarzan, The (1921), **318**, 320, **321**

Adventures of Tom Sawyer, The (1938), 178, 419

Adventures of Wild Bill Hickok, The (television), 375

Aerosmith, 463

Affair to Remember, An (1957), 499

Affairs of Anatol, The (1921), 15

Affleck, Ben, 120, 430

Africa's Elephant Kingdom (1998), 242

After Image (2001), 458

After the Fall, 232

Afterglow (1997), 439

Agee, James, 56

Agent Cody Banks (2003), 417

Aherne, Brian, 425

Aidman, Charles, **232**, 232–33, 240, 532

Airheads (1994), **120**, 464

Airport (1970), 402, 403, 516

Akins, Claude (Claude Marion Akins), 230, 240, 275, 429, **490**, 490–91, 520, 522, 535

Aladdin (1992), 484

Aladdin and the Wonderful Lamp (1917), 317

Alba, Maria, 207

Albert LeClear Photography Studio (Terre Haute), 41

Albertson, Lillian, 527, 533

Alcazar Theater (San Francisco), 30

Alcoa Hour, The (television), 189

Alcoa Theatre (television), 509

Alda, Alan, 429

Alden, Betty, 527, 535

Aldrich Family, The (radio), 215, 307

Aldridge, Kay, 366

Aldrin, Buzz, 275

Aleck, Jim, 528

Alexander, Colin, 276

Alexander, James (Jimmy), 528

Alexander, Scott, 417

Alfred Hitchcock Hour, The (television), 409

Alfred Hitchcock Presents (television), 375

Alhambra Theater (Indianapolis), xii, **xii**

Ali, Muhammad, 275

Alias Jane Doe (radio), 112, 306

Alibi's Tent Show (television), 371

Alice (television), 415

Alice Adams: novel, 146; 1923 film, 411; 1935 film, 411

Alice in Wonderland: 1933 film, 59, 267; 1951 film, 333, 338, 340, 487

All About Eve (1950), **178**, 181, 182, 183, 515

All in the Family (television), 270

All in a Night's Work (1961), 261

All My Children (television), 518, 519, 520

All Over Town (1937), 81

All-Story (magazine), 317

All the King's Men (1949), 261

All the President's Men (1976), 483

All the Young Men (1960), 523

Allbritton, Louise, 297

Allen, Fred, 307, 510

Allen, Jane, 527, 538

Allen, Rex, 211

Allen, Theresa, 527, 535

Allen County War Memorial Coliseum (Fort Wayne), 508

Allez-oop, 245

Allyson, June, 509

Altman, Robert, 409, 493

Amadeus (1984), 486

Ambassadeurs, The, 75

Ambassador Theater (New York), 83

Ambush Bay (1966), 484

Ameche, Don, 252

Amelia Earhart (television), 232

Amendáriz, Pedro, 509

American Academy of Dramatic Arts, 192

American Ballet Theater, 486

American Cinema Editors (ACE), 478

American Film Company (Flying A), 4, 6, 377

American Film Institute, 499

American Film Institute Center for Advanced Film Studies, 406

American Flyers (1985), 419

American Humane Association, 481

American Maid (1917), **38**

American Mutual Film Company, 220

American Radio Syndicate, 324

American Recording Company, 473

American Releasing (studio), 385, 391

American Shakespeare Company, 270

American Society of Composers, Authors and Publishers (ASCAP), 445

American Studios, 202

American Theater (Terre Haute), 256

American Tragedy, An: novel, 424; 1931 film, 424

Americana, 245

Americanization of Emily, The (1964), 515

Americans for Democratic Action, 421

Ames, Leon (Leon Waycoff), **90**, 214, **233**, 233–35, 501, 534

Ames, Leon, Jr., 234

Ames, Shelley, 234

Amos n' Andy Show, The: radio, 97, 237; television, 253

And Stars Remain, 76

Anderson, Bill, 468

Anderson, Eddie "Rochester," 254, 274

Anderson, Gilbert M. "Bronco Billy," 31, 33, 343

Anderson, Hanson H., 507

Anderson, Maxwell, 98, 221, 259, 291

Anderson College, 372

Andrews, Dana, 302

Andrews, Julie, 421

Andrews Sisters, 297

Andy Griffith Show, The (television), 234, 261, 373

Andy Hardy Meets Debutante (1940), 464

Angeli, Pier, **114**

Angels Alone, 417

Angkor Rescue, The, 300

Anna and the King (1999), 445

Anna Karenina (1935), 419

Anna Lucasta (1958), 97

Annabella, 234

Annie, 314

Annie Get Your Gun, 194

Another World (television), 519, 520

Anspaugh, David, 381, 418, 522, 530, 532

Any Woman (1925), 52, **52**

Anything Goes, 461, 496

Apache (1954), 18

Apartment for Peggy (1948), 402

Apollo Theater (New York), 454

Applause, 182; 1929 film, 439

Appointment with Adventure (television), 188

Appolo (studio), 202

April (band), 445

Arab, The (1924), 51

Arabian Nights, The, 518

Arbuckle, Roscoe "Fatty," 29, 57, 282, 479

Arcade Theater (Toledo), 28

Are You Now or Have You Ever Been?, 241

Aristocats, The (1970), 274, 487

Arizona Mahoney (1936), 250

Arkansas Travellers, 369

Arlen, Richard, 242

Arlington High School (Indianapolis), 200

Armat, Thomas, xvii, xviii

Armstrong, Louis, 442

Armstrong, Neil, 275

Armstrong Circle Theater (television), 189

Armstrong's Wife (1915), 39

Arnaz, Desi, **414**, 512

Arnold, Billy, 397, 523

Arnold, Edward, 398, 429

Arnow, Max, 189

Arnt, Charles, **235**, 235–36, 299, 535

Arrowsmith (1931), 495

Arruza, Carlos, 494

Arruza (1972), 494

Arsenal Technical High School (Indianapolis), 332, 335, 337, 425, 507

Arsenio (television), 201

Art Blakey's Jazz Messengers, 451

Artcraft Pictures (studio), 385

Arthur, Charlotte, 49

Arthur, Jean, 98, 154
Arthur Jordan Conservatory (Indianapolis), 298, 435, 451. *See also* Metropolitan School of Music.
Artie Shaw orchestra, 442
As Good As It Gets (1997), **124**, 125, 516
As the World Turns (television), 518, 519, 520
As Thousands Cheer, 75, 136, **137**, 138
Asher, Max, 56
Ashley, Elizabeth, 409
Ask-It Basket, The (radio), 262
Asphalt Jungle, The (1950), 247, 289, 501
Assault of the Killer Bimbos (1988), 123
Associated (studio), 391
Astaire, Adele, 75, 135, 137
Astaire, Fred, 75, 135, 137, 246, 272, 405, 461
Astor, Mary, 234, 397, **397**, 398, 503
Atherton, Gertrude, 22
Atlantic Health and Fitness Center, 300
Atlas Film Corporation, 202
Auntie Mame (1958), 302
Aurora (IN) High School, 421
Austin City Limits (television), 446, 453
Austin High School Gang, 442
Authors League of America, 421
Auto Focus (2002), 125
Autograph Hound, The (1939), 339
Autry, Gene, 18, 210, 211, 344, 350, 358, 359, 360, 364, 367, 369, 370, 371, 372, 377, 393, 451, 462
Avalon (1990), 478, 515
Avalon Time (radio), 90
AVCO Embassy Pictures, 484
Awful Truth, The (1937), 499, 515
Ayres, Lew, 227, 481

B & O Railroad, 186
Babe (television), 279
Babes in Arms (1939), 467
Baby Doll (1956), 507
Bacall, Lauren, **18**, 182, 190, 398, 442
Back Street (1932), 272
Bacon, Irving, 373
Bad and the Beautiful, The (1952), 501
Bad Day at Black Rock (1955), 248
Badlands of Dakota (1941), 211
Baer, Buddy, 373
Bailey, Buster, 467
Bailey, Pearl, 523
Bainter, Fay, 423, 498
Bait (2000), 264

Baker, Carroll, 116, 507
Baker, Charles Graham, 413, 526, 538
Baker, Josephine, 464, 466, 467
Baker, Kenny, 438
Baker, Phil, 307, 465
Baker, Tarkington, 39
Baker, Wendy, 527, 535
Baker-Vawter Steel Company, 12
Baldwin, James, 430
Baldwin, Walter, 45
Baldwin, Walter, Jr., 47
Ball, Lucille, 240, 253, 259, **414**, 415, 512
Ball State University, 300, 413, 496, 524
Ballard, Kaye, 314
Ballard, Michael, 415
Balsam, Martin, 188
Bambi (1942), 338
Bamboola, 472
Bancroft, Anne, 409
Bancroft, George, 284
Band Plays On, The, 448
Bandit King of Texas (1949), 367
Bandits (2001), 478
Bandy, Moe, 446
Bankhead, Tallulah, 179, 258
Bara, Theda, 41, 42, 43
Barbee, Richard, 76, 233, 528, 538
Barbour, Don, 435, **435**, 436, 532
Barbour, Ross Edwin, **435**, 435–36, 532
Barcus, James Solomon, 420, 538
Bard, Sara, 332
Barefoot in the Park (television), 457
Bareikis, Arija, 527, 536
Baretta (television), 496
Barker, Reginald, 52
Barker, The: novel, 427; play, 83, 221–22, 402, 427; 1928 film, 384, 427
Barksdale, Margaret, 295
Barn Dance (radio), 363
Barnard, Mrs. John, 82
Barnard College, 486
Barnes, Billy, 313
Barnes, Joanna, **327**, 328
Barnes, V. L., 526
Barney Miller (television), 271
Baron of Arizona, The (1950), 262
Baroud (1933), 52–53
Barr, Julia, 518, 520, 521, 532
Barrett, Claudia, **367**
Barretts of Wimpole Street, The, 232
Barrows, Leslie S. *See* Baker, Charles Graham.
Barry, Don "Red," 366

Barry, Gene, 188

Barrymore, Ethel, xii, 205

Barrymore, John, xii, 8, 26, 154, 168, 178, 179, 278, 398, **398**, 427, 495

Barrymore, John Drew, 105, 205

Barrymore, Lionel, 4, **18**, 205, 418, 426

Barter Theater (Abingdon, VA), 490

Barthelmess, Richard, 75, 294

Bartlett, Hall, 244, 245

Baseheart, Richard, 189

Basinger, Kim, 512

Baskett, James, 236–38, **237**, 333, 454, 471, 515, 535

Baskett, Margaret, 238

Bataan (1943), 252

Batman (1989), 511–12

Batman, The (1943), 386

Batman and Robin (1997), 200

Batman Returns (1992), 417, 419

Battle at Elderbush Gulch, The (1913), 316

Battle Hymn (1957), 96

Battle of Angels, 263

Bauman, Rabbi Morton, 60

Baxter, Anne, xiii, **73**, **174–75**, 174–85, **176**, **177**, **178**, **179**, **180**, **183**, **184**, 298, **299**, 309, 405, 411, 429, 501, 515, 523, 525, 535

Baxter, Catherine Wright, 175, 176, 181

Baxter, James Stewart, 176

Baxter, Kenneth Stuart, 175, 176

Baxter, Len, 256

Baxter, Richard Tobin, 176, **176**

Baynard and Whitney Troubadours, 471

Beach, Rex, 22, 36

Beach Boys, 436

Beacon Hill (television), 478

Beal, Frank, 522–23

Beat the Clock (television), 112

Beauty and the Beast (1991), 314

Bebout, Amy (Amy Michelle Bebout), 527, 537

Bechet, Sidney, 467

Beckett, Scotty, 252

Bedazzled (2000), 121

Beemer, Brace, 401

Beery, Maxine Jones, **351**, 352

Beery, Noah, Jr., 352

Beery, Wallace, 170, 178

Beggarman, Thief (television), 296

Behind Stone Walls (1932), 63

Beiderbecke, Bix, 441, 447, 486

Belasco, David, 4, 278

Belasco Theater: in Los Angeles, 28; in New York, 4

Bell, C. W., 467

Bell, Hank, 356

Bell, Joshua, 436–37, 536

Bell, Book and Candle (1958), 440, 444

Bellamy, Ralph, 189

Belle of Mayfair, The, 42

Belt, Glenn, 530, 536

Ben Casey (television), 409

Ben-Hur: 1922 film, 22; 1925 film, 209, 347

Ben Vereen: Comin' at Ya (television), 476

Bend of the River (1952), 373, **373**

Bendix, William, 312, 522

Benham, Dorothy, 202, 203, **203**

Benham, Ethyle Cooke, 202, 203, **203**

Benham, Harry, 202, **202**, 203, **203**, 537

Benham, Leland, 202, 203, **203**

Benji (1974), 481

Bennett, Alma, 208

Bennett, Barbara Jane, 218, 219, 220, 221

Bennett, Billie, 214, **238**, 238–39, 538

Bennett, Constance Campbell, 218, 220, 221, 222, **223**, 294

Bennett, George Washington, 217, 218

Bennett, Henry, 217

Bennett, Joan Geraldine, 218, 219, 220, 221, 222, **223**

Bennett, Mabel Adrienne Morrison, 218, **218**, 221, 222

Bennett, Richard (Charles Clarence William Henry Richard Bennett), xiii, 179, **217**, 217–23, **218**, **219**, **222**, **223**, 230, 282, 298, 405, 411, 523, 536

Bennett, Sue (Sue Benjamin), 527, 535

Benny, Jack, 159, 160, 163, 179, 274

Benny Goodman Orchestra, 257

Benrubi, Abraham (Abraham Rubin Hercules Benrubi), 518, 535

Benrubi, Asher, 518

Benrubi, Patricia, 518

Benti, Joseph, 538

Bentzen, Jayne, 520, 538

Bergen, Polly (Nellie Paulina Burgin), **491**, 491–92, 539

Berger, Ludwig, 214

Bergman, Ingrid, 238

Bergman, Richard, 528, 536

Berklee College of Music, 438, 439

Berle, Milton, 82, 250

Berlin, Irving, 137

Bern, Paul, 209

Bernhardt, Sarah, xii

Bernie, Ben, 437

Bernstein, Barbara, 194

Bernstein, Elizabeth, 194

Bernstein, Ira, 194

Bernstein, Joseph, 194

Bernstein, Leonard, 437

Bernstein, Robert, 194

Berry, Ken, **302**

Best, Dorothy, 492

Best, James (Jules Guy), 240, 492, **492**, 538

Best, Janeen, 492

Best Friend Films, 492

Best Man in Grass Creek (1999), 522

Best of the Worst (television), 123

Best People, The, 151

Best Years of Our Lives, The (1946), 181

Betty Crocker (radio), 262

Beulah (television), 254

Bevan, Billy, 208

Beverly, Eddie Jr., 530

Beverly Hillbillies, The (television), 234

Beverly Hills (CA) High School, 519

Beverly Hills 90210 (television), 200

Beverly of Graustark (1926), 427

Bewitched (television), 234

Beyond Our Control (television), 416, 419

Beyond the Horizon: 1920 stage production, 217, **217**, 220; 1926 stage production, 282

B. F. Keith's (Indianapolis), xi

Big Band and Jazz Hall of Fame, 459

Big Boy, 448

Big Brother (novel), 426

Big Cat, The (1949), 447

Big Chill, The (1983), 504

Big Country, The (1958), 430

Big Dan (1923), **346**

Big Ears (1931), 63

Big Fisherman, The (1959), 423

Big Four Railroad, 12, 72

Big Hop, The (1928), 348

Big Payoff, The (television), 297

Big Show, The (1936), 370

Big Sky, The (novel), 425

Big Sleep, The (1946), 398

Big Story (television), 232

Big Town (television), 292, **293**

Big Valley (television), 445

Bigelow Theater (television), 297

Bigfoot (1970), 360

Bijou Theater (Indianapolis), xii, **xii**

Bill Kenny and the Ink Spots, 455. *See also* Ink Spots.

Billboard (magazine), 128, 369

Billings, George A., 383

Billy Barnes People, The, 313

Billy the Kid (1941), 285

Billy Rose Minstrels, 443

Billy Rose's Diamond Horseshoe (New York), 467

Biltmore Theater (New York), 83

Bindley, Scott, 522, 535

Bindley, William, 522, 530, 535

Biograph (studio), 28, 47

Biography (television), 437

Birth of Indiana, The. See *Indiana*.

Birth of a Nation, The (1915), 11, 14, 15, 317

Birthright (1924), 472

Biscuit Eater, The (1940), **286**, 287

Bix Pieces, The (ballet), 486

B. J. and the Bear (television), 491

Black, Karen (Karen Blanche Ziegler), 492–93, **493**, 515, 538

Black Crepe and Diamonds, 42

Black Expo Youth Video Institute, 445

Black Stallion, The (1979), 511

Blackbirds, 236, 278

Blacque, Taurean, 311

Blacula (1972), 98, **99**

Blair, Betsy, 188

Blake, Eubie, xii, 132, 236, 272, 465, 466, 467, 471, 472

Blaker, Eliza, 283

Blane, Sally, 85

Blanford, Larry, 539

Blashfield, Edwin Holand, 277

Blazing Saddles (1974), 279

Bledsoe, Jules, 278

Blessed Event (1932), 509

Blige, Mary J., 445

Bliss School of Electricity (Washington, D.C.), xvii

Blithe Spirit, 76

Blob, The (1958), 106

Block, A. L., xii, 481

Blondell, Joan, 278, 397, 509, **509**

Blondie (radio), 252

Blood and Sand (1941), 493

Bloom Township (IL) High School, 442

Bloomington (IN) High School South, 420

Blue, Barbara Ann, 17

Blue, Betty Jean Munson Mess, 18

Blue, Gladys Erma, 17

Blue, Lousetta Springer, 11, 17

Blue, Monte (Gerard Montgomery Blue), 10–19, **10–11**, **12**, **13**, **14**, **15**, **16**, **17**, **18**, **19**, 148, **148**, 206, 211, 230, 242, 243, 317, 347, 348, 370, 391, 393, 394, 401, 525, 535

Blue, Morris, 11–12

Blue, Richard, 18

Blue, Richard Monte, 17

Blue, Rupert, 11

Blue, Tove Danor (Tove Rosing Johnson), **16**, 17, 18

Blue, Tove Diane, 18

Blue, Rear Admiral Victor, 11

Blue, William Jackson, 11

Blue Bird, The (1940), 438

Blue Chips (1994), 522

Blue Hawaii (1961), 447

Blue Water (book), 83

Bluebird Café (Nashville, TN), 453

Blyth, Ann, 384

Boat Trip (2002), 201

Bob Newhart Show, The (television), 270

Bobby Deerfield (1977), 484

Bobby Hackett orchestra, 442

Bobby Helms Show, 449

Bochco, Steven, 200, 311

Boer War, The (1913), 378

Boetticher, Budd (Oscar Boetticher Jr.), 493–94, **494**, 515, 538

Boetticher, Georgia, 494

Boetticher, Helen, 494

Bogart, Humphrey, 18, 124, **169**, 172, 394, 398, 425, 483, 507, 523

Bogdanovich, Peter, 7, 462

Boheme, La (opera), 74, 226

Bolero (1934), 67

Bolger, Ray, 138, 139

Bombs! (1915), 57

Bon Voyage: novel, 425; 1962 film, 425, 523

Bonanza (television), 373, 503, 519

Bond, Ward, 302, 328

Bondi, Beulah (Beulah Bondy), 230, 240, 489, **494**, 494–96, 515, 523, 525, 537

Bondy, Abraham, 494

Bondy, Eva Marble, 494

Bonnell, Lee (Terry Melmont), 528

Bonyea, Mrs. R. W., 24, 26

Booker, Harry, **28**

Boomerang, The, 420

Booth, Shirley, 177

Booty Call (1997), 200

Bordoni, Irene, 461

Borgnine, Ernest, 188, 490

Born on the Fourth of July (1989), 200

Born Thief, The (screenplay), 423

Born to Dance (1936), 461, 516

Born Yesterday (1950), 181

Borzage, Frank, 92

Boston Conservatory, 519

Boswell Sisters, 307

Bought! (1931), 221

Bounds, Hazel, 336

Bourbon College, 167

Bourbon Street Beat (television), 260

Bow, Clara, 11, 66, 481

Bowers, John (John Elehue Bowersox), 20–26, **20–21**, **22**, **23**, **24**, **25**, **26**, 52, 62, 109, 148, 320, 348, 394, 525, 532

Bowersox, Charles, 26

Bowersox, George A., 21

Bowersox, Ida, 21, 14

Bowie, David, 457

Boy from Indiana, The (1950), 244, **244**

Boy with Green Hair, The (1948), 299

Boyer, Charles, **477**, 509

Boyz II Men, 445

Brace, Annie, 444

Bradley, Jerry, 453

Brady, Alice, 202, 312

Brady, Diamond Jim, 131

Brady, William A., 21

Brady Bunch, The (television), 194

Brando, Jocelyn, 283

Brando, Marlon, 114, 506

Branigin, Gov. Roger, 406

Brazil (IN) Concert Band, 256

Brazil (IN) High School, 256

Bread Loaf Writers Conference, 430

Breakfast at Tiffany's (1961), 481

Breakfast of Champions: novel, 430; 1999 film, 430

Breaking Away (1979), 419, 522

Breaking the Habit (1964), 516

Breen, Bobby, 243

Breen, Joseph, 480

Bremer, Lucille, 234

Brenda Starr: television, 418; 1989 film, 418

Brenda Starr, Reporter (1945), 418

Brent, Evelyn, 65

Brent, George, 312

Brewer, Gene, 420, 533

Brewster's Millions: novel, 132, 427; 1914 film, 427; 1921 film, 427; 1945 film, 427; 1961 film, 427; 1985 film, 427

Brian's Song (1971), 522

Brice, Fanny, 448

Brickert, Carlton (Carl), 526, 537

Bride and Groom (television), 297

Bride Goes Wild, The (1948), 419

Bridges, Jeff, 420

Bridges, Lloyd, 190

Bridges of Madison County, The (1995), 251

Brieux, Eugene, 220

Brigham Young: Frontiersman (1940), 503

Bright Horizon (radio), 518

Bright Victory (1951), 96

Brightman, Homer, 339, 340

Brighty of the Grand Canyon (1967), 85

Bringing Up Baby (1938), 398

British Broadcasting Corporation (BBC), 263

British International Films Corporation, 387

Broad Ripple High School (Indianapolis), 518

Broadway Bill, 309

Broadway Melody, The (1929), 467

Broadway Theater (New York), 319

Broderick, Jack, 243

Broken Violin, The (1927), 472

Bromfield, John (Farron McClain Brumfield),
    239, 239–41, 537

Brooks, Avery (Avery Franklin Brooks), **241**, 241–
    42, 538

Brooks, Garth, 458

Brooks, James L., 125

Brooks, Louise, 220, 370, 379

Brooks, Mel, 279

Brookshire, Adeline. *See* Nall, Adeline Brookshire.

Brough, Candi, 527

Brough, Randi, 527

Brown, Earle, 207

Brown, Hiram S., 366

Brown, Jim, 118

Brown, Joe E., 312, 394, 415

Brown, John Mason, 127

Brown, Johnny Mack, 350, 364, 370, 375, 385

Brown, Karl, 14

Brown, Kay, 178

Brown, Nacio Herb, 467

Brown County (IN) Playhouse, 504

Brown of Harvard, 4

Brown Dots, 455. *See also* Ink Spots.

Brownies, 72

Brownlow, Kevin, 398

Brown's Business College, 392

Brumfield, Cecil, 239

Brumfield, Martha Toner, 239

Brunst, Margaret, 332, 333

Bryan, William Jennings, 145, 420

Bryant, Pamela Jane, 527, 535

Bryn Mawr College, 426

Buchanan, Jack, 135

Buck Benny Rides Again (1940), **273**

Bucking Society (1916), 29

Buckley, William F., 430

Bucks County Playhouse, 216

Buffalo Bill's Wild West and Pawnee Bill's Far East (1910), 379

Buffalo Bill's Wild West Show, 355, 356, 379

Buffy the Vampire Slayer (television), 518

Bulifant, Joyce, 194

Bullet Proof (1920), 377

Bullfighter and the Lady (1951), 493, 494, 515

Bullock, Jim, 437, 438

Bullock, Walter, 437–38, 447, 515, 538

Bunny, John, 413

Burdick, Chrissie, 322

Burdine Department Store (Miami), 284

Burke, Billie, 131, 137

Burke, Eulalia, 243

Burke, Kathleen, **242**, 242–43, 535

Burke, Melville, 494

Burke, Mrs. Reeves, 262

Burke's Law (television), 509

Burlesque, 168

Burnette, Lester Allen "Smiley," 370, 449

Burns, Fred, 356

Burns, Ken, 242

Burnt Offerings (1976), 493

Burroughs, Edgar Rice, 317, 318, 319, 320, 323,
    324, 356

Burstyn, Ellen, 191, 429

Burton, Frederick, 526, 528, 535

Burton, Gary, 438–39, 535

Burton, Martin, 233, 528, 535

Burton, Richard, 423

Burton, Steve, 519, 520, 535

Burton, Tim, 447

Bus Stop, 293

But Is It Art?, 417

Butch Cassidy and the Sundance Kid (1969), 290

Butler, Dan, 528, 532

Butler, Fred J., 243

Butler, Lois, 243–45, **244**, 424, 535

Butler University, 263, 435, 465

Butterworth, Charles, 47, 148, **151**, **245**, 245–46,
    260, 348, 401, 525, 537

Butterworth, Walter T., 528

Buttons, Red, 98

Buttram, Pat, 275, 312, 369

Buzzington, Ezra (Jonathan Harris), 524, 528,
    533

By the Light of the Silvery Moon (1953), 412, 523

Bye Bye Birdie (1963), 297

Byington, Spring, 169, **261**

Caan, James, **399**

Cabaret, 491

Cabin in the Sky, 279

Cable, Bill, 534

Cabot, Meg (Meggin Patricia Cabot), **420**, 420–21, 536

Cactus Flower, 190

Cadle Tabernacle (Indianapolis), 160

Caged Women II (1996), 300

Cagney, James, 189, 282, 397, 507

Cahiers du Cinema, 399

Cain and Mabel (1936), 297

Caine, Michael, 120

Caine Mutiny, The (1954), 376

Calamity Jane (1953), 373

Caldwell, Erskine, 503

California Junior Boys' Republic, 103

Call Me Madam (1953), 258

Callahan, J. Will, 439–40, 532

Calvert, John, 528, 533

Calvet, Corinne, 240

Cameron, Rod, 376

Cameron, Sean, 528, 534

Camino Real (1970 revival), 293

Camp, Joe, 480–81

Campanella, Joseph, 256

Campbell, Barbara, 399

Campbell, Duane, 415

Campbell, Mifflin "Miff," 453, 454. *See also* Ink Spots.

Campbell Soundstage (television), 188

Campus Carmen, The (1928), 209

Campus Sleuth (1948), 464

Can-Can, 461

Canary, David, 343, 519, 520, 521, 535

Cannes Film Festival, 300

Cannon, Pomeroy, 526, 533

Cannon Films, 300

Canova, Judy, 47, 56

Cantor, Eddie, 131, 132, 276, 307, 462, 464, 465

Can't Help Singing (1944), **297**

Cantlon, Shorty, 397, 523

Canutt, Yakima, 378, 391

Canyon of Adventure, The (1928), **355**

Canyon Films, 346

Canyon Passage (1946), 515

Cape Fear (1962), 491

Cape Playhouse Stock Company, 177

Capitol Records, 254, 436, 455, 464

Capone, Al, 485

Cappyboppy (Peet book), 334

Capra, Frank, 154, 249, 309, 387, 389, 447

Captain Blood (1924), **7**, 8

Captain Commanding, 284

Career, 232

Carew, James, 526, 528, 533

Carey, Harry, 366, 377, 378

Carey, Mariah, 445

Carlon, Fran, 518, 520, 535

Carlyle, Dave. *See* Paige, Robert.

Carmel (IN) High School, 201

Carmichael, Hoagy, xii, 262, 433, 436, 440–42, **441**, 482, 515, 522, 525, 536

Carmichael, Howard Clyde, 440

Carmichael, Lida Mary Robinson, 440

Carnegie Hall (New York), 442

Carnegie Institute of Technology, 83, 248, 430

Carnegie Lyceum (New York), 72

Carney, Augustus, 31

Carnival, 314

Caroline in the City (television), 314

Carousel, 248

Carr, Harry, 17

Carradine, John, 237

Carrie (1952), 320

Carrie Nation, 291

Carroll, Bob Jr., 415

Carroll, Diahann, 118

Carroll, Earl, 137, 284

Carroll, Joan, 234

Carroll, Lewis, 473

Carroll, Nancy, 63

Carson, Hudson, 493

Carson, Johnny, 440

Carson, Kit, 493

Carson, Sunset, 377

Carter, Benny, 455

Carter, Frank, 130, 131, 132

Cartwright, Peggy, 310

Caruso, Anthony, **246**, 246–47, 261, 532

Caruso, Tonia Valente, 247

Caruso, Tonio, 247

Casablanca (1942), 59

Case against Brooklyn, The (1958), 449

Cash, Johnny, 449

Casion Gardens (Los Angeles), 464

Cassidy, Hopalong (William Boyd), 211, 367

Cassidy, Maude, 369, 371

Cassidy (IA) Elementary School, 301

Castle, Irene, 74

Castle, Vernon, 74, 134, 142

Casual Sex? (1988), 449

Cat Screams, The, 291

Cates, Phoebe, 504

Cathcart, Dick, 535

Catlett, Sidney "Big Sid," 528, 538

Cat's Cradle (novel), xi, 430

Cat's Meow, The (2001), 462

Catlett, Walter, 309

Cattle Queen of Montana (1954), 247

Cattle Thief (1936), 294, **294**, 359

Caught (1931), 142

Caveman (1981), 198

CBS, 92, 93, 94, 124, 188, 189, 232, 260, 261,
    262, 307, 415, 478, 510

CBS This Morning (television), 437

Celebration of America's Music, A (television), 459

Central High School (Cleveland), 465

Central Presbyterian Church (Terre Haute), 41

Centron Records, 449

Chadwick, Helene, 396

Chalos, Pete, 256

Chamberlain, Philip, 447

Chamberlain, Richard, 373

Champion, Michael (Michael Campbell
    Champion), 528, 535

Champion (1949), 508

Champion College, 448

Champlin, Charles, 150, 164

Champlin Players, 233

Chandler, Raymond, 398

Chaney, Lon, 22, **141**, 386, 419

Chaney, Lon, Jr., 523

Channing, Carol, 314

Chaplin, Charlie, 29, 148, 208, 238, 320, 387,
    394, 482, 506

Charles, Ray, 462–63

Charles & Diana: A Royal Love Story (television), 418

Charles Mayer and Company, 284

Charley's Aunt (1941), 160, 163, 179

Charlie Chan at the Olympics (1937), 365

Charlie Davis Band, 257

Charlie Rose Show, The (television), 437

Charlotte's Web (1973), 512

Chase, Chevy, 124

Chayefsky, Paddy, 188

Chaykin, Maury, 429

Cheaper by the Dozen (1950), 76

Cheating Cheaters, 168

Cheers (television), 198

Chekov, Mikail, 289

Chelde, Mary, 494

Cheney, Alice, 145, 147, 148, 151

Cheney, Jim, 145

Cher, 493

Chess Game, The (television), 248

Cheyenne (television), 252

Chicago Baptist Institute, 95

Chicago Defender (newspaper), 471

Chicago Morning News (newspaper), 420

Chicago Musical College, 448, 497

Chicago Symphony Orchestra, 446

Chicago Tribune (newspaper), 141

Children of the Corn IV: The Gathering (1996), 493

Children of the Night (1991), 493

Children of the Sun, 472

Children's Theater (New York), 72, 73

China Clipper (1936), 394

Chinese Theater (Los Angeles), 142, 476,
    515

Chissell, Noble "Kid," 523, 528, 535

Chisum (1970), 303

Chocolate Dandies, The, 467

Chocolate Soldier, The, 261

Christian, Charlie, 458

Christie, Al, 62

Christie, Julie, 439

Christie Film Company, 62

Christmas in July (1940), 32

Christmas Story, A (1983), 428–29, 524

Christopher Bean (1932), 495

Christy, Ann (Gladys Cronin), **62**, 62–64, **63**,
    481, 532

Chu Chu and the Philly Flash (1981), 484

Cimarron (1931), 498, 515

Cincinnati Conservatory of Music, 444, 497

Cincinnati Post (newspaper), 419

Cinderella (1950), 333, 340

Circle Theater (Indianapolis), xii, **xiii**, 481,
    508–09

Circle Theater Company, 482, 509

Circle Theatre (television), 417

Circus Night in Silvertown (radio), 250

Cisco Kid, The (television), 375, 386, 417

Citizen Kane (1941), xii, 179, 405, 517

Citizens Gas Company, 482

City of Angels (television), 200, 311

Civic Theater, 518

Civilian Conservation Corps, 480

Claire, Ina, 202

Clambake (1967), 447

Clancy in Wall Street (1930), 29, 214

Clark, Nancy Eloise Cross, 375

Clark, Roy, 275

Clark, Steve (Elmer Stephen Clark), 367, 375,
    375, 376, 385, 386, 528, 532

Clark, Susan, 279, **279**

Clark, Wesley Richard, 375

Clarke, John, 528, 537
Clarke, Mae, 427
Claudelle Inglish (1961), 264
Clayburgh, Jill, 430
Claypool Hotel (Indianapolis), 170
Cleese, John, 504
Clement, Clay, 4
Clement, Clay Jr., 4, 6
Clementine (novel), 244
Clements, Roy, 32
Cleopatra Jones (1973), 457
Cleveland, George, **244**
Cleveland Playhouse, 248
Cleveland Press (newspaper), 499
Clift, Montgomery, 178, 426
Climax, The, 213
Cline, Eddie, **280**
Cline, Patsy, 452
Clinging Vine, The, 497
Close Encounters of the Third Kind (1977), 523–24
Close Harmony (1929), 267
Clothes for a Summer Hotel, 519
Clouds Over Europe (1939), 214. See also *Q Planes*.
Clown, The (1953), 419
Club Idaho, 257
Clyde, Andy, 295
CMG Worldwide, 117
CNN, 437
Cobb, Irvin S., 383
Cobb, Lee, Jr., 98
Cocktail (1988), 457
Cocoanut Grove (Los Angeles), 273
Cocoanut Grove Night Club (Boston), 109, 351
Cody, William F. "Buffalo Bill," 11
Coe, Demas, xviii
Coffin, Tris, 366
Cohan, George M., 142, 206, 312
Cohan, Helen, **141**
Cohen, Paul, 448, 449
Cohens and Kellys in Scotland, The (1930), 29
Cohens and Kellys in Trouble, The (1933), 30
Cohn, Harry, 154, 188
Coke Time with Eddie Fisher (television), 194
Colbert, Claudette, 83, 84, **84**, 153, 170, 312
Cole, J. O., 459, 460
Cole, Kate, 459, 461
Cole Brothers Circus, 359, 469
Coleman, Ronald, **155**
Colgate Comedy Hour, The (television), 253, 297
Colgate House Party (radio), 250
College Widow, The, 28, 420, 523; 1927 film, 523
Collier, William, Jr., 523

Colliers (magazine), 425
Collins, Bootsy, 445
Collins, Joan, 384
Collins, Russell, 248, **248**, 503, 535
Collins, Tom, 452
Columbia Club (Indianapolis), 507, 508
Columbia Pictures, 519
Columbia Records, 455, 457
Columbia Studios, 53, 154, 188, 189, 297, 301, 349, 359, 376, 386, 391, 393, 401, 444, 484, 493, 498
Columbia University, 268, 339, 427
Columbian Trio, 128
Columbo, Russ, 154, 163
Columbo (television), 503
Columbus Commercials (basketball team), 362
Columbus (OH) Dispatch (newspaper), 28
Columbus High School (Vevay), 362
Columbus (IN) Republic (newspaper), 359, 360
Come and Get It (1936), 398
Come Back Little Sheba, 234
Come Back to the Five and Dime, Jimmy Dean, Jimmy Dean (1982), 109, 493
Come into the Garden, 182
Come On, Rangers (1938), 211
Comedy Act Theater (Atlanta), 263
Comes Midnight (1940), 236
Como, Perry, 244
Condoli, Conte (Secondo Condoli), 440, 537
Condoli, Pete, 440, 537
Condon, Eddie (Albert Edwin Condon), 433, **442**, 442–43, 537
Coney Island (1943), 401
Confessions of a Queen (1925), 23, 52
Congress of Industrial Organizations, 95
Conklin, Chester, 29, 57
Conn, Maurice, 363, 364
Conn, Terri, 520, 536
Connelly, Marc, 249
Connolly, Maureen, 418
Connors, Chuck, 522
Conqueror, The (1956), 509
Conquering Power, The (1921), 51
Conrad, Con, 462
Constantine, Michael, 275
Converse, Frank, 491
Conway, Curt, 232
Conway, Jack, 396
Conway, Tom, 211
Coogan, Jackie, 478, 486
Cook, Alice Boulders, 250
Cook, Beatrice Helen, 250

Cook, Emily Erskine, 494

Cook, Joe (Joe Lopez Cook), 59, 90, 190, 248–50, **249**, 538

Cooke, Marjorie Benton, 526, 539

Cooksey, Curtis, 526, 528

Cool Hand Luke (1967), 289, 290

Cooper, Gary, 33, **242**, 243, 302, 304, 323, 430, 523

Cooper, Harry, 149

Copperhead, The (1920), 426

Coppola, Francis Ford, 389, 429, 492

Coral Records, 464

Corea, Chick, 437, 439

Corley, Annie, **250**, 250–51, 538

Corley, David, 250

Corley, Sarah, 250

Cornell University, 296, 396, 430

Cornish College of the Arts, 120

Cornwall, Anne, **20–21**, 22

Coronado (1935), 437

Correll, Charles, 237

Corrigan, Ray "Crash," 211, 350, 370, **371**

Cosmopolitan (magazine), 131, 226

Cost, The (novel), 428

Costas, Bob, 124

Costello, Dolores, 523

Costner, Kevin, 518

Cotton, Joseph, 411

Cotton Club (New York), 441, 467

Cotton States Exposition (1895), xvii

Cottrell, William, 335–37, 537

Couch, Rex, III

Coules, Edith, 316

Count Basie Orchestra, 236, 253, 455

Count of Monte Cristo, The (1934), 309

Country (1984), 449

Country Gentlemen (1936), 81

Country Girl, The: play, 402; 1954 film, 402, **402**, 516

Country Kitchen (television), 194

County Chairman, The (1935), 142, 523

Court-Martial of Billy Mitchell, The (1955), 258

Covered Wagon, The (1923), 4, **5**, **6**, 8

Coward, Noël, 75, 76, 77, 182

Cowboy and the Kid, The (1936), 350

Cowboy Needs a Horse, A (1956), 338

Cox, Jane Marie, 430

Coyne, Joe, 218

Crabbe, Buster, 18, 33, **284**, 285, **324**, 325, **325**, 362, **364**, 376

Craddock, Claudia, 527, 534

Cradle Will Rock, 268

Craig, Catherine, 527, 536

Craig, John (Joe E. Cline), 528, 535

Crain, Jeanne, 181, 424

Cramton, Henry, 264

Cramton, Mrs. Henry, 264

Crane, Edith, 251

Crane, Otis O., 251

Crane, Richard, **251**, 251–52, 534

Crane, Vernon, 448

Crawford, Joan, 75, 189, 251–52, 304, 312

Crawford, Julian, 101, 102, 103, 104

Crawford, Samuel Travis, 241

Crazy House (1943), **80**, 81

Crenna, Richard, 522

Crest, The (Detroit), 436

Crichton, Michael, 484

Crime, 214

Crime Doctor's Gamble (1947), 419

Crime Ring (1938), **366**

Crime without Passion (1934), 168

Crisp, Marie (Hazel Stark), 526, 538

Croft, Douglas, 386

Croft, Mary Jane, 252–53, **253**, 304, 518, 535

Cronin, David, 62

Cronin, Hume, 182

Cronin, Laura, 62

Cronin, Leonora, 62

Crosby, Bing, 63, 153, **153**, 154, **159**, 243, 402, **402**, 438, 442, 464

Crosby, Bob, 454

Crothers, Donna, 254

Crothers, Scatman (Benjamin Sherman Crothers), 230, 253–56, **255**, 274, 487, 525, 538

Crow, Sheryl, 458

Crowd Roars, The (1932), xi, 397, 523

Crown Hill Cemetery (Indianapolis)

Cruise, Tom, 198, 522

Crunch and Des (television), 303

Cruze, James, 8

Cryer, Gretchen, 251, 413, **413**, 534

Cryer, John, 413

CTI Records, 451

Cuban Love Song, The (1931), 59

Cukor, George, 251, 278, 328

Cullen, Bill, 189

Culver Military Academy, 143, 493

Cumberland Telephone Company, 127

Cummings, Bob, 312

Cunningham, Merce, 486

Curse of the Cat People, The (1944), 405

Curtis, Alan, 285

Curtis, Dick, 528, 535

Curtiz, Michael, 58
Curucu, Beast of the Amazon (1956), 240
Curwood, James Oliver, 363
Cusack, Joan, 524
Cusack, John, 522
Cutler, Frank, 281
Cutler-Bryant Medicine Show, 281

Daddy Long Legs (1955), 261
Dailey, Dan, **177**, 254, 299, **299**
Dakotas, The (television), 264
Damaged Goods: 219, 220; 1914 film, 220
Dame Chance (1926), 67
Dames (1934), 394
Damon, Matt, 120, 125
Dances with Wolves (1990), 498
Dancing Around, 74
Dancing on a Dime (1940), 297
Dane, Karl, 522
Danger (television), **187**, 188
Danger Girl, The (1926), **25**
Dangerous Curves (television), 293
Daniels, Bebe, 67
Daniels, Jerry, 453, 454. *See also* Ink Spots.
Danner, Braden, 520, 528, 535
Danner, Tasha Louise, 538
Da Pron, Louis, 476, 532
Daring Years, The (1923), 267
Dark Blue (2002), 293
Dark Command (1940), 170, **172**
Dark Victory (1939), 59
Darkest Americans, 472
Darling, Eddie, 43
Darwell, Jane, 495
Dasche, Lili, 284
Daugherty, George, 530, 535
Daugherty, Herschel, 530, 538
Daughters Courageous (1939), 226
Dave and Sugar, 453
David and Bathsheba (1951), 515
David Harum (1934), 142
Davidson, Donald, 345
Davies, Brian, 478, 528, 535
Davies, Marion, 138, 202, **219**, 297, 426, 427
Davis, Art, 256
Davis, Benny, 462
Davis, Bette, 59, 181, 182, 183, 226, 233, 258, **259**, 418, 425, 485
Davis, Charlie, 105, 260, 262, 482, 508, 533
Davis, Elam, 421
Davis, Elmer Holmes, 421, **421**, 532

Davis, Frank T., 530, 539
Davis, Geena, 522
Davis, George W., 515
Davis, Georgia, 91, 92, 93, **93**, 94
Davis, Helene, 439
Davis, J. Gas, 256
Davis, Jane, 309
Davis, Jerry, 508
Davis, Jim, **413**, 413–14, 533
Davis, Johnnie "Scat," 226, 256–57, **257**, 433, 532
Davis, Louise, 421, 423
Davis, Madelyn Pugh, 253, **414**, 414–15, 535
Davis, Matthew, 508
Davis, Miles, 455
Davis, Nelson, 256
Davis, Richard, 415
Davy Crockett, King of the Wild Frontier (television), 85
Dawn, Isabel, 415, 538
Dawn Patrol, The (1930), 399
Dawn Trail, The (1930), 214, **215**
Day, Doris, 373, 412, 439, 523
Day at the Races, A (1937), 401
Day of the Locust (1975), 493
Day the Earth Stood Still, The (1951), 406
Daydreams (1922), **280**
Days of Our Lives (television), 199, 200, 519, 520
DC Comics, 511
Dead End: 169; 1937 film, **169**, 169–70
Dean, Eddie, 359
Dean, Emma, 110
Dean, James, 104, 105, 106, **108–09**, 108–17, **110**, **111**, **113**, **114**, **115**, 186, **187**, 188, 258, 306, 371, 413, 418, 482, 515, 525, 533
Dean, Jimmy, 275
Dean, Mildred, 109, 110
Dean, Phillip Hayes, 241
Dean, Priscilla, **25**, 35, 202
Dean, Winton, 109, 110, 112
Deane, Shirley, 285
Dear God (1996), 124, 125
Dear Wife (1949), **308**
Death Mask (1998), 492
Death on My Hands, 274
Death Takes a Holiday, 95
DeBakey, Michael, 77
De Carlo, Yvonne, 425
De Casseres, Ethel Carmen, 205
Decatur Central High School (IN), 263
Decca Records, 449, 454, 464
December Bride (television), **261**
Dee, Ann, 448

Dee Dee Records, 447

Deele, The (band), 445

Deep Are the Roots, 95, 96

Deer, Susan, 522, 527, 535

Deerslayer (1943), 417

Dees, Julie McWhirter, 484, 527, 535

Def Comedy Jam, 264

Defense Rests, The (1934), 385

DeForest, Lee, 465

De Havilland, Olivia, 430

De Leath, Vaughn, 4

De-Lovely (2004), 461

Del Rio, Dolores, 481

Delta Rhythm Boys, 241

DeMarco, Mario, 356

Demeny, Georges, xvii

Demetrius and the Gladiators (1954), 98, 423

DeMille, Cecil B., 15, 18, 39, 42, 44, 65, 181, 417

Demolition Man (1993), 419

Dench, Judi, 437

Denham, Bertha Rowland, 359, 360

Denham Studios, 214, 389

Deniece Williams Show, The (radio), 473

Dennis, Sandy, 493

Dennis the Menace (television), 216, **216**, 447

Denny, Reginald, 67

Dent, Vernon, 208

Dentler, Mary Ann, 267

De Palma, Ralph, 459–60

DePaul University, 186

DePauw University, 251, 413, 420, 428, 437, 465

Depp, Johnny, 447

Deppe, Doris Townsend, 203

Des Moines Tribune (newspaper), 226

Desert Man, The (1917), 385

Desilu Productions, 240

Desperate Hours (1990), 425, 523

Desperate Hours, The: novel, 425; play, 425; 1955 film, 425, 523

DeSylva, B. G., 448

Detective Story, 293

Dewhurst, Colleen, 519

DeWitt, Joyce, 496, **496**, 536

DeWitt, Norma, 496

DeWitt, Paul, 496

DeWolfe, Billy, 523

Diagnosis Murder (television), 199

Diamond Horseshoe (1945), 401, 402, 427

Diary of Anne Frank, The (1959), 515

Dick Cavett Show, The (television), 352

Dick Powell Show, The (television), 419, 509

Dick Powell Theatre, The. See *Dick Powell Show, The*.

Dickens, Charles, 518

Dickenson, Angie, 429

Dickson, George, xi

Dickson, James, xi

Dickson, John, xi

Didn't You Used to Be What's His Name? (Denny Miller memoir), 329

Dietl, Frank, 528

Dietrich, Marlene, 394

Dillingham, Charles, 133, 134

Dinah Shore Chevrolet Show (television), 447

Diner (1982), 478, 484

Dingle, Bertie Hutton, 258

Dingle, Charles, 258–59, **259**, 523, 539

Dingle, Charles Jr., 258

Dingle, John Crockett, 258

Dingle, John F., 258

Dinner for Three, 390

Dion, Celene, 445

Directors Guild of America, 406

Disappearance of Aimee, The (television), 418

Disciple, The (1915), 391

Disney, Lillian, 336

Disney, Walt, 85, 274, 333, 334, 335, 336, 339, 340

Disney (studio), 124, 234, 236–37, 331–41, 370, 487

Disputed Passage: novel, 423; 1939 film, 423

Diving In (1990), 518

Divorce of Lady X, The (1938), 214, 389

Dix, Richard, 214, 288, 325, 396, 498

Dixie Duo, 466

Dixie Showboat (television), 254

Dixie Syncopaters, The, 273

Dixieland Five, 462

Dobie Gillis Show, The (television), 314

Doctor Bull (1933), 142

Doctor Dolittle (1998), 484

Doctor Hudson's Secret Journal (novel), 423

Doctor Takes a Wife, The (1940), 401

Doctor's Hospital (New York), 138, 139

Dog on Business, A (1910), 31

Dogfight (1991), 120

Doherty, Shannon, 522

Doll's House, A, 188

Dolly Sisters, 75

Don McNeill's Breakfast Club (radio), 486

Donald, Peter, 189

Donald's Lucky Day (1939), 339

Donaldson, Arthur, 486

Donna Reed Show, The (television), 447

Donner, Richard, 409

Dorsey, Jimmy, 307, 441
Dorsey, Lonnie, 149
Dorsey, Tommy, 307, 441
Double Wedding (1937), 285
Douglas, Bessie Porch, 422
Douglas, Helen Gahagan, 76
Douglas, Ileanna, 524
Douglas, Kirk, **441**, 508
Douglas, Lloyd C., 421–23, 539
Douglas, Melvyn, 105, 259
Douglas, Michael, 506
Douglas, Mike, **325**, 496
Douglass, Frederick, 98
Dove, Billie, 481
Dowling, Eddie, 448
Down Beat (magazine), 451
Down Memory Lane (1949), **30**
Down n' Dirty (2000), 300
Downs, Hugh, 187
Downs, Johnny, 437
Doyle, Arthur Conan, 518
Dozier, William, 188
Dr. Christian (radio), 304
Dr. Doolittle 2 (2001), 264
Dr. Hudson's Secret Journal (television), 423
Dr. Kildare (television), 310
Dr. Quinn, Medicine Woman (television), 328, **328**
Dracula's Daughter (1936), 386
Dramatic Life of Abraham Lincoln, The (1924), 383
Draper, Jack (Lauren Draper), 526, 537
Dream Girl, 259
Dreamboat (1952), 76, **76**
Dreamland Theater (Linton), 273
Dreiser, Theodore, xii, **422**, 423–24, 444, 538
Dresser, Louise (Louise Josephine Kerlin), **140**, 140–43, **141**, **142**, **143**, 206, 230, **277**, 278, 444, 515, 523, 525, 538
Dresser, Paul (Johann Paul Dreiser Jr.), 140, 141, 423, **443**, 443–44, 448, 523, 538
Dressler, Marie, 29, 170
Drew, Ellen, **388**
Drew, John, 142
Drew, Sidney, 205
Dreyfuss, Richard, 523–24
Driscoll, Bobby, **237**, 523
Driscoll, Tex (John W. Morris), 526, 528
Drive, He Said (1971), 493
Drury Lane Theater (Chicago), 303
Duane, Michael (Duane McKinney), 528, 534
Du Brey, Claire, 49
Duchin, Eddy, 307
Duckman (television), 419

Dudley Do-Right (1999), 120–21, **121**
Duff, Howard, 304
Duffey, Henry, 304
Duffy's Tavern (radio), 304
Duggan, Andrew, 259–60, **260**, 534
Duggan, Edward, 259
Duggan, Elizabeth, 260
Duke Comes Back, The (1937), 365–66
Duke of Chicago (1949), 267
Dukes of Hazzard, The (television), 446, 492
Dumbo (1941), 333
Dumke, Ralph, 245, 260–61, **261**, 262, **262**, 537
Dunaway, Faye, 418
Dunbar, Dorothy, 323
Duncan, Johnny, 446
Dunham, Henry Clay, 227
Duning, George William, 433, 444–45, 515, 539
Dunlap, Scott, 351
Dunn, Adelaide Antoinette Henry, 497
Dunn, Joseph John, 497
Dunne, Irene (Irene Marie Dunn), 154, 163, 246, 272, 309, 423, 489, **497**, 497–99, **498**, **503**, 515, 525, 534
DuPont Cavalcade Theater (television), 97
Durand of the Bad Lands: novel, 416; 1917 film, 416; 1925 film, 149, 347, 416
Durango Kid, The (1940), **375**
Durante, Jimmy, 438
Durbin, Deanna, 160, 297, **297**
Durham, Kilburn, 424
Durham, Marilyn Wall, 424, **424**, 538
Dusty's Trail (television), 303
Dutch Uncle (novel), 424
Du Valle, Reginald, 440
Dwan, Allen, 7, 8, 148, 206
Dynasty (television), 275

Eagle, The (1925), 142
Eagle-Lion Studio, 243, 447
Eagle Squadron (1942), 252
Eakin, Dorothy, 338
Earlham College, xvii
Earp, Virgil, 64
Earp, Wyatt, 64
Earth, Wind & Fire, 472
East, Ed, 260, 261, **262**, 262–63, 536
East, Mrs. Jimmie, 262
East, Judge Q. Austin, 262
East, Polly, 262
East Chicago Business College, 186
East Chicago Roosevelt High School, 186

East of Eden (1955), 105, **108–09**, 109, 114, 116, 418, 482, 483, 515, 516
Eastern Illinois University, 502
Eastwood, Clint, 251, 525
Easy Rider (1969), 492
Ebb Tide, 168
Eck, Marcia, 478, 533
Ed Sullivan Show, The (television), 194
Ed Wood (1994), 417, 447
Ed Wynn Show, The (radio), 512
Eddie Condon Floor Show, The (television), 442
Edge of Night, The (television), 520
Eddy, Duane, 447
Eddy, Nelson, 244, 272, 438, 478
Eddy Duchin Story, The (1956), 444, 515
Edison, Thomas, xviii, 525
Edmonds, Kenneth "Babyface," 201, 433, 445–46, 535
Edmonds, Tracey, 201, 445
Educational Pictures, 250
Edward Thomas' Male Quartet, 465
Edward Warren Productions, 202
Edwards, Andy, 528, 533
Edwards, Annie, 95
Edwards, Corey, 528, 535
Edwards, Gus, 224
Edwards, James, xiii, **95**, 95–99, **96**, **97**, 533
Edwards, Valley, 95
Egg and I, The (1947), 33, 170, 172, 516
Eggemeyer, George, xviii
Eggerth, Marta (Martha), 439
Eggleston, Edward, 84, 424, **424**, 522, 538
Egyptian Theater (Los Angeles), 476
Eight Is Enough (television), 232
Eight Jelly Rolls (ballet), 486
Eight Men Out (1988), 522
Eight Simple Rules for Dating My Teenage Daughter (television), 199
Eilers, Sally, 149, 150
Eisenhower, Dwight D., 260
Eisenstaedt, Alfred, 158
Eisenstein, Sergei, 424
Eiteljorg-Menke Advertising Agency, 337
El Capitan Theater (Hollywood), 304
El Dorado (1966), **399**
Electric Horseman, The (1979), 410, 483
Elegance, 75
Elf and the Magic Key, The (television), 314
Elias Day Lyceum Arts Conservatory, 503
Ella Enchanted (2004), 201
Ellington, Duke, 253
Elliott, John, **363**

Elliott, "Wild Bill," 366, 377, 393
Ellis Island (television), 429
Elmer, the Great (1933), 206
Elmo, the Mighty (1920), 320
Elmo the Fearless (1920), 320
Elmore, Pearl, 56
Elopement (1951), 76
Elsie, 272
Elwood (IN) High School, 252
Embassy Entertainment, 484
Emerson, Faye, 189
Emge, David, 528, 538
Emhardt, C. J., 263, **263**
Emhardt, Robert Christian, 263, **263**, 535
Eminent Authors, Inc., 22
Emmick, James, 109
Empire Magazine, 101
Enberg, Alexander, 419
Enberg, Dick, 419, 525
Enchanted Hills Playhouse, 518
Encino Man (1992), 120
End, The (1978), 492
End of Days (1999), 463
Enemy Below, The, 248
English, William H., xi
English Hotel (Indianapolis), xi, 469
English Theater (Indianapolis), xi, **xi**, xii, 142, 248
Enright, Ray, 211, 394, 535
Enright, Vern, 394
Envy (2004), 478
Epps, Mike, 263–64, **264**, 535
Epps, Tommy, 263
ER (television), 293, 518
Eric, Fred, 526, 536
Errol, Leon, 294
Escapist, The (1983), 522
ESPN, 437
Esquire Lounge (Dayton), 435
Essanay Company, 4, 31, 32
Eternal Hills Memorial Park (CA), 276
Eubie!, 467
Europe, James Reese, 468
Evangeline, 39
Evans, Augusta J., 316
Evans, Dale, 523
Evans, Madge, 523
Evans, Tom, 373
Evansville College, 276, 424. *See also* University of Evansville.
Evansville and Terre Haute Railroad, 140, 141
Eve of St. Mark, The, 259; 1944 film, **174–75**, 176

Even Break, An (1917), 385
Everett, Chad (Raymond Lee Cramton), 264–66, **265**, 525, 537
Everson, William K., 34, 347, 406
Everywoman, 4
Ev'ry Month (magazine), 423
Ewell, Tom, 501
Ex-Bad Boy (1931), 224
Excuse My Dust (1951), 309
Executive Suite (1954), 406
Eyes of the Underworld (1943), 288
Eyewitness (1981), 419
Eythe, William, **174–75**, 176
Ezra Buzzington and His All Rube Band, 449. *See also* Hoosier Hot Shots.

F Troop (television), 303, **303**
Fables in Slang (book), 420
Fabulous Baker Boys, The (1989), 410
Fairbanks, Douglas, 24, 65, 66, **67**, 133, 142, 148, 157, 205, 206, 207, 208, 396, 415, 476
Fairbanks, Douglas Jr., 75, 384
Falcon and the Snowman, The (1985), 296
Falk, Peter, 406
Falling from Grace (1992), **456**, 457, 522
Family Affair (television), 417
Family Ford, The, 168
Family Theater: Gary, 506; West Lafayette, 55
Family Ties (television), 473
Famous Artists, 384
Famous Ferguson Case, The, 214
Famous Players-Lasky, 205, 206, 423, 482
Famous Robinson Brothers, 462
Fancy Trimmings, 236
Fanny, 194
Fantasia (1940), 333, 338, 340
Fantasticks, The, 519
Far Country, The (1954), 373
Farewell to Shady Glade (children's book), 334
Farm Aid, 457
Farmer, Frances, 211, 309, 398, 438, 535
Farmer's Daughter (television), 445
Farney, Charles, 56
Farnum, Dustin, 411, 416, 522
Farnum, Franklyn, 238, 346
Farnum, William, 36, 37, 207, 211, 347
Fashionable Adventures of Joshua Craig, The (novel), 428
Fashions in Love (1929), 214, 238, **238**
Fast and Loose (1930), 150
Fat Jones Stables, 363
Fatal Vision (television), 506

Father Is a Bachelor (1950), 85
Father Knows Best: radio, 512; television, 447
Father of the Bride (television), 234
Father's Day, 246
Faye, Alice, 274, **274**, 275, 448
Fazenda, F. Nelda Schilling, 55, 58
Fazenda, Jose Altamar, 55, 57
Fazenda, Louise, 22, **28**, 31, **54–55**, 54–61, **56**, **57**, **58**, **59**, 65, 249, 278, 320, 383, 385, 394, 525, 538
FBI in Peace and War, The (radio), 258
FBO (studio), 323, 385, 391
Federal Theater Project, 278
Fellows, Rev. Albion, 426
Fellows, Albion, 426
Fellows, Mary Erskine, 425
Feminist and the Fuzz, The (television), 314
Ferber, Edna, 55, 115, 398
Ferguson, Bianca, 535
Ferguson, Mattie, 526, 535
Ferrar, Jose, 291
Ferrell, Jami, 527, 533
Festival of Indiana Music, 445
Fetchit, Stepin, **373**
Fiandt, Bev, 157
Fiandt, David, 157
Fibber McGee and Molly (radio), 90, 486
Field, Sally, 524
Field Kindley High School (KS), 312
Fields, Albert (Albert Jean Pierre Fields), 528, 534
Fields, Lew, 141, 142
Fields, Madelyn(e), 149–50, 157, 159, 163
Fields, Totie, **325**
Fields, W. C., 58, 131, 137, 160, 206, 267, 415
Fiest, George Byron, 109
Fifty Million Frenchmen, xi, 79, 209, 461
52nd Street (1937), 438
Fighting Shadows (1935), 294
Fighting Sheriff, The (1931), **349**
Fighting Stallion, The (1926), 378
Fighting Thru (1930), 209, 359
File on Thelma Jordon, The (1950), 240
Film Daily Yearbook, 383
Film Fun (magazine), 417
Filmcraft Pictures (studio), 285
Filson, Al W., 526, 539
Fine and Dandy, 249
Fine Madness, A (1966), 483
Fink, Hugh, 535
Fiquero Playhouse (Hollywood), 304
Fireball Fun for All, 82
Firefly (television), 271

First National (studio), 32, 37, 134, 276, 356, 358, 384, 385, 391, 417, 481, 482, 483
Fish Called Wanda, A (1988), 504, 516
Fisher, Margarita, 377
Fisher, Mary, 176
Fisk, Marilyn, 303
Fitzgerald, Geraldine, 387
Fitzmaurice, George, 208
Five and Ten (1931), **219**
Five Easy Pieces (1970), 493, 515
500 Pound Jerk, The (television), 279
Fixed Bayonets! (1951), 112
Flaherty, Robert, 17
Flambard's Confession (novel), 424
Flaming Disk (1920), 320
Flamingo Room (Terre Haute), 257
Flanigan, Bob, 435, **435**, 436, 537
Flash Gordon (1936), **284**, 285, **324**, 325
Fleischman's Hour (radio), 90
Fleming, Victor, 206, 207, 397
Flirtation Walk (1934), 272
Floradora, 38
Flory, Med, 528, 532
Flowing Gold (1940), 309
Flying A. *See* American Film Company.
Flying Colors, 137, 245
Flying High, 246, 307
Flynn, Errol, 373, 423
Fogle, Jared, 528
Foley, Red, 90, 369
Folger Theater (Washington, D.C.), 241
Follies, 491
Follies Mariguy (New York), 74
Follow the River: novel, 429; television, 419
Follow Your Heart (1936), 438
Fonda, Annabella, 208
Fonda, Henry, 189, 208, 289, 291, **477**
Fontaine, Joan, 299
Fool There Was, A (1915), 42
Fools' Parade (1971), **180**
Fools Rush In, 138
Footloose (1984), 457, 473
For Heaven's Sake (1950), 76, 402
For Me and My Gal (1942), 439
Foran, Dick, 297
Forbes, Sheila, 303
Ford, Harrison, **123**, 124, 410
Ford, John, 17, 189, 289, 386, 396, 412, 493, 495
Ford, Nancy, 413
Ford, Ross, 538
Fordson High School (Dearborn, MI), 264

Forest Lawn Cemetery (CA), 137, 163, 173, 208, 256, 360, 424
Forgive Me Father (2001), 300–301
Forgive Us Our Tresspasses (novel), 423
Forsythe, John, 98
Fort Benjamin Harrison (Indianapolis), 246
Fort Dodge Stampede (1951), 373
Fort Wayne Community Theater, 518
40 Guns to Apache Pass (1967), 376
Forty-eighth Street Playhouse (New York), 267
Forty-eighth Street Theater (New York), 21
42nd Street (1933), 276, 509
Forward Pass, The (1929), 365
Foster, Norman (Garland "Nick" Hoeffer), **83**, 83–85, **84**, **85**, 148, 153, 223, **266**, 267, 299, 312, 394, 522
Foster, Stephen, 444
Fountainhead, The (1949), 312
Four Columbians, 128
Four Daughters (1938), **225**, 226
Four Freshmen, 435, **435**, 436, 532
Four Friends (1981), 419, 522
Four Horsemen of the Apocalypse, The (1921), 23, **48–49**, 50, 51, 320
Four Ink Spots, 454. *See also* Ink Spots.
Four Mothers (1941), 226
Four Riff Brothers, 454
Four Star Playhouse (television), 509
Four Star Productions, 105, 509
Four Wives (1939), 226
Fourth Alarm, The (1930), 63
Fowler, Bill, 114, 116
Fox: studio, 37, 42, 43, 47, 65, 142, 148, 149, 150, 224, 347, 362, 365, 384, 385, 386, 391, 397, 398, 413, 438; television network, 201
Fox, Rick, 534
Fox, Sidney, 481
Fox, Vivica, **200**, 200–201, 311, 445, 520, 521, 535
Fox, William, 347
Fox Pantages Theater, 324
Foxtrap (1986), **118**
Frame, Fred, 397, 523
Francis the Talking Mule (1950), 367
Frankeheimer, John, 188, 408
Frankfort Distillers Corporation, 176
Frankie and Johnnie (1936), 462
Franklin College, 45, 167, 172, 259, 272, 404, 406, 421
Franklin (IN) Daily Journal (newspaper), 172
Fraser, Brendan, **119**, 119–21, **120**, **121**, 489, 518, 535

Fraser, Carol, 119

Fraser, Griffin Arthur, 121

Fraser, Holden Fletcher, 121

Fraser, Peter, 119

Frasier (television), 199

Frazee, Jane, 297

Freckles: novel, 429; 1928 film, 429; 1935 film, 429; 1960 film, 429

Freckles Comes Home (1942), 429

Freddie Rose's Song Shop (radio), 462

Frederick, Pauline, 22, 312

Free Willy 3: The Rescue (1997), **250**

Freed, Arthur, 234, 467

Freedman, Hy, 210

Freeman, Ada Mae, 480

Freeman, Earl, 337

Freeman, Ernest, 480

Freeman, Mona, **308**, 428, 523

Freeze Frame (1992), 522

French Line, The (1954), 415

Fresh Prince of Bel-Air, The (television), 200

Freshman, The (1925), 387

Fricke (Frickie), Janie, 446, 539

Friday After Next (2002), 264

Friday the 13th (1980), 191

Friday the 13th, Part 2 (1981), 191

Friday the 13th, Part 3 (1982), 191

Friday the 13th: The Final Chapter (1984), 191

Friedkin, William, 478

Friedman, Irving "Izzy," 446–47, 533

Friendly Persuasion: novel, 430; 1956 film, **171**, 430, 523

Friends of Mr. Sweeney: novel, 421; 1934 film, 421

Friermood, Glenn, 248

Froebel High School (Gary), 118

Frohman, Daniel, 278

Frolics of 1929, The, 43

From Dusk Till Dawn (1996), 118

From Here to Eternity (1953), 444, 490, 515

Frost, Robert, 270

Fugitive, The (television), 275, 409, 503

Fuhr, Charlie, 206

Fuller, Dolores (Eble), 447, **447**, 537

Fuller, Hector, 219

Fuller, Penny, 182

Fuller Brush Man, The (1948), 92

Fulton County (IN) Historical Society, 321

Fun and Fancy Free (1947), 340

Fun and Folly with Ed East and Polly (radio), 262

Funny Face (1957), 515

Funny Girl (1968), 448

Funny Lady (1975), 476

Funny Thing Happened on the Way to the Forum, A, 309, 314

Fuqua, Charlie, 453, 454. *See also* Ink Spots.

Furies, The (1950), 240

Gabet, Sharon, 296, 520, 532

Gable, Clark, **144–45**, 155, **156**, 157, 158, 160, 162, 163, 164, 371, 427, 480, 507, 522

Gable, John Clark, 164

Gaffigan, Jim, 528, 537

Gage, Mary Francis, 499

Gallagher, Anthony J. "Andy," 266

Gallagher, Margaret, 266

Gallagher, Pamela, 267

Gallagher, Richard "Skeets" (Anthony Richard Gallagher), 84, 148, 153, **266**, 266–67, 278, 348, 538

Gallagher, Richard Jr., 267

Gallagher, Sena Simmons, 266, 267

Galloping Dynamite (1937), 364

Galt, Maginel, 182, 183

Galt, Melissa, 182, 183, 184

Galt, Randolph, 181, 182

Galway, James, 453

Gam, Rita, 425

Gamble, Frederick, 377–78, 535

Game of Their Lives, The (2005), 418

Game Old Knight, A (1915), 56

Gandhi, Mahatma, 75

Gang Busters (radio), 291

Gang's All Here, The (1943), 438

Garber, David S., 526, 533

Garbo, Greta, 135, 428

Garden of Allah, The (1927), 52

Garden Theater (New York), 45

Gardner, Jack, 42, 142, 143

Garfield, John, 226

Garfield (comic strip), 413–14

Garfunkel, Art, 473

Garland, Judy, 234, 286, 412, 439, 464, 467, 507

Garner, James, 274

Garragan (1924), 67

Garrett (IN) Clipper (newspaper), 24

Garrettson, Frank, 183

Garrettson, Grace, 183

Gary Roosevelt High School, 98

Gather Ye Rosebuds (novel), 427

Gathering of One, A (television), 518

Gator (1976), 492

Gay Divorcee, The (1934), 137, 461

Gay Musician, The, 202

Gayety Burlesque Theater (Washington, D.C.), 301

Gayle, Crystal, 446, 539

Gaynor, Janet, 142

Gaynor, Mitzi, 295

Gebhart, Charles, 344

Gebhart, Evelyn Showers, 344

Geer, Ellen, 270

Geer, Raleigh, 270

Geer, Will (William Aughe), 233, 268–70, **269**, 343, 518, 522

Gelbart, Larry, 410

Gelms, Joan Reeves, 340

Gems of Poetry, 426

Gene Autry Show, The (television), 375

General Electric Theater, The (television), 97, 325

General Film Company, 482

General Hospital (television), 216, 276, 510, 519, 520

Generations (television), 200, 520

Gentleman from Indiana, The (1915), 411, 522

Gentlemen of the Press (1929), 83

Gentlemen Prefer Blondes, 314

George Burns and Gracie Allen Show, The (television), 308

George Gobel Show, The (television), 308

George of the Jungle (1997), 120, 518

George Washington Bullion Abroad, 472

George Washington High School (Indianapolis), 289

George Washington Slept Here (1942), 163, 258, 312

Georgia Brown Dramatic School, 312

Georgia Minstrels, 278

Geraghty, Carmelita, 66, 67, 148, **204–05**, 205, **207**, **208**, 208–09, **209**, 348, **355**, 359, 379, 387, 415, 481, 537

Geraghty, Gerald, 148, 205, 209–11, **210**, 415, 537

Geraghty, James, 205

Geraghty, Mary Lynch, 205

Geraghty, Maurice, 148, 205, 209–11, **210**, 391, 393, 415, 537

Geraghty, Sheila, 205, 209

Geraghty, Tom (Thomas Jefferson Geraghty), 67, 148, 205–08, 412, 415, 416, **416**, 537

Gerard, Jim, **190**

Gere, Richard, 296

Gertrude and Heathcliffe (Red Skelton book), 93

Getaway, The (1972), 106

Getting Personal (television), 201

Getz, Stan, 437, 439

Ghere, Catherine, 268

Ghere, Roy, 268

Ghost Busters, The (television), 303

Ghost Catchers (1944), 81, **81**, 476

Ghost of Zorro (1959), 375

Ghost-Town Gold (1936), 370

Ghosts, 232

Giant (1956), 106, 114, **115**, 116, 371, 515

Gibson, Charles Dana, 4, 277

Gibson, Hoot, 63, 347, 378, 391, 392

Gibson, James, 526, 537

Gibson, Mel, 99, 525

Gift, Donn, 534

Gift of Life, The, 266

Gilbert, Jack, 67

Gilbert, John, 26

Gilbert and Sullivan, 336

Gillespie, Dizzy, 455

Gilligan's Island (television), 328

Gillilan, Strick, xviii

Gingham Girl, The, 470

Gingold, Josef, 436–37

Girl and the Game, The (1915), 502

Girl Behind the Counter, The, 142

Girl from Havana, The (1929), 224

Girl from His Town, The (1915), 377

Girl in My Soup, A, 518

Girl Named Sooner, A (1975), 522

Girl of the Golden West, The (1938), **33**, 478

Girl of the Limberlost, A: novel, 429; 1934 film, 142, 429

Girl Shy (1924), 387

Girl with the Whooping Cough, The, 42

Girls, The (television), 426

Girls of Gottenberg, The, 142

Gish, Dorothy, 15

Gish, Lillian, 15, **15**, 16, 319

Glad Rag Doll, The (1929), **272**

Glass, Bonnie, 74

Glass, Lethia, 270

Glass, Montague, 142

Glass, Ron, 270–71, **271**, 538

Glass Key, The (1942), 246

Gleason, Jackie, 190

Gleason, James, 336

Glen or Glenda (1953), 447

Glorious Betsy, 272

Glory of His Country, The (novel), 426

Go Get 'Em, 236

Gobel, George, 275, 369

God Bless You, Mr. Rosewater (novel), 430

Gods and Monsters (1998), 121

Goin' to Town, 236

Going All the Way: novel, 430, 522; 1997 film, 430, 522

Gold and the Girl (1925), 149, 347

Gold Diggers of 1933 (1933), 276

Gold Rush, The (1925), 148
Goldbergs, The (1950), 299
Golden Boy, 104
Golden Chance, The (1915), 39
Golden Spiders, The: A Nero Wolfe Mystery (television), 429
Golden West College, 200
Goldsborough, Fitzhugh Colye, 428
Goldwyn, Samuel, 22, 39, 42, 169–70, 398, 495
Goldwyn Associated Distributors, 417
Goldwyn Pictures (studio), 22, 32, 37, 47, 385, 391, 412
Gombel, Minna, **277**
Gondalier, The, 213
Gone Harlem (1939), 236
Gone with the Wind (1939), 154, 158, 159, 389, 480
Good Advice (television), 198
Good Boy, 245
Good Guys Wear Black (1978), 275
Good Morning America (television), 419
Good Morning, Dearie, 132
Good News (1930), 224, 462
Good Night Ladies, 267
Good Scouts (1938), 339
Good Times (television), 270
Goodin, Peggy, 244, 424, 539
Gooding, Cuba Jr., **124**
Goodman, Benny, 441
Goodman, Greer, 527
Goodman, Jenniphr, 527
Goodman Theater (Chicago), 506
Goodrich, Edna, **38**, 38–39, **39**, 416, 532
Goodwin, Nat C., 38
Goodyear Playhouse (television), 189
Goofy Movie, A (1995), 314
Goose Hangs High, The, 83
Goose Woman, The (1925), 142
Gordon, Gordon, 424, 535
Gordon, Major Jonathan W., 272
Gordon, Maude Turner, 272, **272**, 534
Gordon, Mildred, 424
Gordon, Ruth, 309
Gorgeous Hussy, The (1936), 495, 515
Gorman, Rusty, 533
Gosden, Freeman, 237
Gossett, Christine, 234
Gotsch, Nathan, 530, 532
Gould, Billy, 41
Gould, Jay, 145
Goulding, Edmund, 180, 402
Governors, The, 141
Governor's Boss, The, 420
Grable, Betty, 274, **274**

Graham, Billy, 107
Graham, Heather, 524
Graham, Martha, 408, 486
Graham, Mona, 507
Grahame, Gloria, 501
Grand Army of the Republic (GAR), 12
Grand Hotel (1932), 135
Grand National (studio), 359
Grand Ole Opry, 449
Grand Opera House (Terre Haute), 256
Grand Prize, The, 189
Grand Theater (Evansville), 130, 142
Grand Theater (Indianapolis), xi, **xi**
Grand Theatre (Cleveland), 469
Grand Theft Auto: Vice City (video game), 464
Grant, Cary, **155**, 243, 304, 398, 523
Grant, Joe, 335, 336
Grant, Shelby, 266
Grapes of Wrath, The (1940), 495
Graser, Earle W., 401
Grauman, Sid, 142, 208, 476–77, **477**, 515, 525, 535
Graustark: novel, 427; 1915 film, 427; 1925 film, 427
Gray, Glen, 307, 454
Gray, Jerry, 436
Gray, Mark W. Jr., 530, 535
Grease, 314
Great Adventures of Wild Bill Hickok, The (1938), 393
Great American Broadcast, The (1941), 455
Great American Dream Machine, The (television), 419
Great American Fourth of July and Other Disasters, The (television), 429
Great Day in the Morning, 519
Great Divide, The (1925), 52
Great Escape, The (1963), **105**, 106, 107
Great Gatsby, The (1974), 483, 493
Great Gildersleeve, The (radio), 304
Great God Success, The (novel), 428
Great Impersonation, The (1935), 284
Great McGinty, The (1940), 32
Great Moment, The (1944), 32
Great Profile, The (1940), 178–79
Great Train Robbery, The (1903), 343
Great Vacuum Robbery, The (1915), 29
Great Western Producing Company, 319
Great Ziegfeld, The (1936), 138
Greatest, The (1977), 275
Greatest Thing in Life, The (1918), 319
Green, Eddie, 236
Green, Oliver "Slim," 454. *See also* Ink Spots.
Green Acres (television), 295, 480

Green Light: novel, 423; 1937 film, 423
Green Pastures, The, 98, 236, 248, 472
Greenleaf, Raymond, **261**
Greenwich Village Follies, 224
Gregory, Christopher, 530, 532
Gresham, Gloria, 477–78, **478**, 483, 515, 522, 535
Gresham, Stokes, 477
Gresham, Mrs. Stokes, 477
Grey, Zane, 211
Greyhound, 309
Grier, Pam, 118
Griffin, Francis "Frank" D., 498
Griffin, Merv, 496
Griffith, Corinne, 481
Griffith, D. W., 11, 13, 14, 15, 29, 316, 317, 383, 385
Griffith, Gordon, 318
Griffith, Harry, 526
Griffith, William M., 528
Grim Game, The (1919), 15
Grimm, Tim, 528, 532
Griswold, Claire, 410
Gross, Nancy "Slim," 399
Grossman, Joan, 531, 535
Group, The (television), 263
Group Theater (New York), 248, 506
Gruelle, Johnny (John Barton Gruelle), 499–500, 535
Gruelle, Marcella, 500
Gruelle, R. B., 499
Gruelle, Worth, 500
Guedel, John, 531, 534
Guest in the House, 234; 1944 film, 179
Guiding Light, The (television), 518, 520
Gumm, Dorothy, 464
Gumm, Walter, 535
Guns and Roses (band), 463
Gunsmoke (television), 232, 289, 367, 373, 377, 512
Gustin, Sheree, 519
Gutenberg, Steve, 522
Guthrie, Alfred Bertram Jr., 425, 515, 535
Guthrie, Wayne, 354, 362
Guthrie, Woody, 268
Gwenn, Edmund, 402
Gypsy, 314

Haboush, Victor, 338
Hackett, Bobby, 442
Hackman, Gene, 522
Hadleigh, Boze, 168, 169

Hagemeier, Dorothy West, 87, 88
Hagen, Jean (Jean Shirley Verhagen), **89**, **500**, 500–02, **501**, 515, 525, 533
Hagen (television), 266
Hagenbeck-Wallace Circus, 355, 356
Haggard, Merle, 446
Hahn, Jess, 529, 538
Hail the Conquering Hero (1944), 32
Haines, Rhea, 526
Haines, Robert T., 291, 428, 526, 529, 533
Haines, William, 522
Hair (1979), 486
Hal Roach Studios, 493
Hale, Monte, 211
Half a Hero (1953), **89**, **501**
Hall, Adelaide, 464, 468
Hall, Al, 227
Hall, Arsenio, 201
Hall, Dan T., 531, 535
Hall, Gladys, 153, 164
Hall, Ruth, 362
Hal's Harmonizers. *See* Four Freshmen.
Hamid-Morton Circus, 18
Hamill, Mark, 491–92
Hamilton, Boa, 28
Hamilton, Neil, 188
Hamilton School of Dramatic Expression, 167
Hammerstein, Cliff, 266
Hammerstein, Oscar II, 134
Hammerstein's Victoria Theater (New York), 42
Hampden, Walter, **187**, 188
Hampton, Slide, 451
Hancock, Don, 518
Hancock, John D., 522
Hand of Uncle Sam, The (1910), 4
Hanging Tree, The (1959), 483
Hanks, Tom, **197**, 522
Hanley, James Frederick, 448, 534
Hanley, Michael E., 526, 532
Hanley, Michael R., 535
Hanlon, Robert, 227
Hannie Caulder (1971), 290
Hann's Jubile Singers, 465
Hanover College, 175
Hansel, Howell, 531
Hansel and Gretel, 74
Hanson, Blanche Bennett, 220, 221
Happiest Girl in the World, The, 519
Happy Birthday, Wanda June: play, 430; 1971 film, 430
Happy Campers (2001), 419
Happy Landing (1938), 438, 512
Harbach, Otto, 134

Hardcase (television), 279

Harding, Bertita (Bertita Carla Camille Leonarz), 425, 535

Harding, Jack Ellison de, 425

Harding, Warren G., 479

Hardy, Bob, 448

Harlem Is Heaven (1932), 236

Harlem Nights (1989), 293

Harlow, Jean, 155, 209

Harmon, Tom, 529, 534

Harmony Trail (1944), 359, 370

Harold Robbins' 79 Park Avenue (television), 275

Harper's Weekly (magazine), 426

Harpoon (1948), 240

Harrelson, Woody, 522

Harriman, Hope, 532

Harriman, William, 282

Harris, Dollie Wright, 273

Harris, Harry, 273

Harris, John, 472

Harris, Julie, 189, 194

Harris, Marion, 462

Harris, Phil (Wonga Phil Harris), 254, 256, 272–75, **273**, **274**, 301, 334, 433, 484, 487, 515, 525, 533

Harrison, Benjamin, 145

Harrison, Nate, 451. *See also* Hoosier Hot Shots.

Harrison, Richard B., 236

Harry Houdini and Keaton Medicine Show Company, 281

Hart, Lorenz, 497

Hart, Moss, 98, 137

Hart, Sunshine (Lucia Hart), 208, 387, 527, 535

Hart, William S., 344, 347, 349, 360, 365, 366, 385, 391, 412

Hartford, Dee, 399

Harvard University, 296

Harvard University Law School, 460

Harvester, The (novel), 429

Harvey, Ed, 62, 63

Harvey Hart Players, 373

Hasbro, 500

Hastings, Aimee Raisch, 221

Hatch, Dr. Paul, 215

Hatcher, Richard, 228

Hathaway, Anne, 421

Hathaway, Henry, 24, 25, 159

Hatton, Raymond, 344

Haunted Trails (1949), 386

Haunting Shadows (1920), 427

Havana (1990), 484

Have a Heart, 142

Have Gun–Will Travel (television), 232, 289

Haver, June, 139

Haviland Theater (Cincinnati), 27

Having Wonderful Time (1938), 90

Hawaii Calls, 243

Hawaiian Eye (television), 252

Hawkins (television), 289

Hawkins Falls (television), 187

Hawks, David, 399

Hawks, Frank Winchester, 395

Hawks, Grace Louise, 395

Hawks, Gregg, 399

Hawks, Helen Bernice, 295

Hawks, Helen Howard, 395

Hawks, Howard, xi, xii, 149, 153, 154, 159, 206, 284, 348, 383, 395–400, **396**, **398**, **399**, 427, 441, 516, 523, 525, 533

Hawks, Kenneth, 149, 383, 384, 395–400, **397**, 533

Hawks, William Bellinger, 395, 397

Hay, George D., 529, 533

Hay, Mary, 75

Hayes, Bill, 82, 194

Hayes, Helen, 176, 403, 495

Hayes, Isaac, 459

Hayes, Joseph, 425, 523, 535

Hayes, Marrijane Johnston, 425, 523

Hayes, Rutherford B., 145

Hayes, W. Donn, 478, **478**, 539

Hayloft Frolic (television), 448

Haymes, Dick, 304

Haynes, Lloyd (Samuel Lloyd Haynes), **275**, 275–76, 520, 537

Hays, Robert, 519

Hays, Will H., 44, 160, **160**, 161, **479**, 479–80, 525, 538

Hayward, Grace, 526, 538

Hayward, Leland, 189

Hayward, Susan, 509

Hayworth, Rita (Rita Cansino), 252, 370, 379, 418, 444, **477**, 523

Hazards of Helen, The (1914), 502

HBO, 264

Hear That Trumpet, 464

Hearst, William Randolph, 67, 405

Hearst Publishing Syndicate, 44

Heart of the Rockies (1937), **372**

Heart of the Yukon, The (1927), **20–21**, 22

Heartland Film Festival, 507

Hearts and Sparks (1916), 238

Hearts and Spurs (1925), **147**, 149, 347, **348**

Hearts Are Trumps (1920), 50

Hearts of the World (1918), 317

Heater-Quigley Productions, 275

Heather Field, The, 278

Heathers (1989), 419

Heatter, Gabriel, 421

Heavenly Days (1944), 500

Hecht, Ben, 153, 427

Heinzerling, Thais, 21

Held, Anna, 41

Hell Bound (1931), 224

Heller, Franklin, 188

Heller, Grena, 218

Hellman, Lillian, 258

Hello Broadway, 142

Hello Dolly!, 314

Hellzapoppin: 81; 1941 film, **80**, 81, 297

Helms, Bobby, 448–49, 536

Helms Brothers, 448

Hemingway, Mariel, **456**

Henabery, Joseph, 383

Henderson, Dell, 28

Henderson, Eugene, 406

Henderson, Fletcher, 253

Henderson, Florence, 190, **192**, 192–95, **193**, 525, 538

Henderson House (Terre Haute), 280

Henie, Sonja, 285

Henning, Betty, 297

Henri, Robert, 73

Henry, Charlotte, **85**

Henry Miller Theater (New York), 177

Hepburn, Audrey, 481

Hepburn, Katharine, 154, 177, 294, 398, 411

Hepburn, Ralph, 397, 523

Her Husband's Honor (1918), 39, 416

Her Majesty, Love (1931), **126–27**, **136**, 137

Her Majesty the Widow, 312

Her Second Chance (1926), **29**

Her Wild Oat (1927), 67

Herb Shriner Show, The (television), 510

Herb Shriner Time (television), 510

Hercules (1997), 484

Here Come the Nelsons (1952), **374**

Here Comes the Groom (1951), 442, 515

Here We Go Again (1942), 487

Here's Lucy (television), 253

Herman, Woody, 454

Herriman, George, 335

Hershberger, Kevin, 529, 535

Hershey, Barbara, 522

Hersholt, Jean, 238

Hess, Mary Jane, 87

Heston, Charlton, 183

Hiatt, John, 535

Higgins, Joe, 529, 532

High, Wide, and Handsome (1937), 309

High and the Mighty, The (1954), 274

High Lonesome (1950), 244

High Society (1956), 461, 516

Higher and Higher (1943), 387, 389

Highland Lawn Cemetery (Terre Haute), 44

Hilda Crane, 495

Hill, Dru, 445

Hill, George Roy, 188, 289

Hill, James, 529, 532

Hill, Nellie, 467

Hill, Shirley, 111

Hill, Sue, 111

Hill Street Blues (television), 200, 311

Hiller, Arthur, 478

Hilliard, Harriet, 297

Hillyer, Lambert, 211, 347, 375, 381, **385**, 385–86, 537

Hi-Lo Country, The (1998), 469

Hilton, James, 304

Hilton, Lester, 367

Hirschlag, Allison, 518

Hirschlag, Dr. Richard, 518

His Girl Friday (1940), 154, 398

His Kind of Woman (1951), 247

His Last Laugh (1916), 238

His Night Out (1935), 284

His Precious Life (1917), 57

His Unlucky Job (1921), 394

Historic Indiana. See *Indiana*.

Hit Parade of 1937 (1937), 370

Hit Parade of 1941 (1940), 438, 515

Hit the Deck, 365

Hitchcock, Alfred, 159, 178, **183**, 208, 248, 279, 478

Hitchcock, Betty, 303

Hitchy-Koo of 1919, 461

Hixon, Ken, 529, 536

H. Lieber Company, 482

H. M. S. Pinafore, 83

Hodge, Martha, 291

Hodges, Gil, 190

Hodiak, John, 179, **184**

Hodiak, Katrina, 179, 183–84

Hoeffer, Blanche Cummins, 83

Hoeffer, C. Foster, 83

Hoeffer, Rev. Charles W., 83

Hoffman, Dustin, **409**, 410, 483, 522

Hogestyn, Drake, 199, 519, 520, 532

Hold Your Horses, 249
Holden, William, 124, **402**
Holiday, Billie, 442
Holiday Gourmet (television), 453
Hollenbeck, Eliza A. Nichols, 72
Hollenbeck, Ethel Brown, 72
Hollenbeck, Jacob Grant, 71, 72
Hollenbeck, Jacob Wesley, 72
Hollenbeck, James P., 72
Holliday, Judy, 181, 501
Hollywood Chamber of Commerce, 320
Hollywood Forever Memorial Park, 77, 209
Hollywood Hi, 243
Hollywood High School, 208
Hollywood Hotel: radio, 304; 1937 film,
     226, 257
Hollywood Memorial Cemetery, 321–22
Hollywood Playhouse, 304
Hollywood Screen Test (television), 188
Hollywood Spectator (newspaper), 169
Hollywood Squares (television), 314
Holman, Libby, 75, 76
Holmes, Helen, 378, 502, **502**, 537
Holmes, Phillips, 427, 479
Holt, Jack, 63, 211, 284
Holy Cross Cemetery (Hollywood), 267
Holy Family Adoption Services, 247
Home for Christmas (novel), 423
Home in Indiana (1944), 258, 523
Home of the Brave (1949), 96
Home Towners, The (1928), 221
Homecoming, The: A Christmas Story (television), 260,
     260
Homeier, Skip, 189
Homer Peavey's Jazz Bandits, 442
Homestretch, 328
Homicide: Life on the Street (television), 293
Honey Girl, 470
Honeymoon in Vegas (1992), 457
Honeymoon Lane, 448
Honolulu Lu (1941), **302**
Honor of the Range (1934), **357**
Hoofbeats (radio), 350, **351**
Hooper (1978), 492
Hoop-La (1933), 427
Hoosier Holiday (1943), 523
Hoosier Hot Shots, 369, 448–51, **450**, 523
Hoosier Romance, A (1918), 523
Hoosier Schoolboy (1937), 424, 523
Hoosier Schoolboy, The (novel), 424
Hoosier Schoolmaster, The: 1914 film, 424, 522; 1924
     film, 424, 522; 1935 film, 84, **85**, 424, 522

Hoosiers (1986), 418, 522
Hoover, Herbert, 307
Hope, Anthony, 277
Hope, Bob, 92, 246, 412, 508
Hopkins, Anthony, 425, 523
Hopkins, Miriam, 59, 159, 278
Hopper, Dennis, 522
Hopper, DeWolf, 142
Hopper, Hedda, 67, 116, 142
Horne, Lena, 464, **466**, 467
Horse Feathers (1932), 325
Horse Fever, 215
Horton, Robert, 328
Hosford, Maude, 526, 538
Hot Chocolates, 236
Hot Water (1924), 387
Hotel (television), 183
Hotel Deming (Terre Haute), 41
Hotel Universe, 232
Hotel Washington (Indianapolis), 79
Hotwire (1980), 290
Houdini, Harry, 15, 281
Houghton Mifflin (publisher), 423
Hour of the Gun (1967), 232
House Divided, A, 168; 1931 film, 168
House of a Thousand Candles, The: novel, 427; 1915 film,
     427; 1936 film, 427
House of Lies, The (1916), 39
House Party (radio), 262
House Un-American Activities Committee, 96
Houseman, John, 268, 270, 278, 279, 504
Houston, Whitney, 445
Hovey, Alvin J., 276
Hovey, Alvin Peterson, 276
Hovey, Ann (Anna), **276**, 276–77, 481, 537
How Dear to My Heart (book), 426
How the West Was Won: television, 484; 1962 film, 515
How to Lose a Guy in Ten Days (2003), 293
How's the King?, 249
Howard, Bob, 467
Howard, C. W., 395
Howard, Leslie, 158, 304
Howard Roosa Elementary School (Evansville), 293
Howland, Jobyna, **277**, 277–78, 536
Howland, Olin, 278
Hoxie, Jack, 378, 391
Hrunek, Jack, 186, 191
Hrunek, Marie Love, 186
Hrunek, Rudolph Vincent, 186
Hubbard, Bruce, 529, 536
Hubbard, Frederick "Freddie" DeWayne, 451–52,
     536

Hubbard, Kin (Frank McKinney Hubbard), xii, 205
Hubert, Hugh, 376
Hubert's Hair-Raising Adventure (children's book), 334
Hudson, Rock, 116, 117, **177**, **282**, 423, 508
Hudson Hawk (1991), 417, 419
Hudsucker Proxy, The (1994), 524
Huemer, Richard, 335
Huge Harold (children's book), 334
Hulda of Holland (1916), 21
Hull, Henry, 503
Hulman, Tony, 274
Hume-Fogg High School (TN), 273
Hunchback of Notre Dame, The (1939), 320, 389, 405
Hunt, Helen, 125
Hunt, Marsha, 312
Hunted, The (2003), 478
Hunter, Jeffrey, 373
Hunter (television), 310
Hunter, The (1980), **100–01**, 102, 106
Hunting of the Snark, The (television), 473
Huntington Business College, 21
Hurst, Fannie, 44, 226
Husband's Story, The (novel), 428
Husey, Robert, 276
Hustler, The (1961), 291, **292**
Huston, John, 247
Huston, Walter, 236, 312, 495
Hutchins, Scott Andrew, 529, 536
Hutton, Bill, 529, 538
Hutton, Roy, 453
Hutton, Sylvia Kirby, 450, **452**, 452–53, 534
Hutton, Timothy, 429
Hyer, Martha, 60

I, The Jury (1982), 518
I Cover Chinatown (1936), 84
I Dood It (1943), **90**
I Love Lucy (television), 253, 261, 371, 415
I Remember Mama: play, 197, 232; 1948 film, 499, 515
I Spy (television), 328
I Want to Live! (1958), 406, 517
Ice-Capades (1941), 415
Ice Cube, 264
Ice Man Cometh, The, 248
Idler, The (1914), 272
I'll Show You the Town: novel, 421; 1925 film, 421
I'm Getting My Act Together and Taking It on the Road (play), 413
Immigrant, The (1915), 42

Immoralist, The, 114, 258
Importance of Being Earnest, The, 76
In and Out (1997), 524
In the Company of Men (1997), 522
In the Days of the Thundering Herd (1914), 21, 379
In the House (television), 200
In Old Santa Fe (1934), 358, 359, 369
Ince, Thomas, 49, 391
Ince (studio), 32, 49, 50, 385, 394
Independence Day (1996), 200
Indiana (1916), 522–23
Indiana Arts Commission, 271
Indiana Central University, 520
Indiana Historical Society, 523
Indiana Roof Ballroom (Indianapolis), 467
Indiana Soldiers' and Sailors' Orphans Home, 11, 148
Indiana State Baptist Convention Auxiliary, 95
Indiana State Fair, 88, 93, 250, 332
Indiana State Teachers College. *See* Indiana State University.
Indiana State University, 295, 502
Indiana Theater (Indianapolis), 267, 481–82, 509
Indiana University, 95, 186, 201, 232, 233, 241, 248, 256, 259, 262, 266, 292, 323, 326, 362, 364, 415, 417, 418, 419, 427, 428, 436, 440, 446, 477, 485, 490, 499, 504, 511, 512, 522, 523
Indiana University–Purdue University Indianapolis, 216, 419, 520
Indianapolis Civic Theater, 437
Indianapolis Freeman (newspaper), 471
Indianapolis Motor Speedway, 274, 345, 496, 522, 523
Indianapolis News (newspaper), 9, 12, 130, 131, 161, 299, 303, 344, 354, 359, 362, 417
Indianapolis Press Club, 90
Indianapolis Speedway (1939), 397, 523
Indianapolis Star (newspaper), 60, 143, 161, 219, 252, 274, 284, 285, 365, 419, 499
Indianapolis Star Magazine, 55
Indianapolis Sun (newspaper), 499
Indianapolis Symphony Orchestra, 451
Indianapolis Times (newspaper), 14
Ingram, Rex (Reginald Ingram Montgomery Hitchcock), 49, 50, 51, **51**, 52, 53, 157
Ink Spots, 453–55, **454**
Inn, Frank, 480–81, 537
Inner Sanctum (radio), 291
Innocents Abroad, The, 430; television, 430
Intermission (memoir), 182
Intolerance (1916), 14, 15, 317, 318

Invasion of the Body Snatchers, The (1956), 261
Invisible Ray, The (1936), 386
Irene, 497
Ironside (television), 310
Irreconcilable Differences (1984), 198
Irving, Dick, 409
Irwin, Bill, 120
Is Everybody Happy? (1943), 438
Island of Lost Souls (1933), 242–43
Island of Lost Souls, The (novel), 242
Isn't It Romantic? (1948), 428, 523
It Grows on Trees (1952), **498**, 499, **503**
It Happened on Ice, 250
It Happened One Night (1934), 154, 159, 447
It Happened Tomorrow (1944), 298
It Pays to Advertise (1931), 84, 153, **266**, 267
It Pays to Sin, 233
It Runs in the Family (1994), 429, 524
It's a Wonderful Life (1946), 495
It's Alive III: Island of the Alive (1987), 493
It's the Old Army Game (1926), 206
I've Got a Secret (television), 188, 189, 190
Ives, Burl, 268, **502**, 502–03, 523, 538

Jack and Old Mac (1956), 338
Jack O'Grady and the Varsity Entertainers, 256
Jackpot Jitters (1949), 262
Jackson, Jackie, 230
Jackson, Janet, **228**, 230, 525, 534
Jackson, Jermaine, 230
Jackson, Joseph, 228, 230
Jackson, Katherine, 228
Jackson, LaToya, 230
Jackson, Laura Corinne, 282
Jackson, Marlon, 229
Jackson, Michael, 228, 230, 433, 525, 534
Jackson, Orin, 538
Jackson, Randy, 230
Jackson, Rebbie, 230
Jackson, Tito, 230
Jackson Five, 228–30, **229**, **230**, 534
Jackson White, 168
Jacksons, The, 525
Jade, 43
Jagger, Albert, 503
Jagger, Dean, 499, **503**, 503–04, 516, 525
Jamaica Inn (1939), 389
James, Harry, 257, 454
James at 15: novel, 430; television, 430
James Dean Foundation, 306

James Reese Europe's Society Orchestra, 466
Jane Austen in Manhattan (1980), 179
Jane Wyman Theater (television), 312
Janice Meredith (1924), 356
Jarnegan, 221
Jay and Kai, 455
Jazz (2001), 242
Jazz Contemporaries, 449
Jazz Nocturne (television), 257
Jazz Singer, The (1927), xii, 465
J. Edgar Hoover (television), 260
Jealousy (1916), 43
Jean, Gloria, 476
Jenkins, Amasa, xvii, xviii
Jenkins, Atwood, xvii, xviii
Jenkins, C. Francis, **xvii**, xvii–xvix
Jesse James (1927), 325
Jesse L. Lasky Feature Play Company. *See* Lasky Company.
Jessie Bonstelle stock company, 401
Jesus, the Complete Story (television), 242
Jigsaw (1949), 291
Jim Jam Jems, 448
Joan of Lorraine, 232
Joan the Woman (1917), 65
Joe Porter's Serenaders, 465–66
Joel (novel), 426
John, Joyce, 111
John Golden Theater (New York), 114
John Herron Art Institute, 332, 333, 335, 337, 339, 340
John Herron Art Museum, 333
John Houseman Acting Company, 504
John Robinson Circus, 27
Johnny Apollo (1940), 247
Johnny Belinda (1948), 483, 516
Johnny Comes Flying Home (1946), 252
Johnny Eager (1942), 258
Johnny Holiday (1949), 522
Johnny Ringo (television), 509
Johnson, Chic, 79, **79**, 80, 82, 209
Johnson, Chubby (Charles Randolph Johnson), 366, **368**, **373**, 373–74, **374**, 376, 538
Johnson, Eric, 480
Johnson, James Louis "J. J.," 455, 457, 536
Johnson, June, 82
Johnson, Marilyn, 303
Johnson, Paul, 256
Johnson, Van, 191
Johnson, William L., 529, 534
Johnston, Annie Fellows, 425–26, 538
Johnston, John Leroy, 481, 533

Johnston, Julanne, 62, **65**, 65–67, **66**, **67**, **68**, 394, 481, 536
Johnston, Marrijane. *See* Hayes, Marrijane Johnston.
Johnston, Will, 426
Joker Comedies, 56
Jolley, Sandra, 303
Jolson, Al, xii, 24, 43, 74, 140, 250, 463
Jolson Sings Again (1949), 291, 444, 515
Jones, Anissa, 527, 538
Jones, Buck (Charles Frederick Gebhart), 22, 109, **147**, 148, 149, 163, **204–05**, 207, 209, 214, **215**, 284, 343, **344**, 344–53, **346**, **348**, **349**, **350**, **351**, **352**, 354, 356, 359, 365, 375, 385, 386, 393, 416, 483, 525, 534
Jones, Dell (Odille Dorothy Osborne), 345, 346, 347, 348, 350, 351, **351**, 352
Jones, Forrest, 285–86
Jones, Grover, 206, 415–16, 516, 538
Jones, James Earl, 98
Jones, Jennifer (Phyllis Isley), 370, 379
Jones, Ken D., 366
Jones, L. Q., 295
Jones, Maxine, **351**
Jones, Orville "Hoppy," 453, 454, 455. *See also* Ink Spots.
Jones, Phil, 533
Jones, Philly Joe, 451
Jones, Quincy, 451
Jones, Ralph, 206
Jones, Spike, 451. *See also* Hoosier Hot Shots.
Jordan, Jeremy (Donald Henson), 529, 535
Jordan, Jim, 487
Jordan, Marian, 487, 500
Jordan, William, 529, 537
Jory, Victor, 293
Joslin, Margaret, 32
Jourdan, Louis, 114
Journey into Fear (1943), 85, 222
Joy, Jimmy, 256
Joy Riding (1910), 31
Joyce, Peggy Hopkins, 249
Joyce Jordan, Girl Intern (radio), 291, 518
Juarez (1939), 425
Jubliee, 461
Judge (magazine), 417
Judge, The (1916), 57
Judge Horton and the Scottsboro Boys (television), 418
Judith of Bethulia (1914), 317
Juggling Barretts, The, 249
Julia Allen Wild West Show, 345, 346
Julius Caesar, 232

Julliard School of Music, 224, 504
Junction 88 (1947), 467
June Moon, 83
Jungle Book, The (1967), 274, 334, 516
Jungle Mystery (1932), 209
Jupiter Theater (Florida), 492
Jurgeson, Joan, 279
Just Around the Corner (1938), 438
Just Life, 83
Just Off Broadway (1929), 63
Justice, Bill, 337–38, 536
Justice, Maibelle Heikes, 39, 347, 416, 532
Justice for Disney (autobiography), 338
Juwanna Mann (2002), 251

KABC (television), 297
Kaiser, the Beast of Berlin, The (1918), 317
Kalem Pictures, 378, 502
Kallen, Kitty, 464
Kaltenborn, H. V., 421
Kane, Bob, 386
Kapp Records, 449
Kappas, Dr. John, 194
Karaszewski, Larry, 416–17, 419, 537
Karloff, Boris, 98, 323, 386, 481
Karras, Alex, 279, **279**, 534
Katterjohn, Monte, 206, 539
Kaufman, Al, 148
Kaufman, Rita, 148
Kay Kyser's Kollege of Musical Knowledge (radio), 444
Kaye, Danny, 250
Kazan, Chris, 293
Kazan, Elia, 95–96, 114, 116, 293, 418, 506
KBS World Wide (studio), 358
Keaton, Buster, 92, 119, 250, 280, **280**, 281, 282, 387
Keaton, Harry, 281
Keaton, Joe (Joseph Hallie Keaton), **280**, 280–82, **281**, 538
Keaton, Joseph Z., 280
Keaton, Libbie, 280
Keaton, Louise Dresser, 281
Keaton, Michael, 511
Keaton, Myra Cutler, 281
Keefe, Lenore, 527, 536
Keel, Howard, 423
Keeler, Ruby, 509
Keenan, Harry, 526, 539
Keene, Tom, 211
Keeper of the Bees (novel), 429
Keighley, William, 312

Keith, Benjamin F., 41
Keith, Donald, 63
Keith, Robert (Robert Keith Richey), **282**, 282–83, 532
Keith-Orpheum vaudeville circuit, 80, 261
Keith's Theater (Indianapolis), 298
Kekionga Junior High School (Fort Wayne), 195
Kelly, George, 309
Kelly, Grace, 402, **402**
Kelly Kelly (television), 198–99, 519
Keneally, Mel, 397, 523
Kennedy, Adam, 529, 532
Kennedy, Arthur, **373**, 425
Kennedy, Edgar, 29
Kennedy, John F., 323
Kennedy, Joseph P., 323
Kennedy Center (Washington, D.C.), 241
Kenny, Bill, 454, 455. *See also* Ink Spots.
Kenny, Herb, 455. *See also* Ink Spots.
Kent, Barbara, 63
Kent, Dick, 508
Kenton, Stan, 435, 436
Kentuckian, The (1955), 425
Kercheval, Ken, 521, 529, 537
Kerlin, Ida Shaffer, 140
Kerlin, William S., 140, 141
Kern, Jerome, xii, 132, 134, 142, 245, 497
Kerouac, Jack, 430
Kerr, Brook, 520, 536
Kerr, E. (Elaine) Katherine, 527, 536
Kerrigan, Edward, 9
Kerrigan, J. Warren, **2–3**, 2–9, **4**, **5**, **6**, **7**, 206, 392, 393, 413, 427, 533
Kerrigan, John, 3, 6
Kerrigan, Kathleen (Catherine), 3–4, 6, 9, 533
Kerrigan, Robert, 9
Kerrigan, Sarah McLean, 3, 4, 7, 8
Kerrigan, Wallace, 3, 4, 9, 392, 393, 533
Kettering, Frank Delaney, 449, 450–51. *See also* Hoosier Hot Shots.
Kettles on Old MacDonald's Farm, The (1957), 173
Key Largo (1948), 18, **18**
Keystone (studio), 32, 47, 56, 57, 149
Keystone Cops, 29, 32, 80
KGB (radio), 307
KGER (radio), 297
Kid, The (1921), 320
Kid from Brooklyn, The (1946), 416
Kid from Spain, The (1932), 276
Kid Galahad (1962), 447
Kid Rock, 458
Kid Sister, The (1927), 62

Kilbride, Percy, **166**, 168, 170
Kiley, Richard, 189
Kilgallen, Dorothy, 116
Kill Bill: Vol. 1 (2003), 210
Kill Bill: Vol. 2 (2004), 201
Killers, 258
Killers, The (1946), 310
Killer's Club, The (television), 188
Killing of Sister George, The, 518
Kimbrough, Charles, 191
Kimbrough, Emily, 191, 426, **426**, 533
King, Henry, 52
King, John "Dusty," 370
King, Stephen, 532
King and Four Queens, The (1956), 371
King and I, The, 190
King, Jack, and Jester(s), 454
King of Dodge City (1941), 211
King of Jazz, The (1930), 447
King of Kings, The (1927), 44
King of the Jungle (1927), 320
King Solomon's Mines (film), 328
Kinnear, Edward, 122
Kinnear, Greg, **122**, 122–25, **123**, **124**, 410, 516, 532
Kinnear, Lily, 125
Kinnear, Suzanne, 122
Kinsey, Dr. J. H., xviii
Kinzer, William, 504
Kipling, Rudyard, 42
Kirby, Sylvia. *See* Hutton, Sylvia Kirby.
Kirk, Dave, 295
Kirk, Hector, 523
Kiss Me, Kate, 461
Kiss the Blood Off My Hands (1948), 85, 299
Kit Carson's Buffalo Ranch Wild West Show, 355
Klee, David "Duke," 183
Klein, Chris, 524
Kline, Greta, 504
Kline, Kevin, 427, 504–06, **505**, 516, 521, 524, 525, 536
Kline, Owen, 504
Klugman, Jack, 188
KMIC (radio), 307
KMTR (radio), 297, 307
Knickerbocker Holiday, 236
Knickerbocker Theater: Nashville, TN, 273; New York, 142
Knight, Bobby, 275, 522
Knight, Charlie, 145
Knight, Fuzzy, **363**
Knots Landing (television), 191, 520

Knott, Clara, 526
Knott, Lydia, 379, 385, 536
Knowles, Patrick, 428
Knox, Elwood, 471
Knoxville College, 95
Knudsen, Jeanne, 356
KNX (radio), 307
KNXT (television), 371
Kohner, Susan, 423
Kojak (television), 232
Kole, Doc, 218
Kolker, Henry, **52**
Korda, Alexander, 214, 389
Korda, Vincent, 214
Korda, Zolton, 214, 389
Kortlander, Max, 439
Korty, John, 516, 531, 538
Koster and Bial's Music Hall (New York), xviii
Kotch (1971), 232
K-PAX: novel, 420; 2001 film, 420
K-PAX III: The Worlds of Prot (novel), 420
Krafft, John W., 417, 536
Kraft Television Theater (television), 189, 232, 248
Kramer, Stanley, 96
Krasna, Norman, 158–59
Kratzsch, Hal, 435, **435**, 436, 534
Krazy Kat (comic strip), 335
Krebs, Annabelle, 168
Krebs, Dr. Stanley LeFevre, 168, 169
Kruger, Otto, 312
Krupa, Gene, 441, 442
KTAR (radio), 417
KTLA (television), 289
Kyser, Kay, 444, 507

L. A. Law (television), 251
Labdon, Helen, 125
Ladd, Alan, 242, 246, 247, 261, 523
Laddie (novel), 429
Ladies Be Seated (radio), 262
Ladies in Lavender (2004), 437
Ladies of Washington (1944), **298**
Ladies' Man (1931), 152
Lady and Gent (1932), 516
Lady and the Tramp (1955), 338, 487
Lady by Choice (1934), 309
Lady Eve, The (1941), 32
Lady for a Night (1942), 415
Lady of Burlesque (1943), 312
Lady Takes a Chance, A (1943), 298
Laemmle, Carl, 6

Lafayette (IN) Call (newspaper), 420
Lafayette (IN) High School, 32
Lafayette (IN) Jefferson High School, 492
Lafayette Players Stock Company, 236
Lafayette Theater (New York), 472
Laff Capades of 1959, 313
Laffing Room Only, 81
LaFleur, Art, 529, 534
Lait, Jack, 142
Lake, Veronica, 428, 523
Lamb, Arthur J., 470
Lamb, Brian, 538
Lamour, Dorothy, 423
Lancaster, Burt, 299, 310, 408, **512**
Lancer (television), 260
Landes, Grace, 240
Landis, Carole, 370, 379
Landis, Forrest, 529, 536
Landis, Frederick, 426, 532
Lane, Allen "Rocky," 211, 234, 343, **365**, 365–68, **366**, **367**, **368**, 370, 373, 375, 376, 537
Lane, Leota (Leota Mullican), 224, **224**, 226, 227, 536
Lane, Lola (Dorothy Mullican), 224, **224**, **225**, 226, 227, 257, 284, 536
Lane, Priscilla (Priscilla Mullican), 224, **224**, **225**, 226, 227, 257
Lane, Rosemary (Rosemary Mullican), 224, **224**, **225**, 226, 227, 257
Lang, June, 286
Langdon, Harry, 387
Langdon's Legacy (1916), 7, 427
Lange, Eddie, 447, 464
Langford, Edward T., 526
Langford, Frances, 438, **478**
Langham, Rhea, 155, 157
Langtry, Lily, xii
Laramie (television), 328
La Redd, Cora, 467
Lardner, Ring, 206
Laredo (television), 417
Lariat Kid, The (1929), 63
Larwill (IN) High School, 503
Las Vegas Hillbillys, The (1966), 469
Las Vegas Show, 314
Laserhawk (1997), 300
Lasky, Blanche, 42
Lasky, Jesse, 39, 42, 205, 423
Lasky Company, 39, 42, 49
Lass of the Lumberlands, The (1916), 378, 502
Lassie (television), 312
Last Angry Man, The (1959), 189

Last Castle, The (2001), 519
Last Outpost, The (1935), 243
Last Sweet Days of Isaac, The (play), 413
Last Trail, The (1927), **207**
Late Night with Conan O'Brien (television), 437
Later Today (television), 194
Later with Greg Kinnear (television), **122**, 124
Laub, Juell, 512
Laugh, Clown Laugh, 4
Laughton, Charles, 242, 320, 389, **477**
Laura (1944), 76, 517
Laurel and Hardy, 30, 80
Law West of Tombstone, The (1938), 366
Lawless Riders (1935), 294, 359
Lawson, Priscilla Shortridge (Biscella Shortridge), **283**, 283–86, **284**, **324**, 325, 536
Leach, Barbara, 111
Leader of the Pack, 496
Leaf and Bough, 425
League of Their Own, A (1992), 522
Lear, Moya, 82
Lear, Norman, 484
Lee, Billy (Billy Lee Schlensker), 211, 286–88, **287**, **288**, 538
Lee, Canada, 98
Lee, Davey, 24
Lee, Johnny, 237
Lee, Peggy, 447
Lee, Stan, 511
Leedy, Glenn, **237**
Leeper, Mary, 356, 359, **359**
Leigh, Jennifer Jason, 524
Leigh, Vivian, 387, 389
Leisen, Mitchell, **151**
LeMay, Alan, 412
Lemmon, Jack, 189, 283
Lemon Drop Kid, The (1951), 508
Lennon, Julian, 473
Lenox Hill Hospital, 183
Lenox School of Jazz, 455
Leonard, Benny, 148
Leonard, Jim, 532
LeRoy, Mervyn, 159, 189
Leslie, Gladys, 368
Leslie, Lew, 236
Lesser, Sol, 328
Lester, Terry, 520, 521, 536
Lethal Weapon (1987), 449
Letterman, David, 124, 496, 529, 536
Levine, Nat, 210, 358, 359
Levinson, Barry, 478, **478**
Lewis, Forrest, 304, 308, **498**, 499, 518, 529, 534

Lewis, Fulton Jr., 421
Lewis, Jerry, 491
Lewis, Sinclair, 17
Lewis, Ted, 261, 470
Lewton, Val, 406
Liberty radio network, 359
Liberty Theater: New York, 65; Terre Haute, 256
Lieber, Herman, xii, 481–82, 536
Lieber, Herman, Sr., 481
Lieber, Mary Metzger, 481
Lieber, Robert, xii, 481–82, 536
Life: magazine, 106, 158, 417; play, 21
Life Can Be Beautiful (radio), 518
Life of Riley, The (television), 312, 328, 478
Life with Father: play, 303; television, 234
Lighthouse by the Sea, The (1924), 58
Lightnin' (1930), **141**, 142
Li'l Abner, 45
Lillian Bonstelle Playhouse (Dearborn, MI), 264
Lillie, Major Gordon "Pawnee Bill," 354–55, 379, 536
Lillie, May, 379
Lincoln, Elmo (Otto Elmo Linkenhelt), 7, 22, 49, 211, 315, **316**, 316–22, **317**, **318**, **321**, 525, 533
Lincoln, Marci'a Eldora, 316, 321, 322
Lind, Greta, 520, 527, 533
Lindbergh, Anne Morrow, 24
Lindbergh, Charles A., 24
Lingham, Tom (Thomas G. Lingham), 378, 536
Linkenhelt, Don, 316, 319
Linkenhelt, Eldora Hunter, 316, 319
Linkenhelt, Louis R. 316
Linkenhelt, Jay, 322
Linkenhelt, Jeff, 322
Linkenhelt, Maurice, 316, 322
Linkletter, Art, 262, 321
Linton, Betty Hyatt, 233
Linton-Stockton (IN) Elementary School, 273
Linville, Kate, 270
Lion King, The (1994), 306
Lion Man, The (1919), 392
Lion's Claws, The (1918), 378
Little Bo Peep, 218
Little Boy Lost (1953), 402
Little Colonel, The (1935), 426
Little Darlin' Records, 449
Little Foxes, The: play, 95, 258; 1941 film, 258, **259**
Little Lord Fautleroy, 494
Little Men (1940), 413
Little Miss Broadway (1938), 438
Little Miss Brown, 21
Little Mo (television), 418

Little Nashville Opry, 452
Little Night Music, A (novel), 430
Little Orphant Annie (1918), 523
Little Princess, The (1917), 396
Little Rock College, 508
Little Women (stage play), 312
Littlefield, Ralph, 529, 534
Live Oak Memorial Park (CA), 286
Lives of a Bengal Lancer, The (1935), 242, **242**, 516
Living Dolls (television), 200
Livingston, Bob, 325, 350, 364, 370
Lloyd, Harold, 3, 18, 62, 63, **63**, 387, 389
Lloyd, Jake, 522
Lockhart, June, 189
Lockridge, Ross, Jr., 426, **426**, 523, 536
Lofner, Carol, 273
Lofner-Harris Band, 273
Logan, Josh, 194, 291
Logansport (IN) High School, 62, 417
Lombard, Carole (Jane Alice Peters), xii, 36, 67, 84, 109, 132, 138, **144–45**, 144–65, **146**, **147**, **148**, **149**, **151**, **152**, **153**, **155**, **156**, **157**, **160**, **162**, **163**, 175, 195, 209, **235**, 236, 246, **266**, 267, 309, 347, 348, **348**, 379, 387, 398, **398**, 416, 427, 497, 506, 516, 525, 532
Lombard, Etta, 145
Lombard, Harry, 145
London Academy of Dramatic Art, 263
London Calling, 467
London Hippodrome, 130
Lone Ranger, The: radio, 401; television, 375
Lone Rider, The (1930), 349
Lone Star State of Mind (2002), 458
Lonesome Dove (television), 328
Long, Ivadine, 196, 197, 198
Long, Leland, 196, 197, 198
Long, Robert, 529
Long, Shelley, 194, **196**, 196–99, **197**, **199**, 478, 519, 532
Long, Long Trailer, The (1954), 512
Long Beach Poly High School (CA), 246
Long Gray Line, The (1955), **186**, 189
Longacre Theater (New York), 241
Longfellow, Henry Wadsworth, 39
Look for the Silver Lining (1949), 139
Look Who's Laughing (1941), 487
Lopez, Vincent, 447
Lord, Marjorie, 390, 501
Loretta Young Show, The (television), 503
Lorraine, Louise, 320
Los Angeles City College, 313
Los Angeles Civic Opera, 261

Los Angeles High School, 55, 179
Los Angeles Philharmonic Orchestra, 244
Los Angeles Tennis Club, 158
Los Angeles Times (newspaper), 51, 292
Losin' It (1983), 198
Lost Express, The (1917), 378, 502
Lost in the Stars, 98
Lotus Club (London), 130
Lou Grant (television), 232
Loughton, Phyllis, 403
Louis the 14th, 294
Louise, Anita, 423
Louisville Post (newspaper), 4
Louth, William, 190
Love, Clarence, 455
Love Affair (1939), 499, 515
Love Boat, The (television), 198
Love Doctor, The (1929), 214
Love in Morocco. See *Baroud*.
Love is a Many-Splendored Thing (1955), 515
Love Letters, 191
Love Me Tender (1956), 211
Love That Bob (television), 312
Lovely Liar, 142
Lovers? (1927), 52
Lowe, Edmund, 148
Lowell (IN) High School, 313
Lowe's Theater (Indianapolis), 170
Lowe's vaudeville circuit, 224
Loy, Myrna, 76, 154, 209, 278, 285, 480
L. S. Ayres, 284
Lubin, Arthur, 367
Lubitsch, Ernst, 159, 160, 416
Luckee Girl, 498
Lucky Jordan (1942), 261
Lucky Me, 236
Lucy Gallant (1955), 436
Lucy Show, The (television), 253
Ludden, Joanne, 297
Ludlow, Louis, 58
Lugosi, Bela, 233, 242, 386, 447, **447**
Lukens, Victor, 104
Lullabelle and Scotty, 369
Lulu Belle, 278
Lulu in Hollywood (Louise Brooks book), 220
Lumet, Sidney, 188
Lupino, Ida, 509
Lupone, Robert, 519
Lupus, Peter, 522, 529, 536
Lux Radio Theater, 226, 274, 304
Lux Video Theater (television), 189, 260
LVL Club, 435

Lyceum vaudeville circuit, 278
Lyda, John Wesley, 256
Lydia Bailey (1952), 98
Lydon, James, 252
Lyles, Aubrey, 466
Lynch, David, 440
Lynn, Diana, 426
Lynn, Loretta, 446
Lyon, Ben, **126**, 128, 129
Lyon, Madame Clara, 502
Lyric Theater: Indianapolis, 90, 246, 406; Terre
    Haute, 266
Lytell, Bert, 188

Ma and Pa Kettle (1949), **166–67**, 168
Ma and Pa Kettle series, 33, 170–72
Ma Barker's Killer Brood (1960), **305**, 306
Mable's Fables (television), 289
MacArthur, Charles, 153, 427
Macbeth: play, 278, 309, 504; 1948 film, 306
MacDonald, Jeanette, **33**, 272, 438, 478
MacDonald, Kenneth (Kenneth Dollins), 367,
    375, **375**, **376**, 376–77, 385, 534
MacDonald, LaMee Nave, 376
MacDonald, Wallace, 210
Mack, Ollie (Oliver Trumball), 27–28
Mackaill, Dorothy, 66
Mackey, Bernie, 454. *See also* Ink Spots.
MacLaine, Shirley, 522
MacMillan, Florence, 421
MacMurray, Fred, **151**, 170, **235**, 411, 523
MacPherson, Jennie, 44
MacRae, Gordon, 412, 523
Macy (IN) Monitor (newspaper), 224
Mad About You (television), 314
Mad Doctor, The (1941), **388**
Mad Parade, The (1931), 60
Mad Show, The (television), 314
Madame Butterfly (opera), 74, 225
Madame Capet, 177
Madden, Dave, 314, 415, 538
Made in Paris (1966), 266
Madison (2001), 522
Madison (IN) Herald (newspaper), 497
Madison (IN) High School, 497
Madison Square Garden, 38
Madness of Youth (1923), 65
Madonna, 445, 522
Maeterlinck, Maurice, 438
Maffin, Neil, 520, 529
Maggie's First False Step (1917), 57

Magic Fire: novel, 425; 1956 film, 429
Magic Garden, The: novel, 429; 1927 film, 429
Magician, The (1926), 52
Magnificent Ambersons, The: novel, 146, 179, 222; 1925
    film, 411; 1942 film, xiii, 179, 222, **222**, 279,
    405, 411, 523
Magnificent Obsession: novel, 422–23; 1935 film, 423;
    1954 film, 423
Magnificent Seven, The (1960), 106
Mahoney, Jock, **325**, 376
Maidstone (1970), 459
Maier, Sally, 197
Main, Marjorie (Mary Tomlinson), xi, xii, 33,
    166–67, 166–73, **168**, **169**, **170**, **171**, **172**, **173**,
    230, 234, 239, 259, 312, 430, 501, 508, 516,
    523, 535
Main Street (1923), **12**, **14**, 17
Main Street to Broadway (1953), 510, **511**
Major, Charles, 411, 426, **426**, 538
Make Mine Music (1946), 340
Make Room for Daddy (television), 501
Make Way for Tomorrow (1937), 495
Malcolm X (1992), 251
Malden, Karl (Mladen Sekulovich), 489, 503,
    506, 506–07, 515, 516, 525, 534
Male Animal, The, 234
Maltin, Leonard, 164, 195, 500
Mammoth (band), 463
Mamoulian, Rouben, 76, 493
Man Betrayed, A (1941), 415
Man from Brodney's, The: novel, 413; 1923 film, 413
Man Inside, The, 202
Man of Genesis (film), 317
Man of the World (1931), 152
Man on the Moon (1999), 417
Man Who Knew Too Much, The (1956), 523
Man Who Loved Cat Dancing, The: novel, 424; 1973 film,
    424
Man Who Wasn't There, The (2001), 518
Man Whose Name was John, A (television), 418
Manchild (band), 445
Manchurian Candidate, The (1962), 96
Mandrell, Barbara, 446, 452, 453
Manhattan Classic Company, 519
Manhattan Opera House (New York), 21
Manhunt (television), 293
Manhunter (television), 496
Mann, Hank, 29
Mann, May, 373
Mann, Ned, 526, 534
Mannix, Eddie, 163
Manny, Carter, 183

Man's Man, A (1923), 206

Mantz, Paul, 158

Manual Training School (Indianapolis), 12, 248, 263, 417, 471

Marathon Man (1976), 483

Marble, Alice, 158

March, Fredric, 154, 252, 304, 425

March of Time, The (radio), 258, 307

Marchand, Nancy, 188

Marcheta, 213

Marcus Garland (1925), 472

Marcus Welby, MD (television), 310

Mare Nostrum (1926), 52

Margie (1946), 427, 462

Marian Anderson (1991), 241

Mariners, 494

Marion, Francis, 383

Marion (IN) Leader-Tribune (newspaper), 112, 116

Mark Tapor Forum (Los Angeles), 233

Markham, Pigmeat, 467

Marked Woman (1937), 226

Markey, Enid, 49, 318, 319

Markham, Monte, 191

Marlowe, Marilyn. *See* Murray, Marilyn Ann.

Marriage in Transit (1925), 148

Married with Children (television), 518

Mars, Mick, 538

Mars Theater (West Lafayette). *See* Family Theater.

Marshall, Herbert, 180–81

Marshall, William, 98–99, **99**, 275, 534

Marshall Field and Company, 31, 187

Martian Space Party (1972), 484

Martin, Dean, 328, 491

Martin, Helen, 290

Martin, Irene, 267

Martin, Quinn, 415, 506

Martin, Ross, 232

Martin, Strother, **180**, 230, 288–91, **289**, 343, 534

Martin, Tony, 438

Marty: television, 188; 1955 film, 188

Marvel Comics, 511

Marvin, Lee, 290

Marx, Chico, **155**

Marx, Groucho, **155**

Marx Brothers, 30, 80, 325, 401

Mary Lou (1948), 462

Mary Magdalene (Valeska Suratt screenplay), 44

Mary Ware's Promised Land (Annie Fellows Johnston book), **425**

Mascot Pictures (studio), 210, 358, 359

M*A*S*H: television, 232; 1970 film, 118

Mason, Pauline, 267

Masonic Temple Roof Garden (Chicago), 141

Masquerade Party (television), 189, 464

Masquers Club, The, 394

Massey, Curt, 90, 369

Massey, Ilona, 285

Massey, Raymond, **108–09**

Master Key, The, 4

Maternity, 220

Mathis, Johnny, 473

Mathis, June, 209

Matinee Idol, A, 142

Matinee Theater (television), 232

Matlock (television), 200

Matthau, Walter, 189

Matthews, Helen, 77

Mature, Victor, 423, 444, 523

Maugham, W. Somerset, 71

Maund, Mildred, 509

Maurel, Victor, 74

Maverick: television, 236, 252, 373; 1994 film, 99

Maw, Nicholas, 437

Maxwell, Marilyn (Marvel Marilyn Maxwell), **90**, 234, **507**, 507–08, 532

May, Marty, 82

May, Patsy ("Baby"), 527, 537

Mayer, Louis B., 160, 163, 507

Maynard, Bessie, 354, 360

Maynard, Edith, 362, 364

Maynard, Emma May, 354

Maynard, Ken (Kenneth Olin Maynard), 18, 33, 148, 209, 294, **294**, 323, 343, 344, 348, 349, **354**, 354–61, **355**, **356**, **357**, **358**, **359**, **360**, 362, 363, 365, 369, 370, 375, 483, 525, 538

Maynard, Kermit (Kermit Roosevelt Maynard), 148, 211, 323, 348, 354, 358, 360, **362**, 362–64, **363**, **364**, 367, 375, 385, 538

Maynard, Trixie, 354, 360

Maynard, Willa, 354, 360

Maynard, William, 358

Maynard, William H., 354, 355

Mayor of Newtown, The, 472

MBA Music, 455

MCA Records, 457

McAllister, Lon, 244, **244**, 523

McBiggers, George, 369

McCammon, Ernest, 344

McCarey, Leo, 77, 495

McCarthy, Earl, 529, 532

McCarthy, Kevin, 98

McCarthy, Nobu, **92**

McClain, Billy, 529

McClarnon, Kevin, 533

McClintic, Guthrie, 494, 495

McClure, Arthur F., 366

McConnell, Margaret, 533

McCord, Ted (Thamer D. McCord), 482–83, 516, 538

McCormack, Bartlett, 417, 535

McCormick, John, 26

McCormick, Myron, **291**, 291–92, **292**

McCoy, Tim, 294, 325, 349, 350

McCrae, Carmen, 472

McCullough, L. E., 536

McCutcheon, George Barr, 132, 205, 411, 413, 426–27, **427**, 538

McCutcheon, John T., 420

McCutcheon High School (Lafayette), 250

McDaniel, Hattie, 159

McDermott, Eileen, 510

McDonald, Ballard, 448

McElwaine, Don, 148–49

McEvoy, J. P., 245

McFerrin, Bobby, 437

McGaughey, Samuel, 167

McGee, Vonetta, **99**

McGowan, J. P., 392, 502

McGraw, Ali, 106, 107

McGreevey, John, 417–18, 533

McGreevey, Michael, 418

McGuire, Dorothy, **512**, 523

McHugh, Frank, 312

McIntire, John, 328

McKellan, Ian, 121

McKenna (television), 266

McKenney, Ruth, 427, 537

McKeown, Jack, 531

McKinley, William, 12

McKinney, Nina Mae, 236

McKinnon, Mona, 447

McLaglen, Victor, 302

McMurphy, Charles, 529

McMurtry, Larry, 457

McNarny, Judy, 125

McQuade, Henrietta (Murray), 30

McQuade, Tom, 273

McQueen, Bill, 101, 106

McQueen, Butterfly, 159

McQueen, Chad, 107

McQueen, Steve (Terrence Steve McQueen), xi, xiii, **100–01**, 100–07, **102**, **103**, **104**, **105**, **106**, 232, 343, 406, 408, 489, 509, 516, 525, 535

McQueen, Terry, 107

McVey, Courteen Landis, 293

McVey, Patrick, 292–93, **293**, 508, 532

Meadows, Jayne, 189

Meanest Man in the World, The (1943), 163

Medical Center (television), **265**, 266, 503

Meehan, James Leo, 429

Meehan, Jeanette Porter, 429

Meet Me at the Fair (1953), 254

Meet Me in St. Louis (1944), 234

Meet Nero Wolfe (1936), 429

Meet the Dixons (radio), 258

Meet the Missus (radio), 262

Meet the Navy (radio), 487

Meglin, Ethel, 286, 288

Meglin School for Stage Children, 286, 288

Meighan, Thomas, 39, 412

Meisner, Sanford, 104, 232, 408

Mel Blanc Show, The (radio), 252

Mellencamp, John, 433, **456**, 456–58, 522, 534

Melody Cruise (1933), 274

Melody Time (1948), 340

Melting Pot, The, 312

Melville, Pearl (Josephine Smock), 45

Melville, Rose (Rosa Smock), 45–47, **46**, 539

Melville Sisters Stock Company, 45

Member of the Wedding, A (1952), **95**

Memorial Opera House (Valparaiso), 494

Men in War (1957), 96

Men without Law (1930), **204–05**, 207, 209

Mendell, Ada Gebhart, 344, 352

Menjou, Adolphe, 67, 214, 215, **238**, 238–39

Mephisto Waltz, The (1971), 429

Mercer, Frances, **366**

Mercer, Johnny, 257, 442, 444, 515

Merchant, Richard, 286

Mercury (studio), 84

Mercury Records, 457, 464

Meredino, Melissa, 188

Merendino, Dr. Vincent J., 188

Merriman, Randy, 297

Merry Widow, 261

Merry Wives of Windsor, The, 268

Merton of the Movies (1947), **91**, 234

Merv Griffin Show, The (television), 313, 360

Messick, Dale (Dalia), 418, 537

Messmer, Otto, 339

Methodist Hospital (Indianapolis), 17

Metro (studio), 32, 50, 202

Metropolitan Opera, 224, 497

Metropolitan School of Music (Indianapolis), 79

Metropolitan Theater (Los Angeles), 476

MGM (studio), 17, 52, 67, 75, 91, 92, 138, 160, 170, 178, 209, 234, 251, 258, 266, 285, 328, 401, 447, 464, 480, 481, 487, 501, 507
Michael O'Halloran (novel), 429
Micheaux, Oscar, 472
Michele, Michael, 293, **293**, 538
Michigan State Fair, 450–51
Mickey (1948), 244, 424
Middleton, Charles, 285
Midnight and Jeremiah (Sterling North book), 333
Midnight Jamboree (radio), 448
Midsummer Night's Dream, A, 497
Midwestern University, 313
Mignon, 74
Mikado, The, 213
Mike Douglas Show, The (television), **325**
Mike Fritzol's Frolics, 79
Miles, Sarah, 424
Milheim, Keith, 451. *See also* Hoosier Hot Shots.
Miljan, John, 522
Milky Way, The (screenplay), 416
Mill on the Floss, The (1937), 214
Miller, Ann, 286
Miller, Arthur, 232
Miller, Belle Culbert, 176
Miller, Ben W., 326
Miller, Dean, **261**
Miller, Denny, 315, **325**, 326–29, **327**, **328**, **329**, 343, 536
Miller, Flournoy, 466
Miller, Glenn, 454
Miller, Kent, 327
Miller, Marilyn (Marilynn Reynolds), xi, xii, 75, **126–27**, 126–39, **128**, **129**, **130**, **133**, **135**, **136**, **137**, 272, 294, 489, 525, 538
Miller, Martha Alice Linn, 326
Miller, Oscar "Caro," 128, 129, 130, 131
Miller, Reggie, 522
Miller Brothers 101 Ranch, 345
Millholland, Charles Bruce, xii, 153, 427, 539
Million Dollar Theater (Los Angeles), 476
Mills Brothers, 307, 454
Mills of the Gods (1934), 309
Milsap, Ronnie, 446
Minnelli, Liza, 118
Minnelli, Vincente, 234
Minor, Worthington, 188
Minter, Mary Miles, 22, 416
Minty, Barbara, 106, 107
Minzey, Frank, 47
Miracle of Morgan's Creek, The (1944), 32
Miracle on 34th Street (1947), 402, 516

Miracle Rider, The (1935), 211
Mirage (studio), 410
Mirror, Mirror (1990), 493
Mirror Films, 423
Misadventures of Sheriff Lobo, The (television), 491
Miserables, Les (1935), 391
Misleading Lady (1932), 268
Miss Brewster's Millions (1926), 427
Miss Susan (television), 188, 520
Miss Susie Slagle's (1946), 279
Mission: Impossible (television), 522
Mission to Mars (2000), 464
Missionary Baptist Church (Terre Haute), 45
Missouri Legend, 503
Missouri Pacific Railroad Company, 72
Missourian, The, 67
Mister Buddwing (1966), 515
Mister 880 (1950), **512**
Mister Roberts (1955), 189, 282
Mitchell, Geneva, **294**, 294–95, 359, 379, 537
Mitchum, Robert, 246, 247
Mix, Tom, 17, 21, 33, **207**, 208, 211, 344, 347, 350, 354, 356, 365, 366, 378, 385, 391
Mobley, Roger, 529, 538
Mod Squad (television), 457
Modern Day Houdini. See *Escapist, The*.
Modern Screen Magazine, 497
Mohawk Medicine Show, 281
Mohr, Carolyn, 295, 296
Mollycoddle, The (1920), 206
Mona McCluskey (television), 328
Monday Night Football (television), 279
Money Pit, The (1986), **197**, 198
Moneymaker, Kelly, 520
Monkey Business, 80; 1952 film, 312
Monogram (studio), 309, 350, 370
Monroe, Carolyn, 527, 536
Monroeville (IN) Breeze (newspaper), 423
Monsieur Beaucaire: 1924 film, 412; 1946 film, 412
Monster (2003), 251
Mont, Jeffry, 478, 537
Montague's Kentucky Serenaders, 254
Montgomery, Anthony, 529, 536
Montgomery, Buddy, 458
Montgomery, Monk, 451, 458
Montgomery, Robert, 159
Montgomery, Wes (John Leslie Montgomery), 451, 458–59, **458**, 536
Moody, William Vaughn, 537
Moon over Miami (1941), 401
Moon Theater (Vincennes), 87
Moore, Allyson, 295

Moore, Alvy (Jack Alvy Moore), **295**, 295–96, 534

Moore, Barry, 295

Moore, Colleen, 26, 37, 67, 209, 483, 523

Moore, Demi, 201

Moore, Dudley, 121, 225, 296, 429

Moore, Elsie, 295

Moore, Gary, 189

Moore, Janet, 295

Moore, Margo, 536

Moore, Mary Tyler, 429

Moore, Robert, Jr., 63

Moore, Roy, 295

Moore, Tom (Thomas R. Moore), 531, 538

Moore, Victor, 495

Moorehead, Agnes, 509

Moran, Polly, 56

Moreno, Antonio, 427

Morgan, Helen, 245, 439

Morgan, Henry, 189

Morgantown Blues (baseball team), 369

Moriarty, John H., 412

Morning Glory (1933), 294

Morris, Muriel, 91

Morrison Agency, 310

Morse, Theodore, 448

Morton, Jelly Roll, 486

Morton High School (Richmond), 83

Moss, Ethel, 236

Moss, Mary, 242

Mother Night: novel, 430; 1996 film, 430

Motion Picture (magazine), 56, 65, 412

Motion Picture Classic (magazine), 358

Motion Picture Country Home and Hospital, 303, 360

Motion Picture Herald (newspaper), 370

Motion Picture Producers and Distributors of America, 479

Motion Picture Relief Fund, 234

Motion Picture World (magazine), 52

Motte, Marguerite de la, 22, 23, 24, **26**, 62

Moulin Rouge Café (Chicago), 446

Mounted Fury (1931), 24

Movin' On (television), 491

Moving Picture Weekly (magazine), 7, 202

Mr. and Mrs. Smith (1941), 159

Mr. Belvedere Goes to College (1949), 312

Mr. Chump (1938), 227, 257, **257**

Mr. District Attorney (radio), 291

Mr. Ed (television), 234, 367–68

Mr. Novak (television), 503

Mr. Roberts (stage), 248, 282, 295, 313

Mr. Robinson Crusoe (1932), 206, 207

Mr. Sycamore, 298

Mr. Twee Deedle (comic strip), 499

Mr. Wu (1927), **141**

Mrs. O'Malley and Mr. Malone (1951), 262

MTV (network), 457

Mufandi Institute, 98

Mulholland Drive (2001), 440

Muller, Flora, 268

Mullican, Cora B. Hicks, 224, **224**, 226

Mullican, Dr. Lorenzo, 224, 226

Mullican, Martha, 224, 226, 227, 536

Mummy, The (1999), 121

Muncie Central High School (IN), 311

Muncie Civic Theater (Muncie), 252

Muni, Paul, 189, 304, 425

Murat Theater (Indianapolis), 131, 268, 303

Murder, My Sweet (1944), 509

Murder in Texas (television), 418

Murder She Wrote (television), 251

Murder with Music (1941), 467

Murders in the Rue Morgue (1932), 233

Murphy, Eddie, 264, 293

Murphy, Mary, **510**

Murphy, Ryan, 536

Murphy Brown (television), 199

Murphy's Comedians, 304

Murray, Asher, 30

Murray, Bob, 30

Murray, Carver, 30

Murray, Charlie, **27**, 27–30, **28**, **29**, **30**, 31, 56, 57, 58, 214, 238, 278, 385, 533

Murray, Don, 191, 522

Murray, Ed, 30

Murray, Isaac, 27

Murray, Ken, 360

Murray, Mae, **13**, 74, 142

Murray, Marilyn Ann, 360

Murrow, Edward R., 421

Mushett, John, 487

Music Box Theater (New York), 137

Music Corporation of America (MCA), 485

Music for Millions (1944), 438

Music in the Air, 168; 1934 film, 168

Music Man, The: stage production, 303; 1962 film, 215

Musical Legacy of Roland Hayes, The, 241

Mutiny on the Bounty (1962), 515

Mutt and Jeff, 31

Mutual Film Company, 479, 502

My American Wife: novel, 421; 1936 film, 421

My Best Girl (1927), 208, 387

My Favorite Husband (radio), 415

My Gal Sal (1942), 444, 523
My Man Godfrey (1936), 154, 155, 159, 516
My People, 472
My Sister Eileen: 1942 film, 427; 1956 film, 427
My Summer Story. See *It Runs in the Family*.
My Three Sons (television), 417, 480
Mysterious Island (1951), 252
Mysterious Rider, The (1938), 211
Mystery Mountain (1934), 359

Naked City (television), 445
Nall, Adeline Brookshire, 110, 111, 112, 116, 413
Name of the Game (television), 234
Napoleon of Broadway, 153, 427
Nashville (1975), 493
Nation, The (magazine), 430
National Academy of Design, 339
National Academy of Television Arts and Sciences
     Hall of Fame, 94
National Barn Dance (radio), 358, 450, 451
National Black Arts Festival, 242
National Black Caucus of State Legislators, 445
National Comedy Hall of Fame, 94
National Council of the Arts, 430
National Film Corporation of America, 318
National Press Club, 58
Natural, The (1984), 478, 483
Natural Born Killers (1994), 522
Naughty Marietta, 314
Navajo (1952), 85
Navarro, Fats, 455
Naylor Opera House (Terre Haute), 280
NBC (network), 91, 92, 94, 124, 187, 188, 190,
     194, 250, 261, 262, 300, 311, 314, 373, 410,
     440, 447, 454, 486, 491, 511, 518
NBC Comedy Hour, The (television), 487
Neal, Patricia, **260**
Neff, Greg, 529, 535
Negri, Pola, 320
Negro Actors Guild, 467
Neighborhood Playhouse (New York), 104, 232,
     408
Nelson, Ozzie, 307, **374**
Nelson, Willie, 457, 461
Nero Wolfe (television), 429
Nesbit, Evelyn, 38
Never Love a Stranger (1958), 105
Never So Few (1959), 106
New Albany (IN) Daily Ledger (newspaper), 4
New Amsterdam Theater (New York), 131
New Bedford Port Society, 240

New Colonial Theater (New York), 467
New Jack City (1991), 293
New Mexico Military Institute, 291
New Movie Magazine, 398
New Odd Couple, The (television), 271
New York (magazine), 251
New York Globe (newspaper), 131
New York Herald (newspaper), 205, 415
New York in the Fifties, 430
New York Messenger (newspaper), 470–71
New York Peacock, The (1917), 43
New York Times (newspaper), 8, 62, 65, 66, 240,
     245, 319, 389, 421, 430
New York Tribune (newspaper), 205, 415
New York Yankees (baseball team), 519
New Yorker, The (magazine), 427
Newcombe, John, 522
Newman, Alfred, 438
Newman, E. Jack, 274
Newman, Paul, 104, 289, **292**, 522, 524
Newspaper Enterprise Association, 499
Newspaper of the Air (radio), 307
Next Friday (2000), 264, **264**
Niagara (1953), 248, **248**
Nicholas, Denise, 275
Nichols, Red, 257, 440
Nichols, William, 72
Nicholson, Anne Kenyon, 427
Nicholson, Jack, 125, 256, 493, 512
Nicholson, Kenyon, 83, 221, 384, 402, 427, 537
Nicholson, Lucille, 427
Nicholson, Meredith M., 7, 411, **411**, 427, **427**,
     479, 537
Nicholson, Thomas Brown, 427
Nicklo Theater (Linton), 273
Niesse, Carl, 509
Night and Day (1946), 461, 523
Night of the Fourth, The, 420
Night of the Quarter Moon (1959), 97
Night Riders of Montana (1951), **367**, 373
Night Shift (1982), 198
Nine Lives of Elfego Baca, The (television), 85
Niven, David, 509
Nixon, Richard M., 360
No, No, Nanette, 59
No Man of Her Own (1932), **144–45**
No Sad Songs for Me (1950), 444, 515
No Time for Sergeants: 291; 1958 film, 291
No. 2 Smart Set Company, 471
No Way Out. See *One Way Out*.
Noah's Ark: 1929 film, 58; 1959 film, 338
Noble, Emma, 417

Noble Sissle and Eubie Blake Sing Snappy Songs (1923), 465

Noel, Thomas (Tom) R. S., 529, 533

Noises Off, 496

Nolan, Bob, 359

Nolan, Jeannette Covert, 296, 428, **428**, 523, 538

Nolan, Tom, 296, **296**, 428, 536

Nolan, William F., 105

Nolte, Nick, 439, 522

Norliss Tapes, The (television), 429

Normand, Mabel, 47, 56, 149, 502

North, Sterling, 333, 523

North Ain't South, 472

North Central High School (Indianapolis), 445, 477

North High School (IA), 301

North Star (1925), 356

Northern Indiana District Baptist Association Auxiliary, 95

Northwest Mounted Police (1940), 18

Northwest Passage (1940), 328

Northwestern University, 95, 99, 118, 198, 215, 490, 492, 501

Norton, Fletcher, 42, 43

Norvelle, Dr. Lee, 112

Norworth, Jack, 141, 142

Not as a Stranger (1955), 291

Not My Sister (1916), 49

Not Quite Decent (1929), 365

Nothing Sacred (1937), 154, 157, 159

Novarro, Ramón, 22, 51, 52, 347

Now is the Time for All Good Men, 413

Nurse Betty (2000), 125

NYPD Blue (television), 251

Oakie, Jack, 476

Oberlin College, 241, 242, 486

Oberon, Merle, 389

O'Brian, Hugh, 484

O'Brien, Chet, 138

O'Brien, Margaret, 234

O'Brien, Pat, 299, 397, 523

Occasional Bride, 216

O'Connor, Donald, 254, 297, 476

Odds Against Tomorrow (1959), 406

Odet, Clifford, 402

O'Donnell, Chris, 120

Oedipus Rex, 264

Of Human Hearts (1938), 495, 515

Oh, Daddy! (1915), 377

Oh! Joy!, 471, 472

Oh Kay! (1928), 67

Oh Sailor, Behave (1930), 80

O'Hara, Maureen, 194, 387, 389

O'Haver, Tommy, 201, 381, 531, 536

O. Henry's Full House (1952), 438

Ohio State University, 493

Ohio Theater (Indianapolis), 508

Okinawa (1952), 295

Oklahoma!, 194

Old Home Week (1925), 206

Old Maid, The (1939), 59

Old Timer (radio), 373

Ole Olsen Memorial Theater, 82

Oliver, Richard (Rich), 529

Oliver Twist, 73, 218

Oliver Willard Pierce Academy of Fine Arts (Indianapolis), 497

Olivier, Laurence, 178, 320, 389

Ollie Hoopnoodle's Haven of Bliss (television), 429

Olmos, Edward James, 233

Olsen, J. C., 81–82

Olsen, Ole (John Sigvaard Olsen), xi, **79**, 79–82, **80**, **81**, 209, 297, 461, 476, 536

Olympia Theater (Chicago), 142

Olympus on My Mind, 496

On a Beam of Light (novel), 420

On Borrowed Time: play, 114, 418, 495; 1939 film, 418

On Moonlight Bay (1951), 412, 439, 523

On the Banks of the Wabash (1923), 523

On the Twentieth Century, 427, 504

On the Waterfront (1954), 506, 516

On to Fortune, 291

On Your Toes, 138

Once More with Feeling, 190

One Desire (1955), **177**

One Dollar Bid (novel), 206

One Hundred and One Dalmatians (1961), 334, 338

101 Ranch Wild West Show, 345

113 Club (Fort Wayne), 435

One Life to Live (television), 520

One Man's Family (radio), 252, 304, 518

One of the Family, 494

One Way Out (1986), 300

O'Neal, Shaquille, 522

O'Neill, Eugene, 220, 282

O'Neill's, The (radio), 258

Open Range (2003), 518

Orange County (CA) Plain Dealer (newspaper), 335

Orchard School (Indianapolis), 429

Oriental Theater (Chicago), 510

Original Gangstas (1996), 118

Ormand, Julia, 124

Orphans of the Storm (1921), **15**, 15–16, 17

Orpheum Ballroom (Terre Haute), 256

Orpheum vaudeville circuit, 224, 369

Orr, Anna, 267

Osborn, Paul, 114, 418, 495, 516, 538

Osborne, Joan, 458

O'Shea, Jack, 371

Osmond, Jimmy, 453

Osmond Brothers, 453

Osterhage, Jeff, 529, 532

Ostot, Amos, 507

O'Sullivan, Maureen, 234, 328

Othello (television), 98

Other Girl, The, 219

Other Side of the Wind, The (1972), 85

"Our Gang" comedies, 63, 288, 310

Our Hearts Were Growing Up (1946), 426

Our Hearts Were Young and Gay: book, 191, 426; 1944 film, 426

Our Miss Brooks (television), 252

Our Town, 518

Ouspenskaya, Maria, 177

Out All Night (television), 200

Out Goes She, 214

Out of Africa (1985), 410, 516

Out of the Kitchen, 309

Out of the Storm (1920), 22

Out of This World (television), 519

Outrageous Fortune (1987), 198, 478

Over the Goal (1937), 257

Oxford University, 421

Paar, Jack, 194

Pacific Heights (1990), 296

Pagany, 65

Page, Gale, **225**, 226

Page, Geraldine, 114, 519

Pageant Film Company, 312

Paget, Debra, 494

Paid (1930), 312

Paige, Colleen, 297

Paige, Robert (John Arthur Paige), 211, **297**, 297–98, 536

Paige-Ludden Enterprises, 297

Paint Your Wagon, 260

Pajama Game, 104

Pal Joey (1957), 464

Palace Theater (New York), 43

Paley, William S., 307

Palm Beach Story, The (1942), 32

Palm Memorial Gardens (Las Vegas), 82

Palmer, Betsy (Patricia Betsy Hrunek), 113–14, **186**, 186–91, **187**, **188**, **190**, **191**, 283, 520, 534

Pantages vaudeville circuit, 80, 88

Pantages Vaudeville Theater (Kansas City), 88

Panther in the Sky (novel), 429

Paper Lion (1968), 279

Papermill Playhouse (New Jersey), 190

Papp, Joseph, 232

Paralta Studios, 206

Paramount (studio), 32, 43, 52, 63, 83, 150, 151, 214, 242, 246, 267, 285, 297, 364, 385, 391, 397, 402, 417, 419, 424, 442, 481, 498, 503

Parasites, 75

Pardon My Sarong (1942), 297, 455

Paris, 461

Park Central Hotel (New York), 257

Park Theater (Indianapolis), xii, **xii**

Parker, Sarah Jessica, **121**, 447

Parker Lewis Can't Lose (television), 518

Parmalee, Dave, 72

Parmalee, Mabel A., 71, 72, 73, 74, **75**, 76, 77, 134

Parrish, Mitchell, 441

Parseghian, Ara, 118

Parsons, Bill, 318, 319

Parton, Dolly, 452, 468

Pasadena (CA) High School, 395–96

Pasadena Playhouse, 246, 247, 292, 313, 507

Passing of Two-Gun Hicks, The (1914), 391

Passing Show, The, 262

Passing Show of 1914, The, 131

Passing Show of 1915, The, 131

Passion (1921), 320

Passion of Darkly Noon, The (1995), 120

Passions (television), 520

Patch of Blue, A (1965), 515

Patent Leather Kids, 454

Path of Happiness, The (1916), 202

Pathe (studio), 37, 149, 150, 151, 417, 423, 502

Patrick, Corbin, 274, 285

Patrick, Gail, 288

Patton (1970), 97, **97**

Paul, Richard, 240

Paul Taylor Dance Company, 486

Paulsin, George, 529, 535

Pawnee Bill. *See* Lillie, Major Gordon.

Paws, Inc., 414

Payne, John, 178

Peacock Alley (1922), **13**, 17

Peanut Boys, 454

Pearson, Corey, 529, 536

Peavey, Homer, 442

Peck, Gregory, 310, 491
Peckinpah, Sam, 289, 290
Peck's Bad Boy (1921), 478
Pee-Wee's Playhouse (television), 99
Peed, Emma Thorpe, 332, 333
Peed, George, 333, 335, 337, 538
Peed, Orion Hopkins, 332
Peet, Bill (William Bartlett Peed), **332**, 332–34, 335, 337, 338, 339–40, 538
Peet, Bill, Jr., 333
Peet, Steve, 334
Peggy from Paris, 202, 420
Peggy Sue Got Married (1986), 234
Pendleton, Nat, **59**
Pendleton (IN) High School, 310
Penn, Sean, 296
People (Indianapolis tabloid), 499
People (magazine), 201, 437
People Against O'Hara, The (1951), 419
People vs. Larry Flynt, The (1996), 417
People's Choice, The (television), 252, 480
Peppard, George, 525
Pepper Young's Family (radio), 258
Percolating Puppies, 454
Perfect Crime, A (1921), 148, **148**
Perils of Pauline, The (1914), 502
Period of Adjustment (1962), 515
Perkins, Anthony, 523
Perlberg, William, 401
Perry, Roger, 314
Perry Mason (television), 252, 261, 308, 310, 376
Pershing, General John J., 439
Peso, Oro, 355
Pest in the Storm Country, A, 57
Pete and Gladys (television), 295
Peter Pan: 1924 stage production, 133; 1950 stage production, 98; 1953 film, 333, 338, 340, 487
Peters, Elizabeth Knight, 145, 146, 147, 148, **149**, 151, 153, 160, 161
Peters, Frederic, 145, 146, 147, 148, 152, 153
Peters, Frederic, Jr., 146, 150, **152**, 153, 162, 164
Peters, J. C., 145
Peters, Jean, **248**
Peters, Stuart, 146, 150, **152**, 153, 162, 164
Peters, Susan, 188
Petersburg School for Girls (Virginia), 214
Petrakis, Harry Mark, 537
Petrified Forest, The, 95
Petronella (1986), 453
Petticoat Junction (television), 480
Pettijohn, Charles C., 479
Peyton Place (television), 519

Pfaff, Rosemary, 497
P. F. Voland (publisher), 500
Phantom Crown, The: The Story of Maximilian and Carlota of Mexico (novel), 425
Phantom Empire, The (1935), 210, 211, 359
Phantom of the Open Hearth, The (television), 429
Phantom of the Opera, The (1925), 419
Phantom of Santa Fe (1936), 209
Phantom Rider, The (1936), 284
Philadelphia Story, The, 177
Philco TV Playhouse (television), 188, 189, 417
Phil Harris–Alice Faye Show, The (radio), 254
Phil Harris Scholarship Festival, 275, 296
Philadelphia Orchestra, 437
Philliber, John, 298, **298**, 503, 533
Phillips, David Graham, 428, **428**, 534
Phillips Exeter Academy, 395
Phoenix, River, 120
Photoplay (magazine), 6, 8, 41, 49, 51, 60, 523
Pickfair, 65, 133, 206
Pickford, Jack, 67, 75, 131, 133
Pickford, Mary, 15, 21, 65, 66, 75, 131, 132, 142, 157, 160, 206, 207, 208, 387, 396, 476, 482, 507
Pickwick Players, 313
Picnic (1955), 444, 515
Picture-Play (magazine), 66
Pidgeon, Walter, 170, **172**
Piece of Eden, A (2000), 522
Pied Piper Malone (1924), 412
Pied Piper of Malone, The, 282
Pierce, James, 315, **323**, 323–25, **324**, **325**, 362, 392, 534
Pierce, James, Sr., 323
Pierce, Mrs. James, Sr., 323
Pierce, Joan, 325
Pierce, Joan Burroughs, **323**, 324, 325
Pierce, Michael, 325
Pike High School (Indianapolis), 300
Pinafore, 202
Pinnacle Club (New York), 190
Pinnochio (1940), 333, 340
Pinza, Ezio, 244
Piquer, Conchita, 465
Pirates of Penzance, The, 504, **505**
Pitts, Zazu, 65
Pittsburgh. See *Screwed*.
Pivot, The, 300
Pizzo, Angelo, 418, 522
Place in the Sun, A (1951), 424
Plain Man and His Wife, A, **142**
Plainfield (IN) High Schol, 301

Plainsman, The (1936), 18, 416

Players, The, 293

Playhouse 90 (television), 190, 408, 491, 503

Playroom, The, 492

Pleasure Garden, The (1925), 208

Plum Tree, The (novel), 428

Pluto's Judgement Day (1935)

Po'Boy Productions, 118

Poff, Lon, 278, 325, 529, 535

Pointed Heels (1929), 267

Poisoned Flume, The (1911), 7

Poitier, Sidney, 96, 98, 409, 523

Polar Ice and Fuel Company, 337

Police Story (television), 118

Police Woman (television), 232

Policy Man (1938), 236

Politically Incorrect (television), 118

Pollack, Bernie, 483–84, 538

Pollack, David, 408

Pollack, Rebecca Miller, 408

Pollack, Robert, 146

Pollack, Sydney, 124, 232, 328, 381, **408**, 408–
    10, **409**, 483, 516, 525, 538

Pollard, Daphne, 149

Polly Bergen Show, The (television), 491

Polo, Eddie, 538

Pommer, Erich, 389

Poor Nut, The, 83

Pork Chop Hill (1959), 96, 232

Porky's (1982), 484

Port Charles (television), 521

Port of Missing Men, The (1914), 427

Porter, Cole, xi, xii, 74, 75, 76, 79, 137, 209,
    433, 459–61, **460**, 516, 523, 536

Porter, Ed (Edward D. Porter), 530, 532

Porter, Samuel Fenwick, 459

Portia Faces Life (radio), 291, 518

Poston, Tom, 189

Potash and Perlmutter, 142

Potel, Dr. Christian, 31

Potel, Mrs. Christian, 31

Potel, Mildred, 33

Potel, Victor, **31**, 31–33, **32**, **33**, **56**, 65, 278,
    320, 538

Potters, The (1927), 267

Powell, Dick (Richard Ewing Powell), 105, 257,
    298, 304, 394, 482, 508–10, **509**, 525, 536

Powell, Drew, 530, 533

Powell, Eleanor, **90**

Powell, Ellen, 509

Powell, J. Russell, 239, 530, 536

Powell, Michael, 214

Powell, Norman Scott Barnes, 509, **509**

Powell, Pamela, 509

Powell, Richard, Jr., 509

Powell, Russ, 214, **238**

Powell, William, 152, **152**, 153, 154, 155, 189, 283,
    480

Power, Tyrone, 180, 234, 247, 248

Power, Tyrone, Sr., 426

Powers, Maurine (Maureen), 526, 539

Poynter, Beulah, 22

Practice, The (television), 251

Prancer (1989), 522

Precious Jeopardy (novel), 423

Prentiss, Harvey, 299

Prentiss, Mrs. Harvey, 299

Preminger, Otto, 76

Presenting Lily Mars: novel, 412; 1943 film, 412, 507

Presley, Elvis, 211, 446, 447

Pretty Woman (1990), 296

Price, Ray, 449

Prima, Louis, 463

Prime of Miss Jean Brodie, The, 190

Prime Time, The (1960), 492

Prince, Harold, 309

Prince and the Pauper, The, 73

Prince of Central Park, 314

Princess Diaries, The (2001), 421

Princess Diaries 2: Royal Engagement, The (2004), 421

Princess Theater (Hawaii), 273

Princeton (NJ) Packet (newspaper), 430

Princeton University, 236, 291, 428

Principal (studio), 385, 391

Prisoner of Zenda, The: stage production, 278; 1921
    film, 51; 1937 film, 419

Prisoner of Zenda, Rupert of Hentzon, The (book), 277

Private Parts (1997), 464

Proctor, Philip, 484, 520, 530, 533

Producers Releasing Corporation (PRC), 370

Prometheus Unbound, 504

Prowse, Juliet, 328

Prude's Fall, The (1924), 67

Pruitt, Marvin, 435

Public Affair, A (1962), 291

Publisher's Clearing House, 420

Puck, Eva, 465

Puck (magazine), 417

Pulliam, Eugene C., **160**, 161

Pullman Standard Car Company, 95

Purcell, Irene, 527, 535

Purcell, June, 527, 536

Purdue University, 283, 420, 518

Purl, Linda, 522

Purple Lady, The, 43
Purple Road, The, 74
Pushed Too Far (1986), 522
Pyle, Ernie, 190, 428, **428**, 538

Q Planes (1939), 389. See also *Clouds Over Europe.*
Quality Twins, The (radio), 261
Queen Bee (1955), 189
Queen City Four, 377
Queen for a Day (television), 447
Queen's Theater (London), 214
Quick as a Flash (television), 464
Quick Millions (1931), 233
Quicksands (1923), 396
Quincy (television), 232
Quincy Adams Sawyer (1922), 22, **23**, **32**, **33**, **56**, 320

Rabbitt, Eddie, 446
Rachel and the Stranger (1948), 85
Racket, The: play, 83, 417; 1928 film, 267, 417; 1951 film, 417
Rage at Dawn (1955), 390
Raggedy Ann and Andy: A Musical Adventure (1977), 500
Raging Bull (1980), 511
Rags to Royalty, 73
Ragtime (1981), 486
Railroad Raiders, The (1917), 378, 502
Rain (1932), 495
Rain Man (1988), 483, 522
Rain or Shine, 59, 249; 1930 film, 249, 250
Rains, Claude, 423, 425
Raintree County: novel, 426; 1957 film, 248, 426, 523
Ramar of the Jungle (television), 371
Ramis, Harold, 121
Ranch Party (television), 447
Randolph, Amanda, 236–37
Range Feud (1931), **352**
Ranier, Louise, 159
Raposo, Joe, 500
Rascals (1938), 243
Rathbone, Basil, **143**, **388**
Raum, Green, Jr., 72
Rawhide: television, 261; 1951 film, 371
Ray, Nicholas, 116
Ray Rockett Productions, 383
Rayart Film Company, 363
Raymond, Gene, 159
Razor's Edge, The: novel, 71; 1946 film, **73**, 76, 176, 179, 181, 515, 517

RCA, 438, 453, 454, 468, 469
RCA Victor, 254
RCA Victor Show, The (television), 244
Reagan, Ronald, 247
Reardon, Will K., 267
Rebecca (1940), 178, 478
Rebel without a Cause (1955), 116
Rebels, The (television), 302
Rebhorn, James, 520, 521, 535
Record, Billy, 530
Red, Hot and Blue! 461
Red Badge of Courage, The (television), 232
Red Ball Jets (band), 463
Red Buttons Show, The (television), 215, 464
Red Glove, The (1919), 378
Red Raiders, The (1927), 358
Red Rose, The, 42
Red Ryder film series, 366
Red Skelton Show, **92**
Red Violin, The (1998), 437
Redbook (magazine), 425
Reckell, Peter, 519–20, 533
Redford, Robert, 409, 483, 490, 519, 525
Redpath Chautauqua Company, 213
Reed, Leonard, 454. See also Ink Spots.
Reed, Robert, 172
Reeves, Harry, 339–40, 539
Reid, Antonio "L.A.," 445
Reid, Wallace, 39, 317, 479
Reimer, Eddie, 316
Reiner, Rob, 124, 478
Reivers, The (1969), **106**
Remarkable Mr. Pennypacker, The (1959), 76
Rembush, Frank, 479
Remick, Lee, 522
Renoir, Jean, 179
Republic (studio), 81, 302, 325, 350, 364, 365, 366, 370, 375
Republican National Committee, 479
Return to Peyton Place (1961), 376
Revenge of the Creature (1955), 240
Revenge of the Zombies (1943), 237
Revere, Anne, **299**
Reynolds, Burt, 424, 430, 492
Reynolds, Claire, 127, 128, 130, 138
Reynolds, Edwin, 127, 128
Reynolds, Edwin, Jr., 127, 128
Reynolds, Ruth, 127, 128, 129, 130, 138
Rhythm Club, The (radio), 454
Rhythm on the Range (1936), 438
Rialto Theater (Fort Wayne), 507
Rice, Elmer, 495

Rich, Charlie, 446

Rich, Freddie, 307

Rich, Young, and Pretty (1951), 436

Rich Man's Plaything, A (1917), 43

Richardson, Frank, 424

Richardson, Helen, 424

Richardson, Ralph, 389

Richey, Robert Keith, Jr., 282

Richman, Harry, 273, 284

Richmond (IN) High School, 376

Richmond (IN) Palladium (newspaper), xviii, 83

Richmond (IN) Telegraph (newspaper), xvii

Riddle, Nelson, 447

Ride 'em Cowboy (1936), 350

Ride Ranger Ride (1936), 369

Riding High (1950), 309

Rifleman, The (television), 236, 509

Riley, James Whitcomb, xii, 37, 205, 268, 411, **411**, 523, 533

Rin Tin Tin, 58, 394

Rinehart, Mary Roberts, 22

Ringling Brothers Circus, 12, 346, 356

Riskin, Robert, 154

Ritter, John, 496

Ritter, Tex, 211, 325, 449

Ritz Brothers, 80

Ritz Carlton Nights, 224

Riva Records, 457

Riverboat (television), 328

Rivers, Johnny, 447

Riverside Park (Indianapolis), 168

Rivoli Theater (New York), 465

RKO (studio), 179, 274, 366, 389, 404, 405, 406, 498, 499

Roach, Hal, Jr., 493

Road Demon (1938), 523

Road of Life, The (radio), 258

Road to Glory, The: 1926 film, 149, 397; 1936 film, **396**

Road to Nashville, The (1967), 469

Road to Yesterday, The, 4

Roar Like a Dove, 190

Robber Bridegroom, The, 504

Robbins, Tim, 524

Robe, The: novel, 423; 1953 film, 423, 515

Roberts, Lee S., 439

Roberts, Lynn, **372**

Roberts, Pernell, 188, 519

Robeson, Paul, 96, 98, 241, 278, 464

Robin Hood: 1922 film, 65, 205; 1973 film, 274

Robinson, Bill "Bojangles," 236, 426, 467, 523

Robinson, E. G., **477**

Robinson, J. Russel, 461–62, 536

Robinson, Johnny, 462

Robinson, Shari Sue, 298–300, **299**, 536

Rock-a-bye, Baby, 142

Rockett, Al (Albert L.), **383**, 383–84, 534

Rockett, Laura (Lottie), 384

Rockett, Norman, 384

Rockett, Ray, **383**, 383–84, 534

Rockett Film Corporation, 383

Rocky Jones, Space Ranger (television), 252

Rocky Mountain (1950), 373

Rocky Rhodes (1934), 349

Rocky II (1979), 511

Rodgers, Richard, 194, 459, 497

Rogers, Buddy, 507

Rogers, Ginger, **76**, 272, 405

Rogers, Ivan, **300**, 300–01, 536

Rogers, James B., 531, 536

Rogers, Jean, 285

Rogers, Mimi, 425

Rogers, Ola, 300

Rogers, Paul B., 300

Rogers, Robert M., 538

Rogers, Roy, 18, 210, 211, 344, 350, 367

Rogers, Will, 29, 131, 140, 142, 307, 336, 347, 523

Rogue of the Rio Grande (1930), 209

Rollins, Sonny, 451

Romance of Helen Trent, The (radio), 518

Romance of Tarzan, The (1918), 319

Romance of the Utah Pioneers, A (1913), 56

Romberg, Sigmund, 131

Romero, Cesar, 155

Ronstadt, Linda, 468

Room for One More (television), 260

Room 222 (television), 275, **275**

Rooney, Mickey, 160, 286, 523

Roosevelt, Franklin D., 91, 160, 163, 421

Roosevelt, Theodore, 12

Roots: The Next Generation (television), 418

Rorem, Ned, 539

Rosalie, 134; 1937 film, 461

Rosalinda, 261

Rose, Axl (William Rose), 433, 463, **463**, 538

Rose, David, 98, 436

Rose, Fred (Knowles Fred Rose), 462–63, 538

Rose of Washington Square (1939), 446

Rose Tattoo, The, 260, 490

Roseanne (television), 518

Rosebrock, Della Morris, 316

Roseman, Edward, 420, 523, 526, 539

Rosetti and Ryan (television), 98

Rosomme, Alyssa, 125
Ross, Churchill (Ross Weigle), 530, 538
Ross, Ellen, 527, 533
Ross, Diana, 228
Roth, David Lee, **463**, 463–64, 536
Rough Riders, The, 350
'Round Midnight (1986), 451
Roundtree, Richard, 118
Rourke, Michey, 425
Rousters, The (television), 266
Rowan and Martin's Laugh-In (television), 314
Roy Rogers Show, The (television), 480
Royal British Navy Band, 256
Royal Family, The, 218
Royal Scandal, A (1945), 179
Rubin, Benny, 243–44
Ruby and Oswald (television), 418
Rudolph, Marci'a. See Lincoln, Marci'a Eldora.
Rudy (1993), 418, 522
Rugrats (television), 271
Rugrats Movie, The (1998), 484
Ruick, Barbara, 306
Ruick, Mel, 306
Ruler of the Town, The, 471
Rules of Engagement (2000), 478
Runyan, Damon, 167, 284
Rushville (IN) Daily Republican (newspaper), 205, 206, 412
Russell, Gail, 426
Russell, Harold, 181
Russell, Isaac Snookum, 455
Russell, Lillian, 131
Russell, Rosalind, 154, 302
Russell, Todd, 188
Russell, William D., 531, 536
Rust, David, 67
Rutgers University, 241
Ruth, Babe, 63
Ruth of the Rockies (1920), 378
Rutkowski, Chris, 536
Ryan, Sheila, 312, 368
Ryan, Tom, 413
Ryan's Hope (television), 518, 520, 521
Rydell, Mark, 409
Ryder, Winona, 121
Ryerson, Ann, 198

Sabrina (1995), **123**, 124, 410
Sabrina, the Teenage Witch (television), 199, 314
Sabrina Fair, 248
Sabu and the Magic Ring (1957), 98

Sackcloth and Scarlet (1925), 52, 206
Sad Sack, The (radio), 512
Safety Last! (1923), 387
Sailor's Sweetheart, A (1927), **57**
Saint Benedict's Academy (Louisville), 497
Saint Louis Post-Dispatch (newspaper), 232
Sajak, Pat, 188
Sally, xii, 132, 133, 134, 294; 1929 film, **130**, 134–35, 272
Sally, Irene and Mary (1938), 438
Saludos Amigos (1942), 340
Salvation, 168
Sam Houston, 4
Sam Spade (radio), 306
Sam Whiskey (1969), 373
Same Time Next Year, 189, 191
Samson (1914), 6
Samuel French (publisher), 425
San Diego I Love You (1944), 427
San Francisco Beat (television), 312
San Francisco Examiner (newspaper), 232, 347
Sand Pebbles, The (1966), xiii, **105**, 106, 406, 516, 517
Sandburg, Carl, **479**
Sanders, George, **178**, 211
Sanders, Harlan, 530
Sandpiper, The (1965), 97
Sandrich, Mark, 274
Sands of Iwo Jima (1949), 302
Sanford and Son (television), 270
Santa Barbara (television), 521
Santschi, Anna, 34
Santschi, Augusta, 34
Santschi, Bertha, 34
Santschi, John, 34
Santschi, Tom (Paul William Santschi), **34**, 34–37, **35**, **36**, 376, 385, 394, 416, 523, 534
Sarah Scott Junior High School (Terre Haute), 295
Saroyan, William, 190
Sartorius, Herman, 301
Satan Never Sleeps (1962), 77, **77**
Saturday Evening Post (magazine), 428
Saturday Jamboree (radio), 486
Saturday's Children, 494
Savage Dawn (1985), 493
Savalas, Telly, 289
Save the Children, 266
Say It Isn't So (2001), 524
Say It with Songs (1929), 23
Sayers, Loretta, **349**
Saylor, Sid, 364
Sayonara (1957), 114, 418, 516
Scacchi, Greta, 437

Scaia, Stephen, 531, 536

Scalphunters, The (1968), 410

Scammon, Richard, 504

Scapino, 518

Scaramouche (1923), 51

Scarface (1932), 399

Scarlet Empress, The (1934), 142

Scarlet Runner, The (1916), 309

Scarlet Sister Mary, 168

Scarlett, 43

Schaefer, Armand, 210

Schaefer, Mark, 369, 449

Schaffer, Franklin, 188

Scheitlen, Marian G., 205

Schenck, Joe, 208

Schenck, Wade, 536

Schenkel, Chris, 275, 530, 534

Scherrer, Paul (Paul Scherier Jr.), 530, 536

Schickel, Richard, 154

Schlatter, George, 314

Schmidt, Charles, 256

School Daze with Greg Kinnear (radio), 122

School Ties (1992), **119**, 120

Schrab, Mirza Ahmad, 44

Schricker, Henry, **160**, 161, 163

Schrock, Raymond, 419, 421, 533

Schroeder, Carly, 521, 537

Schulthies, Charles, 484, 533

Schwartz, Sherwood, 194

Scorcese, Martin, 389

Scott, George C., **97**

Scott, Gordon, **325**, 328

Scott, Martha, 425

Scott, Randolph, 18, 36, 242, 288, 376, 394, 494, **494**

Scout, The (1994), 120

Scream Blacula Scream! (1973), 98

Screaming Shadow, The (1920), 378

Screen Actors Guild, 6, 234, 310, 364, 394

Screen Extras Guild, 364

Screen Writers Guild, 403

Screwed (2000), 417

Sea Hunt (television), 393

Seabiscuit (2003), 251

Seagram and Sons Company, 176

Seals Brothers Circus, 320

Search for Tomorrow (television), 504, 521

Searchers, The (1956), 412

Searching for Bobby Fischer (1993), 410

Sears, Ted, 340

Season of Passion (1959). See *Summer of the Seventeenth Doll.*

Seasons of the Heart (television), 491

Seaton, George, 401–03, **402**, 515, 516, 525, 537

Second City Improvisational Company, 198

Second City Revue, The, 314

Second Fiddle to a Steel Guitar (1966), 469

Second Generation, The (novel), 428

Secret Agent X-9 (1937), 391

Secret of the Whistler, The (1946), 419

Secret Storm, The (television), 521

Security Risk (1954), 375

See America First, 74, 460

See My Lawyer (1945), 81

See the Jaguar, 113

Seeing It Through (1920), 65

Seegar, Carrie, 213

Seegar, Dorothy, 213, **213**, 214, 216

Seegar, Frank F., 213

Seegar, Helen, 213, **214**, 215

Seegar, Mildred, 213

Seegar, Miriam, 213, **213**, 214, **214**, 215, **215**, 216, **238**, 239, 379, 389, 390, 534

Seegar, Sara(h), 213, 215, **216**, 534

Seen but Not Heard, 177

Seidel, Tom (Emil Seidel), 501, 530, 536

Selby, Norman, 537

Seldes, Gilbert, 245

Selecca, Connie, 183

Selena (1997), 463

Selig Polyscope Company, 4, 35, 36, 37, 523

Selleck, Tom, 524

Selznick, David O., 159, 178, 242, 383, 478

Selznick (studio), 202, 239, 479

Señor Daredevil (1926), 358

Sennett, Mack, 27, 29, 31, 55, 56, 57, 63, 149, 150, 208, 209, 238, 442

Sennett (studio), 394

Sense and Sensibility (1995), 410

September 30, 1955 (1977), 109

Sergeant York (1941), 399, 516

Sesame Street (television), 437, 500

Set My People Free, 98

Set-Up, The, 96; 1949 film, 406

Seven Brides for Seven Brothers (television), 519

Seven Keys to Baldpate (1929), 214

Seven Men from Now (1956), 494, **494**

Seventh Heaven (1927), 142

Seventh Street Christian Church (Richmond), 83

77 Sunset Strip (television), 252

Severin Hotel (Indianapolis), 465

Seville's (Indianapolis), 263

Seward, Billie, **363**

S. H. Dudley's Smart Set Company, 471

Shaft (1971), 455, 457
Shaggy Dog, The (1959), 501
Shane (1953), 425, 515
Shanks, Robert H., 419, 532
Shannon, Frank, **324**
Shannon of the Sixth (1914), 378
Shapera, Florence, 512
Shapiro, Bernstein and Von Tilzer, 470
Shaw, Arnold, 389
Shaw, Artie, 461, 464
Shaw, George Bernard, 268
Shaw, Wilbur, 397, 523
She (1917), 43
She Came, She Saw, She Conquered (1916), 47
Shearer, Norma, 67, 209, 397
Shearing, George, 439, 458
Sheehan, Winfield, 365
Sheen, Charlie, 522
Sheet Steel Products Company, 175
Shell Chateau (radio), 250
Shelter (play), 413
Shepherd, Jean, 428–29, **429**, 524, 535
Shepherd of the Hills, The (1941), 170
Sheridan, Ann, 379, 397, 523
Sheriff of Cochise (television), **239**, 240
Sheriff of Sundown (1944), 370
Sherman, Lowell, 295, 312
Sherwood, Bobby (Robert J. Sherwood Jr.), 464, 536
She's My Baby, 498
Shields, Brooke, 418
Shinnick, Ann, 499
Shinnick, Mark, 499
Ship Comes In, A (1928), 142, 515
Shipman, Helen, 282, 497
Shirk, Bill (William Poorman), 522, 530, 533
Shirley, Bill, 530, 536
Shocking Miss Pilgrim, The (1947), 401, 402
Shoes of the Fisherman, The (1968), 515
Sho-Gun, The, 420
Shore, Dinah, 496
Shore, Pauly, 120
Shortridge, Abram Crum, 283
Shortridge, Elizabeth "Minnie" Hess, 283, 284
Shortridge, Elmer, 283
Shortridge High School (Indianapolis), 283, 415, 429, 430, 461, 465
Shotgun Slade (television), 409
Show of Shows, The (1929), 17, 59
Show of Wonders, The, 131
Show-Off, The, 309; 1946 film, **90**, 508
Showalter, Max, **248**

Showboat, 261, 278, 498
Shriner, Herb (Herbert Arthur Shriner), 189, 489, 510–11, **510**, 520, 532
Shriner, Indy, 510
Shriner, Kin, 510, 520, 521
Shriner, Wil, 510
Shubert, J. J., 131, 132
Shubert, Lee, 130, 131, 132, 282
Shuffle Along, xii, 132, 133, 464–65, 466, 467, 471, 472
Shuffle Along of 1933, 467
Sibley, John, 341, 537
Sideli, Sivia, 263
Sidewalks of London (1938), 214, 389
Sidewalks of New York, 448
Sidney, George, 29
Sidney, Scott, 318
Siegel, Jerry, 224
Sign of Zorro, The (television), 85
Signal Oil Company, 324
Silverado (1985), 504
Silverman, Fred, 491
Silverman, Sime, 42
Simmons, Jean, 423
Simmons, Mrs. Wheeler, 262
Simon, Al, 367
Simon, Melvin, 482–83
Simon and Schuster (publisher), 500
Simpson College, 224
Sims, Autumn, 532
Sin of Harold Diddlebock, The (1947), 32
Sinatra, Frank, 106, 387, 389, 463, 522
Sing, Baby, Sing (1936), 438, 515
Sing Along (television), 194
Singin' in the Rain (1952), 500, 501, 515
Singing Nun, The (1966), 266
Siren, The (1917), 43
Sirens of Titan, The (novel), 430
Siskel, Gene, 124
Sissle, Rev. George A., 465
Sissle, Martha Angeline, 465
Sissle, Noble Lee, xii, 132, 272, **465**, **466**, 464–68, 471, 472, 536
Sister Act, 226
Sisters of the Skillet (radio), 261, 262, **262**
Sitting Pretty (1948), **70–71**, 76, 517
Six Dance Lessons in Six Weeks, 492
Six Million Dollar Man, The (television), 457
Six Weeks (1982), 429
63rd Street Theater (New York), 466
Sixx-Nine (Christopher Harvest), 201
Sjostrom, Victor, 23, 52

Skelton, Chris, 87, 88

Skelton, Ida M. Fields, 88, 94

Skelton, Joseph Elmer, 88

Skelton, Joseph Ismal, 88

Skelton, Paul, 87, 88

Skelton, Richard Freeman, 93, **93**

Skelton, Red (Richard Bernard Skelton), **86–87**, 86–94, **88**, **89**, **90**, **91**, **92**, **93**, 234, 258, 304, 309, 419, **501**, 507, 525, 534

Skelton, Valentina Marie, 92, **93**

Skin Deep (1929), 24

Skin of Our Teeth, 95

Skinner, Cornelia Otis, 426

Skinner, Otis, xii

Sky Gypsies (radio), 325

Skyloft Players, 95

Slap Shot (1977), 290

Slapstick: novel, 430; 1982 film, 430

Slaughterhouse-Five: novel, 430; 1972 film, 430

Slave, The (1917), 43

Sleepers (1996), 478

Sleeping Beauty (1959), 334, 338, 487

Sleepless in Seattle (1993), 499

Slender Thread, The (1965), 409

Slow Burn (television), 300

Slow as Lightning (1923), 376

Sloyan, James J., 530, 536

Small, Edward, 53

Small Circle of Friends, A (1980), 198

Small Productions, 53

Smart Set (magazine), 17

Smarter Set, 471

Smile Like Yours, A (1997), 124

Smiles, 135, **135**

Smiley, Sam, 530, 532

Smiley, Tavis, 534

Smilin' Through (1941), 439

Smiling Irish Eyes (1929), 67

Smith, Afton, 121

Smith, Alexis, 523

Smith, Clifford, 391, 539

Smith, Connie (Constance June Meador), 468–69, 533

Smith, David, **407**, **426**

Smith, Forrest, 243

Smith, Kate, 307–08

Smith, Lucy, **407**

Smith, Maggie, 437

Smith, Noel Mason, 57

Smith, Robert C., 533

Smith, Russell, **466**

Smith, Wil, 200

Smock, Carolyn, 45

Smock, Dinah Wilson, 45

Smock, Ida, 45

Smock, Jacob, 45

Smock, Maud, 45

Smock, William, 45

Smoky (1946), **502**

Snake Pit, The: novel, 430; 1948 film, 430

Snakeville comedy series, **32**, 32–33

Snipes, Wesley, 518

Snow, Jeanne (Jeanne Jones Snow), 527, 534

Snow White and the Seven Dwarfs (1937), 333, 336, 337, 338

So Dear to My Heart (1949), 333, 523

So Proudly We Hail! (1943), 252

So This is Harris! (1933), 274, 515

Soap Opera Update (magazine), 519

Society of Motion Picture Engineers (SMPE), xviii

Soldier of Fortune (1955), 248

Solid Gold Cadillac, The (1956), 261

Some Came Running (1958), 328, 522

Somebody Loves Me (1952), 439

Somebody Up There Likes Me (1956), 104, 406

Somers, Suzanne, 496

Something to Shout About (1943), 516

Something to Think About (1920), 15

Something of Value (1957), 98

Sommers, Mark Berko, 415

Son of Paleface (1952), 308

Son of the Gods (1930), 294

Sondheim, Stephen, 491

Song at Twilight, 182

Song of Bernadette, The (1943), 258, 516

Song of Norway (1970), 192, **193**

Song of the South (1946), 237, **237**, 333, 338, 515

Song of Surrender (1949), 427

Sons of Indiana, 190

Sons of the Pioneers, 359

Sopranos, The (television), 264, 464

Sorry, Wrong Number (1948), 240

Sorting It Out (television), 198

Soul Food (1997), 200, 201, 445

Soul of Broadway, The (1915), 43

Sound of Music, The, 194; 1965 film, 406, 482, 483, 516, 517

South Bend (IN) Central High School, 275, 311

South Bend (IN) Times (newspaper), 245

South Pacific, 190, 291

South Side High School (Fort Wayne), 196

Southern Methodist University, 120

Southern Yankee, A (1948), 92, 258

Space Sluts in the Slammer (film), 123

Spacey, Kevin, 420

Sparrow Records, 473

Speakeasy (1929), 224

Speedway (1929), 522

Speedway (IN) High School, 496

Speedy (1928), 62, **63**

Sphere (1998), 478

Spice of 1922, 43, 448

Spiceland (IN) High School, 413

Spiderman (comic strip), 227

Spike Jones and the City Slickers, 451

Spina, Harold, 438

Spinout (1966), 447

Spoilers, The: 1914 film, 34, 36; 1942 film, 394; 1955 film, 309

Spoon River Anthology, 232

Spooner Stock Company, 4

Sporting Chance, A (1945), **311**

Spring Meeting, 177

Springtime in the Rockies (1942), 438

Squall, The, 214

Squaw Man, The: 1914 film, 42; 1918 film, 15

Squier, Emma-Lindsey, 533

Sssssss (1973), **289**

St. Bonaventure Lyceum (Terre Haute), 443

St. Clair House (Terre Haute), 45

St. Denis, Ruth, 65, 507

St. Elmo (novel), 316

St. Francis Hotel (San Francisco), 273

St. Francis Xavier Academy (New York), 249

St. John, Jill, 418

St. Johns, Adela Rogers, 25, 26, 163, 428

St. Joseph's Academy (Terre Haute), 266

St. Louis Cardinals (baseball team), 519

St. Martin's Lane. See *Sidewalks of London*.

St. Martin's Press (publisher), 421

St. Mary-of-the-Woods College, 45

St. Mary's College (California), 239, 240

St. Mary's Convent (Los Angeles), 55

St. Meinrad's Academy, 443

St. Vincent Catholic Grade School (Logansport), 417

St. Vincent Hospital (Indianapolis), 12

Stack, Robert, 160

Stadt der Versuchung Die (1925), 67

Stahl, John M., 52

Stallone, Sylvester, 483

Stand Up and Cheer! (1934)

Stander, Lionel, 429

Standing, Gordon, 320

Stanley, Helene, 367, 379

Stanwyck, Barbara, 168, 240, 312, 522

Star-Crossed Romance of Josephine Cosnowski, The (television), 429

Star Is Born, A (1937), 21, 25, 26, 109

Star Maker, The (1939), 243

Star Theater (Indianapolis), 461–62

Star Trek (television), 275, 445

Star Trek: Deep Space Nine (television), **241**, 241–42

Star Trek: The Motion Picture (1979), 406

Star Trek: The Next Generation (television), 419

Star Trek: Voyager (television), 419

Star-Wagon, The, 298

Starrett, Charles, 376

Stars in My Crown (1950), 419

Starsky and Hutch (2004), 118

Starting Over: novel, 430; 1979 film, 430

State Fair (1933), 142

State of Grace (1990), 463

Stauber, Liz (Elizabeth), 527, 536

Steel Helmet, The (1951), 96, **96**

Steele, Bob, 349, 371, 375, 378

Steele, Karen, 188

Steiger, Rod, 188

Stein, Jules, 485, 525, 537

Stein, Louis, 485

Stein, Rebecca, 485

Steinbeck, Gwyn, 109

Steinbeck, John, 114

Steinman, Gertrude, 309

Stella Dallas (1937), 439, 462

Step Lively (1944), 387, 389

Stephens, A. S., 38

Stepping Sisters (1932), **277**

Sterling, Andrew B., 470

Sterling, Ford, 56, 57

Stevens, Edwin, 202

Stevens, George, 116, 117, 159, 278, 411, 424

Stevenson, Morton John, 4

Stewart, Anita, **210**

Stewart, Fred Mustard, 429, 535

Stewart, James, 183, 288, 291, 304, 373, **373**, 495, 523

Stewart, Peggy, 361

Stewart, Roberta, 332

Stiller, Ben, 118

Stillman, Harry, 345

Stillwell, Edna, 89, 90, 91, 92, 93

Sting, The (1973), 483

Stock, Barbara, 521, 527, 536

Stock, Dennis, 116

Stocker, Chris, 33

Stockwell, Dean, 299

Stolen Hours (1963), 430

Stone, Ezra, 215
Stone, Francine Lida, 215
Stone, Dr. J. C., 215
Stone, Josef, 215
Stone, Mike, 300
Stooge, The (1953), 491
Stoopnagel and Bud, 307
Stop That Cab (1951), 262
Storey, Robert, 195, 196
Storm, Gale, 237
Storm, T. J., 530
Storm Daughter, The (1924), **35**
Storm in Summer, A (2000), 406
Stormy Weather, 467
Story of G.I. Joe (1945), 428
Stout, Clarence, 88
Stout, Rex, 429, **429**, 533
Stowaway (1936), 365
Stradlin, Izzy (Jeff Isbell), 463
Straight to Heaven (1939), 236
Straight Way, The (1916), 43
Strange Cargo (1929), 417
Strange Invaders (1983), 449
Strangers on a Train (1951), 278
Stranger's Return, The (1933), 495
Strasberg, Lee, 104, 113, 492
Stratton-Porter, Gene, 142, 411, 429, **429**, 539
Streep, Meryl, 251
Street Angel (1928), 142
Street Scene, 495
Streetcar Named Desire, A: play, 506, 518; 1951 film,
     506, 516
Streets of San Francisco, The (television), 506–07
Streisand, Barbra, 448, 468
Stevens, Rock. *See* Lupus, Peter.
Stride (ballet), 486
Stringer, Arthur, 278
Strong Man, The (1926), 387
Stuart Walker Players, 268
Stubblefield, Stubby, 397, 523
Stuck on You (2003), 125
Student Prince, The, 21, 314
Student Tour (1934), 401
Studio Arena Theater (Buffalo, NY), 518
Studio One (television), 105, 113, 188, 189, 417
Stunt Man, The (1980), 484
Sturges, John, 106
Sturges, Preston, 32
Styne, Jule, 438, 515
Subject was Roses, The, 293
Success Story, 248
Such Men are Dangerous (1930), 384, 397

Sudden Bill Dorn (1937), 350
Suez (1938), 234
Sullivan, Helen, 254
Sullivan, Margaret, 291
Sullivan's Travels (1941), 32
Sultan of Sulu, 202, 420
Summer and Smoke (a.k.a. *The Eccentricities of a Nightingale*),
     190, 191
Summer of the Seventeenth Doll (1959), 181
Summers, Marc (Marc Berkowitz), 530, 536
Summerville, Slim, 29
Sunday Dinner for a Soldier (1944), 179
Sunny, 134; 1930 film, **133**, 135
Sunrise (1927), 142
Sunrise at Campobello (1960), 501
Sunshine Comedies, 32
Super Sex, The (1922), 385
Support Your Local Sheriff! (1969), 373
Suratt, Anna, 41
Suratt, Leah, 41
Suratt, Ralph, 41
Suratt, Valeska, **40–41**, 40–44, **42**, **43**, 533
Sure Fire, 83
Surf Party (1964), 252
Surfside Six (television), 252
Susan and God: play, 177; 1940 film, 251–52
Susan Lenox (Her Fall and Rise) (1931), 428
Susan Lenox: Her Rise and Fall: novel, 428; play, 428
Susan Slept Here (1954), 512
Suspense: radio, 274; television, 417
Sutter's Gold (1936), 284
Swain, Mack, 57
Swamp Water (1941), **176**, 179
Swann, Myrtle, 499
Swanson, Gloria, 11, 15, 28, 142, 206, 267
Sweet, Blanche, 22, **23**, 238, 386
Sweet Adeline, 245
Sweet Alyssum: novel, 426; 1915 film, 426
Sweet Sixteen, 213
Sweet Surrender (1935), 284
Sweetheart Time, 497
Sweethearts (1938), 272
Swing, Raymond Gram, 421
Swing Fever (1943), 508
Swing High, Swing Low (1937), **151**, **235**, 236
Swing Your Lady (1938), **59**
Swiss Family Robinson, The (1940), 413
Sword and the Rose, The (1953), 426
Sword in the Stone, The (1963), 334
Symposium on Popular Songs, A (1962), 338
Syncopation (1942), 279
Synthetic Sin (1929), 67

Taaffe, Edna, 49

Taaffe, Ella Thorn, 49

Taaffe, Martin, 49

Taft, William Howard, 420

Take a Chance, 81; 1933 film, 168

Take Care of My Little Girl: novel, 424; 1951 film, 424

Taken (television), 519

Taking of Luke McVane, The (1915), 391

Talbot, George H., 294–95

Tale of Two Cities, A (1935), 419

Tales of the Diamond K (radio), 359

Tales of Hoffman (opera), 74

Taliesin, 183

Talk Soup (television), 123–24

Talmadge, Constance, 67

Talmadge, Norma, 57, 278, 476

Taming of the Shrew, The, 168

Tamiroff, Akim, 423

Tanchuck, Ida Lee, 316

Tandy, Jessica, 182

Tanen, Kitty, 399

Tango and Cash (1989), 483

Tanguay, Eva, 43

Tarantino, Quentin, 118

Taras Bulba (1962), 364

Tarkington, Booth, xii, xiii, 146, 179, 205, 222, 279, 405, **411**, 411–12, 415, 426, 507, 522, 523, 536

Tarzan (television), 275

Tarzan, the Ape Man (1959), 315, 325, **326**, **327**

Tarzan and the Golden Lion (1927), 315, 323, **323**, 392

Tarzan of the Apes (1918), 315, **317**, 318, 319

Tarzan's Magic Fountain (1949), 320

Tarzan's New York Adventure (1942), 320

Tavern, The, 312

Taylor, Elizabeth, 97, 116, 117, 426

Taylor, Gil, 451. *See also* Hoosier Hot Shots.

Taylor, James, 437

Taylor, Jeri Suer, 419, **419**, 538

Taylor, Robert, 423

Taylor, Ruth, 150

Taylor, William Desmond, 39

Tea with a Kick! (1923), 65

Teacher's Pet (1958), 402

Teagarden, Jack, 441, 440

Tech High School (Indianapolis), 263

Tecumseh: The Last Warrior (television), 429

Tell Me More, 81

Tell Me That You Love Me, Junie Moon (1970), 118

Telluride Film Festival, 406

Temple, Shirley, 286, 299, 306, 365, 426, 438

Temple Houston (television), 373

Ten Commandments, The (1956), 181, 376

Ten Nights in a Barroom (1931), **35**, 37

Tennessee Johnson (1942), 258

Tennessee's Partner (1955), 247

Terhune, Donald Roltaire, 369, 371

Terhune, Garrat, 369

Terhune, Mary Swains, 369

Terhune, Max (Robert Max Terhune), 350, 359, 367, **369**, 369–72, **370**, **371**, **372**, 375, 385, 393, 534

Terhune, Maxine, 369

Terhune, Robert Max, Jr., 369, 371

Terminator 2: Judgment Day (1991), 463

Terre Haute Gazette (newspaper), 420

Terre Haute Star (newspaper), 42

Terre Haute Tribune (newspaper), 420

Terror after Midnight: novel, 425; 1962 film, 425

Terror Squad (1987), 522

Terry, Alice (Alice Frances Taaffe), 23, **48–49**, 48–53, **50**, **51**, **52**, **53**, 138, 148, 157, 206, 525, 534

Terry, Tex (Edward E. Terry), 377

Tesich, Steve, 419, 522

Texas (television), 521

Texas Ranger, The (1931), 209

Thalberg, Irving, 67, 383, 401

Thanhouser Film Corporation, 202

Tharp, Twyla, 486, **486**, 534

That Darn Cat: 1965 film, 424; 1997 film, 424

That Night in Rio (1941), 401

That Touch of Mink (1962), 444

That's My Boy (1951), 491

That's the Spirit (1933), 467

Thaw, Harry K., 38

Theater West (Hollywood), 232

Theatricum Botanicum (California), 270

Theodora Goes Wild (1936), 499, 515

Theodora Irvine's School of Theater, 176

There's Always a Breeze, 177, 182, 183

There's No Business Like Show Business (1954), 295

They Died with Their Boots On (1941), 292

They Knew What They Wanted (1940), 506

They Shoot Horses, Don't They? (1969), 409–10, 516

Thief of Bagdad, The: 1924 film, 65, 67, **67**; 1940 film, 214, 389

Thin Man, The (1934), 480

Thing Called Love, The (1993), 296

Thinnes, Roy, 429

Third Best Sport, 260

Third Day, The: novel, 425; 1965 film, 425

This Could Be the Night (1957), 104

This Is It, 299
This Is Tom Jones (television), 314
This Is Your Life (television), 254
This Mad World (1930), **143**
This Property Is Condemned (1966), 409, 483
This Was a Woman (1948), 390
Thom, James Alexander, 429, **430**, 537
Thomas, Danny, 501
Thomas, Ernest, 530, 534
Thomas, Frank, 274
Thomas, Larri, 240
Thomas, Linda Lee, 460, 461
Thomas, Lyn (Jaqueline), 532
Thomas, Olive, 131, 133
Thomas, Richard, **269**, 522
Thomas, Tony, 344
Thompson, Ada, 127, 128, 129, 131
Thompson, Bill, 90, **486**, 486–87, 525, 539
Thompson, Claude, 101, 102, 103, 104
Thompson, Eva, 103
Thompson, Fred, 325, 349
Thompson, Leon, 128
Thompson, Louise, 128
Thompson, Lynn, 127
Thompson, John, 283
Thompson, Mary, 127, 128
Thompson, Randy, 530, 532
Thornhill, Claude, 256, 433, 539
Thoroughly Modern Millie (1967), 446
Those Magnificent Men in Their Flying Machines (1965),
    86–87, 88, 94
Three Caballeros, The (1944), 340
Three for Bedroom C (1952), 267
Three for the Show (1955), 291
Three Little Pigs (1933), 336
Three Little Wolves (1936), 336
Three Men on a Horse, 215
Three Mesquiteers, 350, 370, **371**
Three Orphan Kittens (1935), 336
Three Stooges, 80, 294, 376, 444
Three's a Crowd, 75
Three's Company (television), 496
Thunder Run (1986), 303
Thundering Dawn (1923), **2–3**
Tibbett, Lawrence, **155**
Tierney, Dorothy, 282
Tierney, Gene, 180
Tiffany (studio), 358
Tiger Shark. See Angkor Rescue, The.
Tiger Smiles, The, 291
Tightwad, The, 282
Till the End of Time (1946), 308

Tillie's Punctured Romance: 1914 film, 29, 238; 1928
    film, 58
Tillis, Mel, 446
Tillotson, Mary Ellen, 240, 241
Tim Tyler's Luck (1937), 391
Time (magazine), 445
Time of Your Life, The, 289
Time Out for Ginger, 105
Time to Smile (radio), 307
Times Have Changed: novel, 421; 1923 film, 421
Tin Men (1987), 478
Tin Pan Alley (1940), 439
Tin Star, The (1957), 189
Tinder, Olive, 170
Tip Toes, 81
T. J. Hooker (television), 275
To Be or Not to Be (1942), 159, 163, **163**
To Have and Have Not (1944), 398, 441–42
To Have and to Hold (1922), 208
To Kill a Mockingbird (1962), 310
To Please a Lady (1950), 522
To Tell the Truth (television), 491
Tobacco Road, 234, 268, 503
Toby, 206
Today (television), 190, 194
Todd, Harry, 32
Todd, Thelma, 227
Together We Two, 401
Toland, Greg, 94
Toland, Lothian, 94
Tom Brown's School Days (1940), 413
Tomlinson, Jennie McGaughey, 167
Tomlinson, Rev. Samuel Joseph, 167, 168, 239
Tomorrow the World, 248
Tonight Show, The (television), 437, 440, 446
Tonight We Sing (1953), 312
Tony Randall Show, The (television), 496
Too Much Johnson, 206
Toones, Fred, 288
Toot Sweet, 448
Tootsie (1982), **409**, 410, 483, 484, 516
Top Cat (television), 512
Top of the Heap (1972), 457
Topper (1937), 441
Toppers, The. *See* Four Freshmen.
Torrance, Ernest, 4, **6**, 522
Torres, Antonia, 243
Torres, Donald, 530, 536
Torres, Raquel, **10–11**, 12
Tosca (opera), 74, 226
Touched by an Angel (television), 251
Tougaloo College, 241

Tower of Ivory, The (novel), 22
Tower Realty Company, 482
Tower Theater (Los Angeles), 57
Toy Boat, The, 236
Toy Story (1995), 484
Toy Story 2 (1999), 416–17, 419
Trackdown (television), 105
Tracked by the Police (1927), 394
Tracy, Spencer, 162, 336, 507
Trade Winds (television), 293
Trail of Robin Hood (1950), 211
Trail of the Lonesome Pine (1936), 416
Trails of the Wild (1935), **363**
Tramp, Tramp, Tramp (1926), 387
Tremayne, Les, 390
Trench, Tracey, 531, 539
Trendle, George, 401
Trevlac, John. *See* Calvert, John.
Trevor, Claire, **18**, 169
Triangle (studio), 385, 391
Trianon Ballroom (Terre Haute), 256
Tribute, 189
Tribute to a Bad Man (1956), 406
Trietsch, Bessie, 449
Trietsch, Kenneth Henry, 449–51, 533. *See also* Hoosier Hot Shots.
Trietsch, Paul Edward "Hezzie," 449–51, 533. *See also* Hoosier Hot Shots.
Trilogy of Terror (television), 493
Trip Through Fijiland, A (1935), 404–05
Triumph of X, 282
Troop Beverly Hills (1989), **199**
Trouble in Paradise (1932), 416
Troupers, The, 377
Truant Husband, The (1921), 383
True Grit (1969), 290
True Story of Lynn Stuart, The (1958), **188**, 189
Truex, Ernest, 214
Truffaut, François, 159
Truman, Harry, 467
Trumbauer, Frankie, 447
Truth about Mother Goose, The (1957), 338
Truth or Consequences (radio), 307
Tubb, Ernest, 448
Tucker, Betty, 301
Tucker, Cindy, 303
Tucker, D. D. (Doris), 301
Tucker, Forrest, 301
Tucker, Forrest Meredith, **301**, 301–03, **302**, **303**, 343, 371, 376, 394, 415, 525, 534
Tucker, Pam, 303
Tucker, Sean, 303

Tucker, Sophie, 462, 464
Tucker, Tanya, 447
Tulsa (1949), 447
Tumbleweeds: comic strip, 413; 1925 film, 378
Turn of a Card, The (1918), 206
Turn of the Screw, The, 408
Turner, Alexander, 272
Turner, Emma, 272
Turner, Kathleen, 234
Turner, Nancy Ann Wright, 272
Turner, Roscoe, 398
Tutt, J. Homer, 236, 470–72, 532
Tuttle, Lurene, 112, **304**, 304–06, **305**, 518, 525, 538
Tutton, Jack, 203
Twain, Mark, 430
Twelve O'Clock High: television, 260; 1949 film, 503, 516
Twentieth Century (1934), xii, 153, 154, 398, **398**, 399, 427
Twentieth Century Fox (studio), 84, 124, 139, 178, 179, 252, 299, 401, 402, 448, 498–99, 503
Twenty Million Sweethearts (1934), 394
Twenty Mule Team (1940), 178
20-20 (television), 419
Twilight of Honor (1963), 373, 515
Twilight Zone (television), 232
Twilight's Last Gleaming (1977), 232
Twinkletoes (1926), 67
Two and a Half Men (television), 413
Two Flags West (1950), 308
Two for the Money (television), 510
Two for the Seesaw (1962), 483, 516
Two on an Island, 298
Two Wrongs Make a Right (1987), 300
Tyler, Tom, 209, 211, 238, 349
Tyrone Guthrie Theater (Minneapolis), 270
Tyson, Bruce, 199
Tyson, Juliana, 199
Tyson Studio, 296

Uncle Tom's Cabin (television), 241
Undercover Cat, The (novel), 424
Union Pacific (1939), 18
Union Station (Indianapolis), 170
United Artists, 32, 511
United Media, 500
United Press International, 511
United States Costume Company, 6

Universal (studio), 3, 5, 7, 32, 50, 56, 63, 81, 155,
    170, 202, 282, 284, 285, 297, 319, 325, 346,
    349, 350, 358, 359, 362, 385, 386, 391, 392,
    413, 417, 478, 485, 498
University High School (CA), 327
University of Arizona, 122
University of California at Los Angeles, 306–07,
    311, 327, 328, 496
University of Central Florida, 492
University of Chicago, 268
University of Cincinnati, 519
University of Evansville, 270, 269. *See also*
    Evansville College.
University of Florida, 519
University of Illinois, 3, 422
University of Indianapolis, 520
University of Iowa, 279, 426
University of Kentucky, 278
University of Michigan, 244, 289
University of Mississippi, 492
University of Notre Dame, 175, 245, 365, 416,
    522
University of Southern California, 417
University of Tennessee, 430
University of Vienna, 485
University of West Virginia, 485
University of Wyoming, 478
University Players, 291
University Theater Group, 520
Unsinkable Molly Brown, The (1964), 515
Up and Down, 472
Up the Creek (1984), 296
Up Pops the Devil (1931), 84, 153, 267
Up She Goes, 266
Upper Canada College, 119, 120
Urban Cowboy (1980), 478
U.S. Marshal (television), 240
U.S. Steel Hour, The (television), 188, 189
Uslan, Michael E., **511**, 511–12, 536
Uta Hagen-Herbert Berghof School, 104

Valenti, Jack, 480
Valentine, Karen, 275
Valentino, Rudolph, 23, **48–49**, 50, 51, 74, 140,
    142, 320, 412
Valentino (1951), 53
Vallee, Rudy, 81, 90, 249
Valley of Decision, The (1916), 220
Valley of the Sun (1942), 413
Valparaiso University, 494
Vamping Venus (1928), 58

Vampire, The (painting), 42
Van de Carr, Cecile Bellaire, 176
Van Dyke, W. S., 17, 149
Van Halen, Alex, 463
Van Halen, Eddie, 463
Van Halen (band), 463
Van Ness, Jon (Jon Van Ness Philip), 530
Van Patten, Joyce, 232
Van Peebles, Mario, 293
Van Trees, James, 483
Vance, Vivian, 253
Vandaworker, J. B., 12
Vanilla Sky (2001), 449
Vanishing Dagger, The (1920), 378
Vanities, 137, 249
Variety, 25, 31, 42, 43, 169, 232, 300, 301, 356
Varsity Show (1937), 226, 257
Velez, Lupe, **302**
Venable, Evelyn, 426
Venice (CA) Athletic Club, 239
Venice (CA) High School, 239
Ventresca, Vincent, 530, 536
Venuti, Joe, 441, 447
Vereen, Ben, 476
Vernon, Irene, 527, 537
Verse and Worse (1921), 394
Very Rich Woman, A, 309
Vest Pocket Players, 504
Vick's Open House (radio), 307
Victim, The (1916), 43
Victor Potel Homespun Comedy Company, 32
Victorine Studios, 51
Victory through Air Power (1943), 333
Vidor, Florence, **14**, 386
Vidor, King, 67, 495
Viennese Nights, 59
Vigo County (IN) Historical Society, 444
Vigran, Belle, 512
Vigran, Herb (Herburt Vigran), 512, **512**, 532
Vigran, Richard, 512
Vigran, Robert, 512
View from the Bridge, A, 248
Vincennes (IN) Sun-Commercial (newspaper), 90
Vincent, James, 7
Vincz, Melanie, 520, 527, 536
Violets are Blue (1986), 504
Viper (1988), 522
Visitors, The (1972), 293
Vitagraph (studio), 202
Voice from the Fireplace, A (1910), 4
Voils, Andy, 530, 532

Von Leer, Hunter (Paul Hunter Von Leer), 520, 530, 539

Von Radetz, Count Josef Radetsky, 425

Von Sternberg, Josef, 424

Von Tilzer, Albert (Albert Gumm), 141, 469–70, **470**, 536

Von Tilzer, Harry (Harry Gumm), **469**, 469–70, 536

Von Tilzer, Jack, 470

Vonnegut, Kurt, Jr., xi, 429–30, **430**, 536

Vonnegut, Kurt, Sr., 429

Vonnegut, Mary Lieber, 429

Vonnegut, Theodore, 39

Von Zell, Harry, 306–08, **307**, **308**, 402, 525, 536

Voyage of the Rock Aliens (1988), **296**

Wabash Avenue (1950), 274, **274**

Wabash College, 420, 427, 479, 503, 523

Wabash (IN) High School, 79

Waddleigh High School (New York), 208

Wade, John P. (John Patrick Wade), 526, 530

Wagner, Harrison, 520

Wagner, Jack, 520

Wagner, Kristina (Kristina Crump Wagner), 216, 520, 536

Wagner, Peter, 520

Wagner, Robert, 522

Wagon Train (television), 308, 328, 417

Wagon Wheel Playhouse, 518

Wagon Wheels (1934), 288

Wagons Roll at Night, The (1941), 394

Wagons Westward (1940), 350

Waite, Ralph, **269**

Waiting for Lefty, 268

Wake Up and Dream, 461; 1934 film, 154

Wakefield, Ben H., 430

Wakefield, Brucie Ridge, 430

Wakefield, Dan, xii, 430, 522, 536

Walburn, Raymond, 148, 309, **309**, 348, 536

Waldron (IN) High School, 326

Walker, Bill (William Franklin Walker), 310

Walker, Carrie, 310

Walker, Robert, 310

Walker, Sallie. *See* Brace, Annie.

Walker, Stuart, 494

Walker, William, 535

Walker Theater (Indianapolis), 242

Walking My Baby Back Home (1953), 476

Walking with Dinosaurs (television), 242

Wall, Russell, 424

Wall, Stacy Birdsall, 424

Wallace, Lew, 22, 209, 411, 412, **412**, 533

Wallace, May (May Maddox), 526, 534

Waller, Fats, 442

Waller High School (Chicago), 242, 268

Wallis, Brent, 58, 60

Wallis, Hal B., 57, 58, 59, 60, 135, 137, 240

Walsh, Raoul, 157, 206

Walston, Ray, 291

Walter Baldwin Stock Company, 45

Walton, Tony, 478

Waltons, The (television), 260, 268, 418, 495

Waltz of the Toreadors, 504

Wampas Baby Star, 62, 63, 66, 208, 276, 481

Wanted: Dead or Alive (television), **104**, 105, 106, 509

War and Remembrance (television), 491

War Hunt (1962), 409

War of the Worlds, The (1953), 261, 295

War Song, The, 224

Ward, Athole Shearer, 397, 399

Ward, Baxter, 297

Ward, Charles Otto "Gabe," 449, 450, 535. *See also* Hoosier Hot Shots.

Ward, Jay, 120

Ward, Mary Jane, 430, 533

Ward, Pete, 399–400

Ward and Vokes, 141

Warfield, William, 98

Wariner, Steve, 533

Waring, Fred, 226, 257

Waring, Tom, 226

Warner, Jack, 135, 137

Warner Brothers (studio), 17, 18, 59, 80, 116, 135, 226, 245, 247, 257, 264, 276, 358, 394, 413, 447, 463, 482, 483, 492, 498, 506, 509

Warren, Lesley Ann, 430

Warren, Michael, 200, 201, 311, **311**, 537

Washington-Lee (VA) High School, 301

Wasserman, Lou, 409

Watch the Birdie (1950), 234

Water Hole, The (1928), 63

Waterloo Bridge (1940), 439

Waters, Bob, 300

Waters, Daniel, 417, 419, 537

Waters, Ethel, 137, 279, 471

Waters, Mark, 537

Watkins, Sammy, 256

Watson, Ivory "Deek," 453, 454, 455, 536. *See also* Ink Spots.

Way Out, The (1918), **24**

Way We Were, The (1973), 410, 483

Way West, The (novel), 425

Waycoff, Charles, 233

Waycoff, Cora, 233

Wayne, David, 282–83, 295

Wayne, John, 36, 274, 302, 352, **352**, 370, 371, **371**, 394, **399**, **494**, 509

Wayne State University, 264

WBOW radio, 253, 502

We the People (radio), 307

We Were Soldiers (2002), 125

Weaver Brothers, 369

Web, The (television), 232, 417

Webb, Chris, 416, 419, 537

Webb, Clifton (Webb Parmalee Hollenbeck), xii, 7, **70–71**, 70–78, **72**, **73**, **74**, **75**, **76**, **77**, 116, 134, 137, 181, 245, 402, 460, 461, 489, 498, 517, 525, 536

Webb, Edgar, 216

Webb, George (George Webb Frey), 526, 536

Webb Dance Studio, 74

Webster (television), 279, **279**

WED Enterprises, 336, 338

Weems, Ted, 507

Weintraub, Sy, 328

Weir, Helen, 526, 535

Weismuller, Johnny, **325**, 328

Welles, Orson, 84, 85, 179, 222, 278, 279, 304, 306, 405, 411

Wellington Hotel (Chicago), 41

Wellman, William, 159, 206, 425

Wells, H. G., 242

Wells, Herman B, 499

Wells, Mary K., **293**

Wells Fargo Gunmaster (1951), **368**, 373

Wenzel, Thornoe, 277

We're Not Dressing (1934), 153, **153**, **159**

Werner, Gwen, 82

West, Jessamyn, 430, **430**, 523, 534

West, Mae, 168, 336

West, Roland, 227

West Side Story (1961), 406, 440, 517

West Wing, The (television), 251

Western Associated Motion Picture Advertisers (WAMPAS), 62, 66, 208, 276, 481

Western Courage (1935), 203, 359

Westerner, The (1940), 302

Westminster Grammar School (Venice, CA), 239

Westworld (1973), 484

WFBE (radio), 454

WFBM (radio), 325, 437

WFMK (later WING) (radio), 254

WGBF (radio), 417

WGN, 186, 261

Wharton, Bessie Emerick, 526, 533

What a Wife Learned (1923), 22

What Every Woman Knows, 219

What Men Want (1930), 209

What Price Hollywood? (1932), 25

Wheel of Fortune (television), 188

Wheeler, Burt, 278

Wheeler Dealers, The (1963), 274

Wheeler and Woolsey, 30

Whelan, John, 389

Whelan, Michael, 215

Whelan, Tim, 214, **214**, 215, **387**, 387–90, **388**, **389**, 507, 537

Whelan, Tim, Jr., 215, 389

When Harry Met Sally (1989), 478

When Knighthood Was in Flower: novel, 426; 1908 film, 426; 1922 film, 426

When Knights Were Bold (1929), 214, 389

When the Clouds Roll By (1919), 206

Where Roses Grow Wild (novel), 421

Where the Pavement Ends (1923), 51

Where the Sidewalk Ends (1950), 308

Whispering Smith (1916), 378

Whistling in Brooklyn (1943), 91

Whistling in Dixie (1942), 91

Whistling in the Dark (1941), 91

Whitaker, Charles "Slim," 356

White, Christine, 112–13

White, Dorothy L., 258

White, George, 466–67

White, Jules, 376

White, Maurice, 472, 473

White, Olive (Olive Celeste Moore White), 526, 536

White, Pearl, 36, 147, 378, 502

White, Sam, 376

White, Sammy, 465

White, Sara, 424

White, Stanford, 38

White Banners: novel, 423; 1938 film, 423

White Man's Burden (1995), 296

White Nights (1985), 486

White Shadows in the South Seas (1928), **10–11**, 12, 17

Whited, Sadie, 316

Whiteman, Paul, 307, 447, 454, 486

Whitemore, James, 112

Whiteside, Walker, 526, 532

Whiting, Dick, 257

Whiting, Richard, 438, 515

Whiting Mead Wrecking Company (Los Angeles), 13

Whitman, Ernest, 467–68

Whitney, Salem Tutt, 236, 470–72, 532

Whittemore, Dr. W. Lawrence, 138

WHK (radio), 454

Who are the DeBolts? And Where Did They Get Nineteen Kids? (1977), 516

Who Killed Cock Robin? (1935), 336

Whole Town's Talking, The, 301

Why Do Fools Fall in Love? (1998), 200, 201

Why Worry? (1923), 387

Wife Number Two (1917), 43

Wil Shriner Show, The (television), 510

Wild, Wild West (television), 232, 373

Wild Birds, 494

Wild Boys of the Road (1933), 276

Wild Bull of the Campus (film), 362

Wild Bunch, The (1969), 289, 290

Wilde, Oscar, xii

Wilde, Ted, 63

Wilder, Billy, 214

Wiley, Jan, 379, 527, 533

Wiley High School (Terre Haute), 253, 266, 295

Wilhite, Don, 458

Wilie, Austin, 256

Will and Grace (television), 410

Willard, Shirley K., 321

Willets, Gilson, 522–23

Willett, Clark and Colby (publisher), 423

William H. Block department store (Indianapolis), 41

Williams, Andy, 442

Williams, Brock, 389

Williams, Deniece, 472–73, 534

Williams, Mrs. Durbin, 290

Williams, Grant, **282**

Williams, Hank, 462

Williams, John, 306

Williams, Joseph, 306

Williams, Kathlyn, 36, 147, 416, 426

Williams, Kay, 164

Williams, Mark Towner, 306

Williams, Matt, 531, 538

Williams, Richard, 500

Williams, Tennessee, 190, 191, 293, 519

Williams, Wayne, 162

Williamson, Fred, 118, **118**, 300, 534

Willie Dynamite (1974), 457

Willkie, Wendell, 161, 190

Wills, Chill, 367

Wilmington (OH) High School, 419

Wilson, Anthony, 209

Wilson, Carey, 67, 209

Wilson, Earl, 270

Wilson, Lewis, 386

Wilson, Lois, 4, **5**, 7, 8

Wilson, Nancy, 472

Wilson, Owen, 118

Wilson, "Whip," 386

Wilson, Winslow, 318

Wilson, Woodrow, 132

Winchell, Walter, 83

Winding, Kai, 455

Windom, William, 189

Winds of War, The (television), 491

Windsor Theater (New York), 177

Windust, Bretaigne, 291

Wing and a Prayer (1944), 251, **251**

Winged Victory, 98

Wings: television, 518; 1927 film, 323

Wings of the Morning (1937), 208

Winkler, Otto, 158, 160, 161

Winning (1969), 522

Winona Lake Academy, 485

Winslow, Joan, 110

Winslow, Marcus, 110

Winslow, Ortense, 109, 110

Winter Garden (New York), 43, 131, 282

Winterset, 221, 298; 1936 film, 291

WIRE (radio), 415

Wise, Dave, 404

Wise, Olive Longenecker, 404

Wise, Robert, xiii, 96, 104, 106, 179, 258, 308, **404**, 404–07, **407**, 482, 483, 515, 517, 525, 537

Wise, Robert, Sr., 404

WISH: radio, 477; television, 477

Wish You Were Here, 194

Wishard Hospital (Indianapolis), 263

With Honors (1994), 120

Withers, Edward H., 311–12

Withers, Isabel (Isabella Irene), **311**, 311–13, 535

Withers, Jane, 286

Withers, Minnie Snow, 311–12

Withey, Virginia Philley, 532

Wittenberg College and Seminary, 422

Wiz, The (1978), 478

Wizard of Oz, The (stage), 314

WKBF (radio), 454

WLS (radio), 369, 450

WLW (radio), 454

WNAP (radio), 518

WNDU (television), 416, 417, 419

Wolf Tracks (1920), 392

Wolfe, Elsie de, 74

Woman from Hell, The (1929)

Woman I Love, The (television), 418

Woman-Proof (1923), 206

Woman's Christian Temperance Union, 503

Woman's Home Companion (magazine), 425
Women, The, 169; 1939 film, 170
Wonder, Stevie, 472
Wonder Bar (1934), 59
Wonderful Town, 313
Wonderful World of the Brothers Grimm, The (1962), 515
Wong, Anna May, **67**
Wood, Cornett, 338, 340
Wood, Edward, 447
Wood, Natalie, 116, 409, 483
Wooden, John, 311, 327
Woodland, 202
Woods, T. K., 404
Woodward, Joanne, 522
Woody Herman orchestra, 440
Woolridge, Mrs. John, 238
WOR (radio), 324
Worcester Academy, 459
World According to Garp, The (1982), 419
World Color Printing Company, 499
World of Suzie Wong, The (1960), 114, 418
Worley, Jo Anne, **313**, 313–14, 484, 535
WOWO (radio), 450
Wright, Allen "Sug," 273
Wright, Mrs. Allen "Sug," 273
Wright, Eric Lloyd, 182
Wright, Frank Lloyd, 175, 179, 181, 183, **184**
Wright, Geraldine, 393
Wright, John Lloyd, 175
Wright, Mack V., 6, 211, 375, 392–93, 533
Wright, Maginel, 182
Wright, William H., 419, 501, 529, 532
Written on the Wind (1956), **282**
WTTS (radio), 448
WTTV (television), 448
WXYZ: radio, 401; television, 257
Wyler, William, 398, 430
Wyman, Jane, 423, 442, 523
Wymore, Patricia, 373
Wynn, Ed, 189, 307
Wynter, Dana, 384
Wyoming (1940), 170

Yale University, 459, 460
Yankee Doodle Dandy (1942), 59
Yankee Prince, 142
Yanks (1979), 296
Yellow Mustings, 472
Yes or No, 168

Yes Sir, Mr. Bones (1951), 254
Yolanda: novel, 426; 1924 film, 426
York, Dick, 532
York Music Company, 470
You Asked for It (television), 321
You Can't Take It with You, 111
You Never Can Tell, 268
You Never Know, 76, **76**, 461
You'll Never Get Rich (1941), 516
Youmans, Vincent, 135
Young, Alan, 367, 368
Young, Gig, 189
Young, John S., 250
Young, Loretta, 85
Young, Olga, 82
Young, Polly Ann, 85
Young, Robert, 507
Young, Roger E., 536
Young, Samuel Y., 45
Young and the Restless, The (television), 200, 521
Young in Heart, The (1938), 419
Young Man of Manhattan (1930), 84, **84**
Young Man with a Horn (1950), **441**, 482
Young Savages, The (1961), 408
Youngblood, Rob, 539
You're a Big Boy Now (1966), 492
You're My Everything (1949), **177**, 299, **299**
Yours, Mine, and Ours (1968), 415
You've Got Mail (1998), 125
Yurka, Blanche, 214

Zadora, Pia, **296**
Zaharias, Babe, 279
Zaharias, George, 279
Zane Grey Theater (television), 236, 417, 509
Zanuck, Darryl, 76, 137, 178, 180, 336, 495
Zaring Theater (Indianapolis), 243
Zeb, 45
Zeller's Zouaves, 12
Zelli's Night Club (Paris), 310
Ziegfeld, Florenz, 127, 131, 133, 134, 135, 137, 138, 278, 466
Ziegfeld Follies (1946), 92
Ziegfeld Follies of 1918, The, 131
Ziegfeld Follies of 1919, The, 132
ZigZag (2002), 518
Zoller, Eric, 253
Zoot Suit, 233
Zorro's Fighting Legion (1939), 325